ISBN 978-0-260-98685-6
PIBN 10998106

Wilson Brothers, a Corporation,
Complainant,

vs.

Nathan Grossman et al.,
(Defendants)
Appellees.

In the Appeal of WILSON BROTHERS,
a Corporation, Complainant, and
G. L. CLAUSEN, Trading as CLAUSEN
& Company,
(Intervening Petitioners)
Appellants.

APPEAL FROM CIRCUIT
COURT, COOK COUNTY.

280 I.A. 615

MR. PRESIDING JUSTICE O'CONNOR
DELIVERED THE OPINION OF THE COURT.

The Master in Chancery to whom the case was referred recommended that a decree be entered awarding complainant, Wilson Brothers, a corporation, a lien for $1467.60, and G. L. Clausen, the intervenor, a lien for $1508. The Chancellor disapproved of the Master's report, holding that neither claim should have been allowed. The bill was dismissed for want of equity and this appeal followed.

The record discloses that Nathan Grossman was the owner of a long term lease on property located at 236 South Wabash avenue, Chicago, and Calvin Burr Beach and others, the lessors, owned the fee. A new building was to be constructed on the premises by the tenant. The building was erected, the two claims involved in the instant case are for work done and materials furnished by the claimants on the building.

Wilson Brothers, a corporation, made a contract with the tenant to furnish all labor and material for the plumbing, gas fitting and sewerage work for the building. It completed the work and from time to time was paid on account, the total amount so paid being $10,[illegible], leaving a balance due of $1467.60, the from the Cody Trust Co., being the proceeds of a mortgage on the property, and part of the money was paid out by the Northern Trust Company Bank which was acting as trustee for the owners of the fee. Nilson Brothers, a corporation, completed its contract April 17, 1929, and about June 7, 1929, when it demanded the balance due, the tenant suggested that it was short of money, that it would give its note for the $1467.60, due in thirty days, and that Nilson Brothers should execute its waiver of lien. The record discloses that at that time the 226 Wabash Building Corp. was the tenant, the lease having been assigned to it. August Nilson, president of Nilson Brothers, testified that he talked to Nathan Grossman, an officer of the Building corporation, and demanded the balance of the money; that it was finally agreed that the Building corporation would give its thirty day note for the amount of the claim, to be signed by the Building corporation and William J. Pancoe, individually, who was interested in the leasehold estate. Pancoe, according to his testimony, was the financial adviser and general superintendent of the 226 South Wabash Building Corporation during the period the building was being erected.

The evidence further shows that Nilson Brothers executed its waiver of lien dated June 7, 1929, and the affidavit of its president, August Nilson, acknowleding receipt of the amount it here claims. About three days thereafter Grossman by telephone advised that the note was ready. Nilson thereupon sent a messenger with the waiver of lien and affidavit, to pick up the note, and this was done. When the messenger returned with the note, Nilson testified, he immediately called up Grossman and complained that the note was not made in accordance with their agreement, that it had not been signed by Pancoe, and that Grossman asked for a few days when the note would be paid.

The evidence further shows that after the waiver of lien

from the Cody Trust Co., being the proceeds of a mortgag
property, and part of the money was paid out by the Nort
Company Bank which was acting as trustee for the owners
Wilson Brothers, a corporation, completed its contract a
1929, and about June 7, 1929, when it demanded the balan
tenant suggested that it was short of money, that it wou
note for the $1567.67, due in thirty days, and that Wils
should execute its waiver of lien. The record disclose
that time the 226 Wabash Building Corp. was the tenant,
having been assigned to it. August Wilson, president of
Brothers, testified that he talked to Nathan Grossman, a
of the Building corporation, and demanded the balance of
that it was finally agreed that the Building corporation
its thirty day note for the amount of the claim, to be s
the Building corporation and William J. Pancoe, individu
was interested in the leasehold estate. Pancoe, accordi
testimony, was the financial adviser and general manag
the 226 South Wabash Building Corporation during the per
building was being erected.

The evidence further shows that Wilson Brothers
its waiver of lien dated June 7, 1929, and the affidavit
president, August Wilson, acknowledging receipt of the am
here claims. About three days thereafter Grossman by tel
vised that the note was ready. Wilson thereupon sent a
with the waiver of lien and affidavit, to pick up the not
this was done. When the messenger returned with the not
testified, he immediately called up Grossman and complain
the note was not made in accordance with their agreement,
had not been signed by Pancoe, and that Grossman asked i
when the note would be paid.

The evidence further shows that after the waiver

was delivered by Grossman to the Northern Trust Co., that Bank from time to time paid out money on architect's certificates and waivers of lien, the money having been deposited with the bank by the tenant. Nilson complained repeatedly to Grossman that the note should be signed by Pancoe, as agreed, and there seems to have been considerable negotiations back and forth but nothing ever came of them. The note was not returned, nor was it paid. About June 20th Nilson Brothers learned that the Northern Trust Co. was paying out money on account of work done on the building, and it advised the bank of the circumstances under which the waiver of lien was executed - that Pancoe had not signed the note as it had been agreed he would do, and that the waiver of lien had been wrongfully obtained.

The bank was also notified that a claim for mechanic's lien would be filed unless the note was taken up, and considerable was said and done by Nilson in endeavoring to have the note paid. July 3, 1929, a letter was written by Nilson Brothers, signed by F G. Holm, who was in its employ, to the Wabash Building Corp., advising that the note would be due July 10th and asking for payment, stating that upon receipt of payment the cancelled note would be returned. After this letter was put in evidence Nilson testified that Holm had no authority to write such a letter; that he was their bookkeeper and buyer and had nothing to do toward the collection of the note. Holm was called by plaintiff, Nilson Brothers, and testified but was asked nothing about the letter.

William J. Pancoe testified that he never agreed to sign the note; that he superintended the entire job of constructing the building and letting the contracts; that he hired architects and all men on the job; that he was an officer of the Building corporation, and the broker; that he "sold the property originally for the Northern Trust Company;" that upon receipt of the letter signed by Holm, was delivered by Grossman to the Northern Trust Co., that bank from time to time paid out money on architect's certificates and waivers of lien, the money having been deposited with the bank by the tenant. Nilsen complained repeatedly to Grossman that the note should be signed by Fences, as agreed, and there seems to have been considerable negotiations back and forth but nothing ever came of them. The note was not returned, nor was it paid. About June 20th Nilsen Brothers learned that the Northern Trust Co. was paying out money on account of work done on the building, and it advised the bank of the circumstances under which the waiver of lien was executed - that Fences had not signed the note as it had been agreed he would do, and that the waiver of lien had been wrongfully obtained.

The bank was also notified that a claim for mechanic's lien would be filed unless the note was taken up, and considerable was said and done by Nilsen in endeavoring to have the note paid. July 2, 1929, a letter was written by Nilsen Brothers, signed by F. G. Holm, who was in its employ, to the Wabash Building Corp., advising that the note would be due July 10th and asking for payment, stating that upon receipt of payment the cancelled note would be returned. After this letter was put in evidence Nilsen testified that Holm had no authority to write such a letter; that he was their bookkeeper and buyer and had nothing to do toward the collection of the note. Holm was called by plaintiff, Nilsen Brothers, and testified he was asked nothing about the letter.

William J. Fences testified that he never agreed to sign the note; that he superintended the entire job of constructing the building and letting the contracts; that he hired architects and all men on the job; that he was an officer of the Building corporation, and the broker; that he "sold the property originally for the Northern Trust Company;" that upon receipt of the letter signed by Holm, above mentioned, he asked Nilson that time of payment of the note be extended ninety days, and that Nilson agreed to this provided Pancoe would guarantee the note, which Pancoe refused to do. Grossman, with whom Nilson had his transactions in connection with the making of the note, did not testify.

The Master found the agreement was that Pancoe was to sign the note, that the waiver of lien was fraudulently obtained and that Holm had no authority to write the letter. Apparently the Chancellor did not agree with this finding. In any event, the decree disallowed the lien of Nilson's claim.

We have considered all the evidence in the record and are of opinion that the claim was properly disallowed. Although the waiver of lien and affidavit and the note were exchanged about June 10th, there is no evidence that the note was tendered back nor the return of the waiver demanded from the bank. On the contrary the evidence shows that Nilson Brothers endeavored to collect the note from time to time and is still holding it. If the procuring of the note and waiver of lien were fraudulent, complainant should have rescinded the transaction.

Clausen, who is a licensed structural engineer, claims there is due him $1508 for structural engineering, survey work and labor rendered in connection with the construction of the building, which work was done between June 18, 1928, and January 17, 1929; that he made an oral agreement with Hall, Lawrence & Ratcliffe, the architects of the building, to do this work. There is no dispute in the evidence but that the work was done, nor is the amount of the claim disputed. The defense to this claim was that Clausen did work as a subcontractor of Wendnagel & Co., who had a contract to do certain work on the building and that Clausen did this work and was paid $500 therefor by Wendnagel & Co. The evidence shows that Clausen did work for Wendnagel & Co. and was paid $500, but his above mentioned, he asked Wilson that time of payment of the note be extended ninety days, and that Wilson agreed to this provided Pancoe would guarantee the note, which Pancoe refused to do. Fergus, with whom Wilson had his transactions in connection with the making of the note, did not testify.

The Master found the agreement was that Pancoe was to sign the note; that the waiver of lien was fraudulently obtained and that Hahn had no authority to write the letter. Apparently the Chancellor did not agree with this finding. In any event, the decree disallowed the lien of Wilson's claim.

We have considered all the evidence in the record and are of opinion that the claim was properly disallowed. Although the waiver of lien and affidavit and the note were exchanged about June 10th, there is no evidence that the note was tendered back nor the return of the waiver demanded from the bank. On the contrary the evidence shows that Wilson Brothers endeavored to collect the note from time to time and is still holding it. If the procuring of the note and waiver of lien were fraudulent, complainant should have rescinded the transaction.

Clausen, who is a licensed structural engineer, claims there is due him $1800 for structural engineering, survey work and labor rendered in connection with the construction of the building, which work was done between June 16, 1928, and January 17, 1929; that he made an oral agreement with Hall, Lawrence & Ratcliffe, the architects of the building, to do this work. There is no dispute in the evidence but that the work was done, nor is the amount of the charge disputed. The defense to this claim was that Clausen did work as a subcontractor of Vanderpool & Co., who had a contract to do certain work on the building and that Clausen did this work and was paid $500 therefor by Vanderpool & Co. The evidence shows that Clausen did work for Vanderpool & Co. was paid $300, but claim here is that the work he did was under an oral contract for other work, made between him and the architects as above stated. Clausen testified he made such a contract with Mr. Jones of the firm of Hall, Lawrence & Ratcliff, architects, and Jones corroborates this testimony. The evidence shows that Clausen, from time to time, attempted to collect his bill but was unsuccessful.

We think the evidence sustains the finding of the Master that Clausen made an oral agreement for the work he did and for which he claims the $1508.

Counsel for defendant say that Clausen's itemized bill, which is in evidence, shows that the first work for which he claims payment was done June 18, 1928, and the last September 14, 1928; that the one item appearing on the statement after this last mentioned date is one of $75 for a survey claimed to have been done January 17, 1929; that this item is spurious and is put in solely for the purpose of preventing the claim from being barred because not filed within the time limited by the Mechanic's Lien act. No such contention was made on the hearing when the evidence was offered before the Master, and there is no evidence in the record that in any way tends to sustain this contention, there must be some evidence that this last charge was spurious before the contention could be sustained, and there is none. Moreover, the point seems to have been made for the first time in this court. We think Clausen should be given a lien for his claim.

For the reasons stated the decree of the Superior court of Cook county is affirmed as to Nilson Brothers, a corporation, and it is reversed as to Clausen's claim.

DECREE AFFIRMED IN PART AND DECREE REVERSED IN PART AND REMANDED WITH DIRECTIONS.

McSurely and Matchett, JJ., concur.

claim here is that the work he did was under an oral contract for other work, made between him and the architects as above stated. Clausen testified he made such a contract with Mr. Jones of the firm of Hall, Lawrence & Ratcliff, architects, and Jones corroborates this testimony. The evidence shows that Clausen, from time to time, attempted to collect his bill but was unsuccessful.

We think the evidence sustains the finding of the Master that Clausen made an oral agreement for the work he did and for which he claims the $1609.

Counsel for defendant say that Clausen's itemized bill, which is in evidence, shows that the first work for which he claims payment was done June 16, 1928, and the last September 11, 1928; that the one item appearing on the statement after this last mentioned date is one of $75 for a survey claimed to have been done January 17, 1929; that this item is spurious and is put in solely for the purpose of preventing the claim from being barred because not filed within the time limited by the Mechanic's Lien act. No such contention was made on the hearing when the evidence was offered before the Master, and there is no evidence in the record that in any way tends to sustain this contention; there must be some evidence that this last charge was spurious before the contention could be sustained, and there is none. Moreover, the point seems to have been made for the first time in this court. We think Clausen should be given a lien for his claim.

For the reasons stated the decree of the Superior court of Cook county is affirmed as to William Brothers, a corporation, and it is reversed as to Clausen's claim.

DECREE AFFIRMED IN PART AND DECREE REVERSED
IN PART AND REMANDED WITH DIRECTIONS.

37904

GEORGE SCOTT and KATIE McTEER SCOTT,
Appellants,

vs.

ANNA L. DUNLAP et al.,
Appellees.

APPEAL FROM SUPERIOR COURT OF COOK COUNTY.

280 I.A. 615[2]

MR. PRESIDING JUSTICE O'CONNOR DELIVERED THE OPINION OF THE COURT.

July 7, 1933, complainants filed their bill, designated a petition, to set aside the forfeiture of a real estate contract in which complainants were purchasers and defendants the sellers; they also prayed for an injunction against defendants to restrain the enforcement of a judgment entered in a forcible detainer suit in the Municipal court of Chicago, brought by defendants against the complainants to recover possession of the same premises. After a number of pleadings were filed, complainants filed their amended petition praying for the same relief, defendants answered, there was a hearing before the Chancellor and a decree entered in which a number of findings are made, and it was decreed (1) that the bill be dismissed for want of equity, (2) that the forfeiture of the real estate contract be approved and confirmed, and the real estate contract entered into between the parties be cancelled and held for naught; (3) that the payments made by complainants on account of the purchase price of the property be retained by the defendant Anna L. Dunlap as liquidated damages for breach of the contract by complainants; (4) that the contract dated January 7, 1931, between complainants and Reans was rightfully cancelled by defendant Dunlap, and that it be removed as a cloud on the title to the premises; (5) that complainant George E. Scott pay to defendant Anna L. Dunlap $1010.81, which was the amount in default at the time of the forfeiture of the contract by defendants, and that Anna L. Dunlap have execution therefor; (6) that complainant George E. Scott forthwith vacate

11

37906

GEORGE SCOTT and KATIE McTEER SCOTT,
Appellants,

vs.

ANNA L. DUNLAP et al.,
Appellees.

APPEAL FROM CIRCUIT COURT OF COOK COUNTY.

280 I.A. 615

MR. PRESIDING JUSTICE O'CONNOR DELIVERED THE OPINION OF THE COURT.

July 7, 1933, complainants filed their bill, designated a petition, to set aside the forfeiture of a real estate contract in which complainants were purchasers and defendants the sellers; they also prayed for an injunction against defendants to restrain the enforcement of a judgment entered in a forcible detainer suit in the Municipal court of Chicago, brought by defendants against the complainants to recover possession of the same premises. After a number of pleadings were filed, complainants filed their amended petition praying for the same relief, defendants answered, there was a hearing before the Chancellor and a decree entered in which a number of findings are made, and it was decreed (1) that the bill be dismissed for want of equity, (2) that the forfeiture of the real estate contract be approved and confirmed, and the real estate contract entered into between the parties be cancelled and held for naught; (3) that the payments made by complainants on account of the purchase price of the property be retained by the defendant Anna L. Dunlap as liquidated damages for breach of the contract by complainants; (4) that the contract dated January 7, 1931, between complainants and Rosse was rightfully cancelled by defendant Dunlap, and that it be removed as a cloud on the title to the premises; (5) that complainant George E. Scott pay to defendant Anna L. Dunlap $1010.21, which was the amount in default at the time of the forfeiture of the contract by defendants, and that Anna L. Dunlap have execution therefor; (6) that complainant George E. Scott forthwith vacate the premises, (7) that the order of court appointing Draper & Kramer, Inc., as agents of the premises be vacated and set aside, and that such agents restore possession to defendant Anna L. Dunlap.

The record is confused, but it appears without dispute that on February 7, 1933, complainants were in default in the payment of a number of installments, aggregating $1010.81, that on account of such defaults defendant Anna L. Dunlap on February 23, 1933, served a notice on complainants that unless the payments in default were made within thirty days, steps would be taken to cancel the contract for the purchase and sale of the premises. A number of other notices were served, including notice of forfeiture and demand for possession.

As stated, there is no dispute but that the defaults existed as claimed, nor that complainants made no offer in the bill or on the hearing to pay any amount on account of the defaults. The only contention seems to be that they were unable to make the payments on account of lack of funds.

Complainants contend that defendants waived the time of payment of the installments because the payments were almost always made after they fell due and defendants from time to time accepted partial payments, therefore before defendants would be permitted to declare a forfeiture they must, under the law, give reasonable notice of their intention to insist upon the payments being made as they fell due. This states a correct principle of law but is inapplicable here because, we think, sufficient notice was given before an attempt was made to cancel and forfeit the contract. But in any event this would not require a reversal of the decree because complainants would not be entitled to the relief they prayed for unless they made an offer, either by their pleadings or on the hearing, to pay up the amounts then in default. In these circumstances, the premises; (7) that the order of court appointing Draper Kramer, Inc., as agents of the premises be vacated and set aside, and that such agents restore possession to defendant Anna L. Dunlap.

The record is confused, but it appears without dispute that on February 7, 1933, complainants were in default in the payment of a number of installments, aggregating $1010.81, that on account of such defaults defendant Anna L. Dunlap on February 23, 1933, served a notice on complainants that unless the payments in default were made within thirty days, steps would be taken to forfeit the contract for the purchase and sale of the premises. A number of other notices were served, including notice of forfeiture and demand for possession.

As stated, there is no dispute but that the defaults existed as claimed, nor that complainants made no offer in the bill or on the hearing to pay any amount on account of the defaults. The only contention seems to be that they were unable to make the payments on account of lack of funds.

Complainants contend that defendants waived the time of payment of the installments because the payments were almost always made after they fell due and defendants from time to time accepted partial payments, therefore before defendants would be permitted to declare a forfeiture they must, under the law, give reasonable notice of their intention to insist upon the payments being made as they fell due. This states a correct principle of law but is inapplicable here because, we think, sufficient notice was given before an attempt was made to cancel and forfeit the contract. And in any event this would not require a reversal of the decree because complainants would not be entitled to the relief they prayed [illegible] they make no offer, either by their pleadings or at the [illegible] in default." In which circumstances, obviously the decree dismissing the bill was the only decree that could be entered, and therefore it must be affirmed.

But the decree went much farther than to dismiss the bill. We have above set forth the various matters decreed by the Chancellor. In the absence of a cross bill the Chancellor was wholly unwarranted in finding, in substance, that substantially everything the defendants did in the matter was in accordance with the contract and the law. There was no warrant under the pleadings to decree the cancellation of the contract, that the moneys paid by the complainants to the defendants on account of the purchase price be retained by defendants as liquidated damages, that the defendants be given judgment against complainant George E. Scott for the $1010.81, being the aggregate amount of the defaults at the time the notice of forfeiture was given; nor was there any warrant to decree that the premises be immediately vacated by complainants, or any of the other matters above mentioned.

The decree of the Superior court of Cook county, insofar as it dismissed complainants' bill of complaint, is affirmed, in all other matters it is reversed.

Each party will be required to pay their own costs in this court.

DECREE AFFIRMED IN PART AND REVERSED IN PART.

McSurely and Matchett, JJ., concur.

37926

ROSLYN GIBSON,
Appellee,

vs.

ROBERT EARL GIBSON,
Appellant.

APPEAL FROM CIRCUIT COURT OF COOK COUNTY.

280 I.A. 615

MR. PRESIDING JUSTICE O'CONNOR DELIVERED THE OPINION OF THE COURT.

March 28, 1930, Roslyn Gibson was awarded a decree of divorce from the defendant, Robert Earl Gibson. The decree finds that defendant agreed "to pay to the complainant, on the first of each and every month until her death or re-marriage, the sum of Three Hundred Dollars ($300.00) per month for her support and maintenance, and the additional sum of One Hundred Dollars ($100.00) per month for the support and maintenance of said son, William , until his death or until he shall attain legal age."

March 2, 1933, complainant filed her petition in which it was alleged that the defendant was behind in the payments provided for in the decree and prayed that a rule be entered to show cause why he should not be adjudged in contempt. The contempt proceeding was abandoned and on April 17, 1933, and subsequent thereto, an amended and supplemental petition was filed praying that the court fix the amount the defendant was in arrears. June 16, 1933, defendant filed his petition for a reduction of alimony, that matter was abandoned. The court heard the evidence on the question of whether the defendant was in arrears.

Defendant contended he was not in arrears in the payment of alimony, and evidence on this question was introduced by both sides. The court found defendant was in arrears $2200 but allowed him a credit of $832 which he had paid for tuition and expenses in sending the son to Notre Dame University, leaving a balance of $1368; and it seems to be conceded that afterward the defendant paid $200

37956

EVELYN GIBSON,
Appellee,

vs.

ROBERT EARL GIBSON,
Appellant.

APPEAL FROM CIRCUIT COURT OF COOK COUNTY.

280 I.A. 615

MR. PRESIDING JUSTICE O'CONNOR
DELIVERED THE OPINION OF THE COURT.

March 28, 1930, Evelyn Gibson was awarded a decree of divorce from the defendant, Robert Earl Gibson. The decree finds that defendant agreed "to pay to the complainant, on the first of each and every month until her death or re-marriage, the sum of Three Hundred Dollars ($300.00) per month for her support and maintenance, and the additional sum of One Hundred Dollars ($100.00) per month for the support and maintenance of said son, William, until his death or until he shall attain legal age."

March 2, 1933, complainant filed her petition in which it was alleged that the defendant was behind in the payments provided for in the decree and prayed that a rule be entered to show cause why he should not be adjudged in contempt. The contempt proceeding was abandoned and on April 17, 1933, and subsequent thereto, an amended and supplemental petition was filed praying that the court fix the amount the defendant was in arrears. June 16, 1933, defendant filed his petition for a reduction of alimony; that matter was abandoned. The court heard the evidence on the question of whether the defendant was in arrears.

Defendant contended he was not in arrears in the payment of alimony, and evidence on this question was introduced by both sides. The court found defendant was in arrears $2800 but allowed him a credit of [illegible] which he had paid for tuition and expenses in sending the son to Notre Dame University, leaving a balance of [illegible]; and it seems to be conceded that afterward the defendant paid [illegible] alimony due the wife for her support, leaving $1168 still due. The court also allowed complainant $300 as and for her solicitor's fees and ordered that defendant pay $1468. There seems to be little or no dispute as to the amount of the payments made.

The defendant takes the position that the moneys he paid to complainant and expended on the son from the time of the divorce amounted to more than the $400 provided for in the decree. The evidence shows that for a period of two years after the entry of the decree March 28, 1930, defendant paid the $400 as required by the decree and in addition paid out considerable money in sending the son to camps and for other expenses. During this period of two years he made no claim that he should be given credit on the $400 monthly alimony for such additional expenditures. While the father is to be commended for what he did in this respect, we think such moneys ought not be charged against the mother. We think the Chancellor was correct in not giving credit for such expenditures. As stated above, the defendant was given credit for the $832 which he paid for sending the son to Notre Dame University, and some slight argument is made by counsel for complainant that the court erred in this respect, and therefore the amount found due by the Chancellor should be increased by $832. Upon a consideration of all the evidence in the record, we are of opinion that we would not be justified in disturbing the finding of the Chancellor in this respect.

Counsel for both sides in their respective briefs state a number of times that the decree of divorce was entered by consent. Obviously this is not the fact, as an examination of the record discloses. It is contrary to the law for a husband and wife to consent to a divorce, but the amount of alimony may be agreed upon by the parties. Smith v. Smith, 334 Ill. 370. In the instant case the amount of alimony and the times of payment were by agreement of the parties.

alimony due the wife for her support, leaving $1168 still due. The court also allowed complainant $300 as and for her solicitor's fees and ordered that defendant pay $1468. There seems to be little or no dispute as to the amount of the payments made.

The defendant takes the position that the moneys he paid to complainant and expended on the son from the time of the divorce amounted to more than the $400 provided for in the decree. The evidence shows that for a period of two years after the entry of the decree March 28, 1930, defendant paid the $400 as required by the decree and in addition paid out considerable money in sending the son to camps and for other expenses. During this period of two years he made no claim that he should be given credit on the $400 monthly alimony for such additional expenditures. While the father is to be commended for what he did in this respect, we think such moneys ought not be charged against the mother. We think the Chancellor was correct in not giving credit for such expenditures. As stated above, the defendant was given credit for the $888 which he paid for sending the son to Notre Dame University, and some slight argument is made by counsel for complainant that the court erred in this respect, and therefore the amount found due by the Chancellor should be increased by $888. Upon a consideration of all the evidence in the record, we are of opinion that we would not be justified in disturbing the finding of the Chancellor in this respect.

Counsel for both sides in their respective briefs state a number of times that the decree of divorce was entered by consent. Obviously this is not the fact, as an examination of the record discloses. It is contrary to the law for a husband and wife to consent to a divorce, but the amount of alimony may be agreed upon by the parties. Smith v. Smith, 334 Ill. 370. In the instant case the amount of alimony and the times of payment were by agreement of the parties. [illegible]

Defendant contends that he was entitled to credit for the moneys he had spent on the son because the $400 a month he was required to pay in accordance with the terms of the decree, was not all to be paid to the complainant. There is no merit in this contention. The finding of the decree is plain. By it the court found that the defendant was a man of means and that he had agreed "to pay to the complainant, on the first of each and every month *** ($300.00) per month for her support and maintenance, and the additional sum of One Hundred Dollars ($100.00) per month for the support and maintenance of said son."

A further point made by the defendant is that he was entitled to credit for such moneys which he paid out on behalf of the son because while the decree provided that the custody of the son should be given to the complainant, it further provided that "the care and education of said minor child, William, be and remain with the complainant, Roslyn Gibson, and the defendant, Robert Earl Gibson, jointly, until the further order of this Court." We think this provision does not in any way modify the prior provision of the decree requiring him to pay to complainant $400. This was the construction placed upon the decree by the parties for a period of two years immediately following the entry of the decree.

The judgment and decree of the Circuit court of Cook county is affirmed.

JUDGMENT AND DECREE AFFIRMED.

McSurely and Matchett, JJ., concur.

Defendant contends that he was entitled to credit for the moneys he had spent on the son because the $600 a month he was required to pay in accordance with the terms of the decree, was not all to be paid to the complainant. There is no merit in this contention. The finding of the decree is plain. By it the court found that the defendant was a man of means and that he had agreed "to pay to the complainant, on the first of each and every month *** ($500.00) per month for her support and maintenance, and the additional sum of One Hundred Dollars ($100.00) per month for the support and maintenance of said son."

A further point made by the defendant is that he was entitled to credit for such moneys which he paid out on behalf of the son because while the decree provided that the custody of the son should be given to the complainant, it further provided that "the care and education of said minor child, William, be and remain with the complainant, Roslyn Gibson, and the defendant, Robert Earl Gibson, jointly, until the further order of this Court." We think this provision does not in any way modify the prior provision of the decree requiring him to pay to complainant $400. This was the construction placed upon the decree by the parties for a period of two years immediately following the entry of the decree.

The judgment and decree of the Circuit court of Cook county is affirmed.

JUDGMENT AND DECREE AFFIRMED.

McSurely and Matchett, JJ., concur.

38049

MICHAEL BORNIAK,
Appellant,

vs.

CHICAGO AND WEST SUBURBAN TRANSIT COMPANY and CHICAGO, BURLINGTON & QUINCY RAILROAD COMPANY,
Appellees.

APPEAL FROM SUPERIOR COURT OF COOK COUNTY.

280 I.A. 616

MR. JUSTICE McSURELY DELIVERED THE OPINION OF THE COURT.

Plaintiff appeals from an adverse judgment entered on instructed verdicts as to both defendants in the trial of an action on the case wherein plaintiff sought to recover damages for personal injuries received.

The accident happened on the southern approach to a viaduct running north and south over the railroad tracks of the Burlington Railroad company on 52nd avenue in the town of Cicero, Illinois, on each side of the roadway of the viaduct is a narrow wooden sidewalk, four feet and four inches wide, for the use of pedestrians, there are two lines of street car tracks on the roadway between the sidewalks; from photographs in evidence, counting the approaches on the north and south side, the viaduct is very long. Apparently no witness testified as to its exact length.

About 11:30 p. m. January 29, 1931, plaintiff with Mr. Joseph Habel was walking on the easterly sidewalk, going south on the southerly approach of the viaduct; plaintiff was walking on the outer edge of the sidewalk, Habel at his left; when, according to plaintiff, they were about 100 feet south of the bridge proper, he collided with a northbound street car owned and operated by the Chicago and West Suburban Transit Company, receiving the injuries for which he seeks damages.

In his declaration plaintiff alleged that the railroad company negligently constructed and maintained the approach and sidewalk in such close proximity to the easterly street car rail that

38049

MICHAEL BORNIAK,
Appellant,

vs.

CHICAGO AND WEST SUBURBAN TRANSIT COMPANY and CHICAGO, BURLINGTON & QUINCY RAILROAD COMPANY,
Appellees.

APPEAL FROM SUPERIOR COURT OF COOK COUNTY.

280 I.A. 616

MR. JUSTICE McSURELY DELIVERED THE OPINION OF THE COURT.

Plaintiff appeals from an adverse judgment entered on instructed verdicts as to both defendants in the trial of an action on the case wherein plaintiff sought to recover damages for personal injuries received.

The accident happened on the southern approach to a viaduct running north and south over the railroad tracks of the Burlington Railroad company on 52nd avenue in the town of Cicero, Illinois; on each side of the roadway of the viaduct is a narrow wooden sidewalk, four feet and four inches wide, for the use of pedestrians; there are two lines of street car tracks on the roadway between the sidewalks. From photographs in evidence, counting the approaches on the north and south side, the viaduct is very long. Apparently no witness testified as to its exact length.

About 11:30 p. m. January 29, 1931, plaintiff with Mr. Joseph Habel was walking on the easterly sidewalk, going south on the southerly approach of the viaduct, plaintiff was walking on the outer edge of the sidewalk, Habel at his left; when, according to plaintiff, they were about 100 feet south of the bridge proper, he collided with a northbound street car owned and operated by the Chicago and West Suburban Transit Company, receiving the injuries for which he seeks damages.

In his declaration plaintiff alleged that the railroad company negligently constructed and maintained the approach and sidewalk in such close proximity to the easterly street car rail that the street car overhung the edge of the sidewalk creating a condition dangerous for pedestrians on the sidewalk, that the street car company should have known of this condition but so carelessly operated its street car that it ran upon plaintiff, seriously injuring him.

The evidence on behalf of plaintiff tends to show that the east rail was 24½ inches from the sidewalk, it was two feet from the gauge of the rail to the outside of the car, which would leave one-half inch for clearance between the side of the car and the edge of the sidewalk. Plaintiff argues that these were measurements at a certain point in the tracks which were bowed or bent toward the sidewalk; but it was established by the evidence that this bow or bend in the track was not at the point where plaintiff was struck, so that, at the point of the accident, there was a clearance between the side of the car and the edge of the sidewalk of 2½ inches.

Defendant Burlington Railroad company argues that the evidence fails to shew any breach of any duty on its part which caused the accident in question. Plaintiff invokes certain provisions of an ordinance which provides that the Burlington Railroad company shall maintain the viaduct, to which the Railroad company replies that in many cases it has been held that ordinances of this character are void since the passage of the Public Utilities act. Village of Atwood v. C. I. & W. R. R. Co., 316 Ill. 425; Northern Trust Co. v. Chicago Rys. Co., 318 Ill. 402, City of Chicago v. Commerce Com., 356 Ill. 501.

Moreover, the provisions of the alleged ordinance do not cast any duty on the railroad company with reference to street car tracks over the viaduct. It gives to the railroad company no control over the laying of such tracks nor any right to direct where they shall be laid or to interfere with them in any manner after they have been laid.

the street car overhung the edge of the sidewalk creating a condition dangerous for pedestrians on the sidewalk; that the street car company should have known of this condition but so carelessly operated its street car that it ran upon plaintiff, seriously injuring him.

The evidence on behalf of plaintiff tends to show that the east rail was 24½ inches from the sidewalk; it was two feet from the gauge of the rail to the outside of the car, which would leave one-half inch for clearance between the side of the car and the edge of the sidewalk. Plaintiff argues that these were measurements at a certain point in the tracks which were bowed or bent toward the sidewalk; but it was established by the evidence that this bow or bend in the track was not at the point where plaintiff was struck, so that, at the point of the accident, there was a clearance between the side of the car and the edge of the sidewalk of 2½ inches.

Defendant Burlington Railroad company argues that the evidence fails to show any breach of any duty on its part which caused the accident in question. Plaintiff invokes certain provisions of an ordinance which provides that the Burlington Railroad company shall maintain the viaduct, to which the Railroad company replies that in many cases it has been held that ordinances of this character are void since the passage of the Public Utilities act. Village of Atwood v. C. I. & W. R. R. Co., 316 Ill. 425; Northern Trust Co. v. Chicago Rys. Co., 318 Ill. 402; City of Chicago v. Commerce Com., 356 Ill. 501.

Moreover, the provisions of the alleged ordinance do not cast any duty on the railroad company with reference to street car tracks over the viaduct. It gives to the railroad company no control over the laying of such tracks nor any right to direct where they shall be laid or to interfere with them in any manner after they have been laid.

The street car company also says that there is no evidence that the tracks were improperly constructed or maintained, that from all that appears in the record they were laid and maintained pursuant to authorization of the proper authorities and in full compliance with all laws or ordinances regulating the operation of the street railway. As we have said, the evidence places the point of accident as some distance - about 42 feet - from the alleged bend in the tracks. Moreover, there is no competent evidence that any such bend existed at the time of the accident, which occurred in January, 1931, as the photographs introduced in evidence were taken in September, 1934.

We are of the opinion that the evidence fails to prove that the accident was occasioned by the negligence of the defendants, or either of them. Even if the negligence of defendants might be a close question, we think that the plaintiff was guilty of contributory negligence as a matter of law.

On the night in question plaintiff and Habel had walked the entire length of the viaduct, a distance equal to three or four city blocks, plaintiff was all this time walking alongside the street car track; he said he knew the sidewalk was narrow, and he must have known that the distance between it and the street car track was slight; he said he was talking to Mr. Habel all the time and was not paying any attention as to whether a street car might be coming along or not, he says that he first saw the street car when it was about six feet from him as he was walking on the sidewalk about two or three inches from the edge; there were electric lights along the south approach of the viaduct, and the street car was lighted. Habel testified that after the car passed him he saw it 100 feet away, although there was some smoke which he says obstructed his vision.

If, as plaintiff says, he was walking two or three inches from the edge of the sidewalk, his shoulder and arm must have pro-

The street car company also says that there is no evidence that the tracks were improperly constructed or maintained; that from all that appears in the record they were laid and maintained pursuant to authorization of the proper authorities and in full compliance with all laws or ordinances regulating the operation of the street railway. As we have said, the evidence places the point of accident as some distance - about 48 feet - from the alleged bend in the tracks. Moreover, there is no competent evidence that any such bend existed at the time of the accident, which occurred in January, 1931, as the photographs introduced in evidence were taken in September, 1934.

We are of the opinion that the evidence fails to prove that the accident was occasioned by the negligence of the defendants, or either of them. Even if the negligence of defendants might be a close question, we think that the plaintiff was guilty of contributory negligence as a matter of law.

On the night in question plaintiff and Nebel had walked the entire length of the viaduct, a distance equal to three or four city blocks; plaintiff was all this time walking alongside the street car track; he said he knew the sidewalk was narrow, and he must have known that the distance between it and the street car track was slight; he said he was talking to Mr. Nebel all the time and was not paying any attention as to whether a street car might be coming along or not; he says that he first saw the street car when it was about six feet from him as he was walking on the sidewalk about two or three inches from the edge; there were electric lights along the south approach of the viaduct, and the street car was lighted. Nebel testified that after the car passed him he saw it 100 feet away, although there was some smoke which he says obstructed his vision.

If, as plaintiff says, he was walking two or three inches from the edge of the sidewalk, his shoulder and arm must have pro-truded over the edge. As he was facing the street car, which was approaching on a track close to the sidewalk, prudence would have suggested that he step back so as to avoid being struck His failure to do so, on the ground that he was not paying any attention to the street car, was clearly negligence on his part

There have been many decisions in other jurisdictions involving the overhang of a street car as it rounds a curve. In Matulewicz v. Metropolitan St. Ry. Co., 95 N. Y. S. 7, it was held that plaintiff was guilty of contributory negligence as a matter of law in not stepping back to avoid the overhang of a car as it rounded a curve. In Garvey v. Rhode Island Company, 26 R. I. 80, the court said: "* for one to place himself within reach of the swing or overhang of a car while it is in motion is as much a bar to his recovery in an action against the company as though he had negligently placed himself in front of a moving car and been injured thereby." Other cases are Hering v. City of Detroit, 244 Mich. 293, and Hayden v. Fair Haven & W. R. Co., 76 Conn. 355. In this last case plaintiff was standing about twelve inches from the edge of the sidewalk when he was struck by the running-board of a street car. In Weir v. Railways Co., 108 Kans. 610, it was held that even if the plaintiff did not understand the extent of the overhang of a street car but could see the nearness of the track to the sidewalk curb and took a position so close to it as to be struck and injured, it would be conceded that the injury was the result of her own negligence. See also Beach v. Pacific Northwest Traction Co., 135 Wash. 290.

Plaintiff cites Pell v. J. P. & A. R. R. Co., 238 Ill. 510 There a passenger was sitting on a seat facing the center of the car, with his arm and hand extending outside of the car through an open window, where his hand was caught and injured by a passing car, of the close proximity of which he had no notice or warning. In the truded over the edge. As he was facing the street car, which was approaching on a track close to the sidewalk, prudence would have suggested that he step back so as to avoid being struck. His failure to do so, on the ground that he was not paying any attention to the street car, was clearly negligence on his part.

There have been many decisions in other jurisdictions involving the overhang of a street car as it rounds a curve. In Samuelson v. Metropolitan St. Ry. Co., 95 N. Y. S. 7, it was held that plaintiff was guilty of contributory negligence as a matter of law in not stepping back to avoid the overhang of a car as it rounded a curve. In Garvey v. Rhode Island Comp'y, 26 R. I. 80, the court said: "* For one to place himself within reach of the swing or overhang of a car while it is in motion is as much a bar to his recovery in an action against the company as though he had negligently placed himself in front of a moving car and been injured thereby." Other cases are Herring v. City of Detroit, 244 Mich. 297, and Loyden v. Fair Haven & W. R. Co., 76 Conn. 355. In this last case plaintiff was standing about twelve inches from the edge of the sidewalk when he was struck by the running-board of a street car. In Welz v. Railways Co., 108 Kans. 610, it was held that even if the plaintiff did not understand the extent of the overhang of a street car but could see the nearness of the track to the sidewalk curb and took a position so close to it as to be struck and injured, it would be conceded that the injury was the result of her own negligence. See also Beach v. Pacific Northwest Traction Co., 135 Wash. 290.

Plaintiff cites Pell v. J. P. & A. R. R. Co., 238 Ill. 510, where a passenger was sitting on a seat facing the center of the car, with his arm and hand extending outside of the car through an open window, where his hand was caught and injured by a passing car, of the close proximity of which he had no notice or warning. In the instant case the plaintiff knew of the proximity of the street car tracks to the sidewalk and had ample opportunity to observe the approach of the street car. He testified that he could have seen it if he had looked. In C. M. & St. P. Ry. Co. v. Halsey, 133 Ill. 248, it was held that one who fails to observe due care but walks blindly into danger is guilty of contributory negligence, and that "If he shall permit himself to become absorbed in thought about other matters, and, in consequence, oblivious of his present surroundings, he will do so at his peril."

The abstract furnished by the plaintiff is properly criticized. It is in many respects insufficient. But we prefer to place our conclusion upon the reasons above stated.

We hold that plaintiff failed to prove that the defendants or either of them were guilty of the negligence which caused the accident to plaintiff, and also that plaintiff was guilty of contributory negligence as a matter of law.

The instructions directing a verdict for the defendants were properly given, and the judgment is affirmed.

AFFIRMED.

O'Connor, P. J., and Matchett, J., concur.

instant case the plaintiff knew of the proximity of the street car tracks to the sidewalk and had ample opportunity to observe the approach of the street car. He testified that he could have seen it if he had looked. In C. M. & St. P. Ry. Co. v. Halsey, 133 Ill. 248, it was held that one who fails to observe due care but walks blindly into danger is guilty of contributory negligence, and that "if he shall permit himself to become absorbed in thought about other matters, and, in consequence, oblivious of his present surroundings, he will do so at his peril."

The abstract furnished by the plaintiff is properly criticized. It is in many respects insufficient. But we prefer to place our conclusion upon the reasons above stated.

We hold that plaintiff failed to prove that the defendants or either of them were guilty of the negligence which caused the injury to plaintiff, and also that plaintiff was guilty of contributory negligence as a matter of law.

The instructions directing a verdict for the defendants were properly given, and the judgment is affirmed.

AFFIRMED.

O'Connor, P. J., and Matchett, J., concur.

37907

PEOPLE OF THE STATE OF ILLINOIS,
Defendant in Error,

vs.

LOUIS W. GRUBER,
Plaintiff in Error.

ERROR TO CRIMINAL COURT OF COOK COUNTY.

4/8

280 I.A. 616[2]

MR. JUSTICE MATCHETT DELIVERED THE OPINION OF THE COURT.

Defendant has sued out this writ of error to reverse a judgment of the Criminal court entered upon the verdict of the court finding him guilty on a charge of obtaining signatures to written instruments by means of false pretenses. The indictment contained fifteen counts, and defendant was adjudged guilty upon all of them. On the first seven counts he was sentenced to pay a fine of $10 and to serve one year of imprisonment in the House of Correction, the punishment on the last six counts to run concurrently with that of the first count. On counts eight to fifteen he was sentenced to one year imprisonment and ordered to pay a fine of $10 and costs, the punishment under counts nine to fifteen to run concurrently with that under the eighth count and the punishment under count eight to begin after the expiration of the sentence on count one. In addition to the fines, therefore, defendant was sentenced to two years imprisonment.

The first count of the indictment in substance charges defendant Gruber, also known as "Schrader," pretended to the Great Atlantic & Pacific Tea Co. and to its agent, one Hall, that the Shellmar Products Co. had a subsidiary company named the Monarch Specialties Company, and that it was the custom of the Shellmar Products Company to have its products invoiced and collections made through this subsidiary; that defendant pretended that the selling price of 99,260 doughnut wrappers sold to the Tea Co. and manufactured and printed by the Products Co. was $8.92 per thousand; that an invoice of these doughnut wrappers stating the sale of same

1

37907

PEOPLE OF THE STATE OF ILLINOIS,
Defendant in Error,

vs.

LOUIS W. GRUBER,
Plaintiff in Error.

ERROR TO CRIMINAL COURT OF COOK COUNTY.

280 I.A. 616

MR. JUSTICE MATCHETT DELIVERED THE OPINION OF THE COURT.

Defendant has sued out this writ of error to reverse a judgment of the Criminal court entered upon the verdict of the court finding him guilty on a charge of obtaining signatures to written instruments by means of false pretenses. The indictment contained fifteen counts, and defendant was adjudged guilty upon all of them. On the first seven counts he was sentenced to pay a fine of $10 and to serve one year of imprisonment in the House of Correction, the punishment on the last six counts to run concurrently with that of the first count. On counts eight to fifteen he was sentenced to one year imprisonment and ordered to pay a fine of $10 and costs, the punishment under counts nine to fifteen to run concurrently with that under the eighth count and the punishment under count eight to begin after the expiration of the sentence on count one. In addition to the fines, therefore, defendant was sentenced to two years imprisonment.

The first count of the indictment in substance charges defendant Gruber, also known as "Schrader," pretended to the Great Atlantic & Pacific Tea Co. and to its agent, one Hall, that the Shellmar Products Co. had a subsidiary company named the Monarch Specialties Company, and that it was the custom of the Shellmar Products Company to have its products invoiced and collections made through this subsidiary; that defendant pretended that the selling price of 97,260 doughnut wrappers sold to the Tea Co. and manufactured and printed by the Products Co. was $8.92 per thousand; that an invoice of these doughnut wrappers stating the sale of same by the Monarch Specialties Co. had been made by it as a subsidiary by the Products Co., whereas defendant well knew that the Shellmar Co. had no subsidiary company named Monarch Specialties Co., and that the Monarch Specialties Co. was in fact a name used by defendant under which he transacted business, that defendant knew it was not the practice or custom of the Shellmar Products Co. to have any of its products invoiced or collected for by this alleged subsidiary company, knew that the price of the doughnut wrappers was not $8.92 per thousand but $5.98 per thousand, knew that the invoice was not made by the Specialties Co., but was made by him (defendant) under that name; that defendant knew that these representations were false and were made by him with the design of inducing the Atlantic & Pacific Tea Co., its agents, and its agent, one Hall, to execute a check for $1149.72 and to have the Tea Co., its agents, and one Hall, its agent, deliver the check to defendant after it was signed; that the Tea Co. and Hall, relying on these false pretenses, signed and delivered the check to defendant, and that defendant, with intent to cheat and defraud the Tea Co. out of $303.69, fraudulently and unlawfully obtained the signature of Hall to the written instrument.

The remaining counts were identical except that they described similar offenses on different dates with reference to different purchases, and amounts.

Defendant did not testify at the trial. The only evidence offered in his behalf was that of two character witnesses. There is practically no conflict in the evidence. In 1925 defendant was employed by the Great Atlantic & Pacific Tea Co., which is a large corporation organized in New Jersey in 1869 and which transacts a general business in foods throughout the United States. For convenience in the transaction of its business it has separated the territory into six divisions, the middle western division including Illinois, Iowa, Wisconsin, Minnesota, and parts of Michigan, Indiana, Oklahoma and by the Monarch Specialties Co. had been made by it as a subsidiary by the Products Co., whereas defendant well knew that the Sheilmar Co. had no subsidiary company named Monarch Specialties Co., and that the Monarch Specialties Co. was in fact a name used by defendant under which he transacted business, that defendant knew it was not the practice or custom of the Sheilmar Products Co. to have any of its products invoiced or collected for by this alleged subsidiary company, knew that the price of the doughnut wrappers was not $8.92 per thousand but $5.08 per thousand, knew that the invoice was not made by the Specialties Co., but was made by him (defendant) under that name; that defendant knew that these representations were false and were made by him with the design of inducing the Atlantic & Pacific Tea Co., its agents, and its agent, one Hall, to execute a check for $1149.72 and to have the Tea Co., its agents, and one Hall, its agent, deliver the check to defendant after it was signed; that the Tea Co. and Hall, relying on these false pretenses, signed and delivered the check to defendant, and that defendant, with intent to cheat and defraud the Tea Co. out of $303.69, fraudulently and unlawfully obtained the signature of Hall to the written instrument.

The remaining counts were identical except that they described similar offenses on different dates with reference to different purchases, and amounts.

Defendant did not testify at the trial. The only evidence offered in his behalf was that of two character witnesses. There is practically no conflict in the evidence. In 1928 defendant was employed by the Great Atlantic & Pacific Tea Co., which is a large corporation organized in New Jersey in 1859 and which transacts a general business in foods throughout the United States. For convenience in the transaction of its business it has separated the territory into six divisions, the middle western division including Illinois, Iowa, Wisconsin, Minnesota, and parts of Michigan, Indiana, Oklahoma and

Kansas. The headquarters of this division were in Chicago, where it operated about 800 stores. The Tea Co. also operated warehouses, bakeries and a produce department.

Defendant began his service as a clerk in the order department. He was promoted from time to time until he became assistant purchasing agent. In 1929 he worked under one Holmes, who in turn was under a Mr. Hecht, divisional purchasing agent. This department was known as the supply buying department and purchased for the corporation all commodities which were not intended to be resold. Defendant received a salary of $75 a week, and he continued to work for the Tea Co. as assistant purchasing agent until August, 1933, when he tendered his resignation without stating his reason for doing so.

The Shellmar Products Co. was a printer of cellophane, which was printed in different colors. Mr. Huse, a salesman for the Shellmar Co., went into the offices of the A. & P. to solicit business and through defendant obtained an order for cellophane on October 9, 19[illegible]. Defendant at first gave instructions to ship the cellophane to the A. & P. Co., but before the order was shipped he instructed Huse to bill the material to the Monarch Specialties Co. at 1145 Bryn Mawr and to ship it to the A. & P. Co. Defendant told Mr. Huse that the Monarch Specialties Co. was a packaging department created to handle sliced bacon. Later defendant instructed Mr. Huse to bill the cellophane to the Monarch Specialties Co, at 668 Oakdale avenue, Chicago. Large orders were thereafter given by the A. & P. Co. to the Shellmar Products Co. through defendant. It was customary for him to order a million doughnut or bacon wrappers and direct that they be shipped in one or two hundred thousand lots as needed. By his direction all these goods were billed to the Monarch Specialties Co., and not to the A. & P. Co. By buying in large lots a lower price for the goods was obtained. Defendant and Huse also agreed that as the price of

Kansas. The headquarters of this division were in Chicago, where it operated about 600 stores. The Tea Co. also operated warehouses, bakeries and a produce department.

Defendant began his service as a clerk in the order department. He was promoted from time to time until he became assistant purchasing agent. In 1929 he worked under one Holmes, who in turn was under a Mr. Hecht, divisional purchasing agent. This department was known as the supply buying department and purchased for the corporation all commodities which were not intended to be resold. Defendant received a salary of $75 a week, and he continued to work for the Tea Co. as assistant purchasing agent until August, 1933, when he tendered his resignation without stating his reason for doing so.

The Shellmar Products Co. was a printer of cellophane, which was printed in different colors. Mr. Huse, a salesman for the Shellmar Co., went into the offices of the A. & P. to solicit business and through defendant obtained an order for cellophane on October 9, 1929. Defendant at first gave instructions to ship the cellophane to the A. & P. Co., but before the order was shipped he instructed Huse to bill the material to the Monarch Specialties Co. at 1148 Bryn Mawr and to ship it to the A. & P. Co. Defendant told Mr. Huse that the Monarch Specialties Co. was a packaging department created to handle sliced bacon. Later defendant instructed Mr. Huse to bill the cellophane to the Monarch Specialties Co. at 666 Oakdale avenue, Chicago. Large orders were thereafter given by the A. & P. Co. to the Shellmar Products Co. through defendant. It was customary for him to order a million doughnut or bacon wrappers and direct that they be shipped in one or two hundred thousand lots as needed. By his direction all these goods were billed to the Monarch Specialties Co., and not to the A. & P. Co. By buying in large lots a lower price for the goods was obtained. Defendant and Huse also agreed that as the price of cellophane decreased its sale price would be decreased proportionately, and in this way on numerous occasions the cellophane was billed to the Monarch Specialties Co. at a lower price than the order specified. The Shellmar Co. gave a discount of two per cent if the bills were paid within ten days. The Monarch Specialties Co. took advantage of this discount, as well as occasional decreases in prices, but the Monarch Specialties Co. always charged the A. & P. Co. without reference to such decrease in costs and without allowing the two per cent discount for cash. The orders from defendant to Huse were given orally. Huse did not at any time get a written order from defendant. The Shellmar Products Co. sent out invoices describing the goods. These invoices were paid by the Monarch Specialties Co. by check and all of them discounted within the ten day period. The checks were not signed by the A. & P. Co. but were signed "Monarch Specialties Co." in handwriting.

It was stipulated on the trial that the Shellmar Products Co. received payments on the various invoices from the Monarch Specialties Co.

The State also showed by the testimony of a Dr. Butler, a dentist who had offices at 1145 Bryn Mawr, Chicago, that the Monarch Specialties Co. was located at that address when he came into the building in 1930. A man whom he knew as Mr. Schrader occupied the Monarch Specialties Co. office. He identified this Mr. Schrader as defendant, said that he usually saw him around 9:15 in the evening, and that mail marked "A. & P. Co." for the Monarch Specialties Co. was placed on the table in his reception room. After "Mr.Schrader" moved from the building, the witness saw two letters marked with the forwarding address, 668 Oakdale ave.

Gladys West, a nurse employed by a doctor with offices at 1145 Bryn Mawr, testified that she knew defendant as "Mr. Schrader" and saw him in the offices of the Monarch Specialities Co. She sorted cellophane decreased its sale price would be decreased proportionately, and in this way on numerous occasions the cellophane was billed to the Monarch Specialties Co. at a lower price than the order specified. The Shellmar Co. gave a discount of two per cent if the bills were paid within ten days. The Monarch Specialties Co. took advantage of this discount, as well as occasional decreases in prices, but the Monarch Specialties Co. always charged the A. & P. Co. without reference to such decreases in costs and without allowing the two per cent discount for cash. The orders from defendant to Muse were given orally. Muse did not at any time get a written order from defendant. The Shellmar Products Co. sent its invoices describing the goods. These invoices were paid by the Monarch Specialties Co. by check and all of them discounted within the ten day period. The checks were not signed by the A. & P. Co. but were signed "Monarch Specialties Co." in handwriting.

It was stipulated on the trial that the Shellmar Products Co. received payments on the various invoices from the Monarch Specialties Co.

"The State also showed by the testimony of a Dr. Butler, a dentist who had offices at 1145 Bryn Mawr, Chicago, that the Monarch Specialties Co. was located at that address when he came into the building in 1930. A man whom he knew as Mr. Schroeder occupied the Monarch Specialties Co. office. He identified this Mr. Schroeder as defendant, said that he usually saw him around 9:15 in the evening, and that mail marked "A. & P. Co." for the Monarch Specialties Co. was placed on the table in his reception room. After "Mr. Schroeder" moved from the building, the witness saw two letters marked with the forwarding address, 880 Oakdale ave."

Gladys West, a nurse employed by a doctor with offices at 1145 Bryn Mawr, testified that she knew defendant as "Mr. Schroeder" and saw him in the offices of the Monarch Specialties Co. She sorted the mail and took it to the various offices in the building and delivered the mail for the Specialties Co. She later received an order to forward the mail to Dr. French's office at 668 Oakdale avenue.

Dr. French, whose offices were at 668 Oakdale avenue, testified that he formerly had his office at 1145 Bryn Mawr, that while located there he met a man by the name of Schafer, who had an office in the building; that when the Doctor moved to 668 Oakdale avenue a man came to him and wanted to know if he had desk room to rent, paid him $10 a month to receive his mail, explained that as he was a traveling salesman and was gone for long periods of time he did not want the expense of maintaining a hotel mailing address, that the man told him (Dr. French) that his name was Al Schafer. Dr. French further testified that defendant was not the man who introduced himself as "Al Schafer." This witness was shown a receiving ticket from the Shellmar Products Co. bearing his signature and said he did not remember the occasion when he signed it.

Three witnesses, employees of the Lake View Trust & Savings Bank, testified that defendant introduced himself at their bank as "L. S. Schrader" and opened an account in the name of the Monarch Specialties Co. on September 27, 1930, that he closed it October 16, 1930, reopened it October 17, 1930, and again closed it September 21, 1933. A signature card which bore the name of L. S. Schrader and the addresses 1145 Bryn Mawr and 668 Oakdale, was prepared and kept on file in connection with the Monarch Specialties Co. Defendant, these witnesses said, often came to the bank and would tell the proper officer of the bank beforehand if he was about to withdraw a check of any considerable amount. Defendant under the name of the Monarch Specialties Co. obtained checks from the Great Atlantic & Pacific Tea Co. in payment of these swollen accounts.

It was stipulated on the trial that fifteen checks made out to the Monarch Specialties Co. by the A. & P. Co. were deposited in the mail and took it to the various offices in the building and delivered the mail for the Specialties Co. She later received an order to forward the mail to Dr. French's office at 668 Oakdale avenue.

Dr. French, whose offices were at 665 Oakdale avenue, testified that he formerly had his office at 1145 Bryn Mawr, that while located there he met a man by the name of Schafer, who had an office in the building, that when the Doctor moved to 668 Oakdale avenue a man came to him and wanted to know if he had desk room to rent, paid him $10 a month to receive his mail, explained that as he was a traveling salesman and was gone for long periods of time he did not want the expense of maintaining a hotel mailing address; that the man told him (Dr. French) that his name was Al Schafer. Dr. French further testified that defendant was not the man who introduced himself as "Al Schafer." This witness was shown a receiving ticket from the Chelimar Products Co. bearing his signature and said he did not remember the occasion when he signed it.

Three witnesses, employees of the Lake View Trust & Savings Bank, testified that defendant introduced himself at their bank as "L. S. Schrader" and opened an account in the name of the Monarch Specialties Co. on September 27, 1930, that he closed it October 16, 1930, reopened it October 17, 1930, and again closed it September 21, 1933. A signature card which bore the name of L. S. Schrader and the addresses 1145 Bryn Mawr and 668 Oakdale, was prepared and kept on file in connection with the Monarch Specialties Co. Defendant, these witnesses said, often came to the bank and would tell the proper officer of the bank beforehand if he was about to withdraw a check of any considerable amount. Defendant under the name of the Monarch Specialties Co. obtained checks from the Great Atlantic & Pacific Tea Co. in payment of these swollen accounts.

It was stipulated on the trial that fifteen checks made out to the Monarch Specialties Co. by the A. & P. Co. were deposited in the Lake View Trust & Savings Bank and that the Monarch Specialties Co. account was debited for the fifteen accounts paid by the Specialties Co. to the Shellmar Products Co. as stated in the indictment.

An employee in the real estate office of James B. Waller testified to the execution of a lease renting an office at 1145 Bryn Mawr avenue to L. S. Schrader for the Monarch Specialties Co. in April, 1929.

Many witnesses described the manner in which the financial auditing department and the purchasing department of the Tea Co. were handled. Checks after passing through the financial department in the usual way were signed by Philetus D. Hall, who had been employed by the A. & P. Co. for 53 years. He executed all the checks covering the amounts in the invoices of the Monarch Specialties Co. It was his custom to sign these checks when the invoices accompanying the checks bore certain signatures which meant the checks were O. K. for payment. It was stipulated that the fifteen checks signed by Mr. Hall paid the various invoices of the Monarch Specialties Co. which were offered and received in evidence.

Defendant earnestly contends that the indictment should have been quashed for indefiniteness and uncertainty. The record discloses a written motion to quash the indictment on the ground the grand jury was unlawfully drawn, followed by an oral motion to quash for other reasons which are carefully paragraphed but which do not shew that indefiniteness and uncertainty of the indictment was urged. Not having raised the point then, defendant is not in a position to successfully urge it now. People v. Fox, 346 Ill. 374. However, we think the contention is without merit. It is suggested that the indictment was subject to objection in this respect, in that the instruments upon which it is based are not sufficiently described nor by proper averment connected with the specific false the Lake View Trust & Savings Bank and that the Monarch Specialties Co. account was debited for the fifteen accounts paid by the Specialties Co. to the Shallmar Products Co. as stated in the indictment.

An employee in the real estate office of James R. Waller testified to the execution of a lease renting an office at 1148 [illegible] avenue to L. S. Schroeder for the Monarch Specialties Co. in April, 1930.

Many witnesses described the manner in which the financial auditing department and the purchasing department of the Tea Co. were handled. Checks after passing through the financial department in the usual way were signed by Philetus D. Hall, who had been employed by the A. & P. Co. for 53 years. He executed all the checks covering the amounts in the invoices of the Monarch Specialties Co. It was his custom to sign these checks when the invoices accompanying the checks bore certain signatures which meant the checks were O. K. for payment. It was stipulated that the fifteen checks signed by Mr. Hall paid the various invoices of the Monarch Specialties Co. which were offered and received in evidence.

Defendant earnestly contends that the indictment should have been quashed for indefiniteness and uncertainty. The record discloses a written motion to quash the indictment on the ground the grand jury was unlawfully drawn, followed by an oral motion to quash for other reasons which are carefully paragraphed but which do not show that indefiniteness and uncertainty of the indictment was urged. Not having raised the point then, defendant is not in a position to successfully urge it now. People v. Fox, 346 Ill. 374. Moreover, we think the contention is without merit. It is suggested that the indictment was subject to objection in this respect, in that the instruments upon which it is based are not sufficiently identified nor is proper ownership averred with the specificity which pretenses used to obtain the checks, and that the dates of the particular checks are not given nor set out in full. Defendant says it was necessary to set out the specific instruments either *verbatim* or in substance. The different counts of the indictment described the instruments as to the drawer, drawee, payee and amount. While the respective dates of the same are not mentioned, the indictment does aver the date of the offence which bears closely upon the date of the instruments. This was sufficient. See 25 Corpus Juris 633 and cases there cited. The mere fact that these dates were not stated would not preclude defendant from pleading *autre-fois convict* or *autre-fois acquit* to a subsequent indictment for these same offenses.

It is also urged that the indictment did not show with clearness whether the Monarch Specialties Co. was or was not a subsisting company in fact and in law. There is an averment that this was the name under which defendant did business. This was sufficient in that respect.

It is urged that the indictment is defective in that it is formed on the theory that the obtaining of the signature to each check as set forth in the different counts of the indictment was a separate offense. While in general the acts of defendant as averred showed a similarity of purpose and method, these acts took place at distinct and different times and covered transactions in which distinct and different instruments were obtained and different sums and amounts of money by means of these acts were appropriated to defendant's own use. We think the indictment was not defective, in that it was framed upon the theory that each one of these separate transactions constituted a distinct offense. *People v. Allen*, 352 Ill. 262.

It is also urged that the false representations were not calculated to deceive and accomplish the purpose sought because too pretenses used to obtain the checks, and that the dates of the particular checks are not given nor set out in full. Defendant says it was necessary to set out the specific instruments either verbatim or in substance. The different counts of the indictment described the instruments as to the drawer, drawee, payee and amount. While the respective dates of the same are not mentioned, the indictment does aver the date of the offense which bears closely upon the date of the instruments. This was sufficient. See 26 Corpus Juris 655 and cases there cited. The mere fact that these dates were not stated would not preclude defendant from pleading autrefois convict or autrefois acquit in a subsequent indictment for these same offenses.

It is also urged that the indictment did not show with clearness whether the Research Specialties Co. was or was not a subsisting company in fact and in law. There is no averment that this was the name under which defendant did business. This was sufficient in that respect.

It is urged that the indictment is defective in that it is framed on the theory that the obtaining of the signature to each check as set forth in the different counts of the indictment was a separate offense. While in general the acts of defendant as averred showed a similarity of purpose and method, these acts took place at different and different times and covered transactions in which distinct and different instruments were obtained and different sums and amounts of money by means of these acts were appropriated to defendant's own use. We think the indictment was not defective, in that it was framed upon the theory that each one of these separate transactions constituted a distinct offense. People v. Allen, [illegible] Ill. 362.

It is also urged that the false representations were not [illegible] remote from the offense of obtaining the signatures to the checks. This point requires little attention. Certain oral and written words amounting to representations by defendant were in point of time somewhat remote, but words are not the only means whereby false representations may be conveyed. Actions are just as deceptive - sometimes more so. Indeed, silence may under some circumstances amount to a criminal act, if followed by wrongful appropriation. Jones v. State, 97 Ga. 430. The real point is not the remoteness of the time in which the representations were made but the causal connection between such representations and the obtaining of the property by means of them. We shall not undertake to review the many cases cited by defendant, most of which are from other jurisdictions.

It is further urged that no offense was committed because the Tea Co. made an independent investigation before executing the checks said to have been obtained by false pretenses. Defendant cites People v. Blume, 345 Ill. 524. There is no doubt it is a necessary element of this crime that the person defrauded should have relied on the false representations, but this contention is not based on facts. The Tea Co. made no investigation of defendant's dummy company which was used by him in the perpetration of fraud. In that particular the victim relied, as it had a right to do, upon the supposed honesty of its employee.

Defendant cites People v. Dinenza, 356 Ill. 118, to the point that when the evidence as a whole does not establish guilt beyond a reasonable doubt, the judgment should be reversed. That is the law. We do not entertain any reasonable doubt on this record.

Defendant also contends that there was a substantial variance between the allegation of the indictment and the proofs, in that the indictment alleged that the Monarch Specialties Co. was a subsidiary of the Shellmar Products Co., while the proofs tended remote from the offense of obtaining the signatures to the checks. This point requires little attention. Certain oral and written words amounting to representations by defendant were in point of time somewhat remote, but words are not the only means whereby false representations may be conveyed. Actions are just as deceptive - sometimes more so. Indeed, silence may under some circumstances amount to a criminal act, if followed by wrongful appropriation. Jones v. State, 97 Ga. 430. The real point is not the remoteness of the time in which the representations were made but the causal connection between such representations and the obtaining of the property by means of them. We shall not undertake to review the many cases cited by defendant, most of which are from other jurisdictions.

It is further urged that no offense was committed because the Tea Co. made an independent investigation before executing the checks said to have been obtained by false pretenses. Defendant cites People v. Blume, 345 Ill. 524. There is no doubt it is a necessary element of this crime that the person defrauded should have relied on the false representations, but this contention is not based on facts. The Tea Co. made no investigation of defendant's dummy company which was used by him in the perpetration of fraud. In that particular the victim relied, as it had a right to do, upon the supposed honesty of its employes.

Defendant cites People v. Dinenza, 356 Ill. 118, to the point that when the evidence as a whole does not establish guilt beyond a reasonable doubt, the judgment should be reversed. That is the law. We do not entertain any reasonable doubt on this record.

Defendant also contends that there was a substantial variance between the allegation of the indictment and the proofs, in that the indictment alleged that the Kenneth Specialty Co. was a partnership of [illegible] to show that it was a representative or agent. That objection was not raised on the trial and cannot be urged here. People v. Garamony, 359 Ill. 210.

Objection is made to some of the instructions, but the record fails to show at whose instance they were given and does not disclose any objection or exception to any one of them. We find no error in this respect. People v. Drury, 335 Ill. 539.

It is also urged that it was error to enter judgment and impose sentence on each count. What we have already said with reference to the indictment makes it unnecessary to give this point further consideration. Kroer v. People, 78 Ill. 294, People v. Elliott, 272 Ill. 592, People v. Allen, 357 Ill. 262.

Defendant asserts with apparent confidence that the indictment does not allege, or the facts prove, any offense within the meaning of the statute. (Smith-Hurd's Ill. Rev. Stats., 1933, chap. 38, sec. 96, par. 253). It is said that the facts disclose a business arrangement with which all the parties were satisfied, and that to hold such acts criminal would fill the jails and penitentiaries with victims the legislature never intended to be there. We hesitate to believe that the community generally has departed so far from the standards of primary honesty. People v. Haines, 14 Wend. (N. Y.) 546, 28 Am. Dec. 530. On the contrary, we think the tendency of modern decisions is in the direction of a vigilant enforcement of the law against false pretenses for the protection of the public against swindlers of all kinds. The criminal pretense here did not consist in a single act. It comprised many acts extending over a considerable time. The means by which defendant undertook to appropriate the property of his employer were planned with a degree of care and executed with a diligence worthy of a better cause. To his employer, the Tea Co., he falsely represented that the Monarch Specialties Co. was a subsidiary of the Shellmar to show that it was a representative or agent. That objection was not raised on the trial and cannot be urged here. People v. Garamony, 259 Ill. 246.

Objection is made to some of the instructions, but the record fails to show at whose instance they were given and does not disclose any objection or exception to any one of them. We find no error in this respect. People v. Emery, 335 Ill. 535.

It is also urged that it was error to enter judgment and impose sentence on each count. What we have already said with reference to the indictment makes it unnecessary to give this point further consideration. Kroer v. People, 78 Ill. 294; People v. Elliott, 272 Ill. 592; People v. Allen, 353 Ill. 362.

Defendant asserts with apparent confidence that the indictment does not allege, or the facts prove, any offense within the meaning of the statute. (Smith-Hurd's Ill. Rev. Stats., 1933, chap. 38, sec. 96, par. 253). It is said that the facts disclose a business arrangement with which all the parties were satisfied, and that to hold such acts criminal would fill the jails and penitentiaries with victims the legislature never intended to be there. We hesitate to believe that the community generally has departed so far from the standards of ordinary honesty. People v. Haynes, 14 Wend. (N.Y.) 546, 28 Am. Dec. 530. On the contrary, we think the tendency of modern decisions is in the direction of a vigilant enforcement of the law against false pretenses for the protection of the public against swindlers of all kinds. The criminal pretense here did not consist in a single act. It comprised many acts extending over a considerable time. The means by which defendant undertook to appropriate the property of his employer were planned with a degree of care and executed with a diligence worthy of a better cause. To his employer, the Tea Co., he falsely represented that the Monarch Specialties Co. was a subsidiary of the Shellar

Products Co. He falsely pretended that it was the custom and practice of the Shellmar Co. to invoice and collect for its products through the Monarch Specialties Co. He falsely pretended that the selling price of doughnut and bacon wrappers was more per thousand than the actual price. He pretended that the invoices of these wrappers indicated the sale of the same by the Monarch Specialties Co. to the Great Atlantic & Pacific Tea Co., while to the Shellmar Products Co. he falsely represented that the Monarch Specialties Co. was a division department of the Great Atlantic & Pacific Tea Co. The proof shows that he himself was the Monarch Specialties Co.

By these means and through the confidence reposed in him by his employer he was able secretly, fraudulently, and in disregard of his fiduciary relationship to obtain these checks from his employer and thus cheat the employer out of large sums of money. His actions were in effect just as harmful as if he had embezzled or stolen his employer's money. Defendant has had a fair trial. We do not entertain a doubt of his guilt.

The judgment is affirmed.

AFFIRMED.

O'Connor, P. J., and McSurely, J., concur.

Products Co. He falsely pretended that it was the custom and practice of the Shellmar Co. to invoice and collect for its products through the Monarch Specialties Co. He falsely pretended that the selling prices of cellophane and bread wrappers was more per thousand than the actual prices. He pretended that the invoices of these wrappers indicated the sale of the same by the Monarch Specialties Co. to the Great Atlantic & Pacific Tea Co., while to the Shellmar Products Co. he falsely represented that the Monarch Specialties Co. was a division department of the Great Atlantic & Pacific Tea Co. The proof shows that he himself was the Monarch Specialties [illegible]

[illegible] By these means and through the confidence reposed in him by his employer he was able secretly, fraudulently, and in disregard of his fiduciary relationship to obtain these checks from his employer and thus mulct his employer out of large sums of money. His actions were as criminal just as natural as if he had embezzled or stolen his employer's money. Defendant had had a fair trial. We do not otherwise [illegible] of his guilt.

[illegible] The judgment is affirmed.

[illegible] [illegible] AFFIRMED.

O'Connor, P. J., and [illegible], J., concur.

37950

ROBIN P. ALLEN and FRANCIS M. ALLEN, Doing Business as The Allen Company, Appellants,

vs.

FIRST NATIONAL BANK OF CHICAGO and RELIANCE BANK AND TRUST COMPANY, Appellees.

APPEAL FROM SUPERIOR COURT OF COOK COUNTY

194

280 I.A. 616

MR. JUSTICE MATCHETT DELIVERED THE OPINION OF THE COURT.

Complainants were depositors in the Reliance Bank & Trust Co. to the amount of $3000 on June 18, 1932, when that bank was closed by the Auditor of Public Accounts. They filed their bill on May 23, 1933, undertaking to sue not only for themselves but for all other depositors, none of whom up to this time have joined in their suit.

November 4, 1933, (a demurrer to the original bill having been sustained) complainants filed an amended bill of complaint consisting of twelve paragraphs. They made defendants thereto the Reliance Bank, the First National Bank, through which it cleared, and prayed that an accounting might be taken in connection with collateral, notes, bonds and securities received by the First National from the Reliance bank, and that such collateral, or the proceeds thereof, might be impressed with a trust in favor of complainants, and that the two banks might be held jointly and severally liable upon such accounting for any deficiency in the amount of loss sustained by them as depositors, that the court might find that the two banks had conspired to defraud the depositors, and for general relief.

November 3, 1934, a general demurrer of defendants was sustained, and the cause was dismissed for want of equity. From that order complainants have perfected this appeal. The question for decision is whether the amended bill of complaint states a

34

37950

ROBIN F. ALLEN and FRANCIS M. ALLEN,
Doing Business as The Allen Company,
Appellants,

vs.

FIRST NATIONAL BANK OF CHICAGO and
RELIANCE BANK AND TRUST COMPANY,
Appellees.

APPEAL FROM SUPERIOR
COURT OF COOK COUNTY.

280 I.A. 616

MR. JUSTICE MATCHETT DELIVERED THE OPINION OF THE COURT.

Complainants were de ositors in the Reliance Bank & Trust Co. to the amount of $8000 on June 18, 1932, when that bank was closed by the Auditor of Public Accounts. They filed their bill on May 23, 1933, undertaking to sue not only for themselves but for all other depositors, none of whom up to this time have joined in their suit.

November 4, 1933, (a demurrer to the original bill having been sustained) complainants filed an amended bill of complaint consisting of twelve paragraphs. They made defendants thereto the Reliance Bank, the First National Bank, through which it cleared, and prayed that an accounting might be taken in connection with collateral, notes, bonds and securities received by the First National from the Reliance Bank, and that such collateral, or the proceeds thereof, might be impressed with a trust in favor of complainants, and that the two banks might be held jointly and severally liable upon such accounting for any deficiency in the amount of loss sustained by them as depositors; that the court might find that the two banks had conspired to defraud the depositors, and for general relief.

November 5, 1934, a general demurrer of defendants was sustained, and the cause was dismissed for want of equity. From that order complainants have perfected this appeal. The question for decision is whether the amended bill of complaint states a good cause of action.

The determination of this question requires attention to the fact averments of the amended bill (construed according to the general rule in such cases) most strongly against the pleader Betten V. Williams, 277 Ill. App. 353. The amended bill avers that the Reliance Bank, prior to June 18, 1932, was an Illinois banking corporation, and the First National a national banking corporation, through which the Reliance bank cleared, that complainants were depositors in the Reliance bank to the amount of $3000 on June 18, 1932, when the bank was closed by the Auditor of Public Accounts, that the two banks through their officers, in order to induce depositors to keep their accounts with the Reliance bank represented that it was in a sound and liquid condition, that to that end the First National bank caused a letter to be written, stating that it had investigated the resources and liabilities of the Reliance bank (when or how not averred) and that the Reliance bank was in a sound and liquid condition; that this letter was enlarged and placed in a conspicuous place in the Reliance bank office (when or by whom not stated), and that relying thereon, complainants and others kept their funds in the bank, that on December 29, 1931, the two defendant banks in cooperation caused to be made and published a statement of the resources and liabilities of the Reliance bank at the close of business December 31, 1931. This statement is set up in detail, and it appears therefrom that the amount of cash on hand was stated to be $836,702.75, without any bills payable. The bill further alleges that March 30, 1932, the Reliance bank, with the knowledge and approval of the First National, caused another statement to be made, as of March 31st, purporting to shew cash resources of $418,176.32 and bills payable of $236,582.28, and relying on these statements complainants and other depositors allowed their funds to remain on deposit in the Reliance bank; that good cause of action.

II

The determination of this question requires attention to the fact averments of the amended bill (construed according to the general rule in such cases) most strongly against the pleader. Batten v. Williams, 277 Ill. App. 353. The amended bill avers that the Reliance Bank, prior to June 13, 1932, was an Illinois banking corporation, and the First National a national banking corporation, through which the Reliance bank cleared; that complainants were depositors in the Reliance bank to the amount of $3000 on June 13, 1932, when the bank was closed by the Auditor of Public Accounts, that the two banks through their officers, in order to induce depositors to keep their accounts with the Reliance bank represented that it was in a sound and liquid condition, that to that end the First National bank caused a letter to be written, stating that it had investigated the resources and liabilities of the Reliance bank (when or how not averred) and that the Reliance bank was in a sound and liquid condition, that this letter was enlarged and placed in a conspicuous place in the Reliance bank office (when or by whom not stated), and that relying thereon, complainants and others kept their funds in the bank, that on December 29, 1931, the two defendant banks in cooperation caused to be made and published a statement of the resources and liabilities of the Reliance bank at the close of business December 31, 1931. This statement is set up in detail, and it appears therefrom that the amount of cash on hand was stated to be $556,702.76, without any bills payable. The bill further alleges that March 30, 1932, the Reliance bank, with the knowledge and approval of the First National, caused another statement to be made, as of March 31st, purporting to show cash resources of $418,176.32 and bills payable of $256,383.35, and relying on these statements complainants and other depositors allowed their funds to remain on deposit in the Reliance bank; that these particular statements were untrue, because on December 29, 1931, the Reliance bank arranged with the First National bank for a sale to the First National of certain bonds and securities and credited its account with the proceeds of said sale and used the same to pay the note of the Reliance bank held by the First National; that only thereby was the Reliance bank able to issue the statement of December 30, 1931, to the effect that there were no bills payable; that after the statement was issued, the bonds and securities were turned back to the Reliance bank and the indebtedness re-established; that a similar transaction took place on March 29, 1932, when bills payable due from the Reliance to the First National were in excess of $1,200,000, and again the Reliance bank sold to the First National bonds and securities aggregating $1,043,238.85, again under an agreement that the Reliance bank would repurchase the same, which was carried out.

The amended bill further avers that on May 31, 1933, the receiver of the Reliance bank issued his report, stating that prior to the closing of that bank, in order to meet withdrawals, it borrowed large sums of money from the Reconstruction Finance Co. and the First National bank to the total amount of $1,355,505.28, and that at the time the Reliance bank was closed three-fifths of the bank's assets had been pledged; that the receiver's statement of liabilities from June 18, 1932, to May 31, 1933, shows that on June 18, 1932, the Reliance bank owed on bills payable to the Reconstruction Finance Corporation $703,890 and on bills payable to the First National $651,615.28, that on May 31, 1933, there had been repaid to the Reconstruction Finance Corporation $365,209.31, and to the First National $440,414.74, leaving the balance due to the Finance Corporation $338,680.69, and to the First National Bank $211,200.54; that the receiver's report shows that after payment of preferred claims there would be available for distribution to general credi-

these particular statements were untrue, because on December 30, 1931, the Reliance bank arranged with the First National bank for a sale to the First National of certain bonds and securities and credited its account with the proceeds of said sale and used the same to pay the note of the Reliance bank held by the First National; that only thereby was the Reliance bank able to issue the statement of December 30, 1931, to the effect that there were no bills payable; that after the statement was issued, the bonds and securities were turned back to the Reliance bank and the indebtedness re-established; that a similar transaction took place on March 29, 1932, when bills payable due from the Reliance to the First National were in excess of $1,200,000, and again the Reliance bank sold to the First National bonds and securities aggregating $1,043,288.85, again under an agreement that the Reliance bank would repurchase the same, which was carried out.

The amended bill further avers that on May 31, 1933, the receiver of the Reliance bank issued his report, stating that prior to the closing of that bank, in order to meet withdrawals, it borrowed large sums of money from the Reconstruction Finance Co. and the First National bank to the total amount of $1,365,505.78, and that at the time the Reliance bank was closed three-fifths of the bank's assets had been pledged; that the receiver's statement of liabilities from June 16, 1932, to May 31, 1933, shows that on June 16, 1932, the Reliance bank owed on bills payable to the Reconstruction Finance Corporation $703,000 and on bills payable to the First National $661,618.88; that on May 31, 1933, there had been repaid to the Reconstruction Finance Corporation $565,305.31, and to the First National $460,414.74, leaving the balance due to the Finance Corporation $138,000.00, and to the First National Bank $201,203.84; that the receiver's report shows that after payment of preferred claims there would be available for distribution to general credit-tors the total sum of $362.82 upon total claims of $3,002,429.05.

Item 9 of the bill charges:

"That the item which was carried on the report of March 30, 1932, as an asset consisting of United States securities and bonds subject to repurchase in the amount of $1,043,288.85 is the same item which now appears in the receiver's report under the heading 'Bills Payable,' and that as of May 31, 1933, the sum of $440,414.74 of the cash received by the receiver was paid to the First National Bank of Chicago, and that there was still due it an alleged indebtedness of $651,615.28 for which it held the aforesaid collateral, which was carried on the statement subject to repurchase agreement."

The tenth paragraph avers:

"And your orators further show that it was known to the officers of 'Reliance' and 'First' and to their directors and to the two banks that it was illegal for a national bank to enter into an agreement to purchase bonds and mortgages under an agreement to repurchase, and that the arrangements to carry the item of bonds and securities in the amount of $1,043,288.85 under the heading 'Subject to Repurchase' instead of 'Bills Payable,' tended to deceive the bank depositors and was in violation of the National Banking Act."

This paragraph particularly averred that these agreements were in violation of section 5136 of the United States Revised Statutes as amended February 25, 1927, which provided in substance that the national banks should thereafter be limited to buying and selling investment securities without recourse and under regulations to be prescribed by the comptroller of the currency; also that the agreement was contrary to section 64, paragraph 4 of the Criminal Code of Illinois, providing in substance that it should not be lawful for any incorporated bank or individual doing a banking business to assume the payment of or become liable for and guarantee to pay the principal of, or interest on, any bonds, notes or other evidence of indebtedness on account of any person, persons, company or incorporation, and that any assumption, liability or guarantee, whereby such deposits or trust funds could be jeopardized or impaired should be null and void.

The bill also avers that with the knowledge of the illegality of the acts and for the purpose of deceiving complainants and the other bank depositors, defendants entered into this scheme, tors the total sum of $2352.82 upon total claims of $3,002,429.05.

Item 9 of the bill charges:

"That the item which was carried on the report of March 10, 1932, as an asset consisting of United States securities and bonds subject to repurchase in the amount of $1,043,228.95 is the same item which now appears in the receiver's report under the heading 'Bills Payable,' and that as of May 21, 1932, the sum of $440,414.74 of the cash received by the receiver was paid to the First National Bank of Chicago, and that there was still due it an alleged indebtedness of $651,815.25 for which it held the aforesaid collateral, which was carried on the statement subject to repurchase agreement."

The tenth paragraph avers:

"And your orators further show that it was known to the officers of 'Reliance' and 'First' and to their directors and to the two banks that it was illegal for a national bank to enter into an agreement (to purchase bonds and mortgages under an agreement to repurchase, and that the arrangements to carry the item of bonds and securities in the amount of $1,043,228.95 under the heading 'Subject to Repurchase' instead of 'Bills Payable,' tended to deceive the bank depositors and was in violation of the National Banking Act."

This paragraph particularly averred that these agreements were in violation of section 5136 of the United States Revised Statutes as amended February 25, 1927, which provided in substance that the national banks should thereafter be limited to buying and selling investment securities without recourse and under regulations to be prescribed by the comptroller of the currency, also that the agreement was contrary to section 64, paragraph 4 of the Criminal Code of Illinois, providing in substance that it should not be lawful for any incorporated bank or individual doing a banking business to assume the payment of or become liable for and guarantee to pay the principal of, or interest on, any bonds, notes or other evidence of indebtedness on account of any person, persons, company or incorporation, and that any assumption, liability or guarantee, whereby such deposits or trust funds could be jeopardized or impaired should be null and void.

The bill also avers that with the knowledge of the illegality of the acts and for the purpose of deceiving complainants and the other bank depositors, defendants entered into this scheme, and that complainants and other bank depositors were led to believe that the Reliance bank was solvent and had no bills payable outstanding and were thereby induced to keep their deposits and to continue to make their deposits, as a result of which all the depositors now stand to lose the sum of $3,000,000.

The bill therefore prayed for relief as hereinbefore set forth.

A careful reading of the bill fails to disclose the precise theory upon which complainants rely. It is not easy to identify the particular fund upon which it is insisted a trust should be impressed. The res of the trust, which is, of course, necessary to its existence (Gurnett v. Mutual Life Ins. Co., 268 Ill. App. 518) is hardly visible to the judicial eye, nor are the averments of the bill in this respect entirely consistent. The bill by way of epithet, describes the transactions by which on two occasions bonds and securities were delivered by the Reliance to the First National Bank as only "pretended" transactions, while later in the bill these transactions are both described as real ones which were contrary to the statutes of the United States and the State of Illinois, and being contrary to and against the statute, it is claimed that a trust ex maleficio arises. The averments of the bill, however, are to the effect that in both of these transactions, the securities of the First National bank were returned to the Reliance bank. It is, of course, quite impossible to establish a trust ex maleficio against property in the possession of the First National Bank, while the bill avers of the same property that it was, prior to the appointment of a receiver, returned to the Reliance bank. There is an indefinite assertion in the bill (and it probably was in the mind of the pleader) that the securities upon which the trust should be impressed are those said to be the same ones used on former occasions and afterward deposited and that complainants and other bank depositors were led to believe that the Reliance bank was solvent and had no bills payable outstanding and were thereby induced to keep their deposits and to continue to make their deposits, as a result of which all the depositors now stand to lose the sum of $3,000,000.

The bill therefore prayed for relief as hereinbefore set forth.

A careful reading of the bill fails to disclose the precise theory upon which complainants rely. It is not easy to identify the particular fund upon which it is insisted a trust should be impressed. The *res* of the trust, which is, of course, necessary to its existence (*Gammell v. Mutual Life Ins. Co.*, 248 Ill. App. 182) is hardly visible to the judicial eye, nor are the averments of the bill in this respect entirely consistent. The bill by way of epithet, describes the transactions by which on two occasions bonds and securities were delivered by the Reliance to the First National Bank as only "pretended" transactions, while later in the bill these transactions are both described as real ones which were contrary to the statutes of the United States and the State of Illinois, and being contrary to and against the statute, it is claimed that a trust *ex maleficio* arises. The averments of the bill, however, are to the effect that in both of these transactions, the securities of the First National bank were returned to the Reliance bank. It is, of course, quite impossible to establish a trust *ex maleficio* against property in the possession of the First National Bank, while the bill avers of the same property that it was, prior to the appointment of a receiver, returned to the Reliance bank. There is an indefinite assertion in the bill (and it probably was in the mind of the pleader) that the securities upon which the trust should be impressed are those said to be the same ones used on former occasions and afterward deposited with the First National bank as collateral security for a loan represented by the note of the Reliance bank. This note with the collateral security was in the possession of the First National bank at the time the receiver was appointed. If it is the intention of the pleader to have a trust impressed upon these securities, we must regard the fact averments of the bill as utterly inadequate. It does not aver when the loan was made, or the amount of it. There is no denial in the bill that the Reliance bank received from the First National bank cash to the amount represented by its note, nor, so far as we can ascertain from a careful reading of the bill, is there any assertion of any conduct which was contrary to equity and good conscience in connection with that loan. The principle upon which equity impresses property in the hands of one person with a trust in favor of another, irrespective of any agreement between the parties, is well stated in 65 Corpus Juris, p. 462, where the author says:

> "It is a general principle that one who acquires land or other property by fraud, misrepresentation, imposition, or concealment, or under any other such circumstances as to render it inequitable for him to retain the property, is in equity to be regarded as a trustee _ex maleficio_ therefor for a person who suffers by reason of the fraud or other wrong."

This principle has been followed by the courts in Illinois in cases such as _People v. American Trust & Savings Bank_, 262 Ill. App. 458; _Fetherston v. National Republic Bancorporation_, 272 Ill. App. 500, _Lyons v. 333 North Michigan Ave. Bldg. Corp._, 277 Ill. App. 93; _Streeter v. Gamble_, 298 Ill. 332.

The fact averments of this bill are, however, wholly insufficient to justify the application of that rule, and the averments are too indefinite and uncertain to justify equitable relief. Not only is the fund upon which it is sought to impress a trust indefinite and uncertain, but the bill is insufficient in other respects. There is, for instance, no averment that the Reliance bank was insolvent at the time of the transactions set up in the bill, nor, with the First National bank as collateral security for a loan represented by the note of the Reliance bank. This note with the collateral security was in the possession of the First National bank at the time the receiver was appointed. If it is the intention of the pleader to have a trust impressed upon these securities, we must regard the fact averments of the bill as utterly inadequate. It does not aver when the loan was made, or the amount of it. There is no denial in the bill that the Reliance bank received from the First National bank cash to the amount represented by its note, nor, so far as we can ascertain from a careful reading of the bill, is there any assertion of any conduct which was contrary to equity and good conscience in connection with that loan. The principle upon which equity impresses property in the hands of one person with a trust in favor of another, irrespective of any agreement between the parties, is well stated in 65 Corpus Juris, p. 462, where the author says:

> "It is a general principle that one who acquires land or other property by fraud, misrepresentation, imposition, or concealment, or under any other such circumstances as to render it inequitable for him to retain the property, is in equity to be regarded as a trustee ex maleficio therefor for a person who suffers by reason of the fraud or other wrong."

This principle has been followed by the courts in Illinois in cases such as Ziegler v. American Trust & Savings Bank, 202 Ill. App. 455; Fetherston v. National Republic Bancorporation, 274 Ill. App. 500; Lyons v. 333 North Michigan Ave. Bldg. Corp., 277 Ill. App. 93; Stiefler v. McCullough, 285 Ill. 332.

The fact averments of this bill are, however, wholly insufficient to justify the application of that rule, and the averments are too indefinite and uncertain to justify equitable relief. Not only is the fund upon which it is sought to impress a trust indefinite and uncertain, but the bill is insufficient in other respects. There is, for instance, no averment that the Reliance bank was insolvent at the time of the transactions set up in the bill, ...

indeed, that it is now or ever was insolvent. For aught that appears from the averments of the bill at the time these various transactions which are denounced took place, the Reliance bank was entirely solvent and the loans advanced by the First National to the Reliance bank from time to time may have been of very great benefit to it and to its depositors. Neither are any facts averred which tend in any way to show that the First National bank unduly profited in any way in these transactions with the Reliance bank, or that the loans made by it in any way tended to bring about the subsequent closing of the Reliance bank. There is, therefore, no factual basis for the impression of a trust upon any assets in the possession of the First National Bank. Construing the bill most liberally, it cannot be held to do more than set up a very uncertain cause of action in fraud and deceit for which complainants have a perfect remedy at law, there being no averment that defendants are insolvent.

Nor are the facts averred, in our opinion, sufficient to justify the prosecution of a representative suit, in which complainants act for all the depositors. Whether any cause of action in fraud and deceit exists in favor of particular depositors depends upon the actual facts existing with reference to each one of them. An adjudication of their respective rights cannot be made in this action. Neither they nor defendants can be deprived of their right to trial by jury through the prosecution to a decree by one depositor of a suit of this character. Hale v. Hale, 146 Ill. 227; Brauer v. Laughlin, 235 Ill. 265; Betten v. Williams, 277 Ill.App. 353; Spear v. Green, 246 Mass. 259. Fetherston et al. v. National Republic Bancorporation et al., Gen. No. 37951, opinion this day filed.

The demurrer was properly sustained and the bill was properly dismissed as without equity. For these reasons the decree is affirmed.

AFFIRMED.

O'Connor, P. J., and McSurely, J., concur.

indeed, that it is now or ever was insolvent. For aught that appears from the averments of the bill at the time these various transactions which are complained took place, the Reliance Bank was entirely solvent and the loans advanced by the First National to the Reliance Bank from time to time may have been of very great benefit to it and to its depositors. Neither are any facts averred which tend in any way to show that the First National Bank unduly profited in any way in these transactions with the Reliance Bank, or that the loans made by it in any way tended to bring about the subsequent closing of the Reliance Bank. There is, therefore, no factual basis for the imposition of a trust upon any assets in the possession of the First National Bank. Construing the bill most liberally, it cannot be held to do more than set up a very uncertain cause of action in fraud and deceit for which complainants have a perfect remedy at law, there being no averment that defendants are insolvent.

Nor are the facts averred, in our opinion, sufficient to justify the prosecution of a representative suit, in which complainants act for all the depositors. Whether any cause of action in fraud and deceit exists in favor of particular depositors depends upon the actual facts existing with reference to each one of them. An adjudication of their respective rights cannot be made in this action. Neither may defendants be deprived of their right to trial by jury through the prosecution to a decree by one depositor of a suit of this character. Hale v. Hale, 146 Ill. 227; Brauer v. Laughlin, 235 Ill. 265; Cotton v. Williams, 277 Ill.App. 353; Dover v. Green, 246 Mass. 259; Pettersen et al. v. National Republic Bancorporation et al., Gen. No. 37081, opinion this day filed.

The demurrer was properly sustained and the bill was properly dismissed as without equity. For these reasons the decree is affirmed.

AFFIRMED.

O'Connor, P. J., and McSurely, J., concur.

[illegible]

38013

PEOPLE OF THE STATE OF ILLINOIS ex rel. OSCAR NELSON, Auditor of Public Accounts,

vs.

DEPOSITORS STATE BANK, a Corporation

CLARA L. OPPENHEIMER, SIGMUND WEDELES and CHICAGO TITLE AND TRUST COMPANY, a Corporation, Trustees under the Last Will and Testament of JULIUS OPPENHEIMER, Deceased,

Appellees,

vs.

WILLIAM L. O'CONNELL, as Receiver of Depositors State Bank,

Appellant.

APPEAL FROM CIRCUIT COURT OF COOK COUNTY.

280 I.A. 616

MR. JUSTICE MATCHETT DELIVERED THE OPINION OF THE COURT.

The receiver appeals from an order entered November 16, 1934, on the petition of the trustees of the Estate of Julius Oppenheimer, directing him to pay to the Treasurer of Cook County as part of the expense of administration and prior to the payment of other claims against the estate, certain unpaid taxes, penalties, etc., assessed for the years 1930 and 1931, and a proportionate share of the same taxes for the year 1932, pursuant to the terms of a supplemental agreement entered into between his predecessor in office and Julius Oppenheimer, deceased, as evidenced by an indenture in writing executed and delivered July 16, 1932. The receiver, as we understand it, does not deny that the obligation is due and owing, but argues that it should be allowed only as a general claim against the estate.

The facts in brief are that the trustees were and are the owners of premises which on January 1, 1921, by indenture, Julius Oppenheimer, now deceased, leased for ninety-nine years to L. R Steele Co., a corporation, which thereafter became bankrupt and on June 1, 1923, by its trustees in bankruptcy assigned the leasehold to the Depositors State Bank, which entered and took possession and

38013

PEOPLE OF THE STATE OF ILLINOIS ex rel. OSCAR NELSON, Auditor of Public Accounts,

vs.

DEPOSITORS STATE BANK, a Corporation.

FANNIE L. OPPENHEIMER, ALFRED [illegible] and CHICAGO TITLE AND TRUST COMPANY, as Trustees under the Last Will and Testament of JULIUS OPPENHEIMER, Deceased,

Appellees,

vs.

WILLIAM L. O'CONNELL, as Receiver of Depositors State Bank,

Appellant.

APPEAL FROM CIRCUIT COURT OF COOK COUNTY.

280 I.A. 616

MR. JUSTICE MATCHETT DELIVERED THE OPINION OF THE COURT.

The receiver appeals from an order entered November 15, 1934, on the petition of the trustees of the Estate of Julius Oppenheimer, directing him to pay to the Treasurer of Cook County as part of the expense of administration and prior to the payment of other claims against the estate, certain unpaid taxes, penalties, etc., assessed for the years 1930 and 1931, and a proportionate share of the same taxes for the year 1932, pursuant to the terms of a supplemental agreement entered into between his predecessor in office and Julius Oppenheimer, deceased, as evidenced by an indenture in writing executed and delivered July 16, 1928. The receiver, as we understand it, does not deny that the obligation is due and owing, but argues that it should be allowed only as a general claim against the estate.

The facts in brief are that [illegible] of premises which on January 1, 1921, by indenture, Julius Oppenheimer, now deceased, leased [illegible] Co., a corporation, which thereafter [illegible] 1, 1925, by its trustee in bankruptcy assigned the leasehold to the Depositors State Bank, which entered and took possession and occupied the same until February 9, 1932, when it was closed by the State Auditor of Public Accounts, who appointed Frank L. Webb, receiver, predecessor to the appellant receiver. Webb took possession of the premises and continued to occupy the same until William L. O'Connell was by order of court appointed his successor, July 6, 1933. Article 3 of the original lease provides that as a further consideration for the lease the lessee covenants to pay in due season from time to time, in addition to rent, "all taxes *** which may at any time after the year 1920 and until the expiration of said term be taxed, assessed, charged, levied or imposed on said premises ***" and that the lessee would not suffer said taxes, etc., to become delinquent in respect of payment.

July 16, 1932, Webb as receiver filed a petition in the Circuit court, reciting the history of the lease as above related and stating that the building on the premises was large and valuable and was occupied only in part by the bank and its business; that the second and third floors brought in a substantial income of approximately $5,000 per annum; that the basement brought in a like amount of revenue; that the lease was a valuable part of the assets of the bank "only if and so long as there shall be no default, entitling the lessor to terminate the lease"; that the rent payable under the lease was $15,000 per annum, and that the rent from February, 1932, was unpaid; that if the lessor elected to forfeit, the leasehold estate would be lost and the trust estate in possession of the receiver depleted to the extent of the value of the leasehold; that with the approval of the Auditor of Public Accounts and subject to the approval of the court, the receiver proposed to execute a supplemental indenture with the lessor, whereby he would expressly assume and adopt the said lease and its obligations and acquire a reduction of rent to the amount of $8750 per annum for the term ending April 30, 1934; that by the proposed supplemental indenture occupied the same until February 9, 1933, when it was closed by the State Auditor of Public Accounts, who appointed Frank L. Webb receiver, predecessor to the appellant receiver. Webb took possession of the premises and continued to occupy the same until William A. O'Connell was by order of court appointed his successor, July 8, 1933. Article 3 of the original lease provides that as a further consideration for the lease the lessee covenants to pay in due season from time to time, in addition to rent, "all taxes * which may at any time after the year 1920 and until the expiration of said term be taxed, assessed, charged, levied or imposed on said premises ***and that the lessee would not suffer said taxes, etc., to become delinquent in respect of payment.

July 14, 1933, Webb as receiver filed a petition in the Circuit court, reciting the history of the lease as above related and stating that the building on the premises was large and valuable but was occupied only in part by the bank and its basement; that the second and third floors brought in a substantial income of approximately $5,000 per annum; that the basement brought in a like amount of revenue; that the lease was a valuable part of the assets of the bank "only if and so long as there shall be no default, entitling the lessor to terminate the lease"; that the rent payable under the lease was $16,250 per annum, and that the rent from February, 1933, was unpaid; that if the lessor elected to forfeit, the leasehold estate would be lost and the trust estate in possession of the receiver depleted to the extent of the value of the leasehold; that with the approval of the Auditor of Public Accounts and subject to the approval of the court, the receiver proposed to execute a supplemental indenture with the lessor, whereby he would expressly assume and adopt the said lease and its obligations and acquire a reduction of rent to the amount of $4750 per annum for the term ending April 30, 1934; that by the proposed supplemental indenture he would secure the privilege, in case he should so elect, to terminate the lease on April 30, 1934, and be relieved of all liability under the lease except a liability to pay (in addition to taxes levied prior to such date of termination) one-third of the taxes for 1934; that it seemed necessary in order to conserve the estate to adopt said lease.

July 16, 1932, the court entered an order which recited that due notice had been given and found the facts to be as set forth in the petition, and directed the receiver to execute such supplemental indenture, which was in fact executed and delivered by the trustee and by the receiver on the same day.

April 13, 1934, the trustees filed their petition, upon which the order appealed from was entered. It recites the facts as heretofore related, states that O'Connell has been duly appointed successor of Webb and avers that the amount of "taxes with penalties, interest and costs accrued thereon to date, is the sum of $16,434.11." Copies of the lease and supplemental indenture were attached to the petition and it prayed for the entry of the proper orders. It was duly verified.

The receiver answered the petition, admitting facts as above narrated, but averring that he had served notice of his election to terminate the lease on April 30, 1934, and that he had vacated and surrendered the premises to the trustees. The receiver denied that the rent was due but stated that after the filing of the petition he had paid the quarterly rent in the sum of $2,187.50, for the term ending April 30, 1934. The answer admitted the taxes, penalties and costs against the premises but denied the receiver was liable under the terms of the lease or supplemental indenture, setting up verbatim section 1 of article 6 of the original lease and section 4, page 8, of the supplemental indenture, and stating that if there was any just obligation it should be allowed only as a general claim. The he would secure the privilege, in case he should so elect, to terminate the lease on April 30, 1934, and be relieved of all liability under the lease except a liability to pay (in addition to taxes levied prior to such date of termination) one-third of the taxes for 1934; that it seemed necessary in order to conserve the estate to adopt said lease.

July 16, 1932, the court entered an order which recited that due notice had been given and found the facts to be as set forth in the petition, and directed the receiver to execute such supplemental indenture, which was in fact executed and delivered by the trustee and by the receiver on the same day.

April 13, 1934, the trustees filed their petition, upon which the order appealed from was entered. It recites the facts as heretofore related, states that O'Connell has been duly appointed successor of Webb and avers that the amount of "taxes with penalties, interest and costs accrued thereon to date, is the sum of $16,454.11." Copies of the lease and supplemental indenture were attached to the petition and it prayed for the entry of the proper orders. It was duly verified.

The receiver answered the petition, admitting facts as above narrated, but averring that he had served notice of his election to terminate the lease on April 30, 1934, and that he had vacated and surrendered the premises to the trustees. The receiver denied that the rent was due but stated that after the filing of the petition he had paid the quarterly rent in the sum of $8,187.50, for the term ending April 30, 1934. The answer admitted the taxes, penalties and costs against the premises but denied the receiver was liable under the terms of the lease or supplemental indenture, setting up verbatim section 1 of article 6 of the original lease and section 4, page 8, of the supplemental indenture, and stating that if there was any just obligation it should be allowed only as a general claim. The answer also stated that the leasehold interest was carried on the records of the bank as an asset of $287,000; that it was no longer an asset and asked the same to be charged off the books.

The matter was heard upon the petition, the answer, and a stipulation as to certain facts with reference to the assessment and collection of taxes in Cook county during the period in question. The court entered the order as prayed by the petitioners.

The facts as hereinabove summarized are not fully set forth in the receiver's abstract but appear in the additional abstract filed by petitioners.

The receiver says that the rights and liabilities of creditors and debtors of an insolvent corporation are fixed and determined as of the date the receiver is appointed, citing Hynes v. Ill. Trust & Savings Bank, 226 Ill. 95; Streeter v. Junker, 230 Ill. App. 366, which announce that well settled rule. He further says, citing Streeter v. Junker, that neither the receiver nor the court can change such rights, the power of the court extending only to the construction and adjudication of the rights as they existed when the receiver was appointed; that neither the court nor the receiver can make an obligation incurred by the insolvent corporation prior to the receivership an administrative expense of the receivership; that upon the appointment of the receiver the landlord's claim for rent is in the nature of a general claim, citing Atkinson & Co. v. Aldrich-Clisbee Co., 248 Fed. 134. These propositions also may be conceded, we think, without determining the real questions raised on this record, namely, whether the supplemental indenture was binding upon the receiver, and if binding, whether properly construed it would obligate the receiver to make the payments as authorized and directed by the order from which the receiver has appealed.

The supplemental indenture of July 16, 1932, was based upon

answer also stated that the leasehold interest was carried on the records of the bank as an asset of $227,000; that it was no longer an asset and asked the same to be charged off the books.

The matter was heard upon the petition, the answer, and a stipulation as to certain facts with reference to the assessment collection of taxes in Cook county during the period in question. The court entered the order as prayed by the petitioners.

The facts as hereinabove summarized are not fully set forth in the receiver's abstract but appear in the additional abstract filed by petitioners.

The receiver says that the rights and liabilities of creditors and debtors of an insolvent corporation are fixed and determined as of the date the receiver is appointed, citing Hynes v. Ill. Trust & Savings Bank, 226 Ill. 79; Kreuter v. Junker, 290 Ill. App. 306, which announce that well settled rule. He further says, citing Kreuter v. Junker, that neither the receiver nor the court can change such rights, the power of the court extending only to the construction and adjudication of the rights as they existed when the receiver was appointed; that neither the court nor the receiver can make an obligation incurred by the insolvent corporation prior to the receivership an administrative expense of the receivership; that upon the appointment of the receiver the landlord's claim for rent is in the nature of a general claim, citing Atkinson & Co. v. Aldrich-Clisbee Co., 268 Fed. 126. These propositions also may be conceded, we think, without determining the real questions raised on this record, namely, whether the supplemental indenture was binding upon the receiver, and if binding, whether properly construed it would obligate the receiver to make the payments as authorized and directed by the order from which the receiver has appealed.

The supplemental indenture of July 16, 1935, was based upon

the order of the court entered on that day and pursuant to which the indenture was executed. That order was not appealed from. It recites that notice was given of the hearing upon which it was entered, and no motion has been made to set it aside, nor has the jurisdiction of the court to enter it been at any time directly questioned. The receiver, however, suggests in his fifth point that since the bank itself was without authority to pledge any of its assets to secure the payment of its general deposits, any agreement of this nature made by the receiver in its behalf was void. He cites to this point People v. Seward State Bank, 268 Ill. App. 32; People v. Citizens State Bank, 275 Ill. App. 159; People v. Wiersema State Bank, 276 Ill. App. 21; Hoffman v. Sears Community State Bank, 356 Ill. 598. These authorities are all distinguishable, in that the contracts there held to be ultra vires were made by the respective banks and not by a receiver appointed by the court. It is also to be observed that the attack made upon the contract in each case was direct, rather than collateral. The predecessor of the receiver here having secured the order which directed the execution of the supplemental indenture for the benefit of the estate, it would seem that his successor is estopped to question the validity of that order, and that that issue as between the receiver and the trustees may be regarded as res adjudicata. Central Trust Co. v. 35 S. Wabash Bldg. Corp., 273 Ill. App. 380; Casot v. Hubbel, 36 N. Y. 676; In re Denison, 114 N. Y. 621; 53 Corpus Juris 157. At any rate, such a contract made with the approval and sanction of the court is regarded as inviolable. 53 Corpus Juris 157; DeWolf v. Royal Trust Co., 173 Ill. 435; Atlantic Trust Co. v. Chapman, 208 U. S. 360.

It is contended in behalf of the receiver that the supplemental indenture properly construed does not obligate the receiver to pay these taxes in any manner other than as a general claim for the order of the court entered on that day and pursuant to which the indenture was executed. That order was not appealed from. It recites that notice was given of the hearing upon which it was entered, and no motion has been made to set it aside, nor has the jurisdiction of the court to enter it been at any time directly questioned. The receiver, however, suggests in his fifth point that since the bank itself was without authority to pledge any of its assets to secure the payment of its general deposits, any agreement of this nature made by the receiver in its behalf was void. He cites on this point People v. Harvard State Bank, 262 Ill. App. 32; People v. Illinois State Bank, 272 Ill. App. 159; People v. Wiersema State Bank, 270 Ill. App. 31; Hoffman v. Lenore Community State Bank, 256 Ill. 332. These authorities are all distinguishable, in that the contracts there held to be ultra vires were made by the respective banks and not by a receiver appointed by the court. It is also to be observed that the attack made upon the contract in each case was direct, rather than collateral. The predecessor of the receiver here having secured the order which directed the execution of the supplemental indenture for the benefit of the estate, it would seem that his successor is estopped to question the validity of that order, and that that issue as between the receiver and the trustees may be regarded as res adjudicata. Central Trust Co. v. Lake S. Cabash Bldg. Corp., 275 Ill. App. 392; Swart v. Kuhlig, 38 N. Y. 672; In re Dowlan, 214 N. Y. 433; 34 Corpus Juris 157. At any rate, such a contract made with the approval and sanction of the court is regarded as inviolable. 53 Corpus Juris 157; Selig v. Royal Trust Co., 172 Ill. 482; Atlantic Trust Co. v. Chapman, 208 U. S. 360.

It is contended in behalf of the receiver that the supplemental indenture properly construed does not obligate the receiver to pay these taxes in any manner other than as a general claim for rent past due. It is not denied by the terms of the original lease that the obligation was upon the lessee, or its assignee, to pay such taxes. The first provision of the supplemental indenture provides:

"That said Frank L. Webb, not personally but as Receiver as aforesaid of said Depositors State Bank, does hereby accept and adopt said indenture of lease bearing date the first day of January, 1921, and the leasehold estate thereby created, and does hereby assume and agree to pay all the rent in said lease reserved, now due or hereafter to accrue thereunder, and does hereby assume and agree to perform, keep, observe and be bound by all the covenants, provisions, obligations and conditions of said lease, both in respect to the portion of the term of said lease which has heretofore elapsed and in respect to the unexpired portion of said term."

Clause 4 of the same indenture accords to the receiver the right to elect on April 30, 1934, (upon giving due notice on January 1, 1934) to terminate the lease, and further states:

"And it is agreed that if the Receiver shall exercise said privilege of termination and give notice thereof as hereinbefore provided, the term of said lease shall end absolutely on the thirtieth day of April, 1934, and that thereupon the respective rights and obligations of the lessor and lessee, under said lease, shall in all respects be the same as though the original full term of said lease had then expired by lapse of time; provided, however, always that (in addition to his obligations to pay and discharge all taxes, assessments, levies and charges, taxed, assessed, levied or imposed for or during the term of said lease, or any portion thereof) the Receiver shall be liable to pay and discharge one-third (1/3) of the general taxes for the year 1934, upon said premises (including the improvements thereon) when and so soon as the amount thereof shall have been determined."

The language of these provisions of the indenture seems to be plain and unambiguous. There is no room for construction. The execution of this indenture may have been unwise and unfortunate, but it was apparently executed in good faith and with the approval of the court by the receiver's predecessor. We must therefore hold that the receiver is bound.

The order is affirmed.

ORDER AFFIRMED.

O'Connor, P. J., and McSurely, J., concur.

rent was due. It is not denied by the terms of the original lease that the obligation was upon the lessee, or its assignee, to pay such taxes. The first provision of the supplemental indenture provides:

> "[illegible] said Frank L. Webb, not personally but as receiver as aforesaid of said Depositors State Bank, does hereby accept and adopt said indenture of lease bearing date the first day of January, 1922, and the leasehold estate thereby created, and does hereby assume and agree to pay all the rent in said lease reserved, now due or hereafter to accrue thereunder, and does hereby assume and agree to perform, keep, observe and be bound by all the covenants, provisions, obligations and conditions of said lease, both in respect to the portion of the term of said lease which has heretofore elapsed and in respect to the unexpired portion of said term."

Clause 4 of the same indenture accords to the receiver the right to elect on April 30, 1934, (upon giving due notice on January 1, 1934) to terminate the lease, and further states:

> "And it is agreed that if the Receiver shall exercise such privilege of termination and give notice thereof as hereinbefore provided, the term of said lease shall end absolutely on the thirtieth day of April, 1934, and that thereupon the respective rights and obligations of the lessor and lessee, under said lease, shall be [illegible] to the same as though the original full term of said lease had then expired by lapse of time; provided, however, that [illegible] (in addition to his obligations to pay and discharge all rents, [illegible], taxes and charges, [illegible] accruing, [illegible] for or during the term of said lease, or any portion thereof) the Receiver shall be liable to pay and discharge one-third (1/3) of the general taxes for the year 1934, upon said premises (including the improvements thereon) when and as soon as the amount thereof shall have been determined."

The language of these provisions of the indenture seems to be plain and unambiguous. There is no room for construction. The execution of this indenture may have been unwise and unfortunate, but it was voluntarily executed in good faith and with the approval of the court by the receiver's predecessor. We must therefore hold that the receiver is bound.

The order is affirmed.

[illegible] ORDER AFFIRMED.

[illegible]

[illegible], P. J., and [illegible], J., concur.

to pay these taxes [illegible] as a preferred claim for

37946 - 37947

PEOPLE OF THE STATE OF ILLINOIS, (Plaintiff) Defendant in Error,

vs.

SOPHIE SVIRSKY and GEORGE PATRIS, (Defendants) Plaintiffs in Error.

ERROR TO CRIMINAL COURT OF COOK COUNTY.

277

280 I.A. 617[1]

MR. PRESIDING JUSTICE O'CONNOR DELIVERED THE OPINION OF THE COURT.

Frank Currin, otherwise called Lee Frank, Harry Fitzel, George Patris, John Poulos, John Everick, William Walter and Sophie Svirsky were indicted by the Grand Jury of Cook county, charged with conspiracy to damage and destroy buildings by bombs and to manufacture and sell bombs with intent that they be used to destroy or damage buildings. The jury returned a verdict finding Frank Currin, George Patris and Sophie Svirsky guilty as charged; John Poulos was found not guilty; Currin and Patris were sentenced on the verdict to the penitentiary; and defendant Sophie Svirsky was sentenced to the House of Correction for one year and fined $1000. Harry Fitzel and John Everick were granted a severance, and defendant William Walter during the trial withdrew his plea of not guilty and entered a plea of guilty, but whether he has been sentenced does not appear. Defendant George Patris sued out a writ of error from this court, No. 37946, and defendant Sophie Svirsky sued out another writ of error, and these two have been consolidated for hearing on one set of abstracts and briefs.

The record discloses that defendant George Patris was the secretary of the organization of Restaurateurs of Illinois, with offices at 6 North Clark street, Chicago; that Harry Fitzel, who had attended the University of Illinois College of Pharmacy, was a registered pharmacist; that Frank Currin was a former saloon keeper.

There is further evidence to the effect that about January, 1934, Currin was looking for a job and met Arthur Fry, formerly

37046 - 37047

PEOPLE OF THE STATE OF ILLINOIS,
(Plaintiff) Defendant in Error,

vs.

SOPHIE SVINSKY and GEORGE PATRIS,
(Defendants) Plaintiffs in Error.

ERROR TO CRIMINAL
COURT OF COOK COUNTY

280 I.A. 617

MR. PRESIDING JUSTICE O'CONNOR
DELIVERED THE OPINION OF THE COURT.

Frank Darvin, otherwise called Leo Frank, Henry Pitzel, George Patris, John Poulos, John Everick, William Walter and Sophie Svinsky were indicted by the Grand Jury of Cook county, charged with conspiracy to damage and destroy buildings by bombs and to manufacture and sell bombs with intent that they be used to destroy or damage buildings. The jury returned a verdict finding Frank Darvin, George Patris and Sophie Svinsky guilty as charged; John Poulos was found not guilty; Darvin and Patris were sentenced on the verdict to the penitentiary; and defendant Sophie Svinsky was sentenced to the House of Correction for one year and fined $1000. Henry Pitzel and John Everick were granted a severance, and defendant William Walter during the trial withdrew his plea of not guilty and entered a plea of guilty, but whether he has been sentenced does not appear. Defendant George Patris sued out a writ of error from this court, No. 37046, and defendant Sophie Svinsky sued out another writ of error, and these two have been consolidated for hearing on one set of abstracts and briefs.

The record discloses that defendant George Patris was the secretary of the organization of Restaurateurs of Illinois, with offices at 6 North Clark street, Chicago; that Henry Pitzel, who had attended the University of Illinois College of Pharmacy, was a registered pharmacist; that Frank Darvin was a former saloon keeper.

There is further evidence to the effect that about January, 1934, Darvin was looking for a job and met Arthur Fry, formerly employed at Currin's saloon, and enlisted his aid in getting a job breaking windows or any kind of racket; that Fry took him to defendant John Poulos, who ran a restaurant, and Poulos suggested that Currin see Patris at 6 North Clark street, which Currin later did. Poulos testified that he sent Currin to Patris to see if he could get work in a restaurant.

There is also evidence that Currin and Fitzel drove to Peoria in Fitzel's automobile and bought a quantity of black powder and fuses for the purpose of making bombs, and that Currin afterward bought some steel pipes; that Fitzel made bombs in his room where he lived, which was above the drug store where he worked, in Chicago; that on the night of March 5th Fitzel and Currin with two girls drove out to the South side of Chicago in Fitzel's car, a coupe with a rumble seat; the four sat in the front seat; they drove around and about 3:30 o'clock in the morning of March 6th stopped in the vicinity of 11103 South Michigan avenue; that Currin got out, took a bomb from the rumble seat of the car, intending to light the fuse and throw it in the doorway of the Legion cafe, when a police officer became suspicious; Currin explained to the officer what he was doing in the neighborhood and gave the officer his card, which in a way satisfied the officer; Currin and the others then drove away and the officer looked in a doorway a few doors from the Legion cafe, found the bomb and cut the fuse. Currin was arrested as he was going to his home about 5:30 in the morning; Fitzel also was arrested on that day. At the police station Currin and Fitzel told the police that Fitzel was making bombs and Currin was throwing them in restaurants, that they were doing this for Patris and were being paid by him. Later that same day Patris was taken to the police station. Afterward Patris and Currin were interrogated by the police and an assistant State's attorney; during such interrogation Currin said that on February 12, 1934, he and defendant Walter had borrowed Fitzel's

and John Fonkos, who ran a restaurant, and Tom
Currie see Fakrio at 6 North Clark street, and
Fonkos testified that he sent Currie to Fairia
got work in a restaurant.

There is also evidence that Currie and
Fossie in Pitasi's automobile and bought a qu
[illegible] for the purpose of making bombs,
bought some steel pipes; that Pitasi made bomb
[illegible], which was above the drug store where he
that on the night of March 9th Pitasi and Curr
out to the north side of Chicago in Pitasi's c
[illegible] the four out in the front seat; they
[illegible] o'clock in the morning of March 9th stopp
[illegible] Michigan avenue; that Currie got o
[illegible] out of the car, proceeding to light
it in the doorway of the Legion club, when a p
[illegible] Currie explained to the officer wh
[illegible] gave the officer his name, w
the officer [illegible] and the others then drove
[illegible] in a doorway a few doors from the Legi
[illegible] the fuse. Currie was arrested as he w
[illegible] in the morning; Pitasi also was arr
At the police station Currie and Pitasi told w
[illegible] making bombs and Currie was throwing them
they were doing this for Fairia and were being
that [illegible] Fairia had taken to the police s
Fairia [illegible] by the pol
State's [illegible] Cu
February 17, [illegible] had

car and drove to the North side, 2517 Devon avenue, taking a bomb with them, and about 1:30 p. m., Walter threw the bomb into the doorway of the beauty parlorbelonging to Michael Muller; the bomb exploded and considerable damage was done. Currin stated he did this at the request of Patris, and while Patris was interested only in damaging or destroying restaurants, not beauty parlors, yet he did this job at Patris's request; that Patris said it was a favor he was doing for a friend. Currin also broke a window in the restaurant at 113th Place and South Michigan avenue, for which Patris paid him $5. The evidence further tends to show that at the request of the defendant Sophie Svirsky he on March 3rd and again on March 4th bombed Charles Matucki's Tavern, which was two or three doors from Svirsky's place of business, for which she paid him $40.

Currin, Fitzel and Walter testified before the Grand Jury.

At the beginning of the trial Patris and Svirsky filed separate verified petitions, praying that each be granted a severance, which the court denied. In each of the petitions it was stated on information and belief that Currin and Fitzel had made written confessions, as well as oral admissions, to members of the police department and to assistants of the State's attorney, admitting their guilt and implicating defendants Patris and Svirsky.

Defendant Sophie Svirsky testified in her own behalf, denying that she had anything to do with the bombing of Charles Matucki's Tavern; that she knew nothing about it, and denied any wrongdoing in any of the matters testified to on the hearing.

There is considerable other evidence in the record which we do not mention since we have reached the conclusion that there must be a new trial as to Patris.

Defendant Svirsky contends that the court should have directed a verdict of not guilty, as requested by her, on the ground that the indictment charged that all the defendants jointly conspired to bomb

buildings in Cook county, while all of the evidence, even if believed, tended to show that there were two distinct conspiracies, one conspiracy between Frank Currin, Patris and the other defendants, except herself; that this conspiracy was entered into apparently for the purpose of damaging restaurants so as to make the owners of them join the association of Restaurateurs, of which Patris was the secretary, which was the conspiracy charged in the indictment; that the other conspiracy shown by the evidence was that she had conspired with Currin and Fitzel to bomb the Tavern of her competitor, Matuski, which was not the conspiracy charged in the indictment or sustained by the evidence; that she never knew or heard of any of the other defendants until after the parties were arrested. We think this contention must be sustained. All of the evidence, viewed most favorably for the People, tended to show that there were two separate and distinct conspiracies, having no relation to each other. A conspiracy has been defined by our Supreme court as a combination of two or more persons to accomplish, by some concerted action, some criminal or unlawful purpose, or to accomplish some purpose, not in itself criminal or unlawful, by criminal or unlawful means. Spies v. The People, 122 Ill. 1.

There being one conspiracy charged in the indictment, and all of the evidence tending to show that defendant Svirsky was in no way connected with that conspiracy, a verdict should have been directed in her favor. Tinsley v. U. S., 43 Fed. 2nd, 890.

Defendant Patris denied all charges made against him in toto and contends that the court should have granted his motion for a severance for the reason that in his petition he alleged that the defendants Currin and Fitzel had made confessions and admissions implicating themselves with him, and that he denied he was guilty of any offense as was indicated by such confessions and admission. As a general rule, those indicted jointly for the commission of a buildings in Cook county, while all of the evidence, even if believed, tended to show that there were two distinct conspiracies, the conspiracy between Frank Curvin, Fatria and the other defendants, except herself; that this conspiracy was entered into apparently for the purpose of damaging restaurants so as to make the owners of them join the association of Restaurateurs, of which Fatria was the secretary, which was the conspiracy charged in the indictment; that the other conspiracy shown by the evidence was that she had conspired with Curvin and Fitzel to bomb the tavern of her competitor, Antonell, which was not the conspiracy charged in the indictment or sustained by the evidence; that she never knew or heard of any of the other defendants until after the parties were arrested. We think this contention must be sustained. All of the evidence, viewed most favorably for the People, tended to show that there were two separate and distinct conspiracies having no relation to each other. A conspiracy has been defined by our Supreme court as a combination of two or more persons to accomplish, by some concerted action, some criminal or unlawful purpose, or to accomplish some purpose, not in itself criminal or unlawful, by criminal or unlawful means. Boles v. The People, 133 Ill. 1.

There being one conspiracy charged in the indictment, and all of the evidence tending to show that defendant Evinsky was in no way connected with that conspiracy, a verdict should have been directed in her favor. Sinclair v. U. S., 49 Fed. 2nd, 899.

Defendant Fatria denied all charges made against him in this and contends that the court should have granted his motion for a severance for the reason that in his petition he alleged that the defendants Curvin and Fitzel had made confessions and admissions implicating themselves with him, and that he denied he was guilty of any offense as was indicated by such confessions and admissions. As a general rule, those indicted jointly for the commission of a crime should be tried together (Doyle v. People, 147 Ill. 394) and the matter of granting separate trials is largely in the discretion of the court. People v. Sobzeak, 288 Ill. 157. In view of the state of the record at the time the petitions were presented, we are unable to say that the court abused its discretion in denying Patris a separate trial. But during the hearing it developed that a great deal of the evidence offered against Patris was that given by defendants Currin, Fitzel and Walter in which they admitted their own guilt and implicated Patris. This also appeared from the testimony of police officers who testified (most of which was out of the presence of Patris) as to admissions and confessions made by Currin, Fitzel and Walter to them. And while the court a number of time indicated to the jury that the admissions and confessions made by Currin, Fitzel and Walter, out of the presence of Patris, could not be considered as against him, yet this was not clearly told to the jury. Moreover, at the close of the case the court refused to instruct the jury specifically on this question, as requested by counsel for Patris. We think this was clearly erroneous and that Patris did not have a fair trial.

On the trial the evidence offered was substantially all against defendants Currin, Patris and Svirsky. Currin had pleaded guilty; he had confessed his guilt; Fitzel was granted a severance and he also had confessed his guilt.

Complaint is made that the court unduly restricted the cross examination of defendant Harry Fitzel, who testified for the People. We think there is merit in this contention. Fitzel was an admitted criminal and an alleged accomplice of Patris and considerable latitude should have been given counsel for defendant in his cross examination. Moreover, a number of times Fitzel, on his own motion, refused to answer questions and was sustained in this respect by the court. This was clearly erroneous. Fitzel had admitted his guilt and he should have been required to answer the questions.

crime should be tried together (Doyle v. People, 147 Ill. 394) and the matter of granting separate trials is largely in the discretion of the court. People v. Rohrook, 296 Ill. 167. In view of the state of the record at the time the petitions were presented, we are unable to say that the court abused its discretion in denying Patris a separate trial. But during the hearing it developed that a great deal of the evidence offered against Patris was that given by defendants Garrin, Pitzel and Walter in which they admitted their own guilt and implicated Patris. This also appeared from the testimony of police officers who testified (most of which was out of the presence of Patris) as to admissions and confessions made by Garrin, Pitzel and Walter to them. And while the court a number of times indicated to the jury that the admissions and confessions made by Garrin, Pitzel and Walter, out of the presence of Patris, could not be considered as against him, yet this was not clearly told to the jury. Moreover, at the close of the case the court refused to instruct the jury specifically on this question, as requested by counsel for Patris. We think it was erroneous and that Patris did not have a fair trial.

On the trial the evidence offered was substanti[al] against defendants Garrin, Patris and Sweeny. Garrin had [pleaded] guilty; he had confessed his guilt; Pitzel was granted a sev[erance]; he also had confessed his guilt.

Complaint is made that the court unduly restricted the cross examination of defendant Harry Pitzel, who testified for [the] People. We think there is merit in this contention. Pitzel was an admitted criminal and an alleged accomplice of Patris and considerable latitude should have been given counsel for defendant in his cross examination. Moreover, a number of times Pitzel, on his own motion, refused to answer questions and was sustained in this respect by the court. This was clearly erroneous. Pitzel had admitted his guilt and he should have been required to answer the questions.

Complaint it also made that the court, in other respects which need not be pointed out, unduly limited counsel for defendants in their cross-examination of witnesses. We think there is merit in this contention also. The court should have given considerable leeway owing to the fact that a number of the witnesses testifying for the People were admittedly guilty of the offenses charged in the indictment.

Complaint is also made that the court erred in admitting the confession and admissions of defendant Currin because they were not obtained voluntarily. Before the hearing of evidence the matter of the admission or confession of Currin was heard out of the hearing of the jury, and there is some evidence to the effect that Currin was abused by the police and forced to admit his guilt, and therefore the confession was inadmissible. The police officers denied that they abused Currin or any other defendant or witness, and the evidence is to the effect that Currin's story was fabricated. Whether the admission or confession was voluntary and therefore admissible was for the court, and his decision holding it was voluntary will not be disturbed unless against the manifest weight of the evidence. People v. Bartz, 342 Ill. 56.

For the reasons stated the judgment of the Criminal court of Cook county as to defendant Sophie Svirsky is reversed; and as to defendant George Patris the judgment is reversed and the cause remanded.

JUDGMENT REVERSED AS TO DEFENDANT SOPHIE SVIRSKY AND DEFENDANT GEORGE PATRIS, AND THE CAUSE REMANDED AS TO PATRIS.

McSurely and Matchett, JJ., concur.

37980

JOSEPH E. ROTHSTEIN,
Appellant,

vs.

LONDON GUARANTEE AND ACCIDENT COMPANY, LTD., a Corporation,
Appellee.

APPEAL FROM MUNICIPAL COURT OF CHICAGO.

280 I.A. 617[2]

MR. PRESIDING JUSTICE O'CONNOR DELIVERED THE OPINION OF THE COURT.

Plaintiff brought an action against the defendant on a burglar insurance policy. There was a jury trial and a verdict finding the issues against the plaintiff. Afterward the court awarded a new trial and the defendant filed a record in this court, #37604, and asked for leave to appeal from the order granting a new trial. The leave was denied; there was another jury trial and another verdict finding the issues against plaintiff; judgment was entered on the verdict and plaintiff appeals.

The record discloses that on November 26, 1932, the defendant issued to plaintiff its policy of insurance by which it agreed to indemnify plaintiff for loss by burglary on household goods in plaintiff's apartment in a building known as 911 North Francisco avenue, Chicago, for a period of one year. The policy was for $1000. Afterward, on January 15, 1933, plaintiff claimed his apartment had been burglarized; that the articles stolen cost $1997.95, and it was stipulated that at the time of the burglary they were worth $700.

In his statement of claim plaintiff itemized the articles stolen, which included household goods and clothing belonging to himself and his wife. Defendant filed an affidavit of merits denying that plaintiff's apartment had been burglarized. Plaintiff claims the face of the policy, $1000.

As stated, there was a jury trial and the record discloses

37980

JOSEPH B. [illegible],
Appellant,

vs.

LONDON GUARANTEE AND ACCIDENT COMPANY, LTD., a corporation,
Appellee.

[illegible] COURT OF CHICAGO.

290 I.A. 617

MR. PRESIDING JUSTICE O'CONNOR
DELIVERED THE OPINION OF THE COURT.

Plaintiff brought an action against the defendant on a burglar insurance policy. There was a jury trial and a verdict finding the issues against the plaintiff. Afterward the court awarded a new trial and the defendant filed a record in this court, #37604, and asked for leave to appeal from the order granting a new trial. The leave was denied; there was another jury trial and another verdict finding the issues against plaintiff; judgment was entered on the verdict and plaintiff appeals.

The record discloses that on November 28, 1932, the defendant issued to plaintiff its policy of insurance by which it agreed to indemnify plaintiff for loss by burglary on household goods in plaintiff's apartment in a building known as 911 North Francisco avenue, Chicago, for a period of one year. The policy was for $1000. Afterward, on January 16, 1933, plaintiff claimed his apartment had been burglarized; that the articles stolen cost $1997.98, and it was stipulated that at the time of the burglary they were worth $700.

In his statement of claim plaintiff itemized the articles stolen, which included household goods and clothing belonging to himself and his wife. Defendant filed an affidavit of merits denying that plaintiff's apartment had been burglarized. Plaintiff claims the face of the policy, $1000.

As stated, there was a jury trial and the record discloses

that at the close of all the evidence, and after argument of coun. sel, the court instructed the jury that "there is only one question in this case, and that is: Was there a burglary?" No complaint is made to the instruction.

Plaintiff offered evidence to the effect that about three o'clock in the afternoon of January 15, 1933, himself, his wife and child left the apartment and returned about nine o'clock that night; at that time his wife and child went to the apartment; he went to a lodge meeting and returned about forty-five minutes thereafter, when he discovered that the front door to the apartment had been "jimmied and most of the stuff in the house was gone and little things were laying around the floor. The drawers were all out. Everything was upset. The closets were empty, just the hangers and something like that;" that he telephoned the police; that they came and went through the apartment; that he found the screen on the back window of the apartment was off; some household goods were on the floor of the pantry and porch; some time later he submitted an itemized proof of loss which showed a total loss of $1997.95.

Nathan Roth, plaintiff's former landlord who occupied another apartment in the building at the time in question, called by plaintiff, testified that at about eleven o'clock in the evening he was called to plaintiff's apartment and when he got there he found the lock on the front door "jimmied"; that he went into the apartment and found "the drawers were pulled out and all the clothes were thrown all over the house, like there was something done there, like a burglary;" that he looked at the back door; that one window was open in the kitchen.

A police officer called by plaintiff testified that he received a call at about ten o'clock on the evening of January 15, 1933, and went to plaintiff's apartment with Officer Ferguson; that

that at the close of all the evidence, and after argument of counsel, the court instructed the jury that "there is only one question in this case, and that is: Was there a burglary?" No complaint is made of the instruction.

Plaintiff offered evidence to the effect that about three o'clock in the afternoon of January 15, 1933, himself, his wife and child left the apartment and returned about nine o'clock that night; at that time his wife and child went to the apartment; he went to a lodge meeting and returned about forty-five minutes thereafter, when he discovered that the front door to the apartment had been "jimmied and most of the stuff in the house was gone and little things were laying around the floor. The drawers were all out. Everything was upset. The closets were empty, just the hangers and something like that;" that he telephoned the police; that they came and went through the apartment; that he found the screen on the back window of the apartment was off; some household goods were on the floor of the pantry and porch; some time later he submitted an itemized proof of loss which showed a total loss of [illegible].

Nathan Roth, plaintiff's former landlord who occupied another apartment in the building at the time in question, called by plaintiff, testified that at about eleven o'clock in the evening he was called to plaintiff's apartment and when he got there he found the lock on the front door "jimmied"; that he went into the apartment and found "the drawers were pulled out and all the clothes were thrown all over the house, like there was something done there, like a burglary;" that he looked at the back door; that one window was [illegible].

A police officer called by plaintiff testified that he received [illegible] on the evening of January 15, 1933, and went to plaintiff's apartment [illegible] he noticed "a lot of drawers and clothes upset in the bedrooms;" that he took a report; that plaintiff and his wife stated they had not made a thorough check-up and said that there were some clothes and jewelry missing. "I took a record of the two articles of jewelry that were missing" and told them if there was anything further to get in touch with the police station, that he saw "stuff thrown on the floor, and I examined the doors and windows;" that he did not remember whether the pantry window was open or closed; that he made a written report at the time, which he had with him; that he noted on the report that an entry was made through the pantry window; he found no marks of violence on the doors.

A witness called by defendant testified he was a claim agent of the New York Central Lines and investigated a case which plaintiff's wife had concerning an accident that happened on January 9, 1933; that he called at plaintiff's apartment and talked to Mrs. Rothstein in plaintiff's presence, and in answer to a question he put to Mrs. Rothstein she stated that for two weeks immediately following the accident on January 9th, she was "confined in her bed at home."

In rebuttal plaintiff testified that he was at home when the investigator for the New York Central Lines called, and at that time the representative did not ask his wife how long she was confined at home after the accident. He did not ask her "how long she was confined to her home or any place else."

The evidence further shows that a Mr. Lesman, who rented a room in plaintiff's apartment, had lived there for about three years, paying $15 a month, and that some of his shirts and other belongings were missed at the time of the burglary. This is substantially all the evidence in the record.

The plaintiff contends that the court erred in permitting the investigator for the New York Central Lines to testify to the

[illegible]

[illegible] "a lot of drawers and clothes upset in the bedroom;" that he took a report; that plaintiff and his wife stated they had not made a thorough check-up and said that there were some clothes and jewelry missing. "I took a report of the two articles of jewelry that were missing" and told them if there was anything further to get in touch with the police station; that he saw "some things on the floor, and I examined the doors and windows;" that he did not remember whether the pantry window was open or closed; that he made a written report of the case, which he had with him; that he stated in the report that an entry was made through the pantry window; he found no marks of violence on the doors.

A witness called by defendant testified he was a claim agent of the New York Central Lines and investigated a case which plaintiff's wife had concerning an accident that happened on January 5, 1937; that he called at plaintiff's apartment and talked to Mrs. Rothstein in plaintiff's presence, and in answer to a question he put to Mrs. Rothstein she stated that for two weeks immediately following the accident on January 5th, she was "confined in her bed at home."

In rebuttal plaintiff testified that he was at home when the investigator for the New York Central Lines called, and at that time the representative did not ask his wife how long she was confined at home after the accident. He did not ask her "how long she was confined to her home or any place else."

The evidence further shows that a Mr. Lemmon, who rented a room in plaintiff's apartment, had lived there for about three years, paying $18 a month, and that some of his shirts and other belongings were missing at the time of the burglary. This is substantially all the evidence in the record.

[illegible]

conversation he had with Mrs. Rothstein, over defendant's objection. We think this contention cannot be sustained. Plaintiff was present at the time of the conversation and testified in rebuttal, as above stated. Moreover, it further appears from the itemized list of goods which plaintiff claims were stolen, that many of the items belonged to Mrs. Rothstein. In these circumstances, we think she would have been a competent witness although she was not called, and therefore the conversation testified to by the representative of the Railroad company was competent.

Plaintiff further contends that the finding of the jury is contrary to the manifest weight of the evidence. We have above stated the substance of the evidence, and in view of the fact that there were two jury trials and the further fact that on the second trial the court refused to set aside the verdict, we would not be warranted in disturbing the verdict on the ground that it was against the manifest weight of the evidence. The jury saw and heard the witnesses testify and was in a much better position to determine the truth of the matter in controversy than we are, in a court of review, where we have but the printed page before us.

The judgment of the Municipal court of Chicago is affirmed.

JUDGMENT AFFIRMED.

McSurely and Matchett, JJ., concur.

conversation he had with Mrs. Rothstein, over defendant's objection. We think this contention cannot be sustained. Plaintiff was present at the time of the conversation and testified in rebuttal, as above stated. Moreover, it further appears from the itemized list of goods which plaintiff claims were stolen, that many of the items belonged to Mrs. Rothstein. In these circumstances, we think she would have been a competent witness although she was not called, and therefore the conversation testified to by the representative of the Railroad company was competent.

Defendant further contends that the finding of the jury is contrary to the manifest weight of the evidence. We have above stated the substance of the evidence, and in view of the fact that there were two jury trials and the further fact that on the second trial the court refused to set aside the verdict, we would not be warranted in disturbing the verdict on the ground that it was against the manifest weight of the evidence. The jury saw and heard the witnesses testify and was in a much better position to determine the truth of the matter in controversy than we are, in a court of review, where we have but the printed page before us.

The judgment of the Municipal court of Chicago is affirmed.

JUDGMENT AFFIRMED.

McSurely and Matchett, JJ., concur.

37991

ANTHONY VANAGAITIS,
Plaintiff-Appellee,

vs.

LITHUANIAN NEWS PUBLISHING CO., a Corporation, and PIUS GRIGAITIS, Defendants-Appellants.

APPEAL FROM SUPERIOR COURT OF COOK COUNTY.

29A

280 I.A. 617[3]

MR. PRESIDING JUSTICE O'CONNOR DELIVERED THE OPINION OF THE COURT.

Anthony Vanagaitis brought an action to recover damages for an alleged libel against the Lithuanian News Publishing Co., a corporation, Pius Grigaitis, and Vincent Poska. On motion of plaintiff at the close of plaintiff's case his suit was dismissed as to Poska. There was a jury trial. The court instructed the jury to find a verdict in favor of plaintiff, leaving the question of the amount of damages to be determined by them. A verdict was accordingly returned fixing the damages at $500; judgment was entered on the verdict and defendants appeal.

The record discloses that defendant, Lithuanian News Publishing Co., publishes a daily newspaper in the Lithuanian language, in Chicago, of which defendant, Grigaitis is the editor. Plaintiff charges that he was libelled by an article printed in the defendants' newspaper on December 18, 1931. His position is that he was a musician and public entertainer engaged in the occupation and profession of giving concerts, musical recitals and public entertainments for hire before people of Lithuanian descent and extraction; that he possessed a good name and reputation of ability and talent as a musician, public entertainer and composer of musical and dramatic sketches; that the defendants were engaged in the publication of a daily newspaper having a circulation of over 50,000 copies; that they maliciously conspired to ruin his reputation and to deprive him of following

37991

ANTHONY VANAGAITIS,
Plaintiff-Appellee,

vs.

LITHUANIAN NEWS PUBLISHING CO.,
a corporation, and PIUS GRIGAITIS,
Defendants-Appellants.

APPEAL FROM

OF COOK COUNTY.

280 I.A. 617[3]

MR. PRESIDING JUSTICE O'CONNOR
DELIVERED THE OPINION OF THE COURT.

Anthony Vanagaitis brought an action to recover damages for an alleged libel against the Lithuanian News Publishing Co., a corporation, Pius Grigaitis, and Vincent Duske. On motion of plaintiff at the close of plaintiff's case his suit was dismissed as to Duske. There was a jury trial. The court instructed the jury to find a verdict in favor of plaintiff, leaving the question of the amount of damages to be determined by them. A verdict was accordingly returned fixing the damages at $500; judgment was entered on the verdict and defendants appeal.

The record discloses that defendant, "Lithuanian News Publishing Co.," publishes a daily newspaper in the Lithuanian language, in Chicago, of which defendant, Grigaitis is the editor. Plaintiff charges that he was libeled by an article printed in the defendants' newspaper on December 18, 1931. His position is that he was a musician and public entertainer engaged in the occupation and profession of giving concerts, musical recitals and public entertainments for hire before people of Lithuanian descent and extraction; that he possessed a good name and reputation of ability and talent as a musician, public entertainer and composer of musical and dramatic sketches; that the defendants were engaged in the publication of a daily newspaper having a circulation of over 20,000 copies; that they maliciously contrived to ruin his reputation and to deprive him of following his occupation and profession in earning a livelihood by falsely publishing that he possessed no ability or talent; that he was a "buffoon, zany, harlequin and impostor;" that the printed article in defendants' newspaper concerning the plaintiff stated that plaintiff's intelligence could be clearly seen in plaintiff's publication known as "Margutis" which was a magazine published by plaintiff; that an examination of "Margutis" would disclose that its editor, the plaintiff, had "loose beats" or "loose soup in his head;" that a reading of the matter contained in "Margutis" would disclose that plaintiff was not an artist but had little or no ability a s a composer or entertainer, the occupation or profession which he was following. The article further stated that another way of determining plaintiff's intelligence and ability was shown by the entertainments which from time to time were given by plaintiff or supervised by him. A number of these performances are set forth in the article. Plaintiff's counsel in their brief say that the publication of the article by defendants held plaintiff up to the people who read the article to be an "ignorant, illiterate, vulgar, and obscene buffoon, *** an imposter, falsely and fraudulently posing as a man of education, talent and ability;" that the article was libellous per se.

Plaintiff called defendant, Origaitis, as his first witness. He testified that he was the editor of the paper and supervised its general policy and that the article complained of was published in the issue of December 18, 1931; that he saw the article when it was published but did not direct that it be published and did not know that it had been published until he saw it in print; that defendant Poska supervised putting the article in the paper; that Poska was a subordinate of the witness. The paper had a daily circulation of about 35,000.

A witness translated the article from the Lithuanian

2

his occupation and profession in earning a livelihood by falsely publishing that he possessed no ability or talent, that he was a [illegible], ninny, harlequin and impostor"; that the printed article in defendants' newspaper concerning the plaintiff stated that plaintiff's intelligence could be clearly seen in plaintiff's publication known as "Margutis" which was a magazine published by plaintiff; that an examination of "Margutis" would disclose that its editor, the plaintiff, had "loose boats" or "loose cogs in his head;" that a reading of the matter contained in "Margutis" would disclose that plaintiff was not an artist but had little or no ability as a composer or entertainer, the occupation or profession which he was following. The article further stated that another way of determining plaintiff's intelligence and ability was shown by the entertainments which from time to time were given by plaintiff or supervised by him. A number of these performances are set forth in the article. Plaintiff's counsel in their brief say that the publication of the article by defendants held plaintiff up to the people who read the article to be an "ignorant, illiterate, vulgar, and obscene buffoon, *** an impostor, falsely and fraudulently posing as a man of education, talent and ability;" that the article was libelous per se.

Plaintiff called defendant, Grigaitis, as his first witness. He testified that he was the editor of the paper and supervised its general policy and that the article complained of was published in the issue of December 18, 1951; that he saw the article when it was published but did not direct that it be published and did not know that it had been published until he saw it in print; that defendant Fuchs supervised putting the article in the paper; that Fuchs was a subordinate of the witness. The paper had a daily circulation of about 25,000.

A witness translated the article from the Lithuanian

into the English language and plaintiff testified in his own behalf that he was born in Lithuania and had lived in Chicago ten years; that he was a musician and composer and editor of the Lithuanian "music magazine, Margutis;" that for three years he studied music in conservatories of Europe; that he composed Lithuanian folk songs which were played by the Chicago Symphony Orchestra; that he had given concerts in many large cities of the United States; had produced phonograph records of his compositions, (which seemed to have been played for the edification of the judge and jury.)

Plaintiff also introduced evidence to the effect that defendant publishing company had printed plaintiff's magazine "Margutis" from April, 1928, to November, 1931, and on a number of occasions articles had appeared in their newspaper prepared by some one connected with the paper, extolling plaintiff's virtues as an artist. Six days before the alleged libelous article appeared in defendants' paper, plaintiff had withdrawn the printing of his magazine "Margutis" from defendants; that on December 22, 1931, four days after the libelous article had appeared, and one day before the instant case was brought, another article appeared in defendants' newspaper concerning plaintiff, which plaintiff contends was also libelous, although in some respects the article had admitted some errors had appeared in the article of December 18th. Plaintiff offered no evidence of any specific damages sustained by him on account of the alleged libel.

The defendants filed pleas, among them being one of justification and contend that the article of December 18th stated the truth about plaintiff and that defendants published it "with good motives and for justifiable ends" and that this is a good into the English language and plaintiff testified in his own behalf that he was born in Lithuania and had lived in Chicago ten years; that he was a musician and composer and editor of the Lithuanian music magazine, "Margutis;" that for three years he studied music in conservatories of Europe; that he composed Lithuanian folk songs which were played by the Chicago Symphony Orchestra; that he had given concerts in many large cities of the United States; had produced phonograph records of his compositions, (which seemed to have been played for the edification of the judge and jury.)

Plaintiff also introduced evidence to the effect that defendant publishing company had printed plaintiff's magazine "Margutis" from April, 1928, to November, 1931, and on a number of occasions articles had appeared in their newspaper prepared by a one connected with the paper, extolling plaintiff's virtues as an artist. Six days before the alleged libelous article appeared in defendants' paper, plaintiff had withdrawn the printing of his magazine "Margutis" from defendants; that on December 27, 1931, four days after the libelous article had appeared, and one day before the instant case was brought, another article appeared in defendants' newspaper concerning plaintiff, which plaintiff contends was also libelous, although in some respects the article admitted some errors had appeared in the article of December 193
Plaintiff offered no evidence of any specific damages sustained by him on account of the alleged libel.

defense. They admit that they published lauditory articles concerning plaintiff prior to the time in question but say that plaintiff had changed performances into a degrading, obscene character and vulgar burlesque.

In proof of their plea of justification they offered some of the articles appearing in plaintiff's magazine, "Margutis." They also offered evidence tending to show that some of the alleged entertainments put on by plaintiff were lewd, degrading and obscene. Some of the articles were translated into the English language.

We will not discuss these articles here but are of opinion that whether they indicate or tended to indicate that the author of them had "loose beats" in his head was a question for the jury. As to the alleged entertainments claimed to have been given or supervised by plaintiff, defendants offer evidence as to what took place at those affairs, one of which performance was held at the Oaks picnic grove; another at the Lithuanian auditorium, and of a number of other performances on other occasions and places.

The testimony given by witnesses who attended these performances which were also attended by whole families, is to the effect that they were of a low order, degrading, vulgar and obscene. If their testimony was to be believed, and there was none to the contrary, the plea of justification would have been sustained by the evidence. If the performances were given by plaintiff, of the character testified to by defendants' witnesses, then defendants were performing a public service in calling the attention of the public to the matter so that they would not be further patronized.

It is true that witnesses were called by plaintiff in rebuttal, including plaintiff himself, who apparently intended to testify that the performances were not of the character as testified to by some of defendants' witnesses, but for some

reason, which is not apparent to us, the court excluded such offered testimony. Obviously both sides had a right to be heard on this question.

Whether defendants had sustained their plea of justification was for the jury, and the court erred in instructing the jury that plaintiff was entitled to recover.

The declaration set up the alleged libelous article verbatim in the Lithuanian language and a translation of it into the English language and plaintiff and defendants each called a witness who translated the article into the English language. There are some discrepancies in the translations but we think they are trivial and of no importance. They are substantially the same. The complaint made by defendants that "There are no innuendoes in the Lithuanian article set forth in the declaration," and that this should have been done, we think is clearly without merit.

The judgment of the Superior Court of Cook County is reversed.and cause remanded

JUDGMENT REVERSED.
AND CAUSE REMANDED.

McSurely and Matchett, JJ., concur.

fication was for the jury, and the court erred in instructin[g] the jury that plaintiff was entitled to recover.

The declaration set up the alleged libelous articl[e] verbatim in the Lithuanian language and a translation of it [in] the English language and plaintiff and defendants each calle[d] witnesses who translated the article into the English language. There are some discrepancies in the translations but we thi[nk] they are trivial and of no importance. They are substantia[lly] the same. The complaint made by defendants that "There are inaccuracies in the Lithuanian article and words in the declaration," and that this should have been done, we think is also without merit.

The judgment of the Superior Court of Cook County [is] reversed and cause remanded.

JUDGMENT REVERSED.
AND CAUSE REMANDED.

38020

GUSTAF ADOLF ECKMAN and
EARL DWYER,
Appellants,

vs.

INDEPENDENT ORDER OF SVITHIOD,
a Corporation, HAZEL BERG, ELMER
H. OLSON and CHARLES H. OHREN,
Appellees.

APPEAL FROM MUNICIPAL COURT
OF CHICAGO.

304

280 I.A. 617[4]

MR. PRESIDING JUSTICE O'CONNOR
DELIVERED THE OPINION OF THE COURT.

Plaintiffs, as the only heirs at law and next of kin of Alfred Victor Eckman, deceased, claimed to be the beneficiaries of an insurance certificate issued by the defendant Independent Order of Svithiod, a corporation. They brought suit to recover $1000, the face of the policy. There was a trial before the court without a jury, and on motion of defendant the court dismissed the suit on the ground that the Municipal court of Chicago had no jurisdiction of the case, and plaintiffs appeal.

The record discloses that on May 24, 1919, the defendant, a fraternal insurance company, issued its certificate for $1000 to Alfred Victor Eckman, in which Eckman's wife, Jennie Berg Eckman, was named as beneficiary. While the certificate was in effect the wife died, and later the husband, the insured, died. There was no change of beneficiary.

The certificate provided that where the beneficiary died prior to the death of the insured member, the insurance should be paid in the following order: (1) to the member's surviving wife or husband, (2) to the member's children, and (3) to the next of kin of the member according to the laws of the State of Illinois. There were no surviving children and it is stipulated that a judgment or decree was entered by the Probate court of Cook county finding that plaintiffs, Gustaf Adolf Eckman and Earl Dwyer were the only heirs at law and next of kin of the insured.

[illegible]

GUSTAV ADOLF HEDMAN and
KARL DWYER,
Appellants,

vs.

INDEPENDENT ORDER OF SVITHIOD,
a Corporation, HAZEL BERG, ELMER
E. OLSON and CHARLES E. GREEN,
Appellees.

APPEAL FROM MUNICIPAL
OF CHICAGO.

260 I.A. 617

MR. PRESIDING JUSTICE O'CONNOR
DELIVERED THE OPINION OF THE COURT.

Plaintiffs, as the only heirs at law and next of kin of Alfred Victor Hedman, deceased, claimed to be the beneficiaries of an insurance certificate issued by the defendant Independent Order of Svithiod, a corporation. They brought suit to recover $1000, the face of the policy. There was a trial before the court without a jury, and on motion of defendant the court dismissed the suit on the ground that the Municipal court of Chicago had no jurisdiction of the case, and plaintiffs appeal.

The record discloses that on May 24, 1919, the defendant, a fraternal insurance company, issued its certificate for $1000 to Alfred Victor Hedman, in which Hedman's wife, Jennie Berg Hedman, was named as beneficiary. While the certificate was in effect the wife died, and later the husband, the insured, died. There was no change of beneficiary.

The certificate provided that where the beneficiary died prior to the death of the insured member, the insurance should be paid in the following order: (1) to the member's surviving wife or husband, (2) to the member's children, and (3) to the next of kin of the member according to the laws of the State of Illinois. There were no surviving children and it is stipulated that a judgment or decree was entered by the Probate court of Cook county finding that plaintiffs, Gustaf Adolf Hedman and Karl Dwyer were the only heirs at law and next of kin of the insured.

It appeared that letters of administration in the estate of Alfred Victor Eckman were issued by the Probate court of Cook county and that matter was still pending.

The defendant Independent Order of Svithiod, a corporation, filed an affidavit of merits in which it admitted the issuance of the certificate as alleged, and averred that the certificate was "now held by Hazel Berg, Elmer H. Olson and Charles H. Ogren as security for" debts claimed to be due from the assured Eckman to Berg, Olson and Ogren, and therefore the defendant could not safely pay the $1000 insurance until the claims of the three persons to the insurance were settled.

The affidavit of merits prayed that the three be made parties to the suit and that summons issue against them, which was accordingly done. Each of the three filed an affidavit of merits, Hazel Berg claiming that Eckman, the insured, was indebted to her for $750; Elmer H. Olson claimed $150, and Charles H. Ogren $355.

Since the certificate of insurance provided to whom the $1000 should be paid in case of the death of the insured and of the beneficiary named, obviously the Probate court had nothing to do with the matter. The insurance was not payable to the insured's estate. The Municipal court, not the Probate court, clearly had jurisdiction of the matter.

In their brief counsel for defendant Independent Order of Svithiod, a corporation, say that no costs should be adjudged against it and that it be allowed to deduct its court costs. There is no warrant for such a contention. This defendant in its affidavit of merits alleged that the certificate of insurance was held by Berg, Olson and Ogren as security for debts claimed to be due to them from the insured. There was not a scintilla of evidence introduced to sustain this averment. The liability of the defendant

It appeared that letters of administration in the estate of Alfred Victor Nelson were issued by the Probate court of Cook county and that matter was still pending.

The defendant Independent Order of Svithiod, a corporation, filed an affidavit of merits in which it admitted the issuance of the certificate as alleged, and averred that the certificate was "now held by Hazel Berg, Elmer R. Olson and Charles E. Ogren as security for" debts claimed to be due from the insured Nelson to Berg, Olson and Ogren, and therefore the defendant could not safely pay the $1000 insurance until the claims of the three persons to the insurance were settled.

The affidavit of merits prayed that the three be made parties to the suit and that summons issue against them, which was accordingly done. Each of the three filed an affidavit of merits, Hazel Berg claiming that Nelson, the insured, was indebted to her for $750; Elmer R. Olson claimed $180, and Charles E. Ogren $360.

Since the certificate of insurance provided to whom the $1000 should be paid in case of the death of the insured and of the beneficiary named, obviously the Probate court had nothing to do with the matter. The insurance was not payable to the insured's estate. The Municipal court, not the Probate court, clearly had jurisdiction of the matter.

In their brief counsel for defendant Independent Order of Svithiod, a corporation, say that no costs should be adjudged against it and that it be allowed to deduct its court costs. There is no warrant for such a contention. This defendant in its affidavit of merits alleged that the certificate of insurance was held by Berg, Olson and Ogren as security for debts claimed to be due them by the insured. There was not a scintilla of evidence introduced to sustain this statement. The liability of the defendant to plaintiffs was clear, and the money should have been paid without suit.

The judgment of the Municipal court of Chicago is reversed and judgment will be entered in this court for $1000 in favor of the plaintiffs and against the Independent Order of Svithiod, a corporation.

JUDGMENT REVERSED AND JUDGMENT ENTERED HERE.

McSurely and Matchett, JJ., concur.

37956

VIOLET ALBRECHT,
Appellee,

vs.

METROPOLITAN CREDIT AND DISCOUNT CORPORATION, a Corporation,
Appellant.

APPEAL FROM MUNICIPAL COURT OF CHICAGO.

280 I.A. 618

MR. JUSTICE McSURELY DELIVERED THE OPINION OF THE COURT.

This is an appeal by defendant from a judgment of $375 entered upon the verdict of a jury in an action wherein plaintiff claimed defendant had converted certain property of hers.

John Manzat operated a rooming house in Chicago, known as the Garden Beach Hotel; the defendant held a chattel mortgage on all the furniture. In August, 1932, plaintiff rented a furnished room but in October following left Chicago; she says she left three cardboard boxes containing her personal property in the custody of Mr. Manzat, her landlord. In January, 1933, defendant foreclosed its chattel mortgage on the furniture and moved it from the Garden Beach hotel. Plaintiff says that when she returned to Chicago the following July her boxes were gone, and she claims they were taken and converted by the defendant when it took the furniture.

We are of the opinion that the finding of the jury that the defendant converted the boxes is against the manifest weight of the evidence.

Manzat testified that plaintiff, when she left the rooming house, left the three cardboard boxes in his custody, promising to pay him $1.00 a month for storage; that he placed them with some of his personal property in a storeroom under the stairway, which was locked with a Yale padlock to which he had the key.

Frank Jackey and Edward Leadley were sent by defendant to

37086

Violet Kennedy,
Appellee,

vs.

Metropolitan Credit and Discount Corporation, a Corporation,
Appellant.

APPEAL FROM MUNICIPAL COURT
CHICAGO.

280 I.A. 618

MR. JUSTICE McSURELY DELIVERED THE OPINION OF THE COURT.

This is an appeal by defendant from a judgment of $375 entered upon the verdict of a jury in an action wherein plaintiff claimed defendant had converted certain property of hers.

John Kennet operated a rooming house in Chicago, known as the Garden Ranch Hotel; the defendant held a chattel mortgage on all the furniture. In August, 1932, plaintiff rented a furnished room but in October following left Chicago; she says she left three cardboard boxes containing her personal property in the custody of Mr. Kennet, her landlord. In January, 1933, defendant foreclosed its chattel mortgage on the furniture and moved it from the Garden Ranch hotel. Plaintiff says that when she returned to Chicago the following July her boxes were gone, and she claims they were taken and converted by the defendant when it took the furniture.

We are of the opinion that the finding of the jury that the defendant converted the boxes is against the manifest weight of the evidence.

Kennet testified that plaintiff, when she left the rooming house, left the three cardboard boxes in his custody, promising to pay him $1.00 a month for storage; that he placed them with some of his personal property in a storeroom under the stairway, which was locked with a Yale padlock to which he had the key. Frank Kelley and Edward Lindsey were sent by defendant to the premises to foreclose the chattel mortgage; they asked Mr. Manzat if he wished to renew the mortgage, but on his replying in the negative they handed him the foreclosure notice and took possession of the chattels, checking the articles on the list in the chattel mortgage; they did not take possession of any property except that contained in the list. The articles were the ordinary furnishings of a rooming house - no personal belongings. The boxes and personal property of Mr. Manzat in the storeroom were not disturbed. Headley testified that Mr. Manzat had the only key to the storeroom.

Manzat testified that after defendant took possession he told Jackey of the boxes belonging to plaintiff and wanted to remove them from the storeroom but that Jackey said he could not take the boxes out unless he gave him some telephone slugs. Manzat says he never took the boxes out. Jackey denies this story and testified that Manzat had the only key to the storeroom and that he was told that he could take out any of his personal belongings; that nothing was said about giving the witness any telephone slugs.

After defendant took possession of the furniture it remained in the house for about a month, and as roomers left they were permitted to remove their personal belongings. John Crews was custodian at this time and testified that Mr. Manzat came to the place one evening and took some stuff out of the storeroom; that another man, a Mr. Hoyt, who was a fellow custodian and who has since died, called a police officer who said that Manzat had a right to take the stuff out of the storeroom; that thereupon Manzat took the goods that were there, including the cardboard boxes; that he took all of the articles. Another witness testified that he made an inventory of the property taken under the mortgage, which consisted mostly of furniture; that no boxes were taken. Another witness testified

of furniture [illegible] another chattel [illegible]
[illegible] of the premises [illegible] the mortgage, which consisted mostly
[illegible] of the [illegible] testified that he made up
[illegible] there, including the cupboard boxes; that he took
the stuff out of the storeroom; that thereupon Hannat took the
called a police officer who said that Hannat had a right to take
man, a Mr. Boyd, who was a fellow custodian and who has since died,
one evening and took some stuff out of the storeroom; that another
dian at this time and testified that Mr. Hannat came to the place
mitted to remove their personal belongings. John Crowe was custo-
in the house for about a month, and as roomers left they were per-
this. After defendant took possession of the furniture it remained

telephone slugs.

longings; that nothing was said about giving the witness any
that he was told that he could take out any of his personal be-
and testified that Hannat had the only key to the storeroom and
Hannat says he never took the boxes out. Jenney denies this story
take the boxes out unless he gave him some telephone slugs. Han-
them from the storeroom but that Jenney said he could not
told Jenney of the boxes belonging to plaintiff and wanted to
Hannat testified that after defendant took possession he

only key to the storeroom.

were not disturbed. Lendley testified that Mr. Hannat had the
The boxes and personal property of Mr. Hannat in the storeroom
ordinary furnishings of a rooming house - no personal belongings.
property except that contained in the list. The articles were the
in the chattel mortgage; they did not take possession of any
possession of the chattels, checking the articles on the list
in the negative they handed him the foreclosure notice and took
Hannat if he wished to renew the mortgage, but on his replying
the premises to foreclose the chattel mortgage; they asked Mr.

37954

he was in the moving business and moved the furniture from the Garden Beach hotel to another building, that he was present all the time the goods were loaded; that there were no boxes of any kind taken from the building.

This evidence not only fails to support plaintiff's claim that defendant converted her boxes but supports the claim of defendant that Manzat removed the boxes from the storeroom and took possession of them.

We are inclined to think that the jury was improperly influenced by the remarks of the attorneys for plaintiff and by the court. In arguing to the jury counsel for plaintiff said, "We all know how the Metropolitan - or I mean - a finance company probably forecloses on a mortgage." Such an argument would tend to prejudice a jury against the defendant's method of doing business, and although an objection was sustained to the remark the damage was done.

The trial court, as shown by the record, admitted that he took a greater part in the examination of witnesses than was proper. He constantly interrupted witnesses with comments that had a tendency to influence the jury favorably toward plaintiff. At one time he referred to the plaintiff as "a working girl" who had not much money. He interrogated Crowe, the custodian, as to whether he was "sitting down or standing up" while acting as custodian. Other comments tended to give the jury an unfavorable impression of defendant while plaintiff was presented as an object of sympathy.

Defendant makes other points which are not decisive. Its agents took possession of the goods in the building and any action of its agents with reference to the removal of the goods, or otherwise, would be the action of the principal.

As defendant disclaimed possession of the boxes in question, he was in the moving business and moved the furniture from the Hamden Beach Hotel to another building; that he was present at the time the goods were loaded; that there were no boxes of any kind taken from the building.

This evidence not only fails to support plaintiff's claim that defendant converted her boxes but supports the claim of the defendant that Hansen removed the boxes from the storeroom and took possession of them.

We are inclined to think that the jury was improperly influenced by the remarks of the attorneys for plaintiff and by the court. In arguing to the jury counsel for plaintiff said, "We all know how the Metropolitan -- or I mean -- a finance company probably forecloses on a mortgage." Such an argument would tend to prejudice a jury against the defendant's method of doing business, and although an objection was sustained to the remark the damage was done.

The trial court, as shown by the record, admitted that he took a greater part in the examination of witnesses than was proper. He constantly interrupted witnesses with comments that had a tendency to influence the jury favorably toward plaintiff. At one time he referred to the plaintiff as "a working girl" who had not much money. He interrogated Crowe, the custodian, as to whether he was "sitting down or standing up" while acting as custodian. Other comments tended to give the jury an unfavorable impression of defendant while plaintiff was presented as an object of sympathy.

Defendant makes other points which are not decisive. Its agents took possession of the goods in the building and any action of its agents with reference to the removal of the goods, or otherwise, would be the action of the principal.

As defendant disclaimed possession of the boxes in question, claiming they had been taken away by Kanzat, any demand on it prior to suit would have been unavailing and therefore unnecessary. _Nat. Bond & Investment Co. v. Zakos_, 230 Ill. App. 608; _Kee & Chapell Co. v. Pennsylvania Co._, 291 Ill. 248.

For the reason that the verdict is contrary to the manifest weight of the evidence, the judgment is reversed and the cause remanded.

REVERSED AND REMANDED.

O'Connor, P. J., and Matchett, J., concur.

claiming they had been taken away by Kamsat, any demand on it prior to suit would have been unavailing and therefore unnecessary. *Ext. Land & Investment Co. v. Zakos*, 234 Ill. App. 660; *Lee & Chapell Co. v. Pennsylvania Co.*, 291 Ill. 246.

For the reason that the verdict is contrary to the manifest weight of the evidence, the judgment is reversed and the cause remanded.

REVERSED AND REMANDED.

O'Connor, P. J., and Matchett, J., concur.

37594

CHARLES G. MORGENROTH and MARIE MORGENROTH, Appellees,

vs.

MIDLAND OIL CO., a Corporation, Appellant.

APPEAL FROM SUPERIOR COURT OF COOK COUNTY.

324

280 I.A. 618[2]

MR. JUSTICE MATCHETT DELIVERED THE OPINION OF THE COURT.

This appeal is now before this court on a rehearing granted.

November 14, 1932, a garage belonging to plaintiffs and situated at 4605-09 South Halsted street in Chicago was partly destroyed by fire. Plaintiff brought an action on the case alleging that the fire was caused through the negligence of defendant in delivering gasoline to the tenant who occupied the premises. The declaration alleged that the gasoline was negligently poured into a tank used as a receptacle for it, causing the tank to overflow and the gasoline to run over the floor of the garage, and that the gasoline being highly inflammable ignited, causing the premises to burn, without fault of plaintiffs. There was a plea of the general issue and a special plea that the gasoline was not delivered by any agent or servant of defendant within the scope of his employment or by defendant's authority.

There was a trial by jury and a verdict for plaintiffs in the sum of $3500, on which the court, overruling motions for a new trial and in arrest, entered judgment.

Defendant contends that the verdict was a compromise between the questions of liability and of the amount of damages. It points out that plaintiff Charles Morgenroth gave testimony tending to show damages to the amount of $9418; that this evidence was uncontradicted and says it is therefore apparent that the question of defendant's liability did not receive fair consideration from the jury, and that a new trial should have been granted for that reason. Defendant in its original brief cited Galomneulos v. Petropoulos, 147 Ill. App. 1;

[illegible]

CHARLES G. MORGENROTH and [redacted],
Appellees,

vs.

KIRKLAND OIL CO., a Corporation,
Appellant.

APPEAL FROM SUPERIOR COURT
OF COOK COUNTY.

280 I.A. 618

MR. JUSTICE [redacted] DELIVERED THE OPINION OF THE COURT.

This appeal is now before this court on a rehearing granted.

November 14, 1932, a garage belonging to plaintiffs, and situated at 4605-09 South Halsted street in Chicago was partly destroyed by fire. Plaintiff brought an action on the case alleging that the fire was caused through the negligence of defendant in delivering gasoline to the tenant who occupied the premises. The declaration alleged that the gasoline was negligently poured into a tank used as a receptacle for it, causing the tank to overflow and the gasoline to run over the floor of the garage, and that the gasoline being highly inflammable ignited, causing the premises to burn, without fault of plaintiffs. There was a plea of the general issue and a special plea that the gasoline was not delivered by any agent or servant of defendant within the scope of his employment or by defendant's authority.

There was a trial by jury and a verdict for plaintiffs in the sum of $3500, on which the court, overruling motions for a new trial and in arrest, entered judgment.

Defendant contends that the verdict was a compromise between the questions of liability and of the amount of damages. It points out that plaintiff Charles Morgenroth gave testimony tending to show damages to the amount of $6418; that this evidence was uncontradicted and says it is therefore apparent that the question of defendant's liability did not receive fair consideration from the jury, and that a new trial should have been granted for that reason. Defendant in its original brief cited [illegible] v. [illegible], 147 Ill. App. [illegible]

Selamakas v. Victory Ice & Ice Cream Co., 245 Ill. App. 178; Simmons v. Fish, 210 Mass. 563, 97 N. E. 102, and many like cases from different jurisdictions. In none of the cases cited are the facts similar to those here appearing. In its petition for rehearing defendant complains that the opinion of the court ignored the cases of Lynch v. Kuhlmann Investment Co., 25 Pac. (2nd) 744, and Ecoero v. Demitto, 208 N. Y. S. 601, which were of those cited. In the Lynch case plaintiff claimed actual damages under undisputed evidence amounting to $1503, and also claimed $2000 exemplary damages. The verdict was for $195.54 "actual damages." In the Ecoero case plaintiff's claim was for the value of labor and material, which the undisputed evidence tended to show was worth $2269.77. The verdict was for $100, and it was apparent the jury was confused. This case is clearly distinguishable. Here there were twenty different items of damage, and while the testimony of plaintiffs was uncontradicted by oral testimony in that respect, the nature of the damage sustained was such that the jury had a right to discount the testimony. It may have thought that some of the repairs were unnecessary. It may have thought that the garage as repaired was much more valuable than it was before it was burned.

Moreover, the rule is somewhat modified by a line of cases, such as Meyers v. I. C. R. R. Co., 197 Ill. App. 179, which hold that a defendant ordinarily cannot complain that a judgment against him is too small. The trial Judge saw the witnesses and heard the evidence. Apparently he was of the opinion that the verdict was not one of objectionable compromise. We are not disposed to say that he erred in that respect, or that the record is such as to indicate that the jury did not pass on the question of defendant's liability.

The controlling question in the case is whether the person who delivered the gasoline to the tenant on plaintiffs' premises and who made delivery in such a way as to cause the tanks to overflow,

Bolanowski v. Victory Ice & Ice Cream Co., 244 Ill. App. 178; Simmons v. Fish, 210 Mass. 563, 97 N. E. 102, and many like cases from different jurisdictions. In none of the cases cited are the facts similar to those here appearing. In its petition for rehearing defendant complains that the opinion of the court ignored the cases of Lynch v. Robinson Investment Co., 38 Pac. (2nd) 764, and Romero v. Hamlin, 208 N. Y. S. 601, which were of those cited. In the Lynch case plaintiff claimed actual damages under undisputed evidence amounting to $1005, and also claimed $5000 exemplary damages. The verdict was for $165.54 "actual damages." In the Romero case plaintiff's claim was for the value of labor and material, which the undisputed evidence tended to show was worth $2489.77. The verdict was for $165, and it was apparent the jury was confused. This case is clearly distinguishable. Here there were twenty different items of damage, and while the testimony of plaintiff's was uncontradicted by oral testimony in that respect, the nature of the damage sustained was such that the jury had a right to discount the testimony. It may have thought that some of the repairs were unnecessary. It may have thought that the garage as repaired was much more valuable than it was before it was burned.

Moreover, the rule is somewhat modified by a line of cases, such as Meyers v. I. C. R. R. Co., 107 Ill. App. 179, which hold that a defendant ordinarily cannot complain that a judgment against him is too small. The trial judge saw the witnesses and heard the evidence. Apparently he was of the opinion that the verdict was not one of objectionable compromise. We are not disposed to say that he erred in that respect, or that the record is such as to indicate that the jury did not pass on the question of defendant's liability.

The controlling question in the case is whether the person who delivered the gasoline to the tenant on plaintiffs' premises and who made delivery in such a way as to cause the tanks to overflow, was the servant or agent of defendant in performing that work. The material evidence may be summarized as follows:

In 1930 the owners built on the premises a garage 60 feet wide and 113 feet long. The premises were leased to the Bates Motor Transport Lines. The tenant took possession October 1, 1930, and remained in possession until the day of the fire, November 14, 1932. The tenant operated a freight trucking business. Up to July, 1931, it received its gasoline from the Sinclair Oil Co., which delivered it into tanks furnished by the Sinclair Oil Co. and located in the garage. About that date a new contract for the purchase of gasoline from defendant, Midland Oil Co., was entered into. In the making of this contract defendant was represented by its president, Mr. Ottenhoff. Under the arrangement agreed upon, defendant supplied two tanks into which the oil was to be delivered. Defendant also furnished a "stick," as it was called, by which the oil was to be measured. The evidence shows that the gasoline was delivered by truck every day and was transferred to these tanks by means of a hose through which it ran into a fill pipe just outside the garage.

The evidence is also uncontradicted to the effect that the name "Midland Oil Co." in letters six or eight inches high appeared on both sides of the truck. The inscription "Midland Oil Co." appeared on the back of the truck in smaller letters. It is a fair inference, we think, from all the evidence that there were no other names appearing on the truck. The truck was painted a dark green on both sides and the letters on it were in a kind of white silver. There is also evidence tending to show that the driver of the truck wore a suit bearing the name of the Midland Oil Co., but this is denied.

Each day when the driver delivered the gasoline he also delivered to the customer a bill for the same. This bill was on the regular printed billhead of the Midland Oil Co., and appropriate was the servant or agent of defendant in performing that work. The material evidence may be summarized as follows:

In 1926 the owners built on the premises a garage 60 feet wide and 113 feet long. The premises were leased to the Bates Motor Transport Lines. The tenant took possession October 1, 1930, and remained in possession until the day of the fire, November 14, 1932. The tenant operated a freight trucking business. Up to July, 1931, it received its gasoline from the Sinclair Oil Co., which delivered it into tanks furnished by the Sinclair Oil Co. and located in the garage. About that date a new contract for the purchase of gasoline from defendant, Midland Oil Co., was entered into. In the making of this contract defendant was represented by its president, Mr. Ottensoff. Under the arrangement agreed upon, defendant supplied two tanks into which the oil was to be delivered. Defendant also furnished a "stick," as it was called, by which the oil was to be measured. The evidence shows that the gasoline was delivered by truck every day and was transferred to these tanks by means of a hose through which it ran into a fill pipe just outside the garage.

The evidence is also uncontradicted to the effect that the name "Midland Oil Co." in letters six or eight inches high appeared on both sides of the truck. The inscription "Midland Oil Co." appeared on the back of the truck in smaller letters. It is a fair inference, we think, from all the evidence that there were no other names appearing on the truck. The truck was painted a dark green on both sides and the letters on it were in a kind of white silver. There is also evidence tending to show that the driver of the truck wore a suit bearing the name of the Midland Oil Co., but this is denied.

Each day when the driver delivered the gasoline he also delivered to the customer a bill for the same. This bill was on the regular printed billhead of the Midland Oil Co., and represented blanks were supplied by that company. This driver called daily to deliver defendant's gasoline to the tenant on the premises. No oil or gas was delivered by him except on delivery tickets in the name of defendant company. The contract for the sale of the gas was, however, made between the tenant and defendant, and the contract was for their mutual benefit.

The evidence also tends to show that the ownership of the gasoline remained in defendant company until it was delivered to the customer, and the driver took from the customer receipts for defendant's gasoline so delivered. The delivery of gasoline to these premises was discontinued by defendant after the fire. There was some gasoline left in the tanks, and about six days after the fire Mr. Bates received an envelope addressed to the Bates Motor Transport Lines, on which appeared the name of the sender, the Midland Oil Co., and within the envelope were writings which appeared in evidence as plaintiffs' exhibits 2, 3 and 4, dated November 19, 1931. Exhibit 2 was a printed delivery receipt of the Midland Oil Co., 2205 W. Harrison St., acknowledging receipt of 931 gallons of gasoline and 34 gallons of ethyl. On the receipt in pencil are the words, "Returned for credit," signed by one Goldberg. Plaintiffs' exhibits 3 and 4 are duplicate bills on the billheads of the Midland Oil Co., on which appeared in type, "Credit Memorandum, 931 gallons gasoline at .11c - $102.41, 34 gallons Ethyl. .14 - $4.76, total $107.17." During the time the tenant purchased gasoline from the Midland Oil Co., Mr. Ottenhoff, the president, called at least once a week. Sometimes he inquired about gasoline, at other times he collected checks. Mr. Bates at times complained to Mr. Ottenhoff of the carelessness of "his driver" in delivering the gasoline, but the conversations were erroneously excluded by the court on defendant's objection.

The name of the driver of the truck was John Lananga.

blanks were supplied by that company. This driver called daily to deliver defendant's gasoline to the tenant on the premises. No oil or gas was delivered by him except on delivery tickets in the name of defendant company. The contract for the sale of the gas was, however, made between the tenant and defendant, and the contract was for their mutual benefit.

The evidence also tends to show that the ownership of the gasoline remained in defendant company until it was delivered to the customer, and the driver took from the customer receipts for defendant's gasoline so delivered. The delivery of gasoline to these premises was discontinued by defendant after the fire. There was some gasoline left in the tanks, and about six days after the fire H. R. Bates received an envelope addressed to the Bates Motor Transport Lines, on which appeared the name of the sender, the Midland Oil Co., and within the envelope were writings which appeared in evidence as plaintiffs' exhibits 2, 3 and 4, dated November 19, 1931. Exhibit 2 was a printed delivery receipt of the Midland Oil Co., 2000 W. Harrison St., acknowledging receipt of 931 gallons of gasoline and 14 gallons of ethyl. On the receipt in pencil are the words, "Returned for credit," signed by one Goldberg. Plaintiffs' exhibits 3 and 4 are duplicate bills on the billheads of the Midland Oil Co., on which appeared in type, "Credit Memorandum, 931 gallons gasoline at .11c - $102.41, 14 gallons Ethyl, .34 - $4.76, total $107.17." During the time the tenant purchased gasoline from the Midland Oil Co., Mr. Ottenhoff, the president, called at least once a week. Sometimes he inquired about gasoline, at other times he collected checks. Mr. Bates at times complained to Mr. Ottenhoff of the carelessness of "his driver" in delivering the gasoline, but the conversations were erroneously excluded by the court on defendant's objection.

The name of the driver of the truck was John Lemangue.

Section 2065 of the Busch-Bernstein Revised Chicago Code of 1931 provides in substance that it shall be unlawful for any person, firm or corporation to use or to cause or permit any of his, its or their employees to use any motor vehicle, wagon or other vehicle in the transportation of property upon the streets, alleys or avenues of the city unless the vehicle has the name and owner thereof, and also a serial number distinguishing the vehicle from any other controlled or used by the same person, firm or corporation, plainly painted in letters at least one and a half inches in length in a conspicuous place on the outside of the vehicle. If the cartage company owned the truck, its name with serial number should have been on it. There was no proof that its name was on the truck and it is a fair inference from all the evidence it was not there.

In support of defendant's plea and for the purpose of contradicting the evidence above recited tending to show that the driver of the truck was the agent of defendant, Mr. Ottenhoff, president of defendant corporation, testified that at the time the gasoline was delivered defendant did not own any trucks or motor equipment for the delivery of gasoline, but that this gasoline was delivered to the customers of defendant under an oral contract between defendant and Wierenga Brothers Cartage Co., and that defendant paid the Cartage company once each month for delivering the gasoline. The uncontradicted evidence shows that the office of the Midland Oil Co. was at 2205 W. Harrison street in the office of the Cartage company. The oral contract of the Cartage company had been (according to defendant's evidence) entered into about five years prior to the trial.

There is no evidence showing when or where the truck upon which defendant's name was painted was purchased. Mr. Ottenhoff testified that the custom was that when defendant had a customer for oil or gasoline, defendant notified the Cartage company to make de-

Section 2058 of the Busch-Bernstein Revised Chicago Code of 1931 provides in substance that it shall be unlawful for any person, firm or corporation to use or to cause or permit any of his, its or their employees to use any motor vehicle, wagon or other vehicle in the transportation of property upon the streets, alleys or avenues of the city unless the vehicle has the name and owner thereof, and also a serial number distinguishing the vehicle from any other controlled or used by the same person, firm or corporation, plainly painted in letters at least one and a half inches in length in a conspicuous place on the outside of the vehicle. If the cartage company owned the truck, its name with serial number should have been on it. There was no proof that its name was on the truck and it is a fair inference from all the evidence it was not there.

In support of defendant's plea and for the purpose of contradicting the evidence above recited tending to show that the driver of the truck was the agent of defendant, Mr. Ostendorff, president of defendant corporation, testified that at the time the gasoline was delivered defendant did not own any trucks or motor equipment for the delivery of gasoline, but that this gasoline was delivered to the customers of defendant under an oral contract between defendant and Vlerenga Brothers Cartage Co., and that defendant paid the Cartage company once each month for delivering the gasoline. The uncontradicted evidence shows that the office of the Midland Oil Co. was at 2808 W. Harrison street in the office of the Cartage company. The oral contract of the Cartage company had been (according to defendant's evidence) entered into about five years prior to the trial.

There is no evidence showing when or where the truck upon which defendant's name was painted was purchased. Mr. Ostendorff testified that the custom was that when defendant had a customer for oil or gasoline, defendant notified the Cartage company to make delivery but that he (Ottenhoff) never gave any instructions to the drivers. He said that these drivers took receipt blanks of the defendant company for all oil and gasoline delivered and redelivered them to the Midland Oil Co.; that "We (Midland Oil Co.) instructed Wierenga Brothers Cartage Company to get receipts for us, in fact we had receipts printed. These receipt blanks were used as invoices to our customers whereby Wierenga Brothers got the receipt for us."

The Midland Oil Co. had one desk in the office of the Cartage company but did not pay any rent for the space occupied. This desk was used by Mr. Ottenhoff, the president. The Cartage company, Mr. Ottenhoff said, had three trucks on which the name of defendant company was inscribed, and these trucks seem to have been used exclusively for the delivery of products of defendant.

John Lananga testified that his salary was paid by the Cartage company by check, but it does not appear upon what basis his compensation was computed and no checks were produced. Lananga said he received orders from the manager of the Cartage Co., Ben Wierenga, and Mr. Ottenhoff testified he gave orders to Wierenga, and not to the driver.

Defendant corporation has a capital stock of $10,000, of which Ben Wierenga owns $2000. The terms of the supposed oral agreement between defendant and the Cartage company is vague and uncertain. There is no proof of the amount agreed to be paid to the Cartage company by defendant company for delivery of gasoline to its customers. Mr. Ottenhoff testified that defendant did not own the trucks and that the Cartage company owned "the truck," but no bills of sale or licenses were produced. There is evidence tending to show that the Cartage company did business for other customers and that it was engaged in business prior to the organization of defendant company, but the extent of such business is not definitely

Lively but that he (Ottenhoff) never gave any instructions to the drivers. He said that these drivers took receipt blanks of the defendant company for all oil and gasoline delivered and redelivered them to the Midland Oil Co.; that "We (Midland Oil Co.) instructed Vierenga Brothers Cartage Company to get receipts for us, in fact we had receipts printed. These receipt blanks were used as invoices to our customers whereby Vierenga Brothers got the receipt for us."

The Midland Oil Co. had one desk in the office of the cartage company but did not pay any rent for the space occupied. This desk was used by Mr. Ottenhoff, the president. The Cartage company, Mr. Ottenhoff said, had three trucks on which the name of defendant company was lettered, and these trucks seem to have been used exclusively for the delivery of products of defendant.

John Lemmage testified that his salary was paid by the cartage company by check, but it does not appear upon what basis his compensation was computed and no checks were produced. Lemmage said he received orders from the manager of the Cartage Co., Ben Vierenga, and Mr. Ottenhoff testified he gave orders to Vierenga, and not to the drivers.

Defendant corporation had a capital stock of $10,000, of which Ben Vierenga owns $2000. The terms of the supposed oral agreement between defendant and the Cartage company is vague and uncertain. There is no proof of the amount agreed to be paid to cartage company by defendant company for delivery of gasoline to its customers. Mr. Ottenhoff testified that defendant did not own the trucks and that the cartage company owned "the truck," but no bills of sale or licenses were produced. There is evidence tending to show that the Cartage company did business for other customers and [illegible] prior to the organization of the [illegible] disclosed.

Defendant's contention that the court should have instructed a verdict in its favor at the close of all the evidence is based upon the theory that there were undisputed, affirmative facts disproving the prima facie case made by the proof that defendant's name appeared in three places upon the truck which delivered the gas, and that the Cartage company was therefore an independent contractor and not the agent of defendant. In support of this contention defendant has cited Foster v. Wadsworth Howland Co., 168 Ill. 514; Connelly v. Peoples Gas Light Co., 260 Ill.162; Densby v. Bartlett, 318 Ill. 616, together with similar cases from other jurisdictions. On the other hand, it is contended by plaintiffs that their case rests not alone upon the inference based upon the evidence as to the name which appeared upon the truck, namely, "Midland Oil Co." but also upon the inference of non-ownership of the truck by the Cartage company by reason of the absence of its name, as the ordinance required, if it was the owner, and upon other evidence tending to show that the driver was about defendant's business, and, further, that the evidence offered by defendant on this issue is so improbable in its nature and is contradicted by other facts and circumstances appearing in evidence, to such an extent as to raise an issue of fact, which has been settled adversely to defendant's contention by the verdict of the jury. Plaintiffs rely on Page v. Brink's Chicago City Express Co., 192 Ill. App. 389; Kirn v. Chicago Journal Co., 195 Ill. App. 197; Hartley v. Red Ball Transit Co., 344 Ill. 534, with numerous cases from other jurisdictions.

It is quite impossible to review in detail all the cases called to our attention as bearing on this question. A careful reading of them indicates, we think, that the reason a master is held answerable for the wrongs of his servant in the course of dismissed.

Defendant's contention that the court should have instructed a verdict in its favor at the close of all the evidence is based upon the theory that there were undisputed, affirmative facts disproving the *prima facie* case made by the proof that defendant's name appeared in those places upon the truck which delivered the gas, and that the Garbage company was therefore an independent contractor and not the agent of defendant. In support of this contention defendant has cited Foster v. Wadsworth Howland Co., 168 Ill. 514; Connolly v. Peoples Gas Light Co., 260 Ill. 165; [illegible] v. [illegible], 318 Ill. 616, together with similar cases from other jurisdictions. On the other hand, it is contended by plaintiffs that their case rests not alone upon the inference based upon the evidence as to the name which appeared upon the truck, namely, "Midland Oil Co.," but also upon the inference of non-ownership of the truck by the Garbage company by reason of the absence of its name, as the ordinance required, if it was the owner, and upon other evidence tending to show that the driver was about defendant's business, and, further, that the evidence offered by defendant on this issue is so improbable in its nature and is contradicted by other facts and circumstances appearing in evidence, to such an extent as to raise an issue of fact, which has been settled adversely to defendant's contention by the verdict of the jury. Plaintiffs rely on [illegible] v. Ralph's Chicago City Express Co., 202 Ill. App. [illegible]; [illegible] v. [illegible] Co., 199 Ill. App. 397; Hartley v. Red Ball Transit Co., 344 Ill. 534, with numerous cases from other jurisdictions.

It is quite impossible to review in detail all the cases called to our attention as bearing on this question. A careful reading of them [illegible], we think, that the reason a [illegible] [illegible] his employment has in some cases been put upon too narrow ground. In the petition for rehearing defendant complained that the opinion of the court cited Shannon v. Nightingale, 321 Ill. 168, which was not cited in the briefs. We think, however, that the facts there were not materially unlike those which appear here. In that case, the plaintiff was struck by a truck hauling oil and gasoline and driven by one Pratt. The defendant did not contend that the driver was not negligent but relied on the defense that Pratt "was not their (defendants, who were partners of the Eastern Illinois Oil Co.) servant but was the servant of an independent contractor," one Rose Loux. The evidence showed that Pratt, who drove the truck, received payment from customers of the defendants and took orders for further deliveries to them; that the name of the firm, "Eastern Illinois Oil Co.", was painted on the truck and printed on the memorandum tickets given when orders were delivered or taken; that the trucks, however, belonged to Mrs. Loux and were kept on her premises, and that Pratt and other drivers of the trucks were employed by her. The cause was submitted to the jury which returned a verdict for the plaintiff, upon which judgment was entered, which was affirmed by the Appellate court. Upon review by the Supreme courtit was said that no question of law arose for consideration, except that raised by motion of the defendants to direct a verdict, and that the plea that Pratt was not the servant of the defendants raised an issue of fact; that the jury had found against the defendants on that issue, and that under such state of facts controverted questions of fact were involved. The opinion goes on to state that if the contract with Mrs. Loux had been in writing the question would have become a matter of law, citing Pioneer Construction Co., v. Hansen, 176 Ill. 100; that since the contract was not in writing but could be shown only by parol evidence, the determination of its terms was necessarily left to the jury; that it was his employment has in some cases been put upon too narrow ground.

In the petition for rehearing defendant complained that the opinion of the court cited Shannon v. Nightingale, 321 Ill. 168, which was not cited in the briefs. We think, however, that the facts there were not materially unlike those which appear here. In that case, the plaintiff was struck by a truck hauling oil and gasoline and driven by one Pruitt. The defendant did not contend that the driver was not negligent but relied on the defense that Pruitt "was not their (defendants, who were partners of the Eastern Illinois Oil Co.) servant but was the servant of an independent contractor," one Rosa Lenz. The evidence showed that Pruitt, who drove the truck, received payment from customers of the defendants and took orders for further deliveries to them; that the name of the firm, "Eastern Illinois Oil Co.", was painted on the truck and printed on the memorandum tickets given when orders were delivered or taken; that the trucks, however, belonged to Mrs. Lenz and were kept on her premises, and that Pruitt and other drivers of the trucks were employed by her. The cause was submitted to the jury which returned a verdict for the plaintiff, upon which judgment was entered, which was affirmed by the Appellate court. Upon review by the Supreme court it was said that no question of law arose for consideration, except that raised by motion of the defendants to direct a verdict, and that the plea that Pruitt was not the servant of the defendants raised an issue of fact; that the jury had found against the defendants on that issue, and that under such state of facts controverted questions of fact were involved. The opinion goes on to state that if the contract with Mrs. Lenz had been in writing the question would have become a matter of law, citing Pioneer Construction Co., v. Hansen, 176 Ill. 100; that since the contract was not in writing but could be shown only by parol evidence, the determination of its terms was necessarily left to the jury; that it was properly submitted to the jury under instructions to the court. The court in that opinion also distinguished Danaby v. Bartlett, 318 Ill. 616 (upon which defendant here relies) and said that it was not intended in that case "to overthrow the rule announced in the decisions which have been cited, that the verdict of the jury on such mixed questions of law and fact, approved by the trial court and the Appellate court, is conclusive and not subject to review by this court."

It is true, as defendant points out, that in the later case of Nelson v. Stutz Chicago Factory Branch, 341 Ill. 387, certain language used in the Shannon case with reference to the direction of a verdict was modified. In the Shannon case the court said:

> "If the condition of the evidence at the close of the plaintiff's case does not justify an instruction for a verdict in favor of the defendant, no evidence which the defendant may introduce will justify such instruction except uncontradicted evidence of an affirmative defense. Evidence contradictory of the plaintiff's will not do it."

The opinion in the Nelson case states that this language should be qualified; that "the question is whether there is evidence to sustain every element of the plaintiff's case necessary to be proved to sustain the cause of action," and that for the words "an affirmative defense" should be substituted "facts consistent with every fact which the evidence of the plaintiff tends to prove but showing affirmatively a complete defense." The opinion went on to say: "This is the situation here. There is no contradiction of the plaintiff's evidence and none of the defendant's." Such is not the situation in this case. In the later case of Hartley v. Red Ball Transit Co., 344 Ill. 534, plaintiff sued defendant for alleged negligence of its servant, Thomas Burke, in driving a truck whereby plaintiff was injured. The defense relied on was that Burke was not the servant or employee of defendant but an independent contractor. Defendant introduced in evidence a written contract between properly submitted to the jury under instructions to the court.

The court in that opinion also distinguished Hanley v. Bartlett, 335 Ill. 452 (upon which defendant here relies) and said that it was not intended in that case "to overthrow the rule announced in the decisions which have been cited, that the verdict of the jury on such mixed questions of law and fact, approved by the trial court and the Appellate court, is conclusive and not subject to review by this court."

It is true, as defendant points out, that in the later case of Nelson v. Stutz Chicago Factory Branch, 341 Ill. 387, certain language used in the Hanley case with reference to the direction of a verdict was modified. In the Hanley case the court said:

"If the condition of the evidence at the close of the plaintiff's case does not justify an instruction for a verdict in favor of the defendant, no evidence which the defendant may introduce will justify such instruction except uncontradicted evidence of an affirmative defense. Evidence contradictory of the plaintiff's will not do it."

The opinion in the Nelson case states that this language should be qualified; that "the question is whether there is evidence to sustain every element of the plaintiff's case necessary to be proved to sustain the cause of action," and that for the words "an affirmative defense" should be substituted "facts consistent with every fact which the evidence of the plaintiff tends to prove but showing affirmatively a complete defense." The opinion went on to say: "This is the situation here. There is no contradiction of the plaintiff's evidence and none of the defendant's." Such is not the situation in this case. In the later case of Hartley v. Red Ball Transit Co., 344 Ill. 534, plaintiff sued defendant for alleged negligence of its servant, Thomas Burke, in driving a truck whereby plaintiff was injured. The defense relied on was that Burke was not the servant or employee of defendant but an independent contractor. Defendant introduced in evidence a written contract between itself and Burke, which showed the sale to Burke of a Red Ball motor truck and an agreement to give him work to consist of long distance hauling. The written contract expressly provided that Burke was not an employee of the company, nor in any way or at any time its agent, he being in handling all the shipments an individual contractor and to be considered and treated as such. The contract provided, however, that the truckman should make all collections as directed by the company and turn same in at the first company office he passed and report to all Red Ball offices located in cities through which he was passing, and that he should follow instructions given him by the managers. The court said:

"If the construction of the contract depends not only upon the meaning of the words employed but upon extrinsic facts and circumstances or upon the construction which the parties themselves have placed upon it, which is to be proved like any other fact if such facts are controverted, the inference to be drawn is for the jury, and in such case the whole question as to what the contract was should be submitted to the jury under proper instructions. Turner v. Osgood Art Colortype Co., 223 Ill. 629."

In this case we have not questioned the rule announced in the case of Nelson v. Stutz Chicago Factory Branch, 341 Ill. 387. Defendant contends that this court, contrary to the decision in that case, has held that the *prima facie* case made by proof of the lettering upon the truck could not be overcome by uncontradicted evidence on behalf of defendant that the driver was acting for the Wierenga Brothers Cartage Co., and in no wise in the business of defendant in this case. Defendant misunderstands in this regard. On the contrary, we hold that the facts here do not bring this case within that rule. In the first place, plaintiffs did not rely solely upon the *prima facie* case inferred from the lettering on the truck, but upon that evidence and other evidence which tended to show that the truck was being used in defendant's business. Again, the evidence by which defendant sought to overcome the supposed *prima facie* case is not in our opinion uncontradicted but, on the [illegible] Truck and Burke, which showed the sale to Burke of a Red Ball motor truck and an agreement to give him work to consist of long distance hauling. The written contract expressly provided that Burke was not an employee of the company, nor in any way or at any time its agent, he acting in handling all the shipments an individual contractor and to be considered and treated as such. The contract provided, however, that the truckman should make all collections as directed by the company and turn same in at the first company office he passed and report to all Red Ball offices located in cities through which he was passing, and that he should follow instructions given him by the managers. The court said:

"If the construction of the contract depends not only upon the meaning of the words employed but upon extrinsic facts and circumstances of which the construction which the parties themselves [illegible] is to be proved like any other fact [illegible] the inference to be drawn is for the [illegible] as to what the contract [illegible] to the jury under proper instructions. [illegible] Co., 283 Ill. [illegible]."

In this case we have not questioned the rule announced in the case of [illegible] v. [illegible] Factory Branch, 343 Ill. 287. Defendant contends that this court, contrary to the decision in that case, has held that the prima facie case made by proof of the lettering upon the truck could not be overcome by uncontradicted evidence on behalf of defendant that the driver was acting for the [illegible] Carriage Co., and in no wise in the business of defendant in this case. Defendant misunderstands in this regard. On the contrary, we hold that the facts here do not bring this case within such rule. In the first place, plaintiffs did not rely solely upon the prima facie case inferred from the lettering on the truck, but upon other evidence which tended to show that the truck was used in defendant's business. Again, [illegible] sought to overcome the apparent [illegible] contrary, is in some respects contradicted and in many other respects, highly improbable. There is an abundance of authority to the effect that under such circumstances the question is for the jury. Dennis v. Sinclair Lumber Co., 242 Mich. 89; Ralli v. Peters, 241 N. Y. 177; Glielmi v. Netherland Dairy Co., 254 N. Y. 60; Horowitz v. Daily Mirror, 258 N. Y. S. 39; Callas v. Independent Taxi Owners' Assoc., 66 Fed. (2nd) 192, are a few of the cases which indicate that the controlling question here was for the jury. We take it that it cannot be questioned that plaintiffs having established a prima facie case the burden of proof was upon defendant to produce evidence which would overcome it. There is in plaintiffs' favor the further evidence showing that the drivers of the truck delivered bills to plaintiffs, and we think the jury might also fairly infer from the evidence that they took orders in defendant's behalf. There were circumstances throwing doubt upon the facts to which the president of the defendant company testified. There are the inferences arising from the ordinance; from the lack of proof as to the license for the truck; from the fact that the president of defendant received complaints as to the negligence of the driver.

The jury could reasonably disbelieve much of the testimony offered in defendant's behalf. The evidence as to the terms of the supposed contract was indefinite and uncertain. The evidence of defendant as to the ownership of the trucks is also indefinite and uncertain. Evidence certain and reliable in this respect must have been available.

The testimony of the president of the defendant company to the effect that he never gave directions to the drivers is, under all the facts appearing in the record, quite improbable. The jury apparently did not believe the testimony produced in defendant's behalf. We cannot say that it was unreasonable in so regarding it. The jury has settled the controlling issues of fact in plaintiffs' contrary, is in some respects contradicted and in many other respects, highly improbable. There is an abundance of authority to the effect that under such circumstances the question is for the jury. Ennis v. Sinclair Lumber Co., 242 Mich. 59; Kalil v. Peters, 241 N. Y. 177; Gilmond v. Netherland Dairy Co., 234 N. Y. 44; Horowitz v. Daily Mirror, 256 N. Y. S. 79; Gelina v. Independent Taxi Owners' Assn., 40 Fed. (2nd) 185, are a few of the cases which indicate that the controlling question here was for the jury. We take it that it cannot be questioned that plaintiffs having established a prima facie case the burden of proof was upon defendant to produce evidence which would overcome it. There is in plaintiffs' favor the further evidence showing that the drivers of the truck delivered bills to plaintiffs, and we think the jury might also fairly infer from the evidence that they took orders in defendant's behalf. There were circumstances throwing doubt upon the facts to which the president of the defendant company testified. There are the inferences arising from the ordinance; from the lack of proof as to the license for the truck; from the fact that the president of defendant received complaints as to the negligence of the driver.

The jury could reasonably disbelieve much of the testimony offered in defendant's behalf. The evidence as to the terms of the supposed contract was indefinite and uncertain. The evidence of defendant as to the ownership of the trucks is also indefinite and uncertain. Evidence certain and reliable in this respect must have been available.

The testimony of the president of the defendant company to the effect that he never gave directions to the drivers is, under all the facts appearing in the record, quite improbable. The jury apparently did not believe the testimony produced in defendant's behalf. We cannot say that it was unreasonable in so regarding it. The jury has settled the controlling issues of fact in plaintiffs' favor. The Judge who saw and heard the witnesses has approved the verdict. The judgment is affirmed.

AFFIRMED.

O'Connor, P. J., concurs.

McSurely, J., dissents.

37898

CURT TEICH & COMPANY, INC., a Corporation, Appellee,

vs.

MAX RIGOT SELLING AGENCY, INC., a Corporation, Appellant.

APPEAL FROM SUPERIOR COURT OF COOK COUNTY.

280 I.A. 618[3]

MR. JUSTICE MATCHETT DELIVERED THE OPINION OF THE COURT.

I. Plaintiff sued in assumpsit, filing a declaration of four counts, to which were added the common counts, with an affidavit of claim to the effect that $13,687.47 was due for goods sold and delivered, and $9,871.24 on account of goods manufactured for defendant at its request, which defendant refused to accept. A bill of particulars was also filed showing in detail same items sold and delivered. Defendant filed pleas with an affidavit of merits which stated as to goods sold and delivered it was entitled to credits in the amount of $12,122.13, and as to the claims for goods manufactured upon alleged oral requests by defendant to plaintiff it denied having given any such orders and denied having made any such requests; further, that the alleged oral contracts were unenforceable under the Statute of Frauds. The affidavit of merits admitted liability to the amount of $1,565.34, which it offered to pay, and denied on behalf of defendant any other liability. There was a trial by the court with a finding for plaintiff in the sum of $18,015.62, on which the court entered judgment.

II. Plaintiff is a corporation engaged in the business of printing and lithographing in Chicago. Defendant corporation for more than twenty years was under an oral arrangement with plaintiff as the exclusive jobber for plaintiff's products in the Chicago area. That relationship ended with the year 1933, and this suit is brought by plaintiff to collect the balance claimed by plaintiff to be due from defendant and involves a number of transactions. By

37503

CURT TEICH & COMPANY, INC., a Corporation, Appellee,

vs.

MAX RIGOT SELLING AGENCY, INC., a Corporation, Appellant.

APPEAL FROM SUPERIOR COURT OF COOK COUNTY.

280 I.A. 618

MR. JUSTICE MATCHETT DELIVERED THE OPINION OF THE COURT.

1. Plaintiff sued in assumpsit, filing a declaration of four counts, to which were added the common counts, with an affidavit of claim to the effect that $13,687.47 was due for goods sold and delivered, and $9,872.24 on account of goods manufactured for defendant at its request, which defendant refused to accept. A bill of particulars was also filed showing in detail same items sold and delivered. Defendant filed pleas with an affidavit of merits which stated as to goods sold and delivered it was entitled to credits in the amount of $10,128.11, and as to the claims for goods manufactured upon alleged oral requests by defendant to plaintiff it denied having given any such order and denied having made any such requests; further, that the alleged oral contracts were unenforceable under the Statute of Frauds. The affidavit of merits admitted liability in the amount of $2,565.36, which it offered to pay, and denied on behalf of defendant any other liability. There was a trial by the court with a finding for plaintiff in the sum of $16,619.40, on which the court entered judgment.

2. Plaintiff is a corporation engaged in the business of printing and lithographing in Chicago. Defendant corporation for more than twenty years was under an oral arrangement with plaintiff as the exclusive jobber for plaintiff's products in the Chicago area. That relationship ended with the year 1935, and this suit

the pleadings defendant admits the delivery to it of goods as set up in the bill of particulars to the amount of $13,687.47. As against this defendant claims for profit the difference between plaintiff's cost price and the sale price on more than $35,000 worth of merchandise sold the chain stores, $8,106.17; for damages on account of loss of profits by non-delivery of 50,000 folders, $750, for an alleged overcharge of one cent each on 40,562 view books $405.62. Other claims of defendant for merchandise of defendant claimed to have been converted to plaintiff's use to the amount of $1,173.54, and 2½ cents each on 67,474 World's Fair view books, have been withdrawn. The balance of $1565.34 admitted to be due by the original pleadings is thus increased to $4,435.68.

III. It seems convenient to first dispose of the smaller items which are disconnected with the larger items in controversy. The first of these is defendant's claim for damages on account of failure of plaintiff to deliver 50,000 folders on which it would have realized by resale profits to the amount of $750. June 29, 1933, defendant ordered 25,000 large 18 view folders of Greater Chicago. The order stated, "ship when ready." It was confirmed by plaintiff in the usual way. August 4, 1933, defendant gave an order for 25,000 large view folders of Chicago Parks. The word "rush" appears on this order. It was confirmed and accepted by plaintiff.

Mrs. Riget testified she had calls for these view books every day and could have sold all of them had they been delivered within four or five ~~day~~ weeks of the dates of the orders, which she says would have been the usual and normal time allowed for delivery. The order for the Park folders was cancelled by defendant October 16, 1933. The evidence of Mrs. Riget is to the effect that this merchandise ceased to be salable after October. She says she could have sold "a few anyway; I could have sold more than 1,000."

the pleadings defendant admits the delivery to it of goods as set up in the bill of particulars to the amount of $13,557.47. As against this defendant claims for profit the difference between plaintiff's cost price and the sale price on more than $35,000 worth of merchandise sold the chain stores, $8,106.17; for damages on account of loss of profits by non-delivery of 50,000 folders, $750, for an alleged overcharge of one cent each on 49,562 view books $495.62. Other claims of defendant for merchandise of defendant claimed to have been converted to plaintiff's use to the amount of $1,173.84, and 2½ cents each on 67,474 World's Fair view books, have been withdrawn. The balance of $1565.34 admitted to be due by the original pleadings is thus increased to $4,435.45.

III. It seems convenient to first dispose of the smaller items which are disconnected with the larger issues in controversy. The first of these is defendant's claim for damages on account of failure of plaintiff to deliver 50,000 folders on which it would have realized by resale profits to the amount of $750. June 29, 1933, defendant ordered 25,000 large 12 view folders of Greater Chicago. The order stated, "ship when ready." It was confirmed by plaintiff in the usual way. August 4, 1933, defendant gave an order for 25,000 large view folders of Chicago Parks. The word "rush" appears on this order. It was confirmed and accepted by plaintiff.

Mrs. Higgs testified she had calls for these view books every day and could have sold all of them had they been delivered within four or five weeks of the dates of the orders, which she says would have been the usual and normal time allowed for delivery. The order for the Park folders was cancelled by defendant October 16, 1933. The evidence of Mrs. Higgs is to the effect that this

She testified, however, indefinitely as to only two orders for these books received by her from customers, one September 8, 1933, for 25 folders and another November 28 for 25. Her statement on cross-examination is to the effect that she had no memorandums of orders received by her for these goods between June 29th and October 16th. As a matter of fact the inventory taken in December showed 3500 folders in defendant's stock at the factory, but she says she "was too busy to go out and inspect the merchandise." There is no evidence that defendant turned down any order received by her for these goods, and it is impossible to believe that if there had in fact been an opportunity to sell them, Mrs. Rigot would have failed to insist on delivery. The evidence is not sufficient to establish defendant's claim in this respect or any liability on the part of plaintiff.

Defendant also claims an offset to the amount of $405.62 because, it says, plaintiff charged ten cents a book for 40,562 view books, for which only nine cents should have been charged. The evidence shows that the view books were ordered by defendant and confirmation of the order sent to defendant by plaintiff at ten cents a book. Mrs. Rigot wrote on the confirmation in pencil, changing the price from ten to nine cents, but this was never returned to plaintiff for correction. Evidence for plaintiff is to the effect that if the confirmation had been returned as changed, the order would have been stopped automatically. Max Rigot testified he did not see the invoices or the billings; he said he told Mr. Teich he could not afford to pay more than $90 a thousand, and that Mr. Teich agreed to accept nine cents. Mrs. Rigot testified the price of nine cents was made after a meeting held during her husband's illness; she says she told Mr. Teich the day following receipt of the confirmation to take it back, that she did not want the goods at that price, and that Mr. Teich then issued a credit

She testified, however, indefinitely as to only two orders for these goods received by her from customers, one September 8, 1933, for 10 folders and another November 28 for 25. Her statement on cross-examination is to the effect that she had no memorandum of orders received by her for these goods between June 29th and October 16th. As a matter of fact the inventory taken in December showed 2500 remained in defendant's stock at the factory, but she says she "was too busy to go out and inspect the merchandise." There is no evidence that defendant turned down any order received by her for these goods, and it is impossible to believe that if there had in fact been an opportunity to sell them, Mrs. Rigot would have failed to insist on delivery. The evidence is not sufficient to establish defendant's claim in this respect or any liability on the part of plaintiff.

Defendant also claims an offset to the amount of $400.00 because, she says, plaintiff charged ten cents a book for 40,000 view books, for which only nine cents should have been charged. The evidence shows that the view books were ordered by defendant and confirmation of the order sent to defendant by plaintiff at ten cents a book. Mrs. Rigot wrote on the confirmation in pencil, changing the price from ten to nine cents, but this was never returned to plaintiff for correction. Evidence for plaintiff is to the effect that if the confirmation had been returned as changed, the order would have been stopped automatically. Max Rigot testified he did not see the invoices or the billings; he said he told [illegible] he could not afford to pay more than 900 a thousand, and [illegible] agreed to accept nine cents. Mrs. Rigot testified [illegible] which was made after a meeting held during her bill making the price nine cents; that this came back in the mail several days later and she put it in the files; it was not produced Mrs. Rigot said that the order was given May 8th and that her husbank became ill on the 25th, and that she received the confirmation a few days later. Another order dated June 24, 1933, for the same kind of goods, at the price of ten cents each, however, was produced. Mrs. Rigot acknowledged her signature to this order and admitted she also gave another order on the 30th of the month for a similar item at ten cents a book; her testimony as to this item seems to be inconsistent and contradictory. It is also contradicted by witnesses for defendant. The item ought not, in our opinion, to be allowed.

IV. There remains for consideration two items much disputed by the parties, both of which grow out of a special arrangement entered into during the season of 1933. The evidence shows that under the oral agreement theretofore existing it was customary for defendant to purchase its merchandise from plaintiff and resell it at such price as it might be able to secure. Defendant had an exclusive agency for the sale of plaintiff's products in the Chicago area. As the season of 1933 approached a large trade was anticipated on account of the exposition to be held in Chicago during that year. About the same time the price of paper from which defendant's products were manufactured as a result of federal legislation was doubled. In anticipation of this, plaintiff notified defendant and its other customers that on July 1, 1933, the price of its goods would be increased. When the trade received this information it produced a flood of orders from prospective customers.

Max Rigot was president of defendant corporation, Mrs. Rigot its secretary; both had large experience in the business. Curt Teich, Sr., was president of plaintiff corporation; his son Curt Teich, Jr., was the manager in control of the plant, and another son, Walter, was, as he describes himself, "contact man." The business bill making the price nine cents; that this came back in the mail several days later and she put it in the files; it was not produced. Mrs. Rigot said that the order was given by him and that her husband became ill on the 28th, and that she received the confirmation a few days later. Another order dated June 24, 1933, for the same kind of goods, at the price of ten cents each, however, was produced. Mrs. Rigot acknowledged her signature to this order and admitted she also gave another order on the 30th of the month for a similar item at ten cents a bottle; her testimony as to this item seems to be inconsistent and contradictory. It is also contradicted by witnesses for defendant. The item ought not, in our opinion, to be allowed.

IV. There remain for consideration two items much disputed by the parties, both of which grew out of a special arrangement entered into during the season of 1933. The evidence shows that under the oral agreement theretofore existing it was customary for defendant to purchase its merchandise from plaintiff and resell it at such prices as it might be able to secure. Defendant had an exclusive agency for the sale of plaintiff's products in the Chicago area. As the season of 1933 approached a large trade was anticipated on account of the exposition to be held in Chicago during that year. About the same time the price of paper from which defendant's products were manufactured as a result of federal legislation was doubled. In anticipation of this, plaintiff notified defendant and its other customers that on July 1, 1933, the price of its goods would be increased. When the trade received this information it produced a flood of orders from prospective customers.

V. Max Rigot was president of defendant corporation, Mrs. Rigot the secretary; both had large experience in the business. Curt Teich, Jr., was president of plaintiff corporation; his son Curt of plaintiff had been conducted in Chicago for 36 years, and the factory at this time was at 1755 Irving Park boulevard.

Mr. Rigot was taken seriously ill about May 25th. Mrs. Rigot thereupon took charge of the office; she found it very difficult to arrange to take care of the flood of orders which came in for the reasons above stated. A meeting was arranged between Mr. and Mrs. Rigot, Curt Teich, Jr., and Walter Teich about June 29th at the Edgewater Beach hospital where Mr. Rigot remained during his illness. At this meeting it was proposed in view of the situation which had arisen that plaintiff undertake to deliver orders received by defendant from the chain stores, as they were called, direct from the factory and thus relieve Mrs. Rigot of the burden. Walter Teich testifies he suggested that expenses incurred as a result of this arrangement should be taken out of the profits and what was left over divided fifty-fifty between plaintiff and defendant, that Mr. Rigot said he would be willing to have plaintiff go ahead and make up what plaintiff thought was enough goods to supply the demand, and that defendant would be responsible and pay plaintiff for goods that might be left over at the close of the Fair. Curt Teich, Jr., also says Mr. Rigot suggested that Mrs. Rigot be kept supplied and said that plaintiff should not worry about the goods left over as he would take care of that. He further testified that Mr. Rigot suggested the establishment of a department at plaintiff's plant to be known as Max Rigot Selling Agency, World's Fair Division, so that large orders fro the chain stores might be filled. He quotes Mr. Rigot as saying, "You organize this division and hire whatever help is necessary. The expenses will come out of the max profits and what is left over will be split 50-50 between us."

The three largest chain stores dealt with were Woolworths, Kresges and Walgreens, and under date of June 20th plaintiff mailed to each of them a letter (having first received the written approval of defendant) in which appeared this statement:

of plaintiff had been conducted in Chicago for 36 years, and the factory at this time was at 1755 Irving Park boulevard.

Mr. Rigot was taken seriously ill about May 25th. Mrs. Rigot thereupon took charge of the office; she found it very difficult to arrange to take care of the flood of orders which came in for the reasons above stated. A meeting was arranged between Mr. and Mrs. Rigot, Curt Teich, Jr., and Walter Teich about June 9th at the Edgewater Beach hospital where Mr. Rigot remained during his illness. At this meeting it was proposed in view of the situation which had arisen that plaintiff undertake to deliver orders received by defendant from the chain stores, as they were called, direct from the factory and thus relieve Mrs. Rigot of the burden. Walter Teich testifies he suggested that expenses incurred as a result of this arrangement should be taken out of the profits and what was left over divided fifty-fifty between plaintiff and defendant; that Mr. Rigot said he would be willing to have plaintiff go ahead and make up what plaintiff thought was enough goods to supply the demand, and that defendant would be responsible and pay plaintiff for goods that might be left over at the close of the Fair. Curt Teich, Jr., also says Mr. Rigot suggested that Mrs. Rigot be kept supplied and said that plaintiff should not worry about the goods left over as he would take care of that. He further testified that Mr. Rigot suggested the establishment of a department at plaintiff's plant to be known as Max Rigot Selling Agency, World's Fair Division, so that large orders fro the chain stores might be filled. He quotes Mr. Rigot as saying, "You organize this division and hire whatever help is necessary. The expenses will come out of the ~~gax~~ profits and what is left over will be split 50-50 between us."

The three largest chain stores dealt with were Woolworths, Kresges and Walgreens, and under date of June 29th plaintiff mailed to each of them a letter (having first received the written approval of defendant) in which appeared this statement:

"In order to assist the Max Rigot Selling Agency in maintaining first-class service to your stores, Mr. Rigot has asked us to ship and bill all orders for your stores direct through Curt Teich & Company, Inc., to which we are sure you will have no objection. We want to do this merely as an aid in maintaining the prompt and efficient service given you by the Max Rigot Selling Agency in the past."

Mrs. Rigot denies the conversation as to terms and says in substance that Walter Teich offered to handle these orders for her at the factory to help her out. The arrangement was undoubtedly made for the mutual benefit of plaintiff and defendant, both of whom were interested in keeping the trade and good will of these large customers. Teich, Sr., had been out of the city and when he returned, as the evidence indicates, he and Walter Teich called on Mr. Rigot July 6th or 7th. Both testified in substance that Mr. Rigot said he did not wish to have Mrs. Rigot worried about deliveries and they should go ahead and make goods sufficient to last throughout the summer; that the subject of the merchandise that might be left over at the end of the Fair was gxx again brought up, that Mr. Rigot said he would have ways of dispos ng of it, it was his merchandise and he was responsible and would pay for it. They further testified that Mr. Rigot said he was very anxious to have "the big accounts serviced;" that he was wil.ing to accept ten per cent on cards and twenty per cent on folders. Mr. Rigot was quite ill, and the con versation was ended with a statement by Teich that he would write up the conversation in regular form and submit it to Mrs. Rigot by return mail.

July 7, 1933, plaintiff wrote defendant a letter purporting to comply with this agreement. It recited that all orders received from these three large customers would be filled, shipped and billed by plaintiff direct to their stores, and that on post cards, folders, etc., shipped and billed, defendant should receive a ten per cent commission; that payments for the goods should be made to plaintiff and the commissions credited to defendant as soon as the invoices

"In order to assist the Max Nigot Selling Agency in maintaining first-class service to your stores, Mr. Nigot has asked us to ship and bill all orders for your stores direct through Telch & Company, Inc., to which we are sure you will have no objection. We want to do this merely as an aid in maintaining the prompt and efficient service given you by the Max Nigot Selling Agency in the past."

arrange." Mrs. Nigot denied the conversation as to terms and says in substance that Walter Telch offered to handle these orders for her at the factory to help her out. The arrangement was undoubtedly made for the mutual benefit of plaintiff and defendant, both of whom were interested in keeping the trade and good will of these large customers. Telch, Sr., had been out of the city and when he returned, as the evidence indicates, he and Walter Telch called on Mr. Nigot July 6th or 7th. Both testified in substance that Mr. Nigot said he did not wish to have Mrs. Nigot worried about deliveries and they should go ahead and make goods sufficient to last throughout the summer; that the subject of the merchandise that might be left over at the end of the fair was not again brought up; that Mr. Nigot said he would have ways of disposing of it, it was his merchandise and he was responsible and would pay for it. They further testified that Mr. Nigot said he was very anxious to have "the big accounts serviced;" that he was willing to accept ten per cent on cards and twenty per cent on folders. Mr. Nigot was quite ill, and the conversation was ended with a statement by Telch that he would write up the conversation in regular form and submit it to Mrs. Nigot by return mail.

July 7, 1933, plaintiff wrote defendant a letter purporting to comply with this agreement. It recited that all orders received from these three large customers would be filled, shipped and billed by plaintiff direct to their stores, and that on post cards, folders, etc., shipped and billed, defendant should receive a ten per cent commission; that payments for the goods should be made to plaintiff and the commissions credited to defendant as soon as the invoices were paid; that defendant should be invoiced for all goods actually delivered to these customers; that invoices and delivery slips would accompany each shipment so that any shortage could be reported at once and proper investigation made of claims reported within 48 hours; that the credit extended to defendant should not be over $10,000 at any time, and the final balance due plaintiff should be settled within 30 days after the closing of the Fair at the end of 1933. This letter was apparently sent to defendant by registered mail.

July 8, 1933, Mrs. Rigot handed to Walter Teich a proposed agreement written on the letterhead of the Max Rigot Selling Agency. It is dated Chicago, July 8, 1933, and reads:

> "It is hereby agreed and accepted by Max Rigot Selling Agency and Curt Teich & Co. that on all orders for World's Fair Cards, World's Fair Folders and World's Fair Books, Minature, Sets, etc. which they are shipping, billing and charging direct to the F. W. Woolworth Co., S. S. Kresge Co., Walgreen Co. and others, our commission on all and every one of these orders is and will be 10% on all view cards. 25% on all view folders.
>
> Max Rigot Selling Agency
> Anna Rigot
> Sect.
> Curt Teich & Company
> Curt Teich
> Pres."

In the exhibit offered in evidence the words "and view books" and the words "and Minature Sets" were cancelled, and the testimony is to the effect that the cancellation of these words was made by Curt Teich, Sr., who says that after cancelling the same he called the matter to the attention of Mr. Rigot and told him that commissions could not be allowed on the view books and minature sets.

July 10, 1933, defendant by Max Rigot sent to plaintiff a reply to the registered letter in which he said:

> "There is something rotten in Denmark, or rather at 1755 Irving Park Blvd."

The letter asked why all this "scheming," complained that instead of assisting Mrs. Rigot, plaintiff was antagonizing her, called atten-

were paid; that defendant should be invoiced for all goods actually delivered to these customers; that invoices and delivery slips should accompany each shipment so that any shortage could be reported at once and proper investigation made of claims reported within 48 hours; that the credit extended to defendant would not be over $10,000 at any time, and the final balance due plaintiff should be settled within 30 days after the closing of the Fair at the end of 1933. This letter was apparently sent to defendant by registered mail.

July 8, 1933, Mrs. Higet handed to Walter Teich a proposed agreement written on the letterhead of the Max Higet Selling Agency. It is dated Chicago, July 8, 1933, and reads:

"It is hereby agreed and accepted by Max Higet Selling Agency and Curt Teich & Co. that on all orders for World's Fair Cards, World's Fair folders and World's Fair Books, miniature sets, etc. which they are shipping, billing and charging direct to the F. W. Woolworth Co., S. S. Kresge Co., Walgreen Co. and others, our commission on all and every one of these orders is and will be 10% on all view cards. 20% on all view folders.

Max Higet Selling Agency
Anna Higet
Secy.
Curt Teich & Company
Curt Teich
Pres."

In the exhibit offered in evidence the words "and view books" and the words "and miniature sets" were cancelled, and the testimony is to the effect that the cancellation of these words was made by Curt Teich, Jr., who says that after cancelling the same he called the matter to the attention of Mr. Higet and told him that commissions could not be allowed on the view books and miniature sets.

July 10, 1933, defendant by Max Higet sent to plaintiff a reply to the registered letter in which he said:

"There is something rotten in Denmark, or rather at 1735 Irving Park Blvd."

The letter asked why all this "uproaring," complained that instead of assisting Mrs. Higet, plaintiff was antagonizing her, called attention to the agreement given by Mrs. Rigot to Walter, and added: "You are constantly scheming and changing your mind. What are you afraid of? Have you taken advantage of my sickness, and now is your conscience bothering you?" The letter also said that to "ease your mind" defendant had paid $10,000 in advance and concluded, "Why then try to dictate the terms at your whim?" July 11th plaintiff replied lengthily to this letter, evidently intending to mollify defendant, saying plaintiff was anxious to help defendant, wanted him to regain his health as quickly as possible, and further:

"While the writer was away orders came in so fast to the Max Rigot Selling Agency that Mrs. Rigot asked us to fill these orders direct. We did this, as we felt like you and Mrs. Rigot, that under all conditions the good will of the chain stores must be preserved. The handling of these orders meant extra expense, and in order to handle it right, you as president of Max Rigot Selling Agency and the writer as president of Curt Teich & Company came to an agreement, which was acknowledged by me in our letter of July 7."

The letter protests that plaintiff is not scheming or taking advantage, calls attention to the condition of matters at the paper mills and their cooperation by running day and night and Sundays; says there will be more business than ever the next sixty days; that the parties must "keep our minds free from petty annoyances and be prepared to meet any emergency", etc.; that the writing of letters such as that of July 10, 1933, will not help Mr. Rigot's health or "our nerves;" that that letter would not have been written had it been given due consideration, but that plaintiff would not hold it against defendant; asks that in the future if defendant had anything to say he should not put it in a letter as it had that time, and states that if Mr. Rigot would call up the writer, Curt Teich, he would be glad to talk over the situation with him.

July 12, 1933, Mr. Rigot wrote from the Edgewater Beach hotel that if he had used rather strong language he still felt it was not out of place; that his sickness had kept him from knowing what was going on; that he enclosed an estimate of what was and tion to the agreement given by Mrs. Bigot to Walter, and added: "You are constantly scheming and changing your mind. What are you afraid of? Have you taken advantage of my sickness, and has [illegible] your conscience bothering you?" The letter also said that to "ease your mind" defendant had paid $10,000 in advance and concluded, "Why then try to dictate the terms at your whim?" July 11th plaintiff replied lengthily to this letter, evidently intending mollify defendant, saying plaintiff was anxious to help defendants, wanted him to regain his health as quickly as possible, and further:

"While the writer was away orders came in so fast to the Ben Bigot Selling Agency that Mrs. Bigot asked us to fill these orders direct. We did this, as we felt like you and Mrs. Bigot, that under all conditions the good will of the chain stores must be preserved. The handling of these orders meant extra expense, and in order to handle it right, you as president of Ben Bigot Selling Agency and the writer as president of Curt Teich & Company came to an agreement, which was acknowledged by me in our letter of July 7."

The letter protests that plaintiff is not scheming or taking advantage, calls attention to the condition of matters at the paper mills and their cooperation by running day and night and Sundays; says there will be more business than ever the next sixty days; that the parties must "keep our minds free from petty annoyances and be prepared to meet any emergency", etc.; that the writing of letters such as that of July 10, 1933, will not help Mr. Bigot's health or your nerves;" that that letter would not have been written had it been given due consideration, but that plaintiff would not hold it against defendant, only that in the future if defendant had anything to say he should not put it in a letter as it had that time, and states that if Mr. Bigot would call up the writer, Curt Teich, he would be glad to talk over the situation with him.

July 13, 1933, Mr. Bigot wrote from the Edgewater Beach Hotel that if he had used rather strong language he still felt it was not out of place; that his sickness had kept him from knowing what was going on; that he enclosed an estimate of what was and could be done. The letter complains that if plaintiff had been able to supply the demand for goods, space could have been rented next to defendant's office with a little extra expense - not over two or three hundred dollars and all the orders filled, thus saving many thousands of dollars. The letter states: "Now, Mr. Teich, don't let us waste any more time and energy on writing letters which lead to nothing. Let us get down to work. There's a nice few extra thousand dollars in it for you also." After paying a compliment to Walter Teich, the letter concludes: "As you insisted on a signed agreement-- sign the agreements which Walter delivered to you, and as I hope to be down to work next week, let us pull together in peace and harmony for ~~xx~~ now is the chance to get out of the RED for which we have been waiting for the last three years."

After these letters plaintiff proceeded with the manufacture of the goods as orders were given by Mrs. Rigot. According to the new arrangements the goods sold to the chain stores were billed direct by plaintiff and plaintiff received payment direct for the goods and gave credit to defendant on most of the items at ten per cent.

There is much more evidence conflicting in its nature as to conversations between the parties, but this written evidence conclusively shows, we think, that the contention now made by defendant that it is entitled to credit as under the old arrangement for $8106.17 for profit on merchandise sold for it through plaintiff cannot be sustained. On the contrary, we think that a preponderance of the evidence tends to show (and that the trial court apparently found) that the parties after July 8, 1933, operated under the written agreement which Mrs. Rigot sent by Walter to plaintiff, and that after striking out the words as already indicated, plaintiff (waived its views on these matters and proceeded to carry on the business according to that agreement as originally submitted.

8

could be done. The letter complains that if plaintiff had been able to supply the demand for goods, space could have been rented next to defendant's office with a little extra expense - not over two or three hundred dollars and all the orders filled, thus saving many thousands of dollars. The letter states: "Now, Mr. Telch, don't let us waste any more time and energy on writing letters which lead to nothing. Let us get down to work. There's a nice few extra thousand dollars in it for you also." After paying a compliment to Walter Telch, the letter concludes: "As you insisted on a signed agreement-- sign the agreements which Walter delivered to you, and as I hope to be down to work next week, let us pull together in peace and harmony for as now is the chance to get out of the hole for which we have been waiting for the last three years."

After these letters plaintiff proceeded with the manufacture of the goods as orders were given by Mrs. Sigot. According to the new arrangements the goods sold to the chain stores were billed direct by plaintiff and plaintiff received payment direct for the goods and gave credit to defendant on most of the items at ten per cent.

There is much more evidence conflicting in its nature as to conversations between the parties, but this written evidence conclusively shows, we think, that the contention now made by defendant that it is entitled to credit as under the old arrangement for $3108.17 for profit on merchandise sold for it through plaintiff cannot be sustained. On the contrary, we think that a preponderance of the evidence tends to show (and that the trial court apparently found) that the parties after July 5, 1933, operated under the written agreement which Mrs. Sigot sent by Walter to plaintiff, and that after striking out the words as already indicated, plaintiff waived its views on these matters and proceeded to carry on the business according to that agreement as originally submitted.

This was apparently the view of the trial court. Computing upon the basis of the agreement of July 8, 1933, which was uncancelled, defendant would be entitled (as shown by defendant's exhibit 37) to a total credit by way of commissions of $5118.53, which we think it is apparent was allowed by the trial court and for which we find defendant is entitled to receive credit upon the purchase price of goods sold and delivered amounting to $13,687.47, leaving a balance of $8568.94.

V. Plaintiff claims the amount of $9,871.24 upon the theory that by reason of parol agreements defendant is obligated to pay plaintiff for goods manufactured at its request but not accepted by it. The uncontradicted evidence tends to show that at the close of the season of 1933 there remained in the possession of plaintiff at the factory 418,345 World's Fair cards, 379,318 World's Fair folders, 28,661 World's Fair books and 145,103 World's Fair minatures, upon all of which appeared the imprint of the Max Rigot Sales Agency. The evidence also tends to show that the sales price of these goods amounts to the sum demanded by plaintiff on these items. While it is somewhat difficult to ascertain precisely which items were allowed and which disallowed by the trial Judge, we think it apparent that these items set up in the counts one to four of the declaration, were allowed substantially.

As already stated, the evidence tending to establish these claims rests entirely in parol. Curt Teich, Sr., Curt Teich, Jr. and Walter Teich all testify to oral conversations with Mr. and Mrs. Rigot in which they are in substance said to have promised, that defendant would pay for any goods left over at the end of the season; that these goods would be defendant's goods, in that plaintiff should not concern itself about them. They say that at different times Mr. Rigot requested that Mrs. Rigot during his illness and while the rush was on should be supplied with goods, and that defendant would

This was apparently the view of the trial court. Computing upon the basis of the agreement of July 6, 1933, which was uncancelled, defendant ought to be credited (as shown by defendant's exhibit 37) to a total credit by way of commissions of $8118.63, which we think it is apparent was allowed by the trial court and for which we find the defendant is entitled to receive credit upon the purchase price of goods sold and delivered amounting to $13,687.47, leaving a balance of $[illegible].

Plaintiff claims the amount of $9,871.24 upon the theory that by reason of parol agreements defendant is obligated to pay plaintiff for goods manufactured at its request but not accepted by it. The preponderance of evidence tends to show that at the close of the season of 1933 there remained in the possession of plaintiff at the factory [illegible] World's Fair cards, 570,[illegible] World's Fair Tele-[illegible], [illegible] World's Fair Books and 148,153 World's Fair almanacs, upon all of which appeared the imprint of the Max Rigot Sales Agency. The evidence also tends to show that the sales price of these goods amounts to the sum demanded by plaintiff on these items. While it is somewhat difficult to ascertain precisely which items were allowed and which disallowed by the trial judge, we think it apparent that these items set up in the counts one to four of the declaration, were allowed substantially.

As already stated, the evidence tending to establish these claims [illegible] is parol. Curt Teich, Sr., Curt Teich, Jr. and Ralph Teich and Mrs. [illegible] testify to oral conversations with Mr. Rigot in which [illegible] in substance said to have promised, that defendant would [illegible] any goods left over at the end of the season; that [illegible] for defendant's goods, in that plaintiff should [illegible] [illegible]. They say that at different times [illegible] Mr. Rigot requested that Mrs. [illegible] during his absence [illegible] which was as should be supplied [illegible] and that defendants would pay for any surplus. There is also uncontradicted evidence to the effect that late in the season Mrs. Riget objected to the sale of part of these goods to another customer on the ground that defendant's agency for the sale of the goods was an exclusive one. Mr. Kepner, auditor for plaintiff, also testifies that Mr. Riget made a statement to him to the effect that the goods belonged to defendant and that defendant would pay for them. He says that Mr. Riget said, speaking of these goods, "Don't worry about that, I will take care of it, that is all my stuff."

Relying upon this evidence, plaintiff contends that under section 18, paragraph 2 of the Sales act (Cahill's Ill. Rev. Stats. 1933, chap. 121½) and section 19, rule 4 of the same act, it was the intention of the parties that the title to these goods should pass to defendant. Plaintiff argues that the provisions of the last named section to the effect that where there is a contract to sell unascertained or future goods by description and goods of that description in a deliverable state were unreservedly appropriated to the contract either by the seller with the ~~xxxxxx~~ assent of the buyer, or the buyer with the assent of the seller, the property in the goods thereupon passes to the buyer, and that the assent may be either express or implied and may be given either before or after the appropriation is made. Plaintiff says that delivery of the goods to the buyer in such case is not necessary to pass the title and cites Mechem on Sales, sec. 1674; Rhea v. Riner, 21 Ill. 526; Osgood v. Skinner, 211 Ill. 229; Commonwealth Trust Co. v. Gregson, 303 Ill. 458; Rudin v. King-Richardson Co., 311 Ill. 513; Santa Rosa Vallejo Tan Co. v. Kronauer & Co., 228 Ill. App. 236. Plaintiff also calls attention to the rule that any act done by the buyer of the goods tendered in fulfillment of the contract which he has no right to do, unless he is the owner of the goods, is in itself an acceptance, citing M. Hommel Wine Co.

pay for any surplus. There is also uncontradicted evidence to the effect that late in the season Mrs. Rigot objected to the sale of part of these goods to another customer on the ground that defendant's agency for the sale of the goods was an exclusive one. Mr. Kegner, auditor for plaintiff, also testifies that Mr. Rigot made a statement to him to the effect that the goods belonged to defendant and that defendant would pay for them. He says that Mr. Rigot said, speaking of these goods, "Don't worry about that, I will take care of it, that is all my stuff."

Relying upon this evidence, plaintiff contends that under section 19, paragraph 2 of the Sales act (Cahill's Ill. Rev. Stats. 1933, chap. 121½) and section 19, rule 4 of the same act, it was the intention of the parties that the title to these goods should pass to defendant. Plaintiff argues that the provisions of the last named section to the effect that where there is a contract to sell unascertained or future goods by description and goods of that description in a deliverable state were unreservedly appropriated to the contract either by the seller with the assent of the buyer, or the buyer with the assent of the seller, the property in the goods thereupon passes to the buyer, and that the assent may be either express or implied and may be given either before or after the appropriation is made. Plaintiff says that delivery of the goods to the buyer in such case is not necessary to pass the title and cites Mechem on Sales, sec. 1074; <u>[illegible] v. [illegible]</u>, 81 Ill. 580; <u>Osgood v. Skinner</u>, 211 Ill. 229; <u>Commonwealth Trust Co. v. Gregson</u>, 303 Ill. 486; <u>Austin v. King-Hitchcock Co.</u>, 311 Ill. 413; <u>Santa Rosa Vallejo Tan. Co. v. Kronauer</u>, 133 Ill. App. 328. Plaintiff also calls attention to the rule that any act done by the buyer of the goods tendered in fulfillment of the contract which he has no right to do, unless he is the owner of the goods, is in itself an acceptance, citing <u>H. [illegible] Fish Co.</u>

v. Netter, 197 Ill. App. 382; Wolf Co. v. Monarch Refrigerating Co., 252 Ill. 491. Plaintiff says that in such case replevin or an action for damages in the event of conversion by the seller will lie. The cases cited state well settled law where circumstances are such as to make the rule stated applicable. Defendant, as we understand, does not argue that the law is not as stated, but contends, in the first place, that the supposed contract testified to by plaintiff's witnesses is too ambiguous and uncertain to be enforceable because it is impossible to ascertain from the evidence offered by plaintiff that a definite and certain quantity of goods or articles were sold and no means are shown by which the quantities involved in the contract could be determined. It is urged (plausibly we think) that the supposed contract upon which plaintiff relies is void for uncertainty. 55 Corpus Juris 195; Wolf v. Selig Polyscope Co., 204 Ill. App. 178; Gray v. Cooper, 217 Mo. App. 592; Dixie Portland Flour Co. v. Kelsay-Burns Milling Co., 86 Ind.App. 137.

It is also urged (plausibly, we think) that assuming that the evidence is sufficient to establish a contract, there is a variance between the agreement as alleged in counts 1 to 4, and the supposed agreement proved by the evidence, in that these counts allege verbal orders for specific quantities of specific merchandise while the proof at most tends to show verbal orders for unascertained quantities of specific merchandise. Hamilton Co. v. Channel Chemical Co., 327 Ill. 362; Brodsky v. Frank, 342 Ill. 110; Beaver District v. C. C. C. & St. L. Ry. Co., 347 Ill. 122. However this may be, there remains the controlling question of fact argued at length in defendant's brief to the effect that a preponderance of the evidence compels the inference that there was no such contract or agreement between the parties. So far as the testimony in regard to the oral conversations is concerned, plaintiff, its officers and employees testified to oral conversations as already stated. These conversa-

v. Hudson, 167 Ill. App. 360; Hall Co. v. Monarch Refrigerating Co., 208 Ill. 493. Plaintiff says that in such case replevin or an action for damages in the event of conversion by the seller will lie. The cases cited state well settled law where circumstances are such as to make the rule stated applicable. Defendant, as we understand, does not argue that the law is not as stated, but contends, in the first place, that the supposed contract testified to by plaintiff's witnesses is too ambiguous and uncertain to be enforceable because it is impossible to ascertain from the evidence offered by plaintiff that a definite and certain quantity of goods or materials were sold and no means are shown by which the quantities involved in the contract could be determined. It is urged (plausibly) by defendant that the supposed contract upon which plaintiff relies is void for uncertainty. 35 Corpus Juris 105; Hall v. [illegible] Refrigerating Co., 208 Ill. 493; [illegible] v. [illegible], 217 Mo. App. 502; [illegible] Portland Flour Co. v. [illegible] Milling Co., 58 Ind. App. 137.

It is also urged (plausibly, we think) that assuming that the evidence is sufficient to establish a contract, there is a variance between the agreement as alleged in counts 1 to 4, and the supposed agreement proved by the evidence, in that those counts allege verbal orders for specific quantities of specific merchandise while the proof at most tends to show verbal orders for unascertained quantities of specific merchandise. [illegible] Co. v. [illegible], 257 Ill. 369; [illegible] v. [illegible], 348 Ill. 110; [illegible] v. C. & A. R. R. Co., 247 Ill. 182. However this may be, there remains the controlling question of fact argued at length in defendant's brief to the effect that a preponderance of the evidence shows that [illegible] or otherwise [illegible] the goods. So far as the testimony in regard to the sale [illegible] by the buyer of the goods [illegible] tions are specifically denied by Mr. and Mrs. Rigot, to whom they are attributed. The witnesses on both sides of the controversy seem to be equally interested. Under such circumstances, in weighing the evidence, it is necessary to carefully search the record for the purpose of ascertaining facts and circumstances by which the truth of the issue of fact may be determined. There is first the probability or improbability of the facts as related by the witnesses.

Plaintiff asks us to find that defendant obligated itself to pay unreservedly for an indefinite amount of goods such as plaintiff might see fit to manufacture. Defendant says that it is unreasonable to suppose that defendant would have obligated itself to such an unlimited extent. The argument has much weight. The evidence heretofore recited shows that the Rigots were suspicious of plaintiff and did not seem to have confidence that defendant would be fairly treated by plaintiff in the ususual situation which had arisen. The letter of Max Rigot gave expression to his views that there was something "rotten in Denmark." It seems improbable that under such circumstances he would unreservedly commit himself to plaintiff's good will. Upon the whole, we think the agreements upon which plaintiff relies quite improbable. Again, it will be remembered that on July 7, 1933, Mr. Teich, Sr., after a conference with the Rigots, stated he would write a letter giving his version of the contract between them. The letter of that date appears in evidence and seems to cover the situation fully, but we search the letter in vain for any statement indicating that an agreement had been made that plaintiff might manufacture whatever amount of goods it wished to and that defendant would be obligated to take and pay for them. If such promise had been made, it would seem that Mr. Teich in this letter would have at least mentioned it. Its absence tends strongly to indicate that nosuch agreement was made. Again, the usual custom according to all the evidence was that orders given for goods for which defendant was obligated to pay were com-tions are specifically denied by Mr. and Mrs. Rigot, to whom they are attributed. The witnesses on both sides of the controversy seem to be equally interested. Under such circumstances, in weighing the evidence, it is necessary to carefully search the record for the purpose of ascertaining facts and circumstances by which the truth of the issue of fact may be determined. There is first the probability or improbability of the facts as related by the witnesses.

Plaintiff asks us to find that defendant obligated itself to pay unreservedly for an indefinite amount of goods such as plaintiff might see fit to manufacture. Defendant says that it is unreasonable to suppose that defendant would have obligated itself to such an unlimited extent. The argument has much weight. The evidence heretofore recited shows that the Rigots were suspicious of plaintiff and did not seem to have confidence that defendant would be fairly treated by plaintiff in the unusual situation which had arisen. The letter of Max Rigot gave expression to his views that there was something "rotten in Denmark." It seems improbable that under such circumstances he would unreservedly commit himself to plaintiff's good will. Upon the whole, we think the agreements upon which plaintiff relies quite improbable. Again, it will be remembered that on July 7, 1923, Mr. Teich, Sr., after a conference with the Rigots, stated he would write a letter giving his version of the contract between them. The letter of that date appears in evidence and seems to cover the situation fully, but we search the letter in vain for any statement indicating that an agreement had been made that plaintiff might manufacture whatever amount of goods it wished to and that defendant would be obligated to take and pay for them. If such promise had been made, it would seem that Mr. Teich in this letter would have at least mentioned it. Its absence tends strongly to indicate that no such agreement was made. Again, the usual custom according to all the evidence was that orders given for goods for which defendant was obligated to pay were confirmed in writing. The evidence is all to the effect that such orders would be confirmed and promptly given. There were no confirmations and no bills issued during the ~~[illegible]~~ entire season covering the goods described in counts one to four. The inference, of course, is that these goods were not ordered by defendant and that defendant was not obligated concerning them. Again, plaintiff's books when examined tend strongly to support the theory of defendant. The evidence shows that an examination of these books fails to disclose that plaintiff ever made any charge against defendant for these goods on its books. Again, the proof shows that statements were rendered by plaintiff monthly and sometimes oftener, but no statement was ever rendered by plaintiff tending to show that defendant was to be thus liable. Again, on August 15th plaintiff wrote defendant:

> "No doubt, you are aware of the fact that very shortly a number of your subjects will be sold out completely. It takes three weeks to make up a new edition, and it is to your interest that these orders are started at an early date."

Pertinently, defendant asks if the merchandise now sued for belonged to defendant, what was the necessity for further orders, and why this letter? Again, in September the uncontradicted evidence shows that plaintiff offered to reduce the price to defendant of a part of this merchandise. Why offer to reduce it, if the merchandise had been already sold for a definite price and appropriate it to defendant, as plaintiff now insists? Again, on September 6, 1933, Walter Teich, as the evidence shows, gave Mrs. Higet an inventory of these goods in which in his own handwriting they were designated as a part of the "C. T. World's Fair Cards." Again, on August 21, 1933, Walter Teich, as the evidence shows, gave to Mrs. Higet an inventory of defendant's reserve stock at the factory, which appears in evidence as defendant's exhibit 15, and defendant pertinently asks, why if it was defendant's merchandise, was it put on a separate and distinct list?

firmed in writing. The evidence is all to the effect that such orders would be confirmed and promptly given. There were no confirmations and no bills issued during the entire season covering the goods described in counts one to four. The inference, of course, is that these goods were not ordered by defendant and that defendant was not obligated concerning them. Again, plaintiff's books when examined tend strongly to support the theory of defendant. The evidence shows that an examination of these books fails to disclose that plaintiff ever made any charge against defendant for these goods on its books. Again, the proof shows that statements were rendered by plaintiff monthly and sometimes oftener, but no statement was ever rendered by plaintiff tending to show that defendant was to be thus liable. Again, on August 15th plaintiff wrote defendant:

"No doubt, you are aware of the fact that very shortly a number of your subjects will be sold out completely. It takes three weeks to make up a new edition, and it is to your interest that these orders are started at an early date."

Pertinently, defendant asks if the merchandise now sued for belonged to defendant, what was the necessity for further orders, and why this letter? Again, in September the uncontradicted evidence shows that plaintiff offered to reduce the price to defendant of a part of this merchandise. Why offer to reduce it, if the merchandise had been already sold for a definite price and appropriate it to defendant, as plaintiff now insists? Again, on September 6, 1933, Walter Teich, as the evidence shows, gave Mrs. Hight an inventory of these goods in which in his own handwriting they were designated as a part of the "C. T. World's Fair Cards." Again, on August 21, 1933, Walter Teich, as the evidence shows, gave to Mrs. Hight an inventory of defendant's reserve stock at the factory, which appears in evidence as defendant's exhibit 1, and defendant pertinently asks, why if it was defendant's merchandise, was it put on a separate and distinct list?

Again, it will be remembered that plaintiff has contended that defendant was not to get any commission on view books and minatures -- the items which appear scratched out on plaintiff's exhibit No. 7. Yet in these counts plaintiff seeks to recover for view books and xxx minatures, thus inconsistently and unreasonably taking the position that defendant would be obligated to pay for goods left over, although not entitled to receive any compensation at all for such of the goods as were sold. Defendant reasonably argues that one does not agree to purchase merchandise on which he is to receive no profit or commission. Indeed, Walter Teich in his testimony stated that deliveries were made to a customer, Mr. Hearne, out of this stock remaining, which he described as "out of our stock."

VI. The inference of fact from all these matters is, we think, that defendant did not make a contract by which it agreed to obligate itself to pay for these goods. These items therefore amounting to the sum of $9,871.24 must be disallowed. We have already found that defendant is entitled to commissions not yet credited in the amount of $5,118.53. The total amount due for goods sold and delivered was $13,687.47, and allowing this credit there remains a balance due from defendant to plaintiff of $8,568.94, for which judgment will be entered in this court.

For the reasons indicated the judgment of the trial court is reversed, with judgment here in favor of plaintiff and against defendant for $8,568.94.

REVERSED WITH FINDING OF FACT AND JUDGMENT HERE.

O'Connor, P. J., and McSurely, J., concur.

[illegible]

[illegible] it will be remembered that plaintiff had consented that defendant was not to get any commission on view books and signatures -- the items which appear scratched out on plaintiff's exhibit No. 7. Yet in these counts plaintiff seeks to recover for view books and signatures, thus imposing plainly and unreasonably upon the position that defendant would be obligated to pay for goods sold, although not entitled to receive any compensation at all for most of the goods as were sold. Defendant reasonably argues that one does not agree to purchase merchandise on which he is to receive no profit or commission. Indeed, Walter [illegible] [illegible] stated that deliveries were made to a customer, the balance of this stock remaining, which he described as "[illegible]"

[illegible] of fact from all these matters is, we think, [illegible] a contract by which it agreed to [illegible] [illegible] those goods. These items therefore [illegible] [illegible] of $1,571.21 must be disallowed. We have already [illegible] that defendant is entitled to commissions not yet credited [illegible] of $1,115.55. The total amount due for goods sold [illegible] was $11,[illegible].47, and allowing this credit there re[illegible] a balance due from defendant to plaintiff of $5,566.94, for [illegible] judgment will be entered in this court.

For the reasons indicated the judgment of the trial court [illegible] judgment here in favor of plaintiff and against [illegible] $5,[illegible].94.

[illegible] WITH FINDING OF FACT AND JUDGMENT HERE.

O'Connor, P.J., and [illegible], J., concur.

37953

DELLA FISHER,
Plaintiff in Error,

vs.

GUY A. RICHARDSON, etc., et al., as CHICAGO SURFACE LINES,
Defendants in Error.

ERROR TO SUPERIOR COURT OF COOK COUNTY.

280 I.A. 618[4]

MR. JUSTICE MATCHETT DELIVERED THE OPINION OF THE COURT.

December 24, 1931, plaintiff filed a declaration in case in five counts, the first of which in substance averred that on August 1, 1930, she was a passenger on one of defendant's street cars at or near the intersection of 63rd street and Stony Island avenue in Chicago, and that defendants so negligently managed and propelled the car that while in the exercise of due care plaintiff was thrown upon the rear platform, steps and upon the ground, injuring her. Another count charged defendants with negligence in that while plaintiff was in the act of alighting with care the car was started forward with a violent jerk; another, that plaintiff was about to alight and before she had time to do so, defendants started the car; and yet another count, afterward withdrawn, charged wilful and wanton negligence.

Defendants filed a plea of the general issue. The cause was submitted to a jury which returned a verdict for defendants on which the court, overruling plaintiff's motion for a new trial, entered judgment. It is urged for reversal that the verdict and the judgment are against the manifest weight of the evidence; that the court erred in permitting an exhibit designated as "History Sheet" to be taken to the jury room, and that the court erred in giving certain instructions to the jury at the request of defendants.

The evidence for plaintiff tended to show that on August 1, 1930, she was a passenger on a car of defendants going east on 63rd

37053

[illegible],
Plaintiff in Error,

vs.

[illegible], etc., et al., as [illegible],
Defendants in Error.

ERROR TO SUPERIOR COURT

OF COUNTY.

280 I.A. 618

MR. JUSTICE [illegible] DELIVERED THE OPINION OF THE COURT.

[illegible] 14, 1931, plaintiff filed a declaration in case in five counts, the first of which in substance averred that on August 1, 1930, she was a passenger on one of defendant's street cars at near the intersection of [illegible] street and Stony Island avenue in Chicago, and that defendants so negligently managed and propelled the car that while in the exercise of due care plaintiff was thrown upon the rear platform, steps and upon the ground, injuring her. Another count charged defendants with negligence in that while plaintiff was in the act of alighting with care the car was started forward with a violent jerk; another, that plaintiff was about to alight and before she had time to do so, defendants started the car; and yet another count, afterward withdrawn, charged wilful and wanton negligence.

Defendants filed a plea of the general issue. The cause was submitted to a jury which returned a verdict for defendants on which the court, overruling plaintiff's motion for a new trial, entered judgment. It is urged for reversal that the verdict and the judgment are against the manifest weight of the evidence; that the court erred in permitting an exhibit designated as "History Sheet" to be taken to the jury room, and that the court erred in giving certain instructions to the jury at the request of defendants.

The evidence for plaintiff tended to show that on August 1, 1930, she was a passenger on a car of defendants going east on [illegible] street to her home at 1416 East 54th street; that as the car approached Stony Island avenue (which runs north and south) where she expected to take another car, it stopped; that plaintiff was then out on the rear platform; that a man on the platform just ahead of her got off; that simultaneously a lady boarded the car; that when one of plaintiff's feet was reaching down toward the pavement and the other still on the step of the car, the car started with a quick jerk, throwing plaintiff to the pavement and inflicting very serious injuries upon her.

The evidence for defendants tended to show that plaintiff came to the rear platform of the car and while the car was in motion and before it came to its regular stopping place, she undertook to alight, though warned by the conductor not to do so, and fell off the car.

Plaintiff's narration of the manner in which the accident occurred is corroborated by a single witness, Mr. Olthen. Defendants point out that three eye-witnesses testified positively that plaintiff undertook to alight from the moving car before it reached the usual stopping place, and that three other witnesses testified to other facts inconsistent with plaintiff's theory of the case.

Kramer, the conductor of the car, testified that plaintiff stepped toward the entering part of the car and before he knew it she was off on the ground. The car, he said, had not stopped but was slowing down and went about fifteen feet after she stepped off; that there was no jerking or jarring of the car at the time; that a man stood on the platform and Kramer took his name.

Stanley Peppilars, the man who stood on the platform of the car, was produced as a witness by defendants and testified that he saw plaintiff coming out of the exit door of the street car, walking slowly. While he was looking at her she all at once stepped off the car; the car was then slowing down to a stop and went slowly about almost to her home at 1411 East 54th street; that as the car approached Stony Island avenue (which runs north and south) where she expected to take another car, it stopped; that plaintiff was then out on the rear platform; that a man on the platform just ahead of her got off; that simultaneously a lady boarded the car; that when one of plaintiff's feet was reaching down toward the pavement and the other still on the step of the car, the car started with a quick jerk, throwing plaintiff to the pavement and inflicting very serious injuries upon her.

The evidence for defendants tended to show that plaintiff came to the rear platform of the car and while the car was in motion and before it came to its regular stopping place, she undertook to alight, though warned by the conductor not to do so, and fell off the car.

Plaintiff's narration of the manner in which the accident occurred is corroborated by a single witness, Mr. Olthen. Defendants point out that three eye-witnesses testified positively that plaintiff undertook to alight from the moving car before it reached the usual stopping place, and that three other witnesses testified to other facts inconsistent with plaintiff's theory of the case.

Kramer, the conductor of the car, testified that plaintiff stepped toward the entering part of the car and before he knew it she was off on the ground. The car, he said, had not stopped but was slowing down and went about fifteen feet after she stepped off; that there was no jerking or jarring of the car at the time; that a man stood on the platform and Kramer took his name.

Stanley Poppelaars, the man who stood on the platform of the car, was produced as a witness by defendants and testified that he saw plaintiff coming out of the rear door of street car, walking slowly. While he was looking, her she all at once stepped off the car; the car was then slowing down to a stop and went slowly about fifteen feet after the lady stepped off and then came to a stop. He and the conductor picked her up from the street, "walked her" to the curbstone and over to the drug store and put her in a chair. No one else was alighting from the car when the lady stepped off nor was any woman boarding the car. There was no jerk or jar of the car during the time the lady stepped off. He was in a hurry to get home, and after the lady was in the chair in the drug store he signed the card the conductor gave him and went over to 64th street to catch a car.

At the time of the accident Mr. and Mrs. Newman were walking on the south side of 63rd street. Mrs. Newman says she saw a woman step off the moving car when it was about 75 feet from the corner. Mr. Newman testified his wife made an exclamation; that he looked and saw a woman on the ground; that after the accident the car stopped close to its usual stopping place; that he did not notice the car at first; he noticed the woman.

Headley, the motorman, testified that he was on the front platform of the car which was "drifting to make a stop;" he was about 20 or 30 feet from the corner; he looked back to see what the trouble was and saw the conductor and another man helping plaintiff to the sidewalk from a point ten or fifteen feet to the rear of the car.

Mr. Cameron, a passenger on the car and employed by the Daily News, testified: He noticed that the car stopped a little short of the corner and that the motorman was not in his place. The street car had stopped ten or fifteen feet west of the regular stopping place; he saw the conductor and another man helping a woman across the street to the drug store; at that time he handed his business card to the motorman.

Martin Meehan, a policeman at the Woodlawn station, went to St. Bernard hospital, where plaintiff was taken on the evening of fifteen feet after the lady stepped off and then came to a stop. He and the conductor picked her up from the street, "walked her" to the curbstone and over to the drug store and put her in a chair. No one else was alighting from the car when the lady stepped off nor was any woman boarding the car. There was no jerk or jar of the car during the time the lady stepped off. He was in a hurry to get home, and after the lady was in the chair in the drug store he signed the card the conductor gave him and went over to 63th street to catch a car.

At the time of the accident Mr. and Mrs. Newman were walking on the south side of 63rd street. Mrs. Newman says she saw a woman step off the moving car when it was about 75 feet from the corner. Mr. Newman testified his wife made an exclamation; that he looked and saw a woman on the ground; that after the accident the car stopped close to the usual stopping place; that he did not notice the car at first; he noticed the woman.

Handley, the motorman, testified that he was on the front platform of the car which was "drifting to make a stop;" he was about 30 or 35 feet from the corner; he looked back to see what the trouble was and saw the conductor and another man helping plaintiff to the sidewalk from a point ten or fifteen feet to the rear of the car.

Mr. Cameron, a passenger on the car and employed by the Daily News, testified: He noticed that the car stopped a little short of the corner and that the motorman was not in his place. The street car had stopped ten or fifteen feet west of the regular stopping place; he saw the conductor and another man helping a woman across the street to the drug store; at that time he handed his business card to the motorman.

Martin Keeban, a policeman at the Woodlawn station, went to St. Bernard hospital, where plaintiff was taken on the evening of the day of the accident, for the purpose of making out a report about the accident. He testified that plaintiff told him she was getting off an eastbound 63rd street car and fell while the car was in motion; that she did not tell him that another woman was getting on the car while it was in motion, nor that a man got off the car at the same time.

The witness Olthen testified that he lived on Kimbark avenue and at this time was on his way to the golf grounds at Jackson Park, accompanied by his mother who was then 80 years of age; that at the time of the accident they were standing about 30 or 35 feet west of the drug store at the corner of 63rd street and Stony Island avenue; his mother was tired and asked to stop for a few minutes rest; that in looking out on the street he saw a street car come along; a heavy set man got off and then a woman whom he afterward found to be plaintiff; the street car had stopped at the time the man got off; the man was on the side-step coming over toward the sidewalk, and plaintiff started to get off; as she was getting off the car pulled up about two feet with a jerk and stopped, throwing plaintiff, who fell; the man who got off the car went to plaintiff's assistance; he (Olthen) ran and assisted plaintiff to her feet and got her over to the curb; the man left them at the curb and Olthen took plaintiff to the drug store with the help of a man standing alongside of a taxicab; Olthen went on the back end of the platform of the car and made a memorandum, from which he was able to say the car was numbered 5505 and the conductor's number was 4658, and that the time of day was 3:40; the conductor did not ask him for his name and address, although Olthen went on the car and also talked with the conductor. He took plaintiff to the home of her brother in a Yellow taxicab, his aged mother going with him, and he saw her three times while she was in the hospital when his mother was with him and one time alone.

the day of the accident, for the purpose of making out a report the accident. He testified that plaintiff told him she was getting off an eastbound 63rd street car and fell while the car was in motion; that she did not tell him that another woman was getting on the car while it was in motion, nor that a man got off the car at the same time.

The witness Githen testified that he lived on Kimbark avenue and at that time was on his way to the golf grounds at Jackson Park, accompanied by his mother who was then 80 years of age; that at the time of the accident they were standing about 30 or 35 feet west of the drug store at the corner of 63rd street and Stony Island avenue; his mother was tired and wanted to stop for a few minutes rest; that in looking out on the street he saw a street car come along; a heavy set man got off and then a woman which he afterward found to be plaintiff; the street car had stopped at the time the man got off; the man was on the side-step coming over toward the sidewalk, and plaintiff started to get off; as she was getting off the car pulled up about two feet with a jerk and stopped, throwing plaintiff, who fell; the man who got off the car went to plaintiff's assistance; he (Githen) ran and assisted plaintiff to her feet and got her over to the curb; the man left them at the curb and Githen took plaintiff to the drug store with the help of a man standing alongside of a taxicab; Githen went to the back end of the platform of the car and made a memorandum, from which he was able to say the car was numbered 2508 and the conductor's number was 4880, and that the time of day was 3:40; the conductor did not ask him for his name and address, although Githen went on the car and also talked with the conductor. He took plaintiff to the home of her brother in a Yellow taxicab, his aged mother going with him, and he saw her three times while she was in the hospital when his mother was with him and one time alone.

He did not know plaintiff or her brother prior to this time. Plaintiff and her brother afterward called on him at his home, 6013 Kimbark avenue, in the fall of 1931, and neither of them called again. Plaintiff came to his home in an automobile, but neither at the hospital nor in his home did he talk with her about how the accident happened; he did not get the name of the cabman who assisted him on the day of the accident nor the number of his cab; he did not get the name of the woman who was getting on the car.

Mr. Newman testified that he knew the witness Olthen by sight but did not remember seeing him at the scene of the accident on this particular day, nor does Olthen seem to have been recognized by any of the witnesses except plaintiff.

In their reply brief attorneys for plaintiff undertake to discredit defendants' witnesses because, they say, "all" claimed plaintiff walked into the corner drug store after the accident, while the uncontradicted evidence as to the extent of plaintiff's injuries shows this was impossible. In view of the sweeping character of these assertions in this regard, we have examined all the evidence bearing on this point and find these assertions unwarranted. Two of defendants' witnesses say in substance that she walked to the store with assistance, but none of them says that she went there without assistance.

Having regard to the evidence as recited above, it seems the issues of fact in this case were for the jury, and after seeing and hearing all the witnesses and considering all their material evidence, the jury returned a verdict for defendants. The court, who also saw and heard the witnesses, approved the verdict by entering judgment on it. This court cannot hold, as plaintiff requests, that the verdict of the jury is against the clear preponderance of the evidence.

It is also contended that the court erred in permitting a

He did not know plaintiff or her brother prior to this time. Plaintiff and her brother afterward called on him at his home, 6012 Kimbark avenue, in the fall of 1931, and neither of them called again. Plaintiff came to his home in an automobile, but neither at the hospital nor in his home did he talk with her about how the accident happened; he did not get the name of the cabman who assisted him on the day of the accident nor the number of his cab; he did not get the name of the woman who was getting on the car.

Mr. Newman testified that he knew the witness Olthen by sight but did not remember seeing him at the scene of the accident on this particular day, nor does Olthen seem to have been recognized by any of the witnesses except plaintiff.

In their reply brief attorneys for plaintiff undertake to discredit defendants' witnesses because, they say, "all" claimed plaintiff walked into the corner drug store after the accident, while the uncontradicted evidence as to the extent of plaintiff's injuries shows this was impossible. In view of the sweeping character of these assertions in this regard, we have examined all the evidence bearing on this point and find these assertions unwarranted. Two of defendants' witnesses say in substance that she walked to the store with assistance, but none of them says that she went there without assistance.

Having regard to the evidence as recited above, it seems the issues of fact in this case were for the jury, and after seeing and hearing all the witnesses and considering all their material evidence, the jury returned a verdict for defendants. The court, who also saw and heard the witnesses, approved the verdict by entering judgment on it. This court cannot hold, as plaintiff requests, that the verdict of the jury is against the clear preponderance of the evidence.

It is also contended that the court erred in permitting a

written statement called "History Sheet" to be taken to the jury room by the jury during its deliberations. Plaintiff claims that in this purported copy were words alleged to have been spoken by plaintiff which were contrary to the evidence given by her and cites cases, such as Lawson v. Curtiss, 19 Ill. 455; People v. Sprangler, 314 Ill. 602; Johnson v. N. K. Fairbank Co., 156 Ill. App. 381, to the point that this was reversible error. The exhibit is not abstracted. The record shows that it was plaintiff's exhibit 14 introduced by agreement. Nowhere in the abstract nor so far as we can find by diligent search of the record is it made to appear that this exhibit was in fact taken to its room by the jury. It is for the party complaining to show from the record presented to this court the existence of the supposed error of which he complains. Gerbelman v. Heffman, 328 Ill. 193; Decatur Coal Co. v. Clokey, 332 Ill. 253; Arkansas Sweet Potato Growers' Exchange v. Wignall-Moore Co., 249 Ill. App. 34. Moreover, this case was tried under the Practice act of 1907, and section 76 of that act provides that "papers read in evidence, other than depositions, may be carried from the bar by the jury." The record fails to show reversible error in this respect.

Plaintiff also complains of the instructions given by the court at the request of defendants. She complains of instruction No. 2 by which the jury was told that if it believed from the evidence under the instructions of the court that it was the manner in which plaintiff alighted from the car in question that caused her to fall and not any negligence on the part of defendants as charged, the verdict should be for the defendants. It is objected that the instruction assumed plaintiff alighted in an unusual or extraordinary manner. The criticism is hypercritical. The uncontradicted evidence shows plaintiff did alight from the car. That is an undisputed fact. The manner in which she alighted is material, written statement called "History Sheet" to be taken to the jury room by the jury during its deliberations. Plaintiff claims that in this purported copy were words alleged to have been spoken by plaintiff which were contrary to the evidence given by her and other persons, such as Kernes v. [illegible], 19 Ill. 485; People v. [illegible], 244 Ill. 603; Johnson v. [illegible] Fairbank Co., 186 Ill. App. [illegible], to the point that this was reversible error. The exhibit is not abstracted. The record shows that it was plaintiff's exhibit 14 introduced by agreement. Nowhere in the abstract nor so far as we can find by diligent search of the record is it made to appear that this exhibit was in fact taken to its room by the jury. It is for the party complaining to show from the record presented to this court the existence of the supposed error of which he complains. [illegible] v. [illegible], 328 Ill. 193; Decatur Coal Co. v. [illegible], 232 Ill. 293; Arkansas Sweet Potato Growers' Exchange v. [illegible] Co., 240 Ill. App. 34. Moreover, this case was tried under the Practice act of 1907, and section 76 of that act provides that "papers read in evidence, other than depositions, may be carried from the bar by the jury." The record fails to show reversible error in this respect.

Plaintiff also complains of the instructions given by the court at the request of defendants. She complains of instruction No. 2 by which the jury were told that if it believed from the evidence under the instructions of the court that it was the manner in which plaintiff alighted from the car in question that caused her to fall and not any negligence on the part of defendants as charged, the verdict should be for the defendants. It is objected that the instruction assumed plaintiff alighted in an unusual or [illegible] manner. The criticism is hypercritical. The [illegible] undisputed evidence shows plaintiff did alight from the car. That is an undisputed fact. The manner in which she alighted is disputed.

and that question was by this instruction properly submitted to the jury.

Complaint also is made of defendants' instruction No. 8, which told the jury in substance that the law did not exact or require of a street car railway company that its employees should be all the while upon their guard against unusual or extraordinary conduct on the part of passengers; that the conductor would have a right to presume that plaintiff, if she walked to the rear platform of the car before it came to its usual stopping place, would wait until the car stopped before alighting or attempting to alight therefrom, if the jury should so find from the evidence, and further that if the jury believed plaintiff did step from defendants' car while the car was still in motion and before it came to a stop at its usual stopping place and was thus injured, she could not recover. It is said that this instruction assumed that plaintiff alighted in an unusual and extraordinary manner, and that it amounted to contributory negligence on her part to alight from a moving car. The instruction is not, in our opinion, subject to the first objection for reasons already explained, and the second objection indicates a misunderstanding by plaintiff of the issue. It was not a question of whether plaintiff was or was not guilty of contributory negligence in getting off a moving car. It was not a question of contributory negligence at all, but the issue was whether defendants were guilty of the negligence with which they were charged. Plaintiff presented her case to the jury on the theory that she stepped off the car while it was standing. Defendants' theory is that she got off the car while it was moving. If plaintiff stepped from the moving car and was injured she could not recover, because she failed to prove the negligence alleged against defendants, regardless of the question of whether or not she was guilty of contributory negligence.

did this question was by this instruction properly submitted to the jury.

Complaint also is made of defendants' instruction No. 8, which told the jury in substance that the law did not exact or require of a street car railway company that its employees should be on the watch upon their guard against unusual or extraordinary conduct on the part of passengers; that the conductor would have a right to presume that plaintiff, if she walked to the rear platform of the car before it came to its usual stopping place, would wait until the car stopped before alighting or attempting to alight therefrom. If the jury should so find from the evidence, and further that if the jury believed plaintiff did step from defendants' car while the car was still in motion and before it came to a stop at its usual stopping place and was thus injured, she could not recover. It is said that this instruction assumed that plaintiff alighted in an unusual and extraordinary manner, and that it amounted to contributory negligence on her part to alight from a moving car. The instruction is not, in our opinion, subject to the first objection for reasons already explained, and the second objection indicates a misunderstanding by plaintiff of the issues. It was not a question of whether plaintiff was or was not guilty of contributory negligence in getting off a moving car. It was not a question of contributory negligence at all, but the issue was whether defendants were guilty of the negligence with which they were charged. Plaintiff presented her case to the jury on the theory that she alighted off the car while it was standing. Defendants' theory is that she got off the car while it was moving. If plaintiff stepped off while moving and was injured she could not recover, because [illegible] the negligence charged against defendants. [illegible] of whether or not she was guilty of contributory [illegible]

Plaintiff complains of instruction No. 10, which told the jury that if a preponderance of all the evidence in the case failed to establish the liability of defendants, a verdict should be returned for defendants. The use of the word "establish" in this connection is urged to constitute reversible error, and *Murzon v. Schmitz*, 262 Ill. App. 337, and *Williamson v. Eaton*, 266 Ill. App. 614, are cited. However, as plaintiff used the same word to express the same idea in instructions given at her request, she is not in a position to complain. *Fleming v. E. J. & E. Ry. Co.*, 275 Ill. 486.

Complaint is made of instruction No. 17, by which the jury was told that if a preponderance of the evidence did not show that plaintiff fell and was injured "by reason of the negligence charged," the verdict should be for defendants. Plaintiff contends that this instruction meant that plaintiff was required to prove all the negligence alleged in all the counts in plaintiff's declaration. The instruction does not say so. No intelligent jury would understand it to say so. It was, of course, sufficient to prove the negligence alleged in any good count of the declaration which had not been withdrawn, and the instruction, as we understand it, does not say otherwise.

Complaint is also made of instruction No. 18, by which the jury was told that the happening of an accident did not raise a presumption of negligence. It is urged that this is erroneous because the doctrine of *res ipsa loquitur* was applicable, and *Cohen v. Weinstein*, 231 Ill. App. 34, is cited. Plaintiff did not try her case upon the theory that *res ipsa loquitur* was applicable. Under the decisions of the courts it was not. *Barnes v. Danville St. Ry. & Light Co.*, 235 Ill. 566; *Vischer v. Northwestern Elevated R. R. Co.*, 256 Ill. 572; *Enright v. Chicago City Rys. Co.*, 165 Ill. App. 163; *Ferrier v. Chicago Rys. Co.*, 185 Ill. App. 326; and see *Garvis v. Chicago Railways Co.*, No. 37963, in an opinion filed this day.

Plaintiff complains of instruction No. 16, which told the jury that if a preponderance of all the evidence in the case failed to establish the liability of defendants, a verdict should be returned for defendants. The use of the word "establish" in this connection is urged to constitute reversible error, and Johnson v. Schultz, 262 Ill. App. 337, and Williamson v. Eaton, 260 Ill. App. 614, are cited. However, as plaintiff used the same word to express the same idea in instructions given at her request, she is not in a position to complain. Stevens v. N. J. & A. Ry. Co., 279 Ill. 486.

Complaint is made of instruction No. 17, by which the jury was told that if a preponderance of the evidence did not show that plaintiff fell and was injured "by reason of the negligence charged," the verdict should be for defendants. Plaintiff contends that this instruction meant that plaintiff was required to prove all the negligence alleged in all the counts in plaintiff's declaration. The instruction does not say so. No intelligent jury would understand it to say so. It was, of course, sufficient to prove the negligence alleged in any good count of the declaration which had not been withdrawn, and the instruction, as we understand it, does not say otherwise.

Complaint is also made of instruction No. 19, by which the jury was told that the happening of an accident did not raise a presumption of negligence. It is urged that this is erroneous because the doctrine of res ipsa loquitur was applicable, and Cohen v. Weinstein, 271 Ill. App. 54, is cited. Plaintiff did not try her case upon the theory that res ipsa loquitur was applicable. Under the decisions of the courts it was not. Bahnes v. Danville St. Ry. & Light Co., 235 Ill. 360; Wieder v. Northwestern Elevated R. R. Co., 286 Ill. 272; Bartlett v. Chicago City Ry. Co., 165 Ill. App. 169; Ferrier v. Chicago Rys. Co., 188 Ill. App. 326; and see Darwin v. Chicago Railways Co., No. 37693, in an opinion filed this day.

The most serious contention made as to instructions is that the court erred in giving defendants' instruction No. 10, by which the jury was told:

"The Court instructs you that the ordinance of the City of Chicago offered in evidence in this case to the following effect:

'It shall be unlawful for any person to board or alight from a street car or vehicle while the said street car or vehicle is in motion,'

was at the time and place in question, in force and effect, and if you believe from the evidence, under the instructions of the court, that the plaintiff alighted from a car of the defendants while the said car was in motion, then, if you believe that the failure of the plaintiff to comply as aforesaid with the ordinance in question--if she did fail to comply therewith--proximately contributed to cause the accident in question, you should find your verdict in favor of the defendants."

This instruction is criticized first, because it told the jury that the ordinance was "in force and effect." Plaintiff says that the ordinance is invalid, and that similar ordinances were held invalid in Wice v. C. & N. W. Ry. Co., 193 Ill. 351, and Miller v. Eversole, 184 Ill. App. 362. This contention is made for the first time in this court. The ordinance was admitted in evidence without objection by plaintiff. Plaintiff's objection now that it is invalid comes too late. Jaughn v. Carr, 263 Ill. App. 333, Vonesh v. City of Berwin, 324 Ill. 483. In the cases cited the question of the validity of particular ordinances was raised in the trial court. Plaintiff says in her reply brief that it is not claimed that it was error to admit the ordinance in evidence but that it was error to tell the jury it was in force and effect. If the ordinance was supposed to be invalid, or not in force, at the time and place of the accident, plaintiff should have made her objection when it was offered in evidence. She is not permitted to take a different position in that respect in this court from that taken in the trial court. She may not complain of error to which she consented and which she helped the court to make. The alleged distinction is mere quibbling. Plaintiff further says the instruction is erroneous

The most serious contention made as to instructions is that the court erred in giving defendants' instruction No. 10, by which the jury was told:

"The court instructs you that the ordinance of the City of Chicago offered in evidence in this case to the following effect:

'It shall be unlawful for any person to board or alight from any street car or vehicle while the said street car or vehicle is in motion,'

was at the time and place in question, in force and effect, and if you believe from the evidence, under the instructions of the court, that the plaintiff alighted from a car of the defendants while the said car was in motion, then, if you believe that the failure of the plaintiff to comply as aforesaid with the ordinance in question--if she did fail to comply therewith--proximately contributed to cause the accident in question, you should find your verdict in favor of the defendants."

This instruction is criticized first, because it told the jury that the ordinance was "in force and effect." Plaintiff says that the ordinance is invalid, and that similar ordinances were held invalid in [illegible], 183 Ill. 581, and [illegible] Ill. App. [illegible]. This contention is made for the first time in this court. The ordinance was admitted in evidence without objection by plaintiff. Plaintiff's objection now that it is invalid comes too late. [illegible], 265 Ill. App. 535; [illegible] v. [illegible], 254 Ill. 485. In the cases cited the question of the validity of particular ordinances was raised in the trial court. Plaintiff says in her reply brief that it is not claimed that it was error to admit the ordinance in evidence but that it was error to tell the jury it was in force and effect. If the ordinance was claimed to be invalid, or not in force, at the time and place of the accident, plaintiff should have made her objection when it was offered in evidence. She is not permitted to take a different position on that subject in this court than that taken in the trial court. [illegible] which she helped the court to [illegible]. [illegible] Plaintiff further says the instruction is [illegible] because it told the jury that if plaintiff violated the ordinance in question and if the violation was the proximate cause of the accident, the jury should return a verdict for defendants. Plaintiff argues that this amounted to an assertion that the violation of the ordinance was negligence <u>per se</u> and cites <u>Culver v. Harris</u>, 211 Ill. App. 474; <u>Price v. Ill. Bell Telephone Co.</u>, 260 Ill. App. 581; <u>Tuttle v. Checker Taxi Co.</u>, 274 Ill. App. 535. A careful examination of <u>Culver v. Harris</u> will disclose the distinction between this case and those relied upon. There were three ordinances involved in that case. As to two of the ordinances the opinion states that there was no evidence tending to show a violation of the same. It was therefore held that the giving of the instruction was erroneous and misleading. As to the other ordinance, the opinion states there was evidence which would warrant the giving of it, but the instruction was erroneous in that it assumed that the violation of the ordinance was negligence, while the most that could be said was that such violation was only <u>prima facie</u> evidence of that fact. The question erroneously assumed in that case was here submitted to the jury. Moreover, there are cases which seem to hold that the violation of an ordinance is negligence <u>per se</u>. (<u>Partridge v. Eberstein</u>, 225 Ill. App. 209; <u>T. H. & I. R. R. Co. v. Voelker</u>, 129 Ill. 540; <u>Flynn v. Chicago City Ry. Co.</u>, 250 Ill. 460) but these authorities have no application where the facts appear to be, as here, that the violation of the ordinance would necessarily contribute to the cause of the accident. <u>Becker v. Chicago Rys. Co.</u>, 216 Ill. App. 374.

As we have already said on another point, the question here was not whether it was negligence <u>per se</u> to get on or alight from a moving car. The question at issue was whether defendants were negligent as alleged in plaintiff's declaration, or some count thereof which was submitted to the jury. From that standpoint this instruction is not erroneous.

As we find no reversible error in the record, the judgment is affirmed.

AFFIRMED.

O'Connor, P. J., and McSurely, J., concur.

because it told the jury that if plaintiff violated the ordinance in question and if the violation was the proximate cause of the accident, the jury should return a verdict for defendants. Plaintiff argues that this amounted to an assertion that the violation of the ordinance was negligence per se and cites Culver v. Harris, 211 Ill. App. [illegible]; [illegible] v. [illegible], 280 Ill. App. 58[illegible]; [illegible] v. [illegible] Fuel Co., 274 Ill. App. 523. A careful examination of Culver v. Harris [illegible] discloses the distinction between that case and the [illegible] here. There were three ordinances involved in that case. As to one of the ordinances the opinion states that there was no evidence tending to show a violation of the same. It was therefore held that the giving of the instruction was erroneous and misleading. As to the other ordinance, the opinion states there was evidence which would warrant the giving of it, but the instruction was erroneous because it assumed that the violation of the ordinance was negligence, while the most that could be said was that such violation was only prima facie evidence of that fact. The question [illegible] in that case was [illegible] submitted to the jury. Moreover, there are cases which seem to hold that the violation of an ordinance is negligence per se. (Partridge v. [illegible], 285 Ill. App. [illegible]; [illegible] R. R. Co. v. [illegible], 180 Ill. 540; [illegible] v. [illegible], 200 Ill. 464) but these authorities have no application where the facts appear to be, as here, that the violation of the ordinance could not possibly contribute to the cause of the accident. [illegible] v. [illegible] Co., 216 Ill. App. 364.

[illegible] we have already said on another point, the question here was not whether it was negligence per se to get on or alight from a [illegible]. The question of fact was whether defendants were negligent [illegible] of same [illegible] the jury. [illegible] plaintiff was [illegible] in the record, the judgment is affirmed.

O'Connor, P. J., and McSurely, J. [illegible].

37963

GLORIA CAREVIC,
Appellant,

vs.

GUY A. RICHARDSON, Receiver of Chicago Railways Co., HARVEY B. FLEMING, Receiver of Chicago City Railway Co., Calumet & South Chicago Railway Co., and Southern Street Railway Co., doing business as CHICAGO SURFACE LINES,
Appellees.

APPEAL FROM SUPERIOR COURT OF COOK COUNTY.

280 I.A. 619

MR. JUSTICE MATCHETT DELIVERED THE OPINION OF THE COURT.

Plaintiff's declaration filed January 26, 1933, avers that on September 24, 1932, at the intersection of VanBuren and Clark streets, Chicago, defendants stopped one of their cars for the purpose of allowing plaintiff and others to board the same, and that while she was a passenger and in the act of boarding the car defendants, by their servant, negligently caused the car to be suddenly started with a jerk, whereby she was violently thrown off the car to the street and injured. Defendants filed a plea of the general issue. There was a trial by jury with a verdict for defendants, upon which the court entered judgment.

The evidence upon the trial was very conflicting, that for plaintiff tending to show that when the car stopped she attempted to board it; that when she had one foot on the step of the car and another on the platform, the car was started violently. The evidence for defendants tended to show that plaintiff did not attempt to board the car until after it was started; that she then ran to the entrance of the car and tried to get on and in that way received her injuries.

Plaintiff cites Ohio & Mississippi R. R. Co. v. Muhling, 30 Ill., 9, to the point that a prospective passenger who attempts to enter a street car which has stopped to receive passengers, is deemed in law to be a passenger. That proposition is not questioned. She contends further that the court erred in giving at the request of

37963

GLORIA GARVIC,
Appellant,

vs.

GUY A. RICHARDSON, Receiver of Chicago Railways Co., HARVEY B. HURD, Receiver of Chicago City Railway Co., Calumet & South Chicago Railway Co., and Southern Street Railway Co., doing business as CHICAGO SURFACE LINES,
Appellees.

280 I.A. 619

MR. JUSTICE MATCHETT DELIVERED THE OPINION OF THE COURT.

Plaintiff's declaration filed January 26, 1933, avers that on September 24, 1932, at the intersection of VanBuren and Clark streets, Chicago, defendants stopped one of their cars for the purpose of allowing plaintiff and others to board the same, and that while she was a passenger and in the act of boarding the car defendants, by their servants, negligently caused the car to be suddenly started with a jerk, whereby she was violently thrown off the car to the street and injured. Defendants filed a plea of the general issue. There was a trial by jury with a verdict for defendants, upon which the court entered judgment.

The evidence upon the trial was very conflicting, that for plaintiff tending to show that when the car stopped she attempted to board it; that when she had one foot on the step of the car and another on the platform, the car was started violently. The evidence for defendants tended to show that plaintiff did not attempt to board the car until after it was started; that she then ran to the entrance of the car and tried to get on and in that way received her injuries.

Plaintiff cites Ohio & Mississippi R. R. Co. v. Muhling, 30 Ill., 9, to the point that a prospective passenger who attempts to enter a street car which has stopped to receive passengers, is deemed in law to be a passenger. That proposition is not questioned. She contends further that the court erred in giving at the request of defendants instruction No. 6, which is as follows:

> "The Court instructs the jury that the relation of passenger and carrier does not make the carrier an insurer of the absolute safety of the passenger. The carrier does not guarantee that it will protect passengers against remote, unusual and extraordinary perils not to be foreseen by the exercise of the highest degree of care reasonably consistent with the practical operation of the carrier's business. The carrier is not required to exercise a degree of care which is not practicable in the operation of its business, and if the jury believe from the evidence that the injury to the plaintiff could only have been prevented by a degree of care and caution on the part of the defendants or its employees not reasonably practical in the operation of said defendants' street railroad, then the plaintiff cannot recover against said defendants, and the jury should find said defendants not guilty."

Plaintiff contends, citing Barretta v. Chicago Railways Co., 214 Ill. App. 455, that the giving of this instruction was reversible error under the facts which appear in this case. She says that the effect of the instruction was to compel the jury to find for defendants, even if plaintiff was a passenger, unless she further proved what it was that caused the car to start with a jerk. In other words, as we understand her argument, it is that the doctrine of res ipsa loquitur is applicable under the evidence, but that contrary to that doctrine this instruction required plaintiff to prove what it was that caused the car to start with a jerk.

The point is not well taken. The doctrine of res ipsa loquitur was not applicable to the case at all, - in the first place because plaintiff's declaration charged specific negligence, (West Chicago St. R. R. Co. v. Martin, 154 Ill. 523; Barnes v. Danville St. Ry. & Light Co., 235 Ill. 566; O'Rourke v. Marshall Field & Co., 307 Ill. 197; Crawford v. Chicago Union Traction Co., 137 Ill. App. 163, Enright v. Chicago City Ry. Co., 165 Ill. App. 163) and also because, according to the uncontradicted evidence, in attempting to board the car plaintiff's movements were personal and voluntary. McFadden v. Chicago, Rock Island & Pacific Ry. Co., 149 Ill. App. 298; Ferrier v. Chicago Rys. Co., 185 Ill. App. 326; Piper v. Green, 216 Ill. App. 590.) Moreover, since there was defendants' instruction No. 6, which is as follows:

"The Court instructs the jury that the relation of passenger and carrier does not make the carrier an insurer of the absolute safety of the passenger. The carrier does not guarantee that it will protect passengers against results, unusual and extraordinary [illegible] not to be foreseen by the exercise of the highest degree of care reasonably consistent with the practical operation of the carrier's business. The carrier is not required to exercise a degree of care which is not practicable in the operation of its business, and if the jury believe from the evidence that the injury to the plaintiff could only have been prevented by a degree of care and caution on the part of the defendants or its employees not reasonably practical in the operation of said defendants' street railroad, then the plaintiff cannot recover against said defendants, and the jury should find said defendants not guilty."

Plaintiff contends, citing Merretta v. Chicago Railways Co., 214 Ill. App. 488, that the giving of this instruction was reversible error under the facts which appear in this case. She says that the effect of the instruction was to compel the jury to find for defendants, even if plaintiff was a passenger, unless she further proved that it was that caused the car to start with a jerk. In other words, as we understand her argument, it is that the doctrine of res ipsa loquitur is applicable under the evidence, but that contrary to that doctrine this instruction required plaintiff to prove what it was that caused the car to start with a jerk.

The point is not well taken. The doctrine of res ipsa loquitur was not applicable to the case at all, - in the first place because plaintiff's declaration charged specific negligence, (West Chicago St. R. R. Co. v. Martin, 154 Ill. 523; Morgan v. Danville St. Ry. & Light Co., 238 Ill. 544; Gilmartin v. Marshall Field & Co., 207 Ill. 197; Crawford v. Chicago Union Traction Co., 137 Ill. App. 143; Harlock v. Chicago City Ry. Co., 165 Ill. App. 144) and also because, according to the uncontradicted evidence, in attempting to board the car plaintiff's movements were personal and voluntary. (Skibitsky v. Chicago, Rock Island & Pacific Ry. Co., [illegible] Ill. App. [illegible]; [illegible] v. Chicago [illegible] Co., [illegible] Ill. App. [illegible]; [illegible]) Moreover, since [illegible] of direct evidence on both sides of the issue presented by the pleadings, there was no room for the presumption which arises in cases where res ipsa loquitur is applicable. People v. Tate, 316 Ill. 52; Green v. Acom, 325 Ill. 474. Beard v. Haskell Park Bldg. Corp., 248 Ill. App. 467. Furthermore, the court in instruction No. 11 gave at plaintiff's request an instruction substantially to the same effect as this one of which she complains. Under such circumstances her complaint could not avail even if the instruction were erroneous. Consolidated Coal Co. v. Haenni, 146 Ill. 614; Funk v. Babbitt, 156 Ill. 408; Harney v. Sanitary District, 260 Ill. 84; Fleming v. Elgin, Joliet & Eastern Ry. Co., 275 Ill. 486.

The judgment of the trial court is affirmed.

AFFIRMED.

O'Connor, P. J., and McSurely, J., concur.

direct evidence on both sides of the issue presented by the pleadings, there was no room for the presumption which arises in cases where res ipsa loquitur is applicable. People v. Tate, 316 Ill. 82; Gunch v. Acom, 325 Ill. 474; Hunt v. Kaskell Park Dist. Corp., 249 Ill. App. 467. Furthermore, the court in instruction No. 11 gave at plaintiff's request an instruction substantially to the same effect as this one of which she complains. Under such circumstances her complaint could not avail even if the instruction were erroneous. Consolidated Coal Co. v. Haenni, 146 Ill. 614; Funk v. Babbitt, 156 Ill. 408; Harvey v. Sanitary District, 250 Ill. 84; Fleming v. Elgin, Joliet & Eastern Ry. Co., 275 Ill. 486.

The judgment of the trial court is affirmed.

AFFIRMED.

O'Connor, P. J., and McSurely, J., concur.

37973

PEOPLE OF THE STATE OF ILLINOIS,
Defendant in Error,

vs.

JOE JUTENAS,
Plaintiff in Error.

ERROR TO MUNICIPAL COURT OF CHICAGO.

280 I.A. 619[2]

MR. JUSTICE MATCHETT DELIVERED THE OPINION OF THE COURT.

On June 26, 1934, an information was filed in the municipal court against Joe Jutenas, alleging that on June 13, 1934, he made an assault upon Minnie and Lambert W. Craemer with intent to inflict on their persons bodily injuries. There was a trial by the court and a finding of guilty as charged with judgment thereon. Defendant was sentenced to the House of Correction for ninety days and fined in the sum of $100. The case has been brought to this court upon the common law record alone. The record as at first filed failed to show that defendant was arraigned, that a plea to the information was entered, or that defendant waived his right to be tried by a jury. The conviction on such record could not, of course, be sustained. Cahill's Ill. Rev. Stats., 1933, Criminal Code, division 13, section 3, paragraph 755; People v. Kyenoy, 355 Ill. 451.

A supplemental record has, however, been filed by the State which shows that the record as originally presented to this court was mutilated, and that the true record in fact shows that defendant was arraigned, that he entered a plea of not guilty, and that he waived his right of trial by jury.

The judgment is affirmed.

AFFIRMED.

O'Connor, P. J., and McSurely, J., concur.

37973

PEOPLE OF THE STATE OF ILLINOIS,
Defendant in Error,

vs.

JOE VUTERMAN,
Plaintiff in Error.

ERROR TO MUNICIPAL COURT OF CHICAGO.

200 I.A. 619

MR. JUSTICE MATCHETT DELIVERED THE OPINION OF THE COURT.

On June 26, 1934, an information was filed in the Municipal court against Joe Vuterman, alleging that on June 13, 1934, he made an assault upon Minnie and Lambert F. Graeser with intent to inflict on their persons bodily injuries. There was a trial by the court and a finding of guilty as charged with judgment thereon. Defendant was sentenced to the House of Correction for ninety days and fined in the sum of $100. The case has been brought to this court upon the common law record alone. The record as at first filed failed to show that defendant was arraigned, that a plea to the information was entered, or that defendant waived his right to be tried by a jury. The conviction on such record could not, of course, be sustained. Cahill's Ill. Rev. Stats., 1933, Criminal Code, division 13, section 5, paragraph 765; People v. Kycew, 355 Ill. 451.

A supplemental record has, however, been filed by the State which shows that the record as originally presented to this court was mutilated, and that the true record in fact shows that defendant was arraigned; that he entered a plea of not guilty, and that he waived his right of trial by jury.

The judgment is affirmed.

AFFIRMED.

O'Connor, P. J., and McSurely, J., concur.

38004

WILLIAM L. O'CONNELL, Receiver of Phillip State Bank and Trust Company, Appellant,

vs.

JOHN H. TAFT, CHARLES A. WIGHTMAN and FRANK J. DURHAM, Appellees.

374

APPEAL FROM MUNICIPAL COURT OF CHICAGO.

280 I.A. 619

MR. JUSTICE MATCHETT DELIVERED THE OPINION OF THE COURT.

Plaintiff brought suit in contract based upon an alleged written guaranty executed and delivered June 27, 1929, which stated that defendants guaranteed, with other things, the payment of a loan of $35,000 represented by certain notes and coupons of that date, secured by a trust deed conveying to the Chicago Title & Trust Co. a certain 99-year leasehold estate in premises described. John H. Taft, Charles A. Wightman and Frank J. Durham were named as defendants. Wightman was not served, has since died, and the suit has been dismissed as to him.

The alleged guaranty was delivered to the Illinois State Bank, which on July 11, 1931, closed. Its assets were taken over by the Phillips State Bank, which was also closed, and plaintiff was appointed receiver. The statement of claim sets up the guaranty verbatim and alleges that the Phillips State Bank is the owner of $17,500 of the notes, no part of which has been paid, and that the said principal sum is due with interest. Defendant Taft in his answer admits that he signed the document, a substantial copy of which is set out in plaintiff's statement of claim; denies that the Illinois State bank accepted the alleged guaranty; admits that a trust deed dated June 27, 1929, was made; denies that it was made in pursuance of the guaranty and denies that it was made by John Stone and his associates. Defendant Durham in his affidavit of merits sets up this same defense; admits that he signed the guaranty but denies that he executed it on June 27, 1929, or that the bank

39004.

[illegible], Receiver of [illegible] State Bank and Trust Company, Appellant,

vs.

[illegible] ROBERT A. WIGHTMAN [illegible], Appellee.

APPEAL FROM MUNICIPAL COURT OF CHICAGO.

280 I.A. 619

MR. JUSTICE [illegible] DELIVERED THE OPINION OF THE COURT.

Plaintiff brought suit in contract based upon an alleged written guaranty executed and delivered June 27, 1929, which stated [illegible], with other things, the payment of a [illegible] represented by certain notes and coupons of that [illegible] secured by a trust deed conveying to the Chicago Title & Trust Co. a certain 99-year leasehold estate in premises described. [illegible] A. Wightman and Frank J. [illegible] were named as defendants. Wightman was not served, has since died, and the [illegible] dismissed as to him.

The alleged guaranty was delivered to the Phillips State Bank [illegible] May 11, 1931, closed. Its assets were taken over by the [illegible] which was also closed, and plaintiff [illegible] receiver. The statement of claim sets up the guaranty [illegible] and alleges that the Phillips State Bank is the owner of [illegible] of the notes, no part of which has been paid, and that the said principal sum is due with interest. Defendant [illegible] in his [illegible] that he signed the document, a substantial copy of which is set out in plaintiff's statement of claim; denies that the [illegible] State Bank [illegible] the alleged guaranty; admits that [illegible] June 27, 1929; and denies that it was made [illegible] denies that it was made by [illegible] and his associates. Defendant [illegible] in his affidavit of [illegible] that he signed the guaranty but denies that he [illegible] on August [illegible], 1929, or that the Bank made the loan relying on such guaranty.

The trial began April 12, 1934. At the close of all the evidence each of the defendants presented motions for a directed verdict in his favor and plaintiff presented a motion that the jury should be directed to return a verdict in his favor against both defendants for the sum of $21,247.43. The court by stipulation of the parties submitted the cause to the jury, reserving the right to thereafter determine as a matter of law whether these motions should have been allowed. The jury returned a verdict against plaintiff and in favor of Durham and a verdict in favor of plaintiff and against Taft, with damages assessed at $7,000. Thereafter the court denied plaintiff's motion for a judgment of $21,247.43 against both defendants, allowed the motion of Durham for a judgment on the verdict in his favor against plaintiff, set aside the verdict against defendant Taft, and also entered judgment in his favor against plaintiff for costs. From these orders and judgments plaintiff has taken this appeal. There can, we think, be no doubt as to the material facts established by the evidence, although much evidence not material to any issue was upon the trial allowed to go to the jury and resulted, we think, in confusing it.

In 1929 the Illinois State Bank was doing a banking business in Evanston. Defendant Taft was its president, Wightman, Durham, Hakes, Hogg and others, directors. Hakes was also executive vice-president; he was a brother-in-law of Harry Eugene Kelly, who acted as attorney for the bank. Hogg was cashier and secretary of the board of directors. The by-laws of the Bank provided for monthly meeting of the directors and that at such meeting the directors should examine the loans made by the bank during the preceding month.

At a meeting of the board in January or February, 1929, the making of this loan of $35,000 was suggested. The party most actively interested was Wightman, and Taft, president of the bank, also made the loan relying on such guaranty.

The trial began April 12, 1934. At the close of all the evidence each of the defendants presented motions for a directed verdict in his favor and plaintiff presented a motion that the jury should be directed to return a verdict in his favor against both defendants for the sum of $22,847.43. The court by stipulation of the parties submitted the cause to the jury, reserving the right to thereafter determine as a matter of law whether these motions should have been allowed. The jury returned a verdict against plaintiff and in favor of Durham and a verdict in favor of plaintiff and against Taft, with damages assessed at $7,500. Thereafter the court denied plaintiff's motion for a judgment of $22,847.43 against both defendants, allowed the motion of Durham for a judgment on the verdict in his favor against plaintiff, set aside the verdict against defendant Taft, and also entered judgment in his favor against plaintiff for costs. From these orders and judgments plaintiff has taken this appeal. There can, we think, be no doubt as to the material facts established by the evidence, although much evidence not material to any issue was upon the trial allowed to go to the jury and resulted, we think, in confusing it.

In 1929 the Illinois State Bank was doing a banking business in Evanston. Defendant Taft was its president, Wightman, Durham, Hakes, Hogg and others, directors. Hakes was also executive vice-president; he was a brother-in-law of Henry Magnus Kelly, who acted as attorney for the bank. Hogg was cashier and secretary of the board of directors. The by-laws of the bank provided for monthly meeting of the directors and that at each meeting the directors should examine the loans made by the bank during the preceding month. At a meeting of the board in January February, 1930, the making of this loan of $30,000 was suggested. The party most actively interested was Wightman, but Taft, president of the bank, also indicated a desire that the loan be made. The written guaranty indicates that John Stone for himself and others made an application to the bank for this loan. The application itself has apparently been lost and was not in evidence, but the description in the guaranty would seem to be sufficient. Stone was a clerk in a Chicago law office, and the evidence clearly indicates that he was expected to act as a "dummy" in the transactions, his name being used by others as a matter of convenience. The matter of the proposed loan came before the board of directors at several of its subsequent meetings, and there were objections by some of the directors who thought that the bank should not make a loan of such an amount upon this kind of security. At the April meeting of the board it was agreed that the loan would be made to John Stone provided three of the directors would guarantee it. Mr. Wightman volunteered to guarantee it, Mr. Taft also volunteered, and after both of them had talked further with Durham he said he also would sign the guaranty. The matter was then referred to the attorney, Mr. Kelly, to draw up the necessary papers.

The minutes of the board of directors with reference to this transaction is as follows:

"On motion made by Bruce E. Hakes, seconded by Charles A. Wightman, authority was given to the officers of the bank to make a leasehold loan of $35,000.00 on the property located at 1561-63-65 Sherman avenue, Evanston, Illinois, to John Stone if Messrs. Taft, Durham and Wightman will guarantee to pay the loan in case of default of interest or payment on principal in consideration of the lease being assigned to them in case they are obliged to pay the loan and if the proposed lease shall be approved by the Bank's counsel."

For reasons not disclosed by the record the owners of the premises thereafter decided that Hansen should be substituted for Stone. While this substitution was not formally accepted by resolution of the board at any time, Hakes testified that all the directors were informed of the change and gave their assent thereto. The lease, the trust deed and the notes were all executed by Charles F. and indicated a desire that the loan be made. The written guaranty indicates that John Stone for himself and othe[illegible] an application to the bank for this loan. The application itself had apparently been lost and was not in evidence, but the description in the guaranty would seem to be sufficient. Stone was a clerk in a Chicago law office, and the evidence clearly indicates that he was expected to act as a "dummy" in the transactions, his name being used by others as a matter of convenience. The matter of the proposed loan came before the board of directors at several of its subsequent meetings, and there were objections by some of the directors who thought that the bank should not make a loan of such an amount upon this kind of security. At the April meeting of the board it was agreed that the loan would be made to John Stone provided three of the directors would guarantee it. Mr. Wightman volunteered to guarantee it, Mr. Taft also volunteered, and after both of them had talked further with Durham he said he also would sign the guaranty. The matter was then referred to the attorney, Mr. Kelly, to draw up the necessary papers.

The minutes of the board of directors with reference to this transaction is as follows:

"On motion made by Bruce S. Eaken, seconded Charles A. Wightman, authority was given to the officers of the bank to make a leasehold loan of $25,000.00 on the property located at 1801-[illegible] Sherman avenue, Evanston, Illinois, to John Stone if Messrs. Taft, Durham and Wightman will guarantee to pay the loan in case of default of interest or payment on principal in consideration of the lease being assigned to them in case they are obliged to pay the loan and if the proposed lease shall be approved by the Bank's counsel."

For reasons not disclosed by the record the owners of the premises thereafter decided that Hansen should be substituted for Stone. While this substitution was not formally accepted by resolution of the board at any time, Eaken testified that all the directors were informed of the change and gave their assent thereto. The lease, the trust deed and the notes were all executed by Charles E. and

May E. Hansen and were all dated July 27, 1928. This loan to Hansen was formally approved at a meeting of the board of directors held July 9, 1929, at which defendants were present. The loan was entered in the loan register of the bank as No. 1633. The entry showed the name of Charles F. Hansen as the maker of the notes and trust deed; that the amount of the loan was $35,000, represented by principal notes for $500 each; that the premises were at 1561-63 Sherman avenue. The guaranty, the lease, the trust deed and the notes bear the same date.

Wigatman was in California; he executed the guaranty there and acknowledgedit before a notary public of Los Angeles County on July 1, 1929. Taft signed the guaranty and acknowledged it before a notary public in Cook county July 5th. There is some evidence tending to show that Durham signed on July 5th, but the certificate of the notary shows that he acknowledged the execution of the guaranty August 24, 1929. After signing the guaranty Taft delivered it to attorney Kelly together with a cashier's check of the Illinois State bank for $19,000, payable to the order of C. M. McDonald et al., owners of the premises. Taft, at the time of delivering the check to attorney Kelly directed him in writing to deliver it "when all the papers are in order." Durham testified that he read the guaranty before he signed it, including the clause which stated that the lease was between "Schwall and others as lessors and another as lessee." He made no inquiry as to who this other lessee was.

The evidence shows that both defendants knew that Stone and Hansen were dummies in the transaction who permitted their names to be used for the benefit of others. Hansen thereafter assigned the lease to Taft who held it for the bank as shown by his letter of October 18, 1930, to Mr. Bent, another director, in which he stated:

Roy E. Hansen and were all dated July 27, 1928. This loan to Hansen was formally approved at a meeting of the board of directors held July 9, 1928, at which defendants were present. The loan was entered in the loan register of the bank as No. 1633. The entry showed the name of Charles F. Hansen as the maker of the notes and trust deed; that the amount of the loan was $38,000, represented by principal notes for $500 each; that the premises were at 1561-65 [illegible] avenue. The guaranty, the lease, the trust deed and the notes bear the same date.

Wightman was in California; he executed the guaranty there and acknowledged it before a notary public of Los Angeles County on July 2, 1928. Taft signed the guaranty and acknowledged it before a notary public in Cook county July 5th. There is some evidence tending to show that Durham signed on July 5th, but the certificate of the notary shows that he acknowledged the execution of the guaranty August 24, 1928. After signing the guaranty Taft delivered it to attorney Kelly together with a cashier's check of the Illinois State bank for $18,000, payable to the order of C. W. McDonald et al., owners of the premises. Taft, at the time of delivering the check to attorney Kelly directed him in writing to deliver it "when all the papers are in order." Durham testified that he read the guaranty before he signed it, including the clause which stated that the lease was between "Bagnell and others as lessors and another as lessee." He made no inquiry as to who this other lessee was.

The evidence shows that both defendants knew that Stone and Hansen were dummies in the transaction who permitted their names to be used for the benefit of others. Hansen thereafter assigned the lease to Taft who held it for the bank as shown by his letter of October 18, 1928, to Mr. Kent, another director, in which he stated:

"At the time the bank agreed to make a loan of $35,000 on this property and before any money was paid over, an assignment of this lease was taken from Mr. Hansen and this was put in my name for the protection of the bank and is considered by me as protection for other interested parties in this lease."

In the same letter he also stated, "We have this assignment on record in my name of this lease." April 11, 1931, in response to an inquiry about this loan from Cleveland, Ohio, Mr. Taft wrote:

"The income from the property doesn't take care of all the expenses as the building is old. The intention of the owners is to build a very fine building and at that time will secure a new bonds issue and the present will be paid off. In addition to this there is a personal guarantee by three responsible men offering additional security on the bonds.

Our bank is still holding some of the bonds something like $10,000 and we consider the investment secure. Interest payments will be met as the money deposited from the building is always on hand at this bank."

In view of the argument of defendants that they cannot be held because Hansen was substituted for Stone, the guaranty itself seems to be a necessary part of any adequate statement of the facts. It is as follows:

"Guaranty to the Illinois State Bank of Evanston.
June 27, 1929

Whereas, an application has been made to the Illinois State Bank of Evanston by JOHN STONE, on his own behalf and others, for a loan in the sum of thirty-five thousand dollars ($35,000) to be evidenced by certain notes or bonds, to be secured by a deed of trust, wherein the Chicago Title & Trust Company is to be trustee, conveying, as security for said notes or bonds, a certain leasehold estate created in and by an indenture of lease made by and between ROLAND R. SCHWALL and others, as lessors, and another as lessee, to be presently executed on the premises described as follows:

* * * * * * * * * * * * * *

and

Whereas, each of us is a stockholder in said Illinois State Bank and a director thereof; and

Whereas, as consideration herein, each of us is desir us, on account of the profit that will be realized by said Illinois State Bank, and, in turn, by each of us, that such loan shall be made by said Illinois State Bank, and

Whereas, as additional consideration each of us acknowledges receipt from said Illinois State Bank of one dollar ($1.00), and other good and valuable considerations for the execution hereof; and

Whereas, said Illinois State Bank declines to make such loan without this guaranty by each of us;

Therefore, we jointly and severally hereby, for value received, guarantee to said Illinois State Bank, and to said Illinois State Bank for and on behalf of all subsequent holders of evidences thereof, the payment of said thirty-five thousand

"At the time the bank agreed to make a loan of $35,000 on this property and before any money was paid over, an assignment of this lease was taken from Mr. Hansen and this was put in my name for the protection of the bank and is considered by me as protection for other interested parties in this lease."

In the same letter he also stated, "We have this assignment on record in my name of this lease." April 11, 1931, in response to an inquiry about this loan from Cleveland, Ohio, Mr. Taft wrote:

"The income from the property doesn't take care of all the expenses on the building in 1931. The intention of the owners is to build a very fine building and at that time will secure a new bonds issue and the present will be paid off. In addition to this there is a personal guarantee by three responsible men offering additional security on the bonds.

Our bank is still holding some of the bonds something like $10,000 and we consider the investment secure. Interest payments will be met as the money deposited from the building is always on hand at this bank."

In view of the argument of defendants that they cannot be held because Hansen was substituted for Stone, the guaranty itself seems to be a necessary part of any adequate statement of the facts. It is as follows:

"Guaranty to the Illinois State Bank of Evanston.
June 27, 1929

Whereas, an application has been made to the Illinois State Bank of Evanston by JOHN STONE, on his own behalf and others, for a loan in the sum of thirty-five thousand dollars ($35,000) to be evidenced by certain notes or bonds, to be secured by a deed of trust, wherein the Chicago Title & Trust Company is to be trustee, conveying, as security for said notes or bonds, a certain leasehold estate created in and by an indenture of lease made by and between ROLAND R. CONRAD and others, as lessors, and another as lessee, to be presently executed on the premises described as follows:

* * * * * * * * * * * * * *

and

Whereas, each of us is a stockholder in said Illinois State Bank and a director thereof; and

Whereas, as consideration herein, each of us is desirous, on account of the profit that will be realized by said Illinois State Bank, and, in turn, by each of us, that such loan shall be made by said Illinois State Bank; and

Whereas, as additional consideration each of us acknowledges receipt from said Illinois State Bank of one dollar ($1.00), and other good and valuable considerations for the execution hereof; and

Whereas, said Illinois State Bank declines to loan without this guaranty by each of us;

Therefore, we jointly and severally hereby, for value received, guarantee to said Illinois State Bank, and to said Illinois State Bank for and on behalf of all subsequent holders of evidence thereof, the payment of said thirty-five thousand dollars ($38,000) with the interest thereon specified in said notes or bonds, according to their tenor and the tenor of coupons belonging thereto, as and when they severally shall become due, and the strict observance by such lessee, and by every assignee under said indenture of lease, of all the terms and obligations thereof without default; provided, that in case the lessee or any assignee of the lessee under said indenture of lease, shall make any default in compliance with the terms and obligations of said indenture of lease, or there shall be any default in payment of any of such notes or bonds, we, and each of us, upon our prompt compliance with the terms hereof, shall be subrogated to all of the rights, privileges and security of said Illinois State Bank in said indenture of lease, said deed of trust, and said notes or bonds, with the full value thereof to us and each of us over and above making said Illinois State Bank whole in the premises; in which subrogation said Illinois State Bank hereby agrees to execute any papers, bring any suit or take any action necessary to give complete effect accordingly for the protection of us and each of us.

Therefore, we and each of us hereby covenant and agree, as aforesaid, with said Illinois State Bank and every subsequent holder of each of said notes or bonds.

Charles A. Wightman (Seal)
John H. Taft (Seal)
Frank J. Durham (Seal)

.... (Seal)"

The facts summarized and an analysis of the guaranty, we think compel the inference as a matter of law that plaintiff is entitled in this action to recover the full amount of his claim from both defendants. Their principal contention seems to be based upon the theory that the guaranty was that of a loan to John Stone and that they are not liable because the loan defaulted on was one made to Charles F. Hansen. Even if the oral evidence which makes the facts clear were excluded, this would not be a necessary inference from the language of the guaranty. It is true it recites an application made to the bank by John Stone, but it adds that it was made for others as well as for himself. This recitation in the preamble is not at all inconsistent with the language which appears in the body of the guaranty to the effect that the signers guaranteed the bank the payment of the notes and coupons according to their tenor and the strict observance by the lessee and his assignees of the terms of the lease. Moreover, the preamble distinctly states not that the lease shall run to John Stone but to "another as lessee."

dollars ($25,000) with the interest thereon evidenced by said notes or bonds, according to their tenor and the tenor of the coupons belonging thereto, as and when they severally shall become due, and the strict observance by such lessee, and by every assignee under said indenture of lease, of all the terms and obligations thereof without default; provided, that in case the lessee or any assignee of the lessee under said indenture of lease, shall make any default in compliance with the terms and obligations of said indenture of lease, or there shall be any default in payment of any of such notes or bonds, we, and each of us, upon our prompt compliance with the terms hereof, shall be subrogated to all of the rights, privileges and security of said Illinois State Bank in said indenture of lease, said deed of trust, and said notes or bonds, with the full value thereof to us and each of us over and above holding said Illinois State Bank whole in the premises; in which subrogation said Illinois State Bank hereby agrees to execute any papers, bring any suit or take any action necessary to give complete effect accordingly for the protection of us and each of us.

Wherefore, we and each of us hereby covenant and agree, as aforesaid, with said Illinois State Bank and every subsequent holder of each of said notes or bonds.

Charles A. Wightman (Seal)
John H. Taft (Seal)
Frank J. [illegible] (Seal)

.... (Seal)."

The facts summarized and an analysis of the guaranty, we think compel the inference as a matter of law that plaintiff is entitled in this action to recover the full amount of his claim from both defendants. Their principal contention seems to be based upon the theory that the guaranty was that of a loan to John Stone and that they are not liable because the loan defaulted on was one made to Charles F. Hansen. Even if the oral evidence which makes the facts clear were excluded, this would not be a necessary inference from the language of the guaranty. It is true it recites an application made to the Bank by John Stone, but it adds that it was made for others as well as for himself. This recitation in the preamble is not at all inconsistent with the language which appears in the body of the guaranty to the effect that the signers guaranteed the Bank the payment of the notes and coupons according to their terms and the strict observance by the lessee and his assignees of the terms of the lease. Moreover, the preamble distinctly states not that the loan shall run to John Stone but to "another as lessee."

Parol evidence was admitted to show that this lessee was Hansen, and that evidence was admissible as the many cited cases show. The rule which defendants urge strenuously with reference to the strict construction of a contract of guaranty is not applicable here. The reference in the contract to "another as lessee" would be entirely ambiguous and doubtful without such evidence. It was admissible in order that the intention of the parties to the agreement might be ascertained and carried out. Shreffler v. Nadelhoffer, 133 Ill. 536; Fairbanks v. Owensboro Wagon Co., 72 Ill. App. 530; Mahler Tex. Inc. v. Woodka, 251 Ill. App. 177. The rule is that parol evidence is always admissible in order to ascertain either the identity of the parties to the contract or the subject matter to which a written instrument refers. Platt v. Aetna Ins. Co., 153 Ill. 113; Cumberledge v. Brooks, 235 Ill. 249, Fuchs v. Kittredge & Co., 242 Ill. 88; Peabody v. Dewey, 51 Ill. App. 260, Burge Machine Works v. Mandarin Inn, 225 Ill. App. 358.

Here, the uncontradicted evidence shows that the Illinois State Bank made this loan in full reliance on these three directors who agreed to execute the guaranty. In justness and fair dealing they may not now be allowed to repudiate it. It is conceded that where, as here, both parties move for a directed verdict, it is equivalent to the submission of the case to the court for a trial without a jury. Hungate v. N. Y. Life Ins., 267 Ill. App. 257. Under the law as we view it, defendants are both liable and under the evidence plaintiff is entitled to recover the sum of $17,500 with interest thereon at 6% per cent per annum from June 27, 1930, to the date of the filing of this opinion, amounting to the total sum of $23,000.76, for which judgment will be entered against defendants and in favor of plaintiff in this court.

REVERSED AND JUDGMENT IN FAVOR OF PLAINTIFF AND AGAINST DEFENDANTS FOR $23,000.76.

O'Connor, P. J., and McSurely, J., concur.

Parol evidence was admitted to show that this lessee was [illegible], and that evidence was admissible as the many cited cases show. The rule which defendants urge strenuously with reference to the strict construction of a contract of guaranty is not applicable here. The reference in the contract to "another as lessee" would be entirely ambiguous and doubtful without such evidence. It was admissible in order that the intention of the parties to the agreement might be ascertained and carried out. [illegible] v. [illegible], [illegible] Ill. [illegible]; [illegible] v. [illegible] Co., 72 Ill. App. 330; [illegible] Co. v. [illegible], [illegible] Ill. App. 177. The rule is that parol evidence is always admissible in order to ascertain either the identity of the parties to the contract or the subject matter to which a written instrument refers. Platt v. Aetna Ins. Co., 153 Ill. 113; Gumbertshaw v. Brooks, 235 Ill. 340; Kuhn v. [illegible] & Co., 242 Ill. 88; Peabody v. Dewey, 61 Ill. App. 269; [illegible] v. [illegible] Ins. 223 Ill. App. 380.

[illegible], the uncontradicted evidence shows that the Illinois [illegible] made this loan in full reliance on these three directors [illegible] to execute the guaranty. In justness and fair dealing they may not now be allowed to repudiate it. It is conceded that [illegible], as both parties move for a directed verdict, it is [illegible] to the submission of the case to the court for a trial without a jury. Hannate v. N. Y. Life Ins., 207 Ill. App. 237. [illegible] the law as we view it, defendants are both liable and under the evidence plaintiff is entitled to recover the sum of $17,500 with [illegible] interest at 5% per cent per annum from June 27, 1930, to [illegible] of the filing of this opinion, amounting to the total [illegible], for which judgment will be entered against defendants and in favor of plaintiff in this court.

REVERSED AND JUDGMENT IN FAVOR OF PLAINTIFF AND AGAINST DEFENDANTS FOR $[illegible],000.78.

O'Connor, [illegible], J. concur.

38024

GILBERT MILLER,
Appellant,

vs.

MIRRA L. STURTZ,
Appellee.

APPEAL FROM MUNICIPAL COURT OF CHICAGO.

38 4

280 I.A. 6104

MR. JUSTICE MATCHETT DELIVERED THE OPINION OF THE COURT.

Plaintiff has appealed from an order entered November 24, 1934, on motion of defendant, vacating a judgment theretofore entered on October 11, 1934, setting the cause for hearing on November 27, 1934. The action was begun December 16, 1933, and was in trover for the conversion of certain described personal property. The record shows the default of defendant January 2, 1934, for want of appearance, an order on January 10, 1934, setting the default aside, another default for want of an affidavit of merits on January 29, 1934, judgment against defendant for $2480 which was on February 6th thereafter set aside, and another order of default on March 9th for failure to file an affidavit of merits and judgment on March 12th thereafter for $2480 which was set aside on March 15th.

The record also shows that on October 11, 1934, in the absence of defendant, the cause was tried by jury, a verdict was entered against defendant and plaintiff's damages were assessed at $2480. On November 24th, which was more than 30 days thereafter, a petition was filed purporting to be in support of a motion to set aside the judgment of October 11th. The petition set up in substance that the attorney for plaintiff had agreed to notify attorney for defendant when the case would come up for trial and had failed and neglected to inform him. The petition purports to be verified, but an examination discloses that the verification is only to the effect that the affiant is the petitioner.

38034

GILBERT MILLER,
Appellant,

vs.

ELMER L. STURTZ,
Appellee.

APPEAL FROM MUNICIPAL COURT OF CHICAGO.

280 I.A. 610+

MR. JUSTICE MATCHETT DELIVERED THE OPINION OF THE COURT.

Plaintiff has appealed from an order entered November 24, 1934, on motion of defendant, vacating a judgment theretofore entered on October 11, 1934, setting the cause for hearing on November 27, 1934. The action was begun December 16, 1933, and was in trover for the conversion of certain described personal property. The record shows the default of defendant January 2, 1934, for want of appearance, an order on January 10, 1934, setting the default aside, another default for want of an affidavit of merits on January 29, 1934, judgment against defendant for $8400 which was on February 6th thereafter set aside, and another order of default on March 9th for failure to file an affidavit of merits and judgment on March 12th thereafter for $8450 which was set aside on March 15th.

The record also shows that on October 11, 1934, in the absence of defendant, the cause was tried by jury, a verdict was entered against defendant and plaintiff's damages were assessed at $8480. On November 24th, which was more than 30 days thereafter, a petition was filed purporting to be in support of a motion to set aside the judgment of October 11th. The petition set up in substance that the attorney for plaintiff had agreed to notify attorney for defendant when the case would come up for trial and had failed and neglected to inform him. The petition purports to be verified, but an examination discloses that the verification is only to the effect that the affiant is the petitioner.

The petition does not comply with Section 21 of the Municipal Court act and would not justify the order entered if the judgment of October 11th had not been modified on November 23rd on motion of plaintiff himself. This order is not abstracted but appears in the record and recites that due notice having been served on the attorney of record for defendant and the court having heard arguments of counsel found that it had jurisdiction of the subject matter and the parties thereto, it was ordered that the judgment of October 11, 1934, be corrected and amended so as to read:

"Trial by jury ex parte and non obstante veredicto, the Court finds the defendant, Minna L. Sturtz, guilty as charged in the Statement of claim, damages $2480 in tort. Judgment on finding against the defendant, Minna L. Sturtz, in the sum of $2480 and costs.

"It is further ordered that the Statement and Affidavit of Claim for defendant be and the same hereby is dismissed for want of prosecution."

The effect of this order was to set aside the judgment theretofore entered on the verdict of the jury upon plaintiff's claim and also to adjudicate a claim made against plaintiff by defendant. Plaintiff should not be permitted to stultify himself by taking inconsistent positions. The jurisdiction of the court having been by these proceedings restored, it was, we think, certainly within the discretion of the trial Judge, who was familiar with all the facts, to set aside the former judgment and place the cause again on the trial calendar. In view of the confused record, we think it was well for the parties to begin anew.

The order is therefore affirmed.

ORDER AFFIRMED.

O'Connor, P. J., and McSurely, J., concur.

2

The petition does not comply with Section 21 of the Municipal Court Act and would not justify the order entered if the judgment of October 11th had not been modified on November 23rd on motion of plaintiff himself. This order is not abstracted but appears in the record and recites that due notice having been served on the attorney of record for defendant and the court having heard arguments of counsel found that it had jurisdiction of the subject matter and the parties thereto, it was ordered that the judgment of October 11, 1934, be corrected and amended as to read:

"Trial by jury ex parte and non obstante veredicto, the jury finds the defendant, Hans L. Sturts, guilty as charged in the statement of claim, damages $2150 in tort. Judgment on finding against the defendant, Hans L. Sturts, in the sum of $2150 and costs.

"It is further ordered that the statement and affidavit of claim for defendant be and the same hereby is dismissed for want of prosecution."

The effect of this order was to set aside the judgment theretofore entered on the verdict of the jury upon plaintiff's claim and also to adjudicate a claim made against plaintiff by defendants. Plaintiff should not be permitted to stultify himself by taking inconsistent positions. The jurisdiction of the court having been by these proceedings restored, it was, we think, certainly within the discretion of the trial judge, who was familiar with all the facts, to set aside the former judgment and place the cause again on the trial calendar. In view of the confused record, we think it was well for the parties to begin anew.

The order is therefore affirmed.

ORDER AFFIRMED.

38046

LILLIAN RAINA,
Appellant,

vs.

CHARLES P. SCHWARTZ and LAVINIA S. SCHWARTZ, his wife,
Appellees.

APPEAL FROM MUNICIPAL COURT OF CHICAGO.

39 A

280 I.A. 620

MR. JUSTICE MATCHETT DELIVERED THE OPINION OF THE COURT.

October 17, 1933, plaintiff sued on three principal notes with interest notes attached. The principal notes were dated at Chicago, October 25, 1928, were for $500 each and numbered 11, 12, and 13, respectively, payable to bearer, with interest at the rate of six per cent per annum, payable on the 25th day of October and April each year, according to coupons attached. Both principal and interest were payable at the Noel State Bank, Chicago. Notes Nos. 11 and 12 by their terms matured October 25, 1934, and note No. 13 on October 25, 1935. Each of the notes provided that after maturity it would draw interest at the rate of 7 per cent per annum, and that in case of default in payment of interest and the continuance of such default for three days, the legal owner might at his election declare the principal amount to be due and payable. Each of the notes also stated that it was secured by a trust deed of even date to the Noel State Bank, trustee, on real estate in Cook county, Illinois.

Plaintiff alleged in her statement of claim that she was the bona fide and legal holder and owner of said notes in due course. She alleged default in the payment of interest on October 25, 1932, and her election to declare the principal amount due. Copies of the notes and coupons were attached to her statement of claim, and in an affidavit she stated the nature of her claim and that there was due, after allowing just credits and set-offs, $1677.50.

The time of defendants for filing an affidavit of merits

2

[illegible]

LILLIAN MATHER,
Appellant,

vs.

CHARLES P. SCHWARTZ and LAVINIA S. SCHWARTZ, his wife,
Appellees.

APPEAL FROM MUNICIPAL COURT OF CHICAGO.

280 I.A. 620'

MR. JUSTICE HEBEL DELIVERED THE OPINION OF THE COURT.

October 17, 1935, plaintiff sued on three principal notes with interest notes attached. The principal notes were dated at Chicago, October 25, 1928, were for $500 each and numbered 11, 12 and 13, respectively, payable to bearer with interest at the rate of six per cent per annum, payable on the 25th day of October and April each year, according to coupons attached. Both principals and interest were payable at the Kaal State Bank, Chicago. Notes Nos. 11 and 12 by their terms matured October 25, 1934, and note No. 13 on October 25, 1935. Each of the notes provided that after maturity it should bear interest at the rate of 6 per cent per annum, and that in case of default in payment of interest and the continuance of such default for three days, the legal owner might at his election declare the principal amount to be due and payable. Each of the notes also stated that it was secured by a trust deed of even date to the Kaal State Bank, trustee, on real estate in Cook county, Illinois.

Plaintiff alleged in her statement of claim that she was the bona fide and legal holder and owner of said notes in due course, the alleged default in the payment of interest on October 25, 1932, and her election to declare the principal amount due. Copies of the notes and coupons were attached to her statement of claim, and in the affidavit she stated the nature of her claim and that there was due, after allowing just credits and set-offs, $1697.50.

Motion of defendants for filing an affidavit of merits

was extended from time to time. Defaults entered were set aside by stipulation, etc., until on September 8, 1934, defendants filed an amended affidavit of merits, verified by Charles P. Schwartz. This affidavit of merits denied that plaintiff was the legal owner and holder before maturity of these notes, but averred that neither the notes nor coupons had been presented to Charles P. Schwartz or any other defendant for payment; that the Noel State Bank had closed its doors prior to October 25, 1932; that neither plaintiff nor any one in her behalf had given notice in writing of the place where the notes would be presented for payment. The affidavit averred that defendants were and always had been ready, able and willing to pay the interest and would pay it if plaintiff would notify them of the place of payment. The affidavit denied plaintiff's right to accelerate the payment of the notes and denied that plaintiff was entitled to $1627.50, or any other sum.

A motion to strike the affidavit of merits was denied. The cause was submitted to a jury which returned a verdict for defendants, upon which the court, overruling motions for a new trial, entered judgment. Plaintiff urges for reversal that the verdict of the jury and the judgment are contrary to the manifest weight of the evidence, and this is the controlling question in the case.

At the beginning of the trial defendants tendered $135 interest admitted to be due. It was refused justifiably, we think, since on the theory of either plaintiff or defendants it was insufficient because it did not include the costs of suit. Kahbash v. Byers, 164 Ill. App. 449; Sweetland v. Tuthill, 54 Ill. 215. Plaintiff then proved the genuineness of the signatures of defendants to the instrument sued on, and plaintiff gave testimony (which is uncontradicted) showing that she was a bona fide holder in due course before the maturity of the notes and coupons, which were then offered and received in evidence.

has extended from time to time. Defaults entered ... aside by stipulation, etc., until on September 8, 1936, defendants filed an amended affidavit of merits, verified by Charles F. Schwartz. This affidavit of merits denied that plaintiff was the legal owner and holder before maturity of these notes, but averred that neither the notes nor coupons had been presented to Charles F. Schwartz or any other defendant for payment; that the Noel State Bank had closed its doors prior to October 28, 1932; that neither plaintiff nor any one in her behalf had given notice in writing of the place where the notes would be presented for payment. The affidavit averred that defendants were and always had been ready, able and willing to pay the interest and would pay it if plaintiff would notify them of the place of payment. The affidavit denied plaintiff's right to accelerate the payment of the notes and denied that plaintiff was entitled to $4,374.68, or any other sum.

A motion to strike the affidavit of merits was denied. The cause was submitted to a jury which returned a verdict for defendants, upon which the court, overruling motions for a new trial, entered judgment. Plaintiff urges for reversal that the verdict of the jury and the judgment are contrary to the manifest weight of the evidence, and this is the controlling question in the case.

At the beginning of the trial defendants tendered $155 interest admitted to be due. It was refused justifiably, we think, since on the theory of either plaintiff or defendants it was insufficient because it did not include the costs of suit. Gehlbach v. Brown, 186 Ill. App. 462; Kirkland v. Kirkland, 86 Ill. 215. Plaintiff then proved the genuineness of the signatures of defendants to the instruments sued on, and plaintiff gave testimony (which is uncontradicted) showing that she was a bona fide holder in due course before the maturity of the notes and coupons, which were then offered and received in evidence.

Other evidence for plaintiff tended to show that she lives in Chicago; that she received these notes from her sister who lives in Minnesota, and that just before the interest was due in October, 1932, she turned the notes and coupons over to her brother, Arthur Maina, an attorney of Chicago, in order that he might gibe them attention. The evidence also shows that these three principal notes were of a series for the total amount of $32,000, secured by the same trust deed. The evidence also shows that on October 29, 1932, the attorney for plaintiff filed a bill to foreclose this trust deed. The Noel State Bank was before that time closed by the Auditor of Public Accounts. It was therefore not possible to present the notes and coupons to it for payment, and plaintiff claims that it was not necessary to do so, citing New Hope Delaware Bridge Co. v. Perry, 11 Ill. 467; Yeats v. Berney, 62 Ill. 61; Barber v. Bell, 77 Ill. 490. Defendants on the contrary rely on section 70 of the Negotiable Instrument act (Cahill's Ill. Rev. Stats., 1933, chap. 98, par. 91, p. 1921), which in substance provides that presentment for payment of a negotiable instrument is not necessary in order to charge the person primarily liable, except in case of bank notes, but that if the instrument is payable at a special place and the debtor is able and willing to pay it there at maturity, such ability and willingness are equivalent to a tender of payment. Charles A. Schwartz testified that defendants were always willing and able to pay the interest, and defendants argue that this was, under the circumstances, equivalent to a tender on their part.

The evidence considered as a whole, we think, does not sustain this contention. As already stated, the Noel State Bank was closed when the interest fell due. A willingness to pay in a place not in existence did not amount to a tender. The evidence shows that on October 29, 1932 - four days after the interest matured - a bill was filed to foreclose the trust deed. Attorney Maina testified

Other evidence for plaintiff tended to show that she lives in Chicago; that she received these notes from her sister who lives in Minnesota, and that just before the interest was due in October, 1932, she turned the notes and coupons over to her brother, Arthur Kahn, an attorney of Chicago, in order that he might give them attention. The evidence also shows that these three principal notes were of a series for the total amount of $38,000, secured by the same trust deed. The evidence also shows that on October 29, 1932, the attorney for plaintiff filed a bill to foreclose this trust deed. The Real State Bank was before that time closed by the Auditor of Public Accounts. It was therefore not possible to present the notes and coupons to it for payment, and plaintiff claims that it was not necessary to do so, citing New Hope Delaware Bridge Co. v. Perry, 11 Ill. 467; Yeats v. Ferney, 68 Ill. 81; Bunker v. Hall, 77 Ill. 490. Defendants on the contrary rely on section 70 of the Negotiable Instrument act (Cahill's Ill. Rev. Stats., 1933, chap. 98, par. 91, p. 1961), which in substance provides that presentment for payment of a negotiable instrument is not necessary in order to charge the person primarily liable, except in case of bank notes, but that if the instrument is payable at a special place and the debtor is able and willing to pay it there at maturity, such ability and willingness are equivalent to a tender of payment. Charles F. Edwards testified that defendants were always willing and able to pay the interest, and defendants argue that this was, under the circumstances, equivalent to a tender on their part.

The evidence considered as a whole, we think, does not sustain this contention. As already stated, the Real State Bank was closed when the interest fell due. A willingness to pay in a place not in existence did not amount to a tender. The evidence shows that on October 29, 1932 - four days after the interest matured - a bill was filed to foreclose the trust deed. Attorney Kahn testified (and his evidence is not contradicted) that on October 30th thereafter Mr. Schwartz called him by 'phone and told him he was glad the bill was filed; that if he, Maina, had not done so someone else would have filed it. Attorney Maina then told him that all plaintiff wanted was her interest, and that the reason for filing the bill was that Mr. Schwartz had written a letter to all the holders of the notes telling them that he was going to pay only three per cent interest. Mr. Maina told Mr. Schwartz that his client would not accept three per cent; that the notes were in his office, and when he was ready to pay six per cent he should bring over the money and he would receive the notes. Mr. Schwartz asked Mr. Maina to come and see him and they would talk it over, that most people were taking three per cent.

Mr. Maina also testified (and in this respect also his testimony is not contradicted) that in May, 1933, he went to the office of Mr. Schwartz and that at that time Mr. Schwartz showed him a list of holders of these securities who, he said, were accepting three per cent. Mr. Maina testified:

> "I told him my client wants six per cent; that she is a working girl, and the notes were sold to her on the representation that he was a wealthy man; that all she wanted is her interest.
> He said he was trying to extend all the notes, and asked whether I will extend this also. I said I did not know if she will extend it; I had no authority to extend any notes. He asked me about one note holder, they could not find her. I told him all I knew was my sister owns these three notes. He said it would be embarrassing if he paid six per cent. I told him he contracted to pay six per cent."

Mr. Maina also testified to another conversation with Mr. Schwartz in August, 1933, when he told him he was going to start a suit at law; that the back taxes had not been paid since 1929; that Mr. Schwartz had not kept his promises and had brought him into court five times on a demurrer. He says. "I told him I had no more confidence in him; that he never offered to pay a dime on these notes; all he offered to pay was three per cent, and that I was going to sue on the notes."

(and his affidavit is not contradicted) that on October 14th there-

after, Schwarz called him by 'phone and was glad

the bill was filed; that if Mr. Kalina had not done so someone else

would have filed it. Attorney Kalina then told him that all plain-

tiff wanted was her interest, and that the reason for filing the

bill was that Mr. Schwarz had written a letter to all the holders

of the notes telling them that he was going to pay only three per

cent interest; Mr. Kalina told Mr. Schwarz that his client would

not accept three per cent; that the notes were in his office, and

that he was ready to pay six per cent if he should bring over the

[illegible] would receive the notes. Mr. Schwarz asked Mr. Kalina

[illegible] and they would talk it over, that most people

were taking three per cent.

III. Mr. Kalina also testified (and in this respect also his testimony is not contradicted) that in May, 1933, he went to the office of Mr. Schwarz and that at that time Mr. Schwarz showed him a list of holders of these securities who, he said, were accepting three per cent. Mr. Kalina testified:

"I told him my client wants six per cent; that she is a working girl, and the notes were sold to her on the representation that he was a wealthy man; that all she wanted is her interest. He said he was trying to extend all the notes, and asked whether I will accept this also. I said I did not know if she will accept it; I had no authority to extend any notes. He asked me about the note holder, they could not find her. I told him all I knew was my client gets about three notes. He said it would be outstanding if he paid six per cent. I told him he contracted to pay six per cent."

Mr. Kalina also testified to another conversation with Mr. Schwarz in August, 1933, when he told him he was going to start a suit at law; that the back taxes had not been paid since 1930; that Mr. Schwarz had not kept his promises and had brought him into court. [illegible] He said: "I told him I had no more confidence in him, that he never offered to pay a dime on these notes; [illegible] and that I was going to sue on the notes."

Mr. Schwartz testified that he "always offered" the interest if Mr. Maina would present the notes. He does not specifically deny the conversations above recited. On cross-examination he said, however, that he did not remember whether what he offered was three or six per cent; that Mr. Maina "wouldn't accept three per cent because it would cancel the foreclosure", further:

"He wouldn't take the six; he refused to surrender the notes that were due; he was willing to take six per cent, but he wouldn't cancel the due notes, and I couldn't give him any money because the money was deposited with me by the owners. The three per cent was the proposition of reorganization. He worked that out with Karlin; I thought that was a reasonable basis. I testified that most of the rest of them got their interest, the notes are cancelled; they are in the office. I think they got three per cent. No one got six per cent, but we offered it to Maina; that was in my office before this lawsuit was started. I do not remember the exact date."

The uncontradicted evidence in this case shows that the interest was due, and there can be no dispute that plaintiff was entitled to a judgment for at least that amount. The uncontradicted evidence also shows that defendants knew where the notes were, and that at no time did they tender any money in payment of either interest or principal.

The verdict was manifestly against the evidence and the motion for a new trial should have been granted.

For the reasons indicated the judgment is reversed and the cause remanded.

REVERSED AND REMANDED.

O'Connor, P. J., and McSurely, J., concur.

38244

BESSIE SUCHY, BOHUMIL HAJICEK, CHARLES HAJICEK, LOUIS HAJICEK, JOHN FRANTA, Sr., JOHN FRANTA, Jr., ELSIE FRANTA and MARIE KOVARIK,
Appellees,

vs.

JOHN HAJICEK, CHRISTINA HAJICEK, LILLIAN NOVOTNY and WILLIAM FRANTA,
Defendants.

JOHN HAJICEK,
Appellant.

INTERLOCUTORY APPEAL FROM SUPERIOR COURT OF COOK COUNTY.

280 I.A. 620

MR. JUSTICE McSURELY DELIVERED THE OPINION OF THE COURT.

Plaintiffs filed their complaint seeking a decree that John Hajicek, one of the defendants, held the legal title to certain real estate as trustee for the plaintiffs, and also that he be held to an account for rents of such premises. The complaint also alleged that he has instituted forcible detainer proceedings in the Municipal court of Chicago against Bessie Suchy, one of the plaintiffs, to oust her from one of the apartments in the building on the premises, and plaintiffs asked for a temporary injunction restraining John Hajicek from proceeding with this forcible detainer action or from instituting or maintaining any other suit for rent or possession of the premises until the further order of the court. The temporary injunction was granted and defendant John Hajicek appeals.

The complaint alleges that Marie Hajicek, the mother of the plaintiffs and defendants, and the grandmother of the Frantas, had owned the property in question in fee simple, that when she was seventy years of age and in good health, and desirous of transferring her worldly possessions during her lifetime for the benefit of her children, she executed a deed of the premises, without consideration, to Bohumil C. Bartik, and at the same time Bartik conveyed the premises by deed to Marie Hajicek and her son John Hajicek, as

36844

BESSIE BUCHY, DOMINIK HAJICEK,
CHARLES HAJICEK, LOUIS HAJICEK,
JOHN VRANTA, Sr., JOHN VRANTA, Jr.,
ELSIE VRANTA and MARIE KOVARIK,
Appellees,

v.

JOHN HAJICEK, CHRISTINA HAJICEK,
LILLIAN NOVOTNY and WILLIAM VRANTA,
Defendants.

JOHN HAJICEK,
Appellant.

INTERLOCUTORY
APPEAL FROM SUPERIOR
COURT OF COOK COUNTY.

280 I.A. 620

MR. JUSTICE McSURELY DELIVERED THE OPINION OF THE COURT.

Plaintiffs filed their complaint seeking a decree that John Hajicek, one of the defendants, held the legal title to certain real estate as trustee for the plaintiffs, and also that he be held to an account for rents of such premises. The complaint also alleged that he has instituted forcible detainer proceedings in the municipal court of Chicago against Bessie Buchy, one of the plaintiffs, to oust her from one of the apartments in the building on the premises, and plaintiffs asked for a temporary injunction restraining John Hajicek from proceeding with this forcible detainer action or from instituting or maintaining any other suit for rent or possession of the premises until the further order of the court. The temporary injunction was granted and defendant John Hajicek appeals.

The complaint alleges that Marie Hajicek, the mother of the plaintiffs and defendants, and the grandmother of the Vrantas, had owned the property in question in fee simple, that when she was seventy years of age and in good health, and desirous of transferring her worldly possessions during her lifetime for the benefit of her children, she executed a deed of the premises, without consideration, to Joseph G. Kartik, and at the same time Kartik conveyed the premises by deed to Marie Hajicek and her son John Hajicek, as joint tenants; that it was expressly understood and agreed between John and his mother, Marie, that John would hold the legal title to the property for the benefit of all the children and that the profits from the property should be for the benefit of all of the children.

That Marie Hajicek subsequently died, and thereafter John was in possession of the premises, which consists of a lot and a two-story frame building comprising three apartments, and plaintiff Bessie Suchy was in possession of one of the apartments, that John Hajicek has instituted forcible detainer proceedings in the Municipal court of Chicago against Bessie Suchy and threatens to oust her from possession of her apartment, which, if carried out, plaintiff Bessie Suchy will suffer irreparable loss.

Defendant appealing, questions the allegations of the complaint, and further argues that the relation of landlord and tenant exists between John Hajicek and Bessie Suchy, and that a tenant cannot question the title of his landlord.

As we have said in McDougall Co. v. Woods, 247 Ill. App. 170, in appeals from interlocutory orders it is not our province to determine the rights of the parties in the subject matter of the litigation. If a complaint states facts which prima facie give a right to a preliminary injunction it will have no more effect than the mere maintenance of the status quo. An appeal from such an interlocutory injunction is to permit a review of the exercise of the discretion lodged in the chancellor with the purpose of determining whether the interlocutory order was necessary to maintain the status quo and preserve the equitable rights of the parties.

The injunction in this case was properly entered to maintain the status quo pending final disposition of the cause. It hardly requires argument to demonstrate that should Bessie Suchy, the daughter of Marie Hajicek, be ousted from possession of the

2

16244

joint tenants; that it was expressly understood and agreed between John and his mother, Marie, that John would hold the legal title to the property for the benefit of all the children and that the profits from the property should be for the benefit of all of the children.

That Marie Hajicek subsequently died, and thereafter John was in possession of the premises, which consists of a lot and a two-story frame building comprising three apartments, and plaintiff Bessie Suchy was in possession of one of the apartments; that John Hajicek has instituted forcible detainer proceedings in the Municipal Court of Chicago against Bessie Suchy and threatens to oust her from possession of her apartment; which, if carried out, plaintiff Bessie Suchy will suffer irreparable loss.

Defendant appealing, questions the allegations of the complaint, and further argues that the relation of landlord and tenant exists between John Hajicek and Bessie Suchy, and that a tenant cannot question the title of his landlord.

As we have said in McDougall Co. v. Woods, 247 Ill. App. 170, in appeals from interlocutory orders it is not our province to determine the rights of the parties in the subject matter of the litigation. If a complaint states facts which prima facie give a right to a preliminary injunction it will have no more effect than the mere maintenance of the status quo. An appeal from such an interlocutory injunction is to permit a review of the exercise of the discretion lodged in the chancellor with the purpose of determining whether the interlocutory order was necessary to maintain the status quo and preserve the equitable rights of the parties.

The injunction in this case was properly entered to maintain the status quo pending final disposition of the cause. It would, upon the record, be inequitable that should Bessie Suchy, the daughter of Marie Hajicek, be ousted from possession of the premises which she occupied before the death of her parents, that she would suffer irreparable damages should it be subsequently decreed that John Hajicek held title to the property in trust for the benefit of Bessie Suchy and the other plaintiffs.

It is also true that a party in possession, even though he recognizes the title in another, may afterward set up title in himself if he shows that his recognition was based upon misapprehension. Wright v. Stice, 173 Ill. 571. The complaint in the instant case alleges that plaintiff did not know of the agreement between Marie and John Hajicek until after John threatened ouster proceedings against her.

Among the cases approving temporary injunctions under somewhat similar circumstances are Penkala v. Tomczyk, 317 Ill. 356; Funk v. Fowler, 179 Ill. App. 356; Cordell v. Solomon, 234 Ill. App. 430; Kulwin v. Harsh, 232 Ill. App. 419.

For the reasons indicated the temporary injunction is affirmed.

AFFIRMED.

O'Connor, P. J., and Matchett, J., concur.

premises which she occupied before the death of her parents, that she would suffer irreparable damages should it be subsequently decreed that John Hajicek held title to the property in trust for the benefit of Bessie Suchy and the other plaintiffs.

It is also true that a party in possession, even though he recognizes the title in another, may afterward set up title in himself if he shows that his recognition was based upon misapprehension. Wright v. Stice, 173 Ill. 571. The complaint in the instant case alleges that plaintiff did not know of the agreement between Marie and John Hajicek until after John threatened ouster proceedings against her.

Among the cases approving temporary injunctions under somewhat similar circumstances are Fenkola v. Tomczyk, 317 Ill. 356; Funk v. Fenley, 179 Ill. App. 586; Cordell v. Solomon, 234 Ill. App. 580; Kelvin v. Harsh, 232 Ill. App. 419.

For the reasons indicated the temporary injunction is affirmed.

AFFIRMED.

O'Connor, P. J., and Matchett, J., concur.

Filed alone May 22, 1935

38017

THE NATIONAL BANK OF THE REPUBLIC OF CHICAGO, as Trustee, etc., Appellee,

vs.

168 ADAMS BUILDING CORPORATION, THE MIDLAND CLUB, DUFFY-NOONAN CONSTRUCTION COMPANY, a Corporation, etc., Appellants.

DUFFY-NOONAN CONSTRUCTION COMPANY, a Corporation, and CARPENTER, RUMBAUGH and DEAN, Appellants.

APPEAL FROM CIRCUIT COURT OF COOK COUNTY.

280 I.A. 620[3]

MR. JUSTICE McSURELY DELIVERED THE OPINION OF THE COURT.

Complainant, as Trustee, filed its bill to foreclose a trust deed executed by the 168 Adams Building Corporation to secure a bond issue of $3,250,000. The Duffy-Noonan Construction Company, a defendant, as holder of second mortgage bonds, by its cross-bill attacked the validity of the corporate organization of the 168 Adams Building Corporation, denied the validity of the trust deed sought to be foreclosed and asserted that if the holders of the bonds have any rights their remedy is as general creditors only. Certain defendants also claimed mechanics' liens against the premises.

The cause was referred to a master who heard evidence and reported, finding against the contention of the Construction company and in favor of the mechanics' lien claimants, and recommended a decree as prayed for by complainant and that the cross-bill of the Construction company be dismissed. The chancellor sustained the master and entered a decree accordingly. Benjamin F. Langworthy, a bondholder, prosecuted an appeal to the Supreme court, asserting that the amounts allowed for fees were excessive, but his appeal was dismissed by stipulation. Cross-appeals were prosecuted to the Supreme court by the Construction Company; M. R. Carpenter, Samuel

Filed alone May 22, 1935.

[illegible]

THE NATIONAL BANK OF THE REPUBLIC OF [illegible], as Trustee, etc.,
Appellee,

[illegible]

vs.

THE ADAMS BUILDING CORPORATION, [illegible] DUFFY-MOORMAN CONSTRUCTION COMPANY, a corporation, etc.,
Appellants.

[illegible]

[illegible] CONSTRUCTION COMPANY, [illegible] and [illegible],
Appellants.

APPEAL FROM CIRCUIT COURT, COOK COUNTY.

280 I.A. 620

MR. JUSTICE McSURELY DELIVERED THE OPINION OF THE COURT.

Complainant, as Trustee, filed its bill to foreclose a trust deed executed by the 166 Adams Building Corporation to secure first mortgage bonds. The Duffy-Moorman Construction Company, [illegible], the holders of [illegible] second mortgage bonds, by its cross-bill attacked the validity of the corporate organization of the 166 Adams Building Corporation, denied the validity of the trust deed sought to be foreclosed and asserted that if the holders of the bonds have any rights their remedy is as general creditors only. Certain defendants also claimed mechanics' liens against the premises.

The cause was referred to a master who heard evidence and reported, finding against the contention of the Construction company and in favor of the mechanics' lien claimants, and recommended a decree as prayed for by complainant and that the cross-bill of [illegible] the Construction company be dismissed. The chancellor sustained the report and entered a decree accordingly. Benjamin F. Langworthy, a [illegible] prosecuted an appeal to the Supreme court, asserting [illegible] for [illegible] companies, but his appeal was

E. Dean and Richard L. Rumbaugh, also defendants, prosecuted a cross-appeal, claiming certain interest in the property of the Midland Club, the complainant asserted cross-errors as to the allowance of mechanics' liens. In Bank of Republic v. Adams Bld. Corp., 359 Ill. 27, it was held that the appeal should not have been taken to the Supreme court and the cause was transferred to the Appellate court.

The cross-bill of the Construction company asserts that the trust deed recites that The Midland Club is a corporation organized and existing under the laws of Illinois and that all of the stock of the Building Corporation is owned or controlled by The Midland Club, which, it is argued, is in violation of secs. 1, 2 and 3 of the General Corporation Act, Illinois Statutes (Cahill), which provides that building corporations may be organized only for acquiring or operating "only one building and the site therefor and for no other purpose," and section 8, which prohibits any corporation from purchasing or holding the stock of a building corporation.

To consider this point it is necessary to narrate some of the facts. In 1923 The Midland Club was organized and incorporated under the Illinois laws as a corporation for social purposes, not for profit; it had a list of upwards of 1000 members, classified as life members; it bought the real estate in question and early in 1926 was planning to acquire a building to accommodate the Club's activities; the plan adopted was that a building corporation would be formed under the Illinois laws by the members of The Midland Club, the stock of this building corporation would be issued to the incorporators and held by them for the benefit of the life members of the Club, the Club would convey its real estate to the building corporation and the latter would issue first mortgage bonds to the amount of $3,250,000 and its second mortgage bonds to the amount of $1,000,000 to be sold to the public, and out of the proceeds the

See.

M. Pong and Richard L. Rumbaugh, also defendants, prosecuted a cross-appeal, claiming certain interest in the property of the Midland Club; the complainant asserted cross-errors as to the allowance of mechanics' liens. In Bank of Republic v. Adams Bldg. Corp., 339 Ill. [illegible], it was held that the appeal should not have been taken to the Supreme court and the cause was transferred to the Appellate court.

The cross-bill of the Construction company asserts that the trust deed recites that The Midland Club is a corporation organized and existing under the laws of Illinois and that all of the stock of the building corporation is owned or controlled by The Midland Club, which, it is argued, is in violation of secs. 1, 2 and 8 of the General Corporation Act, Illinois Statutes ((Cahill), which provides that building corporations may be organized only for acquiring or promoting "only one building and the site therefor and for no other purpose," and section 8, which prohibits any corporation from purchasing or holding the stock of a building corporation.

To consider this point it is necessary to narrate some of the facts. In 1923 the Midland Club was organized and incorporated under the Illinois laws as a corporation for social purposes, not for profit; it had a list of upwards of 1000 members, classified as life members; it bought the real estate in question and early in 1925 was planning to acquire a building to accommodate the Club's activities; the plan adopted was that a building corporation would be formed under the Illinois laws by the members of The Midland Club, the stock of this building corporation would be issued to the incorporators and held by them for the benefit of the life members of the Club. The Club would convey its real estate to the building corporation and the latter would issue first mortgage bonds in the amount of $3,250,000 and its second mortgage bonds to the amount of $1,000,000 to be sold to the public, and out of the proceeds the building corporation would erect a twenty-two story building upon the site conveyed to it and lease to The Midland Club space therein for its quarters.

This was done, and in October, 1926, the charter of the 168 Adams Building Corporation was issued upon the application of Charles E. Schlytern, Richard P. Garrett and LeRoy Tolzein, members of The Midland Club, and the stock was issued in their names; in the same month The Midland Club conveyed to the Building Corporation the real estate and on November 1, 1926, the Building Corporation made and executed its first mortgage bonds and trust deed now sought to be foreclosed; November 15, 1926, the Building Corporation executed its second mortgage bonds in the amount of $1,000,000.

The Duffy-Noonan Construction Company was a general contractor; Joseph J. Duffy and John P. Noonan owned all the stock except one share; these men were both members of The Midland Club in 1926; the Duffy-Noonan Construction Company by bid obtained the contract for the construction of the twenty-two story building and on November 1, 1926, entered into a written contract with the Building Corporation to this end. The contract provided that the Construction Company should receive $2,039,335 in cash and $547,200 in the second mortgage bonds of the Building Corporation as compensation for constructing the building. The building was constructed and the Construction Company received $2,026,341.20 in cash, out of the proceeds of the sale of the first mortgage bonds to the public and $619,100 of the second mortgage bonds, the excess being due to additional work not specified in the contract.

A copy of the trust deed sought to be foreclosed was delivered to Mr. Noonan at the time his corporation entered into the contract and was examined by the attorney for the Construction Corporation. The second mortgage bonds had stamped on their face, "This is a junior mortgage," and it was understood that these second building corporation would erect a twenty-two story building upon the site conveyed to it and lease to The Midland Club space therein for its quarters.

This was done, and in October, 1926, the charter of the 188 Adams Building Corporation was issued upon the application of Charles H. McIntyre, Richard P. Garrett and LeRoy Tolstein, members of The Midland Club, and the stock was issued in their names; in the same month The Midland Club conveyed to the Building Corporation the real estate and on November 1, 1926, the Building Corporation made and executed its first mortgage bonds and trust deed now sought to be foreclosed; November 15, 1926, the Building Corporation executed its second mortgage bonds in the amount of $1,000,000.

The Duffy-Noonan Construction Company was a general contractor; Joseph J. Duffy and John P. Noonan owned all the stock except one share; these men were both members of The Midland Club in 1926; the Duffy-Noonan Construction Company by bid obtained the contract for the construction of the twenty-two story building and on November 1, 1926, entered into a written contract with the Building Corporation to this end. The contract provided that the Construction Company should receive $2,050,535 in cash and $547,200 in the second mortgage bonds of the Building Corporation as compensation for constructing the building. The building was constructed and the Construction Company received $2,026,341.30 in cash, out of the proceeds of the sale of the first mortgage bonds to the public and $619,100 of the second mortgage bonds, the excess being due to additional work not specified in the contract.

A copy of the trust deed sought to be foreclosed was delivered to Mr. Noonan at the time his corporation entered into the contract and was examined by the attorney for the Construction Corporation. The second mortgage bonds had stamped on their face, "This is a junior mortgage," and it was understood that these would mortgage bonds taken by the Construction Company in part payment for constructing the building should be subordinate to the claims of the holders of the first mortgage bonds.

The Midland Club joined in the execution of the first trust deed and guaranteed the payment of the first mortgage bonds, and also by the same instrument conveyed unto the complainant-trustee and its successors all its right, title and interest in and to the real estate in question.

The Construction Company employed various sub-contractors in constructing the building and gave them for their services over $300,000 of the second mortgage bonds it had received.

We are of the opinion that the trust deed sought to be foreclosed is valid, for the following reasons. Even if it were conceded that the stock of the Building Corporation was held and owned by The Midland Club, and for that reason the Building Corporation charter was void, still the trust deed would be a valid mortgage upon the mortgaged premises as the property of The Midland Club. This Club owned the premises prior to the making of the trust deed in question and had a right to mortgage the same.

The argument is that the 168 Adams Building Corporation, because its stock was, as alleged, owned by The Midland Club, was not a valid de jure or de facto corporation, and therefore there was no grantee in the deed from The Midland Club. If this were so then The Midland Club was the owner of the real estate on November 1, 1926, when the trust deed in question was executed by the Club as well as by the Building Corporation. The right of The Midland Club to mortgage its property cannot be questioned.

Defendants say that it was planned to use only five stories of the twenty-two story building for club purposes and to rent the balance to various tenants. It is urged that a corporation organized not for profit cannot rent such excess space. This might be an mortgage bonds taken by the Construction Company in part payment for constructing the building should be subordinate to the claims of the holders of the first mortgage bonds.

The Midland Club joined in the execution of the first trust deed and guaranteed the payment of the first mortgage bonds, and also by the same instrument conveyed unto the complainant-trustee and its successors all its right, title and interest in and to the real estate in question.

The Construction Company employed various sub-contractors in constructing the building and gave them for their services over $200,000 of the second mortgage bonds it had received.

We are of the opinion that the trust deed sought to be foreclosed is valid, for the following reasons. Even if it were conceded that the stock of the Building Corporation was held and owned by The Midland Club, and for that reason the Building Corporation charter was void, still the trust deed would be a valid mortgage upon the mortgaged premises as the property of The Midland Club. This Club owned the premises prior to the making of the trust deed in question and had a right to mortgage the same.

The argument is that the 168 Adams Building Corporation, because its stock was, as alleged, owned by The Midland Club, was not a valid de jure or de facto corporation, and therefore there was no grantee in the deed from The Midland Club. If this were so then The Midland Club was the owner of the real estate on November 1, 1926, when the trust deed in question was executed by the Club as well as by the Building Corporation. The right of The Midland Club to mortgage its property cannot be questioned.

Defendants say that it was planned to use only five stories of the twenty-two story building for club purposes and to rent the balance to various tenants. It is urged that a corporation organized not for profit cannot rent such excess space. This might be an abuse of power granted to the corporation, but this cannot be raised as a defense in a collateral proceeding, and can be questioned only by the State. Rector v. Hartford Deposit Co., 190 Ill. 380; Alexander v. Tolleston Club, 110 Ill. 65, Wolff v. Schwill & Co., 351 Ill. 28.

It is a matter of common knowledge that clubs of a social or religious nature own and maintain buildings and lease some portion of them to others, thus receiving rentals to reduce their own cost of operation for the benefits of their members. We know of no cases that hold that this is against public policy. A corporation organized for pecuniary profit means for the pecuniary profit of its stockholders, ordinarily in the shape of dividends. The record does not show that The Midland Club planned to or did receive any rentals as dividends.

It is also a matter of common knowledge that many corporations organized for profit, which have power to own and improve real estate for their own offices or quarters, are not restricted to such improvements as will only accommodate their absolute requirements. This question was considered in Brown v. Schleier, 118 Fed. 981, which involved the question of the right of a national bank to construct and operate a building which included space largely in excess of the actual needs of the bank. It was held that there was no law or policy which prevented this so long as the corporation acted in good faith.

A further consideration against the position of the Duffy-Noonan Construction Company is that it is estopped to deny the validity of the trust deed sought to be foreclosed and the validity of the Adams Building Corporation. Duffy and Noonan were members of The Midland Club and had full knowledge of its plans to create the Adams Building Corporation, of the making of the first mortgage and abuse of power granted to the corporation, but this cannot be raised as a defense in a collateral proceeding, and can be questioned only by the State. Hunter v. Hartford Deposit Co., 190 Ill. 389; Alexander v. Tullerton Club, 112 Ill. 63; Wolff v. Cappelli & Co., 391 Ill. 88.

It is a matter of common knowledge that clubs of a social or religious nature own and maintain buildings and lease some portion of them to others, thus receiving rentals to reduce their own cost of operation for the benefits of their members. We know of no cases that hold that this is against public policy. A corporation organized for pecuniary profit means for the pecuniary profit of its stockholders, ordinarily in the shape of dividends. The record does not show that The Midland Club planned to or did receive any rentals as dividends.

It is also a matter of common knowledge that many corporations organized for profit, which have power to own and improve real estate for their own offices or quarters, are not restricted to such improvements as will only accommodate their absolute requirements. This question was considered in Brown v. Schleier, 118 Fed. 981, which involves the question of the right of a national bank to construct and operate a building which included space largely in excess of the actual needs of the bank. It was held that there was no law or policy which prevented this so long as the corporation acted in good faith.

A further consideration against the position of the Duffy-Noonan Construction Company is that it is estopped to deny the validity of the trust deed sought to be foreclosed and the validity of the Adams Building Corporation. Duffy and Noonan were members of the Midland Club and had full knowledge of its plans to create the Adams Building Corporation, of the making of the first mortgage and of the second mortgage; the Construction Company agreed that as compensation for constructing the building it would take over $2,000,000 in cash out of the sale to the public of the first mortgage bonds and would accept over $500,000 of the second mortgage bonds in part payment for constructing the building, the record shows that in fact it did receive more than these sums and in turn gave these second mortgage bonds in excess of $300,000 to sub-contractors who worked on the building for the Construction Company. The Midland Club, Adams Building Corporation and the Duffy-Noonan Construction Company understood fully how the money was to be raised to pay for the construction of the building, and the agreement was carried out fully. Under such circumstances the construction company will not now be heard to claim that both the first and second mortgages are void, and will not be permitted to repudiate its contract entered into with full knowledge of the facts and carried out pursuant to the agreement.

A further consideration is that although the Construction Company asserted in its cross-bill that the entire amount of the second mortgage bonds - $619,100 - was under its control and it offered to surrender the same upon the equities of all the parties to this proceeding being adjudicated upon the basis of a quantum meruit, the evidence shows that over $300,000 of these bonds given to sub-contractors were beyond the power of the Construction Company to recall or control. So that if its theory should prevail these sub-contractors would hold as compensation for their services void second mortgage bonds and would have no claim against either The Midland Club or the 168 Adams Building Corporation, but could look only to the Construction Company for compensation. It is well settled that a party who has contracted with a corporation de facto cannot be permitted, after having received the benefits of his con-

[illegible] second mortgage; the Construction Company agreed that as [illegible] for constructing the building it would take over $1,000,000 in cash out of the sale to the public of the first mortgage bonds and would accept over $300,000 of the second mortgage bonds in part payment for constructing the building; the record shows that in fact it did receive more than those sums and in turn [illegible] those second mortgage bonds in excess of $300,000 to sub-contractors who worked on the building for the Construction Company; the [illegible] Club, Adams Building Corporation and the Duffy-Rosene Construction Company understood fully how the money was to be applied to pay for the construction of the building, and the agreement was carried out fully. Under such circumstances the Construction Company will now not be heard to claim that both the first and second mortgages are valid, and will not be permitted to repudiate its contract entered into with full knowledge of the facts and [illegible] pursuant to the agreement.

A further consideration is that although the Construction Company asserted in its cross-bill that the entire amount of the [illegible] bonds - $333,100 - was under its control and it [illegible] the same upon the equities of all the parties [illegible] being adjudicated upon the basis of a [illegible], the evidence shows that over $300,000 of these bonds, [illegible] to sub-contractors were beyond the power of the Construction Company to recall or control. So that if its theory should prevail these sub-contractors [illegible] as compensation for their services said second mortgage bonds [illegible] would have no claim against either the Midland [illegible] Building Corporation, but would look only to the Construction Company for compensation. It is [illegible] settled that a party who has [illegible] a corporation [illegible] tract, to allege any defect in the organization of the corporation as affecting its capacity to enforce such contract. Winget v. Quincy Bldg. Assoc., 128 Ill. 67; Eckert v. Cleveland, 138 Ill. App. 434; Gilmer Creamery Assoc. v. Quentin, 142 Ill. App. 448.

The record justifies the conclusion that the 168 Adams Building Corporation was a valid de jure corporation. It was organized in proper form for the purpose of erecting, leasing and operating a building; there is no defect or omission in the steps of the organization.

But defendants say that it is apparent on the face of the trust deed and in other writings that it was organized as a part of an unlawful plan under which the stock was to be owned by The Midland Club, in violation of section 8 of the General Corporation Act, Illinois Statutes (Cahill). There is certain language used in the various recitals in the records of The Midland Club and other documents which seem to bear out the claim that the stock of the Building Corporation was owned by The Midland Club. In the trust deed there is language to this effect. But there was abundant evidence to support the findings of the master that the stock was not owned by the Club but was held for the benefit of the life members of The Midland Club. The stock of the Building Corporation was never issued to the Club but was issued to Schlytern, Garrett and Tolzein; a resolution was adopted by these subscribers to the capital stock which recites that the shares of capital stock are "for the benefit of the life membership of said Midland Club;" and Garrett testified that the subscribers to the stock took the certificates for the benefit of the life members of the Club. Other witnesses testified without contradiction that this was the fact. Moreover, it appears that those subscribers assigned the certificates of stock to certain trustees, to be held by the trustees under the terms of a trust agreement which declared that the trustees held the stock of the trust, to allege any defect in the organization of the corporation as affecting its capacity to enforce such contract. Winget v. Quincy Bldg. Assoc., 128 Ill. 67; Hoggatt v. Cleveland, 154 Ill. App. 434; Gilmer Creamery Assoc. v. Quinlin, 142 Ill. App. 445.

The record justifies the conclusion that the 180 Adams Building Corporation was a valid de jure corporation. It was organized in proper form for the purpose of erecting, leasing and operating a building; there is no defect or omission in the steps of the organization.

But defendants say that it is apparent on the face of the trust deed and in other writings that it was organized as a part of an unlawful plan under which the stock was to be owned by the Midland Club, in violation of section 6 of the General Corporation Act, Illinois Statutes (Cahill). There is certain language used in the various recitals in the records of the Midland Club and other documents which seem to bear out the claim that the stock of the Building Corporation was owned by the Midland Club. In the trust deed there is language to this effect. But there was abundant evidence to support the findings of the master that the stock was not owned by the Club but was held for the benefit of the life members of the Midland Club. The stock of the Building Corporation was never issued to the Club but was issued to Schlytern, Garrett and Tolsein; a resolution was adopted by these subscribers to the capital stock which recites that the shares of capital stock are "for the benefit of the life membership of said Midland Club;" and Garrett testified that the subscribers to the stock took the certificates for the benefit of the life members of the Club. Other witnesses testified without contradiction that this was the fact. Moreover, it appears that these subscribers assigned the certificates of stock to certain trustees, to be held by the trustees under the terms of a trust agreement which declared that the trustees held the stock of the

Building Corporation for the life members of The Midland Club.

Even if the evidence did not establish this fact, as a matter of law the life members would be the equitable owners of the stock of the Building Corporation, for if The Midland Club could not own the stock it would belong to the members of the Club. Walker v. Taylor, 252 Ill. 424; Wolf v. DeWolf & Co., 53 Fed. (2d) 999. We hold that the 168 Adams Building Corporation was both de facto and de jure a valid corporation, and that also the mortgage sought to be foreclosed herein is valid.

Defendants R. A. Carpenter, Richard L. Rumbaugh and Samuel M. Dean claim that they were members of The Midland Club during all of the aforesaid transactions and that by virtue of such membership they have an undivided proportionate interest in all the property held for and on behalf of the Club, as they did not authorize the conveyance of the real estate to the Building Corporation, nor the mortgage. This claim cannot be maintained. The real estate was the property of The Midland Club and not that of the members of the Club, although they may have equities in it as evidenced by the membership certificates. But the corporation acts through its board of directors and officers and its property is not subject to the control of its members or its stockholders. National Brake Beam Co. v. Equipment Co., 226 Ill. 28; Sellers v. Greer, 172 Ill. 549; Bloom v. Vehon Co., 341 Ill. 200.

The decree held that Anderson & Lind Manufacturing Company had a mechanic's lien on the premises for $3908.90 on account of millwork delivered and used in the construction of the building. Complainant says that the evidence does not show a single continuous contract for all millwork but only separate orders and deliveries made at separate and different times, and that claimant is entitled to a lien for the last item only, which was the only delivery within four months before the claim was filed. Sec. 7

Building Corporation for the life members of the Midland Club.

Even if the evidence did not establish this fact, as a matter of law the life members would be the equitable owners of the stock of the Building Corporation, for if the Midland Club could not own the stock it would belong to the members of the Club. *Parker v. Taylor*, 202 Ill. 424; *Hall v. McNeil & Co.*, 53 Fed. (2d) 979. We hold that the 100 Adams Building Corporation was both *de facto* and *de jure* a valid corporation, and that also the mortgage sought to be foreclosed herein is valid.

Defendants A. R. Carpenter, Richard L. Kavanagh and August H. Dean claim that they were members of the Midland Club during all of the aforesaid transactions and that by virtue of such membership they have an undivided proportionate interest in all the property held for and on behalf of the Club, as they did not authorize the conveyance of the real estate to the Building Corporation, nor the mortgage. This claim cannot be maintained. The real estate was the property of the Midland Club and not that of the members of the Club, although they may have equities in it as evidenced by the membership certificates. But the corporation acts through its board of directors and officers and its property is not subject to the control of its members or its stockholders. *National Bank Home Co. v. Equipment Co.*, 206 Ill. 58; *Hollins v. Greer*, 173 Ill. 549; *Bloom v. Vehon Co.*, 341 Ill. 200.

The decree held that Anderson & Lind Manufacturing Company had a mechanic's lien on the premises for $5998.90 on account of millwork delivered and used in the construction of the building. Complainant says that the evidence does not show a single continuous contract for all millwork but only separate orders and deliveries made at separate and different times, and that claimant is entitled to a lien for the last item only, which was the only delivery within four months before the claim was filed. Sec. 7

Mechanics' Lien Act. We hold that the master properly found a single, continuous contract. A witness testified on behalf of the Manufacturing Company that he was requested to figure on all of the material that might be needed on the building and that if the price was right the Manufacturing Company would receive orders from time to time. Figures were submitted and accepted, and the Company was told to enter the order and that written orders for material as needed would be sent. The purchase of the material was a single transaction, with a series of orders for successive deliveries. Under such circumstances the claim was filed within apt time from the last delivery. Love on Mechanic's Liens, p. 184, Illinois Malleable Iron Co. v. Brennan, 174 Ill. App. 38; Weil v. Bonash, 237 Ill. App. 544. We hold that the decree allowing this claim was proper.

The Dearborn Electrical Construction Company was allowed a mechanic's lien for electrical work to the amount of $7,000, and in the proportion that this amount bears to $4,717,000 it was decreed to be entitled to a first and prior lien on the proceeds of sale of the real estate. The master and the decree found that on September 9, 1927, this lien claimant entered into a written contract with 163 Adams Building Corporation to furnish and install complete electric light fixtures, and that subsequently an additional contract was made for additional work, the last work being completed May 15, 1928, and that on September 7, 1928, the lien claim was properly filed in the Circuit court of Cook county. The complainant argues that the evidence shows that the work was completed prior to May 7, 1928, and therefore the claim was not filed within four months thereafter. The lien claimant introduced evidence to the contrary. There was thus submitted a question of fact, and we cannot say that the master was not justified in finding with the claimant. It is unnecessary to detail the evidence, which would

Mechanics' Lien Act. We hold that the master properly found a single, continuous contract. A witness testified on behalf of the Manufacturing Company that he was requested to figure on all of the material that might be needed on the building and that if the price was right the Manufacturing Company would receive orders from time to time. Figures were submitted and accepted, and the Company was told to enter the order and that written orders for material as needed would be sent. The purchase of the material was a single transaction, with a series of orders for successive deliveries. Under such circumstances the claim was filed within due time from the last delivery. Love on Mechanic's Liens, p. 164. Illinois Hydraulic Iron Co. v. Bryant, 174 Ill. App. 56; Wolf v. Romech, 222 Ill. App. 266. We hold that the decree allowing this claim was proper.

The Bourbon Electrical Construction Company was allowed a mechanic's lien for electrical work to the amount of $7,000, and in the proportion that this amount bears to $6,717,000 it was decreed to be entitled to a first and prior lien on the proceeds of sale of the real estate. The master and the decree found that on September 2, 1927, the lien claimant entered into a written contract with 100 Adams Building Corporation to furnish and install complete electric light fixtures, and that subsequently an additional contract was made for additional work, the last work being completed May 15, 1928, and that on September 7, 1928, the lien claim was properly filed in the circuit court of Cook county. The complainant argues that the evidence shows that the work was completed prior to May 7, 1928, and therefore the claim was not filed within four months thereafter. The lien claimant introduced evidence to the contrary. There was thus presented a question of fact, and we cannot say that the master was not justified in finding with the claimant. It is unnecessary to detail the evidence, which would only unduly lengthen this opinion. The decree of the court in this respect will be affirmed.

We have not discussed all the points and arguments made upon this appeal but have stated the affirmative reasons for our conclusion.

We hold that the record fully justified the decree in all respects and it is affirmed.

AFFIRMED.

O'Connor, P. J., and Matchett, J., concur.

10

[redacted] this opinion. The decree of the court in this respect will be affirmed.

[redacted] We have not discussed all the points and arguments made [redacted] this appeal but have stated the affirmative reasons for our [redacted]

We hold that the record fully justified the decree in all respects and it is affirmed.

[redacted] AFFIRMED.

O'Connor, [illegible] and Kitchell, JJ., concur.

36166

KATHERINE M. RAUSCH,
Appellee,

vs.

WALTER C. CLEAVE and HAZEL M CLEAVE,
Appellants.

APPEAL FROM MUNICIPAL COURT OF CHICAGO.

47

280 I.A. 620[4]

MR. JUSTICE McSURELY DELIVERED THE OPINION OF THE COURT.

Plaintiff brought suit upon a promissory note for $1800, executed by the defendants, and upon trial the jury found for the defendants. The trial court granted the motion of plaintiff for a new trial and defendants moved this court for leave to appeal from that order. This was granted and briefs have been filed upon the appeal.

The issue presented by the pleadings was whether plaintiff was the legal owner of the note and whether the holder, for a consideration received, agreed to cancel the note. The trial court was of the opinion that the verdict for defendants was against the greater weight of the evidence, and allowed a new trial.

In December, 1928, defendants borrowed $1500 from Joseph J. Rausch, the husband of plaintiff, and executed the note in question together with a trust deed conveying real estate in Niles Center as security; the note was due December 5, 1930. In April, 1930, pursuant to a written contract, defendants conveyed the real estate to Edwin L. Stafford and his wife Ellen. The interest falling due June 5, 1930, was not paid, and the following April Joseph Rausch inquired of the defendant Walter C. Cleave over the telephone as to what might be done about paying the note; it was agreed that a conference should be held to discuss the matter; this conference was attended by Joseph J. Rausch, Walter C. Cleave, Edwin L. Stafford and a Mr. Norman, a real estate broker in whose office the conference was held; Rausch demanded payment of the note and Stafford and Cleave said they were without funds and were unable to pay.

There is some conflict in the testimony as to what was further said. Cleave and Norman testified that Rausch thereupon proposed that if Stafford would convey the property secured by the trust deed to him, Rausch would pay Stafford $100 and cancel and release the note and mortgage. Rausch denied that he made this offer and testified that he said that if Stafford would make a reasonable price he, Rausch, would get somebody to buy the title. Stafford testified that Rausch's offer was $75 and that Stafford wanted more. There is no denial of the fact that thereafter Stafford and his wife conveyed the property to Joseph J. Rausch and Alexander Baim, who were in business as partners, and $100 was paid to Stafford.

When the note was introduced in evidence on behalf of plaintiff it was prima facie evidence that she was the legal owner, but there was evidence which tended to overcome this presumption. Joseph Rausch testified that his wife owned the note; that it had been in her possession and that she took it out of her box where she kept it and handed it to him. This was contradicted by the testimony of plaintiff, herself, who said that she had never seen the note before it was shown to her upon the trial. Walter C. Cleave testified that Joseph Rausch told him in 1931 that he still owned this note. Norman, the real estate broker, testified that at the conference in his office in the spring of 1931 Joseph Rausch stated that he owned the note. There was other evidence tending to show that Joseph Rausch claimed to own the note. A party having the legal title to a promissory note must sue in his own name. Collins v. Ogden, 323 Ill. 594. We are of the opinion the greater weight of the evidence proved that Joseph J. Rausch, at the time of the suit, was the legal owner of the note and not the plaintiff.

But even if the plaintiff was the legal owner of the note, her husband was acting as her agent when he attended the conference in

Kerman's office and entered into the agreement there made.

The trial court expressed the opinion that the evidence was conflicting. Under such circumstances it is the peculiar province of the jury to weigh the variant stories and to judge the credibility of the witnesses and to render a verdict accordingly. In Wright v. Stinger, 269 Ill. App. 224, the court said, "Where the evidence is sharply conflicting, courts rarely feel warranted in holding a verdict manifestly wrong."

We hold that not only was the verdict of the jury in the instant case not against the manifest weight of the evidence, but on the contrary, the verdict was in accord with the weight of the testimony. The jury could properly conclude that Rausch, in consideration of receiving a conveyance of the mortgaged real estate, agreed not only to pay Stafford $100 but also to cancel the note and mortgage. The conveyance was made, Stafford received his $100, and Rausch was, in justice, bound to carry out his further agreement to cancel the note. It would be manifestly unjust to permit the holder of the note to receive title to the premises which was mortgaged to secure the note, and also at the same time to permit the holder to have judgment against defendants for the amount of the note.

The verdict of the jury did substantial justice between the parties and the trial court erred in setting it aside and granting a new trial. This order will therefore be reversed and the cause remanded with directions to the trial court to enter judgment on the verdict.

REVERSED AND REMANDED
WITH DIRECTIONS.

O'Connor, P. J., and Matchett, J., concur.

Herman's office and entered into the agreement there made.

The trial court expressed the opinion that the evidence was conflicting. [illegible] of the jury to [illegible] bility of the witnesses and to render a verdict accordingly. In [illegible]

[illegible]

[illegible]

[illegible]

[illegible]

[illegible]

testimony. The jury could properly conclude that [illegible] [illegible]

[illegible]

mortgage. The conveyance was made, Kinsler received his $100, and Hanneh was, in justice, bound to carry out his further agreement to cancel the note. It would be manifestly unjust to permit the holder of the note to recover title to the premises which was mortgaged to secure the note, and also at the same time to permit the holder to have judgment against defendants for the amount of the note.

The verdict of the jury did substantial justice between the parties and the trial court erred in setting it aside and granting a new trial. This order will therefore be reversed and the cause remanded with directions to the trial court to enter judgment on the verdict.

REVERSED AND REMANDED
WITH DIRECTIONS.

O'Connor, P. J., and Hatchett, J., concur.

46 A

37601

HERBERT PARSONS,
Appellee,

v.

PERCY W. STEPHENS, doing business as United States Utilities,
Appellant.

APPEAL FROM MUNICIPAL COURT OF CHICAGO.

280 I.A. 621

MR. PRESIDING JUSTICE FRIEND DELIVERED THE OPINION OF THE COURT.

Plaintiff brought a tort action in the municipal court to recover damages for certain alleged fraudulent acts by defendant arising out of a sales contract between the parties. The jury returned a verdict for $1,185.58, on which judgment was duly entered. This appeal followed. Plaintiff filed no brief to defend his record.

Plaintiff's statement of claim alleges in substance that September 29, 1933, he entered into a written agreement with defendant, wherein the latter undertook to furnish certain items of merchandise to plaintiff at listed prices, subject to certain discounts, and sold to plaintiff the exclusive right to sell said items of merchandise in the following described territories:

"That territory in the State of Illinois north of and including the counties named: Henderson, Warren, Knox, Peoria, Tazewell, McLean and Ford and Iroquois but not east of Western Avenue in Chicago, nor the Wieboldt Store in Evanston."

It is further alleged that in consideration of the sale of said merchandise in the territories designated, plaintiff paid to defendant the sum of $1,023.58, and expended the further sum of $385 in developing said territories, besides devoting his entire time to the enterprise; and defendant expressly warranted to plaintiff that there was no other contract in existence covering said territory or any part thereof, but notwithstanding said implied and express warranties,

37601

HERBERT PARSONS,
Appellee,

v.

PERCY W. STEPHENS, doing business as United States Utilities,
Appellant.

APPEAL FROM MUNICIPAL COURT OF CHICAGO.

280 I.A. 621

MR. PRESIDING JUSTICE FRIEND DELIVERED THE OPINION OF THE COURT.

Plaintiff brought a tort action in the municipal court to recover damages for certain alleged fraudulent acts by defendant arising out of a sales contract between the parties. The jury returned a verdict for $1,165.35, on which judgment was duly entered. This appeal followed. Plaintiff filed no brief to defend his record.

Plaintiff's statement of claim alleges in substance that September 20, 1935, he entered into a written agreement with defendant, wherein the latter undertook to furnish certain items of merchandise to plaintiff at listed prices, subject to certain discounts, and sold to plaintiff the exclusive right to sell said items of merchandise in the following described territories:

"That territory in the State of Illinois north of and including the counties named: Henderson, Warren, Knox, Peoria, Tazewell, McLean and Ford and Iroquois but not east of Western Avenue in Chicago, nor the Wieboldt Store in Evanston."

It is further alleged that in consideration of the sale of said merchandise in the territories designated, plaintiff paid to defendant the sum of $1,025.35, and expended the further sum of $388 in developing said territories, besides devoting his entire time to the enterprise; and defendant expressly warranted to plaintiff that there was no other contract in existence covering said territory or any part thereof, but notwithstanding said implied and express warranties, defendant had in existence, full operation and effect a contract for the territory described as:

"That section of Cook County, State of Illinois north of Madison Street, in the City of Chicago, running west from Lake Michigan to Austin Avenue, then north to North Avenue and continuing west on North Avenue to Western limits of Cook County, State of Illinois,"

dated April 19, 1933, by and between defendant and one Jerome S. Sherry, for the sale and distribution of identical articles as listed in the contract entered into with plaintiff; that when defendant sold plaintiff the exclusive territory designated, he impliedly warranted that there was not at the time of the signing of said contract, nor would there be at any time in the future during the continuation thereof, any merchandise enumerated in said contract within the territories specified, other than that furnished by plaintiff; that defendant, through his active, wilful, intentional and malicious fraud, obtained from plaintiff the said sum of $1,023.58, and in addition thereto plaintiff had incurred and paid expenses amounting to $385, and his time which is reasonably worth $200; that when plaintiff learned of the existence of the contract between defendant and Sherry he immediately notified defendant of the breach of warranties and fraud, demanded the return of all moneys paid by him together with his expenses and offered to return the merchandise. The last allegation was by agreement of the parties stricken from the statement of claim.

The affidavit of merits admitted the signing of the agreement, but denied the sale to plaintiff of the exclusive rights to sell said merchandise in the territory designated, and averred that defendant merely gave plaintiff the distributing rights thereto; denied that plaintiff paid defendant the sum of $1,023.58 in consideration of the sale of the items of merchandise and territories specified, but stated that said sum was paid to defendant in consideration of merchandise sold and delivered to plaintiff; denied that defendant had in existence, full operation and effect a contract for the territory described as:

"That section of Cook County, State of Illinois, north of Madison street, in the City of Chicago, running west from Lake Michigan to Austin Avenue, then north to North Avenue and continuing west on North Avenue to Western limits of Cook County, State of Illinois."

dated April 19, 1933, by and between defendant and one Jerome S. Sherry, for the sale and distribution of identical articles as listed in the contract entered into with plaintiff; that when defendant sold plaintiff the exclusive territory designated, he impliedly warranted that there was not at the time of the signing of said contract, nor would there be at any time in the future during the continuation thereof, any merchandise enumerated in said contract within the territories specified, other than that furnished by plaintiff; that defendant, through his active, wilful, intentional and malicious fraud, obtained from plaintiff the said sum of $1,083.58, and in addition thereto plaintiff had incurred and paid expenses amounting to $385, and his time which is reasonably worth [illegible]; that when plaintiff learned of the existence of the contract between defendant and Sherry he immediately notified defendant of his breach of warranties and fraud, demanded the return of his money paid by him together with his expenses and offered to return the merchandise. The last allegation was by agreement of the parties stricken from the statement of claim.

The affidavit of merits admitted the making of the agreement, but denied the sale to plaintiff of the exclusive rights to sell said merchandise in the territory indicated, and averred that defendant merely gave plaintiff the distributing rights thereto; denied that plaintiff paid defendant the sum of $1,083.58 in consideration of the sale of the items of merchandise and territories specified, but stated that said sum was paid to defendant in consideration of merchandise sold and delivered to plaintiff; denied that plaintiff had expended the sum of $385 in developing said territories and that there existed any implied or express warranty to plaintiff with reference to other contracts covering said territory. Defendant admitted that he entered into a contract with Sherry, but averred that the same was for the sale and distribution of only part of the articles of the kind listed in plaintiff's contract, and that Sherry's contract had been terminated prior to the entering into of said agreement with plaintiff, that Sherry had secured a position with the Metropolitan Life Insurance Company and had discontinued acting as distributor under such contract. Defendant denied any active, wilful, intentional or malicious fraud on his part, or that plaintiff was entitled to any sum whatsoever.

The contract entered into between the parties is as follows:

"Distributors' Agreement and Contract
U. S. UTILITIES
2750-2752 West Van Buren Street
Chicago
Distributor
Herbert Parsons
Chicago
Northern Illinois
Agreement and Distributors' Contract

This agreement and contract made in duplicate this 29th day of September, 1933, by and between U. S. Utilities (Percy W. Stephens) with general offices at 2750 West Van Buren Street in the City of Chicago, State of Illinois, hereinafter called First Party:

And Herbert Parsons of 1027 No. Lawndale Avenue, Chicago, Illinois, hereinafter called Second Party:

Witnesseth as Follows: In consideration of the mutual covenants herein contained and in further consideration of the purchase from First Party by Second Party of the initial shipment described below, at prices and discounts as herein stated, First Party does hereby give to Second Party the distributing rights on these utilities in the following territory and agrees to turn over to second party all orders it received from said territory for these utilities during the life of this agreement, and first party will not knowingly make any shipment into said territory other than by virtue of this agreement during the life of this agreement.

Territory: That territory in the State of Illinois north of and including the counties named: Henderson, Warren, Knox, Peoria, Tazewell, McLean, Ford and Iroquois, but not East of Western Avenue in Chicago, nor the Wiebeldt Store in Evanston, P. W. S. H. S. P.

plaintiff had expended the sum of $885 in developing said territories and that there existed any implied or express warranty to plaintiff with reference to other contracts covering said territory. Defendant admitted that he entered into a contract with Sherry, but averred that the same was for the sale and distribution of only part of the articles of the kind listed in plaintiff's contract, and that Sherry's contract had been terminated prior to the entering into of said agreement with plaintiff; that Sherry had secured a position with the Metropolitan Life Insurance Company and had discontinued acting as distributor under such contract. Defendant denied any active, wilful, intentional or malicious fraud on his part, or that plaintiff was entitled to any sum whatsoever.

The contract entered into between the parties is as follows:

"Distributors' Agreement and Contract
U. S. UTILITIES
2700-2702 West Van Buren Street
Chicago
Distributor
Herbert Parsons
Chicago
Northern Illinois
Agreement and Distributors' Contract

This agreement and contract made in duplicate this 20th day of September, 1933, by and between U. S. Utilities (Percy V. Stephens) with general offices at 2700 West Van Buren Street in the City of Chicago, State of Illinois, hereinafter called First Party;

And Herbert Parsons of 1027 No. Lawndale Avenue, Chicago, Illinois, hereinafter called Second Party;

Witnesseth as follows: In consideration of the mutual covenants herein contained and in further consideration of the purchase from First Party by Second Party of the initial shipment described below, at prices and discounts as herein stated, First Party does hereby give to Second Party the distributing rights on those utilities in the following territory and agrees to turn over to Second party all orders it received from said territory for these utilities during the life of this agreement, and first party will not knowingly make any shipment into said territory other than by virtue of this agreement during the life of this agreement.

Territory: That territory in the State of Illinois north of and including the counties named: Henderson, Warren, Knox, Peoria, Tazewell, McLean, Ford and Iroquois, but not east of Western Avenue in Chicago, nor the Wieboldt Store in Evanston, [illegible]

The utilities purchased from first party by second party under this agreement and the retail list prices at which they are to be sold are as follows:

Quantity	Utilities	Individual Retail Prices
4	Gross Rock Crystal Spotting Brush for 3 ounce bottle of fluid @	.30
4	Gross Rock Crystal Spotting Fluid in 3 ounce bottles @	.20
2	Gross Rock Crystal Spotting Fluid 1 ounce bottles @	.10
½	Gross Rock Crystal Spotting Fluid in 8 ounce bottles @	.45
½	Gross Rock Krystal Dry Cleaning Fluid Refill, 80 ounce size	1.95
1	Gross Rock Crystal Dry Cleaning Machine with one refill @	9.75
½	Gross Rock Crystal Purifying Powder in single cartons @	.20
2	Gross Rock Crystal Cleaning Crystals in cartons @	.15
2	Gross OPE-N-WAY Letter Scale and Desk Service @	.50
(2)	2 Gross Utilities Opening Tool @	.25
2	Gross Aluminum Rosette molds with handle and plate	.35
2	Gross Utilities Rubber Holder for steel wool @	.10
2	Gross Aluminum World's Fair 1933 molds with handle	.25

Total net price to Distributer $1,023.58. Amount paid with agreement $750.00. Ship soon as possible FOB Chicago. Balance due Cash 9/31/33 $273.58.

Discounts. The base discount to second party on above retail price is: 40% then 10% and 20%. In addition to these discounts first party agrees that whenever shipments to second party during any calendar month beginning with the date of this agreement shall exceed a total net cost to second party of not less than the amounts indicated below, then first party will give second party a further discount from said net prices, to be applied on all shipments made by first party to second party during the next calendar month immediately following that during which it was earned, this additional discount being 10% when the net price of shipments to second party is between $125.00 and $250.00, 20% when the net price of shipments to second party is between $250.00 and $375.00, 30% when the net price of shipments to second party is over $375.00. These additional discounts will be figured on all shipments to second party beginning with the date of this agreement and including the initial shipment ordered herein. J. W. S. H. S. P.

Advertising. First party will supply free of charge an amount of advertising material it considers reasonable and will supply at its cost whatever additional advertising materials second party needs. First party also agrees that with its approval second party may spend any month for general advertising an amount equal to 2-1/2% of the net cost of its purchases during the preceding month which percentage second party might deduct from its purchases during the next month immediately following until the full approved allowance has been thus credited, but each credit shall be for only 2-1/2% of the net invoice value of shipments as made.

New Products. It is understood and agreed that first

party may modify, change and/or improve its utilities and second party agrees to accept on future shipments whatever changes, etc., first party may make. First party further agrees that whatever new utilities it produces during the life of this agreement will be first presented to second party to handle in accordance with the policy adopted by first party and first party will not offer same for sale in the territory covered by this agreement until they have been thus offered to second party to handle.

Guarantee. First party guarantees its products as to materials and workmanship and accepts no other responsibility and second party has examined and tested these products and is entirely satisfied with them in every respect. It is further agreed that second party shall not and cannot make contracts nor incur any liability or obligation which will in any way involve first party without the written consent of first party, and first party has made and makes no representations or warranties, and assumes no responsibility other than as specifically set forth in this agreement.

Cancellation of this agreement. To all intents and purposes this agreement shall be a continuing one and it will be continued by first party so long as second party shall take from first party on its general terms and at the net cost to second party not less than $250.00 worth of its utilities during the first period of sixty days of the life of this agreement and not less than $500 worth during the next period of sixty days and not less than $750.0 during each sixty days period thereafter. However, second party might cancel the continuation of this agreement by giving written notice to first party in which event second party shall have the right at that time to sell its business and its utilities then on hand to a successor at any price second party might set, but this successor and new distributor is to be approved by first party before the distributing rights herein contained are transferred. In the event that second party does not itself appoint a successor, then second party hereby agrees to so notify first party in writing, at the same time giving first party full right, power and authority for a reasonable time to appoint another distributor or successor for second party to whom first party shall be fully authorized and empowered to sell and transfer for second party whatever utilities, display material, advertising materials, etc. that second party may have on hand and/or on display at that time, the sale and transfer to be at the same net price at which second party purchased said utilities and materials at from first party.

Price Maintenance. Second party agrees to maintain the list price set by first party for the sale of its utilities and first party agrees to supply second party with its utilities in accordance with the discounts hereinbefore stated and at the retail list prices hereinbefore set forth subject to changes in costs of materials, labor, transportation, etc., and other causes beyond the control of first party. This agreement is made in accordance with the laws of the State of Illinois and shall be so interpreted. Second party agrees to give first party the best distribution of which it is capable, and furthermore agrees to do everything in its power and to the best of its ability to promote the sale of these utilities in the territory hereinbefore set forth.

U. . UTILITIES
(Signed) Herbert Parsons
First Party.
H. S. Wankwell
(Signed) Percy W. Stephens,
Second Party."

party may modify, change and/or improve its utilities and second party agrees to accept on future shipments whatever changes, etc., first party may make. First party further agrees that whatever new utilities it produces during the life of this agreement will be first presented to second party to handle in accordance with the policy adopted by first party and first party will not same for sale in the territory covered by this agreement un- have been, thus offered to second party to handle.

Guarantee. First party guarantees its products as to materials and workmanship and accepts no other responsibility and second party has examined and tested these products and is entirely satisfied with them in every respect. It is further agreed that second party shall not and cannot make contracts nor incur any liability or obligation which will in any way involve first party without the written consent of first party, and first party has made and makes no representations or warranties, and assumes no responsibility other than as specifically set forth in this agreement.

Cancellation of this agreement. To all intents and purposes this agreement shall be a continuing one and it will be continued by first party so long as second party shall take from first party on its general terms and at the net cost to second party not less than $250.00 worth of its utilities during the first period of sixty days of the life of this agreement and not less than $50 in during the next period of sixty days and not less than $750.00 during each sixty days period thereafter. However, second party might cancel the continuation of this agreement by giving written notice to fi in which event second party shall have the right at this t its business and its utilities then on hand t at any price second party might set, but this successor and new distributor is to be approved by first party before the distributing rights herein contained are transferred. In the event that second party does not itself appoint a successor, then second party hereby agrees to so notify first party in writing, at the same time giving first party full right, power and authority for a reasonable time to appoint another distributor or successor for second party to whom first party shall be fully authorized and empow transfer for party whatever utilities, display material, advertising materials, etc. that second party may have on hand and/or on display at that time, the sale and transfer to be at the same net price at which second party purchased said utilities and materials at from first party.

Price Maintenance. Second party agrees to maintain the list price set by first party for the sale of its utilities and first party agrees to supply second party with its utilities in accordance with the discounts heretofore stated and at the retail list prices heretofore set forth subject to changes in costs of materials, labor, transportation, etc., and other causes beyond the control of first party. This agreement is made in accordance with the laws of the State of Illinois and shall be so interpreted. Second party agrees to give first party the best distribution of which it is capable, and furthermore agrees to do everything in its power and to the best of its ability to promote the sale of these utilities in the territory hereinbefore set forth.

U. S. UTILITIES
(Signed) Herbert Parsons
<u>First Party.</u>
H. S. Mansell
Signed) Percy V. Stephens.
<u>Second Party.</u>"

Defendant insists that the verdict of the jury and the judgment of the court are contrary to the law and evidence, and that a new trial should have been granted. As a basis for this contention it is first urged that plaintiff's contract was not an exclusive one. It appears to us, however, that the language of the third paragraph of the agreement indicates clearly that plaintiff was awarded certain exclusive rights within the designated territory; that the contract was not merely one for the sale of merchandise, but was also for the exclusive right to sell the merchandise within the designated territory. It appears from a careful examination of the record that the Sherry contract had been made prior to the time that plaintiff paid defendant the sum of $1,023.58 and entered into the contract with him, and that no mention thereof was made to plaintiff when defendant received this sum. It also appears reasonably clear from the testimony of plaintiff, Sherry and defendant himself, that Sherry's contract had never been terminated by defendant or Sherry, and that it was operative at the time plaintiff purchased the rights claimed under his contract. After plaintiff had perfected an organization for the distribution of merchandise purchased from defendant he found that identical items of merchandise had been placed for sale by Sherry's organization in various parts of the territory allotted to plaintiff, and it was then that he and Sherry together confronted defendant, who was unable to, and did not, deny that there were two distributors in the territory. Defendant takes the position that Sherry had accepted employment with the Metropolitan Life Insurance Company prior to September 29, 1933, and had abandoned the contract, but the evidence does not justify this conclusion. There is testimony tending to prove that Sherry's wife had, with defendant's consent, carried on Sherry's business during a portion of the time. Moreover, although defendant had the apparent right to cancel Sherry's contract, he took no steps to do so, and the same was in fact never formally cancelled.

Defendant insists that the verdict of the jury and the judgment of the court are contrary to the law and evidence, and that a new trial should have been granted. As a basis for this contention it is first urged that plaintiff's contract was not an exclusive one. It appears to us, however, that the language of the third paragraph of the agreement indicates clearly that plaintiff was awarded certain exclusive rights within the designated territory; that the contract was not merely one for the sale of merchandise, but was also for the exclusive right to sell the merchandise within the designated territory. It appears from a careful examination of the record that the Sherry contract had been made prior to the time that plaintiff paid defendant the sum of $1,222.28 and entered into the contract with him, and that no mention thereof was made to plaintiff when defendant received this sum. It also appears reasonably clear from the testimony of plaintiff, Sherry and defendant himself, that Sherry's contract had never been terminated by defendant or Sherry, and that it was operative at the time plaintiff purchased the rights claimed under his contract. After plaintiff had perfected an organization for the distribution of merchandise purchased from defendant he found that identical items of merchandise had been placed for sale by Sherry's organization in various parts of the territory allotted to plaintiff, and it was then that he and Sherry together confronted defendant, who was unable to, and did not, deny that there were two distributors in the territory. Defendant takes the position that Sherry had accepted employment with the Metropolitan Life Insurance Company prior to September 29, 1935, and had abandoned the contract, but the evidence does not justify this conclusion. There is testimony tending to prove that Sherry's wife had, with defendant's consent, carried on Sherry's business during a portion of the time. Moreover, although defendant had the apparent right to cancel Sherry's contract, he took no steps to do so, and the same was in fact never formally cancelled.

Defendant takes the further position that there were no express or implied warranties contained in plaintiff's contract. We believe that the language employed justifies the conclusion that under the terms of the contract plaintiff was given certain rights for the distribution of defendant's product, which by implication excluded the giving of those same rights to any other. Good faith between the parties required that defendant apprise plaintiff of Sherry's contract, and his failure so to do justified the court and jury in finding that there was an element of fraud perpetrated by defendant on plaintiff. Plaintiff acted promptly when he learned of Sherry's contract and that some of the identical goods were being distributed by Sherry in his territory, and immediately offered to rescind. We do not understand why the parties struck out the last paragraph of plaintiff's statement of claim, under which he alleges that when he learned of the existence of Sherry's contract he immediately notified defendant of his breach of warranties and fraud, demanded the return of his money, and offered to return the merchandise then in plaintiff's possession. That, it seems to us, was the salient part of plaintiff's statement of claim.

However, having stricken that portion of his pleading, plaintiff proceeded to prove damages sustained by him, but evidently proceeded upon the wrong theory. He was at the time of the trial in possession of the goods, and the court gave him a judgment for the full amount paid by him plus expenses claimed to have been incurred by him in developing the territory. There is no order requiring him to return the goods, and we assume that in addition to his judgment he still possesses the merchandise, and obviously he cannot have both. Under the present state of the pleadings, as we understand the rule plaintiff would be entitled to recover as damages only the difference between the value of the property as it was and what it would have been worth if the representations made by defendant had been true.

[illegible]

Sherry's contract, [illegible]

jury in finding [illegible] by

defendant on plaintiff [illegible]

Sherry's contract [illegible]

distributed by Sherry in [illegible] to

resale. [illegible] do not understand [illegible]

paragraph of plaintiff's statement of claim [illegible]

that [illegible] Sherry's contract [illegible]

immediately notified [illegible]

[illegible]

than in plaintiff's possession. [illegible]

part of plaintiff's statement of claim.

However, having stricken [illegible]

plaintiff [illegible]

proceeded upon the wrong theory. [illegible]

possession of the goods, and [illegible]

[illegible]

in developing the territory [illegible]

return the goods, and we assume [illegible] he

still possesses the merchandise, and [illegible] both.

Under the present state of the pleadings, [illegible] the rule

plaintiff would be entitled to recover as damages only the difference

between the value of the property as it was and what it would have

been worth if the representations made by defendant had been true.

(McDowell v. Hield, Appellate Court, First District, General No. 36474, opinion filed October 10, 1933, unpublished.) No such proof was made, however, and no competent evidence of damages was adduced to sustain the verdict and judgment.

We are reluctant to reverse the judgment, as we are of the opinion that upon the merits of the case plaintiff was entitled to a verdict, but having failed to make proper proof of damages, the judgment will have to be reversed and the cause remanded, and it is so ordered.

REVERSED AND REMANDED.

Scanlan and Sullivan, JJ., concur.

47

37668

PETER C. McARDLE, Appellant,	)	APPEAL FROM CIRCUIT COURT,
v.	)	COOK COUNTY.
CITY OF CHICAGO et al., Appellees.	)	280 I.A. 621[2]

MR. PRESIDING JUSTICE FRIEND DELIVERED THE OPINION OF THE COURT.

This appeal presents the sequel to a long, protracted controversy between the parties, dating back more than thirty years. After the adoption of the civil service law by the city, and the creation of a civil service commission, the city of Chicago maintained in its public works department a branch or bureau termed "Testing Laboratory," in charge of one Charles J. Kelly, as a temporary employee. He had sole charge of the laboratory, and his official designation was "cement tester," although he was called "chief cement tester."

In April, 1898, the civil service commission called an examination of applicants for appointment to fill in the classified service of the city for cement tester, and McArdle, petitioner herein, offered himself as a candidate, successfully passed the examination, and was duly notified that he had qualified for appointment in the official service as "cement tester." January 1, 1898, the commissioner of public works made requisition on the commission for a person eligible for appointment and McArdle was certified and assigned to the position of cement tester to take Kelly's place, and the latter was directed to turn over to him all records and paraphernalia pertaining to his duties.

37568

PETER C. McARDLE,
Appellant,

v.

CITY OF CHICAGO et al.,
Appellees.

APPEAL FROM CIRCUIT COURT,

COOK COUNTY.

280 I.A. 621

MR. PRESIDING JUSTICE McSURELY DELIVERED THE OPINION OF THE COURT.

This appeal presents the sequel to a long, protracted controversy between the parties, dating back more than thirty years. After the adoption of the civil service law by the city, and the creation of a civil service commission, the city of Chicago maintained in its public works department a branch or bureau termed "Testing Laboratory," in charge of one Charles J. Kelly, as a temporary employee. He had sole charge of the laboratory, and his official designation was "cement tester," although he was called "chief cement tester."

In April, 1898, the civil service commission called an examination of applicants for appointment to fill in the classified service of the city for cement tester, and McArdle, petitioner herein, offered himself as a candidate, successfully passed the examination, and was duly notified that he had qualified for appointment in the official service as "cement tester." January 1, 1899, the commissioner of public works made requisition on the commission for a person eligible for appointment and McArdle was certified and assigned to the position of cement tester to take Kelly's place, and the latter was directed to turn over to him all records and paraphernalia pertaining to his duties.

McArdle took charge of the laboratory, and the one assistant then assigned to the office, and continued in charge until March 12, 1908. With the city's growth, the work of the laboratory was enlarged and the testing of materials gradually increased, so that in 1908 it embraced the testing of oils, metals and other materials, and its work was conducted by a staff of seven assistants under the superintendence of McArdle.

In December, 1905, when further additions to the work of the laboratory were first contemplated, petitioner applied for an increase in salary because of the increased work and responsibility, and it was decided by his superiors to increase his salary from $125 to $250 a month. This decision was reduced to writing by the then acting city engineer. The report effecting the change gave the petitioner the title of "Cement Tester, Bureau of Engineering." In pursuance of this decision, and conforming to the acts and rules of the commission, the appointing officer of the department reported the change in title to the civil service commission, which spread the report on the minutes of its records as of December 18, 1905. From that date to February, 1908, appellant was paid his salary on the payrolls made and certified by the department and the civil service commission.

In February, 1908, the city engineer notified petitioner that in the name of the deputy commissioner of public works his resignation was demanded, or that in the alternative charges would be preferred against him. No charges were filed, however, and the following month the city engineer notified petitioner that the commissioner of public works had instructed him to select an engineer to take his place, and gave him a letter dated March 12, 1908, stating that one Parkes had been appointed to the position of chief tester in charge of the testing division, and requesting petitioner to turn over all paraphernalia and records to the new incumbent. The

Mcardle took charge of the laboratory, and the one assistant then assigned to the office, and continued in charge until March 12, 1908. With the city's growth, the work of the laboratory was enlarged and the testing of materials gradually increased, so that in 1908 it embraced the testing of oils, metals and other materials, and its work was conducted by a staff of seven assistants under the superintendence of McArdle.

In December, 1905, when further additions to the work of the laboratory were first contemplated, petitioner applied for an increase in salary because of the increased work and responsibility, and it was decided by his superiors to increase his salary from $125 to $150 a month. This decision was reduced to writing by the then acting city engineer. The report effecting the change gave the petitioner the title of "Cement Tester, Bureau of Engineering." In pursuance of this decision, and conforming to the acts and rules of the commission, the appointing officer of the department reported the change in title to the civil service commission, which spread the report on the minutes of its records as of December 12, 1905. From that date to February, 1908, appellant was paid his salary on the payrolls made and certified by the department and the civil service commission.

In February, 1908, the city engineer notified petitioner that in the name of the deputy commissioner of public works his resignation was demanded, or that in the alternative charges would be preferred against him. No charges were filed, however, and the following month the city engineer notified petitioner that the commissioner of public works had instructed him to select an engineer to take his place, and gave him a letter dated March 12, 1908, stating that one Parkes had been appointed to the position of chief tester in charge of the testing division, and requesting petitioner to turn over all paraphernalia and records to the new incumbent. The notification directed petitioner to assume his former duties as cement tester and to report to Parkes. The next day, when the commissioner of public works reported to the civil service commission that McArdle's salary had been reduced from $3,000 per annum to $1,500, in accordance with the annual appropriation bill, petitioner protested to the various officials, but without avail, and shortly thereafter filed his first petition for mandamus.

The review of the order of the circuit court dismissing the petition on demurrer is reported in McArdle v. City of Chicago, 172 Ill. App. 142, filed August, 1912. We then held in effect that when McArdle's duties as cement tester were increased in volume by placing him in charge of testing oils, brass and iron castings, brick, sand, paints, varnishes and other materials used in the construction of buildings, etc., and his salary increased, that this did not constitute the creation of a new office, and when the civil service commission approved and certified the increased payroll attached to his office without requiring any additional examination it amounted to a finding that the change in salary did not involve such a change in his duties as to require an examination, and that under the circumstances he had been improperly discharged, and was entitled to the position under a different name. Certiorari was denied by the Supreme Court.

During the pendency of that suit in this court changes were taking place in relation to petitioner's rights to his office and salary, and when the case was redocketed in the trial court new questions were presented which led the court below of its own motion to order petitioner to file a new petition, bringing the facts down to date. This was done, and the cause xxx finally came on for hearing beforethe court without a jury on issues of fact and a series of requests by petitioner to hold various propositions of law. The court denied most of these requests and found the certification directed petitioner to assume his former duties as [illegible] foreman and to report to Parker. The next day, when the commissioner of public works reported to the civil service commission that Panella's salary had been reduced from $3,[illegible] per annum to $2,900, in accordance with the annual appropriation bill, petitioner protested to the various officials, but without avail, and shortly thereafter filed his first petition for mandamus.

The review of the order of the circuit court dismissing the petition on demurrer is reported in Panella v. City of Chicago, 309 Ill. App. [illegible], filed August 1942. We there held in effect that while Panella's duties as [illegible] foreman were increased in volume by placing him in charge of testing oils, [illegible] and iron castings, [illegible], paint, [illegible] and other materials used in the construction of buildings, etc., and his salary increased, that this did not constitute the creation of a new office, and when the civil service commission approved and certified the increased payroll allotted to his office without requiring any additional examination it amounted to a finding that the change in salary did not involve such a change in his duties as to require an examination, and that under the circumstances he had been improperly discharged, and was entitled to the position under a different name. Certiorari was denied by the Supreme Court.

[illegible] that in during the pendency of that suit in this court changes were taking place in relation to petitioner's rights to his office and salary, and when the case was redocketed in the trial court new circumstances were presented which led the court below of its own motion to order petitioner to file a new petition, bringing the facts down to date. This was done, and the cause [illegible] finally came on for hearing before the [illegible] a jury [illegible] a series of requests by [illegible] propositions of law. The court denied most of [illegible] issues for the city, holding that petitioner's duties were confined exclusively to the testing of cement. Another appeal was prosecuted to this court and the judgment of the lower court was again reversed and the cause remanded in McArdle v. City of Chicago, 216 Ill. App. 343. In an opinion filed January, 1920, we held (1) as to petitioner's title that he became an officer of the City of Chicago and his office was properly designated as "cement tester;" (2) that in March, 1908, he still held the office of cement tester, and was entitled to the salary of $250 a month; (3) that when Parkes was put in his place and petitioner sent to the Chicago pumping station at a reduced salary the attempted demotion failed and in law he still retained the only office he had ever had; (4) that he was neither legally demoted nor laid off; and (5) that since under the law civil service reinstatement and recovery of salary may be accomplished in one proceeding, the right of petitioner both as to his salary and office was clear. The remanding order directed the issuance of a peremptory writ to restore petitioner "to the office or position" from which he had been illegally removed at $250 a month and back salary.

Certiorari was again denied by the Supreme Court, and upon the filing of the mandate of this court the cause was redocketed and assigned to another judge, who entered judgment in accordance with the mandate, restoring petitioner to his office at the salary provided and for back salary, commanding city officials to make necessary appropriations therefor, and commanding and enjoining defendants "that they pay his salary according to the rules in force in relation to the payment of officers' salaries, so long as he shall remain the incumbent of said office of cement tester, by whatever name, style or title the City of Chicago or its officials may hereafter choose to establish or designate for the office, doing in the future such work as petitioner had prior to issues for the city, holding that petitioner's duties were confined exclusively to the testing of cement. Another appeal was prosecuted to this court and the judgment of the lower court was again reversed and the cause remanded in Malkin v. City of Chicago, 218 Ill. App. 545. In an opinion filed January, 1920, we held (1) as to petitioner's title that he became an officer of the City of Chicago and his office was properly designated as "cement tester"; (2) that in March, 1909, he still held the office of cement tester, and was entitled to the salary of $250 a month; (3) that when Durkee was put in his place and petitioner sent to the Chicago pumping station at a reduced salary the attempted demotion failed and in law he still retained the only office he had ever had; (4) that he was neither legally demoted nor laid off; and (5) that since under the law civil service reinstatement and recovery of salary may be accomplished in one proceeding, the right of petitioner both as to his salary and office was clear. The remanding order directed the issuance of a peremptory writ to restore petitioner "to the office or position" from which he had been illegally removed at $250 a month and back salary.

Certiorari was again denied by the Supreme Court, and upon the filing of the mandate of this court the cause was redocketed and assigned to another judge, who entered judgment in accordance with the mandate, restoring petitioner to his office at the salary provided and for back salary, commanding city officials to make necessary appropriations therefor, and commanding and enjoining defendants "that they pay his salary according to the rules in force in relation to the payment of officers' salaries, so long as he shall remain the incumbent of said office of cement tester, by whatever name, style or title the City of Chicago or its officials may hereafter choose to establish or designate for the office, doing in the future such work as petitioner had prior to

March 12, 1908." The order also granted petitioner leave to apply to the court, as future occasions might require, for the issuance of peremptory writs of mandamus "to any and all future officials of the City of Chicago."

Again the city appealed, and on review the judgment of the court was affirmed and later certiorari was denied in the Supreme Court. Upon filing of the mandate in the circuit court the writ issued, following the language of the judgment, and its commands were obeyed up to the appropriation period of 1932. When the annual appropriations for that year were before the city authorities, upon recommendation of the finance committee, an appropriation was made for only six months of petitioner's salary, ending June 30, 1933. The mayor vetoed this item and recommended $420 a month to July 1 and $210 a month thereafter, which was less than the salary applying to the office or position. Many changes had occurred in the offices of mayor and aldermen between 1920 and 1932, so petitioner availed himself of the leave reserved to him in the last judgment order and applied for the issuance of a writ "to any and all future officials of the city." Judgment was again entered in his favor, and a fourth appeal taken to this court, which was likewise affirmed in McArdle v. City of Chicago, (unreported opinion No. 36903, filed December 11, 1933.) The writ issued commanded respondents to implicitly obey the commands of the writ issued July, 1920.

All of the foregoing proceedings are set forth in the petition now before us, and it is averred that March 9, 1934, the peremptory writ on the judgment of December, 1933, was issued and served on all the then present respondents. Preparatory to the consideration of the 1934 appropriation ordinance, the commissioner of public works and city engineer reported to the council petitioner's salary as $5,040, and this was the amount fixed by council

March 13, 1926." The order also granted petitioner leave to apply to the court, as future occasions might require, for the issuance of peremptory writs of mandamus "to any and all future officials of the City of Chicago."

Again the city appealed, and on review the judgment of the court was affirmed and later certiorari was denied in the Supreme Court. Upon filing of the mandate in the circuit court the writ issued, following the language of the judgment, and its commands were obeyed up to the appropriation period of 1933. When the annual appropriations for that year were before the city authorities, upon recommendation of the finance committee, an appropriation was made for only six months of petitioner's salary, ending June 30, 1933. The mayor vetoed this item and recommended [illegible] a month to July 1 and $220 a month thereafter, which was less than the salary applying to the office or position. Many changes had occurred in the offices of mayor and aldermen between 1930 and 1933, so petitioner availed himself of the leave reserved to him in the last judgment order and applied for the issuance of a writ "to any and all future officials of the city." Judgment was again entered in his favor, and a fourth appeal taken to this court, which was likewise affirmed in [illegible] v. City of Chicago, (unreported opinion No. [illegible], filed December 11, 1933.) The writ issued commanded respondents to implicitly obey the commands of the writ issued July, 1926.

All of the foregoing proceedings are set forth in the petition now before us, and it is averred that March 9, 1934, the peremptory writ on the judgment of December, 1933, was issued and served on all the then present respondents; preparatory to the consideration of the 1934 appropriation ordinance, the commissioner of public works and city engineer [illegible] to the council petitioner's [illegible] the amount fixed by council proceedings. The committee made up a tentative ordinance reporting for cement tester, three months, ending March 31, 1934, at the rate of $420 a month, thus failing to report for the remainder of the year. The finance committee met on March 12, 1934. Its chairman stated that the committee had been advised by the assistant corporation counsel that the appropriation for 1934 for petitioner's salary at $5,040 per annum should be made. The committee acted on the advice, included the salary at $5,040 for the year 1934, and reported the bill. March 14, 1934, the city council met in regular session and resolved itself into a committee of the whole to consider the report. The mayor relinquished the gavel to the chairman of the finance committee, who presided. When the item of petitioner's salary was reached, the mayor suggested that the office of petitioner be abolished. Thereupon the assistant corporation counsel and the chairman of the finance committee advised that if the purpose of abolishing the office was to get rid of petitioner it would be necessary also to get rid of all the employees under the petitioner, because of the court orders theretofore entered and the writs placing petitioner in charge of the testing department. The mayor thereupon advised the transfer of these employees to another division. The committee took the mayor's advice and amended the ordinance by striking therefrom the words, "Inspecting and Testing Division, Administrative Unit," and provided for these employees, to the exclusion of petitioner, under "Department of Public Works, City Engineer's Office." The ordinance was passed by the council in that form and signed by the mayor. Petitioner charges that this action of the mayor and council constituted a flagrant and direct violation and disobedience of the commands in said orders and writs and was a direct contempt of the orders of the circuit court.

Respondents filed an answer setting out the material portions of the writs of mandamus which petitioner claims they refused proceedings. The committee [illegible] evidence [illegible] for cement tester, three months, ending [illegible] of $[illegible] a month, thus failing to report for the [illegible] year. The finance committee met on [illegible] its chairman stated that the committee had been advised by the assistant corporation counsel that the appropriation for 1934 for [illegible]'s salary at $3,040 per annum should be made. The committee voted on the advice, included the salary at $3,040 for the year 1934, and reported the bill. March 14, 1934, the city council met in regular session and resolved itself into a committee of the whole to consider the report. The mayor [illegible] the maximum of the finance committee, who [illegible]. [illegible] the item of petitioner's salary was reached, the mayor [illegible] that the office of petitioner be abolished. Throughout the [illegible] counsel and the chairman of the finance committee [illegible] the purpose of abolishing the office was to get rid of petitioner [illegible] it would be necessary also to get rid of all the employees under the petitioner, because of the court order then in force entered and the writs placing petitioner in charge of the [illegible]. The mayor thereupon advised the transfer of these employees to another division. The committee took the mayor's advice and amended the ordinance by striking therefrom the words, "[illegible] Testing Division, Administrative Unit," and providing for the employees, to the exclusion of petitioner, as part of the [illegible] Engineer's Office." The ordinance was [illegible] in that form and signed by the mayor. Petitioner charges that this action of the mayor and council constitutes a flagrant violation and disobedience of the commands in said writs [illegible] direct contempt of the orders of the circuit court.

Respondents filed an answer setting out the facts [illegible] portions of the writs of mandamus which petitioner claims they refused to obey, as well as the provisions of the Revised Chicago Code of 1931, affecting the Department of Public Works. It is averred in the answer and claimed by respondents that they were required to appropriate for petitioner's salary only so long as petitioner remains an incumbent of or entitled to hold the office of cement tester; that at no time in the history of the city was there any ordinance providing for an "office" known as cement tester, or head of the testing division of the City of Chicago, or providing for such an office by any other name; that the place of employment or office of cement tester was abolished in good faith for the purpose of reducing the cost of government and because said position, place of employment or office was no longer essential to the proper operation and management of the department of public works, and that these averments cannot be overcome by allegations in the petition as to what transpired before the finance committee of the city council on the question of appropriating for the position of cement tester in the annual appropriation bill for the year 1934.

Numerous questions are raised by the briefs filed but the controversy, as respondents contend, resolves itself mainly to the following propositions:

(1) If the position of cement tester were an office which had been established by an ordinance providing that it should be filled by an appointment by the mayor, with the approval of the council, as required by Section 2, Article 6, of the Cities & Villages Act, (1933 Cahill's Rev. Stats.) then under the further provision in section 2 that office could be abolished only by an ordinance or resolution to take effect at the end of the fiscal year.

(2) If the position of cement tester were a place of employment under the Civil Service law, then by virtue of the decisions of our Supreme Court the position could be dropped at any time without the formality of an ordinance or resolution.

Petitioner takes the position that the respondents are forever foreclosed from questioning the existence of the office of cement tester because of the original judgment entered in the McArdle case. In that case there was no issue of fact as to the to obey, as well as the provisions of the Revised Chicago Code of 1931, affecting the Department of Public Works. It is averred in the answer and claimed by respondents that they were required to appropriate for petitioner's salary only so long as petitioner remains an incumbent of or entitled to hold the office of cement tester; that at no time in the history of the city was there any ordinance providing for an "office" known as cement tester, as head of the testing division of the city of Chicago, or providing for such an office by any other name; that the place of employment or office of cement tester was abolished in good faith for the purpose of reducing the cost of government and because said position, place of employment or office was no longer essential to the proper operation and management of the department of public works; and that these averments cannot be overcome by allegations in the petition as to what transpired before the finance committee of the city council on the question of appropriating for the position of cement tester in the annual appropriation bill for the year 1934.

Numerous questions are raised by the briefs filed but the controversy, as respondents contend, resolves itself mainly to the following propositions:

(1) If the position of cement tester were an office which had been established by an ordinance providing that it should be filled by an appointment by the mayor, with the approval of the council, as required by section 9, article 6, of the Cities & Villages act, (1933 Cahill's Rev. Stats.) then under the further provision in section 2 that office could be abolished only by an ordinance or resolution to take effect at the end of the fiscal year.

(2) If the position of cement tester were a place of employment under the Civil Service law, then by virtue of the decisions of our Supreme Court the position could be dropped at any time without the formality of an ordinance or resolution.

Petitioner takes the position that the respondents are forever foreclosed from questioning the existence of the office of cement tester because of the original judgment entered in the Kenrick case. In that case there was no issue of fact as to the existence of the office of cement tester. It was decided upon a petition for a writ of mandamus and a demurrer to the petition, and the controversy arose by reason of the reduction in the salary of petitioner from $250 a month to $125 a month and substituting another person in his place as chief tester in charge of the testing division, in violation of the civil service law. It is apparent from the decision that petitioner in his original suit did not claim an office which was created by statute or ordinance, but he claimed only a position to which he was appointed pursuant to the civil service law. The court in its opinion used the term "office" as synonymous with the "position" classified pursuant to the civil service law and the rules of the commission. It is obvious that the court did not base its opinion that petitioner became an officer of the City of Chicago upon the fact that the office of cement tester was created by any statute or ordinance, for there is no such statute and there never has been.

When the first McArdle case was decided the distinction between an "office" and a "place of employment" had not yet been made in the leading civil service cases before the courts. In People v. Loeffler, 175 Ill. 585, the court in discussing the civil service act, said (at p. 601):

"In a certain sense, therefore, the positions, to which the Civil Service act has reference in the city government, are places of employment rather than offices in the strict meaning of the latter term."

Following this decision the Supreme Court in City of Chicago v. Luthardt, 191 Ill. 516, in discussing the question under consideration by the court in the case of People v. Loeffler, supra, held that the offices or positions provided for under the civil service act, "while not strictly offices within the meaning of the constitutional provision, were in a sense municipal offices." In that case no ordinance was pleaded, and plaintiff relied for the creation of his office entirely upon the civil service act, the rules of the existence of the office of cement tester. It was decided upon a petition for a writ of mandamus and a demurrer to the petition, and the controversy arose by reason of the reduction in the salary of petitioner from $200 a month to $125 a month and substituting another person in his place as chief tester in charge of the testing division, in violation of the civil service law. It is apparent from the decision that petitioner in his original suit did not claim an office which was created by statute or ordinance, but he claimed only a position to which he was appointed pursuant to the civil service law. The court in its opinion used the term "office" as synonymous with the "position" classified pursuant to the civil service law and the rules of the commission. It is obvious that the court did not base its opinion that petitioner became an officer of the City of Chicago upon the fact that the office of cement tester was created by any statute or ordinance, for there is no such statute and there never has been.

When the first Kenneally case was decided the distinction between an "office" and a "place of employment" had not yet been made in the leading civil service cases before the courts. In People v. Loeffler, 175 Ill. 585, the court in discussing the civil service act, said (at p. 601):

> "In a certain sense, therefore, the positions, to which the Civil Service act has reference in the city government, are places of employment rather than offices in the strict meaning of the latter term."

Following this decision the Supreme Court in City of Chicago v. Luthardt, 191 Ill. 516, in discussing the question under consideration by the court in the case of People v. Loeffler, supra, held that the offices or positions provided for under the civil service act, "while not strictly offices within the meaning of the constitutional provision, were in a sense municipal offices." In that case no ordinance was pleaded, and plaintiff relied for the creation of his office entirely upon the civil service act, the rules of the commission thereunder, the civil service classification, the officer's examination, the department's requisition and his certification and appointment to the office. The court held that this was sufficient evidence of the existence of, and his appointment to, the office, and did so on the authority of People v. Loeffler, supra.

In Ptacek v. People, 194 Ill. 125, quo warranto proceedings were instituted and the plea set forth the rules of the commission, the calling of an examination, the successful passing by the applicant, the placing of Ptacek's name on the eligible list and his subsequent appointment to and taking of the office of assistant superintendent of police, and demurrer was filed to the plea. The incumbent contended that his position was not an office. The court, although holding that the question was not before it, said (p. 129): "We are, however, clearly of the opinion that the position falls within the definition of an office."

In Hughes v. Traeger, 264 Ill. 612, which was decided in 1914, the validity of the municipal employees' pension act was involved, whereby a portion of all civil service employees' salaries was required to be withheld for the pension fund and its validity depended upon the question whether employees were officers or merely holding contracts with the city for a year, protected against legislative interference or change by the constitutions of the state and of the United States. The court said (p. 615) that by section 1 of the Pension Fund Act its provisions did not apply to temporary or probationary employees, but "it applies, therefore, only to those holding permanent positions, and these positions, whether called offices or places of employment, have substantially the same characteristics, without regard to the character of the services rendered."

It was not until 1918, when the case of People ex rel.

examination thereunder, the civil service classification, the officer's examination, the department's requisition and his certification and appointment to the office. The court held that this was sufficient evidence of the existence of, and his appointment to, the office, and did so on the authority of People v. [illegible], supra.

In [illegible] v. People, 164 Ill. 125, quo warranto proceedings were instituted and the plea set forth the rules of the commission, the holding of an examination, the successful passing by the applicants, the placing of [illegible]'s name on the eligible list, and his subsequent appointment to and taking of the office of assistant superintendent of police; and demurrer was filed to the plea. The respondent contended that his position was not an office. The court, although holding that the question was not before it, said (p. [illegible]): "We are, however, clearly of the opinion that the position falls within the definition of an office."

In Hughes v. Traeger, 264 Ill. 612, which was decided in 1914, the validity of the municipal employees' pension act was involved, whereby a portion of all civil service employees' salaries was required to be withheld for the pension fund and its validity depended upon the question whether employees were officers or merely holding contracts with the city for a year, protected against legislative interference or change by the constitutions of the state and of the United States. The court said (p. [illegible]) that by section 1 of the Pension Fund Act its provisions did not apply to temporary or probationary employees, but "it applies, therefore, only to those holding permanent positions, and these positions, whether called offices or places of employment, have substantially the same characteristics, without regard to the character of the services rendered."

[illegible] the case of People ex rel.

Jacobs v. Coffin, 282 Ill. 599, was decided that our Supreme Court recognized the distinction between an "office," and a "position" or "place of employment" under the civil service law. In that case Jacobs had filed a petition for mandamus to restore him to his position as an expert on system and organization. The respondents demurred to the petition upon the ground that Jacobs was seeking to be reinstated to an office and that there was no general law or statute providing for an expert on system and organization. The court held that petitioner was not claiming an office, but a position or place of employment in the classified civil service of the city to which he had been regularly appointed pursuant to the civil service law, and that one claiming such a position was not required to show that it was created by statute or ordinance, as in the case of one claiming an office. In a long line of cases previous to the Jacobs case, the Supreme Court had held that one seeking by mandamus to compel a restoration to an office must show that the office legally exists, and where the office claimed was unknown to the common law it could exist only when created by statute or by municipal ordinance adopted by authority of the statute. (Stott v. City of Chicago, 205 Ill. 281; People ex rel. v. City of Chicago, 210 Ill. 479; Moon v. The Mayor, 214 Ill. 40; Gersch v. City of Chicago, 250 Ill. 551.) In all of these cases the allegations of the petitioner were that plaintiff had been an officer of the city and was wrongfully removed, and not, as in the original petition in the McArdle case, that he had held a position in the classified civil service of the city. In the Jacobs case the Supreme Court expressly recognized for the first time that a position which is in the nature of a permanent employment may, in the absence of statutory or charter provisions, be created without the requirement of a formal ordinance, by-law or resolution, and said (p. 607): "There is no statute in this State that prescribes the manner or method of creating a position or an employment by a city."

Jacobs v. Coffin, 282 Ill. 609, it was decided that our Supreme Court recognized the distinction between an "office," and a "position" or "place of employment" under the civil service law. In that case Jacobs had filed a petition for mandamus to restore him to his position as an expert on system and organization. The respondents demurred to the petition upon the ground that Jacobs was seeking to be reinstated to an office and that there was no general law or statute providing for an expert on system and organization. The court held that petitioner was not claiming an office, but a position or place of employment in the classified civil service of the city to which he had been regularly appointed pursuant to the civil service law, and that one claiming such a position was not required to show that it was created by statute or ordinance, as in the case of one claiming an office. In a long line of cases previous to the Jacobs case, the Supreme Court had held that one seeking by mandamus to compel a restoration to an office must show that the office legally exists, and where the office claimed was unknown to the common law it could exist only when created by statute or by municipal ordinance adopted by authority of the statute. (Stott v. City of Chicago, 205 Ill. 281; People ex rel. v. City of Chicago, 210 Ill. 479; Moon v. The Mayor, 214 Ill. 40; Gunnell v. City of Chicago, 280 Ill. 583.) In all of those cases the allegations of the petitioner were that plaintiff had been an officer of the city and was wrongfully removed, and not, as in the original petition in the [illegible] case, that he had held a position in the classified civil service of the city. In the Jacobs case the Supreme Court expressly recognized for the first time that a position which is in the nature of a permanent employment may, in the absence of statutory or charter provisions, be created without the requirement of a formal ordinance, by-law or resolution, and said (p. 607): "There is no statute in this State that prescribes the manner or method of creating a position or an employment by a city."

The Jacobs case was followed by People ex rel. Lunderdale v. City of Chicago, 327 Ill. 62, in which it was averred that petitioner took the civil service examination for the "office or position of paving inspector," and throughout the petition the place to which petitioner sought to be restored was characterized as an "office," and "office or position," and a "position or office." Upon this branch of the case the court said: (p. 67)

"This is not an allegation that the employment is either an office or a position, and there is nothing in the petition which would distinguish it as either. While there is no statutory requirement prescribing the manner or method of creating a position or an employment by a city, offices other than those named in the statute must be created by an ordinance of the city, passed by a two-thirds vote of all the aldermen elected, as provided by section 2 of article 6 of the Cities and Villages Act."

The court then proceeds to state, "As there is a well defined distinction between an office and a position as they are considered in law, the petitioner will not be allowed to say that he has been filling one or the other. His employment has been in one or the other. His petition should state which, and if the former, should show the legal existence thereof by pleading the ordinance creating the same."

The respondents herein do not attack the validity of the original judgment in the McArdle case, nor the subsequent decisions, but argue that the use of the term "office" in the first opinion, when, under all the circumstances in that case, the court might more accurately have spoken of the position as a "place of employment" which petitioner claimed and to which he was at the time undoubtedly entitled under the law, underlies the difficulties since encountered. Prior to the Jacobs case courts used the terms synonymously, without drawing any distinction between "offices," "positions," and "places of employment." Since then the difference has been clarified. From a careful examination of the later decisions we are satisfied that petitioner held only a position or place of employment which could be and was abolished by omitting it from the appropriation bill for 1934.

The *Jacobs* case was followed by *People ex rel. Hogan v. City of Chicago*, 287 Ill. 46, in which it was averred that petitioner took the civil service examination for the "office or position of paving inspector," and throughout the petition the place to which petitioner sought to be restored was characterized as an "office," and "office or position," and a "position or office." Upon this branch of the case the court said: (p. 47)

"This is not an allegation that the employment is either an office or a position, and there is nothing in the petition which would distinguish it as either. While there is no statutory requirement prescribing the manner or method of creating a position of an employee, municipal officers other than those named in the statute must be created by an ordinance of the city, passed by a two-thirds vote of all the aldermen elected, as provided by section 2 of article 6 of the Cities and Villages Act."

The court then proceeds to state, "As there is a well defined distinction between an office and a position as they are considered in law, the petitioner will not be allowed to say that he has been filling one or the other. His employment has been in one or the other. His petition should state which, and if the former, should show the legal existence thereof by pleading the ordinance creating the same."

The respondents herein do not attack the validity of the original judgment in the *McArdle* case, nor the subsequent decisions, but argue that the use of the term "office" in the first opinion, where, under all the circumstances in that case, the court might more appropriately have spoken of the position as a "place of employment" which petitioner claimed and to which he was at the time undoubtedly entitled under the law, underlies the difficulties since encountered. Prior to the *Jacobs* case courts used the terms synonymously, without drawing any distinction between "offices," "positions," and "places of employment." Since then the difference has been clarified. From a careful consideration of the later decisions we are satisfied that petitioner held only a position or place of employment which could be and was abolished by omitting it from the appropriation bill for 1934.

In recent years efforts have been made by various municipalities and other branches of government to consolidate or simplify the organization of various departments so as to eliminate subheads thereof without discontinuing the functions of a particular subdivision of the department. This they obviously had the right to do, and we find nothing in the language of any of the McArdle cases or in the judgments of the circuit court which would prevent transfers of employees calculated to eliminate an unnecessary subhead within the department or bureau, such as a cement tester. The principal advantage of such consolidations is the elimination of overhead costs of operation of the various branches of service, and that is precisely what was done in the annual appropriation ordinance for the year 1934 in respect of the bureau of engineering, department of public works. The function of testing materials used in construction work was continued under the direct supervision of an engineer instead of indirectly through the office of cement tester, which was abolished. What the city officials did in 1934 is unlike any of the situations that arose in connection with the controversies in which McArdle's position had theretofore been involved. This case presents the first attempt to abolish as a separate division of the bureau of engineering the function of testing building materials and to abolish the position of cement tester as unnecessary by reason of the consolidation of the testing division with other branches of service under the direct supervision of the city engineer.

Petitioner takes the position by his brief and contended upon oral argument that the commands of the judgment and writ of 1933 provided that the annual appropriation be made "from the entry of the judgment until the further order of the court," and that thereby it was commanded to preserve the status quo of the office and its incumbent as fixed by the judgments until the court should

In recent years efforts have been made by various municipalities and other branches of government to consolidate or simplify the organization of various departments so as to eliminate subheads thereof without discontinuing the functions of a particular subdivision of the department. This they obviously had the right to do, and we find nothing in the language of any of the Mandamus cases or in the judgments of the circuit court which would prevent transfers of employees calculated to eliminate an unnecessary subhead within the department or bureau, such as a cement tester. The principal advantage of such consolidations is the elimination of overhead costs of operation of the various branches of service, and that is precisely what was done in the annual appropriation ordinance for the year 1934 in respect of the bureau of engineering, department of public works. The function of testing materials used in construction work was continued under the direct supervision of an engineer instead of indirectly through the office of cement tester, which was abolished. What the city officials did in 1934 is unlike any of the situations that arose in connection with the controversies in which [illegible]'s position had theretofore been involved. This case presents the first attempt to abolish as a separate division of the bureau of engineering the function of testing building materials and to abolish the position of cement tester as unnecessary by reason of the consolidation of the testing division with other branches of service under the direct supervision of the city engineer.

Petitioner takes the position by his brief and contended upon oral argument that the command of the judgment and writ of 1933 provided that the annual appropriation be made "from the entry of the judgment until the further order of the court," and that thereby it was commanded to preserve the [illegible] of the office and its incumbent as fi[illegible] sanction a change or abolition of the office. We do not believe there was any such sweeping adjudication by said writ. The legislative branch of the government has the power to abolish a position if it proceeds in the proper way, and in this instance it took the necessary and proper steps to effect the change. If petitioner's employment were a legally existing office established by ordinance which had been filled by appointment by the mayor with the approval of the council, as required by the Cities and Villages Act, then of course it could not be abolished except by ordinance or resolution to take effect at the end of the then fiscal year, but, being a position under the civil service law as defined by the later authorities of the Supreme Court, it could be dropped at any time without the formality of an ordinance or resolution, and this is precisely the course pursued by the city authorities in the instant case.

None of the prior McArdle decisions involved the right, power or authority of a city council to abolish the testing and inspection laboratory as a division of the bureau of engineering, department of public works, or to abolish the position designated as cement tester which was classified by the civil service commission as the head office in the testing division. All of the prior litigation involved either an attempt to replace McArdle in the performance of the duties of his position with a person who was not entitled to perform those duties, in violation of the civil service law, or to reduce the salary of McArdle below that of positions of similar rank in violation of the civil service law. The writs of mandamus issued in 1920 and 1933, which petitioner claims were violated by the city authorities when they failed to appropriate for cement tester for the year 1934, each contained provisions commanding the corporate authorities of the city to appropriate annually for the salary of that position only "so long as McArdle remains the sanction a change or abolition of the office. We do not believe there was any such sweeping adjudication by said writ. The legislative branch of the government has the power to abolish a position if it proceeds in the proper way, and in this instance it took the necessary and proper steps to effect the change. If petitioner's employment were a legally existing office established by ordinance which has been filled by appointment by the mayor with the approval of the council, as required by the Cities and Villages Act, then of course it could not be abolished except by ordinance or resolution to take effect at the end of the then fiscal year, but, being a position under the civil service law as defined by the later authorities of the Supreme Court, it could be dropped at any time without the formality of an ordinance or resolution, and this is precisely the course pursued by the city authorities in the instant case.

None of the prior Hezdle decisions involved the right, power or authority of a city council to abolish the testing and inspection laboratory as a division of the bureau of engineering, department of public works, or to abolish the position designated as cement tester which was classified by the civil service commission as the head office in the testing division. All of the prior litigation involved either an attempt to replace Hezdle in the performance of the duties of his position with a person who was not entitled to perform those duties, in violation of the civil service law, or to reduce the salary of Hezdle below that of positions of similar rank in violation of the civil service law. The writs of mandamus issued in 1929 and 1932, which petitioner claims were violated by the city authorities when they failed to appropriate for cement tester for the year 1934, each contained provisions commanding the corporate authorities of the city to appropriate annually for the salary of that position only "so long as Hezdle remains the incumbent of or entitled to hold said office of cement tester," and having been in 1934 legally and properly divested of his office, he was no longer "entitled to hold" the same and respondents cannot be held in contempt under the present petition.

On oral argument petitioner took the position that McArdle's employment could not be abolished without first making an application to the court which issued the various writs, but we regard this contention as untenable. Unless the city officials first abolished the position, their application to a court would present a moot question which the court could not entertain, and there would be nothing for the court to determine. Moreover, in our view of the circumstances, and the law applicable thereto, the court would not be justified in interfering with the city council in the proper exercise of its legislative functions.

For the reasons stated, we are of the opinion that the petition for contempt filed in the circuit court was properly dismissed, and the order will therefore be affirmed.

AFFIRMED.

Scanlan and Sullivan, JJ., concur.

48 4

37796

PEOPLE OF THE STATE OF ILLINOIS ex rel. JOHN RUSCH, Defendant in Error,

v.

HENRY LYNCH, L. E. GARBONE and JOHN LIDRA, Plaintiffs in Error.

ERROR TO COUNTY COURT, COOK COUNTY.

280 I.A. 621[3]

MR. PRESIDING JUSTICE FRIEND DELIVERED THE OPINION OF THE COURT.

This is a writ of error sued out from an order of the county court adjudging defendants guilty of contempt and criminal practices committed by them as officials of the court while acting as judges and clerks of election on November 4, 1934.

March 5, 1935, the bill of exceptions was stricken from the record. All of the assignments of error filed in this court and the points relied upon for reversal of the judgment are based upon matters contained in the bill of exceptions, and not upon anything appearing in the common law record. The bill of exceptions having been stricken the judgment of the county court is affirmed. (People v. Rosenwald, 266 Ill. 548, 556.)

AFFIRMED.

Scanlan and Sullivan, JJ., concur.

37796

PEOPLE OF THE STATE OF ILLINOIS)
ex rel. JOHN RUSCH,
Defendant in Error,

v.

[illegible] and
JOHN LIDKA,
Plaintiffs in Error.)

280 I.A. 621

MR. [illegible] DELIVERED THE OPINION OF THE COURT.

This is a writ of error sued out from an order of the county court adjudging defendants guilty of contempt and criminal practices committed by them as officials of the court while acting as judges and clerks of election on November 6, 1934.

March 6, 1935, the bill of exceptions was stricken from the record. All of the assignments of error filed in this court and the points relied upon for reversal of the judgment are based upon matters contained in the bill of exceptions, and not upon anything appearing in the common law record. The bill of exceptions having been stricken the judgment of the county court is affirmed. ([illegible])

Scanlan and Sullivan, JJ., concur.

37803

49 A

LOUIS MEYSKENS,
Appellant,

v.

GEORGE M. STEVENS, BLANCHE M. STEVENS, WILLIAM T. BLUE and LYDIA T. BLUE,
Appellees.

APPEAL FROM MUNICIPAL COURT OF CHICAGO.

280 I.A. 621[4]

MR. PRESIDING JUSTICE FRIEND DELIVERED THE OPINION OF THE COURT.

Plaintiff brought an action of the 4th class in the municipal court against George M. Stevens and others, jointly, to recover $281.81 alleged to be due for janitor services for the period from December 1, 1932, to August 10, 1933. The court dismissed the suit on motion of defendants, without hearing any evidence, and this appeal followed.

Plaintiff first filed his suit against George M. Stevens alone. Summons was issued and the bailiff returned the summons "not found." Later, pursuant to leave of court, plaintiff filed an amended statement of claim, naming George M. Stevens, Blanche M. Stevens, William T. Blue, Lydia T. Blue and Chicago Title & Trust Co., a corporation, as trustee, defendants in the cause.

Thereafter, George M. Stevens, one of the defendants, acting as attorney for himself and the defendants William T. Blue, Lydia T. Blue and Chicago Title & Trust Company, filed an affidavit of merits denying liability and also a statement of claim of set-off on behalf of these three defendants, claiming $118. When the cause was called for trial plaintiff appeared with his witnesses and offered to produce evidence to support his statement of claim. The defendants, by their attorneys, moved the court to dismiss the suit on the

37803

[illegible],
Appellant,

v.

[illegible]
and [illegible],
Appellees.

[illegible] OHIO 10.

280 I.A. 621

[illegible]

Plaintiff brought an action of the 4th class in the municipal court against George M. Stevens and others, jointly, to recover $281.21 alleged to be due for janitor services in the period from November 1, 1932, to August 10, 1933. The court dismissed the suit on motion of defendants, without hearing any evidence, and this appeal followed.

Plaintiff first filed his suit against George M. Stevens alone. Summons was issued and the bailiff returned the summons "Not found." [illegible] an amended statement of claim, [illegible] George M. Stevens, Lenthe H. Stevens, William [illegible], Lydia [illegible] and [illegible] Title & Trust Co., a corporation, [illegible] defendants. [illegible] acting as attorney for [illegible] William [illegible], Lydia [illegible] and [illegible] filed an affidavit of merits denying liability [illegible] on behalf of these [illegible] [illegible] to produce evidence to support his statement of claim. The defendants, [illegible] ground that defendant Blanche H. Stevens had not been served with process and that on motion of plaintiff the defendant Chicago Title & Trust Co. had been dismissed. The court entered the motion and continued the hearing thereof to a subsequent date, when plaintiff again appeared with his witnesses and by his counsel offered to produce evidence in support of his statement of claim. The offer was rejected, and defendants, after obtaining leave to withdraw their set-off, renewed their motion to dismiss the suit on the same ground theretofore stated, which was allowed, and the suit dismissed.

It is first urged on behalf of plaintiff that the affidavit of merits and statement of claim of set-off were filed on behalf of Blanche H. Stevens, as well as the other defendants; that the motion to dismiss the cause was likewise made on her behalf, along with the other defendants; and that she therefore appeared in the cause generally, so as to give the court jurisdiction of her person. However, we find that the affidavit of merits contains the following averment:

"George M. Stevens makes oath and says that he is one of the defendants and agent for William T. Blue, Lydia T. Blue and Chicago Title & Trust Co., a corporation, as trustee, defendants in the above entitled cause."

From this it would appear that George M. Stevens did not purport to represent Blanche H. Stevens. He alleges that he is agent for William T. Blue, Lydia T. Blue and Chicago Title & Trust Company, but there is no allegation or showing in the affidavit to sustain the claim that he also represented Blanche H. Stevens. Therefore, it cannot be presumed that she was included among the defendants on whose behalf the affidavit of merits and set-off were filed; nor can it be held that the motion to dismiss the suit by George M. Stevens, as attorney for "the defendants in the case," would, by implication, include Blanche H. Stevens among the defendants for whom counsel appeared and made the motion. The record discloses that Blanche H. Stevens was not served with summons, and that she did not enter her appearance

-2-

ground
that defendant Blanche H. Stevens was not [illegible]
and that on motion of [illegible] the [illegible]
Co. had been dismissed. [illegible]
the hearing thereof [illegible]
appeared with his witnesses [illegible]
evidence in support of his [illegible] of claims. [illegible]
and defendants, after obtaining leave to withdraw [illegible]
made their motion to dismiss the suit on the same ground heretofore
stated, which was allowed, and this writ [illegible]

It is first urged on behalf of [illegible]
of [illegible] and the [illegible] of claim of [illegible] on behalf of
Blanche H. Stevens, as well as the other defendants [illegible] motion
to dismiss the cause was filed [illegible] on her behalf, [illegible] the
other defendants, and that she therefore [illegible] the cause
generally, so as to give the court jurisdiction of her person. However, we find that the affidavit of merits contains the following
statement:

"[illegible] defendants [illegible]
the above entitled cause."

From this it would [illegible]
represent Blanche H. Stevens [illegible] William
T. Blue, Lydia [illegible] and there is
no allegation or showing in the [illegible]
he also represented all [illegible] Stevens [illegible] therefore, [illegible] be
presumed that she [illegible]
the affidavit of [illegible]
that the motion to dismiss [illegible] as attorney
for "the defendants in the case," could, by implication, include
Blanche H. Stevens among the defendants for whom counsel appeared and
made the motion. The record discloses that Blanche [illegible] Stevens was
not served with summons, and that she did not enter her appearance

personally, and since George M. Stevens purported to represent only the defendants named in the affidavit, there is no basis on which the court could have acquired jurisdiction of the person of Blanche H. Stevens.

We have examined the cases relied on by plaintiff to support the contention made, but find them inapplicable to the facts of this case. All of the decisions cited indicate that the parties involved took some position or action which the courts in the particular cases considered sufficient to call for an exercise of jurisdiction. Nothing appears upon the record in this case to show that Blanche H. Stevens did any of the things on which the courts in the cases relied on had based their rulings. The question sometimes arises as to whether an attorney has authority to enter the appearance of a party to a suit. Where he has done so, his authority will be presumed from the fact that he entered the appearance, until the want of authority is made to appear. This was the situation in the case of Cizler v. Keinath, 167 Ill. App. 65, cited by plaintiff, but it has no application here. From the foregoing, we conclude that as to the first contention made the court did not have jurisdiction of the person of Blanche H. Stevens.

The procedure in this case falls under the Civil Practice act (Cahill's Ill. Rev. St., 1933, ch. 110). Plaintiff relies principally on section 27 of the act, which is similar to section 14 of the Practice act of 1907, and provides that "when several joint debtors are sued, and any one or more of them shall not be served with process, the pendency of such suit or the recovery of a judgment against the parties served shall not be a bar to a recovery on the original cause of action against such as are not served, in any action which may be thereafter brought." It was held under section 14 of the Practice act of 1907 that judgment taken against one of several defendants, sued as partners, is valid (Sherburne

-2-

presumably, and since Dougherty [illegible]

only the defendants named in [illegible] of Illinois, there is no basis on which the court could have acquired jurisdiction [illegible] of the person of Charles H. Stevens.

We have examined the cases relied on by plaintiff to support the contention [illegible] but [illegible] in the facts of this case. All of the decisions [illegible] is that the parti[illegible] involved took some position or action [illegible]

[illegible]

arises as to whether an attorney has authority [illegible] appear- ance of a party to a suit. [illegible] no authority [illegible]

[illegible]

writ of authority is made to appear [illegible] in the case of [illegible] v. [illegible] [illegible] no application [illegible]

so the first contention [illegible] we have [illegible] of the person of Charles H. Stevens.

The procedure in this case [illegible]

act (Cahill's Ill. Rev. St., [illegible]) [illegible]

[illegible]

14 of the Practice Act of 1907, [illegible]

joint debtors [illegible]

served with process. [illegible]

a judgment against the party [illegible] shall not [illegible] recovery on the original cause of action [illegible] in any action which may be thereafter brought. [illegible] held under section 14 of the Practice act of 1907 that a judgment against one of several defendants, sued as partners, is valid; [illegible]

v. Hyde, 185 Ill. 580 and Mulligan v. Olsen, 222 Ill. App. 615), and a summons in the nature of a scire facias may make a defendant not served a party to the judgment in a suit against partners, as in cases of other joint debtors. So far as Blanche M. Stevens was concerned, plaintiff could have availed himself of this practice and procedure.

It is contended, however, that the dismissal of Chicago Title & Trust Co. as a party precluded plaintiff from proceeding with his action. This was a fourth class action in the municipal court where written pleadings were not required. As to such action it has been generally held to be "the well settled practice that in such courts the party suing need not even name his action, or if misnamed, that will not affect his rights, if upon hearing the evidence he appears to be entitled to recover and the court had jurisdiction of the defendant and of the subject matter of the litigation." (Edgerton v. C. R. I. & P. Ry., 240 Ill. 311, 313; Hehm v. Halverson, 197 Ill. 378; Bruner v. Grand Trunk W. R. Co., 319 Ill. 421, 425.) Since plaintiff was not permitted to introduce any evidence it is impossible to know what his proof would disclose. A cause of action was set forth in his statement of claim and he may have been able to make a case against the three parties who were before the court. In that event he would have been permitted, under the practice in the municipal court, to dismiss Chicago Title & Trust Co. after hearing and have judgment against those defendants over whom the court had jurisdiction. In that situation the court should have allowed him to produce his evidence instead of dismissing the suit on the pleadings. Accordingly, the judgment of the municipal court will be reversed and the cause remanded with directions to proceed in accordance with the views herein expressed.

REVERSED AND REMANDED WITH DIRECTIONS.

Scanlan and Sullivan, JJ., concur.

v. Tully, [illegible] Ill. [illegible]; Phillips v. [illegible] [illegible]

and a mandamus in the nature of a [illegible] may [illegible]

not served a party to the judgment in a suit against partners, as

in cases of other joint debts. [illegible] none [illegible]

was concerned, plaintiff could have availed himself of this practice

and procedure.

It is contended, however, that the dismissal as to Chicago Title & Trust Co. as a party precluded plaintiff from proceeding with his action. This was a fourth class action in the municipal court where written pleadings were not required. [illegible] it has been generally held [illegible] such [illegible] course the party [illegible] his action, [illegible] that will not [illegible] his rights, if upon [illegible] appears to be only led to recover and the court [illegible] jurisdiction of the defendants and of the subject matter of the litigation." Edgerton v. C., R. I. & P. Ry., 240 Ill. 311, 315; [illegible] v. [illegible] 147 Ill. 570; Brandt v. [illegible] 219 Ill. [illegible]. [illegible] plaintiff was not permitted to introduce [illegible] know what his proof would disclose [illegible] in his statement of claim and he may have [illegible] against the three parties [illegible] he would have been permitted, under the practice in the municipal court, to dismiss Chicago Title [illegible] judgment against those [illegible]. In that situation the court should [illegible] evidence instead of dismissing the [illegible]. Accordingly, the judgment of the municipal court will be reversed and the cause remanded with directions to proceed in accordance with the views herein expressed.

REVERSED AND REMANDED WITH DIRECTIONS.

Scanlan and Sullivan, JJ., concur.

37813

ROBBINS MUSIC CORPORATION,
a corporation,
Appellant,

v.

SEPIA GUILD PLAYERS, Inc.,
a corporation,
Defendant.

BALABAN & KATZ CORPORATION,
a corporation,
Appellee.

APPEAL FROM MUNICIPAL COURT OF CHICAGO.

280 I.A. 622[1]

MR. PRESIDING JUSTICE FRIEND DELIVERED THE OPINION OF THE COURT.

Robbins Music Corporation (hereinafter referred to as plaintiff) instituted attachment proceedings against Sepia Guild Players, Inc., a nonresident New York corporation, to recover $2,500 due for money loaned, and Balaban & Katz Corporation (hereinafter referred to as defendant) was served as garnishee April 3, 1934. April 18, 1934, judgment was entered against Sepia Guild Players, Inc., and in favor of plaintiff for the sum claimed, the court sustaining the attachment. April 6, 1934, defendant answered "no funds". Contest on the answer was set for May 21, 1934. Upon hearing the court found the issues against plaintiff and discharged defendant as garnishee. Motion for new trial was overruled and judgment entered on the finding from which plaintiff appeals.

The facts disclose that Sepia Guild Players, Inc., was employed to furnish its services to defendant at the Chicago theatre for one week, beginning March 30, 1934, at a compensation of $7,500, with deductions of $250 for expenses of stage hands and a 5% commission to be paid to the booking agency for procuring the

37813

[illegible] CORPORATION,
a corporation,
Appellant,

v.

[illegible] PLAYERS, INC.,
a corporation,
Defendant.

[illegible] & [illegible] CORPORATION,
a corporation,
Appellee.

MR. PRESIDING JUSTICE [illegible] DELIVERED THE OPINION OF THE COURT.

[illegible] Music Corporation (hereinafter referred to as plaintiff) instituted attachment proceedings [illegible] Players, Inc., a nonresident New York corporation, to recover $2,500 due for money loaned and Balaban & Katz Corporation (hereinafter referred to as defendant) was served as garnishee April 4, 1934. April 11, 1934, judgment was entered against [illegible] Players, Inc., and in favor of plaintiff for the amount claimed, the court sustaining the attachment. April 11, 1934, defendant answered "no funds". Contest on the answer was set for May 21, 1934. Upon hearing the court found that [illegible] plaintiff [illegible] and charged defendant as garnishee. Motion for new trial was overruled and judgment entered on the finding from which [illegible] appeals.

The facts disclose that [illegible] Players, Inc., was employed to furnish its services to defendant at the Chicago theatre for one week, beginning March 30, 1934, at a compensation of $7,500, with deductions of $250 for expenses of stage hands and a 5% commission to be paid to the booking agency for procuring the engagement.

Upon the hearing on the contest of defendant's answer plaintiff called Myrtle Carlson as a witness and introduced certain exhibits numbered 1 to 13, inclusive. Exhibit 1 was the contract between defendant and Sepia Guild Players, Inc. Exhibits 2 and 3 were letters assigning the indebtedness to William Morris Agency, Inc. Exhibits 4 to 12 were checks, representing payments made under the assignments. Exhibit 13 was an additional assignment to William Morris Agency, Inc., of $1,500. The witness called by plaintiff had charge of defendant's payroll and testified that defendant received the assignments by air mail from New York a few days before the show opened March 30, 1934. Exhibits 2 and 3, both dated March 27, 1934, and exhibit 13 dated March 22, 1934, read as follows:

"Mar. 27th, 1934.

William Morris Agency, Inc.
701 Seventh Avenue
New York City.

Gentlemen:
We hereby acknowledge our indebtedness to you in the amount of Six Thousand Eight Hundred Eighty-Seven Dollars and Fifty Cents ($6,887.50).
We hereby authorize the management of the Chicago Theatre, Chicago, to deduct the sum of Six Thousand Eight Hundred Eighty-Seven Dollars and Fifty Cents ($6,887.50) from the salary of Lew Leslie's 'Blackbirds' the week ending April 5th, 1934, and remit to you.

Very truly yours,
Sepia Guild Players, Inc.
by Irene Leslie, Treas."

"Mar. 27th, 1934.

William Morris Agency, Inc.
701 Seventh Avenue,
New York City.

Gentlemen:
It is understood and agreed that out of the monies to be collected by you on account of the engagement of Lew Leslie's 'Blackbirds' at the Chicago Theatre, Chicago, week of March 30th, 1934, that you agree to pay any and all salaries and/or other obligations or expenditures incurred by the show during that week and retain any balance over and above the salaries and expenses for the week in order to reimburse you for advances and commissions due you.

Very truly yours,
Sepia Guild Players, Inc.
By Irene Leslie, Treas.

-15-

engagement.

Upon the basis of the contents of [illegible]

plaintiff called Kystle [illegible] as a witness [illegible]

[illegible]

2 and 3 were letters [illegible]

[illegible]

ment to William Morris Agency, Inc. [illegible]

[illegible]

dated March 17, 1934, [illegible]

as follows.

March 17th, 1934.

William Morris Agency, Inc.
701 Seventh Avenue
New York City.

Gentlemen:

[illegible] the amount of Six [illegible] [illegible] 8th, 1934, and remit to you.

Very truly yours,
[illegible] Players, Inc.
By Irene Leslie, Treas.

March 17th, 1934.

William Morris Agency, Inc.
701 Seventh Avenue,
New York City.

Gentlemen:

It is understood and agreed that out of the monies to be collected by you on account of the engagement of Lew Leslie's "Blackbirds" at the Chicago Theatre [illegible] of March 30th, 1934, that you agree to pay any and all salaries and/or other obligations or expenditures incurred by the show during that week and retain any balance over and above the salaries and expenses for the week in order to reimburse you for advances and commissions due you.

Very truly yours,
[illegible] Players, Inc.
By Irene Leslie, Treas.

Accepted:
William Morris Agency, Inc.
By Nat Lefkowitz."

"Mar. 22nd, 1934.

William Morris Agency, Inc.
701 Seventh Avenue
New York City.

Gentlemen:
We hereby authorize the management of the Chicago Theatre, Chicago, Ill., to deduct the sum of Fifteen Hundred ($1500.00) Dollars from the salary of Lew Leslie's Blackbirds, the week ending April 5th, 1934, and remit to you on account of our indebtedness to you.

Very truly yours,
Sepia Guild Players, Inc.
By Irene Leslie, Treas."

Exhibits 4 to 12, inclusive, represent checks stated by Miss Carlson to have been issued by defendant in pursuance of the foregoing assignments, on the dates and in the amounts following:

Exhibit 4 - Check, dated April 2, 1934, issued to William Morris Theatrical Agency, Inc. for $3923.10, endorsed by payee, by M. . Silver, Balaban & Katz Corporation and Chicago Theatre, paid through Chicago Clearing House on April 3, 1934.

Exhibit 5 - Check, dated April 5, 1934, issued to Pennsylvania R. R. Co. for $264.40, endorsed for deposit by payee and paid through Chicago Clearing House April 11, 1934.

Exhibit 6 - Check, dated April 5, 1934, issued to William Morris Agency for $362.50, endorsed by payee and deposited with Irving Trust Co. on April 18, 1934.

Exhibit 7 - Check, dated April 5, 1934, issued to Balaban & Katz Vacation Account for $1,000 endorsed by payee and paid through Clearings on April 14, 1934.

Exhibit 8 - Check, dated March 24, 1934, issued to R. O. Bruder for $1,000, endorsed by payee and Balaban & Katz Corporation, showing payment through Clearing on March 26, 1934.

Exhibit 9 - Check, dated April 5, 1934, issued to William Morris Agency for $1500, endorsed by payee and received by or deposited with Irving Trust Co. on April 30, 1934.

Exhibit 10- Check dated April 5, 1934, issued to Balaban & Katz Corporation Vacation Account for $200, endorsed by payee and paid on April 14, 1934.

Exhibit 11- Check, dated March 23, 1934, issued to Pennsylvania Greyhound Lines for $200 and paid on March 31, 1934.

Exhibit 12- Check, dated April 5, 1934, issued to Balaban & Katz Corporation for $250, and Cleared on May 1, 1934.

The record contains a statement by the trial judge reciting

-2-

Gentlemen:

[illegible] hereby authorize the management of the Chicago [illegible]

Theatre, Chicago, Ill., to deduct the [illegible]

[illegible]

of our indebtedness to you.

Very truly yours,

[illegible]

Accepted:
William Morris Agency, Inc.
By Nat L. Lewis

William Morris Agency, Inc.
[illegible] Seventh Avenue
New York City.

Exhibits 4 to 14, inclusive, [illegible]

Miss Garrison to have been issued [illegible]

foregoing assignments, [illegible]

Exhibit 4 - Check, [illegible] William Morris Theatrical Agency, Inc. [illegible]

Exhibit 5 - Check [illegible]

Exhibit [illegible] - Check, [illegible]

Exhibit 7 - Check, dated April [illegible]

Exhibit 8 - Check, [illegible]
March [illegible]

Exhibit 9 - Check, [illegible]
or deposited [illegible]

Exhibit 10 - [illegible]
Corporation Vacation Account [illegible]

Exhibit 11 - Check, dated March [illegible]

Exhibit 12 - Check, dated April [illegible], 1954, [illegible]
Corporation for $[illegible], and cleared on [illegible], 1954.

The record contains a statement by the trial judge [illegible] the commencement of the attachment suit, service on defendant as garnishee, the filing of its answer denying that it was indebted to Sepia Guild Players, Inc., or had any money in its possession, charge or control which belonged to the judgment debtor, showing a judgment entered against Sepia Guild Players, Inc., in favor of plaintiff for $2,500, and finding from the evidence adduced and the exhibits offered in evidence that:

(1) Sepia Guild Players, Inc., was entitled to receive the sum of $7500 for services rendered for the week beginning March 30, 1934.

(2) That exhibits 2 and 3 constituted an assignment by Sepia Guild Players, Inc., to William Morris Agency, Inc., of $6,887 50 of the compensation to which it was entitled from defendant pursuant to the contract for services between the parties.

(3) That pursuant to exhibit 4 the sum of $3,923.10 was paid by defendant to William Morris Theatrical Agency, Inc., prior to the service of the garnishment writ, said payment being made pursuant to the assignments (exhibits 2 and 3) and that defendant had the right to take credit for this amount against the compensation due from it to Sepia Guild Players, Inc., under its contract of employment.

(4) That pursuant to exhibit 5 the sum of $264.40 was paid to Pennsylvania Railroad Co. after the date the garnishment writ was served upon the garnishee, but that said sum was paid to apply upon the compensation due Sepia Guild Players, Inc., and that defendant, by reason of exhibits 2 and 3, had the right to take credit for said sum.

(5) That pursuant to paragraph 21 of exhibit 1, which was the contract between the parties, the sum of $362.50, representing commissions due William Morris Agency, was paid by defendant after the date of the service of the garnishment writ on defendant, but that said sum was paid pursuant to the contract and therefore the garnishee was entitled to take credit for the amount by reason of the provisions of the contract.

(6) That pursuant to exhibit 7 the sum of $1,000 was paid to defendant as a matter of bookkeeping, after the date of the service of the garnishment writ, to reimburse defendant for an advance of $1,000 made by it on March 24, 1934, as evidenced by exhibit 8, which represented cash paid Leslie's Blackbirds' show, controlled or produced by Sepia Guild Players, Inc., and that therefore defendant, by reason of exhibits 2 and 3, was entitled to take credit for this sum under the contract.

(7) That pursuant to exhibit 9 the sum of $1500 was paid to William Morris Agency after the date of the service of the garnishment writ on defendant, but by virtue of exhibits 2 and 3 defendant had the right to take credit for said payment under the contract.

the commencement of the attachment suit, service on the garnishee, the filing of its answer denying that it was indebted to Sepia Guild Players, Inc., or had any money in its possession, charge or control which belonged to the judgment debtor, showing a judgment entered against Sepia Guild Players, Inc., in favor of plaintiff for $2,500, and finding from the evidence adduced and the exhibits offered in evidence that:

(1) Sepia Guild Players, Inc., was entitled to receive the sum of $7500 for services rendered for the week beginning March 30, 1934.

(2) That exhibits 2 and 3 constituted an assignment by Sepia Guild Players, Inc., to William Morris Agency, Inc., of $6,887.50 of the compensation to which it was entitled from defendant pursuant to the contract of services between the parties.

(3) That pursuant to exhibit 4 the sum of $3,643.10 was paid by defendant to William Morris Theatrical Agency, Inc., prior to the service of the garnishment writ, said payment being made pursuant to the assignments (exhibits 2 and 3) and that defendant had the right to take credit for this amount against the compensation due from it to Sepia Guild Players, Inc., under its contract of employment.

(4) That pursuant to exhibit 5 the sum of $264.45 was paid to Pennsylvania Railroad Co. after the date the garnishment writ was served upon the garnishee, but that said sum was paid to apply upon the compensation due Sepia Guild Players, Inc., and that defendant, by reason of exhibits 2 and 3, had the right to take credit for said sum.

(5) That pursuant to paragraph XI of exhibit 1, which was the contract between the parties, the sum of $362.5 , representing commissions due William Morris Agency, was paid by defendant after the date of the service of the garnishment writ on defendant, but that said sum was paid pursuant to the contract and therefore the garnishee was entitled to take credit for the amount by reason of the provisions of the contract.

(6) That pursuant to exhibit 7 the sum of $1,0 0 was paid to defendant as a matter of bookkeeping, after the date of the service of the garnishment writ, to reimburse defendant for an advance of $1,000 made by it on March 24, 193 , as evidenced by exhibit 8, which represented cash paid Leslie's Blackbirds' show, controlled or produced by Sepia Guild Players, Inc., and that therefore defendant, by reason of exhibits 2 and 3, was entitled to take credit for this sum under the contract.

(7) That pursuant to exhibit 9 the sum of $1500 was paid to William Morris Agency after the date of the service of the garnishment writ on defendant, but by virtue of exhibits 2 and 3 defendant had the right to take credit for said payment under the contract.

(8) That exhibit 10 represented the sum of $200 repaid to defendant as a matter of bookkeeping, after the date of the service of the garnishment writ, to repay an advancement made on March 23, 1934, to Pennsylvania Greyhound Lines in the sum of $200, as evidenced by exhibit 11, and that defendant had the right to take credit therefor under the provisions of the contract.

(9) That pursuant to exhibit 12 the sum of $250 was paid to defendant for the amount due stage hands under the contract between the parties, and that defendant had the right to take credit for this amount pursuant to the contract.

(10) That the foregoing sums paid by defendant amounted to $7500; that it had the right by virtue of exhibits 2 and 3 to charge all said amounts so paid by it against the compensation of $7500 required to be paid by it to Sepia Guild Players, Inc., pursuant to exhibit 1; and that at the date of the service of the garnishment writ on defendant, the latter was not indebted to Sepia Guild Players, Inc., in any amount whatever, and did not havein its possession, charge or control any moneys or credits owed by or to Sepia Guild Players, Inc.

It is urged that the assignments relied upon by defendant were invalid, in that (1) they were not supported by a valid consideration; (2) they were executed by one purporting to be the treasurer of the judgment debtor, without any evidence as to the genuineness of the signature or the authority of the treasurer to execute the assignments; (3) that they did not constitute a present transfer of any fund or claim, nor vest in the assignee any interest in the claim of the assignor against defendant. (4) that they did not deprive the assignor of control over the claim or the power to revoke the same; and (5) that, construing them together, it appears no assignment was intended, but that they provided for an arrangement under which the assignor controlled the claim or received its benefits, in fraud of the rights of creditors. Plaintiff introduced these assignments in evidence and it is defendant's principal contention that by so doing it is now precluded from challenging the validity of the assignments. It has been held that a party remaining silent when an instrument pertinent to the case is offered in evidence, cannot on appeal be heard to object that proof was not made of its proper execution. (Lake v. Brown, 116 Ill. 83); or that the official seal did not appear on the certificate of acknowledgment of the notary. (Baker v. Baker, to defendant, as a matter of books ... of the service ... garnishment writ, ... on March 22, 193... Pennsylvania Greyhound ... the sum of ..., as evidenced by ... and that ... has the

to ... not ... until the date of ... between the parties ... credit for this ... amount ... collected.

to 175 ; that it ... the right by ...

garnishment writ on ...

oved by or to ... with ...

... that the ... by ... ment

erstion; (2) they are executed by one ..., to be the treasurer of the judgment debtor, without any evidence as to the genuineness of the signature or the authority of the treasurer to execute the assignments; (3) that they ... not contain ... transfer ...

assignor ... of ... the ... and of the rights of creditor ... latest ... in

It is now provided from ...

pertinent to the ... in ... Ward

the certificate of acknowledgment of the notary, ...

169 Ill. 394, 398); or that no proof was made of the genuineness of the names of persons mentioned as vendees in a sheriff's deed. (Gardner v. Eberhart, 82 Ill. 316.) The obvious reason for the rule is that, had objection been made when the instruments were offered, necessary proof could perhaps have been supplied to overcome the objection, and, as applicable to this case, defendant may have been able to show proper execution of the assignments and the authority of the assignor to make them.

Plaintiff takes the position, however, that by offering these documents in evidence it did not acquiesce in their legal sufficiency, and that it may, on appeal, impeach their validity on any legal ground. It has been held that "a party introducing a document in evidence is not precluded from impeaching it by evidence which goes to its validity or which tends to show that it has not in law the effect that it purports to have." (10 Ruling Case Law, 1089, sec. 289; 17 Amer. & Eng. Ann. Cases, 381; Cassel v. First Nat. Bank, 169 Ill. 380.) The reasons most strongly urged for the validity of the assignments are that they were not supported by a valuable consideration, and that, taking into account the circumstances under which they were given, the language employed and the close proximity of the dates they bear to the impending engagement of Sepia Guild Players, Inc., by defendant, indicates an arrangement between the parties calculated to defraud plaintiff. These considerations may be discussed together. The assignments were given shortly before the Sepia Guild Players, Inc., were to open their engagement in Chicago at defendant's theatre, and at a time when it was indebted to plaintiff in the sum of $2,500. The record issilent as to any reason for the assignments. Not being under seal, they import no consideration, and none is shown by any of the evidence adduced. While it is true that, in order to constitute a valid assignment of a debt or other chose in action, no particular form is necessary and

120 Ill. 284, 286); or that no proof was made of the genuineness of the names of persons mentioned as vendees in a sheriff's deed. (Tarver v. Eberhart, 88 Ill. 316.) The obvious reason for the rule is that, had objection been made when the instruments were offered, necessary proof could perhaps have been supplied to overcome the objection, and, as applicable to this case, defendant may have been able to show proper execution of the assignments and the authority of the assignor to make them.

Plaintiff takes the position, however, that by offering these documents in evidence it did not acquiesce in their legal sufficiency, and that it may, on appeal, impeach their validity on any legal ground. It has been held that "a party introducing a document in evidence is not precluded from impeaching it by evidence which goes to its validity or which tends to show that it has not in law the effect that it purports to have." (10 Ruling Case Law, 1009, sec. 180; 17 Amer. & Eng. Ann. Cases, 561; Gassel v. First Nat. Bank, 155 Ill. 280.) The reasons most strongly urged for the validity of the assignments are that they were not supported by a valuable consideration, and that, taking into account the circumstances under which they were given, the language employed and the close proximity of the dates they bear to the impending engagement of Sapia Guild Players, Inc., by defendant, indicates an arrangement between the parties calculated to defraud plaintiff. These considerations may be discussed together. The assignments were given shortly before the Sapia Guild Players, Inc., were to open their engagement in Chicago at defendant's theatre, and at a time when it was indebted to plaintiff in the sum of $2,000. The record is silent as to any reason for the assignments. Not being under seal, they import no consideration, and none is shown by any of the evidence adduced. While it is true that, in order to constitute a valid assignment of a debt or other chose in action, no particular form is necessary and any words are sufficient which show an intention of transferring or appropriating the debt to the assignee, the authorities hold that the transfer must be supported by a valuable consideration. (Savage v. Gregg, 150 Ill. 161, 168; 2 Am. & Eng. Ency. of Law, (2nd Ed.) p. 1031.)

The record discloses that exhibits 6 and 9, aggregating $1,862.50, were checks issued to William Morris Agency, Inc., shortly after the service of the garnishment summons, and paid through Clearing House long thereafter. It is contended by defendant, and the court found, that exhibit 6 represented commissions due William Morris Agency, Inc., pursuant to par. 21 of the contract between the parties. The paragraph referred to provides for a commission to be paid "to the Artists Booking Office, Inc.," and there is nothing to indicate why it was not paid to it instead of to the assignee. Exhibit 9 represents a payment of $1,500 made by check, dated April 5, 1934, to William Morris Agency, Inc., subsequent to the service of the summons. The $1,000 compensation represented by Exhibit 7 was not paid to the William Morris Agency, Inc., but was made on March 24, 1934, for the benefit of Sepia Guild Players, Inc., and only three days thereafter the assignments were executed, for an amount of $6,337.50, which apparently included the $1,000 previously paid the assignor, as evidenced by exhibit 7. These and other circumstances are suspicious on their face and require some explanation. The transfer of funds by assignment must be made in good faith, and, when so made, if supported by an adequate consideration, the garnishee will be protected. (Born v. Staaden, 24 Ill. 320, 323.) However, where no consideration is shown, parties cannot by mere assignment of the debt defeat the rights of a garnisheeing creditor under circumstances which, unexplained, appear upon theirface to be suspicious.

Sec. 11, chap. 62, Cahill's 1933 Ill. Rev. Statutes, provides:

any words are sufficient which show an intention of transferring or appropriating the debt to the assignee, the authorities hold that the transfer must be supported by a valuable consideration. (Savage v. Gregg, 150 Ill. 161, 169; 5 Am. & Eng. Ency. of Law, (2nd Ed.) p. 1051.)

The record discloses that exhibits 6 and 9, aggregating $1,242.50, were checks issued to William Morris Agency, Inc., shortly after the service of the garnishment summons, and paid through Clearing House long thereafter. It is contended by defendant, and the court found, that exhibit 6 represented commissions due William Morris Agency, Inc., pursuant to par. 21 of the contract between the parties. The paragraph referred to provides for a commission to be paid "to the Artists Booking Office, Inc.," and there is nothing to indicate why it was not paid to it instead of to the assignee. Exhibit 9 represents a payment of $1,200 made by check, dated April 5, 1934, to William Morris Agency, Inc., subsequent to the service of the summons. The $1,000 compensation represented by Exhibit 7 was not paid to the William Morris Agency, Inc., but was made on March 24, 1934, for the benefit of Nipla Guild Players, Inc., and only three days thereafter the assignments were executed, for an amount of $6,857.60, which apparently included the $1,000 previously paid the assignor, as evidenced by exhibit 7. These and other circumstances are suspicious on their face and require some explanation. The transfer of funds by assignment must be made in good faith, and, when so made, if supported by an adequate consideration, the garnishee will be protected. (Born v. Staaden, 24 Ill. 320, 323.) However, where no consideration is shown, parties cannot by mere assignment of the debt defeat the rights of a garnishing creditor under circumstances which, unexplained, appear upon their face to be suspicious.

Sec. 11, chap. 62, Cahill's 1933 Ill. Rev. Statutes, provides:

"If it appears that any goods, chattels, choses in action, credits or effects in the hands of a garnishee are claimed by any other person, by force of an assignment from the defendant, or otherwise, the court or justice of peace shall permit such claimant to appear and maintain his right. If he does not voluntarily appear, notice for that purpose shall be issued and served on him in such manner as the court or justice shall direct."

This section of the statute, and section 12 following, which relates to the trial of adverse claims, were manifestly designed to determine the rights of assignees and other adverse claimants and thus protect garnishees from double liability. Under these provisions, if defendant had desired to proceed with caution and prudence, it could in its answer have disclosed the fact that it was indebted to the judgment debtor but that the indebtedness had been assigned, setting forth the assignments relied upon. In that situation the assignee could have been impleaded in the garnishment proceeding, or the court could have required the assignee to file its intervening petition or to be served with notice of the pending litigation, and, upon a full hearing, have determined the validity of the assignments and entered judgment accordingly, thus fully protecting defendant in the payments made both prior to the service of the garnishment summons and subsequent thereto. However, defendant saw fit not to disclose the fact that the debt had been assigned, and chose to recognize the assignments as valid and made payments of large sums of money to the assignee and others after service of the garnishment summons. The garnishee under the law is a mere stakeholder, and should, after he has been served with summons, make no further payments without order of court. If he does so, such payments are made at his peril. (Gorham v. Massillon Iron & Steel Co., 209 Ill. App. 606, 612, affirmed in 284 Ill. 594.)

Drake on Attachments (7th Ed.) p. 562, par. 630, says:

"It is incumbent upon a garnishee for his own protection, to state in his answer, every fact within his knowledge which had destroyed or would affect the relation of debtor and creditor between him and the defendant, or which would show that he ought not to be charged."

"If it appears that any goods, chattels, choses in action, credits or effects in the hands of a garnishee are claimed by any other person, by force of an assignment from the defendant, or otherwise, the court or justice of peace shall permit such claimant to appear and maintain his right. If he does not voluntarily appear, notice for that purpose shall be issued and served on him in such manner as the court or justice shall direct."

This section of the statute, and section 12 following, which relates to the trial of adverse claims, were manifestly designed to determine the rights of assignees and other adverse claimants and thus protect garnishees from double liability. Under these provisions, if defendant had desired to proceed with caution and prudence, it could in its answer have disclosed the fact that it was indebted to the judgment debtor but that the indebtedness had been assigned, setting forth the assignments relied upon. In that situation the assignee could have been impleaded in the garnishment proceeding, or the court could have required the assignee to file its intervening petition or to be served with notice of the pending litigation, and, upon a full hearing, have determined the validity of the assignments and entered judgment accordingly, thus fully protecting defendant in the payments made both prior to the service of the garnishment summons and subsequent thereto. However, defendant saw fit not to disclose the fact that the debt had been assigned, and chose to recognize the assignments as valid and made payments of large sums of money to the assignees and others after service of the garnishment summons. The garnishee under the law is a mere stakeholder, and should, after he has been served with summons, make no further payments without order of court. If he does so, such payments are made at his peril. (Gorham v. Massillon Iron & Steel Co., 209 Ill. pp. 606, 612, affirmed in 284 Ill. 594.)

Drake on Attachments (7th Ed.) p. 562, par. 650, says:

"It is incumbent upon a garnishee for his own protection, to state in his answer, every fact within his knowledge which had destroyed or would affect the relation of debtor and creditor between him and the defendant, or which would show that he ought not to be charged."

In par. 630-a it is said:

> "If the garnishee fail in thus presenting the facts, and in consequence thereof, more judgments are entered against him than the debt owing or the effects held by him authorized, he is wholly remediless; he brings upon himself a double liability by his own negligence, and the law will not protect a negligent garnishee."

In Chott v. Tivoli Amusement Co., 82 Ill. App. 244, it was sought to subject to garnishment the unpaid subscription for stock of garnishee. The court held that if the garnishee had notice that the liability for the unpaid subscription of stock had been sold or assigned, "appellant (garnishee) was bound for his own protection to disclose this in his answer," and further said (p. 248):

> "If the garnishee has notice or information that a third party claims an interest in the fund or property in controversy, he must, if he would protect himself against such claim, disclose it by his answer, even though he cannot, of his own knowledge, swear to the existence of the claim or its precise nature."

In the instant case the garnishee not only had notice of the assignments, but had acted upon them by paying out funds thereunder, and when served with garnishment summons should have brought the assignments to the attention of the court so that if any questions were raised as to their validity the assignee could be brought into court to justify them.

Defendant insists all through its brief that the assignments cannot successfully be contested in the reviewing court, because they were admitted to be valid by plaintiff, who offered them in evidence as its exhibits, and that the chose in action having been validly assigned, as counsel says, is not thereafter subject to garnishment, and its answer "no funds", unless disproved, makes it unnecessary to set out any evidentiary facts to support the answer. This argument assumes the validity of the assignments. As hereinbefore stated, the assignments recite no consideration, and none was shown. In that situation plaintiff has the right to urge that the

In par. 650-a it is said:

> "If the garnishee fail in thus presenting the facts, and in consequence thereof, more judgments are entered against him than the debt owing or the effects held by him authorized, he is wholly remediless; he brings upon himself a double liability by his own negligence, and the law will not protect a negligent garnishee."

In Chott v. Tivoli Amusement Co., 82 Ill. App. 244, it was sought to subject to garnishment the unpaid subscription for stock of garnishee. The court held that if the garnishee had notice that the liability for the unpaid subscription of stock had been sold or assigned, "appellant (garnishee) was bound for his own protection to disclose this in his answer," and further said (p. 248):

> "If the garnishee has notice or information that a third party claims an interest in the fund or property in controversy, he must, if he would protect himself against such claim, disclose it by his answer, even though he cannot, of his own knowledge, swear to the existence of the claim or its precise nature."

In the instant case the garnishee not only had notice of the assignments, but had acted upon them by paying out funds thereunder, and when served with garnishment summons should have brought the assignments to the attention of the court so that if any questions were raised as to their validity the assignee could be brought into court to justify them.

Defendant insists all through its brief that the assignments cannot successfully be contested in the reviewing court, because they were admitted to be valid by plaintiff, who offered them in evidence as its exhibits, and that the choses in action having been validly assigned, as counsel says, is not thereafter subject to garnishment, and its answer "no funds", unless disproved, makes it unnecessary to set out any evidentiary facts to support the answer. This argument assumes the validity of the assignments. As hereinbefore stated, the assignments recite no consideration, and none was shown. In that situation plaintiff has the right to urge that the lack of consideration, the language of the assignments and the circumstances under which they were given, as disclosed by the record, render the assignments invalid, and therefore the answer of "no funds" by defendant does not have the conclusive effect contended for by defendant.

We are not satisfied from the record in this case that the assignments were supported by the necessary consideration, or that the entire transaction is stamped with the good faith required by law. Plaintiff should be given an opportunity to implead the assignee and determine from it all pertinent facts relating to the assignments and the consideration, if any, therefor.

The judgment of the municipal court in favor of defendant, garnishee, will be reversed, and the cause remanded for a new trial on the objections of plaintiff to defendant's answer and for such other proceedings as may be consistent with the views herein expressed.

REVERSED AND REMANDED.

Scanlan and Sullivan, JJ., concur.

lack of consideration, the language of th[illegible]
the evidence under which they were [illegible] as disclosed by the
record, [illegible] the instruments invalid, and therefore the absence
of "no trade" by defendants does not have the conclusive effect
contended for by defendants.

We are not satisfied from the record in this case that
the mechanics were supported by the necessary consideration, or
that the entire transaction [illegible]
by law. Plaintiff should be given an opportunity to defend the
mortgage and [illegible] all [illegible] facts relating to the
assignments and the consideration, if any, thereof.

The judgment of the municipal court, in favor of defendants,
[illegible], will be reversed, and the cause remanded for a new trial
on the objections of plaintiff to defendants' answer and for
other proceedings as may be consistent with the views herein
stated.

[illegible]

[illegible] and Sullivan, JJ., concur.

5/A

37287

AMERICAN NATIONAL INSURANCE COMPANY, a corporation, Appellant, v. MARY ANTON, Appellee.	)	APPEAL FROM SUPERIOR COURT, COOK COUNTY.

280 I.A. 322[2]

MR. PRESIDING JUSTICE FRIEND DELIVERED THE OPINION OF THE COURT.

Complainant filed a bill to foreclose a trust deed on premises improved with a two-story brick building, containing a basement, store and an apartment, occupied by defendant. A receiver was appointed on motion of complainant, April 8, 1932, and empowered and directed by the chancellor's order to "take possession of, rent and collect the rents, issues and profits of said premises, to keep and maintain said premises in a state of good repair, to keep and maintain said premises insured against loss by fire and other casualty, and to pay all taxes thereon that are in default." Thereafter, August 5, 1932, a decree of sale was entered, finding that there was due and owing to complainant the sum of $14,841.25, and a sale ordered in the event said sum was not paid within one day after the entry of the decree.

August 30, 1932, a sale was held, pursuant to the terms of the decree, and the premises were bid in and purchased by complainant, leaving a deficiency of $500. Report of sale was thereafter duly approved, and December 6, 1933, there having been no redemption, master's deed issued to complainant.

February 26, 1934, pursuant to notice served, the final account and report of the receiver was filed and approved, showing

37837

AMERICAN NATIONAL INSURANCE COMPANY, a corporation, Appellant, v. MARY ANTON, Appellee.	[illegible] COURT, COOK COUNTY. 280 I.A. 622

MR. PRESIDING JUSTICE WILSON DELIVERED THE OPINION OF THE COURT.

Complainant filed a bill to foreclose a trust deed on premises improved with a two-story brick building, containing a basement, store and an apartment, occupied by defendant. A receiver was appointed on motion of complainant, April 8, 1932, and empowered and directed by the chancellor's order to 'take possession of, rent and collect the rents, issues and profits of said premises, to keep and maintain said premises in a state of good repair, to keep and maintain said premises insured against loss by fire and other casualty, and to pay all taxes thereon that are in default." Thereafter, August [illegible], 1933, a decree of sale was entered, finding that there was due and owing to complainant the sum of $14,841.25, and a sale ordered in the event said sum was not paid within one day after the entry of the decree.

August 30, 1933, a sale was held, pursuant to the terms of the decree, and the premises were bid in and purchased by complainant, leaving a deficiency of $500. Report of sale was thereafter duly approved, and December 6, 1933, there having been no redemption, master's deed issued to complainant.

February 26, 1934, pursuant to notice served, the final account and report of the receiver was filed and approved, showing that the total collections during the period of receivership amounted to $262.50, the total disbursements being $179.57, leaving a balance on hand of $82.93, which by order of court was divided between the receiver and his attorney. The store was vacant during the entire period of the receivership and redemption, except for seven months thereof, as shown by the receiver's report and account.

May 24, 1934, complainant, who had become the holder of the master's deed, filed a verified petition for a writ of assistance, containing the usual allegations, and averring that defendant, who still was in possession of the premises, had declined to vacate the same or to pay rent therefor, because, as she contended, certain disbursements for coal, janitor services and other charges had been made by her which were in excess of the reasonable rental for the premises.

To this petition, defendant filed an answer, admitting the foreclosure, the issuance of the master's deed and that she had been and was still in possession of the premises, and setting forth an itemized statement, aggregating $620, alleged to have been expended by her for coal, janitor services, plumbing, lights and repairs, since the appointment of the receiver, and that the receiver had failed to pay said sums to her and was liable therefor.

The petition and answer came on for hearing before the chancellor June 5, 1934, and an order was entered decreeing that a writ of assistance issue instanter against defendant and that the cause be referred to a master to take testimony and report the same to the court together with his conclusions of fact relating to the issues made up by the petition and answer. There was substantially no conflict in the testimony, and in July, 1934, the master made his report, specifying the various items shown to have been expended by defendant and finding also that the premises were equipped with a one-unit heating plant, so that the second floor apartment could not be heated without also heating the first floor; that neither the that the total collections during the period of receivership amounted to $262.50, the total disbursements being $179.87, leaving a balance on hand of $82.63, which by order of court was divided between the receiver and his attorney. The store was vacant during the entire period of the receivership and redemption, except for seven months thereof, as shown by the receiver's report and account.

May 24, 1934, complainant, who had become the holder of the master's deed, filed a verified petition for a writ of assistance, containing the usual allegations, and averring that defendant, who still was in possession of the premises, had declined to vacate the same or to pay rent therefor, because, as she contended, certain disbursements for coal, janitor services and other charges had been made by her which were in excess of the reasonable rental for the premises.

To this petition, defendant filed an answer, admitting the foreclosure, the issuance of the master's deed and that she had been and was still in possession of the premises, and setting forth an itemized statement, aggregating $488, alleged to have been expended by her for coal, janitor services, plumbing, lights and repairs, since the appointment of the receiver, and that the receiver had failed to pay said sums to her and was liable therefor.

The petition and answer came on for hearing before the chancellor June 5, 1934, and an order was entered decreeing that a writ of assistance issue instanter against defendant and that the cause be referred to a master to take testimony and report the same to the court together with his conclusions of fact relating to the issues made up by the petition and answer. There was substantially no conflict in the testimony, and in July, 1934, the master made his report, specifying the various items shown to have been expended by defendant, and finding also that the premises were equipped with a separate heating plant, so that the second floor apartment could not be heated without also heating the first floor; that neither the receiver nor complainant furnished any coal for the premises during the years 1932, 1933 and 1934, and that defendant paid for all the coal that was used on the premises; that neither the receiver nor complainant furnished any janitor services during the entire period of foreclosure and redemption, and that defendant paid $15 a month, in room and board, to the janitor for looking after the premises. The master made no recommendations as to the law applicable to the facts, merely stating his conclusions as heretofore shown.

August 7, 1934, pursuant to notice duly served on complainant, defendant presented to the court an order which was entered specifically finding complainant personally liable for the expenditures found by the master to have been made by defendant, and rendering judgment for defendant and against complainant for 727.63, from which this appeal was prosecuted.

Defendant takes the position that the expenditures were necessary for "the use and enjoyment of the premises which the law gave her," and that she was entitled to the judgment against complainant on the theory of unjust enrichment. This was not a homestead. Whatever rights of homestead defendant may have had in the premises were waived under the terms of the trust deed and were forfeited when defaults occurred thereunder. Her right to possession and to the rents, issues and profits of the premises were sequestered in the course of the foreclosure proceeding through the appointment of a receiver. Thereafter she continued to occupy the premises, not through any claim of right, but by sufferance of complainant, and therefore "the law gave her" no right "to the use and enjoyment of the premises" upon which the theory of unjust enrichment could be predicated. That doctrine is based on the law of quasi contracts, and is applicable, not to facts such as these, but to cases where one person has been compelled to pay money which another ought to have paid, and which he is allowed to recover from the latter in an action received [illegible] plaintiff furnishing [illegible] during the years 1929, 1930 and 1931, and that defendant paid [illegible] the cash that was used on the premises; that neither the [illegible] was complainant furnished any janitor service during the said periods of receivership and [illegible]; that defendant paid [illegible] in room and board, to the janitor for looking after the premises. The master made no recommendations as to the law applicable to the facts, merely stating his conclusions as hereinbefore shown.

August 7, 1933, pursuant to notice duly served on complainant, defendant presented to the court an [illegible] which was entered specifically finding complainant personally liable for the expenditures found by the master to have been made by [illegible] and rendering judgment for defendant and against complainant for $237.65, from which this appeal was prosecuted.

Defendant takes the position that the [illegible] expenditures were necessary for "the [illegible] enjoyment of the premises, which the law gave him," and that [illegible] entitled to the judgment against complainant on the theory of unjust enrichment. [illegible] tends. [illegible] premises [illegible] forced [illegible] and to the [illegible] of a receiver. There [illegible] through any of [illegible], but by [illegible] there are [illegible] the premises, upon which [illegible] unjust [illegible] be predicated. That doctrine is [illegible] and is applicable, not to facts such as these, but to cases where one person has been compelled to pay money which another ought to have paid, and which he is allowed to recover from the latter in an action of assumpsit for money paid to her use. 13 Corpus Juris 244. The record discloses that the store in the building was vacant during the entire period of more than two and one-half years, except seven months thereof. Therefore, substantially all the coal paid for by defendant was used to heat her own apartment, and not for the benefit of any other tenant. The janitor services claimed likewise inured to her own benefit, and the same may be said of the repairs, substantially all of which were made in the apartment occupied by her.

Defendant's counsel cites Knickerbocker v. McKindley Coal Co., 172 Ill. 535, and Atlantic Trust Co. v. Chapman, 208 U. S. 360, in support of the proposition that the party at whose instance a receiver is appointed will be required to meet the expenses of the receivership when the fund is ascertained to be insufficient for that purpose. Both of these cases were decided under facts constituting unusual circumstances, and as the court stated in the Atlantic Trust Co. case, *supra*, (p. 375), "Cases may arise in which, because of their special circumstances, it is equitable to require the parties, at whose instance a receiver of property was appointed, to meet the expenses of the receivership," when the fund is not sufficient for that purpose. There were no such special circumstances in this case, and the analogy is not applicable. Defendant was never a creditor of the receiver, there was no express or implied contract with either the receiver or complainant to justify the expenditure of these funds, and in fact neither the complainant nor the receiver knew of the expenditures until long after the receivership had been terminated and the master's deed had issued. During the entire period of the foreclosure and redemption defendant occupied the apartment without the payment of rent, and according to her own appraisal the apartment was reasonably worth $25 a month. Defendant waited until after the receiver had filed his final report and account and had been disof assumpsit for money paid to her use. 15 Corpus Juris 364. The record discloses that the store in the building was vacant during the entire period of more than two and one-half years, except seven months thereof. Therefore, substantially all the coal paid for by defendant was used to heat her own apartment, and not for the benefit of any other tenant. The janitor services claimed likewise inured to her own benefit, and the same may be said of the repairs, substantially all of which were made in the apartment occupied by her.

Defendant's counsel cites Knickerbocker v. McKinley Coal Co., 172 Ill. 535, and Atlantic Trust Co. v. Chapman, 208 U. S. 360, in support of the proposition that the party at whose instance a receiver is appointed will be required to meet the expenses of the receivership when the fund is ascertained to be insufficient for that purpose. Both of these cases were decided under facts constituting unusual circumstances, and as the court stated in the Atlantic Trust Co. case, supra, (p. 375), "Cases may arise in which, because of their special circumstances, it is equitable to require the parties, at whose instance a receiver of property was appointed, to meet the expenses of the receivership," when the fund is not sufficient for that purpose. There were no such special circumstances in this case, and the analogy is not applicable. Defendant was never a creditor of the receiver, there was no express or implied contract with either the receiver or complainant to justify the expenditure of these funds, and in fact neither the complainant nor the receiver knew of the expenditures until long after the receivership had been terminated and the master's deed had issued. During the entire period of the foreclosure and redemption defendant occupied the apartment without the payment of rent, and according to her own appraisal the apartment was reasonably worth $85 a month. Defendant waited until after the receiver had filed his final report and account and had been discharged, and she permitted the small fund which might have been available for the payment of part of her claim, if she had a claim, to be paid on account of receiver's and attorney's fees. Under all the circumstances of the case, we fail to find any ground upon which this judgment can stand, and the same will therefore be reversed.

REVERSED.

Scanlan and Sullivan, JJ., concur.

charged, and she permitted the small fund which might have been available for the payment of part of her claim, if she had a claim, to be paid on account of receiver's and attorney's fees. Under all the circumstances of the case, we fail to find any ground upon which this judgment can stand, and the same will therefore be reversed.

REVERSED.

Scanlan and Sullivan, JJ., concur.

37899

BELL AUTO REPAIR & PAINT COMPANY, a corporation, Appellant, v. GUSTAVE F. TUFO, Appellee.	)	APPEAL FROM MUNICIPAL COURT OF CHICAGO. 280 I.A. 622[3]

MR. PRESIDING JUSTICE FRIEND DELIVERED THE OPINION OF THE COURT.

Plaintiff brought an action in replevin to recover possession of an automobile under the provisions of a chattel mortgage of which it was the owner and holder. The cause was tried by the court without a jury, resulting in a finding that defendant have possession of the property replevied, and that a writ of retorno habendo issue for the return of the property to defendant.

To support the affidavit in replevin plaintiff filed a bill of particulars alleging that it was lawfully entitled to the possession of the automobile under the provisions of a certain chattel mortgage executed by defendant; that plaintiff was at the time of the transaction licensed by the director of trade and commerce to engage in the business of loaning money in the sum of $300 or less; that Tufo, being indebted to plaintiff in the sum of $226.80, executed the chattel mortgage and note in question, and agreed to pay the sum owing in installments of $18.90 each month thereafter, together with interest at 3-1/2% a month on the unpaid balance; that defendant had defaulted in the payment of certain installments on the note and mortgage, by reason whereof plaintiff was entitled to possession of the property.

RYLL AUTO REPAIR & PAINT COMPANY,
a corporation,
Appellant,

v.

OSCAR V. ...,
Appellee.

Plaintiff brought an action in replevin to recover possession of an automobile under the provisions of a chattel mortgage of which it was the owner and holder. The cause was tried by the court without a jury, resulting in a finding that defendant have possession of the property replevied, and that a writ of *retorno habendo* issue for the return of the property to defendant.

To support the affidavit in replevin plaintiff filed a bill of particulars alleging that it was lawfully entitled to the possession of the automobile under the provisions of a certain chattel mortgage executed by defendant; that plaintiff at the time of the transaction licensed by the director of trade and commerce to engage in the business of loaning money in the sum of $300 or less; that [defendant], being indebted to plaintiff in the sum of $226.80, executed the chattel mortgage and note in question, and agreed to pay the sum owing in installments of $18.90 each month thereafter, together with interest at 3-1/2% a month on the unpaid balance; that defendant had defaulted in the payment of certain installments on the note and mortgage, by reason whereof plaintiff was entitled to possession of the property.

Defendant filed his affidavit of merits alleging ownership of the car replevied and admitting that he executed the chattel mortgage and note and that the plaintiff was the owner and holder thereof. He averred that plaintiff had made certain repairs to his car, and that the chattel mortgage was given to secure the payment of the amount due for such repairs; averred that he did not receive any money from plaintiff, that he paid a total of $135.49 on the mortgage, which included principal and interest, denied that he was in default in any of the installment payments on the note, and that the sum of $226.80 was not for moneys leaned to him by plaintiff, but represented the cost of the repairs to the automobile. The affidavit further charged that the contract with plaintiff was usurious, and therefore illegal and void; and that plaintiff was not authorized by law to loan money and charge 3-1/2% a month.

To support its statement of claim plaintiff offered the chattel mortgage and note in evidence and proved by the testimony of John K. Saunders, its secretary in charge of the books and records pertaining to the account, that defendant was in default in certain installments mentioned in the note and chattel mortgage. At the close of plaintiff's case defendant moved for a finding and the court sustained his motion and entered the judgment from which this appeal is prosecuted.

It is urged on behalf of plaintiff that a prima facie case was made when its note and chattel mortgage were admitted in evidence and uncontroverted proof offered and received to establish defaults in the terms and provisions of the note and chattel mortgage, and that the court erred in finding for defendant without requiring evidence to sustain the defense interposed in his affidavit of merits.

Defendant takes the position that the transaction constituted a loan, appearing on its face to be tainted with usury, and that even though the statement of claim alleged that plaintiff

Defendant filed his affidavit of merits alleging ownership of the car replevied and admitting that he executed the chattel mortgage and note and that the plaintiff was the owner and holder thereof. He averred that plaintiff had made certain repairs to his car, and that the chattel mortgage was given to secure the payment of the amount due for such repairs; averred that he did not receive any money from plaintiff, that he paid a total of $138.49 on the mortgage, which included principal and interest, denied that he was in default in any of the installment payments on the note, and that the sum of $226.60 was not for moneys loaned to him by plaintiff, but represented the cost of the repairs to the automobile. The affidavit further charged that the contract with plaintiff was usurious, and therefore illegal and void; and that plaintiff was not authorized by law to loan money and charge 3-1/2% a month.

To support its statement of claim plaintiff offered the chattel mortgage and note in evidence and proved by the testimony of John K. Saunders, its secretary in charge of the books and records pertaining to the account, that defendant was in default in certain installments mentioned in the note and chattel mortgage. At the close of plaintiff's case defendant moved for a finding and the court sustained his motion and entered the judgment from which this appeal is prosecuted.

It is urged on behalf of plaintiff that a *prima facie* case was made when its note and chattel mortgage were admitted in evidence and uncontroverted proof offered and received to establish defaults in the terms and provisions of the note and chattel mortgage, and that the court erred in finding for defendant without requiring evidence to sustain the defense interposed in his affidavit of merits.

Defendant takes the position that the transaction constituted a loan, appearing on its face to be tainted with usury, and that even though the statement of claim alleged that plaintiff was licensed under the Small Loans act, (Cahill's Ill. Rev. St., 1933, ch. 74, par. 27, et seq.) nevertheless there was no evidence to support the allegation and therefore no prima facie case was made requiring him to interpose a defense. The court evidently proceeded upon the same theory, holding the transaction to be a loan at a usurious rate of interest by one who had not proved its authority to make loans under the statute.

The various contentions raised by the parties are all based upon the construction of the Small Loans act, which was carefully considered in the case of People v. Morse, 270 Ill. App. 207, and which we regard as controlling. In that case defendant was charged with having violated the act and was found guilty and fined. The specific charge in the information was that defendant, without a license such as the act requires, made a loan of money to the complaining witness at a rate of interest greater than 7% per annum. The facts are strikingly similar to those of the instant case, and in fact defendant was an officer of the Bell Auto Repair & Paint Company, the plaintiff herein. The evidence in that case disclosed that the complaining witness had signed a note secured by chattel mortgage on his car in payment for repairs made by the defendant, and thereafter failed to pay any of the installments due on the note and mortgage. Defendant testified that he did not lend the complaining witness any money, but did the work and took the note and chattel mortgage in payment for same, charging 3% a month because the complaining witness could not pay all the charges at one time. We reversed the judgment and held that no money was loaned; that the transaction was the ordinary one where the debtor is unable to pay in full in cash and an arrangement was made whereby he could pay in installments, and said (p. 210):

"It is a matter of common knowledge that under such circumstances the debtor generally obligates himself for a larger amount than he would pay on a cash on delivery basis. A special reason for was licensed under the Small Loans act, (Cahill's Ill. Rev. St., 1933, ch. 74, par. 27, et seq.) nevertheless there was no evidence to support the allegation and therefore no prima facie case was made requiring him to interpose a defense. The court evidently proceeded upon the same theory, holding the transaction to be a loan at a usurious rate of interest by one who had not proved its authority to make loans under the statute.

The various contentions raised by the parties are all based upon the construction of the Small Loans act, which was carefully considered in the case of People v. Morris, 270 Ill. App. 207, and which we regard as controlling. In that case defendant was charged with having violated the act and was found guilty and fined. The specific charge in the information was that defendant, without a license such as the act requires, made a loan of money to the complaining witness at a rate of interest greater than 7% per annum. The facts are strikingly similar to those of the instant case, and in fact defendant was an officer of the Bell Auto Repair & Paint Company, the plaintiff herein. The evidence in that case disclosed that the complaining witness had signed a note secured by chattel mortgage on his car in payment for repairs made by the defendant, and thereafter failed to pay any of the installments due on the note and mortgage. Defendant testified that he did not lend the complaining witness any money, but did the work and took the note and chattel mortgage in payment for same, charging 3% a month because the complaining witness could not pay all the charges at one time. We reversed the judgment and held that no money was loaned; that the transaction was the ordinary one where the debtor is unable to pay in full in cash and an arrangement was made whereby he could pay in installments, and said (p. 210):

"It is a matter of common knowledge that under such circumstances the debtor generally obligates himself for a larger amount than he would pay on a cash on delivery basis. A special reason for this exists with reference to a bill for automobile repairs, payable in installments, where the debtor is given possession of the automobile and is likely to depreciate its value by use or accident.

"The statute is clearly applicable only to a case involving the loaning of money. It should not be enlarged by construction so as to include an arrangement whereby a bill for repairs may be paid in installments."

It was not necessary for plaintiff in the instant case to prove that it had been licensed under the act to engage in the business of loaning money, because it contends that this was not a <u>loan</u>. If defendant had introduced evidence to show that it was a loan, plaintiff would still have had an opportunity to prove that it was licensed. Therefore, the underlying question necessary for determination, so far as this appeal is concerned, is whether or not the transaction constituted a loan. If it did not, the statutory provision relating to small loans is not involved, and the mere fact that the note on its face showed interest exceeding the statutory rate would not justify the court in assuming that it was a loan and hold that plaintiff had failed to make a case by omitting proof to show it was licensed. Plaintiff offered sufficient evidence to disclose the nature of the transaction, and since the question as to whether or not this constituted a loan became a pertinent issue, defendant should have offered evidence in support of his contention that it was a loan, so that the court could pass on that issue of fact. In the <u>Morse</u> case, <u>supra</u>, the defendant, under like circumstances, testified that interest at the rate of 3% a month had been charged on the indebtedness. Notwithstanding this evidence, the court held that the transaction was not a <u>loan</u>, and that the interest rate charged was not usurious.

In view of this conclusion upon what appears to be the principal point in the case the judgment of the municipal court will be reversed and the cause remanded for a new trial.

REVERSED AND REMANDED.

Scanlan and Sullivan, JJ., concur.

this exists with reference to a bill for automobile repairs, payable in installments, where the debtor is given possession of the automobile and is likely to depreciate its value by use or accident.

"The statute is clearly applicable only to a case involving the loaning of money. It should not be enlarged by construction so as to include an arrangement whereby a bill for repairs may be paid in installments."

It was not necessary for plaintiff in the instant case to prove that it had been licensed under the act to engage in the business of loaning money, because it contends that this was not a loan. If defendant had introduced evidence to show that it was a loan, plaintiff would still have had an opportunity to prove that it was licensed. Therefore, the underlying question necessary for determination, so far as this appeal is concerned, is whether or not the transaction constituted a loan. If it did not, the statutory provision relating to small loans is not involved, and the mere fact that the note on its face showed interest exceeding the statutory rate would not justify the court in assuming that it was a loan and hold that plaintiff had failed to make a case by omitting proof to show it was licensed. Plaintiff offered sufficient evidence to disclose the nature of the transaction, and since the question as to whether or not this constituted a loan became a pertinent issue, defendant should have offered evidence in support of his contention that it was a loan, so that the court could pass on that issue of fact. In the Morse case, supra, the defendant, under like circumstances, testified that interest at the rate of 3% a month had been charged on the indebtedness. Notwithstanding this evidence, the court held that the transaction was not a loan, and that the interest rate charged was not usurious.

In view of this conclusion upon what appears to be the principal point in the case the judgment of the municipal court will be reversed and the cause remanded for a new trial.

REVERSED AND REMANDED.

Scanlan and Sullivan, JJ., concur.

53 H

37655

LOUIS H. FREISE,
Appellant,

v.

MID-CITY TRUST AND SAVINGS BANK OF CHICAGO, a banking corporation, and MID-CITY NATIONAL BANK OF CHICAGO, a banking corporation,
Defendants.

MID-CITY NATIONAL BANK OF CHICAGO,
Appellee.

APPEAL FROM SUPERIOR COURT OF COOK COUNTY.

280 I.A. 622[4]

MR. JUSTICE SCANLAN DELIVERED THE OPINION OF THE COURT.

Complainant filed his amended bill against Mid-City Trust and Savings Bank of Chicago, a banking corporation (hereinafter called Savings Bank), and Mid-City National Bank of Chicago, a banking corporation (hereinafter called National Bank). Each defendant filed a general and special demurrer to the bill. The chancellor overruled the demurrer of Savings Bank, and sustained the demurrer of National Bank and dismissed the bill as to it for want of equity. Complainant prays an appeal from that portion of the decree dismissing the bill as to National Bank.

The amended bill alleges that complainant was a duly appointed, qualified and acting real estate and insurance broker, licensed by the state of Illinois and by the city of Chicago, and entitled to act as such in said city and state and to charge and receive fees therefor; that during the period set forth in the bill Savings Bank was an Illinois banking corporation and National Bank was and is a national banking corporation, both doing business in

Chicago; that about May 3, 193 , Savings Bank entered into a contract with National Bank whereby the former conveyed to the latter all of its assets and National Bank assumed all of the liabilities of Savings Bank; that said contract provides, inter alia:

"B. Purchaser Agrees:

"1. To and does hereby guarantee to pay, in accordance with the terms thereof, all of the liabilities of the Seller of every kind, nature and description, including all liabilities growing out of any trust relationships assumed by Seller as a result of the operation of its trust department, but excluding its liabilities to its stockholders as such."

That on the same date National Bank took over the banking quarters formerly occupied by Savings Bank, together with all books, records and property belonging to the latter, and has since continued the banking business, as well as the entire business of Savings Bank; that in connection with its banking business Savings Bank desired to have complainant conduct a real estate loan and insurance Department for the purpose of making real estate loans to applicants therefor out of the bank's deposits and charging commissions therefor, for buying and selling real estate mortgages for others, for the conduct of a general real estate brokerage business, and for writing fire, tornado and casualty insurance for others and charging a commission therefor; that the charter of Savings Bank provides that it may loan its own money on personal and real estate security, but that it cannot under said charter and the provisions of Chapters 17A and 73 of Cahill's Illinois Statutes, engage in real estate and insurance brokerage and loan business and charge commissions therefor; that Savings Bank never obtained a license to act as a real estate or insurance broker under said chapters; that during the period commencing June 1, 1924, and ending March 23, 1933, complainant was a duly licensed real estate and insurance broker under the laws of Illinois and entitled to act as broker for others in the negotiating

Old agot [illegible]

contract with [illegible]

latter all of its assets [illegible]

[illegible]

[illegible]

[illegible] March [illegible], 1933:

"[illegible]
with the terms thereof, all of the liabilities [illegible] of
[illegible]
growing out of any trust relation [illegible] assumed by [illegible] as a
result of any operation of its trust [illegible]
its liabilities to its stockholders as such."

That on the same date National [illegible] charters

[illegible]

and property belonging [illegible] since continued the

banking business, [illegible] of savings [illegible]

that in connection with its [illegible] savings bank [illegible]

[illegible]

rent for the [illegible] has

therefor out of the bank' [illegible] commission [illegible],

[illegible]

[illegible]

[illegible]

[illegible]

[illegible]

that it [illegible] 174

and 75 of [illegible] Illinois [illegible]

Insurance [illegible]

for; that [illegible]

[illegible]

period commencing June 1, 1933, [illegible], 193[illegible], complainant

[illegible]

Illinois and entitle to act as broker for other [illegible] the negotiating and sale of real estate loans and for the purpose of selling insurance for commissions; that on and after January 1, 1924, Savings Bank requested complainant to procure licenses from the city of Chicago and state of Illinois entitling him to act as a real estate and insurance broker and requested complainant to manage and conduct a real estate loan and insurance brokerage business in connection with said bank in the name of complainant under the several licenses issued to him from year to year; that during the period commencing June 1, 1924, and ending March 2[illegible], 193[illegible], complainant at the request of Savings Bank, procured such licenses from said state and city that entitled him to act as such real estate and insurance broker, and during said years, at the request of Savings Bank, complainant managed and conducted, in his name and in connection with said Savings Bank, an extensive real estate loan and insurance brokerage business; that Savings Bank collected from various of its customers and others, and retained, large commissions and fees therefor belonging to complainant, all of which should have been paid to him by reason of the fact that Savings Bank could not lawfully carry on such a brokerage business and had no licenses therefor; that Savings Bank made certain payments on account of such commissions to complainant from time to time and provided for him, without charge, desk room on the premises of said bank, as well as stationery, telephone, stenographic and clerical services, and caused records to be kept of all transactions covering the collection of fees and commissions earned by complainant, as well as the payments made to complainant on account thereof as such real estate loan and insurance broker, all of which records are now in the possession of defendants, or one of them; that complainant did not keep an itemized statement or record of charges for such fees or payments made by Savings Bank to him, but, having confidence in and relying upon the integrity of the officers of said bank, depended upon it to keep an accurate account of the payments made by its customers for such services and sale of real estate loans and for the purpose of selling insurance for commissions; that on and after January 1, 1924, Savings Bank requested complainant to procure licenses from the city of Chicago and state of Illinois entitling him to act as a real estate and insurance broker and requested complainant to manage and conduct a real estate loan and insurance brokerage business in connection with said bank in the name of complainant under the several licenses issued to him from year to year; that during the period commencing June 1, 1924, and ending March 25, 1932, complainant at the request of Savings Bank, procured such licenses from said state and city that entitled him to act as such real estate and insurance broker, and during said years, at the request of Savings Bank, complainant managed and conducted, in his name and in connection with said Savings Bank, an extensive real estate loan and insurance brokerage business; that Savings Bank collected from various of its customers and others, and retained, large commissions and fees therefor belonging to complainant, all of which should have been paid to him by reason of the fact that Savings Bank could not lawfully carry on such a brokerage business and had no licenses therefor; that Savings Bank made certain payments on account of such commissions to complainant from time to time and provided for him, without charge, desk room on the premises of said bank, as well as stationery, telephone, stenographic and clerical services, and caused records to be kept of all transactions covering the collection of fees and commissions earned by complainant, as well as the payments made to complainant on account thereof as such real estate loan and insurance broker, all of which records are now in the possession of defendants, or one of them; that complainant did not keep an itemized statement or record of charges for such fees or payments made by Savings Bank to him, but, having confidence in and relying upon the integrity of the officers of said bank, depended upon it to keep an accurate account of the payments made by its customers for such services rendered by complainant to said customers of said bank as well as payments made to complainant from time to time, all of which records said bank kept, and said bank and National Bank now have in their possession accurate records showing said brokerage fees collected by Savings Bank, as well as payments made to complainant; that complainant has no record in his possession or under his control from which he can ascertain the amount of money due and payable to him by said defendants or either of them by reason of the said brokerage services rendered by complainant to the customers of Savings Bank at its request; that defendants have refused and now refuse to deliver to complainant a statement of said moneys so received for complainant's services; that without reference to the records of defendants and further access to their books and accounts complainant is unable to state specifically the amount of such fees due him or the amounts of the credits due defendants; that the moneys from time to time due complainant from Savings Bank varied in proportion to the amount of commissions and fees collected by Savings Bank on complainant's behalf, but the aggregate sum of approximately $750,000 was collected by Savings Bank for complainant and is now withheld by said defendants, all of which indebtedness National Bank has under the terms of the above-mentioned contract assumed; that during the period in question complainant was the manager of the real estate loan departments conducted in connection with the business of Savings Bank and for compensation he rendered no service to said bank during such period other than as a real estate, loan or insurance broker for the purposes and in the manner in said bill set forth; that complainant has demanded of defendants an accounting of the moneys due him, which accounting has been refused, and complainant has also demanded of said defendants a correct statement showing the specific items of fees collected by defendants from their customers for services rendered by complainant to the customers, but defendants now claim

-4-

rendered by complainant to said de[illegible]
[illegible] agreements made to complainant from time to time [illegible]
said bank kept, and said books and [illegible] Bank now [illegible] to which
possession accurate records showing said [illegible]
by foreign banks [illegible]
plainant has no record in his possession or in [illegible]
which he can ascertain the amount of money [illegible]
said defendants or either of them by reason o[illegible]
services rendered by complainant to th[illegible]
at its request; that defendants have [illegible]
deliver to complainant a statement of said [illegible]
complainant services that without [illegible] reference to th[illegible]
defendants and further [illegible] to their books [illegible]
is unable to state specifically, [illegible]
the amounts of the credits due defendant [illegible] that the moneys [illegible]
to [illegible] complaint [illegible] in proportion [illegible]
amount of commissions [illegible] collected by [illegible] on complainant's behalf, but th[illegible]
collected [illegible]
[illegible]
of the above-mentioned [illegible]
complaint [illegible]
mentioned [illegible]
for compensation [illegible] such
period [illegible] the
purposes [illegible]
has demanded of defendants an accounting [illegible] which
accounting has been refused, [illegible] of
said defendants a correct [illegible] of
fees collected by defendants [illegible] services
rendered by complainant to the customers, but [illegible] he has now claim

all of said fees so collected by Savings Bank; that complainant is unable to specifically set forth the payments made by Savings Bank to him, having no record in his possession from which a statement thereof can be made; that defendants have in their possession complete records showing such items; that defendants have refused to permit complainant to see and inspect their books of account and have refused to render to him an account of the moneys earned by him, as well as moneys paid to him; that upon a just and true accounting between complainant and defendants there will be due him the approximate sum of $750,000; that complainant offers to do equity and more particularly to allow defendants credit for all sums which may be lawfully charged against him, and prays for an answer by defendants, not under oath, for a just and true account of the specific items of brokerage services rendered by complainant, an itemized statement of moneys collected by Savings Bank from its customers for such brokerage services so rendered by complainant at the request of Savings Bank, an itemized statement of payments by Savings Bank to complainant on account of his said services, an itemized statement of moneys withheld by Savings Bank from complainant, a general accounting and adjustment of the respective rights of complainant and defendants and an order on defendants to pay complainant the amount found to be due him, and for further relief.

Complainant contends that the chancellor erred in sustaining the demurrer of National Bank to the bill and in dismissing the bill as to said bank for want of equity. National Bank contends that the decree should be affirmed, upon the following grounds:

"Complainant was a salaried employee of the savings bank, and as such, has no claim against the savings bank, and therefore could have none against the national bank.

"If complainant has, or ever had such a claim against the savings bank, he should have asserted it long ago and not permitted the officers, directors and stockholders of the savings bank, for a period of nine years, to be unadvised as to such a claim.

all of said fees so collected by Savings Bank; that complainant is unable to specifically set forth the payments made by Savings Bank to him, having no record in his possession from which a statement thereof can be made; that defendants have in their possession complete records showing such items; that defendants have refused to permit complainant to see and inspect their books of account and have refused to render to him an account of the moneys earned by him, as well as moneys paid to him; that upon a just and true accounting between complainant and defendants there will be due him the approximate sum of $750,000; that complainant offers to do equity and more particularly to allow defendants credit for all sums which may be lawfully charged against him, and prays for an answer by defendants, not under oath, for a just and true account of the specific items of brokerage services rendered by complainant, an itemized statement of moneys collected by Savings Bank from its customers for such brokerage services so rendered by complainant at the request of Savings Bank, an itemized statement of payments by Savings Bank to complainant on account of his said services, an itemized statement of moneys withheld by Savings Bank from complainant, a general accounting and adjustment of the respective rights of complainant and defendants and an order on defendants to pay complainant the amount found to be due him, and for further relief.

Complainant contends that the chancellor erred in sustaining the demurrer of National Bank to the bill and in dismissing the bill as to said bank for want of equity. National Bank contends that the decree should be affirmed, upon the following grounds:

"Complainant was a salaried employee of the savings bank, and as such, has no claim against the savings bank, and therefore could have none against the national bank.

"If complainant has, or ever had such a claim against the savings bank, he should have asserted it long ago and not permitted the officers, directors and stockholders of the savings bank, for a period of nine years, to be unadvised as to such a claim.

"The national bank never assumed any such claim, because it would have been unable to do so as the Comptroller of Currency would not have given it a charter or permitted it to take over the assets of the savings bank and assume the liability, which, according to complainant's claim, amounts to three-quarters of a million dollars.

"Complainant is equitably estopped to claim as against the national bank because he, as an employee of the savings bank, should have asserted such claim, if any he had, long before he did.

"Were a court of equity to allow complainant to assert his claim after such a long delay, it not only would be inequitable as against the national bank, but as against all of its depositors as well.

"If the national bank knew there was any such claim, it would not and could not have assumed the liabilities of the savings bank; but, rather, the depositors of the savings bank would have to share the assets with the complainant, if he has any such claim.

"If complainant had any such claim, by asserting it many years ago he could have greatly, if not totally, reduced it.

"Complainant should not be permitted to stand idly by for nine years, permitting the auditor of public accounts of the State of Illinois, the depositors, other creditors, the officers, directors and stockholders of the savings bank to be misled as to its financial condition and then after his employment with the savings bank is terminated, to assert any such claim against the purchaser of its assets.

"Complainant was a party to the transaction with the savings bank and if the agreement between him and the savings bank were illegal, a court of equity leaves the parties where it may find them, under the maxim of ex facto illicito non oritur actio.

"At least so far as the national bank is concerned, the complainant was guilty of laches and his claim is barred.

"Complainant should not be permitted to obtain any aid in a court of equity on the basis of the claim set out in his bill of complaint.

"Complainant should be equitably estopped from now asserting his claim against the national bank."

The settled rule of pleading is that all of the facts well pleaded in the bill are admitted by the demurrer and must be taken as true for all purposes. A number of the aforesaid grounds are based upon the unwarranted assumption that under the allegations of the bill "apparently everything he (complainant) did, he did as an employee of the savings bank." The bill is not predicated upon the theory that complainant performed the brokerage services for Savings Bank, nor that he received any compensation from Savings Bank for such services, nor that any compensation was agreed upon for such services,

"The national bank never assumes [illegible]
it would have been unable [illegible]
would not have given it a [illegible]
[illegible]
ing to complainant's claim, amounting to [illegible] dollars.

"Complainant is [illegible]
the national bank because he, [illegible] of the savings bank, [illegible]
[illegible]

"Were a court of equity to allow complainant to [illegible]
his claim after such a long delay, it not only would be inequitable as against the national bank, but [illegible] of its [illegible] as well.

"If the national bank [illegible], such claim, it would not and could not [illegible] assume the liabilities of the [illegible] bank; but, rather, the [illegible] of the savings bank would have to share the assets with the complainant, if he has any such claim.

"If complainant had any such claim, [illegible]
years ago he could have [illegible]

"Complainant [illegible] by for nine years, permitting [illegible] state of Illinois, [illegible]
[illegible]
bank is terminated, [illegible]
of its assets.

"Complainant [illegible]
[illegible]
them, under the maxim of [illegible]

"At least so far [illegible], the complainant [illegible]

In a court of [illegible]
of complaint

"Complainant [illegible]
asserting his claim [illegible]

The settled rule of [illegible]
in the bill are [illegible]
for all purposes [illegible]
the unwarranted [illegible] that [illegible]
"apparently everything he (complainant) did, [illegible]
of the savings bank." The bill is not [illegible]
that complainant performed [illegible]
nor that he received any compensation from [illegible] for such
services, nor that any compensation was agreed upon for such services.

When its allegations are reasonably construe the theory of fact of the bill is that complainant operated the business in his own name under licenses issued to him, that Savings Bank collected the fees due him, made certain payments on account of the same to him, but has withheld large sums of money rightfully belonging to him. The bill alleges that complainant was the one who could charge for such services, and that the bank had no authority or power to perform such services or to charge for them. There is no allegation to the effect that the bank, as employer of complainant, charged its customers for fees or operated the brokerage business; nor is there any merit in the argument that the customers were not complainant's clients and that therefore he could not collect from them. Complainant, a licensed broker, conducted a brokerage business, rendered services to certain persons, some of whom were customers of the bank, and the payments made by said persons to the bank were for his services. The allegations, reasonably construed, do not warrant the argument that complainant was compensated by Savings Bank for acting as a broker. The bill alleges that Savings Bank "made certain payments on account of such commissions to complainant from time to time." The demurrer admits this. It is sufficient to say, as to the argument that complainant made no claim for money "when he left the employ of the bank," that the bill alleges, and the demurrer admits, that complainant has demanded of defendants an accounting of the moneys due him and a correct statement showing the specific items of fees collected by defendants from their customers for services rendered by complainant to said customers, and that defendants have refused to permit complainant to see and inspect their books of account and have refused to render to complainant an account of the moneys earned by him, as well as moneys paid to him. Until March 23, 1933, complainant conducted a brokerage business in the bank. On May 8, 1933, National Bank entered into the contract with Savings Bank. On June 22, 1933, the original bill was filed.

-7-

[illegible]

has withheld large sums [illegible]

due him, made [illegible]

until [illegible] issued [illegible]

services, and [illegible]

services or to [illegible] for them. [illegible]

[illegible]

fees or operated the brokerage business [illegible]

[illegible]

certain [illegible]

[illegible]

allegations, [illegible] commonly conc[illegible]

[illegible]

bank," that the bill [illegible]

has demand [illegible] of defendants [illegible]

[illegible]

and to see and inspect the books of [illegible]

render to complainant an account of the moneys [illegible]

as moneys paid to him. Until March 23, [illegible] complainant conducted a

brokerage business [illegible] the bank. On May 6, [illegible] entered

into the contract with Savings Bank. On June 22, [illegible] the original

bill was filed.

A number of the grounds most strongly urged by National Bank in support of the decree are based upon supposed facts that have no basis under the allegations of the bill. National Bank contends that "complainant was a party to the transaction with the savings bank and if the agreement between him and the savings bank were illegal, a court of equity leaves the parties where it may find them, under the maxim of ex facto illicito non oritur actio." It is a sufficient answer to this contention to say that complainant's bill is not based upon the theory of fact that he entered into any illegal agreement with Savings Bank. Nor is there any allegation to the effect that complainant waived any of his rights to the commissions collected by the bank. Complainant alleges, in substance, that Savings Bank collected commissions belonging to him and has wrongfully converted them.

Arguments that the claim is "ridiculous," "unbelievable," that if it "were true," the auditor of public accounts of Illinois would have closed Savings Bank long since; that the public officials would not have permitted the contract between the two banks to be consummated if they knew of complainant's claim; that it would be a "gross injustice not only to all of the depositors of the savings bank but to all who are interested either as depositors, stockholders, directors or officers of the national bank" to allow the claim, have no weight in determining the sufficiency of complainant's amended bill.

The chancellor was justified, in our judgment, in overruling the demurrer of Savings Bank to the bill. By the terms of the contract between the two banks National Bank assumed and agreed to pay all of the liabilities "of every kind, nature and description," of Savings Bank, save "its liabilities to its stockholders as such." In return National Bank took over all of the assets of Savings Bank. The record does not show the special ground upon which the chancellor sustained the demurrer of National Bank.

Two special grounds are here urged why that demurrer should

[illegible]

them, under [illegible]

[illegible]

that if it "were true," the [illegible]

[illegible]

would not have permitted the court of [illegible] to be

consummated if they knew of complainant's [illegible]

"gross injustice" not only to all [illegible]

bank but to all who are interested [illegible]

[illegible]

The [illegible] justified, [illegible] in overruling

the demurrer of [illegible] to the bill [illegible] the con-

tract between the two banks [illegible] any

all of the liabilities of every kind, [illegible]

Savings Bank, [illegible]

return National Bank took over all of the [illegible]

The record does not show the special ground upon which the chancellor

sustained the demurrer of [illegible]

[illegible]

be sustained: (a) "Complainant is equitably estopped from asserting any claim against national bank;" and (b), as far as National Bank is concerned, "complainant is guilty of laches and his claim against the national bank is barred." As to point (a): There are no allegations in the bill that tend to show that National Bank, in making the contract, relied upon any acts or representations of complainant, nor is there any allegation to support the contention that complainant stood idly by and allowed National Bank to purchase the assets of Savings Bank without advising that bank of his claim. Indeed, there is no allegation from which it could be reasonably argued that complainant had any knowledge that National Bank contemplated the purchase of the assets of Savings Bank. As we have heretofore stated, the bill alleges that Savings Bank kept a record "of all transactions covering the collection of fees and commissions earned by complainant, as well as payments made to complainant on account of such fees as such real estate loan and insurance broker." An examination of the books of Savings Bank by National Bank would have furnished the latter with full information as to complainant's claim. We find no merit in the claim of equitable estoppel.

Nor do we find any merit in the claim of laches. The rule is that laches must appear on the face of the bill before the question can be raised by demurrer. Complainant did not cease doing business until March 23, 1933, his bill was filed June 22, 1933, and it is a sufficient answer to the claim of laches that under no possible theory could complainant be charged with laches as to that portion of his claim that accrued within the period immediately preceding the date of filing the bill.

That portion of the dec ee sustaining the demurrer of National Bank to the amended bill and dismissing it for want of equity is reversed, and the cause is remanded with directions to overrule the demurrer of National Bank to the amended bill, and for further proceedings not inconsistent with this opinion.

DECREE REVERSED IN PART, AND CAUSE REMANDED WITH DIRECTIONS.

Friend, P.J., and Sullivan, J., concur.

-9-

be sustained. (a) [illegible] is a wholly [illegible]

[illegible]

Bank to [illegible] is guilty [illegible]

against the National Bank [illegible] "ferred," [illegible]

no allegations in the bill that [illegible]

[illegible]

[illegible]

that complaint would fully [illegible]

the records of [illegible] Bank without [illegible]

Indeed, there is no [illegible]

[illegible]

[illegible]

[illegible]

[illegible]

account of such fees [illegible]

[illegible]

[illegible]

claims. We find no merit in the claim of [illegible]

For the [illegible]

[illegible]

can be raised by demurrer [illegible]

until March [illegible]

[illegible]

[illegible]

claim that accrued within the [illegible]

of filing the bill.

[illegible]

National Bank to the [illegible] bill [illegible] of equity

[illegible]

[illegible] of National Bank to the amended bill, and for further proceedings not inconsistent with this opinion.

[illegible] REMANDED WITH
[illegible].

Friend, P.J., and Sullivan, J., concur.

574

37682

IN THE MATTER OF THE ESTATE OF DANIEL M. JACKSON, Deceased.

CLAIMS OF HARRY E. STRICKLAND and KATHRYN STRICKLAND, for the use of WILLIAM G. PACKARD, (Claimants) Appellees,

v.

CHARLES S. JACKSON, as Executor of the Estate of DANIEL M. JACKSON, Deceased, (Defendant) Appellant.

APPEAL FROM CIRCUIT COURT, COOK COUNTY.

280 I.A. 623[1]

MR. JUSTICE SCANLAN DELIVERED THE OPINION OF THE COURT.

This is an appeal from a judgment in favor of Harry E. Strickland and Kathryn Strickland, for the use of William G. Packard, and against the Estate of Daniel M. Jackson, Deceased, in the sum of $3,250, to be paid as a sixth class claim in due course of administration.

The Stricklands filed two claims in the Probate court against the estate, one for $2,000 for "accrued rent of premises Number 3139 Michigan Avenue, Chicago, for months of June,1929 to and including January, 1930, at $250.00 per month, under written lease dated November 24, 1926 for term expiring June 30, 1931," and one for $1,250 for accrued rent of the same premises "for months of February to June, 1930, inclusive, at $250.00 per month," under the same lease. The claims were allowed and an appeal was taken to the Circuit court, where the cause was tried de novo by the court. During that trial the claims were amended on the face thereof by inserting after the names of claimants the words "for use of William G. Packard."

and a [illegible], for [illegible]
(claimants) appellees,

[illegible]

Deceased,
[illegible] appellant.

260 I.A. 623

[illegible]

This is an appeal from a judgment in favor of [illegible] [illegible] in the sum of $3,290, to be paid in a [illegible] course of administration.

[illegible] against the estate, one for [illegible] Number 5159 Michigan avenue, Chicago, [illegible] and including January, 1950, at [illegible] per [illegible] lease dated November 26, 1946 [illegible] and one for $1,380 for accrued rent at [illegible] months of February to June, 1950, [illegible] per month, under the same lease. The claims were [illegible] taken to the Circuit court, where [illegible] by the court. During that trial the claims were amended on the face thereof by inserting after the names of claimants the words "for use of [illegible]"

The errors relied upon for a reversal of the judgment are: "1. That the Court erred in not finding that the premises were rented by Jackson for gambling purposes. 2. That the Court erred in not finding that the claimants knew that said premises were being rented by Jackson for gambling purposes. 3. That the findings and decision of the Court, are against the weight of the evidence." The law bearing upon a case of this kind is well settled. (See In re Estate of Jackson, 269 Ill. App. 34. Certierari denied by the Supreme court.) Briefly stated, the law is that when premises are rented by the lessee for gambling purposes and this is known to the lessor there can be no recovery for rent; that an illegal agreement may be tacit as well as express, and its existence may be established by proof of facts and circumstances showing coincidences which can be accounted for under no other assumption than that such original understanding existed. The determination of this appeal turns upon the evidence.

From July 1, 1911, until January 1, 1927, the Stricklands conducted in the premises in question the business of making and selling ladies' dresses, and they resided on the fourth floor of the building. Prior to November, 1926, they placed a For Rent sign in one of the windows of the building. Lewis G. Bradford testified that he had known Jackson for about fifteen years; that the latter was a keeper of gambling houses and a "fixer," that is, if anyone wanted to open a gambling house in the district they had to see Jackson and, if satisfactory arrangements were made, he would fix the police so that the gambling house could be operated; that at the time in question the witness had been employed by Jackson for six years "as outside man, looking after his outside interests, making collections, hired men and discharged them in work in gambling houses;" that in November, 1926, he saw the For Rent sign at 3130 Michigan avenue and after speaking to Jackson in reference to the

The errors relied upon for a reversal of the judgment are: "1. That the Court erred in not finding that the premises were rented by Jackson for gambling purposes. 2. That the Court erred in not finding that the claimants knew that said premises were being rented by Jackson for gambling purposes. 3. That the findings and decision of the Court, are against the weight of the evidence." The law bearing upon a case of this kind is well settled. (See In re Estate of Jackson, 308 Ill. App. 34. Certiorari denied by the Supreme court.) Briefly stated, the law is that when premises are rented by the lessee for gambling purposes and this is known to the lessor there can be no recovery for rent; that an illegal agreement may be tacit as well as express, and its existence may be established by proof of facts and circumstances showing coincidences which can be accounted for under no other assumption than that such original understanding existed. The determination of this appeal turns upon the evidence.

From July 1, 1911, until January 1, 1927, the Stricklands conducted in the premises in question the business of making and selling ladies' dresses, and they resided on the fourth floor of the building. Prior to November, 1926, they placed a For Rent sign in one of the windows of the building. Lewis G. Bradford testified that he had known Jackson for about fifteen years; that the latter was a keeper of gambling houses and a "fixer," that is, if anyone wanted to open a gambling house in the district they had to see Jackson and, if satisfactory arrangements were made, he would fix the police so that the gambling house could be operated; that at the time in question the witness had been employed by Jackson for six years "as outside man, looking after his outside interests, making collections, hired men and discharged them in work in gambling houses;" that in November, 1926, he saw the For Rent sign at 3159 Michigan avenue and after speaking to Jackson in reference to the place he went there, saw Strickland, and asked him how much rent he wanted for the place and how long a lease he could give; that Strickland said "$250.00 and he said he could give us four and one-half years from first of January;" that later in the day the witness, together with Harry Lewis, called again at the place and Strickland took them through the house; that Strickland "asked me what we wanted it for, I said a Club; he wanted to know 'Going to do any gambling', I said 'Yes.' Q. Did he ask you what kind of gambling? A. I told him cards, craps * * * card games and crap games. Q. What did he say? A. He didn't say a word. He asked what reference we could give him. I said 'J. B. Mallers of the Maller Building, and Leibrandt of the Lincoln State Bank,' that's all the conversation I had." George F. Leibrandt, president of an investment company which dealt in real estate, bonds and mortgages, testified that he had been in the real estate business in Chicago for thirty-five years and that from May, 1912, to June, 1931, he was president of Lincoln State Bank of Chicago; that he had known Strickland, by reputation, for twenty years; that in the latter part of 1926 Strickland called at the bank and stated to him that Jackson wanted to rent the premises at 3139 Michigan avenue and he "wanted to know as to his responsibility;" that he told Strickland that he had known Jackson a good many years "and he was perfectly responsible." "Was anything else said in that conversation? A. I asked Mr. Strickland what he was going to occupy it for, he said he didn't know. I said 'I understand, you know Mr. Jackson is going to use it for club purposes.' Q. What did Mr. Strickland say? A. Well, he was more interested in the responsibility of Mr. Jackson. Q. Is that the language you used club purposes? A. I told him he was going to use it for gambling house, he had one up the street, I presumed he was going to use this for the same thing. Mr. Lamborn (attorney for claimants): I move that be stricken. The Court:

place he went there, saw Strickland, and asked him how much rent he wanted for the place and how long a lease he would give; that Strickland said "$250.00 and he said he could give us four and one-half years from first of January;" that later in the day the witness, together with Harry Lewis, called again at the place and Strickland took them through the house; that Strickland "asked me what we wanted it for, I said a Club; he wanted to know 'Going to do any gambling', I said 'Yes.' Q. Did he ask you what kind of gambling? A. I told him cards, craps * * * card games and crap games. Q. What did he say? A. He didn't say a word. He asked what reference we could give him. I said 'J. E. Kellers of the Miller Building, and Leibrandt of the Lincoln State Bank,' that's all the conversation I had." George F. Leibrandt, president of an investment company which deals in real estate, bonds and mortgages, testified that he had been in the real estate business in Chicago for thirty-five years and that from May, 1912, to June, 1921, he was president of Lincoln State Bank of Chicago; that he had known Strickland, by reputation, for twenty years; that in the latter part of 1926 Strickland called at the bank and stated to him that Jackson wanted to rent the premises at 2130 Michigan avenue and he "wanted to know as to his responsibility;" that he told Strickland that he had known Jackson a good many years "and he was perfectly responsible." "Was anything else said in that conversation? A. I asked Mr. Strickland what he was going to occupy it for, he said he didn't know. I said 'I understand, you know Mr. Jackson is going to use it for club purposes.' Q. What did Mr. Strickland say? A. Well, he was more interested in the responsibility of Mr. Jackson. Q. Is that the language you used club purposes? A. I told him he was going to use it for gambling house, he had one up the street. I presumed he was going to use this for the same thing. Mr. Lamborn (attorney for claimants): I move that be stricken. The Court:

Sustained. * * * The Court: Was there anything further said? A. No, only I thought it was my duty to tell Mr. Strickland he wasn't going to use it for any residential purposes. * * * The Court: Was anything else said? A. Not outside of saying he was going to use for club purposes and card games." Upon cross-examination the witness stated that Strickland told him that he came to see him about the financial responsibility of Jackson; that the latter sent him to the witness; that he told Strickland that Jackson was going to use the place for club purposes, "for club purpose, card rooms, gambling house;" that "I told Mr. Strickland at that time as to his responsibility he was perfectly all right, he wasn't going to use for residential purposes, he was going to use it for a club, he was going to have a club up the street and you might as well understand what he was going to use it for, so he couldn't come back and say I misled him;" that he did not telephone Strickland to come to see him; that he imagined Jackson told him "to see me."

Shortly thereafter a lease, prepared by claimants' real estate firm, was signed in Strickland's office. By the terms of the same the Stricklands rented the premises to Jackson for a term commencing January 2, 1927, and terminating June 30, 1931, at a monthly rental of $250, to be used "for residence purposes and for no other purpose whatsoever." The lease provided that the lessors should be given free access at all reasonable hours for purposes of examining or exhibiting the same, and that the lessee would not permit the premises to be used for any unlawful purposes or purposes that would injure the reputation of the same or the building of which they are a part. A rider attached to the lease and made a part of it contains the following provisions:

"Lessor reserves the privilege of terminating this lease at any time by giving to Lessee or leaving with some person on the premises or posting thereon a written notice of their intention so

Sustained. * * * The Court: Was there anything further said? A. No, only I thought it was my duty to tell Mr. Strickland he wasn't going to use it for any residential purposes. * * * The Court: Was anything else said? A. Not outside of saying he was going to use for club purposes and card games." Upon cross-examination the witness stated that Strickland told him that he came to see him about the financial responsibility of Jackson; that the latter sent him to the witness; that he told Strickland that Jackson was going to use the place for club purposes, "for club purposes, card rooms, gambling house;" that "I told Mr. Strickland at that time as to his responsibility he was perfectly all right, he wasn't going to use for residential purposes, he was going to use it for a club, he was going to have a club up the street and you might as well understand what he was going to use it for, so he couldn't come back and say I misled him;" that he did not telephone Strickland to come to see him; that he imagined Jackson told him the see me."

Shortly thereafter a lease, prepared by claimants' real estate firm, was signed in Strickland's office. By the terms of the same the Stricklands rented the premises to Jackson for a term commencing January 2, 1927, and terminating June 30, 1931, at a monthly rental of $250, to be used "for residence purposes and for no other purpose whatsoever." The lease provided that the lessors should be given free access at all reasonable hours for purposes of examining or exhibiting the same, and that the lessee would not permit the premises to be used for any unlawful purposes or purposes that would injure the reputation of the same or the building of which they are a part. A rider attached to the lease and made a part of it contains the following provisions:

"Lessor reserves the privilege of terminating this lease at any time by giving to Lessee or leaving with some person on the premises or posting thereon a written notice of their intention so to do at least sixty (60) days in advance. * * *

"Said lessee further covenants and agrees to make, at his own expense, any and all changes, additions, improvements and or repairs of demised premises he may deem necessary and or may be required by the Board of Insurance Underwriters of Chicago, the municipal authorities of the City of Chicago and or any other lawful authorities because of his occupation of the demised premises or of the kind of business conducted therein." (Italics ours.)

Jackson took possession of the building January 1, 1927, and for four or five months repaired, remodeled and redecorated the same, "got it ready for a gambling house." There was an iron door at the front entrance and a "peep hole" in a second door. There were "steel folding gates" leading to the second floor. About June 1, 1927, he commenced to operate a gambling house in the premises, where faro, roulette, craps and games of chance were played by the public for money. Jackson used the fourth floor as a residence and Bradford occupied a few rooms in the rear of the third floor as his living quarters. At the time that Jackson opened the premises as a gambling house cards were passed around the district upon which was printed a notice that the "3130 Club" was opened at 3130 Michigan avenue. "The best people in Chicago patronized this place. All white, no colored people." The proof is overwhelming that Jackson was well known in the vicinity as a professional gambler and an operator of gambling houses. Numerous gambling houses in the neighborhood were operated by various individuals under the supervision of Jackson. "He was the boss of the underworld in that district - gambling and vice. If anyone wanted to run anything in the district, gambling or anything like that, they had to see Dan Jackson before they could operate." Numerous gambling places were supervised by Jackson and every day he received from each place a check for "a percentage of the gross - some places twenty-five per cent and some places as high as fifty per cent." He was also a "boss" in the politics of the ward. At the time the lease was executed Jackson was running a gambling house, where only colored people were admitted, to do at least sixty (60) days in advance. * * *

"Said lessee further covenants and agrees to make, at his own expense, any and all changes, additions, improvements and or repairs of demised premises he may deem necessary and or may be required by the Board of Insurance Underwriters of Chicago, the municipal authorities of the City of Chicago and or any other lawful authorities because of his occupation of the demised premises or of the kind of business conducted therein." (Italics ours.)

Jackson took possession of the building January 1, 1927, and for four or five months repaired, remodeled and redecorated the same, "got it ready for a gambling house." There was an iron door at the front entrance and a "peep hole" in a second door. There were "steel folding gates" leading to the second floor. About June 1, 1927, he commenced to operate a gambling house in the premises, where faro, roulette, craps and games of chance were played by the public for money. Jackson used the fourth floor as a residence and Bradford occupied a few rooms in the rear of the third floor as his living quarters. At the time that Jackson opened the premises as a gambling house cards were passed around the district upon which was printed a notice that the "3159 Club" was opened at 3159 Michigan avenue. "The best people in Chicago patronized this place. All white, no colored people." The proof is overwhelming that Jackson was well known in the vicinity as a professional gambler and an operator of gambling houses. Numerous gambling houses in the neighborhood were operated by various individuals under the supervision of Jackson. "He was the boss of the underworld in that district - gambling and vice. If anyone wanted to run anything in the district, gambling or anything like that, they had to see Dan Jackson before they could operate." Numerous gambling places were supervised by Jackson and every day he received from such place a check for "a percentage of the gross - some places twenty-five per cent and some places as high as fifty per cent." He was also a "boss" in the politics of the ward. At the time the lease was executed Jackson was running a gambling house, where only colored people were admitted.

at 3445 South Michigan avenue, which he had been operating since 1924. Our former opinion, In re Estate of Jackson, supra, relates to the last mentioned place. From the time that Jackson opened the premises in question they were known to the police and the public as the Allegheny Club. The evidence is undisputed that until his death, in the spring of 1929, he conducted an open and notorious gambling house therein. Gambling started at 8 p. m. "We ran until they got ready to go home, 3:00 o'clock, 4:00 o'clock, 5:00 o'clock," in the morning. In June, 1927, approximately two hundred people gambled in the place daily. When complaints were made that there was gambling going on in the premises the police would visit the same "for the purpose of investigating," and although they would find evidence that the premises were being conducted as a gambling house they would make no arrests nor complaints "because gambling was not going on at the time" that they visited. The following testimony, given by a lieutenant of police, shows how Jackson was protected from any serious trouble with the police. The lieutenant testified that upon visiting the place, after a complaint had been made to the police, he found gambling paraphernalia there and Jackson in possession of the premises; that he knew that Jackson ran gambling houses but as he found no persons gambling at the time of the visit he made no arrests. "Q. What did Jackson say about that place? Did he say anything about it? A. Well, I remember Jackson saying that things would be straightened out in a short while. * * * He wouldn't operate until things were straightened out. Q. Did you ask him if he was running a gambling place there? A. Yes. Q. What did he say? A. Well, he said he closed because things were hot. Q. I didn't understand that? A. That he closed the gambling because things were hot. * * * Q. What did he promise, anything as to the future? A. He said he wouldn't operate until things blow over, may operate again, possibly operate, things to that effect. Q. What did you understand he meant at 3448 South Michigan avenue, which he had been operating since 1924. Our former opinion, *In re Estate of Jackson*, supra, relates to the last mentioned place. From the time that Jackson opened the premises in question they were known to the police and the public as the Allegheny Club. The evidence is undisputed that until his death, in the spring of 1930, he conducted an open and notorious gambling house therein. Gambling started at 8 p. m. "We ran until they got ready to go home, 2:00 o'clock, 4:00 o'clock, 8:00 o'clock, in the morning. In June, 1927, approximately two hundred people gambled in the place daily. When complaints were made that there was gambling going on in the premises the police would visit the same "for the purpose of investigating," and although they would find evidence that the premises were being conducted as a gambling house they would make no arrests nor complaints "because gambling was not going on at the time" that they visited. The following testimony, given by a lieutenant of police, shows how Jackson was protected from any serious trouble with the police. The lieutenant testified that upon visiting the place, after a complaint had been made to the police, he found gambling paraphernalia there and Jackson in possession of the premises; that he knew that Jackson ran gambling houses but as he found no persons gambling at the time of the visit he made no arrests. "Q. What did Jackson say about that place? Did he say anything about it? A. Well, I remember Jackson saying that things would be straightened out in a short while. * * * He wouldn't operate until things were straightened out. Q. Did you ask him if he was running a gambling place there? A. Yes. Q. What did he say? A. Well, he said he closed because things were hot. Q. I didn't understand that? A. That he closed the gambling because things were hot. * * Q. What did he promise, anything as to the future? A. He said he wouldn't operate until things blew over, may operate again, possibly operate, things to that effect. Q. What did you understand he meant by that? A. Well, that's the common words of the gamblers 'things were hot'. Q. How could they play there if Police knew about it? A. Well, they did blow over. It is common knowledge gambling exists at times and sometimes it don't. * * * with the knowledge of the Police." A number of police officers and policemen testified that the police department knew that gambling was being conducted in the place. Bradford testified that the place was "protected;" that the police "weren't supposed to go in there at all." Bradford also testified that in June, 1927, he saw Strickland talking to Henry, the janitor, on the sidewalk, and then both walked into the building. John Hardy testified that in December, 1926, he went with Jackson to 3130 Michigan avenue for the purpose of renting the building; that Jackson had an appointment with Strickland through Bradford; that they there met Strickland; that there were also present at the conversation that followed Carter Hayes and "a fellow" that was working in the place for Strickland; that Jackson said to Strickland, "Well, I guess you know what I want this place for; I guess Brad has explained to you," and Strickland said, "I think I do," and Jackson said, "Yes, I want to run a first class gambling house here, roulette and poker and might be little faro and black jack - run a first class place under the name of the Allegheny Club;" that Strickland then said "He didn't care what he run there as long as he got his rent. * * * Well, he told Mr. Jackson he had heard quite a bit about him and he never had the pleasure of meeting him before and Mr. Jackson smiled and says 'Yes, I guess I am well known out in this District, I have been in it quite a few years.'" The witness further testified that after the place commenced to operate as a gambling house he saw Strickland in the place; that "one afternoon the boy at the door - you see there was an iron gate that closed and he came to the door and said 'Mr. Strickland there,' and Mr. Jackson said 'To show him in', and they came in and shook hands and they went into Mr. Jackson's by that? A. Well, that's the common words of the gamblers 'things were hot'. Q. How could they play there if Police knew about it? A. Well, they did blow over. It is common knowledge gambling exists at times and sometimes it don't. * * * With the knowledge of the Police." A number of police officers and policemen testified that the police department knew that gambling was being conducted in the place. Bradford testified that the place was "protected"; that the police "weren't supposed to go in there at all." Bradford also testified that in June, 1927, he saw Strickland talking to Henry, the janitor, on the sidewalk, and then both walked into the building. John Hardy testified that in December, 1926, he went with Jackson to 2138 Michigan avenue for the purpose of renting the building; that Jackson had an appointment with Strickland through Bradford; that they there met Strickland; that there were also present at the conversation that followed Carter Hayes and "a fellow" that was working in the place for Strickland; that Jackson said to Strickland, "Well, I guess you know what I want this place for; I guess Brad has explained to you," and Strickland said, "I think I do," and Jackson said, "Yes, I want to run a first class gambling house here, roulette and poker and might be little faro and black jack - run a first class place under the name of the Allegheny Club." that Strickland then said he didn't care what he ran there so long as he got his rent. * * * Well, he told Mr. Jackson he had heard quite a bit about him and he never had the pleasure of meeting him before and Mr. Jackson smiled and says 'Yes, I guess I am well known out in this District, I have been in it quite a few years.'" The witness further testified that after the place commenced to operate as a gambling house he saw Strickland in the place; that "one afternoon the boy at the door - you see there was an iron gate that closed and he came to the door and said 'Mr. Strickland there', and Mr. Jackson said 'To show him in', and they came in and shook hands and they went into Mr. Jackson's office. Mr. Frank (counsel for defendant): Where was that office? A. As you come into the door and go up on the first floor as you go in the door and go up a few stairs facing Michigan venue and was a big bay window there in it, and they shook hands and talked and Mr. Jackson said to Mr. Strickland 'Come on I want to show you through the place since I have got it arranged', and they left and they were gone a half hour or so before they came back;" that at the time gambling was going on in the place.

Philip Parker, an employee of Jackson, testified that he saw Strickland in the building several times; that on each occasion he would take him to Jackson's office and that in reaching the office they passed three games, roulette, stud poker and faro, that were then going on. A witness for the estate testified that the rental value of the premises in question for residential purposes at the time of the making of the lease was "about $125 to $150 a month." The evidence for the estate also showed that the neighborhood in question had changed for the worse. In addition to the fact that gambling houses were operated in the neighborhood there were notorious houses of prostitution at 3115, 3324, 3340 and 3440 Michigan avenue.

The sole evidence introduced by claimants in rebuttal of the defense made by the estate was the testimony of Strickland. He testified that he had a conversation with Leibrandt in the latter's private office at the bank in the latter part of November, 1926; that "Mr. Leibrandt stated that he understood my building was for rent. He said he understood the neighborhood had gone down a bit, or it was changing and that I was leaving and I said 'That's right.' He said 'Would you have any objection to renting to colored people'. I said I didn't think I would if they were responsible.' Mr. Leibrandt asked me if I knew Dan Jackson I told him I did not, I told him I had heard of him, that I understood he was a politician,

that I knew he had an Undertaking place at 34th and Michigan Avenue because his sign was out and I passed there almost daily. He stated that he was talking for Mr. Jackson, he said Mr. Jackson might be interested in renting that property as a residence and he might use it as a Gun Club for some of his friends. I told Mr. Leibrandt I was not interested in renting to a club but provided Mr. Jackson was financially responsible I would consider renting to him. Mr. Leibrandt told me that Mr. Jackson was worth Two to Two Hundred Fifty Thousand Dollars, that he was very responsible, his reputation was very good, I would be very lucky if I get him for a tenant. Outside of that there was no further conversation relative to that transaction. Q. Was there anything said by Mr. Leibrandt about using the place as a card club? A. Nothing at all. Q. Or a gambling place? A. Nothing at all. Q. Was there anything said by Mr. Leibrandt about the reputation of Jackson? A. Not at all." The witness further testified that at the time of the conversation with Leibrandt he had never met Jackson; "I didn't know him. * * * didn't know anything about him. I took Mr. Leibrandt as the reference, President of the Bank;" that he never heard that Jackson ran gambling houses; "I had never heard anything about him;" that after he put up the For Rent sign on the building "I talked with this Mr. Bradford at the doorway of my reception room in that building. He wanted to know the building was for rent, I told him 'Yes', and the first thing he asked how much I wanted, I told him $250.00 a month, and he said 'Is the whole building for rent', 'Yes'. He said 'What do you want to rent it for', 'Well', I said, 'I want to see what do you want to use it for', he says, 'Well, I have got a party in mind that might be interested'. He says 'Can I go through the property', I said 'No, I am running my business here and I don't want to be disturbed showing the property now but if you come back later on I will show it to you'. As I recall that I knew he had an Undertaking Place at 36th and Michigan Avenue because his sign was out and I passed there almost daily. He stated that he was talking for Mr. Jackson, he said Mr. Jackson might be interested in renting that property as a residence and he might use it as a Gun Club for some of his friends. I told Mr. Leibrandt I was not interested in renting to a club but provided Mr. Jackson was financially responsible I would consider renting to him. Mr. Leibrandt told me that Mr. Jackson was worth Two to Two Hundred Fifty Thousand Dollars, that he was very responsible, his reputation was very good, I would be very lucky if I got him for a tenant. Outside of that there was no further conversation relative to that transaction. Q. Was there anything said by Mr. Leibrandt about using the place as a card club? A. Nothing at all. Q. Or a gambling place? A. Nothing at all. Q. Was there anything said by Mr. Leibrandt about the reputation of Jackson? A. Not at all." The witness further testified that at the time of the conversation with Leibrandt he had never met Jackson; "I didn't know him. * * * didn't know anything about him. I took Mr. Leibrandt as the reference, President of the Bank;" that he never heard that Jackson ran gambling houses; "I had never heard anything about him;" that after he put up the For Rent sign on the building "I talked with this Mr. Bradford at the doorway of my reception room in that building. He wanted to know the building was for rent, I told him 'Yes', and the first thing he asked how much I wanted, I told him $300.00 a month, and he said 'Is the whole building for rent', 'Yes'. He said 'What do you want to rent it for', 'Well', I said, 'I want to see what do you want to use it for', he says, 'Well, I have got a party in mind that might be interested', he says 'Can I go through the property', I said 'No, I am running my business here and I don't want to be disturbed showing the property now but if you come back later on I will show it to you'. As I recall he came back about five o'clock or after my place was closed that evening, a little after five o'clock, he had already told me that he wasn't going to rent it. I had my housekeeper show him through the main floor, the first floor, and I told him that the rest of the building was as he could see from that floor, and that was as far as he went. That was my dealing with Bradford." The witness further testified that he saw Bradford later "with a man named Lewis who I understood was Dan Jackson's Secretary, a man I had dealings with * * * within ten days afterwards;" that at no time did Bradford tell him that the premises were to be used for gambling; that he did say they were to be used as a club; that Bradford never came to his place with Hardy, Hayes and Lewis; that he had no recollection of ever seeing Hardy or Hayes; that he had no knowledge that Jackson was going to use the place for gambling purposes; that after Jackson took possession on January 1, 1927, he never entered the building until after Jackson's death, nor did he even "go to the building." Upon cross-examination Strickland testified that when he met Jackson in reference to a lease he did not ask him for references, nor did he ever ask him for references; that he considered the reference of Leibrandt sufficient; that while he knew John B. Mallers, Jr., well, he did not deem it necessary to inquire of him as to Jackson; that the lease was prepared by the witness' real estate firm; that he knew from hearsay that Jackson was a politician and an undertaker; that the witness had occupied 3139 Michigan avenue from July 1, 1911, until Jackson took possession; that he knew some of his neighbors "all the way down to 35th street;" that he knew that Jackson had an undertaking establishment at 34th street and Michigan avenue; that when he first moved into the premises he was told that Dan Jackson was the alderman of the ward. During the evidence for the claimants, in chief, Strickland testified that after he left 3139 Michigan avenue he opened a place at 675 North Michigan avenue; that after the death of Jackson he went to 3139 in May, 1930;

he came back about five o'clock or after my place was closed that evening, a little after five o'clock, he had already told me that he wasn't going to rent it. I had my housekeeper show him through the main floor, the first floor, and I told him that the rest of the building was as he could see from that floor, and that was as far as he went. That was my dealing with Bradford." The witness further testified that he saw Bradford later "with a man named Lewis who I understood was Dan Jackson's secretary, a man I had dealings with * * * within ten days afterwards"; that at no time did Bradford tell him that the premises were to be used for gambling; that he did say they were to be used as a club; that Bradford never came to his place with Hardy, Hayes and Lewis; that he had no recollection of ever seeing Hardy or Hayes; that he had no knowledge that Jackson was going to use the place for gambling purposes; that after Jackson took possession on January 1, 1927, he never entered the building until after Jackson's death; nor did he even "go to the building." Upon cross-examination Strickland testified that when he met Jackson in reference to a lease he did not ask him for references, nor did he ever ask him for references; that he considered the reference of Leibrandt sufficient; that while he knew John R. Walters, Jr., well, he did not deem it necessary to inquire of him as to Jackson; that the lease was prepared by the witness' real estate firm; that he knew from hearsay that Jackson was a politician and an undertaker; that the witness had occupied 3159 Michigan avenue from July 1, 1911, until Jackson took possession; that he knew some of his neighbors "all the way down to 35th street"; that he knew that Jackson had an undertaking establishment at 35th street and Michigan avenue; that when he first moved into the premises he was told that Dan Jackson was the alderman of the ward. During the evidence for the claimants, in chief, Strickland testified that after he left 3159 Michigan avenue he opened a place at 478 North Michigan avenue; that after the death of Jackson he went to 3159 in May, 1930;

that after the lease was executed he did not question Jackson as to whether the latter would make repairs and alterations in the building and that he never went back to see what repairs and alterations had been made; that at the time Jackson came to his office to close the deal the former stated that he would probably use the rooms on the first floor for a gun club, the Allegheny Gun Club, and that he was going to live in the witness' apartment upstairs; that he did not say what he was going to use the second floor for, and that the provision in the lease that the premises were to be used for residential purposes was inserted because Jackson said that he was going to live in the premises; that Jackson said it would be a shooting club; that "there was a crowd of sportsmen went hunting and that sort of thing and that would be their club house."

There are certain mountain peaks in the evidence that tend very strongly to support the defendant's theory of fact. By the rider attached to the lease Jackson was given the right "to make, at his own expense, any and all changes, additions, improvements and or repairs of demised premises he may deem necessary * * *," and for four or five months he repaired, remodeled and redecorated the building, "got it ready for a gambling house," and still, by another provision in the rider, the Stricklands had the right to terminate the lease at any time by giving to Jackson a written notice of their intention so to do sixty days in advance. The claimants did not call the real estate man who prepared the lease for Strickland. Strickland testified that from the time that Jackson took possession on January 1, 1927, he (Strickland) never entered the premises until after Jackson's death, nor did he even "go to the building;" that he never went back to the place to see what repairs and alterations had been made, and although he talked with Jackson over the telephone several times he never questioned him as to the repairs and alterations that had been made. It also appears that Jackson kept as his janitor an that after the lease was executed he did not question Jackson as to whether the latter would make repairs and alterations in the building, and that he never went back to see what repairs and alterations had been made; that at the time Jackson came to his office to close the deal the former stated that he would probably use the rooms on the first floor for a gun club, the [illegible] Gun Club, and that he was going to live in the witness' apartment upstairs; that he did not say what he was going to use the second floor for, and that the provision in the lease that the premises were to be used for residential purposes was inserted because Jackson said that he was going to live in the premises; that Jackson said it would be a shooting club; that "there was a crowd of sportsmen went hunting and that sort of thing, and that would be their club house."

There are certain uncertain points in the evidence that tend strongly to support the defendant's theory of fact. By the rider attached to the lease Jackson was given the right "to make at his own expense, any and all changes, additions, improvements and/or repairs of and to said premises as he may deem necessary * * *," and for three or four months he repaired, remodeled and redecorated the building, but it wasn't for a gambling house," and still, by another provision in the rider, the plaintiffs had the right to terminate the lease at any time by giving to Jackson a written notice of their intention so to do sixty days in advance. The claimants did not call the real estate man who procured the lease for plaintiffs. Strickland testified that from the time that Jackson took possession on January 1, 1927, he (Strickland) never entered the premises until after Jackson's death, nor did he even "go to the building;" that he never went back to the place to see what repairs and alterations had been made, and although he talked with Jackson over the telephone several times he never questioned him as to the repairs and alterations that old employee of the Stricklands. When Jackson died the payment of rent ceased, and then, for the first time, Strickland, according to his testimony, visited the place. Strickland admits that Jackson told him that "he would probably use the rooms on the first floor for a gun club. * * * There was a crowd of sportsmen went hunting and that sort of thing and that would be their clubhouse." Yet, in the lease he provided that the premises were to be used "for residence purposes and for no other purpose whatsoever." It is conceded that the character of the neighborhood had been changing for a number of years, and the undisputed evidence shows that gambling houses and notorious houses of prostitution were being operated in the vicinity. A lieutenant of police testifie that "it was known all throughout the community that from 31st to 35th Street on Michigan, houses of ill fame and gambling houses were being operated." Strickland testified that he did not ask Jackson for any references and that he made no inquiries concerning him of anyone save Leibrandt. From Strickland's evidence in reference to his conversation with Leibrandt it would seem that he was interested solely in the financial responsibility of Jackson. Had he made the slightest inquiry in the neighborhood as to the reputation and business of Jackson he would have learned the facts in connection with the same. It would be contrary to human experience and common knowledge to hold that the events that we have cited could have happened without the knowledge of the Stricklands. We have made a somewhat lengthy statement as to the character of the place in question, the happenings there, the general reputation of Jackson and the nature of the businesses in which he was engaged, because such evidence bears upon the question as to the good faith of the claimants when they made the lease and their knowledge of the use made of the premises by Jackson.

After a careful consideration of all of the facts and circumstances we have reached the conclusion that the premises [illegible] the [illegible] him that "he would prob[illegible] [illegible] lease he [illegible] [illegible] land's [illegible] could seem [illegible] and common [illegible] the nature of the business [illegible]

premises by Jackson.

After a careful consideration of all of the facts and circumstances we have reached the conclusion that the premises were rented by the Stricklands for gambling purposes and that they knew during the entire period that the lesser occupied the premises that they were being used for gambling purposes. Under such a state of facts the claimants cannot recover under the lease.

The judgment of the Circuit court of Cook county is reversed.

JUDGMENT REVERSED.

Friend, P. J., and Sullivan, J., concur.

premises that they were being used for gambling purposes. O

such a state of facts the claimants cannot recover under the

statute.

The judgment of the circuit court of Cook county i

reversed.

JUDGMENT REVERSED.

Hebel, P. J., and Sullivan, J., concur.

554

37694

HERMAN H. GOODFRIEND, Plaintiff in Error, v. GUSTAV POLLOCK, Defendant in Error.	)	ERROR TO MUNICIPAL COURT OF CHICAGO.

260 I.A. 623[2]

MR. JUSTICE SCANLAN DELIVERED THE OPINION OF THE COURT.

Plaintiff brought an action against defendant in the Municipal court of Chicago to recover $600 alleged to be due under a contract of guaranty. The cause was tried by the court, there was a finding against plaintiff, and he has sued out this writ of error from a judgment entered upon the finding.

Plaintiff's statement of claim alleges that on March 24, 1932, there was in full force and effect a lease dated March 14, 1930, entered into between him, as lessor, and Mark H. Tauber and M. S. Mittelman, as lessees, devising certain premises located at 3513 Lawrence avenue, Chicago, for a term commencing April 1, 1930, and ending April 30, 1933; that the lease provided for the payment of rent for the period commencing May 1, 1932, to the end of the term, at the rate of $250 per month, but that he had been accepting from the lessees the sum of $200 each month; that on March 24, 1932, the lessees were in default in the payment of rent for the month of March, 1932; that plaintiff advised the lessees that unless said rent was paid in full he would take steps to dispossess them from the premises and would also institute proceedings to enforce collection of the rent; that thereupon the lessees proposed to plaintiff that if he would waive the payment of the sum of $200, the amount which they were in arrears for the

37694

HERMAN H. GOODFRIEND,
Plaintiff in Error,

v.

GUSTAV POLLOCK,
Defendant in Error.

ERROR TO MUNICIPAL
COURT OF CHICAGO.

260 I.A. 623

MR. JUSTICE SCANLAN DELIVERED THE OPINION OF THE COURT.

Plaintiff brought an action against defendant in the municipal court of Chicago to recover $600 alleged to be due under a contract of guaranty. The cause was tried by the court, there was a finding against plaintiff, and he has sued out this writ of error from a judgment entered upon the finding.

Plaintiff's statement of claim alleges that on March 24, 1932, there was in full force and effect a lease dated March 14, 1930, entered into between him, as lessor, and Mark H. Tauber and M. S. Mittelman, as lessees, devising certain premises located at 3513 Lawrence avenue, Chicago, for a term commencing April 1, 1930, and ending April 30, 1933; that the lease provided for the payment of rent for the period commencing May 1, 1932, to the end of the term, at the rate of $280 per month, but that he had been accepting from the lessees the sum of $200 each month; that on March 24, 1932, the lessees were in default in the payment of rent for the month of March, 1932; that plaintiff advised the lessees that unless said rent was paid in full he would take steps to dispossess them from the premises and would also institute proceedings to enforce collection of the rent; that thereupon the lessees proposed to plaintiff that if he would waive the payment of the sum of $200, the amount which they were in arrears for the month of March, 1932, and would forbear instituting proceedings to dispossess them, they would procure for the benefit of plaintiff a guaranty in writing signed by defendant, Gustav Pollock, guaranteeing the prompt payment of the rent reserved in the lease for three months during the balance of the term, which proposal was accepted by plaintiff, and thereupon defendant executed and delivered his xxxxxx guaranty in writing to plaintiff, in words and figures as follows:

"GUARANTEE

"For value received the undersigned hereby guarantees the payment of three months' rent and performance of the covenants by Lessee, his heirs, executors, administrators or assigns in the within Lease contained in manner and form as in said lease provided.

"Witness the hand and seal of the undersigned Guarantor this 24 day of March, A. D. 19

"Gustav Pollock (Seal)"

Plaintiff further alleges that in consideration of the delivery to him of said guaranty he waived the payment of the arrears in rent, forebore from instituting legal proceedings for the collection of said sum, and forbore from instituting proceedings to dispossess the lessees from the premises; that thereafter the lessees became and were, and still are in arrears in the payment of their rent for the premises, as follows:

"September 1932, balance due on rent . .	$114.45
October, November, December 1932 and January, 1933 - 4 months @ $200.00 per month	800.00
Total arrearage in said rent	$914.45

which amount said lessees have failed, refused and neglected to pay to plaintiff." Plaintiff further alleges that since the said default in the payment of rent defendant has been notified of the default and payment has been demanded of him to the extent of $600, in accordance with the terms of the written guaranty, but that defendant has refused to pay that sum or any part thereof, to the damage of plaintiff in the sum of $600. Defendant, in his affidavit of merits, admits the execution of the contract of guaranty as alleged, month of March, 1932, and would forbear instituting proceedings to dispossess them, they would procure for the benefit of plaintiff a guaranty in writing signed by defendant, Gustav Pollock, guaranteeing the prompt payment of the rent reserved in the lease for three months during the balance of the term, which proposal was accepted by plaintiff, and thereupon defendant executed and delivered his written guaranty in writing to plaintiff, in words and figures as follows:

"GUARANTEE"

"For value received the undersigned hereby guarantees the payment of three months' rent and performance of the covenants by Lessee, his heirs, executors, administrators or assigns in the within Lease contained in manner and form as in said lease provided.

"Witness the hand and seal of the undersigned Guarantor this 24 day of March, A. D. 19

"Gustav Pollock (Seal)"

Plaintiff further alleges that in consideration of the delivery to him of said guaranty he waived the payment of the arrears in rent, forebore from instituting legal proceedings for the collection of said sum, and forbore from instituting proceedings to dispossess the lessees from the premises; that thereafter the lessees became and were, and still are in arrears in the payment of their rent for the premises as follows:

"September 1932, balance due on rent . .	$114.48
October, November, December 1932 and January, 1933 - 4 months @ $200.00 per month	800.00
Total arrearages in said rent	$914.48

which amount said lessees have failed, refused and neglected to pay to plaintiff." Plaintiff further alleges that since the said default in the payment of rent defendant has been notified of the default and payment has been demanded of him to the extent of $600, in accordance with the terms of the written guaranty, but that defendant has refused to pay that sum or any part thereof, to the damage of plaintiff in the sum of $600. Defendant, in his affidavit of merits, denies the execution of the contract of guaranty as alleged.

but avers that the guaranty was to be valid for a period of three months after the signing thereof, that none of the rents sought to be recovered from him accrued within such three months, and that therefore he is not indebted to plaintiff in any sum whatever.

Upon the trial defendant contended that there was an oral agreement made at the time the guaranty was executed which limited the liability of defendant for the payment of rent to the next three months after the date of the guaranty, and that as the rent for that period had been paid by the lessees he owed plaintiff nothing. Plaintiff contended that the written guaranty was clear and unambiguous and was a guaranty by defendant of three months' rent, or $600, of the $2,600 rent to accrue under the lease, and that to admit oral evidence to the effect that defendant agreed to guarantee only the rent for the first three months would violate the rule which prohibits the introduction of parol evidence to contradict or vary the terms of a written contract, and that plaintiff was entitled to a judgment upon the face of the pleadings. The trial court held that defendant might put in testimony "to show what three months" were intended, and over the objections of plaintiff defendant was allowed to introduce evidence to the effect that defendant told plaintiff that he would guarantee the rent for the next three months and that plaintiff said, "Sign on the dotted line," and that thereupon he signed the guaranty.

The form of guaranty used is the standard printed form found on the backs of leases. As printed it reads: "For value received the undersigned hereby guarantees the payment of rent and the performance of the covenants by lessee * * * in the within lease * * *." The words "three months" in the guaranty were written in by the defendant before he signed the instrument. He was a brother-in-law of Tauber, one of the lessees. Had the guaranty as printed upon the back of the lease been signed without change there could be no question but that it would have been continuing in time, and have applied to but avers that the guaranty was to be valid for a period of three months after the signing thereof, that none of the rents sought to be recovered from him accrued within such three months, and that therefore he is not indebted to plaintiff in any sum whatever.

Upon the trial defendant contended that there was an oral agreement made at the time the guaranty was executed which limited the liability of defendant for the payment of rent to the next three months after the date of the guaranty, and that as the rent for that period had been paid by the lessees he owed plaintiff nothing. Plaintiff contended that the written guaranty was clear and unambiguous and was a guaranty by defendant of three months' rent, or $600, of the $2,600 rent to accrue under the lease, and that to admit oral evidence to the effect that defendant agreed to guarantee only the rent for the first three months would violate the rule which prohibits the introduction of parol evidence to contradict or vary the terms of a written contract, and that plaintiff was entitled to a judgment upon the face of the pleadings. The trial court held that defendant might put in testimony "to show what three months" were intended, but over the objections of plaintiff defendant was allowed to introduce evidence to the effect that defendant told plaintiff that he would guarantee the rent for the next three months and that plaintiff said, "sign on the dotted line," and that thereupon he signed the guaranty.

The form of guaranty used is the standard printed form found on the backs of leases. As printed it reads: "For value received the undersigned hereby guarantees the payment of rent and the performance of the covenants by lessee * * * in the within lease * * *." The words "three months" in the guaranty were written in by the defendant before he signed the instrument. He was a brother-in-law of Tauber, one of the lessees. Had the guaranty as printed upon the back of the lease been signed without change there could be no question but that it would have been continuing in time, and have applied to all rent that would accrue under the lease after the date of signing. The result of the change made by defendant merely limited his liability to three months' rent of the thirteen months' rent remaining to accrue. Defendant, in his modification of the printed form, did not limit his liability in point of time as he did in the matter of amount. Not having limited the time of liability it remained a continuing liability for the period of thirteen months as a matter of law. In Frost v. Standard Metal Co., 116 Ill. App. 642, the guaranty was:

"Chicago, July 19, 1901.

"Standard Metal Co.
"Gentlemen: I hereby guarantee the purchase account of George K. Harrington & Co. for fifteen hundred dollars ($1,500).
"R. Chester Frost,
167 Wabash Ave."

Upon the strength of this guaranty the plaintiff sold goods to Harrington & Co. until February, 1902, when that company was put into voluntary bankruptcy. During the period in question the aggregate purchases of Harrington & Co. from appellee were $9,789.27, and the aggregate payments thereon were $7,168.76, leaving due and unpaid upon the account at the time of the bringing of the suit, $2,620.51. The court held that as the guaranty contained no limitation as to time it indicated that it contemplated a succession of credits for the ultimate liquidation of which appellant would be liable to an amount not exceeding $1,500. In support of its conclusion the court said:

"In Tootle v. Elgutter, 14 Neb. 158, the words of the guaranty were: 'Please let Mr. John Newman have credit for goods to the amount of $100, and for the payment of which I hold myself responsible.' The court say: 'In our opinion, the guaranty in this case was a continuing one, and the limitation therein was as to the extent of the defendant's liability, and not as to the credit to be given to Newman.'

"In Rindge v. Judson, 24 N. Y. 64, a contract to be 'accountable to you that Mr. Butler will pay you for a credit on glass, paints, etc., which he may require in his business, to the extent of $50,' is a continuing guaranty, the court saying: 'Had the guarantor desired or intended to limit his responsibility to a single transaction, or to several transactions not exceeding all rent that would accrue under the lease after the date of signing. The result of the change made by defendant merely limited his liability to three months' rent of the thirteen months' rent remaining to accrue. Defendant, in his modification of the printed form, did not limit his liability in point of time as he did in the matter of amount. Not having limited the time of liability it remained a continuing liability for the period of thirteen months as a matter of law. In Freek v. Standard Metal Co., 116 Ill. App. 642, the guaranty was:

"Chicago, July 19, 1901.

"Standard Metal Co.
"Gentlemen: I hereby guarantee the purchase account of George K. Harrington & Co. for fifteen hundred dollars ($1,500).
"R. Chester Trost,
167 Wabash Ave."

Upon the strength of this guaranty the plaintiff sold goods to Harrington & Co. until February, 1902, when that company was put into voluntary bankruptcy. During the period in question the aggregate purchases of Harrington & Co. from appellee were $9,789.87, and the aggregate payments thereon were $7,168.76, leaving due and unpaid upon the account at the time of the bringing of the suit, $2,620.51. The court held that as the guaranty contained no limitation as to time it indicated that it contemplated a succession of credits for the ultimate liquidation of which appellant would be liable to an amount not exceeding $1,500. In support of its conclusion the court said:

"In Foote v. Figuster, 14 Neb. 188, the words of the guaranty were: 'Please let Mr. John Newman have credit for goods to the amount of $100, and for the payment of which I hold myself responsible.' The court say: 'In our opinion, the guaranty in this case was a continuing one, and the limitation therein was as to the extent of the defendant's liability, and not as to the credit to be given to Newman.'

"In Hindge v. Judson, 24 N. Y. 64, a contract to be 'accountable to you that Mr. Butler will pay you for a credit on glass, paints, etc., which he may require in his business, to the extent of $50,' is a continuing guaranty, the court saying: 'Had the guarantor desired or intended to limit his responsibility to a single transaction, or to several transactions not exceeding that sum in all, it was so easy to have said it in plain and unmistakable terms, that if he failed to do so, and by equivocal language induced the guarantee to part with his goods, he should abide the consequences.'

"Unless the words in which the guaranty is expressed fairly imply that the liability of the guarantor is to be limited, the guaranty will be regarded as continuing until revoked. Wright v. Griffith, 121 Ind. 478.

"An instrument reading: 'The bearer is going to start a peddling route to sell cigars and tobacco. He wishes to buy goods of your firm. We, the undersigned, will be his security to the amount of $1,000,' held to be a continuing guaranty. Sickle v. Marsh, 44 How. Pr. 91."

(See also Taussig v. Reid, 145 Ill. 488; Malleable Iron Range Co. v. Pusey, 244 Ill. 184.) Defendant does not attempt to answer those cases, cited by plaintiff, but assumes that the guaranty is ambiguous and cites cases in support of the well known principle of law that where the terms used by the parties to a contract are ambiguous in meaning, parol evidence is admissible to show the true intent and undertaking of the parties. But in the instant case the guaranty is not ambiguous, and the settled rule governing such an instrument is that its legal effect will be enforced as written. In Taussig v. Reid, supra, the court said (p. 497):

"It can not be said that the cases are entirely harmonious as to the principles which govern in the construction of this class of instruments. But the weight of authority seems to be in favor of construing them by rules at least as favorable to the creditor as those applied to other written contracts, notwithstanding the guarantor is, in a sense, to be regarded as a surety. In Mason v. Prichard, supra, it is held, that the words are to be taken as strongly against the party giving the guaranty as the sense of them will admit. The same general principle is held, more or less directly, in Drummond v. Prestmond, 12 Wheat. 515; Douglass v. Reynolds, supra; Lawrence v. McCalmont, 2 How. 426; Bell v. Bruin, 1 How. 69; Dobbins v. Bradley, 17 Wend. 422; Mayer v. Isaacs, 6 Mees. & Welsb. 605."

To the same effect are Frost v. Standard Metal Co., supra; Swisher v. Deering, 204 Ill. 203, 205; The Heberling Medicine & Extract Co. v. Smith, 201 Ill. App. 126, 131, Castle v. Powell, 261 Ill. App. 132, 141; Mahler Textiles, Inc. v. Woodka, 281 Ill. App. 177, 181. That the contract of guaranty was changed by the action of the court in allowing the parol evidence and in giving a finding and judgment based on such evidence is obvious.

that sum in all, it was so easy to have said it in plain and unmistakable terms, that if he failed to do so, and by equivocal language induced the guarantee to part with his goods, he should abide the consequences.'

"Unless the words in which the guaranty is expressed fairly imply that the liability of the guarantor is to be limited, the guaranty will be regarded as continuing until revoked. Wright v. Griffith, 121 Ind. 478.

"An instrument reading: 'The bearer is going to start a peddling route to sell cigars and tobacco. He wishes to buy goods of your firm. We, the undersigned, will be his security to the amount of $1,000,' held to be a continuing guaranty. Gleske v. Marsh, 44 Nebr. 77. 21.4."

(See also Taussig v. Reid, 145 Ill. 488; Malleable Iron Range Co. v. Pusey, 244 Ill. 184.) Defendant does not attempt to answer these cases, cited by plaintiff, but assumes that the guaranty is ambiguous and cites cases in support of the well known principle of law that where the terms used by the parties to a contract are ambiguous in meaning, parol evidence is admissible to show the true intent and understanding of the parties. But in the instant case the guaranty is not ambiguous, and the settled rule governing such an instrument is that its legal effect will be enforced as written.

In Taussig v. Reid, supra, the court said (p. 497):

"It can not be said that the cases are entirely harmonious as to the principles which govern in the construction of this class of instruments. But the weight of authority seems to be in favor of construing them by rules at least as favorable to the creditor as those applied to other written contracts, notwithstanding the guarantor is, in a sense, to be regarded as a surety. In Mason v. Pritchard, supra, it is held, that the words are to be taken as strongly against the party giving the guaranty as the sense of them will admit. The same general principle is held, more or less directly, in Drummond v. Prestmond, 12 Wheat. 515; Douglass v. Reynolds, supra; Lawrence v. McCalmont, 2 How. 426; Bell v. Bruen, 1 How. 69; Dobbins v. Bradley, 17 Wend. 422; Mayer v. Isaacs, 6 Mees. & Welsb. 605."

To the same effect are Frost v. Standard Metal Co., supra; Wisner v. Deering, 204 Ill. 263, 283; The Heberling Medicine & Extract Co. v. Smith, 201 Ill. App. 126, 131; Castle v. Powell, 241 Ill. App. 132, 141; Kohler Textiles, Inc. v. Gordon, 281 Ill. App. 177, 181. That the contract of guaranty was changed by the action of the court in allowing the parol evidence and in giving a finding and judgment based on such evidence is obvious.

After the court had permitted the defendant to introduce the oral testimony plaintiff also introduced oral testimony in rebuttal of the same, and he strenuously contends that upon a consideration of all of the oral testimony it will be found that the finding of the court as to the alleged oral understanding was against the manifest weight of the evidence. While there is force in this contention we do not deem it necessary to pass upon the same. If we are correct in holding that the court erred in admitting the oral testimony, it is clear that plaintiff was entitled to judgment.

The judgment of the Municipal court of Chicago is reversed and judgment will be entered here in favor of the plaintiff and against the defendant in the sum of $600.

JUDGMENT REVERSED AND JUDGMENT HERE IN FAVOR OF PLAINTIFF AND AGAINST DEFENDANT IN THE SUM OF $600.

Friend, P. J., and Sullivan, J., concur.

-3-

After the court had permitted the defendant to introduce the oral testimony plaintiff [illegible] introduced [illegible] in rebuttal of the [illegible], and he erroneously contends that upon a consideration of all of the oral testimony it will be seen that the finding of the court as to the alleged oral understanding was against the manifest weight of the evidence. While there is force in this contention we do not deem it necessary to pass upon the point. If we are correct in holding that the court erred in admitting the oral testimony, it is clear that plaintiff was entitled to judgment.

The judgment of the Municipal court of Chicago is reversed and judgment will be entered here in favor of the plaintiff and against the defendant in the sum of $600.

JUDGMENT REVERSED AND JUDGMENT HERE
IN [illegible]
[illegible] IN THE SUM OF $600.

Friend, P. J., and Sullivan, J., concur.

36 A

37699

J. A. KFLPSCH,
Defendant in Error,

v.

MARY NOREIKO,
Plaintiff in Error.

ERROR TO MUNICIPAL COURT OF CHICAGO.

280 I.A. 623[3]

MR. JUSTICE SCANLAN DELIVERED THE OPINION OF THE COURT.

Plaintiff sued Joseph Noreiko and Mary Noreiko upon a promissory note signed by them, dated June 25, 1931, for the sum of $2,000, payable to the order of plaintiff one year after date with interest at six per cent per annum. Mary Noreiko sues out this writ of error to reverse a judgment against her in the sum of $2,167.50.

Defendants' amended affidavit of merits states that about June 25, 1929, they were indebted to plaintiff in the sum of $3,000, and that they then gave to plaintiff their note for said sum, due and payable one year after the date thereof; that about September 1, 1929, plaintiff occupied certain premises belonging to defendants, known as 2085 Lunt avenue, Chicago, consisting of a building and a garage; that at that time it was agreed between plaintiff and defendants that plaintiff was to pay to defendants a fair and reasonable rental for the use and occupation of the premises, but that no definite rental was fixed therefor; that it was further agreed that the fixing of the amount of the rent and the payment of it should be considered at the time the said note became due; that plaintiff used and occupied the premises from about September 1, 1929, to about September 1, 1931; that about June 25, 1930, defendants paid to plaintiff on account

37699

J. A. Kerl [illegible],
Defendant in Error,

v.

[illegible],
Plaintiff in Error.

Error to Municipal Court of Chicago.

280 I.A. 632

Plaintiff sued Joseph Koretko and Mary Koretko upon a promissory note signed by them, dated June 25, 1929, for the sum of $2,000, payable to the order of plaintiff one year after date with interest at six per cent per annum. Mary Koretko sues out this writ of error to reverse a judgment against her in the sum of $2,167.50.

Defendants' amended affidavit of merits states that about June 25, 1929, they were indebted to plaintiff in the sum of $3,000, and that they then gave to plaintiff their note for said sum, due and payable one year after the date thereof; that about September 1, 1929, plaintiff occupied certain premises belonging to defendants, known as 2008 [illegible] avenue, Chicago, consisting of a building and a garage; that at the time it was agreed between plaintiff and defendants that plaintiff [illegible] to pay to defendants [illegible] occupation of the premises [illegible] therefore; that it was mutually agreed that [illegible] amount of the rent and the payment of it should be considered [illegible] at time the said note became due; that plaintiff used and occupied the premises from about September 1, 1929, to about September 1, 1931; that about June 25, 1930, defendants paid to plaintiff on account of the said note the sum of $1,000, and they then executed and delivered to plaintiff another note of the said date for the sum of $2,000, due one year thereafter; that it was then "agreed that the rental question of the premises * * * and the amount due as rent thereon should be held in abeyance until the final settlement of the note then executed;" that the customary and reasonable rental of the premises during the period from September 1, 1929, to September 1, 1931, was $90 a month, and that there is now due the sum of $2,160 as the reasonable and usual rental of the said premises, and "that there is nothing due to the plaintiff from defendants on the note sued upon." Defendants also filed an amended "statement and affidavit of claim on set-off," which sets up practically the same facts as are set up in the amended affidavit of merits. The original affidavit of merits and the original statement of claim on set-off had been stricken from the files for insufficiency upon motion of plaintiff. Defendants' original pleadings set up the same defense as was raised in their amended pleadings.

On November 17, 1932, plaintiff suggested to the court the death of defendant Joseph Noreiko, and an order was entered that the "cause proceed in the name of Mary Noreiko, the surviving defendant herein." Plaintiff then moved to strike defendants' amended statement and affidavit of claim on set-off from the files, and the trial court, after a hearing of the motion, entered an order striking the said pleadings from the files. Thereupon defendant Mary Noreiko moved for leave to file an individual second amended affidavit of merits, which motion was denied. An order of default was then entered against her for want of an affidavit of merits and judgment was entered in favor of plaintiff and against her for the sum of $2,167.50 and costs. She sues out this writ of error.

Defendant contends (a) "The Court erred in striking defendants' amended affidavit of merits from the files," and (b) of the said note the sum of $1,000, and they then executed and delivered to Plaintiff another note of the said date for the sum of $2,000, due one year thereafter; that it was then "agreed that the rental question of the premises * * * and the amount due as rent thereon should be held in abeyance until the final settlement of the note then executed"; that the customary and reasonable rental of the premises during the period from September 1, 1929, to September 1, 1931, was $90 a month, and that there is now due the sum of $2,160 as the reasonable and usual rental of the said premises, and "that there is nothing due to the plaintiff from defendants on the note sued upon." Defendants also filed an amended "statement and affidavit of claim on set-off," which sets up practically the same facts as are set up in the amended affidavit of merits. The original affidavit of merits and the original statement of claim on set-off had been stricken from the files for insufficiency upon motion of plaintiff. Defendants' original pleadings set up the same defense as was raised in their amended pleadings.

On November 17, 1932, plaintiff suggested to the court the death of defendant Joseph Moretko, and an order was entered that the "cause proceed in the name of Mary Moretko, the surviving defendant herein." Plaintiff then moved to strike defendants' amended statement and affidavit of claim on set-off from the files, and the trial court, after a hearing of the motion, entered an order striking the said pleadings from the files. Thereupon defendant Mary Moretko moved for leave to file an individual second amended affidavit of merits, which motion was denied. An order of default was then entered against her for want of an affidavit of merits and judgment was entered in favor of plaintiff and against her for the sum of $2,147.50 and costs. She sues out this writ of error.

Defendant contends (a) "The Court erred in striking defendants' amended affidavit of merits from the files," and (b)

"The Court erred in striking the defendants' amended statement of claim from the files." The affidavit of merits required to be filed in the Municipal court of Chicago must set up sufficient facts which, if true, would constitute a good defense to the plaintiff's action. Defendants' amended affidavit of merits, as defendant admits, sets up the same facts as are set up in the amended statement and affidavit of claim on set-off. If the trial court ruled correctly upon the motion to strike the amended statement and affidavit of claim on set-off, it follows that defendants' amended affidavit of merits is insufficient. In Duncan Lumber Co. v. Leonard Lumber Co., 332 Ill. 104, the court said (pp. 106-7):

> "Our statute (Cahill's Stat. 1927, chap. 110, sec. 47 p. 1948,) authorizes a defendant 'having claims or demands against the plaintiff in such action,' to plead the same, etc. That statute has been construed in numerous cases by this court to not authorize unliquidated damages arising out of a contract, not connected with the subject matter of the plaintiff's suit, to be set off against the plaintiff's claim. (Hawks v. Lands, 3 Gilm. 227; Sargeant v. Kellogg, 5 id. 273; DeForrest v. Oder, 42 Ill. 500; Robison v. Hibbs, 48 id. 408; Clark v. Dutton, 69 id. 521; Clause v. Bulleck Printing Press Co., 118 id. 612; Higbie v. Rust, 211 id. 333.)"

A defendant may not set off claims for unliquidated damages growing out of transactions not connected with the transaction sued on. (Duncan Lumber Co. v. Leonard Lumber Co., supra.) In Citizens Trust & Savings Bank v. Blair, 259 Ill. App. 294, the court said (pp. 299-300):

> "In the case of Duncan Lumber Co. v. Leonard Lumber Co., 332 Ill. 104, the court goes still further in holding that section 47 of the Practice Act, Cahill's St. ch. 110, par. 47, does not authorize unliquidated damages arising out of a contract not connected with the subject matter of the plaintiff's suit, notwithstanding the nonresidence of the plaintiff; and in Benedict v. Bear, 252 Ill. App. 439, this court in a recent decision adopts a like construction of the Practice Act. In the absence of any special equitable ground, such as the insolvency of the complainant, we are of the opinion that Smith's unliquidated claim, however meritorious, could not be set off against the mortgage debt."

Defendant's claim for use and occupation, because of the absence of an agreement as to amount of rent to be paid, is an unliquidated claim. Carter v. Joseph, 48 Mich. 610, is a case directly in point. As the opinion in that case is very short, we quote it in full:

-4-

"The Court erred in striking the defendants' amended statement of claim from the files." The affidavit of merits required to be filed in the Municipal court of Chicago must set up sufficient facts which, if true, would constitute a good defense to the plaintiff's action. Defendants' amended affidavit of merits, as defendant admits, sets up the same facts as are set up in the amended statement and affidavit of claim on set-off. If the trial court ruled correctly upon the motion to strike the amended statement and affidavit of claim on set-off, it follows that defendants' amended affidavit of merits is insufficient. In Duncan Lumber Co. v. Leonard Lumber Co., 238 Ill. 104, the court said (pp. 106-7):

"The statute (Cahill's Stat. 1927, chap. 110, sec. 47 par. 1948,) authorizes a defendant 'having claims or demands against the plaintiff in such action,' to plead the same, etc. That statute has been construed in numerous cases by this court to not authorize unliquidated damages arising out of a contract, not connected with the subject matter of the plaintiff's suits to be set off against the plaintiff's claim. (Hawks v. Lands, 3 Gilm. 227; Sargeant v. Kellogg, 5 id. 273; Deforrest v. Oder, 42 Ill. 500; Robison v. Hibbs, 48 id. 408; Clark v. Dutton, 69 id. 521; Gluese v. Bullock Printing Press Co., 115 id. 612; Ribble v. Hunt, 211 id. 333.)"

A defendant may not set off claims for unliquidated damages growing out of transactions not connected with the transaction sued on. (Duncan Lumber Co. v. Leonard Lumber Co., supra.) In Citizens Trust & Savings Bank v. Blair, 238 Ill. App. 294, the court said (pp. 299-300):

"In the case of Duncan Lumber Co. v. Leonard Lumber Co., 238 Ill. 104, the court goes still further in holding that section 47 of the Practice Act, Cahill's St. ch. 110, par. 47, does not authorize unliquidated damages arising out of a contract not connected with the subject matter of the plaintiff's suit, notwithstanding the insolvency of the plaintiff; and in Benedict v. Hess, 209 Ill. App. 239, this court in a recent decision adopts a like construction of the Practice Act. In the absence of any special equitable ground, such as the insolvency of the complainant, we are of the opinion that [illegible]'s unliquidated claims, however meritorious, could not be set off against the mortgage debt."

Defendant's claim for use and occupation, because of the absence of an agreement as to amount of rent to be paid, is an unliquidated claim. Carley v. [illegible] Mass. 429, is a case directly in point. As the opinion in that case is very short, we quote it in full:

"Marston, J. The only question in this case, is whether the defendant in an action can set off a claim for rent and for horse pasture, where the amount had not been agreed upon or fixed in any way by the parties, and we are of opinion that within the rule laid down in Smith v. Warner, 14 Mich. 157, the court properly rejected the same.

"What would be a reasonable rent, and what would be a reasonable compensation to be paid for pasturing a horse, could not be arrived at by any mere mathematical process, but would have to be determined from the conflicting opinions of witnesses. The claim was therefore neither liquidated nor capable of being ascertained by calculation, and therefore not such an one as the statute permits to be the subject of a set-off, not coming under any of the other statutory provisions.

"The judgment must be affirmed with costs."

In Falkenau v. Smedley, 200 Ill. App. 6, suit was brought by the plaintiff against the defendant in the Municipal court of Chicago on a promissory note. The defendant filed an affidavit of merits and a statement of set-off setting forth as the basis of his claim the following items:

"Keep, care and feed of one horse on farm six months, $30 per month, $180; care and feed of one collie dog on farm six months, $15 per month, $90; storage of wine, eight months, $30 per month, $240; use of part of house and storage of furniture, six months, $100 per month, $600; total $1,110."

The Appellate court in affirming the judgment of the Municipal court held that the defendant's claim on set-off was not for a liquidated amount and did not arise out of the subject matter of the plaintiff's suit and was, therefore, not the proper subject of a set-off. In the instant case defendant admits in her pleadings that no definite rental was fixed at the time plaintiff went into possession of the premises, and there is no allegation that a definite rental was ever agreed upon between the parties. While the pleadings state what, in the opinion of defendant, would constitute a reasonable rental, this is not sufficient to make the claim a liquidated one. Nor did defendant's unliquidated claim arise out of the subject matter of plaintiff's suit. The subject matter of plaintiff's suit is the note sued on, dated June 25, 1931. Defendant's claim is one for use and occupation of certain premises and it arose on or about

"Marston, J. The only question in this case, is whether the defendant in an action can set off a claim for rent and for horse pasture, where the amount had not been agreed upon or fixed in any way by the parties, and we are of opinion that within the rule laid down in Smith v. Warner, 14 Mich. 157, the court properly rejected the same.

"What would be a reasonable rent, and what would be a reasonable compensation to be paid for pasturing a horse, could not be arrived at by any mere mathematical process, but would have to be determined from the conflicting opinions of witnesses. The claim was therefore neither liquidated nor capable of being ascertained by calculation, and therefore not such an one as the statute permits to be the subject of a set-off, not coming under any of the other statutory provisions.

"The judgment must be affirmed with costs."

In Feldman v. Medley, 200 Ill. App. 6, suit was brought by the plaintiff against the defendant in the Municipal court of Chicago on a promissory note. The defendant filed an affidavit of merits and a statement of set-off setting forth as the basis of his claim the following items:

"Keep, care and feed of one horse on farm six months, $30 per month, $180; care and feed of one collie dog on farm six months, $15 per month, $90; storage of wine, eight months, $30 per month, $240; use of part of house and storage of furniture, six months, $100 per month, $600; total $1,110."

The Appellate court in affirming the judgment of the Municipal court held that the defendant's claim on set-off was not for a liquidated amount and did not arise out of the subject matter of the plaintiff's suit and was, therefore, not the proper subject of a set-off. In the instant case defendant admits in her pleadings that no definite rental was fixed at the time plaintiff went into possession of the premises, and there is no allegation that a definite rental was ever agreed upon between the parties. While the pleadings state what, in the opinion of defendant, would constitute a reasonable rental, this is not sufficient to make the claim a liquidated one. Nor did defendant's unliquidated claim arise out of the subject matter of plaintiff's suit. The subject matter of plaintiff's suit is the note sued on, dated June 25, 1921. Defendant's claim is one for use and occupation of certain premises and it arose on or about

September 1, 1929. That they were entirely separate transactions at their inception is obvious. Nor do we think that the allegations as to the agreement to fix the rent connect defendant's claim with the subject matter of plaintiff's suit within the meaning of the rule announced in the Duncan Lumber Co. case. Defendant cites Sandow Motor Truck Co. v. Brown, 216 Ill. App. 103, in support of her contention. In that case the plaintiff brought an action in contract to recover the balance claimed to be due on the sale of a truck sold to the defendant, and the latter filed an affidavit of meritssetting up a breach of warranty and he also filed a claim for set-off claiming damages in the sum of $500 because of the breach of warranty. This court properly held that the claim of set-off interposed by the defendant arose out of the same subject matter as the claim of the plaintiff. Hawks v. Lands, 3 Gilm. 227, is also cited by defendant. There it was held that unliquidated damages arising out of covenants, contracts, or torts totally disconnected with the subject matter of the plaintiff's claim, are not such claims or demands as constitute the subject matter of set-off under the statute. That case is against defendant's position.

Defendant alleges that the trial court erred in refusing to grant defendant Mary Nereiko leave to file her individual affidavit of merits after the death of the defendant Joseph Nereiko was suggested. Defendant was represented by able counsel at the hearing. From the bill of exceptions it appears that the trial court called attention to the fact that defendants' original affidavit of merits and original statement and affidavit of claim on set-off had also been stricken "for want of sufficiency." Counsel for defendant did not present to the court any pleading, nor did he even suggest to the court that the defendant had any defense other than the one presented in the second amended affidavit of merits. Indeed, defendant's counsel did not ask the court for leave to file a

September 1, 1929. That they were entirely separate transactions at their inception is obvious. Nor do we think that the allegations as to the agreement to fix the rent connect defendant's claim with the subject matter of plaintiff's suit within the meaning of the rule announced in the Duncan Lumber Co. case. Defendant cites Sandow Motor Truck Co. v. Frong, 216 Ill. App. 103, in support of her contention. In that case the plaintiff brought an action in contract to recover the balance claimed to be due on the sale of a truck sold to the defendant, and the latter filed an affidavit of merits setting up a breach of warranty and he also filed a claim for set-off claiming damages in the sum of $500 because of the breach of warranty. This court properly held that the claim of set-off interposed by the defendant arose out of the same subject matter as the claim of the plaintiff. Hawks v. Lands, 3 Gilm. 227, is also cited by defendant. There it was held that unliquidated damages arising out of covenants, contracts, or torts totally disconnected with the subject matter of the plaintiff's claim, are not such claims or demands as constitute the subject matter of set-off under the statute. That case is against defendant's position.

Defendant alleges that the trial court erred in refusing to grant defendant Mary Noretko leave to file her individual affidavit of merits after the death of the defendant Joseph Noretko was suggested. Defendant was represented by able counsel at the hearing. From the bill of exceptions it appears that the trial court called attention to the fact that defendants' original affidavit of merits and original statement and affidavit of claim on set-off had also been stricken "for want of sufficiency." Counsel for defendant did not present to the court any pleading, nor did he even suggest to the court that the defendant had any defense other than the one presented in the second amended affidavit of merits. Indeed, defendant's counsel did not ask the court for leave to file a second amended statement and affidavit of claim on set-off. Had the counsel made any showing to the court that a different defense could be interposed in her behalf there might be some merit in the instant contention. Under the state of the record we cannot hold that the trial court abused its discretion in refusing leave to file, at a future day, "an individual second amended affidavit of merits."

The judgment of the Municipal court of Chicago is affirmed.

AFFIRMED.

Friend, P. J., and Sullivan, J., concur.

second amended statement and affidavit of claim or set-off. Had the counsel made any showing to the court that a different defense could be interposed in her behalf there might be some merit in the instant contention. Under the state of the record we cannot hold that the trial court abused its discretion in refusing leave to file, at a future day, "an individual second amended affidavit of merits."

The judgment of the Municipal court of Chicago is affirmed.

AFFIRMED.

Friend, P.J., and Sullivan, J., concur.

37834

DAVID RUTTENBERG, LOUIS FISHMAN and HARRY FISHMAN, for use of JOHN DAHMKE, Appellees,

v.

UNITED STATES FIDELITY & GUARANTY COMPANY, a corporation, Appellant.

APPEAL FROM SUPERIOR COURT, COOK COUNTY.

280 I.A. 623[4]

MR. JUSTICE SCANLAN DELIVERED THE OPINION OF THE COURT.

John Dahmke sued David Ruttenberg, Harry Fishman and Louis Fishman to recover damages for personal injuries, claiming that he had been shot and injured by defendant David Ruttenberg, an employee of the Fishmans, and that Ruttenberg at the time of the shooting was acting within the scope of his authority. A jury returned a verdict finding all of the defendants guilty and assessing plaintiff's damages at $20,000. The three defendants sued out, in this court, a writ of error to reverse the judgment entered upon the verdict. (See John Dahmke v. David Ruttenberg, Harry Fishman & Louis Fishman, Gen. No. 37657.) To enforce the judgment garnishment proceedings were instituted by Dahmke against United States Fidelity & Guaranty Company, a corporation, as garnishee. The garnishee defendant had issued a public liability policy of insurance to defendant "Louis Fishman, Lessee for Fargo Hotel," and it was the theory of Dahmke, in the garnishment proceeding, that this policy covered the act of Ruttenberg. In a trial by the court there was a finding for the plaintiff and against the garnishee defendant in the sum of $5,135 and judgment was entered upon the finding. The instant appeal followed.

Pending the appeal in the garnishment matter the first

37834

DAVID RUTTENBERG, LOUIS FISHMAN and HARRY FISHMAN, for use of JOHN DAHMKE,
Appellees,

v.

UNITED STATES FIDELITY & GUARANTY COMPANY, a corporation,
Appellant.

APPEAL FROM SUPERIOR COURT, COOK COUNTY.

280 I.A. 623

MR. JUSTICE SCANLAN DELIVERED THE OPINION OF THE COURT.

John Dahmke sued David Ruttenberg, Harry Fishman and Louis Fishman to recover damages for personal injuries, claiming that he had been shot and injured by defendant David Ruttenberg, an employee of the Fishmans, and that Ruttenberg at the time of the shooting was acting within the scope of his authority. A jury returned a verdict finding all of the defendants guilty and assessing plaintiff's damages at $30,000. The three defendants sued out, in this court, a writ of error to reverse the judgment entered upon the verdict. (See John Dahmke v. David Ruttenberg, Harry Fishman & Louis Fishman, Gen. No. 37657.) To enforce the judgment garnishment proceedings were instituted by Dahmke against United States Fidelity & Guaranty Company, a corporation, as garnishee. The garnishee defendant had issued a public liability policy of insurance to defendant "Louis Fishman, Lessee for Paige Hotel," and it was the theory of Dahmke, in the garnishment proceeding, that this policy covered the act of Ruttenberg. In a trial by the court there was a finding for the plaintiff and against the garnishee defendant in the sum of $6,135 and judgment was entered upon the finding. The instant appeal followed.

Pending the appeal in the garnishment matter the first

division of this court decided the writ of error in the personal injury case. The court held that Ruttenberg, at the time that he shot Dahmke, was not acting within the scope of his authority, and the judgment of the trial court as to the defendants Harry Fishman and Louis Fishman was reversed and the judgment against the defendant David Ruttenberg was affirmed. Thereafter Dahmke filed, in the Supreme court, his petition for leave to appeal from the order of reversal entered in this court, and on April 18, 1935, his petition was denied. The garnishee defendant in the instant appeal has now filed in this court a motion to reverse the judgment against it as garnishee. It contends that, as the judgment against it was entered solely because of the issuance of the public liability policy to Louis Fishman and as there is now no judgment against the defendants Harry Fishman and Louis Fishman, there is no longer any judgment to support the garnishment proceeding and that therefore the garnishment judgment against it should be reversed. Dahmke has not seen fit to contest the instant motion and it is clear that it is a meritorious one. (See First Nat. Bank v. Hahnemann Inst., 356 Ill. 366.)

The judgment order of the Superior court of Cook county appealed from is therefore reversed.

REVERSED.

Friend, P. J., and Sullivan, J., concur.

division of this court recalled the writ of error in [illegible] court injury case. The court held that Feinberg, at the time [illegible] was driving, was not acting within the scope of his authority, and the judgment of the trial court as to the defendants Harry Fishman and Louis Fishman was reversed, and the judgment [illegible] as to defendant David [illegible] was affirmed. Thereafter Fishman filed, in the Supreme court, his petition for leave to appeal from the order of reversal entered in this court, and on April 13, [illegible], his petition was denied. The garnishee defendant in the instant appeal has now filed in this court a motion to reverse the judgment against it as garnishee. It contends that, as the judgment upon which it was entered solely because of the liability of the public liability policy to Louis Fishman and as there is now no judgment against the defendants Harry Fishman and Louis Fishman, there is no longer any judgment to support the garnishment proceeding and that therefore the garnishment judgment against it should be reversed. Fishman has not seen fit to contest the instant motion and it is clear that it is a meritorious one. (See First Nat. Bank v. [illegible], [illegible] Ill. [illegible].)

The judgment order of the Superior court of Cook county appealed from is therefore reversed.

Friend, P. J., and Sullivan, J., concur.

5877

37908

TONY MASINSKI and
KATIE MASINSKI,
Appellees,

v.

TOM DULAK and WALTER H.
FISHER,
Appellants.

APPEAL FROM SUPERIOR
COURT, COOK COUNTY.

280 I.A. 623

MR. JUSTICE SCANLAN DELIVERED THE OPINION OF THE COURT.

Tony Masinski and Katie Masinski, his wife, sued Tom Dulak and Walter H. Fisher in an action of fraud and deceit. The case was tried by the court without a jury, both defendants were found guilty, and plaintiffs' damages were assessed in the sum of $1,614.40.

The declaration alleged, in substance, that plaintiffs were induced to convey to James Volney and Anna Volney, his wife, their farm in Wisconsin in exchange for certain real estate in Chicago by false and fraudulent representations made by defendants to plaintiffs in reference to the Chicago property, whereby plaintiffs were deceived and damaged.

Defendants earnestly contend that they were not given a fair and impartial trial by the court, and in support of this contention they call our attention to a great many parts of the bill of exceptions. It would unduly lengthen this opinion and serve no useful purpose for us to cite the many parts of the bill that clearly support the contention and which have forced us to the conclusion that a due regard for the orderly and proper administration of justice requires that this action be retried.

The judgment of the Superior court of Cook county is reversed and the cause is remanded.

REVERSED AND REMANDED.

Friend, P.J., and Sullivan, J., concur.

[illegible]

TONY MAZURKI and
KAFIA MAZURKI,
Appellees,

v.

TOM [illegible] and [illegible]
FISHER,
Appellants.

280 I.A. 629

MR. [illegible] DELIVERED THE OPINION OF THE COURT.

Tony Mazurki and Kafia Mazurki, his wife, sued [illegible] in an action of fraud and deceit. The case was tried by the court without a jury, both defendants were found guilty, and plaintiffs' damages were assessed in the sum of $[illegible].

The declaration alleged, in substance, that plaintiffs were induced to convey to defendant [illegible] their farm in Wisconsin in exchange for certain real estate in Chicago by false and fraudulent representations [illegible] to plaintiffs in reference to the [illegible] plaintiffs were deceived and damaged.

[illegible] fair and impartial trial by the court [illegible] of exceptions. It would unduly lengthen this opinion [illegible] support the contention and which have forced us to the conclusion that a due regard for the orderly and proper administration of justice requires that this cause be retried.

The judgment of the superior court of Cook county is reversed and the cause is remanded.

[illegible]

[illegible], P.J., and Sullivan, J., concur.

574

37922

ILONA JANCSIK and JOE JANCSIK,
Appellees,

v.

SOVEREIGN CAMP OF THE WOODMEN OF THE WORLD, a corporation,
Appellant.

APPEAL FROM MUNICIPAL COURT OF CHICAGO.

280 I.A. 624[1]

MR. JUSTICE SCANLAN DELIVERED THE OPINION OF THE COURT.

This is an action at law upon an insurance certificate. The case was tried on a stipulation of facts before the court, without a jury. Judgment was entered for plaintiffs in the sum of $918.50.

On December 14, 1916, defendant, a fraternal insurance association, issued to John Jancsik an insurance certificate which provided for a $1,000 death benefit, payable at his death to "Ilona & Joe" Jancsik, for which the insured was to pay $1.25 monthly. On July 10, 1931, the following letter was sent by the "Sovereign Clerk" (National Secretary) of defendant to Jancsik:

"Sovereign Camp, Woodmen of the World
Omaha, Neb.

Office of
John T. Yates, Sovereign Clerk
W.O.W Building

July 10, 1931.

		Annually	Monthly
174 Ind.	$1,000.00	$26.76	$2.32
	Monument	2.68	.23
J. Janisik		$29.44	$2.55

Esteemed Sovereign:

I am in receipt of your letter of recent date wherein you make inquiry relative to exchanging your present certificate for the Ordinary Whole Life certificate.

35982

ILONA JANCSIK and JOE JANCSIK,
Appellees,

v.

SOVEREIGN CAMP OF THE WOODMEN OF THE WORLD, a corporation,
Appellant.

APPEAL FROM MUNICIPAL COURT OF CHICAGO.

280 I.A. 624

MR. JUSTICE SCANLAN DELIVERED THE OPINION OF THE COURT.

This is an action at law upon an insurance certificate. The case was tried on a stipulation of facts before the court, without a jury. Judgment was entered for plaintiffs in the sum of $918.50.

On December 14, 1916, defendant, a fraternal insurance association, issued to John Jancsik an insurance certificate which provided for a $1,000 death benefit, payable at his death to "Ilona A Joe" Jancsik, for which the insured was to pay $1.28 monthly. On July 10, 1931, the following letter was sent by the "Sovereign Clerk" (National Secretary) of defendant to Jancsik:

"Sovereign Camp, Woodmen of the World
Omaha, Neb.

Office of
John T. Yates, Sovereign Clerk
W.O.W Building

July 10, 1931.

			Annually	Monthly
174 Ind.	$1,000.00		$26.76	$2.28
	Monument		2.60	.23
J. Janisik			[illegible]	[illegible]

Esteemed Sovereign:

I am in receipt of your letter of recent date wherein you make inquiry relative to exchanging your present certificate for the Ordinary Whole Life certificate.

You have sufficient credit to enable us to issue to you an Ordinary Whole Life Certificate for $1,000.00 dated back 11 years which of course means that the Paid-Up, Extended Insurance and Cash Surrender values will be effective for the number of years the certificate is dated back.

The rate you will be required to pay on the certificate will be the rate as fixed for the dated back age which is $29.44 annually or $2.55 monthly as specified for age 41. Your attention is called to the fact that a period of three years must elapse from the date of the issuance of the new certificate before the cash surrender or loan values will be available to you.

Fraternally yours,

J. T. Yates
Sovereign Clerk,
Camp 174 Ind.
J. Janisik
Liable 31/7"

JTY-DDM-OL PU70

On the face of that letter Janosik replied as follows:

"John T. Yates,
Sovereign Clerk,
Woodmen of the World.

Esteemed Sovereign Clerk:

I am desirous of accepting the proposition as outlined in the above letter. Enclosed herewith please find my old certificate. Kindly issue me a new certificate as above described.

X John Yanosik
Member"

On July 31, 1931, a new certificate was issued in the name of Janosik. On the first page of the certificate appears the following:

"Participating

Ordinary-Whole Life Certificate

Rates

Age
41

Monthly
$ 2.55

Certificate No.
W-1066293-L

The Sovereign Camp
of the
Woodmen of the World

Quarterly
$ 7.58

Semi-Annually
$ 15.02

Annually
$ 29.44

A Fraternal Beneficiary Association Incorporated
Under the Laws of the State of Nebraska
Referred to Herein as the Association

Hereby Issues this certificate to John Janosik, a member

You have sufficient credit to enable us to issue to you an Ordinary Whole Life Certificate for $1,000.00 dated back 11 years which of course means that the Paid-Up, Extended Insurance and Cash Surrender values will be effective for the number of years the certificate is dated back.

The rate you will be required to pay on the certificate will be the rate as fixed for the dated back age which is $29.44 annually or $2.55 monthly as specified for age 41. Your attention is called to the fact that a period of three years must elapse from the date of the issuance of the new certificate before the cash surrender or loan values will be available to you.

Fraternally yours,

J. T. Yates
Sovereign Clerk,
Camp 174 Ind.
J. Janisik
Kieble 31/7"

JTY-IDM-OL PUTO

On the face of that letter Janesik replied as follows:

"John T. Yates,
Sovereign Clerk,
Woodmen of the World.

Esteemed Sovereign Clerk:

I am desirous of accepting the proposition as outlined in the above letter. Enclosed herewith please find my old certificate. Kindly issue me a new certificate as above described.

X John Yanosik
Member"

On July 31, 1951, a new certificate was issued in the name of Janesik. On the first page of the certificate appears the following:

"Participating

Ordinary-Whole Life Certificate

Rates

Monthly $2.55

Quarterly $7.58

Semi-Annually $15.02

Annually $29.44

Age 41

Certificate No.
W-1066293-L

The Sovereign Camp
of the
Woodmen of the World

A Fraternal Beneficiary Association Incorporated
Under the Laws of the State of Nebraska
Referred to Herein as the Association

Hereby issues this certificate to John Janesik, a member

of Camp No. 174, State of Indiana, and upon receipt of satisfactory proof of death of the said member, while in good standing, the Association

Death Benefit:
Will Pay One Thousand dollars ($1,000.00) to Ilona and Joe Jancsik -- Wife and son, the beneficiary or beneficiaries under this certificate; or

Cash Surrender:
Will Pay the Cash Surrender Value according to paragraph 2, page 2 hereof; or

Automatic Premium Loan:
Will Advance Automatic Premium Loans as set forth in paragraph 3, page 2 hereof; or

Paid-Up or Extended Insurance:
Will Grant Paid-Up or Extended Insurance in accordance with paragraph 2, page 2 hereof.

This certificate is issued in consideration of the warranties and agreements contained in the application for membership, the application for exchange of certificates, and in further consideration of the payment to the Association of the sum of $2.55 for the month in which this certificate is dated and the payment to the Association of $2.55 on or before the last day of each month thereafter, except as provided in the non-forfeiture options on page 2 hereof.

This certificate is issued and accepted with the express agreement that the provisions and benefits contained on this and the three succeeding pages hereof, and in any authenticated riders attached hereto, form a part of this contract as fully as if recited over the signatures hereto affixed.

The values as set out in Table A, page 3 hereof, shall apply to this certificate as if issued on the 1st day of July, 1920, but such values shall not be available to the member until after three years from the date this certificate is issued.

This certificate is issued at Omaha, Nebraska, this 31st day of July, 1931.

W. A. Fraser
President.

____
(Inspected and countersigned.)

Attest:
J. T. Yates
Secretary.

I have read the above certificate and accept the same, and warrant that I am now in good health and have not been sick or injured since the date of my application.

) This, the _____day of _________________________, 19______

____
(Member)

Ordinary
Whole Life

Witness: _________________________
Financial Secretary."

of Camp No. 174, State of Indiana, and upon receipt of satisfactory proof of death of the said member, while in good standing, the Association

Death Benefits:
Will Pay One Thousand dollars ($1,000.00) to Ilona and Joe Janesik -- Wife and son, the beneficiary or beneficiaries under this certificate; or

Cash Surrender:
Will Pay the Cash Surrender Value according to paragraph 2, page 2 hereof; or

Automatic Premium Loan:
Will Advance Automatic Premium Loans as set forth in paragraph 3, page 2 hereof; or

Paid-Up or Extended Insurance:
Will Grant Paid-Up or Extended Insurance in accordance with paragraph 2, page 2 hereof.

This certificate is issued in consideration of the warranties and agreements contained in the application for membership, the application for exchange of certificates, and in further consideration of the payment to the Association of the sum of $2.56 for the month in which this certificate is dated and the payment to the Association of $2.55 on or before the last day of each month thereafter, except as provided in the non-forfeiture options on page 2 hereof.

This certificate is issued and accepted with the express agreement that the provisions and benefits contained in this and the three succeeding pages hereof, and in any authenticated rid attached hereto, form a part of this contract as fully as if recited over the signatures hereto affixed.

The values as set out in Table A, page 4 hereof, shall apply to this certificate as if issued on the 1st day of July, 1920, but such values shall not be available to the member until after three years from the date this certificate is issued.

This certificate is issued at Omaha, Nebraska, this 31st day of July, 1951.

W. A. Fraser
President.

____
(Inspected and countersigned.)

W-106

Attest:
J. T. Yates
Secretary.

I have read the above certificate and accept the same, and warrant that I am now in good health and have not been sick or injured since the date of my application.

This, the ____ day of ____________, 19____

____
(Member)

Ordinary Whole Life

Witness: ____________________
Financial Secretary.

The second page of the certificate contains "Special Provisions and Conditions," but only the second and third need be mentioned. The second is as follows:

"2. Cash Surrender, Loan Value, Paid-Up and Extended Insurance: After thirty-six monthly payments shall have been made on this certificate and after three years from the date of the issuance of this certificate to the member, should the member fail to pay any subsequent monthly payments, the member, within three months after due date of the monthly payment in default, but not later, upon written application and legal surrender of this certificate, may select one of the following non-forfeiture options:

Option (a). The Cash Surrender Value set forth in Column 1 of Table A on page 3 hereof for the period at the end of which premiums have been paid in full, or in lieu thereof the loan value set forth in said table, with interest at the rate of not more than 6 per cent per annum, payable annually in advance.

Option (b). A Paid-Up Certificate for the amount set forth in Column 2 of Table A on page 3 hereof for the period to the end of which premiums have been paid in full.

Option (c). Extended insurance from such due date, for the amount of the death benefit on page 1 hereof, but without Total and Permanent Disability Benefits, for the period specified in Column 3 of Table A on page 3 hereof for the period to the end of which premiums have been paid in full.

If there be any indebtedness against this certificate, the cash surrender value set forth in Column 1 of Table A on page 3 hereof shall be reduced thereby, and the value of the options above named shall be decreased proportionately."

The third is as follows:

"3. Automatic Premium Loan: After thirty-six monthly payments on this certificate shall have been paid, if any subsequent monthly payment be not paid on or before its due date, and if the member has not, prior to such due date, selected one of the options available under the non-forfeiture provisions of this certificate, the Association will, without any action on the part of the member, advance as a loan to the said member the amount of the monthly payments required to maintain this certificate in force from month to month until such time as the accumulated loans, together with compound interest thereon at the rate of five per cent per annum, and any other indebtedness hereon to the Association, equal the cash value hereof at the date of default in the payment of the monthly payments. When the said cash value has been consumed in loans advanced and interest thereon, then this certificate shall become null and void; provided, that while this certificate is continued in force under this provision, the member may resume the payment of monthly payments without furnishing evidence of insurability, and the accumulated loans and interest thereon shall become a lien upon this certificate and shall continue to bear interest at the same rate. Provided further, that such lien may be paid in whole or in part at any time by the member, but if not paid said loan and accumulated interest thereon shall be deducted upon any settlement with the member, or from the amount payable at the death of the member."

The second page of the certificate contains "Special Provisions and Conditions," but only the second and third need be mentioned.

The second is as follows:

"2. Cash Surrender, Loan Value, Paid-Up and Extended Insurance: After thirty-six monthly payments shall have been made on this certificate and after three years from the date of the issuance of this certificate to the member, should the member fail to pay any subsequent monthly payments, the member, within three months after due date of the monthly payment in default, but not later, upon written application and legal surrender of this certificate, may select one of the following non-forfeiture options:

Option (a). The Cash Surrender Value set forth in Column 1 of Table A on page 3 hereof for the period at the end of which premiums have been paid in full, or in lieu thereof the loan value set forth in said table, with interest at the rate of not more than 6 per cent per annum, payable annually in advance.

Option (b). A Paid-Up Certificate for the amount set forth in Column 2 of Table A on page 3 hereof for the period to the end of which premiums have been paid in full.

Option (c). Extended Insurance from such due date, for the amount of the death benefit on page 1 hereof, without Total and Permanent Disability Benefits, for the period specified in Column 3 of Table A on page 3 hereof for the period to the end of which premiums have been paid in full.

If there be any indebtedness against this certificate, the cash surrender value set forth in Column 1 of Table A on page 3 hereof shall be reduced thereby, and the value of the options above named shall be decreased proportionately."

The third is as follows:

"3. Automatic Premium Loan: After thirty-six monthly payments on this certificate shall have been paid, if any subsequent monthly payment be not paid on or before its due date, and if the member has not, prior to such due date, selected one of the options available under the non-forfeiture provisions of this certificate, the Association will, without any action on the part of the member, advance as a loan to the said member the amount of the monthly payments required to maintain this certificate in force from month to month until such time as the accumulated loans, together with compound interest thereon at the rate of five per cent per annum, and any other indebtedness hereon to the Association, equal the cash value hereof at the date of default in the payment of the monthly payments. When the said cash value has been consumed in loans advanced and interest thereon, then this certificate shall become null and void; provided, that while this certificate is continued in force under this provision, the member may resume the payment of monthly payments without furnishing evidence of insurability, and the accumulated loans and interest thereon shall become a lien upon this certificate and shall continue to bear interest at the same rate. Provided further, that such lien may be paid in whole or in part at any time by the member, but if not paid said loan and accumulated interest thereon shall be deducted upon any settlement with the member, or from the amount payable at the death of the member."

On page three of the certificate is contained "Table A Cash Surrender, Paid-Up and Extended Insurance and Loan Values Available in Accordance With the Provisions of This Certificate." The table sets forth, in respective columns, the "Cash or Loan Value," the "Paid-Up Insurance" and "Extended Insurance" at the end of each certificate year. Janesik ceased paying dues after November, 1931.

Plaintiffs contend that the extended insurance feature of the agreement between the parties was still in full force and effect at the time of Janesik's death.

Defendant states its theory as follows: "Plaintiffs' decedent in becoming a member of the defendant agreed to make monthly payments of $1.25; the first certificate contained the defendant's promise of a death benefit only; that a second certificate was issued on July 31, 1931, in exchange for the first certificate. The second certificate required the decedent to make a monthly payment of $2.55. It granted certain cash, surrender and extended insurance values, but it provided that 'such values shall not be available to the member until after three years from the date this certificate is issued.' Decedent paid no assessment after November, 1931, and was suspended therefor ipso facto on January 1, 1932; that when decedent died on November 11, 1933, he had been suspended from the defendant association and his certificate was void."

Defendant admits that a number of courts of last resort "have construed a prior and differently worded contract of insurance (issued by this defendant at a previous date) against the defendant, on the matter of extended insurance," but it contends that Janesik did not get the same kind of certificate that was involved in those cases. The cases referred to are Higgins v. Sovereign Camp, W. O. W., 141 So. (Ala.) 562; Jones v. Sovereign Camp, W. O. W., 67 S. W. (2d) (Tenn.) 159; Daly v. Sovereign Camp, W. O. W., 44 S. W. (2d) (Mo.) 229; Sovereign Camp, W. O. W. v. Hasley, 69 S. W. (2d) (Ark. 273;

On page three of the certificate is contained "Table A Cash Surrender, Paid-Up and Extended Insurance and Loan Values Available in Accordance With the Provisions of This Certificate." The table sets forth, in respective columns, the "Cash or Loan Value," the "Paid-Up Insurance" and "Extended Insurance" at the end of each certificate year. Janesik ceased paying dues after November, 1931.

Plaintiffs contend that the extended insurance feature of the agreement between the parties was still in full force and effect at the time of Janesik's death.

Defendant states its theory as follows: "Plaintiffs' decedent in becoming a member of the defendant agreed to make monthly payments of $[illegible]; the first certificate contained the defendant's promise of a death benefit only; that a second certificate was issued on July 31, 1931, in exchange for the first certificate. The second certificate required the decedent to make a monthly payment of $2.55. It granted certain cash, surrender and extended insurance values, but it provided that 'such values shall not be available to the member until after three years from the date this certificate is issued.' Decedent paid no assessment after November, 1931, and was suspended therefor ipso facto on January 1, 1932; that when decedent died on November 11, 1935, he had been suspended from the defendant association and his certificate was void."

Defendant admits that a number of courts of last resort have construed a prior and differently worded contract of insurance (issued by this defendant at a previous date) against the defendant, on the matter of extended insurance," but it contends that Janesik did not get the same kind of certificate that was involved in those cases. The cases referred to are Rimkus v. Sovereign Camp, W. O. W., 141 So. (Ala.) 663; Jones v. Sovereign Camp, W. O. W., 67 S. W. (2d) (Tenn.) 159; Daley v. Sovereign Camp, W. O. W., 44 S. W. (2d) (Mo.) 229; Sovereign Camp, W. O. W. v. Henley, 60 S. W. (2d) (Ark.) 675;

the death of the member,"

Sovereign Camp, W. O. W. v. Hardee, 66 S. W. (2d) (Ark.) 648.

Defendant further contends that the case involves only the construction of the second certificate of insurance. Plaintiffs contend that there is involved not only a construction of the second certificate but the letter of July 10, which contains the offer from defendant and the signed acceptance thereof by Janosik. As paragraph six of the second certificate specifically provides that the application for exchange of certificates is a part of the agreement, both the certificate and the letter of July 10 must be considered in determining the contract between the parties. But aside from the fact that defendant made the letter a part of the agreement, defendant's argument, when carefully analyzed, amounts to no more than that the contract is susceptible of two interpretations, and even if such is the situation the contract must be given the construction most favorable to the insured; and, further, if the present certificate is ambiguous the letter would be proper evidence to aid in determining what was the actual agreement between the parties. That the rule of construction that if the terms of the contract of insurance are ambiguous the contract must be given that construction most favorable to the insured applies to fraternal insurance associations, see Daly v. Sovereign Camp, W. O. W., supra, p. 232. The letter of July 10, in our judgment, has weight in determining the contract between the parties. Defendant, in its reply brief, argues that plaintiffs' statement of claim is based upon the certificate, alone, and that therefore the letter of July 10 cannot be considered as a part of the contract. It is sufficient to say, in response thereto, that a case, like the instant one, in the Municipal court of Chicago is what the evidence makes it, and that this rule prevails in first class cases as well as fourth class cases. (See the late case of Heilig v. Continental Casualty Co., App. Ct. Gen. No. 37895.)

Defendant, in its reply brief, argues: "That the whole

Sovereign Camp, W. O. W. v. Hardee, 66 S.W.(2d) (Ark.) 646.

Defendant further contends that the case involves only the construction of the second certificate of insurance. Plaintiffs contend that there is involved not only a construction of the second certificate but the letter of July 10, which contains the offer from defendant and the signed acceptance thereof by Janacek. As paragraph six of the second certificate specifically provides that the application for exchange of certificates is a part of the agreement, both the certificate and the letter of July 10 must be considered in determining the contract between the parties. But aside from the fact that defendant made the letter a part of the agreement, defendant's argument, when carefully analyzed, amounts to no more than that the contract is susceptible of two interpretations, and even if such is the situation the contract must be given the construction most favorable to the insured; and, further, if the present certificate is ambiguous the letter would be proper evidence to aid in determining what was the actual agreement between the parties. That the rule of construction that if the terms of the contract of insurance are ambiguous the contract must be given that construction most favorable to the insured applies to fraternal insurance associations, see Daly v. Sovereign Camp, W. O. W., supra, p. 232. The letter of July 10, in our judgment, has weight in determining the contract between the parties. Defendant, in its reply brief, argues that plaintiffs' statement of claim is based upon the certificate, alone, and that therefore the letter of July 10 cannot be considered as a part of the contract. It is sufficient to say, in response thereto, that a case, like the instant one, in the municipal court of Chicago is made as the evidence makes it, and that this rule prevails in first class cases as well as fourth class cases. (See the late case of [illegible] v. [illegible] App. Ct. Gen. No. 37605.)

Defendant, in its reply brief, argues: "That the whole

case turns on the language used on the first page of the certificate * * * where the clear conclusion is that no values shall be available until after 'three years from the date this certificate is issued. This certificate is issued this 31st day of July, 1931.'"

Defendant relies upon the italicized words of the following paragraph of the second certificate:

> "The values as set out in Table A, page 3 hereof, shall apply to this certificate as if issued on the 1st day of July, 1920, *but such values shall not be available to the member until after three years from the date this certificate is issued.*" (Italics ours.)

In our judgment these words refer to the withdrawal privileges available to the insured ("the member") only, and not to the keeping of the insurance alive for a certain period while insured is living nor to the rights of the beneficiaries after the insured's death. The cases to which defendant has called our attention support this interpretation. To cite again the two important paragraphs of the letter sent to Jancsik by defendant on July 10, 1931:

> "You have sufficient credit to enable us to issue to you an Ordinary Whole Life Certificate for $1,000.00 dated back 11 years which of course means that the Paid-Up, Extended Insurance, and Cash Surrender values will be effective for the number of years the certificate is dated back.
>
> "The rate you will be required to pay on the certificate will be the rate as fixed for the dated back age which is $29.44 annually or $2.55 monthly as specified for age 41. *Your attention is called to the fact that a period of three years must elapse from the date of the issuance of the new certificate before the cash surrender or loan values will be available to you.*" (Italics ours.)

In the first paragraph it states "that the Paid-Up, *Extended Insurance*, and Cash Surrender values will be effective," etc., but in the italicized portion of the second paragraph the extended insurance feature is omitted. The italicized words in the paragraph of the second certificate, upon which defendant relies, state that the values set out in the table shall apply to the certificate as if issued on July 1, 1920, "but such values shall not be available *to the member* until after three years from the date this certificate is issued." When the whole agreement between the parties, the letter of July 10 and the contained in the language used on the first page of the certificate * * * where the other conclusion is that no values shall be available until after three years from the date this certificate is issued. This certificate is issued this 31st day of July, 1931.'"

Defendant relies upon the italicized words of the following paragraph of the second certificate:

"The values as set out in Table A, page 3 hereof, shall apply to this certificate as if issued on the 1st day of July, 1920, except that values shall not be available to the member until after three years from the date this certificate is issued." (Italics ours.)

In our judgment these words refer to the withdrawal privileges available to the insured ("the member") only, and not to the keeping of the insurance alive for a certain period while insured is living nor to the rights of the beneficiaries after the insured's death. The cases to which defendant has called our attention support this interpretation. To cite again the two important paragraphs of the letter sent to Janesik by defendant on July 10, 1931:

"You have sufficient credit to enable us to issue to you an Ordinary Whole Life Certificate for $1,000.00 dated back 11 years which of course means that the Paid-Up, Extended Insurance, and Cash Surrender values will be effective for the number of years the certificate is dated back.

"The rate you will be required to pay on the certificate will be the rate as fixed for the dated back age which is $30.48 annually or $2.58 monthly as specified for age 41. Your attention is called to the fact that a period of three years must elapse from the date of the issuance of the new certificate before the cash surrender or loan values will be available to you." (Italics ours.)

In the first paragraph it states "that the Paid-Up, Extended Insurance, and Cash Surrender values will be effective," etc., but in the italicized portion of the second paragraph the extended insurance feature is omitted. The italicized words in the paragraph of the second certificate, upon which defendant relies, state that the values set second certificate, is considered, it seems reasonably clear to us, especially in the light of the aforesaid decisions of the sister states, that the agreement differentiates between privileges granted "to the member" (Janosik) and rights granted to the beneficiaries under the certificate. The letter of July 10 states that Janosik had sufficient credit to enable defendant to issue to him an ordinary whole life certificate for $1,000 "dated back 11 years which of course means that the Paid-Up, Extended Insurance, and Cash Surrender values will be effective for the number of years the certificate is dated back." Under the old policy the rate was $1.25 per month, while under the new policy it was $2.55 per month. At the time of the issuance of the second certificate, according to the dated back provision, it was in its eleventh year, and according to the extended insurance table (Table A) the policy had more than ten years to run after November 30, 1931. Janosik died on November 11, 1933.

The judgment of the Municipal court of Chicago is affirmed.

AFFIRMED.

Friend, P. J., and Sullivan, J., concur.

second certificate, is considered, it seems reasonably clear to us, especially in the light of the aforesaid decisions of the sister states, that the agreement differentiates between privileges granted "to the member" (Janosik) and rights granted to the beneficiaries under the certificate. The letter of July 10 states that Janosik had sufficient credit to enable defendant to issue to him an ordinary whole life certificate for $1,000 "dated back 11 years which of course means that the Paid-Up, Extended Insurance, and Cash Surrender values will be effective for the number of years the certificate is dated back." Under the old policy the rate was $1.68 per month, while under the new policy it was $2.68 per month. At the time of the issuance of the second certificate, according to the dated back provision, it was in its eleventh year, and according to the extended insurance table (Table A) the policy had more than ten years to run after November 30, 1931. Janosik died on November 11, 1933.

The judgment of the Municipal court of Chicago is affirmed.

AFFIRMED.

Friend, P. J., and Sullivan, J., concur.

604

37714

HARRY FRAIMAN,
Appellant,

v.

CONNELLA BAKING COMPANY,
a corporation,
Appellee.

APPEAL FROM SUPERIOR COURT, COOK COUNTY.

280 I.A. 624[2]

MR. JUSTICE SULLIVAN DELIVERED THE OPINION OF THE COURT.

This appeal seeks the reversal of a judgment for defendant entered in an action brought by plaintiff, Harry Fraiman, for personal injuries alleged to have been received by him when his horse-drawn wagon was struck by defendant's automobile truck. No question arises on the pleadings.

Harold Pederson, the only eyewitness to the accident testified in plaintiff's behalf that, while standing as a passenger on the front platform of a southbound Western avenue car on the morning of November 29, 1932, he passed plaintiff driving his horse and wagon at Grand avenue, which was about two blocks north of the accident; that at that time there was a lighted lantern on the rear of plaintiff's wagon, but it had no red globe on it; that he alighted from the street car as he approached Fulton street to go to his place of employment at 300 North Western avenue; that when he reached the building where he was employed it was 6 a.m. and "dusk," and that he could distinguish objects at a distance of 400 feet; that Western avenue was a paved street and it was dry that morning; that the east curb was 15 or 20 feet from the east rail of the street car tracks, and the west curb 8 or 10 feet from the west rail; that there was an extensive railroad viaduct several hundred feet north of Fulton street, under which traffic

37714

HARRY PRAIMAN,
Appellant,

v.

GONNELLA BAKING COMPANY,
a corporation,
Appellee.

APPEAL FROM SUPERIOR COURT, COOK COUNTY.

280 I.A. 624

MR. JUSTICE SULLIVAN DELIVERED THE OPINION OF THE COURT.

This appeal seeks the reversal of a judgment for defendant entered in an action brought by plaintiff, Harry Praiman, for personal injuries alleged to have been received by him when his horse-drawn wagon was struck by defendant's automobile truck. No question arises on the pleadings.

Harold Pederson, the only eyewitness to the accident testified in plaintiff's behalf that, while standing as a passenger on the front platform of a southbound Western avenue car on the morning of November 20, 1933, he passed plaintiff driving his horse and wagon at Grand avenue, which was about two blocks north of the accident; that at that time there was a lighted lantern on the rear of plaintiff's wagon, but it had no red globe on it; that he alighted from the street car as he approached Fulton street to go to his place of employment at 280 North Western avenue; that when he reached the building where he was employed it was 6 a.m. and "dusk," and that he could distinguish objects at a distance of 400 feet; that Western avenue was a paved street and it was dry that morning; that the east curb was 15 or 20 feet from the east rail of the street car tracks, and the west curb 8 or 10 feet from the west rail; that there was an extensive railroad viaduct several hundred feet north of Fulton street, under which traffic on Western avenue passed; that the upgrade from the south end of the viaduct to the street level of Western avenue was about 175 feet; that, as he stood in front of his place of employment, his attention was attracted by the clatter of plaintiff's horse's hoofs on the pavement; that he turned to the north and saw plaintiff driving his horse in the southbound street car track at about eight or ten miles an hour; that he saw defendant's truck, also coming south at thirty-five miles an hour, straddling the west street car rail and about 75 feet behind plaintiff's wagon; that he heard no noise or sound from the truck, and that the truck struck plaintiff's wagon in the rear, about 200 feet south of the viaduct or about 25 feet after reaching the street level of Western avenue; and that plaintiff was thrown to the street from the seat of his wagon and was taken unconscious to the hospital.

Pedersen testified further that he was standing about 75 feet from the point of impact; that from the viaduct to that point the buildings on both sides of Western avenue are five or six stories in height; that he did not see a lighted lantern on the wagon after he passed the wagon at Grand avenue on the street car; and that the lantern was out after the accident, but was warm when he felt it.

Plaintiff testified on direct examination that he was driving south on Western avenue, approaching Fulton street, at 6 a.m. on the morning in question when his wagon was struck; and that he was thrown from it and he regained consciousness in the hospital a day or two later. He testified further on rebuttal that he went to his stable at 5:40 a.m. that morning and spent about fifteen minutes harnessing his horse and cleaning his lantern; and that, after lighting his lantern, he drove from the stable at 5:55 a.m. and traveled about a mile and a half to where the accident happened.

Police officer John F. O'Brien testified in defendant's behalf that he reached the scene of the accident at 5:55 a.m. and on [illegible] that the upgrade from the north [illegible] of the [illegible] to the street level of Western Avenue [illegible] this [illegible] stood in front of his place of employment [illegible] was [illegible] by the [illegible] of plaintiff's horse's hoofs on the pave- [illegible]

[illegible]

miles an hour, [illegible] street [illegible] feet [illegible]

street [illegible]

street from [illegible] hospital.

[illegible]

feet from the [illegible] buildings on both sides of Western Avenue are five or six stories in [illegible] passed the wagon [illegible] term [illegible]

[illegible] south on Western Avenue [illegible]

[illegible] at 6:40 a.m. the morning [illegible] about fifty [illegible] wearing his horse [illegible] lan- tern, he drove from the stable at 6:05 a.m. and traveled [illegible] mile and a half to where the accident happened.

Police officer John F. O'Brien testified on plaintiff's behalf that he reached the scene of the accident at 6:15 a.m. and that it was dark; that he found both the wagon and the truck on the street level, the truck about 15 feet south of the top of the incline and the wagon south of it; that the left front fender of the truck was dented in and the right rear wheel of the wagon damaged; that at least three electric street lamps were lighted, one on the east side of the street, about 35 or 40 feet south of the viaduct, one on the west side of the street, between the viaduct and the top of the incline, and one at the top of the incline; that the lights on the truck were working; that there was a lantern with a white globe hanging by a wire from the rear axle of the wagon, but that it was out and cold; and that the lantern was caked with mud, with its bottom 6 or 8 inches from the pavement.

Officer McNamara, who arrived with officer O'Brien, testified that it was 5:55 or 6 a.m. when they reached the scene, and dark; and that the lantern on the wagon was out and very dirty.

Nicholas Marcuessei, an officer of defendant company, testified that he saw the lantern on the wagon several hours after the accident and that it was dirty. The driver of defendant's truck was not a witness, being in Europe at the time of the trial.

It is conceded by plaintiff that there was no red globe on the lantern on the rear of his wagon.

Defendant introduced in evidence the following section of the 1931 Revised Municipal Code of Chicago:

> "Section 2045. White and Red Lights to be Displayed. When upon any streets, alleys or public places within the city during the period from sunset to one hour before sunrise every motor bicycle and every horse drawn vehicle shall carry one lighted lamp and every other motor vehicle two lighted lamps showing white lights visible at least two hundred feet in the direction toward which such motorcycle, horse drawn vehicle or other motor vehicle is proceeding, and shall also exhibit at least one lighted lamp, which shall be so lighted as to throw a red light visible in the reverse direction; provided, however, that no motor vehicle or horse drawn vehicle shall maintain any light other than a white light or lights visible in the direction in which such motor vehicle or horse drawn vehicle is traveling; and provided, further, that no light other than a red light or lights * * * shall be visible from the rear of such motor vehicle or horse drawn vehicle. * * *"

that it was dark; that he found both the wagon and the truck on the street level, the truck about 15 feet south of the top of the incline and the wagon south of it; that the left front fender of the truck was dented in and the right rear wheel of the wagon damaged; that at least three electric street lamps were lighted, one on the east side of the street, about 35 or 40 feet south of the viaduct, one on the west side of the street, between the viaduct and the top of the incline, and one at the top of the incline; that the lights on the truck were working; that there was a lantern with a white globe hanging by a wire from the rear axle of the wagon, but that it was out and cold; and that the lantern was caked with mud, with its bottom 6 or 8 inches from the pavement.

Officer McNamara, who arrived with officer O'Brien, testified that it was 5:50 or 6 a.m. when they reached the scene, and dark; and that the lantern on the wagon was out and very dirty.

Nicholas Mavrascoi, an officer of defendant company, testified that he saw the lantern on the wagon several hours after the accident and that it was dirty. The driver of defendant's truck was not a witness, being in Europe at the time of the trial.

It is conceded by plaintiff that there was no red globe on the lantern on the rear of his wagon.

Defendant introduced in evidence the following section of the 1931 Revised Municipal Code of Chicago:

"Section 3045. White and Red Lights to be Displayed. When upon any streets, alleys or public places within the city during the period from sunset to one hour before sunrise every motor bicycle and every horse drawn vehicle shall carry one lighted lamp and every other motor vehicle two lighted lamps showing white lights visible at least two hundred feet in the direction toward which such motorcycle, horse drawn vehicle or other motor vehicle is proceeding, and shall also exhibit at least one lighted lamp, which shall be so lighted as to throw a red light visible in the reverse direction; provided, however, that no motor vehicle or horse drawn vehicle shall maintain any light other than a white light or lights visible in the direction in which such motor vehicle or horse drawn vehicle is traveling; and provided, further, that no light other than a red light or lights * * * shall be visible from the rear of such motor vehicle or horse drawn vehicle. * * *"

Defendant also offered and the trial court allowed in evidence a monthly meteorological summary of the United States Department of Agriculture, weather bureau, for the month of November, 1932, which showed that on November 29, 1932, the hour of sunrise in Chicago was 6:56 a.m.

Plaintiff insists that the admission in evidence of the city ordinance and the weather chart constitute prejudicial error and that neither of these exhibits tended to prove any issue in the case. He cites no authority in support of this contention and we think it is without merit.

Under its terms the ordinance did not require plaintiff to exhibit a red light on the rear of his wagon after 5:56 a.m. on the morning in question. While plaintiff's evidence tended to establish the time of the accident at 6 a.m. or later, defendant offered evidence to the effect that it occurred shortly before 5:55 a.m. With this conflict in the evidence as to the time of the accident, even though it concerned only a matter of minutes, the weather chart (C. & E. I. R. R. Co. v. Rapp, 209 Ill. 339) and the ordinance were clearly competent. (Johnson v. Prendergast, 308 Ill. 255; Cahill's Ill. Rev. St., 1933, ch. 51, par. 57, sec. 1.)

Plaintiff complains that the trial court erroneously excluded a written statement signed by his witness Pedersen, consistent with his testimony. The statement was clearly inadmissible and the court properly excluded it. (Chicago City Ry. Co. v. Matthiesen, 212 Ill. 292; Stolp v. Blair, 68 Ill. 541.)

Plaintiff urges that, regardless of any conflict that there may have been in the testimony as to the time of the accident, defendant was estopped to deny facts on the trial which it admitted in response to notice served upon it to "admit facts" under par. 2 of rule 18, rules of practice of the Supreme Court of Illinois. Plaintiff's notice was to admit the following among other facts:

Defendant also offered and the trial court allowed in evidence a monthly meteorological summary of the United States Department of Agriculture, weather bureau, for the month of November, 1932, which showed that on November 20, 1932, the hour of sunrise in Chicago was 6:56 a.m.

Plaintiff insists that the admission in evidence of the city ordinance and the weather chart constitute prejudicial error and that neither of these exhibits tended to prove any issue in the case. He cites no authority in support of this contention and we think it is without merit.

Under its terms the ordinance did not require plaintiff to exhibit a red light on the rear of his wagon after 5:56 a.m. on the morning in question. While plaintiff's evidence tended to establish the time of the accident at 6 a.m. or later, defendant offered evidence to the effect that it occurred shortly before 5:55 a.m. With this conflict in the evidence as to the time of the accident, even though it concerned only a matter of minutes, the weather chart (C. & E. I. R. R. Co. v. Mann, 200 Ill. 230) and the ordinance were clearly competent. (Johnson v. Prendergast, 308 Ill. 255; Cahill's Ill. Rev. St., 1933, ch. 51, par. 57, sec. 1.)

Plaintiff complains that the trial court erroneously excluded a written statement signed by his witness Pedersen, consistent with his testimony. The statement was clearly inadmissible and the court properly excluded it. (Chicago City Ry. Co. v. Matthieson, 212 Ill. 292; Stolp v. Blair, 68 Ill. 541.)

Plaintiff urges that, regardless of any conflict that there may have been in the testimony as to the time of the accident, defendant was estopped to deny facts on the trial which it admitted in response to notice served upon it to "admit facts" under par. 9 of rule 18, rules of practice of the Supreme Court of Illinois. Plaintiff's notice was to admit the following among other facts:

"Notice to Admit Facts.

That the Gonella Baking Company, a corporation, was the owner of a certain automobile commonly known and described as a Ford Truck, then bearing License Number M27524, propelled and operated by one Bruno Bertolimo on Western Avenue, at or near its intersection with Fulton Avenue, in Chicago, Illinois, on the 29th day of November, A. D. 1932, at the hour of to-wit; 6:00 A.M.

That on November 29, 1932, Bruno Bartoloni was then and there employed by the Gonella Baking Company, a corporation, in the operation of said automobile or Ford Truck, on and along said Western Avenue at to-wit; its intersection with Fulton Avenue in Chicago, Illinois, at to-wit: 6:00 A.M."

Pursuant to the notice defendant admitted the facts as stated and the question presented for our consideration is whether it is bound by its admission of the time of the accident (6 a.m.), as set forth under a videlicet, as it was here. We are constrained to hold that it was not so bound. If plaintiff's purpose was to bind defendant as to the exact time of the accident in his notice to admit facts, he should have definitely set forth the time in his notice. The office of the videlicet is to indicate that the party does not undertake to prove the precise circumstances alleged, and in such cases he is not required to prove them. (Bouvier's Law Dictionary, vol. 3, page 3400; Brown v. Berry, 47 Ill. 175.) Inasmuch as the notice to admit facts is in the nature of a pleading, in our opinion the same rule applies to facts set forth under a videlicet and defendant can only be held to have admitted that the accident occurred at or about 6 a.m.

Plaintiff urges that under the facts and circumstances in evidence, including the physical facts, his violation of the city ordinance, if there was a violation, could not possibly have contribute to the accident. While the law is well settled that a violation of a city ordinance is prima facie evidence of negligence, the mere fact that plaintiff was violating the law at the time he was injured will not bar his right to recover unless the unlawful act in some way proximately contributed to the accident in which he was injured. (Star Brewery Co. v. Hauck, 222 Ill. 348; Graham v. Hagmann, 270 Ill. 252.)

"Notice to Admit Facts.

That the Gonella Baking Company, a corporation, was the owner of a certain automobile commonly known and described as a Ford Truck, then bearing License Number 237324, propelled and operated by one Bruno Bertoloni on Western Avenue, at or near its intersection with Fulton Avenue, in Chicago, Illinois, on the 29th day of November, A. D. 1932, at the hour of to-wit: 6:00 A.M.

That on November 29, 1932, Bruno Bertoloni was then and there employed by the Gonella Baking Company, a corporation, in the operation of said automobile or Ford Truck, on and along said Western Avenue at to-wit: its intersection with Fulton Avenue in Chicago, Illinois, at to-wit: 6:00 A.M."

Pursuant to the notice defendant admitted the facts as stated and the question presented for our consideration is whether it is bound by its admission of the time of the accident (6 a.m.), as set forth under a _videlicet_, as it was here. We are constrained to hold that it was not so bound. If plaintiff's purpose was to bind defendant as to the exact time of the accident in his notice to admit facts, he should have definitely set forth the time in his notice. The office of the _videlicet_ is to indicate that the party does not undertake to prove the precise circumstances alleged, and in such cases he is not required to prove them. (Bouvier's Law Dictionary, vol. 3, page 3400; _Kuhn_ v. _Henry_, 47 Ill. 179.) Inasmuch as the notice to admit facts is in the nature of a pleading, in our opinion the same rule applies to facts set forth under a _videlicet_ and defendant can only be held to have admitted that the accident occurred at or about 6 a.m.

Plaintiff urges that under the facts and circumstances in evidence, including the physical facts, his violation of the city ordinance, if there was a violation, could not possibly have contributed to the accident. While the law is well settled that a violation of a city ordinance is _prima facie_ evidence of negligence, the mere fact that plaintiff was violating the law at the time he was injured will not bar his right to recover unless the unlawful act in some way proximately contributed to the accident in which he was injured. (_Star Brewery Co._ v. _Hauck_, 222 Ill. 348; _Graham_ v. _Hagmann_, 270 Ill. 252.)

It was incumbent upon plaintiff to show affirmatively that defendant was guilty of the negligence charged; that such negligence was the proximate cause of the injury in question; and that just prior to and at the time of said injury Fraiman was in the exercise of ordinary care for his own safety. Under the record presented on this appeal the questions as to the time of the accident, whether plaintiff was violating the city ordinance at such time, whether, if he were, such violation proximately contributed to the accident, and negligence and contributory negligence, were properly submitted by the court to the jury.

Plaintiff earnestly contends that the verdict is clearly and manifestly against the weight of the evidence. Inasmuch as this case must be retried for reasons hereafter shown, it is not our purpose nor would it be proper for us to discuss this contention, the evidence in the record, or the credibility of the witnesses.

It is urged as a ground for reversal that in the course of the direct examination of Dr. J. L. Davenport, a medical witness for plaintiff, the trial court made improper remarks to the witness which were prejudicial to plaintiff. The court said to the witness in the presence of the jury: "Do you want me to send you to jail?" That portion of the witness' examination immediately preceding the court's remark was as follows:

"Q. You did a spinal puncture to him, and will you describe what you mean, Doctor, by a spinal puncture?
A. Well we did a spinal puncture on him, and took out a slight bit of the spinal fluid.
Q. Will you repeat it?
A. Did a spinal puncture and took off pressure and eased it on him, which after being punctured and running a bit remained practically normal excepting as to the noise in the head and ear. After we did the spinal puncture he said he felt much better.
Mr. Hinshaw: I object, and move it be stricken.
Mr. Herzon: (Addressing witness) No you cannot.
Mr. Hinshaw: I am sorry, I am sorry, I am making objection when you get through. I object. Let the witness be instructed to follow -
The Witness: I am a human being all the same, and you don't know it all."

While it is the duty of the court to preserve its own

-6-

It was incumbent upon plaintiff to show affirmatively that defendant was guilty of the negligence charged; that such negligence was the proximate cause of the injury in question; and that just prior to and at the time of said injury Krahnman was in the exercise of ordinary care for his own safety. Under the record presented on this appeal the questions as to the time of the accident, whether plaintiff was violating the city ordinance at such time, whether, if he were, such violation proximately contributed to the accident, and negligence and contributory negligence, were properly submitted by the court to the jury. etc.

Plaintiff earnestly contends that the verdict is clearly and manifestly against the weight of the evidence. Inasmuch as this case must be reversed for reasons hereafter shown, it is not our purpose nor would it be proper for us to discuss this contention, the evidence in the record, or the credibility of the witnesses.

It is urged as a ground for reversal that in the course of the direct examination of Dr. J. L. Davenport, a medical witness for plaintiff, the trial court made improper remarks to the witness which were prejudicial to plaintiff. The court said to the witness in the presence of the jury: "Do you want me to send you to jail?" That portion of the witness' examination immediately preceding the court's remark was as follows:

"Q. You did a spinal puncture to him, and will you describe what you mean, Doctor, by a spinal puncture?

A. Well we did a spinal puncture on him, and took out a slight bit of the spinal fluid.

Q. Will you repeat it?

A. Did a spinal puncture and took off pressure and eased it on him, which after being punctured and running a bit remained practically normal excepting as to the noise in the head and ear. After we did the spinal puncture he said he felt much better.

Mr. Hinshaw: I object, and move it be stricken.

Mr. Gordon: (Addressing witness) Do you remember.

Mr. Hinshaw: I am sorry, I am sorry, I am making objection when you get through. I object. Let the witness be instructed to follow -

The Witness: I am a human being all the same, and you don't know it all."

While it is the duty of the court to preserve its own

Ill. 288.)

dignity and the respect due to the courts and the administration of the law by not allowing a witness to overstep the bounds of proper decorum, we fail to perceive in the witness's conduct or in his statement obviously directed to defendant's attorney, who he apparently felt was mistreating him, sufficient to justify the court's threat in the presence of the jury to send the witness, a reputable physician, to jail. A much less extreme and satisfactory method could certainly have been adopted by the court to advise the witness of the rules necessary to be observed and to admonish him to conform to them. Appreciating that jurors are prone to be influenced by any act or word of the presiding judge, we think that the evident effect of the court's language was to cause them to be prejudiced against plaintiff's witness and plaintiff's case. But defendant's counsel say that no objection was taken to the remark of the court and therefore the point cannot be urged here. With this we are unable to agree. The briefs of both parties indicate that when this incident occurred the atmosphere of the court room was not conducive to interference by counsel for plaintiff in behalf of the witness, and we are inclined to think that an objection by him, under the circumstances, would have only aggravated the situation and have been considered by the jury as an affront and display of disrespect to the court, simply tending to further excite the prejudice of the jury.

The following question to which objection was made and overruled, and of which complaint is now made, was asked of plaintiff's witness, Pedersen, by defendant's counsel. "Isn't it a fact that you had a conversation with Mr. Straketh, - a conversation with a man who came to see you from the office of the attorney for plaintiff, from the office of the attorney who represents Harry Fraiman, and isn't it a fact that you were asked to testify to a set of facts to help this man get some money out of the Baking Company?" We think that this question was highly improper and could only have tended to dignity and the respect due to the courts and this spirit is not of the law by not allowing a witness to overstep the bounds of proper decorum, we fail to perceive in the witness's conduct or in his statement obviously directed to defendant's attorney, who he apparently felt was mistreating him, sufficient to justify the court's threat in the presence of the jury to send the witness, a reputable physician, to jail. Much less extreme and satisfactory methods could certainly have been adopted by the court to advise the witness of the rules necessary to be observed and to admonish him to conform to them. Appreciating that jurors are prone to be influenced by any act or word of the presiding judge, we think that the evident effect of the court's language was to cause them to be prejudiced against plaintiff's witness and plaintiff's case. But defendant's counsel say that no objection was taken to the remark of the court and therefore the point cannot be urged here. With this we are unable to agree. The briefs of both parties indicate that when this incident occurred the atmosphere of the court room was not conducive to interference by counsel for plaintiff in behalf of the witness, and we are inclined to think that an objection by him, under the circumstances, would have only aggravated the situation and have been considered by the jury as an affront and display of disrespect to the court, simply tending to further excite the prejudices of the jury.

The following question to which objection was made and overruled, and of which complaint is now made, was asked of plaintiff's witness, Pedersen, by defendant's counsel. "Isn't it a fact that you had a conversation with Mr. Strakety, - a conversation with a man who came to see you from the office of the attorney for plaintiff, from the office of the attorney who represents Harry Friedman, and isn't it a fact that you were asked to testify to a set of facts to help this man get some money out of the Baking Company?" We think that this question was highly improper and could only have tended to produce an inference in the minds of the jurors that the witness was actuated, in testifying, by ulterior motives. Counsel attempts to justify his conduct in asking this question by stating in his brief that he had before him, at the time, copies of statements made by Pedersen directly contrary to his testimony at the trial. Counsel does not state or even pretend that the statements in his possession contained any information that the witness was asked "to testify to a set of facts to help this man get some money out of the Baking Company." He did call two of his investigators to testify in an attempt to impeach Pedersen on other matters, but no attempt was made through them to impeach him on the subject matter of this question. The question was clearly prejudicial to plaintiff. (City of Centralia v. Ayres, 133 Ill. App. 290; Marshall v. Davis, 147 Ill. App. 137.)

Other incidents, more or less prejudicial in their character, are charged by counsel for plaintiff, but in the view we take of this appeal we deem it unnecessary to discuss them.

The evidence was in sharp conflict on many of the material questions of fact and it was essential in order to afford both litigants a dispassionate and impartial trial that both court and counsel conduct themselves so as not to prejudice either party to the cause.

Convinced that the ends of justice will be best served by a retrial of this case, the judgment of the Superior court is reversed and the cause is remanded.

REVERSED AND REMANDED.

Friend, P. J., and Scanlan, J., concur.

produce an inference in the minds of the jurors that the witness was actuated, in testifying, by ulterior motives. Counsel attempts to justify his conduct in asking this question by stating in his brief that he had before him, at the time, copies of statements made by Pedersen directly contrary to his testimony at the trial. Counsel does not state or even pretend that the statements in his possession contained any information that the witness was asked "to testify to a set of facts to help this man get some money out of the Baking Company." He did call two of his investigators to testify in an attempt to impeach Pedersen on other matters, but no attempt was made through them to impeach him on the subject matter of this question. The question was clearly prejudicial to plaintiff. (City of Centralia v. Ayres, 133 Ill. App. 290; Marshall v. Davis, 147 Ill. App. 137.)

Other incidents, more or less prejudicial in their character, are charged by counsel for plaintiff, but in the view we take of this appeal we deem it unnecessary to discuss them.

The evidence was in sharp conflict on many of the material questions of fact and it was essential in order to afford both litigants a dispassionate and impartial trial that both court and counsel conduct themselves so as not to prejudice either party to the cause.

Convinced that the ends of justice will be best served by a retrial of this case, the judgment of the Superior court is reversed and the cause is remanded.

REVERSED AND REMANDED.

Friend, P. J., and Scanlan, J., concur.

61 H

37792

EDITH C. SHAMBAUGH,
Appellee,

v.

DAN U. CAMERON,
Appellant.

APPEAL FROM MUNICIPAL COURT OF CHICAGO.

280 I.A. 624[3]

MR. JUSTICE SULLIVAN DELIVERED THE OPINION OF THE COURT.

By this appeal the defendant, Dan U. Cameron, seeks to reverse a judgment for $473 rendered against him in a fourth class contract action in the Municipal court, tried by the court without a jury.

Plaintiff's statement of claim filed December 22, 1933, alleges in substance that she is the owner of five $1,000 bonds; that all of such bonds were executed by defendant April 1, 1925, and bear interest at the rate of 6% per annum, payable semiannually on April 1 and October 1 of each year, as evidenced by interest coupons in the sum of $30 each; that defendant failed and refused to pay the interest which became due and payable October 1, 1932, April 1, 1933, and October 1, 1933; and that he is indebted to plaintiff in the amount of $473.03 on said interest coupons together with interest thereon at 7% since their several maturities, as therein provided.

In his affidavit of merits defendant did not deny his execution of the bonds and interest coupons nor that the interest coupons were unpaid, but alleged that the principal bonds which were secured by a trust deed made reference to the trust deed for a recital of the rights of the bondholders; and that under the terms of the trust deed, plaintiff was precluded from instituting

37792

EDITH C. SHAMBAUGH,
Appellee,

v.

DAN U. CAMERON,
Appellant.

APPEAL FROM MUNICIPAL COURT

OF CHICAGO.

280 I.A. 624[3]

MR. JUSTICE SULLIVAN DELIVERED THE OPINION OF THE COURT.

By this appeal the defendant, Dan U. Cameron, seeks to reverse a judgment for $475 rendered against him in a fourth class contract action in the municipal court, tried by the court without a jury.

Plaintiff's statement of claim filed December 22, 1933, alleges in substance that she is the owner of five $1,000 bonds; that all of such bonds were executed by defendant April 1, 1926, and bear interest at the rate of 6% per annum, payable semiannually on April 1 and October 1 of each year, as evidenced by interest coupons in the sum of $30 each; that defendant failed and refused to pay the interest which became due and payable October 1, 1932, April 1, 1933, and October 1, 1933; and that he is indebted to plaintiff in the amount of $475.03 on said interest coupons together with interest thereon at 5% since their several maturities, as therein provided.

In his affidavit of merits defendant did not deny his execution of the bonds and interest coupons nor that the interest coupons were unpaid, but alleged that the principal bonds which were secured by a trust deed made reference to the trust deed for a recital of the rights of the bondholders; and that under the terms of the trust deed, plaintiff was precluded from instituting an action at law in her own name on her interest coupons.

Defendant contends that the rights of the holders of the interest coupons are determined by the provisions of the bonds to which they had been theretofore attached, especially where both the bonds and the interest coupons are owned by the same person, as they are here; that, by the express provisions of the bonds and the conditions in the trust deed to which they make reference, plaintiff, who did not comply with these conditions, is barred from maintaining this action; and that the reference in the bonds to the trust deed is sufficiently explicit to incorporate into them its terms, at least to the extent that plaintiff was put on notice of the provisions of the trust deed which limited her right to bring this suit.

The trust deed under which the bonds and interest coupons were issued in this case containsthe following provision:

"Section 11. No holder of any bond or coupon secured hereby shall have any right to institute any suit, action or proceeding in equity or at law for the foreclosure of this indenture, or for the execution of any trust hereof or for the appointment of a receiver or for any other remedy hereunder, unless such holder shall previously have given to the Trustee written notice of such default and of the continuance thereof as hereinbefore provided, nor unless, also, the holders of one-fifth (1/5) in principal amount of the bonds issued hereunder, then outstanding, shall have made written request to the Trustee, and shall have offered to it a reasonable opportunity either to proceed to exercise the powers hereinbefore granted or to institute such action, suit or proceeding in its own name, and the Trustee shall have refused or unreasonably delayed to comply with such request, nor unless, else, they or some one or more of the holders of said bonds shall have offered to the Trustee security and indemnity to the satisfaction of the Trustee against the cost, expenses and liabilities to be incurred therein or thereby, and such notification, request and offer of indemnity are hereby declared, in every such case, at the option of the Trustee, to be conditions precedent to the execution of the powers and trusts of this indenture for the benefit of the bondholders, and to any action or cause of action for foreclosure, or for the appointment of a receiver, or for any other remedy hereunder, it being understood and intended that no one or more holders of bonds and coupons shall have any right, in any manner whatsoever, by his or their action to effect disturb or prejudice the lien of this indenture, or to enforce any right hereunder, except in the manner herein provided, and that all proceedings at law or in equity shall be instituted, had and maintained in the manner herein provided, and for the equal benefit of all holders of such outstanding bonds and coupons."

The recitals contained in the bonds, upon which defendant

an action at law in her own name on her interest coupons.

Defendant contends that the rights of the holders of the interest coupons are determined by the provisions of the bonds to which they had been theretofore attached, especially where both the bonds and the interest coupons are owned by the same person, as they are here; that, by the express provisions of the bonds and the conditions in the trust deed to which they make reference, plaintiff, who did not comply with those conditions, is barred from maintaining this action; and that the reference in the bonds to the trust deed is sufficiently explicit to incorporate into them its terms, at least to the extent that plaintiff was put on notice of the provisions of the trust deed which limited her right to bring this suit.

The trust deed under which the bonds and interest coupons were issued in this case containsthe following provision:

"Section 11. No holder of any bond or coupon secured hereby shall have any right to institute any suit, action or proceeding in equity or at law for the foreclosure of this indenture, or for the execution of any trust hereof or for the appointment of a receiver or for any other remedy hereunder, unless such holder shall previously have given to the Trustee written notice of such default and of the continuance thereof as hereinbefore provided, nor unless, also, the holders of one-fifth (1/5) in principal amount of the bonds issued hereunder, then outstanding, shall have made written request to the Trustee, and shall have offered to it a reasonable opportunity either to proceed to exercise the powers hereinbefore granted or to institute such action, suit or proceeding in its own name, and the Trustee shall have refused or unreasonably delayed to comply with such request, nor unless, also, they or some one or more of the holders of said bonds shall have offered to the Trustee security and indemnity to the satisfaction of the Trustee against the cost, expenses and liabilities to be incurred therein or thereby, and such notification, request and offer of indemnity are hereby declared, in every such case, at the option of the Trustee, to be conditions precedent to the execution of the powers and trusts of this indenture for the benefit of the bondholders, and to any action or cause of action for foreclosure, or for the appointment of a receiver, or for any other remedy hereunder, it being understood and intended that no one or more holders of bonds and coupons shall have any right, in any manner whatsoever, by his or their action to affect disturb or prejudice the lien of this indenture, or to enforce any right hereunder, except in the manner herein provided, and that all proceedings at law or in equity shall be instituted, had and maintained in the manner herein provided, and for the equal benefit of all holders of such outstanding bonds and coupons."

a x (t) The recitals contained in the bonds, upon which defendant

terms of [illegible]

relies as adequately incorporating into the bonds by reference the above provisions of the trust deed containing the so-called no action clause, are as follows:

"* * * Reference being hereby made to said deed of trust for the number and description of the premises conveyed and mortgaged, the nature and extent of the security thereby created, the nature of the rights of the holders of said bonds and of the Trustee in respect of such security."

Two questions are presented for our consideration on this appeal. 1. Assuming that the bonds in question contain adequate and clear reference to all the restrictions contained in the trust deed, is there any limitation in any provision of the trust deed of plaintiff's right to maintain this action at law? 2. Has plaintiff a right to sue at law for the recovery of the amount of her interest coupons or is she relegated to the provisions of the no action clause in the trust deed? (Meyer v. Ludlow Typograph Company, No. 37537, Appellate Court, First district, opinion not published.)

In answer to the first question it is sufficient to say that there is nothing in the trust deed that expressly forbids individual holders of bonds or interest coupons to bring actions at law thereon. The only restrictive provisions in the trust deed limiting an individual's right to proceed to enforce payment of his interest coupons in case of default are those heretofore set forth. Examination of these provisions demonstrates that such terms, conditions and limitations as are therein imposed apply only to proceedings brought under the trust deed itself.

We are clearly of the opinion that under the facts in the instant case the purpose of the restrictions contained in section 11 of the trust deed was to limit individual action only in the institution of foreclosure proceedings or other actions at law or in equity under the trust deed and not in the commencement of an action to recover upon the personal obligation of defendant, and that plaintiff had the right to sue the mortgagor for a judgment on his personal [illegible] so adequately [illegible] than the words by reference the above provisions of the trust deed contain [illegible] so-called no action clause, are as follows:

"[illegible] each holder [illegible] hereby [illegible] to this deed of trust for the nature and description of the premises conveyed and mortgaged, the nature and extent of the security thus [illegible], the rights of the holders of said bonds and of the trustee in respect of such security."

Two questions are presented for our [illegible] in this appeal. 1. Assuming that the bonds in question contain adequate and clear reference to all the restrictive provisions in the trust deed, is there any limitation in any provision of the trust deed of plaintiff's right to maintain this action at law? 2. Has plaintiff a right to sue at law for the recovery of the amount of the interest coupons or is she relegated to the provisions of the no-action clause in the trust deed? (Henry v. [illegible] Company, No. 27537, Appellate Court, First District, opinion not published.)

In answer to the first question it is sufficient to say that there is nothing in the trust deed that expressly prohibits individual holders of bonds or interest coupons to bring actions at law thereon. The only restrictive provisions in the trust deed limiting an individual's right to sue [illegible] to enforce payment of his interest coupons in case of default [illegible] the examination of those provisions demonstrates that such terms, conditions and limitations as are therein imposed apply only to proceedings brought under the trust deed itself.

[illegible] clearly [illegible] the opinion [illegible] in the instant case the purpose of the [illegible] provision [illegible] of the trust deed was to limit [illegible] in the institution of foreclosure proceedings [illegible] other [illegible] in equity under the trust deed, and not in the common case of an action to recover upon the personal obligation of a defendant, as that plaintiff had the right to sue the mortgagor for a judgment on his personal obligation. (Schatzakis v. Rosenwald & Weil, 267 Ill. App. 169; Aeskad v. Thorgersen and Ericksen, No. 37549, Appellate Court, First District, opinion not published.)

If we assume that the quoted provisions of the trust deed are such as to limit the right of bondholders or holders of interest coupons to sue at law, are they incorporated into the bonds expressly or by such clear reference as to bar plaintiff's right to maintain this action?

Even if the trust deed does contain a so-called no action clause, it is readily apparent that the language in the bonds heretofore referred to contains no adequate reference thereto, but simply constitutes a reference to the description, nature and extent of the security and the rights of the bondholders and trustee thereunder. The description of the property and security constitute the subject matter of the clause and to hold that the provisions of the trust deed limiting the right to sue at law was thus included by reference is to bind the bondholder by a stipulation of the trust deed of which the bonds gave him no warning or notice. (Oswianza v. Wengler & Mandell, 358 Ill. 302; Cummings v. Michigan-Lake Bldg. Corp., 277 Ill. App. 470; Aeskad v. Thorgersen and Ericksen, supra; Meyer v. Ludlow Typograph Company, supra.) In the Oswianza case, which is the latest expression of our Supreme Court on the subject, the court said:

"It follows that if there be read into the bonds in this case the no-action provisions of the trust deed it must be by an appropriate reference found in the bond. * * * This case resolves itself into the question whether there is in the bond language which may reasonably be said to incorporate therein, by reference, the no-action clause of the trust deed. * * * The language is so phrased and arrangedas to strongly indicate that the obligor was speaking solely of the security. The purchaser of these bonds would not be impressed with any other thought. It would not occur to him, from this language, that in case the bonds were defaulted on maturity, as is true here, he might be unable to collect because of some provision in the trust deed limiting his power to sue at law. Enforcement against the security and a suit at law are matters of radically different import, and to destroy the right to sue at law, a Provision of such character in the trust deed must be included in the bond, expressly or by clear reference thereto. Sturgis Nat. Bank v. Harris Trust and Savings Bank, (351 Ill. 465); Enoch v.

obligation. (Schmidt v. Rosenwald & Weil, 267 Ill. App. 169; Aenked v. Thorgersen and Erickson, No. 37549, Appellate Court, First District, opinion not published.)

If we assume that the quoted provisions of the trust deed are such as to limit the right of bondholders or holders of interest coupons to sue at law, are they incorporated into the bonds expressly or by such clear reference as to bar plaintiff's right to maintain this action?

Even if the trust deed does contain a so-called no action clause, it is readily apparent that the language in the bonds heretofore referred to contains no adequate reference thereto, but simply constitutes a reference to the description, nature and extent of the security and the rights of the bondholders and trustee thereunder. The description of the property and security constitute the subject matter of the clause and to hold that the provisions of the trust deed limiting the right to sue at law was thus included by reference is to bind the bondholder by a stipulation of the trust deed of which the bonds gave him no warning or notice. (Cunningham v. Wengler & Mendell, 358 Ill. 308; Cummings v. Michigan-Lake Bldg. Corp., 277 Ill. App. 470; Aenked v. Thorgersen and Erickson, supra; Mayer v. Ludlow Typograph Company, supra.) In the Cunningham case, which is the latest expression of our Supreme Court on the subject, the court said:

"It follows that if there be read into the bonds in this case the no-action provisions of the trust deed it must be by an appropriate reference found in the bond. * * * This case resolves itself into the question whether there is in the bond language which may reasonably be said to incorporate therein, by reference, the no-action clause of the trust deed. * * * The language is so phrased and arranged as to strongly indicate that the obligor was speaking solely of the security. The purchaser of these bonds would not be impressed with any other thought. It would not occur to him, from this language, that in case the bonds were defaulted on maturity, as is true here, he might be unable to collect because of some provision in the trust deed limiting his power to sue at law. Enforcement against the security and a suit at law are matters of radically different import, and to destroy the right to sue at law, a provision of such character in the trust deed must be included in the bond, expressly or by clear reference thereto. Sturgis Nat. Bank v. Harris Trust and Savings Bank, (351 Ill. 465); Enoch v.

Brandon, 249 N. Y. 263, 164 N. E. 45. * * * The importance of bonds of this character as commercial paper requires that limitation on the right to sue, appearing in another instrument, be so clearly referred to in the bond that the purchaser of the bond will not be deceived but will be notified that he is to look further to know his rights as a bondholder. If a principle of public policy be invoked, it is quite important that in the traffic of bonds the prospective purchaser thereof know from the bond what search of the trust deed or mortgage is necessary in order to learn his rights. * * * If the common law rights of the holder are to be limited it must be done by appropriate reference in the bond to the provisions of the trust deed or mortgage, that he may have warning that his right to sue in case of default is limited by something not appearing in the bond itself."

Something is said here about the negotiability of the interest coupons. The question of the negotiability of the bonds was raised in the Oswianza case and the court said: "It does not follow, however, that all notes or bonds on which a right to sue exists are negotiable instruments and so negotiability is not a primary factor in determining whether a right to sue at law exists here."

Our decision, as were the decisions in the Cummings, Meyer and Asabad cases, is controlled by the Oswianza case, inasmuch as the reference in the bonds here to the restrictions in the trust deed is limited to the description, nature and extent of the security as it was in that case.

For the reasons indicated herein the judgment of the Municipal court is affirmed.

AFFIRMED.

Friend, P. J., and Scanlan, J., concur.

Brandon, 249 N. Y. 263, 164 N. E. 45. * * * The importance of bonds of this character as commercial paper requires that limitation on the right to sue, appearing in another instrument, be so clearly referred to in the bond that the purchaser of the bond will not be deceived but will be notified that he is to look further to know his rights as a bondholder. If a principle of public policy be invoked, it is quite important that in the traffic of bonds the prospective purchaser thereof know from the bond what search of the trust deed or mortgage is necessary in order to learn his rights. * * * If the common law rights of the holder are to be limited it must be done by appropriate reference in the bond to the provisions of the trust deed or mortgage, that he may have warning that his right to sue in case of default is limited by something not appearing in the bond itself."

Something is said here about the negotiability of the interest coupons. The question of the negotiability of the bonds was raised in the Gavlanes case and the court said: "It does not follow, however, that all notes or bonds on which a right to sue exists are negotiable instruments and so negotiability is not a primary factor in determining whether a right to sue at law exists here."

Our decision, as were the decisions in the Cummings, Mayer and Ascher cases, is controlled by the Gavlanes case, inasmuch as the reference in the bonds here to the restrictions in the trust deed is limited to the description, nature and extent of the security as it was in that case.

For the reasons indicated herein the judgment of the Municipal court is affirmed.

AFFIRMED.

Friend, P. J., and Scanlan, J., concur.

624

37849

IRWIN S. MAZE,
Appellant,

v.

ROBERT H. GORE et al.,
Defendants below.

HOWARD F. BISHOP,
Appellee.

APPEAL FROM MUNICIPAL COURT OF CHICAGO.

280 I.A. 6244

MR. JUSTICE SULLIVAN DELIVERED THE OPINION OF THE COURT.

October 9, 1929, plaintiff brought an action in assumpsit against Robert H. Gore and Howard F. Bishop to recover for labor and materials purported to have been furnished at their request in the matter of tree surgery on and the landscaping of certain premises at Lake Zurich, Illinois, alleged to have been owned by defendants. Bishop, the defendant involved in this proceeding (hereinafter for convenience referred to as defendant), was served with an alias summons October 25, 1929. An appearance was filed in his behalf October 29, 1929. Thereafter, November 13, 1929, Bishop was defaulted for want of an affidavit of merits, damages of $564.51 were assessed on plaintiff's affidavit of claim, and judgment entered against him for that amount. June 30, 1934, Bishop filed his written motion in the nature of a petition for a writ of error coram nobis, supported by his verified petition, to vacate the default judgment of November 13, 1929. July 3, 1934, pursuant to order of court to answer within five days, plaintiff filed "motion of plaintiff to strike petition of defendant, Howard F. Bishop, and dismiss and deny same." After a hearing on the above motions the trial court entered

37960

IRWIN G. HANE,
Appellant,

v.

ROBERT H. GORE et al.,
Defendants below.

HOWARD F. BISHOP,
Appellee.

APPEAL FROM MUNICIPAL
COURT OF CHICAGO.

280 I.A. 624

MR. JUSTICE SULLIVAN DELIVERED THE OPINION OF THE COURT.

October 9, 1929, plaintiff brought an action in assumpsit against Robert H. Gore and Howard F. Bishop to recover for labor and materials purported to have been furnished at their request in the matter of tree surgery on and the landscaping of certain premises at Lake Zurich, Illinois, alleged to have been owned by defendants. Bishop, the defendant involved in this proceeding (hereinafter for convenience referred to as defendant), was served with an alias summons October 25, 1929. An appearance was filed in his behalf October 29, 1929. Thereafter, November 13, 1929, Bishop was defaulted for want of an affidavit of merits, damages of $664.51 were assessed on plaintiff's affidavit of claim, and judgment entered against him for that amount. June 30, 1934, Bishop filed his written motion in the nature of a petition for a writ of error coram nobis, supported by his verified petition, to vacate the default judgment of November 13, 1929. July 5, 1934, pursuant to order of court to answer within five days, plaintiff filed "motion of plaintiff to strike petition of defendant, Howard F. Bishop, and dismiss and deny same." After a hearing on the above motions the trial court entered an order July 6, 1934, overruling plaintiff's motion to strike and dismiss defendant's motion and sustaining defendant's motion to vacate the default judgment theretofore rendered. This appeal seeks to reverse that order.

After setting forth that he had a meritorious defense to plaintiff's claim in that he did not own the premises in question and that he did not request plaintiff to furnish the labor and materials upon which his claim was based or receive any benefit therefrom, defendant charged inter alia in his motion to vacate the judgment that upon being served with summons he requested of Edmund P. Kelly, the then attorney for plaintiff, an indefinite extension of time to file his affidavit of merits to plaintiff's statement of claim until his codefendant, Gore, was served with summons; that attorney Kelly said that he would grant such extension and that he would advise defendant when Gore had been served; that, contrary to his agreement, Kelly had an order entered extending the time for filing defendant's affidavit of merits only ten days from October 30, 1929, that the default judgment was entered November 13, 1929, either without the knowledge or through an error of attorney Kelly, or with his knowledge and contrary to his agreement; that no notice of any nature was given defendant of the entry of the judgment until after it was too late under the law to sue out a writ of error; that, when he did learn of the judgment, an arrangement was made with plaintiff's new attorney that he would proceed to bring in Gore, the other defendant; and that such attorney kept faith with defendant, finally succeeding in getting service on Gore and trying the case against him March 31, 1934.

Plaintiff in his motion to strike Bishop's petition and to dismiss and deny same, not only questioned the legal sufficiency of such petition because of its alleged failure to state the ground for the vacation of the judgment within the purview of section 72, par. 200, chap. 110, Cahill's Ill. Rev. St., 1933 (section 89 of an order July 6, 1934, overruling plaintiff's motion to strike and dismiss defendant's motion and sustaining defendant's motion to vacate the default judgment theretofore rendered. This appeal seeks to reverse that order.

After setting forth that he had a meritorious defense to plaintiff's claim in that he did not own the premises in question and that he did not request plaintiff to furnish the labor and materials upon which his claim was based or receive any benefit therefrom, defendant charged inter alia in his motion to vacate the judgment that upon being served with summons he requested of Edmund P. Kelly, the then attorney for plaintiff, an indefinite extension of time to file his affidavit of merits to plaintiff's statement of claim until his codefendant, Gore, was served with summons; that attorney Kelly said that he would grant such extension and that he would advise defendant when Gore had been served; that, contrary to his agreement, Kelly had an order entered extending the time for filing defendant's affidavit of merits only ten days from October 30, 1929, that the default judgment was entered November 13, 1929, either without the knowledge or through an error of attorney Kelly, or with his knowledge and contrary to his agreement; that no notice of any nature was given defendant of the entry of the judgment until after it was too late under the law to sue out a writ of error; that, when he did learn of the judgment, an arrangement was made with plaintiff's new attorney that he would proceed to bring in Gore, the other defendant; and that such attorney kept faith with defendant, finally succeeding in getting service on Gore and trying the case against him March 21, 1934.

Plaintiff in his motion to strike Bishop's petition and to dismiss and deny same, not only questioned the legal sufficiency of such petition because of its alleged failure to state the ground for the vacation of the judgment within the purview of section 72, par. 200, chap. 110, Cahill's Ill. Rev. St., 1933 (section 89 of the Practice Act in force prior to January 1, 1934), but raised issues of fact by his traverse of the material allegations of defendant's motion, and by his allegation of new matter in confession and avoidance.

It has been distinctly and definitely held that a motion, such as that made here, in the nature of a petition for a writ of error coram nobis, under the statute, is the commencement of a new action at law in which new issues are made up, and that such suit is independent of the proceeding in which the judgment sought to be set aside was rendered and an entirely new suit at law. (Harris v. Chicago House Wrecking Co., 314 Ill. 500.)

Under the rules of the Municipal court the legal sufficiency of defendant's motion to vacate could be properly tested only by a motion to strike or dismiss same. While plaintiff in his motion questioned the legal sufficiency of defendant's motion to vacate the judgment, he did not stop there but proceeded to traverse the material allegations of same, and also to allege certain affirmative facts as a defense to such motion. It was on the issues of fact thus made that the cause proceeded to hearing. Plaintiff's motion concluded with a verification; it is apparent that it partook both of the nature of a motion to strike or dismiss, which raised only issues of law, and of an affidavit of defense on the merits, raising only issues of fact. That it could not be both and must be held to be one or the other requires no citation of authorities.

A motion to strike or dismiss is in the nature of a demurrer and when a plea or an affidavit of meritorious defense is filed, while a demurrer or motion to dismiss is pending, the demurrer or motion to dismiss is waived. (McNulty v. White, 248 Ill. App. 572.) By pleading to the merits of defendant's motion to vacate the judgment plaintiff must be held to have waived the question of its legal sufficiency. (Klefski v. Railroad Supply Co., 235 Ill. 146; Smith v. Rutledge, 332 the Practice Act in force prior to January 1, 1934), but raised issues of fact by his traverse of the material allegations of defendant's motion, and by his allegation of new matter in confession and avoidance.

It has been distinctly and definitely held that a motion, such as that made here, in the nature of a petition for a writ of error coram nobis, under the statute, is the commencement of a new action at law in which new issues are made up, and that such suit is independent of the proceeding in which the judgment sought to be set aside was rendered and an entirely new suit at law. (Harris v. Chicago House Wrecking Co., 314 Ill. 500.)

Under the rules of the Municipal court the legal sufficiency of defendant's motion to vacate could be properly tested only by a motion to strike or dismiss same. While plaintiff in his motion questioned the legal sufficiency of defendant's motion to vacate the judgment, he did not stop there but proceeded to traverse the material allegations of same, and also to allege certain affirmative facts as a defense to such motion. It was on the issues of fact thus made that the cause proceeded to hearing. Plaintiff's motion concluded with a verification; it is apparent that it partook both of the nature of a motion to strike or dismiss, which raised only issues of law, and of an affidavit of defense on the merits, raising only issues of fact. That it could not be both and must be held to be one or the other requires no citation of authorities.

A motion to strike or dismiss is in the nature of a demurrer and when a plea or an affidavit of meritorious defense is filed, while a demurrer or motion to dismiss is pending, the demurrer or motion to dismiss is waived. (McNulty v. White, 248 Ill. App. 572.) By pleading to the merits of defendant's motion to vacate the judgment plaintiff must be held to have waived the question of its legal sufficiency. (Kiefer v. Railroad Supply Co., 225 Ill. 146; Smith v. Rutledge, 332 id. 150; Ide v. Fratcher, 194 id. 552.)

It is conceded that evidence was heard by the trial court on its hearing on the motions of plaintiff and defendant, but it was not preserved by a bill of exceptions. There being no bill of exceptions we must indulge the presumption that defendant introduced proof sufficient to justify the entry of the order appealed from. (Hagan Paper Co. v. East St. Louis Pub. Co., 269 Ill. 535.)

The order appealed from was the judgment of the court in the new proceeding to vacate the judgment theretofore entered, and the record brought to this court in this cause discloses that plaintiff also failed to present a motion in arrest of the order or judgment. In Smythe v. Fargo, 307 Ill. 300, where a petition in the nature of a writ of error coram nobis to vacate a judgment was filed under section 89 of the Practice Act (identical with section 72 of the Civil Practice Act, supra), and an answer was filed denying the material allegations of such petition, the court, in discussing the nature of the proceeding and the proper mode of procedure to preserve for review the question of the legal sufficiency of the petition, said at p. 304:

"The questions here raised were considered in Domitski v. American Linseed Co., 221 Ill. 161. That was a proceeding under what is now section 89 of the Practice act, to vacate and set aside a judgment previously rendered. The complaining party filed a motion for that purpose, setting up the reasons relied on. It does not appear that the opposite party filed anything in reply, but objected to the motion on the ground the term at which the judgment was rendered had expired and the court had no jurisdiction. Affidavits were read in support of the motion, to all of which a general objection was made. The court sustained the motion and vacated the former judgment, to which exceptions were taken. This court said, in substance, that filing the motion to vacate the former judgment was the commencement of a new suit, in which new issues are made up, on which there must be a finding and judgment, and the motion stands in place of a declaration. It is a suit at law independent of the proceeding in which the judgment sought to be set aside was rendered, and unless an issue of law is made on the motion in the trial court, the question passed upon by that court is one of fact whether or not the court in the former proceeding committed any error in fact. The plaintiff in error in that case contended in this court that the motion did not, on its face, disclose any error in fact and that the court erred in assuming jurisdiction of it. The court held that was a question of law, which should have been saved in some appropriate way recognized by law. As that was not done and no motion in arrest of judgment was made, the question whether the motion

Id. 13 [illegible] v. [illegible], 19 Id. 532.)

It is conceded that evidence was heard [illegible] on its hearing on the motions of plaintiff and [illegible], as it was not preserved by a bill of exceptions. There being no bill of exceptions we must indulge the presumption that defendant introduced proof sufficient to justify the entry of the order appealed from. [illegible] ([illegible] v. [illegible], 207 Ill. 229.)

The order appealed from was the judgment of the court in the new proceeding to vacate the judgment theretofore entered, and the errors brought to this court in this cause discussed that plaintiff also failed to present a motion in arrest of the original judgment. In [illegible] v. [illegible], 207 Ill. [illegible], where a petition in the nature of a writ of error coram nobis to vacate a judgment was filed under section 89 of the Practice act (ch. 110 [illegible] section 7 of the Civil Practice act, supra), and an answer was filed [illegible] material allegations of such petition, the court, in discussing the nature of the proceeding and the proper mode of presenting for review the question of the legal sufficiency of the petition, said at p. 306:

[illegible]

[illegible] trial court, the [illegible] motion [illegible] in fact. The plaintiff in error [illegible] that the motion did not [illegible] that the court erred in assuming jurisdiction [illegible] that was a question of law, which should have been [illegible] appropriate way recognized by law. [illegible] that was not done and no motion in arrest of judgment was made, the [illegible] motion [illegible] on its face disclosed any error in fact was not preserved for review. ***

"The issues made by the answer of plaintiffs in error, which may properly be treated as their plea, were issues of fact. By pleading to the merits of the declaration or motion they waived any question as to its sufficiency, and it will here be treated as properly stating a cause of action." (Italics ours.)

As the case stands no question of law is presented on this record, either as to defendant's motion to vacate the judgment or as to the sufficiency of the evidence. It was purely a question of fact as to whether or not there was an error of fact committed by the court which culminated in the judgment sought to be vacated, and plaintiff has preserved no record entitling him to review or question the facts. There is, therefore, no question properly before this court as to whether or not defendant's motion stated, or whether the evidence proved, within the contemplation of section 72 of the Civil Practice Act, an error of fact in the former proceedings in support of the judgment or order. (Harris v. Chicago House Wrecking Co., supra.)

For the reasons indicated the order or judgment of the Municipal court is affirmed.

AFFIRMED.

Friend, P. J., and Scanlan, J., concur.

on its face disclosed any error in fact was not preserved for review. * * *

> "The issues made by the answer of plaintiffs in error, which may properly be treated as their pl , were issues of fact. By pleading to the merits of the declaration or motion they waived any question as to its sufficiency, and it will here be treated as properly stating a cause of action." (Italics ours.)

As the case stands no question of law is presented on this record, either as to defendant's motion to vacate the judgment or as to the sufficiency of the evidence. It was purely a question of fact as to whether or not there was an error of fact committed by the court which culminated in the judgment sought to be vacated, and plaintiff has preserved no record entitling him to revise or question the facts. There is, therefore, no question properly before this court as to whether or not defendant's motion stated, or whether the evidence proved, within the contemplation of section 72 of the Civil Practice Act, an error of fact in the former proceedings in support of the judgment or order. (Harris v. Chicago House Wrecking Co., supra.)

For the reasons indicated the order or judgment of the Municipal court is affirmed.

AFFIRMED.

Friend, P. J., and Scanlan, J., concur.

634

37889

PEOPLE OF THE STATE OF ILLINOIS,
Defendant in Error,

v.

FRANK GUARDINO,
Plaintiff in Error.

ERROR TO MUNICIPAL COURT OF CHICAGO.

280 I.A. 625

MR. JUSTICE SULLIVAN DELIVERED THE OPINION OF THE COURT.

An information was filed June 28, 1934, charging defendant with violation of par. 439 of chap. 38, Smith-Hurd's 1931 Ill. Rev. Statutes. On the same day defendant was arraigned and entered a plea of not guilty. A trial by jury having been waived the cause was submitted to the court. There was a finding of guilty in manner and form as charged in the information and the court entered judgment on the finding, sentencing defendant to a term of one year at labor in the house of correction and to pay a fine of $10 and costs amounting to $6.50. This writ of error seeks to reverse the judgment.

Defendant contends that the information is fatally defective in that it failed to charge any crime and that the judgment and mittimus issued pursuant thereto are void by reason of the invalidity of the information.

The theory is very feebly advanced by counsel for the state that although not carefully drawn the information "defectively states an offense" in that it "follows the language of the heading of the statute and the language of the caption, showing why this legislation was * * * enacted," and that, inasmuch as no motion was made in the trial court either for a bill of particulars, to quash the information or in arrest of judgment, objection on the ground of the

37380

PEOPLE OF THE STATE OF ILLINOIS,
Defendant in Error,

v.

FRANK GUARDINO,
Plaintiff in Error.

ERROR TO MUNICIPAL
COURT OF CHICAGO.

280 I.A. 628

MR. JUSTICE SULLIVAN DELIVERED THE OPINION OF THE COURT.

An information was filed June 25, 1934, charging defendant with violation of par. 459 of chap. 38, Smith-Hurd's 1931 Ill. Rev. Statutes. On the same day defendant was arraigned and entered a plea of not guilty. A trial by jury having been waived the cause was submitted to the court. There was a finding of guilty in manner and form as charged in the information and the court entered judgment on the finding, sentencing defendant to a term of one year at labor in the house of correction and to pay a fine of $10 and costs amounting to $6.50. This writ of error seeks to reverse the judgment.

Defendant contends that the information is fatally defective in that it failed to charge any crime and that the judgment and mittimus issued pursuant thereto are void by reason of the invalidity of the information.

The theory is very feebly advanced by counsel for the state that although not carefully drawn the information "defectively states an offense" in that it "follows the language of the heading of the statute and the language of the caption, showing why this legislation was * * * enacted," and that, inasmuch as no motion was made in the trial court either for a bill of particulars, to quash the information or in arrest of judgment, objection on the ground of the insufficiency of the information may not be availed of on writ of error.

The statute, supra, creating and defining the offenses which constitute tampering with an automobile, with the violation of which it was sought to charge defendant, is as follows:

"TAMPERING WITH ANY MOTOR VEHICLE. Be it enacted by the People of the State of Illinois, represented in the General Assembly: That it shall be unlawful for any person, intentionally and without authority from the owner, to start or cause to be started the motor of any motor vehicle, or to maliciously shift or change the starting device or gears of a standing motor vehicle, to a position other than that in which it was left by the owner or driver of said motor vehicle; and it shall be unlawful to intentionally cut, mark, scratch or damage the chassis, running gear, body, sides, top, covering or upholstering of any motor vehicle, the property of another, or to intentionally cut, mash, mark, destroy or damage such motor vehicle, or any of the accessories, equipment, appurtenances or attachments thereof, or any spare or extra parts thereon being or thereto attached, without the permission of the owner thereof, or to intentionally release the break upon any standing motor vehicle, with intent to injure said machine or cause the same to be removed without the consent of the owner."

The information filed against defendant in this case (omitting the formal parts) charged that defendant

"Did then and there wilfully and unlawfully tamper with an automobile, towit: One Ford Roadster, Motor No. A-4407474, the property of the said Max Evans without permission from the said Max Evans then and there so to do. Viol. par. 439 of Chap. 38, Smith-Hurd's Revised Statute of 1931 A. D."

A mere inspection of this information clearly demonstrates its insufficiency to charge any of the offenses enumerated in the foregoing statute, either in the words contained therein creating such offenses or in equivalent language.

An indictment or information charging an offense defined by statute should be as descriptive of the offense as is the language of the statute and should allege every substantial element of the defense as defined by the statute. (People v. Sheldon, 322 Ill. 70; People v. Martin, 314 id. 110; People v. Barnes, 314 id. 140; Sokel v. People, 212 id. 238; Cannady v. People, 17 id. 158; People v. O'Brien, 251 Ill. App. 314.) It is fundamental that an information must allege all the facts necessary to constitute the crime with which the defendant insufficiency of the information may not be availed of on writ of error.

The statute, supra, creating and defining the offenses which constitute tampering with an automobile, with the violation of which it was sought to charge defendant, is as follows:

"TAMPERING WITH ANY MOTOR VEHICLE. Be it enacted by the People of the State of Illinois, represented in the General Assembly: That it shall be unlawful for any person, intentionally and without authority from the owner, to start or cause to be started the motor of any motor vehicle, or to maliciously shift or change the starting device or gears of a standing motor vehicle, to a position other than that in which it was left by the owner or driver of said motor vehicle; and it shall be unlawful to intentionally cut, mark, scratch or damage the chassis, running gear, body, sides, top, covering or upholstering of any motor vehicle, the property of another, or to intentionally cut, mash, mark, destroy or damage such motor vehicle, or any of the accessories, equipment, appurtenances or attachments thereof, or any spare or extra parts thereon being or thereto attached, without the permission of the owner thereof, or to intentionally release the brake upon any standing motor vehicle, with intent to injure said machine or cause the same to be removed without the consent of the owner."

The information filed against defendant in this case (omitting the formal parts) charged that defendant

"did then and there wilfully and unlawfully tamper with an automobile, to-wit: One Ford Roadster, Motor No. A-4407674, the property of the said Max Evans without permission from the said Max Evans then and there so to do. Viol. par. 459 of Chap. 38, Smith-Hurd's Revised Statutes of 1931 A. D."

A mere inspection of this information clearly demonstrates its insufficiency to charge any of the offenses enumerated in the foregoing statute, either in the words contained therein creating such offenses or in equivalent language.

An indictment or information charging an offense defined by statute should be as descriptive of the offense as in the language of the statute and should allege every substantial element of the offense as defined by the statute. (People v. Sheldon, 322 Ill. 70; People v. Martin, 314 id. 110; People v. Barnes, 314 id. 140; Sokel v. People, 212 id. 238; Kennedy v. People, 17 id. 158; People v. O'Brien, 231 Ill. App. 314.) It is fundamental that an information must allege all the facts necessary to constitute the crime with which the defendant is charged and if it does not set forth such facts with sufficient certainty it will not support a conviction. (People v. Steyan, 280 Ill. 300; People v. Blue, 222 Ill. App. 255.)

The allegations in the information in the instant case charging that defendant "did * * * tamper with an automobile," without a description of any of the acts defined as criminal by the statute, is but a conclusion. The information failed to distinctly charge defendant with any offense specified in the act. The word "tamper" is not found in the statute itself, but only in its caption, and is there used to indicate the general purpose for which it was enacted. The acts which shall constitute tampering and under what circumstances within the contemplation of the act are set forth therein, and defendant was clearly entitled to be definitely advised as to the offense with which he was charged.

We are impelled to hold that the information in question fell short of charging defendant with any offense known to the law, and counsel for the state concede that where an information charges no offense at all its insufficiency may be questioned by writ of error, even though such ground of objection was not urged in the trial court.

In the event that the state's attorney proceeds to file a properly amended information and again try this case, we assume that the trial court will take cognizance of the fact that defendant has served three months of the one year sentence imposed upon him under the judgment reversed herein.

For the reasons indicated the judgment of the municipal court is reversed and the cause remanded.

REVERSED AND REMANDED.

Friend, P. J., and Scanlan, J., concur.

is charged and if it does not set forth such facts with sufficient certainty it will not support a conviction. (People v. Stoyan, 280 Ill. 300; People v. Ellis, 282 Ill. App. 255.)

The allegations in the information in the instant case charging that defendant "did * * * tamper with an automobile," without a description of any of the acts defined as criminal by the statute, is but a conclusion. The information failed to distinctly charge defendant with any offense specified in the act. The word "tamper" is not found in the statute itself, but only in its caption, and is there used to indicate the general purpose for which it was enacted. The acts which shall constitute tampering and under what circumstances within the contemplation of the act are set forth therein, and defendant was clearly entitled to be definitely advised as to the offense with which he was charged.

We are impelled to hold that the information in question fell short of charging defendant with any offense known to the law, and counsel for the state concede that where an information charges no offense at all its insufficiency may be questioned by writ of error, even though such ground of objection was not urged in the trial court.

In the event that the state's attorney proceeds to file a properly amended information and again try this case, we assume that the trial court will take cognizance of the fact that defendant has served three months of the one year sentence imposed upon him under the judgment reversed herein.

For the reasons indicated the judgment of the municipal court is reversed and the cause remanded.

REVERSED AND REMANDED.

Friend, P. J., and Scanlan, J., concur.

64 A

37912

JOSEPH HEIDINGER,
Appellant,

v.

GEORGE HEATLEY,
Appellee.

APPEAL FROM CIRCUIT COURT,
COOK COUNTY.

280 I.A. 625[2]

MR. JUSTICE SULLIVAN DELIVERED THE OPINION OF THE COURT.

A judgment in trover for $235 was entered by the circuit court April 9, 1934, in favor of plaintiff, Joseph Heidinger, and against defendant, George Heatley. On motion of defendant an order was entered June 18, 1934, vacating the judgment. This appeal seeks to reverse that order.

Plaintiff brought a replevin action before a justice of the peace against defendant, a constable, for the possession of an automobile which defendant had seized under a writ of attachment in another proceeding brought by William Roll of Blue Island, Illinois, against one Mrs. R. E. Ross, its alleged owner. The writ of replevin having been returned "no property found," the cause was tried as an action in trover, and judgment entered for defendant, from which plaintiff appealed to the circuit court, where, after a trial by the court without a jury, the issues were found in plaintiff's favor. After overruling defendant's motion for a new trial and in arrest of judgment, the circuit court entered judgment April 9, 1934, as heretofore stated. Defendant prayed an appeal from the judgment, which was not perfected.

Thereafter, on May 22, 1934, more than thirty days after the entry of the judgment, defendant filed a written motion to vacate

37012

JOSEPH [illegible],
Appellant,

v.

GEORGE H [illegible],
Appellee.

MR. JUSTICE SULLIVAN DELIVERED THE OPINION [illegible]

A judgment in trover for $158 was entered by the circuit court April 9, 1934, in favor of plaintiff, Joseph [illegible], and against defendant, George [illegible]. On motion of defendant an order was entered June 15, 1934, vacating the judgment. This appeal seeks to reverse that order.

Plaintiff brought a replevin action before a justice of the peace against defendant, a constable, for the possession of an automobile which defendant had seized under a writ of attachment in another proceeding brought by William [illegible] of Blue Island, Illinois, against one [illegible] The writ of replevin having been returned "no property found," the cause was tried as an action in trover, and judgment [illegible] defendants, from which plaintiff appealed to the circuit court, where, after a trial by the court without a jury, [illegible] in plaintiff's favor. After [illegible] trial and [illegible] April 9, 1934, [illegible] from the judgment, which was not prayed.

Thereafter, on May 22, 1934, more than thirty days after entry of the judgment, defendant filed a written motion to vacate same and for a new trial, and in support thereof a verified petition accompanied by affidavits of both of his attorneys and Mrs. Rose, purporting to set forth the discovery of new evidence (particularly the ownership of the automobile in question by Mrs. Rose), and charging plaintiff with perjury in his testimony on the trial of the cause as to his ownership of the automobile and his attorney with misconduct in that he advised Mrs. Rose to remain out of the state so that she would not be available as a witness to testify as to who was the real owner of the car.

Two questions present themselves on this record: First, Were the facts set forth in the affidavits and petition filed by defendant sufficient to authorize the court to vacate the judgment of April 9, 1934, on the ground of plaintiff's alleged fraud and perjury? Second, Was the order entered June 18, 1934, upon defendant's motion of May 22, 1934, to vacate the judgment an appealable order?

Par. 82, ch. 77, Smith-Hurd's 1933 XXXX Rev. Statutes of Illinois is as follows:

> "Hereafter every judgment, decree or order, final in its nature, of any court of record in any civil or criminal proceeding shall have the same force and effect as a conclusive adjudication upon the expiration of thirty days from the date of its rendition as, under the law heretofore in force, it has had upon the expiration of the term of court at which it was rendered."

Defendant does not question the general rule that under the Civil Practice act a court is without jurisdiction to vacate or set aside its judgment after the expiration of thirty days from the date of its entry. He expressly states that his motion to vacate the judgment was not filed as a motion in the nature of a writ of error coram nobis pursuant to the terms of par. 196, sec. 72, ch. 110, of the Civil Practice act, to correct errors of fact within the contemplation of that section of the act, but he asserts that his motion was grounded on a recognized exception to the general rule, i.e., that judgments procured by fraud may be vacated at any time, same end for a new trial, and in support thereof a verified petition accompanied by affidavits of both of his attorneys and Mrs. Rose, purporting to set forth the discovery of new evidence (particularly the ownership of the automobile in question by Mrs. Rose), and charging plaintiff with perjury in his testimony on the trial of the cause as to his ownership of the automobile and his attorney with misconduct in that he advised Mrs. Rose to remain out of the state so that she would not be available as a witness to testify as to who was the real owner of the car.

Two questions present themselves on this record: First, were the facts set forth in the affidavits and petition filed by defendant sufficient to authorize the court to vacate the judgment of April 9, 1934, on the ground of plaintiff's alleged fraud and perjury? Second, was the order entered June 18, 1934, upon defendant's motion of May 22, 1934, to vacate the judgment an appealable order?

Par. 82, ch. 77, Smith-Hurd's 1933 XXXX Rev. Statutes of Illinois is as follows:

"Hereafter every judgment, decree or order, final in its nature, of any court of record in any civil or criminal proceeding shall have the same force and effect as a conclusive adjudication upon the expiration of thirty days from the date of its rendition as, under the law heretofore in force, it has had upon the expiration of the term of court at which it was rendered."

Defendant does not question the general rule that under the Civil Practice act a court is without jurisdiction to vacate or set aside its judgment after the expiration of thirty days from the date of its entry. He expressly states that his motion to vacate the judgment was not filed as a motion in the nature of a writ of error coram nobis pursuant to the terms of par. 196, sec. 72, ch. 110, of the Civil Practice act, to correct errors of fact within the contemplation of that section of the act, but he asserts that his motion was grounded on a recognized exception to the general rule, i.e., that judgments procured by fraud may be vacated at any time.

even subsequent to the expiration of thirty days from the date of their entry, by a proper showing of such fraud to the court. The fraud relied upon by defendant in his motion to vacate the judgment was the alleged perjury of plaintiff in his testimony as to the ownership of the automobile, and the alleged fraud of plaintiff's attorney in advising or inducing Mrs. Rose to remain outside of the State of Illinois so that she would not be available for the service of process upon her to procure her testimony as to the true ownership of the automobile.

The law is settled that a court has no power to vacate a judgment after the expiration of thirty days from the date of its entry because of the perjury of a witness or witnesses on the trial of the case. (Conway v. Gill, 257 Ill. App. 606; People v. Drysch, 311 Ill. 342.) As to the fraud that would constitute a sufficient reason for vacating a judgment after the expiration of thirty days from the date of its rendition, it has been held that it must be fraud committed by one of the parties on the court.

Defendant cites Wright v. Simpson, 200 Ill. 56; Pease v. Roberts, 16 Ill. App. 634, and City of Chicago v. Nodeck, 202 Ill. 257, in support of his contention that the fraud alleged in the instant case was sufficient to authorize the trial court to vacate the judgment.

We have carefully examined these cases and in none of them are the facts comparable to the facts in this case. It is true that in these cases the judgments were vacated subsequent to the terms at which they were entered, but the order in each case was authorized because of want of jurisdiction of the court to enter the judgment or because of palpable fraud perpetrated directly upon the court to secure the entry of the judgment. It naturally followed in each of these cases that the fraud on the court resulted in injury to the aggrieved party or to one who should have been made a party but was not.

even subsequent to the expiration of thirty days from the date of their entry, by a proper showing of such fraud to the court. The fraud relied upon by defendant in his motion to vacate the judgment was the alleged perjury of plaintiff in his testimony as to the ownership of the automobile, and the alleged fraud of plaintiff's attorney in advising or inducing Mrs. Ross to remain outside of the State of Illinois so that she would not be available for the service of process upon her to procure her testimony as to the true ownership of the automobile.

The law is settled that a court has no power to vacate a judgment after the expiration of thirty days from the date of its entry because of the perjury of a witness or witnesses on the trial of the case. (Conway v. Gill, 257 Ill. App. 406; People v. Myreck, 311 Ill. 542.) As to the fraud that would constitute a sufficient reason for vacating a judgment after the expiration of thirty days from the date of its rendition, it has been held that it must be fraud committed by one of the parties on the court.

Defendant cites Wright v. Simpson, 200 Ill. 56; Kamm v. Roberts, 16 Ill. App. 634, and City of Chicago v. Nodock, 202 Ill. 257, in support of his contention that the fraud alleged in the instant case was sufficient to authorize the trial court to vacate the judgment.

We have carefully examined these cases and in none of them are the facts comparable to the facts in this case. It is true that in these cases the judgments were vacated subsequent to the terms at which they were entered, but the error in each case was authorized because of want of jurisdiction of the court to enter the judgment or because of palpable fraud perpetrated directly upon the court to secure the entry of the judgment. It naturally followed in each of these cases that the fraud on the court resulted in injury to the aggrieved party or to one who should have been made a party but was not.

Here both parties were before the court and participated in a full hearing on the merits. Although defendant alleges in his petition to vacate that he moved for a continuance of the trial because of his failure to locate Mrs. Rose, a material witness, the record discloses no such motion as having been made. Granting that plaintiff is chargeable with the conduct of his attorney, the only fraud asserted is that said attorney advised Mrs. Rose to remain out of the jurisdiction. Can this be held to be such a direct fraud upon the court itself as would empower it to vacate the judgment after the expiration of thirty days? We think not. While the conduct of plaintiff, as alleged, might be considered reprehensible, and of his counsel sharp practice in depriving defendant of evidence that would aid his cause, the element of "direct fraud upon the court" is entirely lacking.

In order to come within the exception to the fundamental rule that, where a final judgment has been rendered in a cause and thirty days have elapsed from the date of its entry, the court no longer has jurisdiction to vacate or change its judgment, the fraud that would vitiate and authorize the court to vacate a judgment after it had become a "conclusive adjudication" must be such as affected the court's jurisdiction to render it, or entered as an element into the judgment itself.

The motion to vacate in this case was not addressed to the equitable powers of the court and plaintiff was afforded no opportunity to raise an issue upon the facts alleged in defendant's petition and affidavits. If defendant has a meritorious complaint, by reason of plaintiff's purported fraud, he has an appropriate remedy in a court of equity.

In discussing this question in Bowman v. Wilson, 64 Ill. 75, the court said at pp. 78 and 79:

Here both parties were before the court and participated in a full hearing on the merits. Although defendant alleges in his petition to vacate that he moved for a continuance of the trial because of his failure to locate Mrs. Rose, a material witness, the record discloses no such motion as having been made. Granting that plaintiff is chargeable with the conduct of his attorney, the only fraud asserted is that said attorney advised Mrs. Rose to remain out of the jurisdiction. Can this be held to be such a direct fraud upon the court itself as would empower it to vacate the judgment after the expiration of thirty days? We think not. While the conduct of plaintiff, as alleged, might be considered reprehensible, and of his counsel sharp practice in depriving defendant of evidence that would aid his cause, the element of "direct fraud upon the court" is entirely lacking.

In order to come within the exception to the fundamental rule that, where a final judgment has been rendered in a cause and thirty days have elapsed from the date of its entry, the court no longer has jurisdiction to vacate or change its judgment, the fraud that would vitiate and authorize the court to vacate a judgment after it had become a "conclusive adjudication" must be such as affected the court's jurisdiction to render it, or entered as an element into the judgment itself.

The motion to vacate in this case was not addressed to the equitable powers of the court and plaintiff was afforded no opportunity to raise an issue upon the facts alleged in defendant's petition and affidavits. If defendant has a meritorious complaint, by reason of plaintiff's purported fraud, he has an appropriate remedy in a court of equity.

In discussing this question in Hoomman v. Wilson, 64 Ill. 75, the court said at pp. 78 and 79:

"It is truly said, generally, that fraud vitiates everything, judgments included, into which it effectively enters. But this is said only of fraud properly alleged and duly shown in a proper proceeding. A court of law may set aside its own judgment obtained by fraud upon itself, but not for fraud practised only upon the adverse party, where he has had his day in court, or opportunity to have it, or has waived it, and his adversary has obtained judgment upon competent and sufficient evidence, however false and fraudulent. The court of law rendering it can not in such case set it aside or review it. Public interest requires that there should be an end of litigation. Errors of law or fact may be corrected by a court of review; and a court of equity, upon a proper showing by a defeated party, of newly discovered evidence which should produce a different result, unknown to him before or at the time of trial, without his fault, may award a new trial in the court of law; but we know of no authority or principle upon which the judgment of a court having jurisdiction of the subject-matter and parties can be otherwise attacked collaterally or be disregarded by any other, or even by the court which rendered it, except as to judgments by confession upon warrant of attorney, over which it is held to have an equitable control by virtue of which it may, upon a proper showing, let the defendant in to plead, leaving the judgment to stand as security for the outcome. We understand these propositions to be so well established and familiar as to require no extended citation of authority."

We are clearly of the opinion that the trial court erred in vacating the judgment, which was a "conclusive adjudication", according to the statutes, of the rights of the parties at the time it was set aside, and that the order vacating same is void. As to defendant's contention that the order vacating the judgment was merely interlocutory and not a final appealable order, it is sufficient to say that the recognized law of this state holds to the contrary. In discussing this question in Conway v. Gill, supra, this court, speaking through Justice Scanlan, said at pp. 612 and 613:

"Defendant in error contends that 'the plaintiffs in error can raise the point, that the judgment was improperly set aside, only by proceeding again to trial in the case which is pending and prosecuting a writ of error from whatever judgment might be rendered on the second trial of the case.' There is no merit in this contention. As the trial court was without jurisdiction or power to vacate the judgment of June 14, 1928, for alleged perjury committed on the trial of the case, the judgment of March 5, 1929, was a void order and plaintiffs in error had the right to sue out a writ of error to set aside the same."

For the reasons indicated herein the order of the circuit court of June 18, 1934, vacating the judgment of April 9, 1934, is reversed.

REVERSED.

Friend, P. J., and Scanlan, J., concur.

38145

CARL J. HALLBERG,
Appellee,

vs.

GOLDBLATT BROS., INC., SHOPPING NEWS, INC., et al.,
Appellants.

INTERLOCUTORY APPEAL FROM SUPERIOR COURT OF COOK COUNTY.

280 I.A. 625

MR. JUSTICE MATCHETT DELIVERED THE OPINION OF THE COURT.

This is an appeal from an interlocutory order granting a preliminary injunction.

Complainant has moved this court to dismiss the appeal on the ground that section 78 of the Civil Practice Act of 1933, under which this appeal was taken, is unconstitutional. This court in appeals from interlocutory orders may pass upon constitutional questions presented. Klever Shampay Karpet Kleaners v. City of Chicago, 238 Ill. App. 291.

Section 78 of the present Practice Act is substantially the same as section 123 of the Practice Act of 1907, which was held constitutional in Bagdonas v. Liberty Land & Invest. Co., 309 Ill. 103. Complainant points out two distinctions between the present statute and the prior one, which he says make the present statute unconstitutional. The present statute provides that the force and effect of the interlocutory order may be stayed upon order of the Appellate court or a judge thereof in vacation. Section 123 of the Practice Act of 1907 contains no such provision. It has been held that the legislature may regulate the power of the courts to grant a supersedeas or stay order without violating the constitutional rights of the litigants. Bryant v. The People, 71 Ill. 32; Public Utilities Com. v. C. & W. T. Ry., 275 Ill. 555.

Counsel for plaintiff also says that the new statute permits an appeal from an interlocutory order to any district of the

38145

CARL J. [illegible], Appellee,

vs.

GOLDBLATT BROS., INC., [illegible] NEWS, INC., et al., Appellants.

INTERLOCUTORY APPEAL FROM CIRCUIT COURT OF COOK COUNTY.

280 I.A. 625

MR. JUSTICE HATCHETT DELIVERED THE OPINION OF THE COURT.

This is an appeal from an interlocutory order granting a preliminary injunction.

Complainant has moved this court to dismiss the appeal on the ground that section 78 of the Civil Practice Act of 1933, under which this appeal was taken, is unconstitutional. This court in appeals from interlocutory orders may pass upon constitutional questions presented. Clever Shampoo Carpet Cleaners v. City of Chicago, 338 Ill. App. 201.

Section 78 of the present Practice Act is substantially the same as section 123 of the Practice Act of 1907, which was held constitutional in [illegible] 309 Ill. 103. Complainant points out two distinctions between the present statute and the prior one, which he says make the present statute unconstitutional. The present statute provides that the force and effect of the interlocutory order may be stayed upon order of the appellate court or a judge thereof in vacation. Section 123 of the Practice Act of 1907 contains no such provision. It has been held that the legislature may regulate the power of the courts to grant a supersedeas or stay order without violating the constitutional rights of litigants. [illegible] R. T. Ry., 275 Ill. 555.

Counsel for plaintiff also says that the new statute permits an appeal from an interlocutory order to any district of the

Appellate court throughout the State. Par. 48, chap. 37, Cahill's statutes of 1933, provides that appeals and writs of error may be taken to the Appellate court in the district in which the case is decided, or by consent, to any other district, furthermore, the question to which district of the Appellate court an appeal shall be taken is not a constitutional question. The defendants have appealed to the Appellate court for the district in which the trial court was located. We hold that the points made against the constitutionality of section 73, chapter 110 of the statutes of 1933 are without merit, and the motion to dismiss the appeal on the ground of the unconstitutionality of the section is denied.

The injunction complained of was granted upon the prayer of an amended bill filed March 11, 1935. The bill consists of 12 paragraphs and is verified by complainant Hallberg, who declares that he is a citizen and taxpayer of the city and brings the suit in behalf of himself and others.

By the injunction Goldblatt Bros., Inc., is restrained from distributing and placing on the streets of the City of Chicago and on the stairways, porches and at the entrances or doors of houses, stores, and places of business in Chicago, printed matter known as "Goldblatt Bros. Shopping News" or similar matter "unless said advertising matter shall be so securely fastened that it cannot be scattered by the wind on the public streets, alleys or sidewalks of the City of Chicago."

A similar injunction was issued against the distribution of "Downtown Shopping News" (a publication similar in character to the Goldblatt publication) issued by defendant Shopping News, Inc., which is substantially of the same size and appearance as the daily newspapers which are distributed in Chicago.

Both injunctions were issued without bond.

The amended bill as verified, upon which the motion for

Appellate court throughout the State. Par. 48, chap. 37, Cahill's statutes of 1933, provides that appeals and writs of error may be taken to the Appellate court in the district in which the case is decided, or by consent, to any other district; furthermore, the question to which district of the Appellate court an appeal shall be taken is not a constitutional question. The defendants have appealed to the Appellate court for the district in which the trial court was located. We hold t at the points made against the constitutionality of section 78, chapter 110 of the statutes of 1933 are without merit, and the motion to dismiss the appeal on the ground of the unconstitutionality of the section is denied.

The injunction complained of was granted upon the prayer of an amended bill filed March 11, 1935. The bill consists of 12 paragraphs and is verified by complainant Hallberg, who declares that he is a citizen and taxpayer of the city and brings the suit in behalf of himself and others.

By the injunction Goldblatt Bros., Inc., is restrained from distributing and placing on the streets of the City of Chicago and on the stairways, porches and at the entrances or doors of houses, stores, and places of business in Chicago, printed matter known as "Goldblatt Bros. Shopping News" or similar matter "unless said advertising matter shall be so securely fastened that it cannot be scattered by the wind on the public streets, alleys or sidewalks of the City of Chicago."

A similar injunction was issued against the distribution of "Downtown Shopping News" (a publication similar in character to the Goldblatt publication) issued by defendant Shopping News, Inc., which is substantially of the same size and appearance as the daily newspapers which are distributed in Chicago.

Both injunctions were issued without bond.

The amended bill as verified, upon which the motion for an appeal from [illegible] these injunctions was based, set up that these publications were distributed in violation of the provisions of a city ordinance regulating the distribution of advertising matter. The amended bill set up the ordinance verbatim and asserted that the manner of distribution was such as to become a danger to the health of the community and annoyance to complainant and a detriment to him in a financial way, since as a taxpayer he was required to contribute to the cost of cleaning the streets. The amended bill asserts that the City of Chicago has not been diligent to enforce the ordinance. The City was made a defendant and the bill prayed for an injunction restraining the City from encouraging and promoting the distribution of such circulars and advertising matter and for a mandatory injunction commanding it to enforce the ordinance against such distribution, and restraining Goldblatt Bros., Inc., Shopping News, Inc., and the City from circulating or distributing the circulars and other advertising matters known as "Goldblatt Bros. Shopping News" and "Downtown Shopping News", and from permitting the same to be distributed upon any of the streets, alleys, sidewalks or public houses in Chicago, or at any houses, stores, or places of business in the city. The City of Chicago has not appeared in this court.

The amended bill was filed March 11, 1935. Defendants Shopping News, Inc., and Goldblatt Bros., Inc., filed full and complete answers under oath on the following day, denying in detail each and every material averment of the amended bill. The answer of Shopping News, Inc., was supported by affidavits of 173 persons belonging to the class for which complainant undertook to sue. These affidavits denied material averments of the amended bill with reference to the distribution of this printed matter.

Defendant Goldblatt Bros., by its verified answer, likewise denied all the material averments of the amended bill, denied that its publication was distributed in violation of the ordinance of these injunctions was based, set up that these publications were distributed in violation of the provisions of a city ordinance regulating the distribution of advertising matter. The amended bill set up the ordinance verbatim and asserted that the manner of distribution was such as to become a danger to the health of the community and annoyance to complainant and a detriment to him in a financial way, since as a taxpayer he was required to contribute to the cost of cleaning the streets. The amended bill asserts that the City of Chicago has not been diligent to enforce the ordinance. The City was made a defendant and the bill prayed for an injunction restraining the City from encouraging and promoting the distribution of such circulars and advertising matter and for a mandatory injunction commanding it to enforce the ordinance against such distribution, and restraining Goldblatt Bros., Inc., Shopping News, Inc., and the City from circulating or distributing the circulars and other advertising matters known as "Goldblatt Bros. Shopping News" and "Downtown Shopping News", and from permitting the same to be distributed upon any of the streets, alleys, sidewalks or public houses in Chicago, or at any houses, stores, or places of business in the city. The City of Chicago has not appeared in this court.

The amended bill was filed March 11, 1935. Defendants Shopping News, Inc., and Goldblatt Bros., Inc., filed full and complete answers under oath on the following day, denying in detail each and every material averment of the amended bill. The answer of Shopping News, Inc., was supported by affidavits of 173 persons belonging to the class for which complainant undertook to sue. These affidavits denied material averments of the amended bill with reference to the distribution of this printed matter.

Defendant Goldblatt Bros., by its verified answer, likewise denied all the material averments of the amended bill, denied that its publication was distributed in violation of the ordinance of the City or that distribution was made in the manner described in the amended bill, or in any such manner as would cause hazard to health, danger of fire or expense in the way of cleaning the streets. This answer is supported by approximately 85 affidavits of persons who also are of the class for which complainant undertakes to sue, and these affidavits deny material averments of the amended bill with reference to the manner in which this printed matter is circulated.

The answer also set up affirmative matter which is not denied. The answer of Goldblatt Bros., Inc., shows that the distribution of its publication has been continued for eighteen years, and the answer of Shopping News, Inc , that its publication had been continued for three years. Among the persons filing affidavits in support of these answers are two tenants of the flat building of which complainant is part owner. These affidavits specifically deny that the distribution of defendant's publication has in any way created a nuisance or the other supposed dangers so elaborately described in the amended bill.

The answers deny that the publications are scattered by gusts of wind over the sidewalks, streets and alleys of the city, and deny that the distribution of these publications constitutes a fire hazard. The standing of complainant as a taxpayer is challenged, and the facts averred seem to be undisputed that for several years prior to the filing of the amended bill he did not pay either personal taxes or taxes levied against the real estate which he says he owns. Significantly, his bill fails to allege that he ever prior to the filing of the bill demanded the enforcement of the ordinance in question by the City of Chicago, or ever made complaint to defendants about the manner in which their productions were distributed. It is quite apparent that his interest in this suit does not arise out of any fear of harm to his property or annoyance to himself.

the City or that distribution was made in the manner described in the amended bill, or in any such manner as would cause hazard to health, danger of fire or expense in the way of cleaning the streets. This answer is supported by approximately 85 affidavits of persons who also are of the class for which complainant undertakes to sue, and these affidavits deny material averments of the amended bill with reference to the manner in which this printed matter is circulated.

The answer also set up affirmative matter which is not denied. The answer of Goldblatt Bros., Inc., shows that the distribution of its publication has been continued for eighteen years, and the answer of Shopping News, Inc., that its publication had been continued for three years. Among the persons filing affidavits in support of these answers are two tenants of the flat building of which complainant is part owner. These affidavits specifically deny that the distribution of defendant's publication has in any way created a nuisance or the other supposed dangers so elaborately described in the amended bill.

The answers deny that the publications are scattered by gusts of wind over the sidewalks, streets and alleys of the city, and deny that the distribution of these publications constitutes a fire hazard. The standing of complainant as a taxpayer is challenged, and the facts averred seem to be undisputed that for several years prior to the filing of the amended bill he did not pay either personal taxes or taxes levied against the real estate which he says he owns. Significantly, his bill fails to allege that he ever prior to the filing of the bill demanded the enforcement of the ordinance in question by the City of Chicago, or ever made complaint to defendants about the manner in which their productions were distributed. It is quite apparent that his interest in this suit does not arise out of any fear of harm to his property or annoyance to himself.

The answers of defendants set up other material and uncontradicted facts with reference to the injury which will result to the business of defendants from these injunctions. The answer of Shopping News, Inc., sets up that it is a corporation organized under the laws of the State of Illinois, that its capital stock is held by the Boston Store, Carson Pirie Scott & Co., The Fair, Marshall Field & Co.; that the purpose of its organization was the publication and distribution of a paper containing news items of local interest and advertising, that it began business in September, 1932, and at present has contracts for advertising for the period from March 1, 1935, to September 1, 1936, which provide for the payment to it of the sum of $1,106, 197. The names of the business houses with which defendant has these contracts are given in detail. The answer also avers that on the basis of income for the last six months the expected additional revenue from the customers named over their contract requirements will equal $220,850, for the period from March 1, 1935, to September 1, 1936, and that the expected revenue of defendant from all sources based on figures for the year 1934 for this period will equal $1,539,483.71. This defendant says that the distribution of its paper is effected by 2,000 persons; that defendant now employs directly 1,333 carriers, who in turn employ 900 helpers, besides the many other employees whose numbers and duties are set up in detail. The publication of defendant is delivered in Chicago twice a week and approximately 600,000 papers are distributed at each delivery. Defendant says that the injunction tends to destroy the business of defendant and render it unable to collect the sum of $1,106,197 for advertising for the period ending September 1, 1936, which contractors for advertising had agreed to pay, that it is unable to make delivery through the United States mails, as the approximate cost of delivery by mail would be $27,000, whereas the cost of delivery by carriers does not exceed $2,600, and that

The answers of defendants set up other [illegible] uncontradicted facts with reference to the injury that [illegible]
the business of defendant [illegible] the [illegible] answer of
Chicago [illegible], Inc., sets up that it is a corporation organized
under the laws of the State of Illinois, that its capital stock is
held by the Boston [illegible] Marshall Field & Co., that the [illegible] the
publication and distribution of [illegible] of
local interest and advertising [illegible] in September,
1930, and at present has contracts for advertising for the period
from March 1, 1931, to September 1, 1936, which provide for the
payment to it of the sum of $4,106,197. [illegible] the
houses with which defendant has these contracts are given in detail.
The answer also avers that on the basis of its income for the last six
months the expected additional revenue from the customers under
their contract requirements will equal $290, [illegible] for the period
from March 1, 1931, to September 1, 1936, and that the expected revenue of defendant from all sources [illegible] for [illegible]
for this period will equal $1,[illegible],[illegible]5.71. [illegible] at
the distribution of its paper is [illegible] by [illegible] defendant now employs directly 1,153 carriers, who in turn [illegible] 900
helpers, [illegible]
are set up in detail. The [illegible] delivered in
Chicago [illegible]
at each delivery. Defendant says that the injunction [illegible] destroy
the business of defendant and render it unable to collect the sum of
$4,106,197 for advertising for the period ending [illegible] 1, 1936,
which contractors for advertising had agreed to pay, that it is
unable to make delivery through the United States mails, as the
approximate cost of delivery by mail would be $27,000, whereas the
cost of delivery by carriers does not exceed $[illegible], and that

delivery by mail is impracticable for the reason that postal authorities will not agree to make delivery on any certain day, that any contract with the U. S. mail for the delivery of a publication such as this must allow from one to three days for delivery.

The answer of Goldblatt Bros., Inc., states that in the year 1933 it paid taxes to the city, county and state in excess of $500,000; that it and its predecessor company have been engaged in the department store business for eighteen years, that business has grown until defendant now operates five department stores, which in 1934 did a gross business of $24,000,000, that its business at the present time represents a capital investment of more than $7,000,000; that the expansion and growth of the business had largely been due to the use of such publications, that it has invested in equipment and fixtures incidental to the publication approximately $200,000, is under contract to purchase 5,000 tons of paper at $40 a ton during the balance of the calendar year of 1935; that it has on hand large quantities of publication for current distribution; that even if restrained for a short period it will lose thousands of customers, that its sales business and profits will greatly decrease; that its capital investment will be greatly impaired and depreciated, that it will be irreparably injured and its property rights destroyed.

The answer of Goldblatt Bros., Inc., further states that it employs in the distribution of these publications from seven to eight hundred persons; in addition, there are from five to six hundred people, wholly or in part, dependent for their livelihood upon the continued publication and distribution, and that if defendant is compelled to desist, many of these employees will be compelled to resort to charity.

After making every possible allowance for exaggeration of prospective damages, it is apparent that the financial interest of delivery by mail is impracticable for the reason that postal authorities will not agree to make delivery on any certain day, that any contract with the U. S. mail for the delivery of a publication such as this must allow from one to three days for delivery.

The answer of Goldblatt Bros., Inc., states that in the year 1933 it paid taxes to the city, county and state in excess of $500,000; that it and its predecessor company have been engaged in the department store business for eighteen years, that business has grown until defendant now operates five department stores, which in 1934 did a gross business of $24,000,000, that its business at the present time represents a capital investment of more than $7,000,000; that the expansion and growth of the business had largely been due to the use of such publications, that it has invested in equipment and fixtures incidental to the publication approximately $200,000, is under contract to purchase 5,000 tons of paper at $40 a ton during the balance of the calendar year of 1935; that it has on hand large quantities of publication for current distribution; that even if restrained for a short period it will lose thousands of customers; that its sales business and profits will greatly decr-ase; that its capital investment will be greatly impaired and depreciated; that it will be irreparably injured and its property rights destroyed.

The answer of Goldblatt Bros., Inc., further states that it employs in the distribution of these publications from seven to eight hundred persons; in addition, there are from five to six hundred people, wholly or in part, dependent for their livelihood upon the continued publication and distribution, and that if defendant is compelled to desist, many of these employees will be compelled to resort to charity.

After making every possible allowance for exaggeration of prospective damages, it is apparent that the financial interest of complainant in this suit is infinitesimal compared with the actual damage with which the business of these two defendants is threatened by this injunction. It was stated upon oral argument (and not controverted) that the restrictions imposed by the injunction required the expenditure by defendant of at least $300 a week.

The briefs of defendants challenge the right of complainant to maintain a bill to restrain the continuance of the alleged public nuisance in the absence of a showing of a special injury peculiar to himself and cite authorities such as High on Injunction (1905), vol. 1, sec. 762; Milligan v. Nelson, 51 Ill. App. 441, affirmed in 151 Ill. 462; Joseph v. Wieland Dairy Co., 297 Ill. 574; Koehler v. Century of Progress, 354 Ill. 347, and many other cases. Complainant relies on Hoyt v. McLaughlin, 250 Ill. 442, and similar cases. The Hoyt case involved the right of a property owner to have an unlicensed saloon enjoined. The facts are clearly distinguishable. However, this issue may well await the taking of the evidence upon a trial of the merits. The precise controversy here concerns the issuance of this injunction before any trial on the merits and without any bond being given to indemnify defendants, notwithstanding sworn answers were on file denying each and every material fact upon which complainant relied. Complainant in his motion for the injunction relied solely upon the verified bill of complaint. It was formerly the rule that upon a motion to dissolve an injunction upon bill and answer, the answer so far as it was responsive to the bill was taken as true, and when it fully and unequivocally denied the material allegations of the bill upon which complainant's equity rested, the court would dissolve the injunction. See High on Injunctions, 1905, vol. 2, sec. 1505. That rule has been modified by statute in Illinois. See Cahill's Ill. Rev. Stats. 1933, chap. 69, secs. 16 and 17, which in substance provides that upon a motion to dissolve an injunction after complainant in this suit is infinitesimal compared with the actual damage with which the business of these two defendants is threatened by this injunction. It was stated upon oral argument (and not controverted) that the restrictions imposed by the injunction required the expenditure by defendant of at least $300 a week.

The briefs of defendants challenge the right of complainant to maintain a bill to restrain the continuance of the alleged public nuisance in the absence of a showing of a special injury peculiar to himself and cite authorities such as High on Injunction (1905), vol. 1, sec. 762, Williams v. Wilson, 51 Ill. App. 441, affirmed in 151 Ill. 462, Joseph v. Wieland Dairy Co., 297 Ill. 574; Kessler v. Century of Progress, 354 Ill. 547, and many other cases. Complainant relies on Hoyt v. McLaughlin, 250 Ill. 442, and similar cases. The Hoyt case involved the right of a property owner to have an unlicensed saloon enjoined. The facts are clearly distinguishable. However, this issue may well await the taking of the evidence upon a trial of the merits. The precise controversy here concerns the issuance of this injunction before any trial on the merits and without any bond being given to indemnify defendants, notwithstanding sworn answers were on file denying each and every material fact upon which complainant relied. Complainant in his motion for the injunction relied solely upon the verified bill of complaint. It was formerly the rule that upon a motion to dissolve an injunction upon bill and answer, the answer so far as it was responsive to the bill was taken as true, and when it fully and unequivocally denied the material allegations of the bill upon which complainant's equity rested, the court would dissolve the injunction. See High on Injunctions, 1905, vol. 2, sec. 1505. That rule has been modified by statute in Illinois. See Cahill's Ill. Rev. Stats. 1933, chap. 69, secs. 16 and 17, which in substance provides that upon a motion to dissolve an injunction after answer, the court shall not be bound to take the answer as absolutely true but shall decide the motion upon the weight of the testimony, and that complainant may support his bill and defendant his answer by affidavits filed with the same which may be read in evidence on the hearing of the motion to dissolve the injunction. While the statute has modified the ancient rule, it has not abolished the reason upon which it rests, and while the statute enlarges the power of the court, it also extends the duty of the chancellor to exercise wise discretion and carefully weigh the testimony and consider the entire situation, to the end that persons may not be deprived of their rights or property without a full, fair and impartial trial according to the law of the land.

Here, the material averments of the bill were absolutely contradicted by the verified answers of both defendants, and these answers were supported by more than 200 affidavits of persons who were of the class in whose behalf complainant averred he filed his bill. If the testimony was to be weighed, there could be no doubt the preponderance of it was in favor of defendants. For that reason the injunction ought not to have been granted and should have been dissolved. That conclusion is much strengthened by the fact that the uncontradicted evidence shows that the issuance of these injunctions very seriously interferes with the property rights of defendants, and that the damages which may and will probably result from a continuance of the injunction will far outweigh any inconvenience or damage complainant might sustain through the continuance of the business of defendants to which he objects.

It is no answer for complainant to say that the injunction does defendants no harm because the order enjoined defendants from distributing or placing on the stairways, porches, and at the entrances or doors of houses, stores and places of business the answer, the court shall not be bound to take the answer as absolutely true but shall decide the motion upon a consideration of the testimony, and that complainant may support his bill and defendant his answer by affidavits filed with the same which may be read in evidence on the hearing of the motion to dissolve the injunction. While the statute has modified the ancient rule, it has not abolished the reason upon which it rests, and while the statute enlarges the power of the court, it also extends the duty of the chancellor to exercise wise discretion and carefully weigh the testimony and consider the entire situation, to the end that persons may not be deprived of their rights or property without a full, fair and impartial trial according to the law of the land.

Here, the material averments of the bill were absolutely contradicted by the verified answers of both defendants, and these answers were supported by more than 200 affidavits of persons who were of the class in whose behalf complainant averred he filed his bill. If the testimony was to be weighed, there could be no doubt the preponderance of it was in favor of defendants. For that reason the injunction ought not to have been granted and should have been dissolved. That conclusion is much strengthened by the fact that the uncontradicted evidence shows that the issuance of these injunctions very seriously interferes with the property rights of defendants, and that the damages which may and will probably result from a continuance of the injunction will far outweigh any inconvenience or damage complainant might sustain through the continuance of the business of defendants to which he objects.

It is no answer for complainant to say that the injunction does defendants no harm because the order only enjoins defendants from distributing or placing on the stairways, porches, and at the entrances or doors of houses, stores and places of business the publications unless they were so securely fastened that they could not be scattered by the wind on the public streets, alleys or sidewalks of the city. Defendants deny that their publications were so scattered, and it was error to enjoin them from doing that which the preponderance of the evidence in the record showed they were not doing.

It would seem that if an injunction were to issue, at least a bond to protect defendants from such damages should have been required. They should not have been subjected to expensive and costly litigation in order to maintain their rights without the protection of a bond. The issuance of the injunction without a bond, even had no answer been on file at the time it issued, would have been unwarranted. No duties which a chancellor is ever called upon to perform require the exercise of finer judicial qualities than those in which these preliminary interlocutory orders are decided. They are entirely justifiable in many cases where it is apparent on the facts presented that little, if any, injury would result and where the effect is to preserve the status until such time as the court may pass upon the case on its merits.

In the very nature of things, this order was not of that kind or character. It does not preserve the status. On the contrary it destroys the status. It does not preserve the subject matter of the litigation until such time as the court may pass upon it, and the parties be heard according to the law of the land, but, on the contrary, proceeded to adjudge the case against defendants without a hearing on the merits. The injunction should not have been issued upon the showing made, and it should have been dissolved upon defendants' motion.

For these reasons the order awarding the injunction and the order refusing to dissolve it will both be reversed.

ORDERS REVERSED.

O'Connor, P. J., concurs.
McSurely, J., dissents. (See next page.)

publications unless they were so securely fastened that they could not be scattered by the wind on the public streets, alleys or sidewalks of the city. Defendants deny that their publications were so scattered, and it was error to enjoin them from doing that which the preponderance of the evidence in the record showed they were not doing.

It would seem that if an injunction were to issue, at least a bond to protect defendants from such damages should have been required. They should not have been subjected to expensive and costly litigation in order to maintain their rights without the protection of a bond. The issuance of the injunction without a bond, even had no answer been on file at the time it issued, would have been unwarranted. No duties which a chancellor is ever called upon to perform require the exercise of finer judicial qualities than those in which these preliminary interlocutory orders are decided. They are entirely justifiable in many cases where it is apparent on the facts presented that little, if any, injury would result and where the effect is to preserve the status until such time as the court may pass upon the case on its merits.

In the very nature of things, this order was not of that kind or character. It does not preserve the status. On the contrary it destroys the status. It does not preserve the subject matter of the litigation until such time as the court may pass upon it, and the parties be heard according to the law of the land, but, on the contrary, proceeded to adjudge the case at that date and without a hearing on the merits. The injunction should not have been issued upon the showing made, and it should have been dissolved upon defendants' motion.

For these reasons the order granting the injunction and the order refusing to dissolve it will both be reversed.

ORDER REVERSED.

O'Connor, P. J., concurs.
McSurely, J., dissents. (See next page.)

38145

MR. JUSTICE McSURELY Dissenting.

The order does not restrain the distribution of circulars but permits this if they are so fastened that they cannot be scattered by the wind into the public streets, alleys or sidewalks of the city of Chicago. In my opinion this is a harmless and reasonable limitation and preserves the status quo so as to protect the public. To reverse the injunctional order would permit the distribution of circulars without any attempt to prevent them from being scattered. I respectfully dissent from the majority opinion.

25148

Mr. JUSTICE McMURRAY Dissenting.

The order does not restrain the distribution of circulars but permits this if they are so fastened that they cannot be scattered by the wind into the public streets, alley or sidewalks of the city of Chicago. In my opinion this is a sensible and reasonable limitation and preserves the status quo so as to protect the public. To reverse the injunction order would permit the distribution of circulars [illegible] prevent them from being scattered. I respectfully dissent from the majority opinion.

74 H

37698

PEOPLE OF THE STATE OF ILLINOIS ex rel. ULYSSES J. GRIM, Appellee,

v.

HARRY S. GRADLE and S. W. PAROWSKI et al., Appellants.

APPEAL FROM SUPERIOR COURT OF COOK COUNTY.

280 I.A. 625[4]

MR. PRESIDING JUSTICE FRIEND DELIVERED THE OPINION OF THE COURT.

The superior court of Cook county directed the issuance of the writ of mandamus against Rodney H. Brandon, director of the department of public works of the State of Illinois; Dorothy L. Kay, assistant director; A. L. Bowen, superintendent of charities; Sidney D. Wilgus, M.D., alienist; John C. Weigel, fiscal superintendent; Frank D. Whipp, superintendent of prisons; Paul L. Schroeder, M. D., criminologist; W. C. Jones, superintendent of parole, all members of the department of public welfare; Harry S. Gradle; S. W. Parowski, managing officer; and W. Emery Lancaster, Ernest Hoover and John V. Clinnin, members of the state civil service commission of the State of Illinois.

To the petition for mandamus, as variously and finally amended January 16, 1934, (hereinafter referred to as the petition) defendants interposed a general and special demurrer, which was overruled. Defendants elected to stand by their demurrer and thereupon the court directed the issuance of the mandamus writ, from which two of the defendants, Harry S Gradle and S. W. Parowski, have prosecuted this appeal.

Various questions are raised as to the sufficiency of the

PEOPLE OF THE STATE OF ILLINOIS
ex rel. ULYSSES J. GRIM,
Appellee,

v.

HENRY S. GRADLE and S. W. PAROWSKI
et al.,
Appellants.

APPEAL FROM SUPERIOR
COURT OF COOK COUNTY.

280 I.A. 625[1]

MR. PRESIDING JUSTICE FRIEND DELIVERED THE OPINION OF THE COURT.

The superior court of Cook county directed the issuance of the writ of mandamus against Rodney H. Brandon, director of the department of public works of the State of Illinois; Dorothy L. Kay, assistant director; A. L. Bowen, superintendent of charities; Sidney D. Wilgus, M.D., alienist; John C. Weigel, fiscal superintendent; Frank D. Whipp, superintendent of prisons; Paul L. Schroeder, M. D., criminologist; W. C. Jones, superintendent of parole, all members of the department of public welfare; Henry S. Gradle; S. W. Parowski, managing officer; and W. Emery Lancaster, Ernest Hoover and John V. Clinnin, members of the state civil service commission of the State of Illinois.

To the petition for mandamus, as variously and finally amended January 16, 1934, (hereinafter referred to as the petition) defendants interposed a general and special demurrer, which was overruled. Defendants elected to stand by their demurrer and thereupon the court directed the issuance of the mandamus writ, from which two of the defendants, Henry S. Gradle and S. W. Parowski, have prosecuted this appeal.

Various questions are raised as to the sufficiency of the

petition, which is quite voluminous and alleges in substance that Ulysses J. Grim, the relater, is a physician and surgeon, licensed to practice medicine in the State of Illinois, and has so practiced for thirty years; that he is a professor and head of the department of oto-laryngology at Loyola University; and that his practice has been confined to the city of Chicago; that in 1871 the general assembly of this state enacted legislation to take over the Chicago Eye & Ear Infirmary, which prior thereto had existed as a private corporation, and directed the governor to accept the transfer of all its assets by the State of Illinois, thus creating a state institution, designated by said act as the Illinois Charitable Eye & Ear Infirmary, which has since that time been conducted and operated to provide gratuitous medical and surgical treatment for all indigent residents of Illinois afflicted with diseases of the eye and ear, in conformity with the objects of its creation as set forth in the act of incorporation; that examinations under the civil service law have been heretofore held for physicians on the medical staff of the infirmary, and that positions were classified as senior and assistant eye surgeon and senior and assistant ear surgeon.

It is further alleged that June 11, 1912, the general assembly of this state placed supervision of charitable institutions, including the Illinois Charitable Eye & Ear Infirmary, in a charities commission and a board of administration; that on March 7, 1917, the general assembly created the department of public welfare, in the place and stead of the charities commission and board of administration, and provided for a director thereof, and for various other officers, among them being an assistant director, alienist, criminologist, fiscal supervisor and superintendent of charities, for the purposes of administration; that except for temporary appointments the lawfully chosen medical staff heretofore connected with the infirmary has been petition, which is quite voluminous and alleges in substance that Ulysses J. Grim, the relator, is a physician and surgeon, licensed to practice medicine in the State of Illinois, and has so practiced for thirty years; that he is a professor and head of the department of oto-laryngology at Loyola University; and that his practice has been confined to the city of Chicago; that in 1871 the general assembly of this state enacted legislation to take over the Chicago Eye & Ear Infirmary, which prior thereto had existed as a private corporation, and directed the governor to accept the transfer of all its assets by the State of Illinois, thus creating a state institution, designated by said act as the Illinois Charitable Eye & Ear Infirmary, which has since that time been conducted and operated to provide gratuitous medical and surgical treatment for all indigent residents of Illinois afflicted with diseases of the eye and ear, in conformity with the objects of its creation as set forth in the act of incorporation; that examinations under the civil service law have been heretofore held for physicians on the medical staff of the infirmary, and that positions were classified as senior and assistant eye surgeon and senior and assistant ear surgeon.

It is further alleged that June 11, 1913, the general assembly of this state placed supervision of charitable institutions, including the Illinois Charitable Eye & Ear Infirmary, in a charities commission and a board of administration; that on March 7, 1917, the general assembly created the department of public welfare, in the place and stead of the charities commission and board of administration, and provided for a director thereof, and for various other officers, among them being an assistant director, alienist, criminologist, fiscal supervisor and superintendent of charities, for the purpose of administration; that except for temporary appointments the lawfully chosen medical staff heretofore connected with the infirmary has been selected in accordance with the statutes of this state by competitive civil service examinations, and that the said institution has been operated successfully for many years by its staff of physicians and surgeons, who are alleged to be competent and experienced practitioners of medicine of high standing in their profession.

It is averred that May 11, 1905, the general assembly passed an act to regulate the civil service of this state, which became effective November 1, 1905, and was amended June 10, 1911, and again July 1, 1919, in accordance with which the governor appointed as members of the state civil service commission W. Emery Lancaster, Ernest Hoover and John V. Clinnin, who accepted said offices, qualified and are now acting as members of said commission; that in the year 1921 relator took the examinations duly prescribed under the rules and regulations of said commission in accordance with the statutes of this state for senior ear surgeon, successfully passed such examination, and since 1923 has been functioning as assistant surgeon on the medical staff of the infirmary, performing his duties as ear surgeon until he was "by the illegal scheme of the defendants, deprived of the opportunity to function as hereinafter set forth;" that said office is still in existence and relator has been a member of the classified civil service since the time of his appointment.

The petition avers that April 19, 1918, the civil service commission adopted certain rules and by rule 1 thereof classified the position occupied by relator; that on July 1, 1933, he received the following communication on the letterhead of the State of Illinois, department of public welfare, signed by defendant S. W. Parowski, as managing officer of the infirmary:

"Dr. U. J. Grim,
Chicago, Illinois.

Dear Doctor:

As Managing Officer at the Illinois Eye and Ear Infirmary, I desire to notify you that I have official notice from the Department selected in accordance with the statutes of this state by competitive civil service examinations, and that the said institution has been operated successfully for many years by its staff of physicians and surgeons, who are alleged to be competent and experienced practitioners of medicine of high standing in their profession.

It is averred that May 11, 1905, the general assembly passed an act to regulate the civil service of this state, which became effective November 1, 1905, and was amended June 10, 1911, and again July 1, 1919, in accordance with which the governor appointed as members of the state civil service commission W. Emery Lancaster, Ernest Hoover and John V. Clinnin, who accepted said offices, qualified and are now acting as members of said commission; that in the year 1921 relator took the examinations duly prescribed under the rules and regulations of said commission in accordance with the statutes of this state for senior ear surgeon, successfully passed such examination, and since 1922 has been functioning as assistant surgeon on the medical staff of the infirmary, performing his duties as ear surgeon until he was "by the illegal scheme of the defendants, deprived of the opportunity to function as hereinafter set forth;" that said office is still in existence and relator has been a member of the classified civil service since the time of his appointment.

The petition avers that April 19, 1918, the civil service commission adopted certain rules and by rule 1 thereof classified the position occupied by relator; that on July 1, 1933, he received the following communication on the letterhead of the State of Illinois, department of public welfare, signed by defendant A. L. Dorowski, as managing officer of the infirmary:

"Dr. U. J. Grim,
Chicago, Illinois.

Dear Doctor:

As Managing Officer of the Illinois Eye and Ear Infirmary, I desire to notify you that I have official notice from the Department of Public Welfare at Springfield, Illinois, that the Illinois State Civil Service Commission, has, for the first time, classified the positions to be held as members of the medical staff of the Illinois Eye and Ear Infirmary.

Dr. Harry Gradle has been appointed Chief of Staff, effective June 27th, 1933, pursuant to Special Order No. 4545.

The members of the staff to fill the new classifications have now been chosen and they will take over their respective duties of care of patients at the Infirmary on July 1, 1933.

I am notifying all professional men who have done work at the institution, regardless of whether or not they have been selected members of the new staff in order that they may govern themselves accordingly.

Any professional men, being Civil Service employees, will retain their Civil Service status to the Classification for which they have been certified by the Commission.

The new staff may call upon the members of the profession for work at the Institution in the future."

It is alleged that the foregoing communication was made "in accordance with a scheme" whereby one Harry Gradle, purporting to have been appointed chief of staff, induced the department of public welfare, the civil service commissioners and S. . Parowski to serve his purposes of evading the civil service laws and for the purpose of diverting the said Illinois Eye & Ear Infirmary from the purposes for which it had been created; that the allegation in said communication stating that the Illinois State Civil Service Commission had for the first time classified the positions to be held by members of the medical staff of the infirmary, is not in accordance with the facts; that relator is not in a position to know what the purported classification has been, but that said positions of eye and ear surgeons and their assistants were classified as averred in the petition and that relator took the examination for said classified position and is entitled to continue therein.

It is alleged that after receiving the foregoing communication relator proceeded to the building occupied by the infirmary for his usual duties, and thereupon was told that there was no work for him and that various other members of said staff had been likewise informed, and that this was all done in pursuance of said illegal scheme, fostered for the purpose of furthering the illegal aims and wishes of of Paul   at Springfield, Illinois, that the Illinois State Civil Service Commission, has, for the first time, classified the positions to be held as members of the medical staff of the Illinois Eye and Ear Infirmary.

Dr. Harry Gradle has been appointed Chief of Staff, effective June 27th, 1933, pursuant to Special Order No. 4565.

The members of the staff to fill the new classifics have now been chosen and they will take over their respective duties of care of patients at the Infirmary on July 1, 1933.

I am notifying all professional men who have done work at the institution, regardless of whether or not they have been selected members of the new staff in order that they may govern themselves accordingly.

Any professional men, being Civil Service employees, will retain their Civil Service status to the Classification for which they have been certified by the Commission.

The new staff may call upon the members of the profession for work at the institution in the future."

It is alleged that the foregoing communication was made "in accordance with a scheme" whereby one Harry Gradle, purporting to have been appointed chief of staff, induced the department of public welfare, the civil service commissioners and S. . Parowski to serve his purposes of evading the civil service laws and for the purpose of diverting the said Illinois Eye & Ear Infirmary from the purposes for which it had been created; that the allegation in said communication stating that the Illinois State Civil Service Commission had for the first time classified the positions to be held by members of the medical staff of the infirmary, is not in accordance with the facts; that relator is not in a position to know what the purported classification has been, but that said positions of eye and ear surgeons and their assistants were classified as averred in the petition and that relator took the examination for said classified position and is entitled to continue therein.

It is alleged that after receiving the foregoing communication relator proceeded to the building occupied by the infirmary for his usual duties, and thereupon was told that there was no work for him and that various other members of said staff had been likewise informed, and that this was all done in pursuance of said illegal scheme, fostered for the purpose of furthering the illegal aims and wishes of said Gradle and various other appointees not qualified under the civil service laws; that the position of "chief of staff" to which Gradle was appointed is not warranted in law, and that the court should find such position to be legally non-existent; that the examination of July 1, 1933, was "a mere sham and merely a device" for the purpose of accomplishing the ends of the illegal scheme referred to; that it was not contemplated by the general assembly that the position occupied by relator should be filled in any other manner than as heretofore done in accordance with the civil service statutes and rules of the commission; that defendants have at no time caused any charges to be filed or preferred against him, and desire to remove him and by means of subterfuge, and contrary to law, replace him and others in positions occupied by him and his colleagues. The petition sets forth at great length the rules of the civil service commission, effective April 19, 1918, and prays for the issuance of a writ of mandamus commanding the defendants named in the petition to forthwith restore relator to the classified civil service as "ear surgeon," sometimes known as "senior ear surgeon," in the infirmary, and commanding defendants to cease and desist from disturbing him in the exercise of his duties as such ear surgeon and from in any way unlawfully preventing him from functioning in that capacity at the infirmary; and commanding defendants and each of them forthwith to remove from the medical and surgical staff of the infirmary all members of said staff who have not been qualified therefor in conformity with the civil service laws of the state, and commanding Gradle to cease and desist from interfering with the proper functioning of relator or his associates chosen under the civil service laws as members of the staff of the infirmary.

To the foregoing petition defendants interposed a general and special demurrer, assigning in substance the following grounds:

(1) That the petition is insufficient in law;

said Gradle and various other appointees as [illegible] civil service list; that the position of "chief [illegible] Gradle was appointed is not warranted in law, and that [illegible] should find such position to be legally non-existent [illegible] examination of July 1, [illegible], was "a mere sham and merely a device for the purpose of accomplishing the ends of the illegal scheme referred to; that it was not contemplated by the general [illegible] that the position occupied by relator should be filled in any other manner than as heretofore done in accordance with the civil service statutes and rules of the commission; that defendants [illegible] at no time caused any charges to be filed or preferred against him, and [illegible] him and others in positions occupied by him on his roll [illegible] petition sets forth at great length the rules of the civil service commission, effective April 1, [illegible], and prays [illegible] a writ of mandamus commanding the defendants named in the petition [illegible] forthwith restore relator to the classified civil service as "a surgeon," sometimes known as "senior eye surgeon," in the [illegible] and commanding defendants to cease and desist [illegible] the exercise of his duties as such eye surgeon [illegible] unlawfully preventing him from functioning in [illegible] capacity [illegible] the infirmary; and commanding defendants [illegible] remove from the medical and surgical staff of [illegible] members of said staff who have not been certified [illegible] formity with the civil service law [illegible] Gradle to cease and desist from [illegible] of relator or his associates [illegible] members of the staff of the infirmary.

To the foregoing petition defendants interposed a general and special demurrer, assigning in substance the following grounds:

(1) That the petition is insufficient in law;

(2) That the petition is defective in failing to aver who was the proper appointing officer to the position claimed by relator;

(3) That the act sought to be compelled by relator by mandamus being, in any event, the enforcement of a private right, a demand must first be made upon the appropriate public officer for the performance of such act, and that the petition does not allege a demand upon or a refusal by the proper officer or officers;

(4) That the petition does not aver facts sufficient to show a wrongful discharge from, or a demand and refusal to reinstate the relator in, a position in the State Classified Civil Service;

(5) That the averments of the petition are ambiguous, inconsistent and contradictory;

(6) That the petition does not show that either Gradle or Parowski have or ever had any authority to appoint, discharge or reinstate a member of the State Classified Civil Service, and any demand on either of them to so appoint, discharge or reinstate a member of the State Classified Civil Service would be unavailing;

(7) That the petition abounds in mere conclusions of the pleader which cannot be taken as the proper pleading of facts essential to make out a case entitling petitioner to the relief prayed for;

(8) That the petition does not aver facts showing any duties prescribed or imposed by law upon Gradle or Parowski, and accordingly no mandamus can issue against them;

(9) That the petition does not aver sufficient facts to justify the issuance of the writ prayed for, but in effect requires the court to ascertain and determine the facts, which is contrary to the office of a writ of mandamus.

It is urged that the court erred, as a matter of law, in overruling the demurrer and directing the issuance of the writ. The writ of mandamus is a summary writ, issued from a court of competent jurisdiction, commanding the officer to whom it is addressed to perform some specific duty which the relator is entitled of right to have performed and which the party owing the duty has failed to perform. (Fergus v. Marks, 321 Ill. 510.) It has been repeatedly held that one petitioning for such writ must show a clear and undoubted right to the relief sought. (People v. Nelson, 346 Ill. 247, 251; People v. Board of Review, 351 Ill. 301, 314.) In the latter case the court said that it ought not to issue in any case unless the party applying therefor shows a clear and undeniable right to the thing sought to be done and in the manner and by the person or body sought to be coerced, (citing People v. Hatch, 33 Ill. 9; People v. Sweitzer, 339 Ill. 28,) and that the court will not order it in doubtful cases. (Kenneally v. City of Chicago, 220 Ill. 485, 503.)

(2) That the petition is defective in failing to aver who was the proper appointing officer to the position claimed by relator;

(3) That the act sought to be compelled by relator by mandamus being, in any event, the enforcement of a private right, a demand must first be made upon the appropriate public officer for the performance of such act, and that the petition does not allege a demand upon or a refusal by the proper officer or officers;

(4) That the petition does not aver facts sufficient to show a wrongful discharge from, or a demand and refusal to reinstate the relator in, a position in the State Classified Civil Service;

(5) That the averments of the petition are ambiguous, inconsistent and contradictory;

(6) That the petition does not show that either Gredis or Perowski have or ever had any authority to appoint, discharge or reinstate a member of the State Classified Civil Service, and any demand on either of them to so appoint, discharge or reinstate a member of the State Classified Civil Service would be unavailing;

(7) That the petition abounds in mere conclusions of the pleader which cannot be taken as the proper pleading of facts essential to make out a case entitling petitioner to the relief prayed for;

(8) That the petition does not aver facts showing any duties prescribed or imposed by law upon Gredis or Perowski, and accordingly no mandamus can issue against them;

(9) That the petition does not aver sufficient facts to justify the issuance of the writ prayed for, but in effect requires the court to ascertain and determine the facts, which is contrary to the office of a writ of mandamus.

It is urged that the court erred, as a matter of law, in overruling the demurrer and directing the issuance of the writ. The writ of mandamus is a summary writ, issued from a court of competent jurisdiction, commanding the officer to whom it is addressed to perform some specific duty which the relator is entitled of right to have performed and which the party owing the duty has failed to perform. (Fergus v. Marks, 321 Ill. 510.) It has been repeatedly held that one petitioning for such writ must show a clear and undoubted right to the relief sought. (People v. Nelson, 346 Ill. 247, 251; People v. Board of Review, 331 Ill. 301, 314.) In the latter case the court said that it ought not to issue in any case unless the party applying therefor shows a clear and undeniable right to the thing sought to be done and in the manner and by the person or body sought to be coerced. (citing People v. Hatch, 33 Ill. 9; People v. Kreitzer, 320 Ill. 28,) and that the court will not order it in doubtful cases. (Kennelly v. City of Chicago, 220 Ill. 485, 505.)

Plaintiff seems to take no issue with these propositions, but insists that his right to the relief demanded is sufficiently averred in the petition. In harmony with these authorities it was incumbent upon the relator in this proceeding to show by clear and specific allegations that he was a member of the classified civil service, specifying his classification and the exact duties prescribed thereunder; that he was ousted from the position and had an unquestioned right thereto; that he had demanded of the proper officer or officers his restoration to the position in the classified civil service, and that such demand had been refused.

According to the petition the classification of the position claimed by petitioner as existing prior to 1933 was "ear surgeon," whose duties were "medical and surgical treatment of ear cases, usually at the Illinois Eye & Ear Infirmary." The petition fails to specify more definitely what the performance of these duties entailed. It carried no salary, and there is nothing to show whether the incumbent was required to examine one or more patients a day, a month or a year, or when he was to perform his services. Under the classification of May 11, 1933, there is no such position as "ear surgeon," the equivalent word used being oto-laryngologist. The duties of "Attending Oto-Laryngologist" are to "have entire charge of the medical and surgical treatment of ear, nose and throat patients" at the infirmary, and "be responsible for the adequate instruction of internes and residents." This is clearly a supervisory position, and not the equivalent of "ear surgeon" in the old classification, which contained no element of instruction or executive responsibility; it is a different position. The duties of "Associate Oto-Laryngologist" in the reclassification are to "assist the Attending Oto-Laryngologist in the medical and surgical treatment of ear, nose and throat patients" at the infirmary. The duties of "Adjunct Oto-Laryngologist" in the

Plaintiff seems to take no issue with these propositions, but insists that his right to the relief demanded is sufficiently averred in the petition. In harmony with these authorities it was incumbent upon the relator in this proceeding to show by clear and specific allegations that he was a member of the classified civil service, specifying his classification and the exact duties prescribed thereunder; that he was ousted from the position and had an unquestioned right thereto; that he had demanded of the proper officer or officers his restoration to the position in the classified civil service, and that such demand had been refused.

According to the petition the classification of the position claimed by petitioner as existing prior to 1932 was "ear surgeon," whose duties were "medical and surgical treatment of ear cases, usually at the Illinois Eye & Ear Infirmary." The petition fails to specify more definitely what the performance of these duties entailed. It carried no salary, and there is nothing to show whether the incumbent was required to examine one or more patients a day, a month or a year, or when he was to perform his services. Under the classification of May 11, 1932, there is no such position as "ear surgeon," the equivalent word used being oto-laryngologist. The duties of "Attending Oto-Laryngologist" are to "have entire charge of the medical and surgical treatment of ear, nose and throat patients" at the infirmary, and "be responsible for the adequate instruction of internes and residents." This is clearly a supervisory position, and not the equivalent of "ear surgeon" in the old classification, which contained no element of instruction or executive responsibility; it is a different position. The duties of "Associate Oto-Laryngologist" in the reclassification are to "assist the Attending Oto-Laryngologist in the medical and surgical treatment of ear, nose and throat patients" at the infirmary. The duties of "Adjunct Oto-Laryngologist" in the reclassification are to "assist in the medical and surgical treatment of ear, nose and throat patients" at the infirmary, "under the direct supervision of the Attending or Associate Oto-Laryngologist." While the latter two classifications may be the equivalent of ear surgeon and assistant ear surgeon in the old classification, there is nothing in the new, any more than there was in the old, to indicate the amount of work that either the associate or adjunct Oto-Laryngologist is required to do, or when he is to do it. Obviously the executive departments of the government had the right and power under the state civil service act to make the reclassification and place Gradle in the position of attending oto-laryngologist, which is entirely different from the position of "ear surgeon," claimed by petitioner and to which he seeks to be restored. Therefore, aside from any other defects in the petition, it appears that no showing is made of a "clear and undoubted right to the relief sought," as required under the repeated holding of the cases in this state.

From an examination of the petition it appears that averment of certain factual acts required by statute to precede, accompany and follow the examinations taken under the civil service act are entirely lacking. (Civil Service act, chap. 126a, Cahill's 1933 Illinois Revised Statutes.) The petition fails to disclose that a public competitive examination was held for the position of "ear surgeon," which was free to all the citizens of the United States (sec. 6, chap. 126a); that the qualifications of the applicants to perform the duties of the position were prescribed by rule in advance of such examination (sec. 6); that the examinations related to matters fairly testing the relative capacity of the persons examined to discharge the duties of such position (sec. 6); that the civil service commissioners or examiners appointed by them controlled said examination (sec. 6); that if examiners were appointed to conduct such examination, reclassification are to "assist in the medical and surgical treatment of ear, nose and throat patients" at the infirmary, "under the direct supervision of the Attending or Associate Oto-Laryngologist." While the latter two classifications may be the equivalent of ear surgeon and assistant ear surgeon in the old classification, there is nothing in the new, any more than there was in the old, to indicate the amount of work that either the associate or adjunct Oto-Laryngologist is required to do, or when he is to do it. Obviously the executive departments of the government had the right and power under the state civil service act to make the reclassification and place Gradle in the position of attending oto-laryngologist, which is entirely different from the position of "ear surgeon," claimed by petitioner and to which he seeks to be restored. Therefore, aside from any other defects in the petition, it appears that no showing is made of a "clear and undoubted right to the relief sought," as required under the repeated holding of the cases in this state.

From an examination of the petition it appears that averment of certain factual acts required by statute to precede, accompany and follow the examinations taken under the civil service act are entirely lacking. (Civil Service act, chap. 126a, Cahill's 1933 Illinois Revised Statutes.) The petition fails to disclose that a public competitive examination was held for the position of "ear surgeon," which was free to all the citizens of the United States (sec. 6, chap. 126a); that the qualifications of the applicants to perform the duties of the position were prescribed by rule in advance of such examination (sec. 6); that the examinations related to matters fairly testing the relative capacity of the persons examined to discharge the duties of such position. (sec. 6); that the civil service commissioners or examiners appointed by them controlled said examination (sec. 6); that if examiners were appointed to conduct such examination.

said examiners made a return or report thereof to the civil service commissioners (sec. 6); that a vacancy existed in the position of ear surgeon in the infirmary (sec. 10); that the proper appointing officer made a requisition upon the civil service commission for an eligible to fill a vacancy existing in the position of ear surgeon at the infirmary (sec. 10); that the name and address of the relator stood highest upon the register of eligibles for the position of ear surgeon, and that he was certified by the state civil service commission to the appointing officer to such position (sec. 10). These allegations were essential to show petitioner's undeniable right to the position.

We find in the petition many vague and general allegations, which defendants insist are mere conclusions of the pleader. The petition does not specifically state that there is in existence such a position as he claims, nor who the appointing officer is to such position, nor that such appointing officer made a requisition upon the state civil service commission for an eligible to fill a vacancy then existing. Plaintiff asserts that it is not necessary for the petition to make these allegations specifically, contending that they are encompassed in the general allegation that relator was certified by the Illinois Civil Service Commission to the position of "Ear Surgeon," and was "properly appointed thereto." It was held in Kenneally v. City of Chicago, 220 Ill. 485, 498, that allegations of a general nature such as these, relating to the creation of the office of police patrolman and the appointment of petitioner thereto, were mere conclusions of the pleader, and not sufficient to support the claim of petitioner. (Citing Stott v. City of Chicago, 205 Ill. 281.) We find all through the petition averments of a general nature, which under the authorities cited in defendants' brief, have been held obnoxious to demurrer. (Quinn v. City of Chicago, 178 Ill. App. 115, 118; City of Chicago v. Gray, 210 Ill. 84, 89; Taylor v. Filler, said examiners made a return or report thereof to the civil service commissioners (sec. 6); that a vacancy existed in the position of ear surgeon in the infirmary (sec. 10); that the proper appointing officer made a requisition upon the civil service commission for an eligible to fill a vacancy existing in the position of ear surgeon at the infirmary (sec. 10); that the name and address of the relator stood highest upon the register of eligibles for the position of ear surgeon, and that he was certified by the state civil service commission to the appointing officer to such position (sec. 10). These allegations were essential to show petitioner's undeniable right to the position.

We find in the petition many vague and general allegations, which defendants insist are mere conclusions of the pleader. The petition does not specifically state that there is in existence such a position as he claims, nor who the appointing officer is to such position, nor that such appointing officer made a requisition upon the state civil service commission for an eligible to fill a vacancy then existing. Plaintiff asserts that it is not necessary for the petition to make these allegations specifically, contending that they are encompassed in the general allegation that relator was certified by the Illinois Civil Service Commission to the position of "ear surgeon," and was "properly appointed thereto." It was held in Kenneally v. City of Chicago, 220 Ill. 485, 498, that allegations of a general nature such as these, relating to the creation of the office of police patrolman and the appointment of petitioner thereto, were mere conclusions of the pleader, and not sufficient to support the claim of petitioner. (Citing Swift v. City of Chicago, 208 Ill. 284.) We find all through the petition averments of a general nature, which under the authorities cited in defendants' brief, have been held obnoxious to demurrer. (Quinn v. City of Chicago, 178 Ill. App. 113, 118; City of Chicago v. Gray, 216 Ill. 84, 89; Taylor v. Tilli-

318 Ill. 356, 359.)

Plaintiff states in his brief that "the entire theory of the case is that Gradle and Parowski had no right to appoint or to discharge, but actually did in connection with, and authorized thereto by the other defendants, physically exclude the relator from his duties." In connection with this statement we find in the petition charges, without the statement of any supporting or surrounding facts, that the letter of July 1, 1933, hereinabove quoted, was a "sham and a device" for the purpose of accomplishing the ends of an illegal scheme, and that the reclassification of the state civil service commission of May 11, 1933, is "illegal and void." Averments of this nature are merely conclusions of the pleader, and are clearly bad on demurrer and cannot be considered in connection with the other averments of the petition in determining whether a case for mandatory relief exists. Moreover, Parowski's letter to petitioner is set out in haec verba in the petition, and a careful reading thereof rebuts these allegations of "sham and fraud". The letter states the reasons for the reclassification, which was evidently carried out in accordance with the spirit and letter of the state civil service act. Furthermore, the letter advises petitioner that "any professional men, being civil service employees, will retain their Civil Service Status to the Classification for which they have been certified by the Commission." There is nothing in this statement to indicate bad faith or that petitioner was ousted from his position.

It also appears from the petition that the only officers having to do with certifications to positions within the classified civil service are the civil service commissioners; the only officers having to do with appointments to such positions, after certification, are the members of the Department of Public Welfare; the only officers who could "restore" relator to a classified civil service position are the

312 Ill. 356, 359.)

Plaintiff states in his brief that "the entire theory of the case is that Gradle and Parowski had no right to appoint or to discharge, but actually did in connection with, and authorized thereto by the other defendants, physically exclude the relator from his duties." In connection with this statement we find in the petition charges, without the statement of any supporting or surrounding facts, that the letter of July 1, 1935, hereinabove quoted, was a "sham and a device" for the purpose of accomplishing the ends of an illegal scheme, and that the reclassification of the state civil service commission of May 11, 1935, is "illegal and void." Averments of this nature are merely conclusions of the pleader, and are clearly bad on demurrer and cannot be considered in connection with the other averments of the petition in determining whether a case for mandatory relief exists. Moreover, Parowski's letter to petitioner is set out in haec verba in the petition, and a careful reading thereof rebuts these allegations of "sham and fraud". The letter states the reasons for the reclassification, which was evidently carried out in accordance with the spirit and letter of the state civil service act. Furthermore, the letter advises petitioner that "any professional men, being civil service employees, will retain their Civil Service Status to the Classification for which they have been certified by the Commission." There is nothing in this statement to indicate bad faith or that petitioner was ousted from his position.

It also appears from the petition that the only officers having to do with certifications to positions within the classified civil service are the civil service commissioners; the only officers having to do with appointments to such positions, after certification, are the members of the Department of Public Welfare; the only officers who could "restore" relator to a classified civil service position are the same. City of Chicago v. O'Hare ...

civil service commissioners and the members of the Department of Public Welfare. Nowhere in the petition is there an averment that any demand was made upon any of these officers. The petition alleges that the "Civil Service Commission purported to delegate to Dr. Gradle entire supervision of the members of the staff of the Illinois Eye & Ear Infirmary," and that any demand on respondents would be futile. It is obvious, of course, that the civil service commission could not, and therefore did not, delegate its powers to Dr. Gradle, and that such purported act would not excuse a demand on the legally constituted officers to perform the official act later made the object of mandamus. It is stated in High on Extraordinary Legal Remedies (3rd ed.) sec. 13, that

> "When the person aggrieved claims the immediate and personal benefit of the act or duty whose performance is sought, demand and refusal are held to be necessary as a condition precedent to relief by mandamus * * * in cases where demand and refusal are held necessary it is not sufficient that the demand be couched in merely general terms but it should be express and distinct, and should clearly designate the precise thing which is required."

Illinois cases so holding are People v. Mt. Morris, 137 Ill. 576, 579 and People v. Dunne, 258 Ill. 441, 447.

The reclassification of May 11, 1933, is fully set forth in the petition. From a reading thereof it clearly appears that it was obviously the result of an attempt to organize the infirmary in such a way as to bring to its personnel the most highly qualified eye and ear specialists obtainable, and provide ample service to the public. As indicating the good faith of those who were responsible for the reclassification, the letter to petitioner of July 1, 1933, and the minutes of the State Civil Service Commission, as set forth in the petition, are fairly convincing. The minutes recite that President Lancaster reported to the commission a conference with Dr. Gradle at the State School for the Blind at Jacksonville, regarding the classifications, and that after an extensive research and investigation of the civil service records, with full information civil service commissioners and the minutes of the [illegible] of Public Welfare. [illegible] in the petition [illegible] that any demand was made upon any of these officers. The petition alleges that the "Civil Service classification purposes" [illegible] the entire supervision of the [illegible] could be fulfilled. [illegible] civil service commission could not, and therefore [illegible] the legally constituted officers to perform [illegible] the object of mandamus. [illegible] legal [illegible] that

"[illegible] the person aggrieved [illegible] personal benefit of [illegible] distinct, and should clearly designate [illegible] is required."

[illegible]

The reclassification of [illegible] in the petition. [illegible] that it was obviously the result of [illegible] such a way as to bring [illegible] public. [illegible] for the reclassification [illegible] the minutes of the [illegible] civil service [illegible] in the petition, are fairly [illegible] President Lancaster reported to the commission [illegible] Dr. Grade at the State School for the Blind [illegible] regarding the classifications, and that after an extensive research and investigation of the civil service records, with full information he made a trip to Chicago in April, 1933, to consult Dr. Gradle; that the investigation conducted by Lancaster disclosed: (1) That there are a number of physicians and surgeons certified as eye surgeon, ear surgeon, assistant eye surgeon, assistant ear surgeon at the infirmary; that these classifications have not been nor will be changed by the adoption of the reclassification; and that there will be no impairment of the civil service status of persons certified to the reclassification. (2) That Dr. Gradle desired to undertake the work of the infirmary only in case he could have an efficient staff that meets his requirements and the approval of the best minds of the medical profession as applicable to the infirmary. (3) That it is imperative and essential that the new classifications as set forth be approved and adopted by the commission; that the qualifications set forth in the requirements for the various positions are very high, and applicants who are able to measure up to the classifications will, under the direction of Gradle, be competent to place the infirmary in the highest rank of similar institutions throughout the country. There is certainly nothing in the reclassification itself, or in the minutes of the Civil Service Commission, indicating a lack of good faith, or "a mere sham and device, or "illegal scheme" to deprive petitioner of his legal rights.

The order of the court, after overruling the demurrer, directs that a writ of mandamus issue against the respondents, including Parewski and Gradle, "commanding said defendants and each of them to restore relator, Grim, to his functions and duties as ear surgeon, and to restore him to his position as ear surgeon without obstructing or hindering him in his said duties." As heretofore stated, the only respondent officials who have any legal duty to perform which concerns appointment or restoration to the civil service position in the infirmary are the members of the civil service commission, who certify eligibles, and members of the department of

public welfare, who are required by law to appoint eligibles certified to them by the commissioners. Farowski and Greble are neither civil service commissioners nor members of the department of public welfare, and therefore have no legal duty in any way related to the appointment or restoration of relator to his alleged position. Moreover, the order is bad as to all respondents, because it directs a writ of mandamus "to restore relator to his functions and duties," without any specification of what those duties are. The only allegation in the petition as to relator's duties is contained in the classification, which defines the duties of his position to give "medical and surgical treatment of ear cases." There is no averment as to how much time these duties require, or when they are to be performed. A writ of mandamus should be sufficiently definite to permit a clear determination by the court of what facts will constitute a disobedience thereof and a contempt of court. As a matter of fact, there is pending before us, as shown by the notice of appeal to this court (in cause No. 37999) an appeal from an order dismissing a petition for a rule to show cause against these petitioners, based on the inability of the court, after a hearing of the evidence offered by petitioner and respondents, to determine whether or not there had been a violation of the mandamus order. In High on Extraordinary Legal Remedies (3rd ed.) sec. 538, it is said that

> "The writ should also call the attention of the respondent with especial certainty and particularity to the precise thing which he is required to do,"

and in section 542, it is stated that

> "The general rule is that it should be directed to those, and to those only, who are to obey it, and a disregard of this rule is sufficient ground for sustaining a motion to quash."

Section 561 states:

> "Great particularity is necessary in stating in the peremptory writ the precise thing which is required, in order that the respondent may be definitely apprised of all that he is commanded to do. And when a peremptory mandamus has been awarded to compel the treasurer of a school district to pay certain orders against the district, but the writ contains no description of the orders, either by

public welfare, who are required by law to appoint eligibles certified to them by the commissioners. Purcell and Grable are neither civil service commissioners nor members of the department of public welfare, and therefore have no legal duty in any way related to the appointment or restoration of relator to his alleged position. Moreover, the order is bad as to all respondents, because it directs a writ of mandamus "to restore relator to his functions and duties," without any specification of what those duties are. The only allegation in the petition as to relator's duties is contained in the classification, which defines the duties of his position to give "medical and surgical treatment of ear cases." There is no averment as to how much time these duties require, or when they are to be performed. A writ of mandamus should be sufficiently definite to permit a clear determination by the court of what facts will constitute a disobedience thereof and a contempt of court. As a matter of fact, there is pending before us, as shown by the motion of appeal to this court (in cause No. 37999) an appeal from an order dismissing a petition for a rule to show cause against these petitioners, based on the inability of the courts after a hearing of the evidence offered by petitioner and respondents, to determine whether or not there had been a violation of the mandamus order. In High on Extraordinary Legal Remedies (3rd ed.) sec. 538, it is said that

"The writ should also call the attention of the respondent with especial certainty and particularity to the precise thing which he is required to do."

and in section 542, it is stated that

"The general rule is that it should be directed to those, and to those only, who are to obey it, and a disregard of this rule is sufficient ground for sustaining a motion to quash."

Section 561 states:

"Great particularity is necessary in stating in the peremptory writ the precise thing which is required, in order that the respondents may be definitely apprised of all that he is commanded to do. And when a peremptory mandamus had been awarded to compel the Treasurer of a school district to pay certain orders against the district, but the writ contained no description of the orders, either by number or amount, and this does not appear in any of the pleadings or other proceedings, the defect is fatal and will warrant the reversal of the judgment."

In People v. Brooks, 57 Ill. 142, 143, the court said:

"We think the writ defective, too, for lack of certainty. The writ must clearly show upon its face that it is the defendant's duty to execute it, and must, with great certainty, call the attention of the defendant to his duty. Tapping on Mandamus, 322."

These rules are well settled and we find no authority to the contrary in plaintiff's brief. In consonance with these rules the order is bad because it commands Gradle and Parowski, who are not required by law either to appoint or to certify eligibles, to restore the relator to his functions and duties, and also because it fails to specify with any particularity, as the authorities hold it should, what these duties are, so as to permit a clear determination later of what facts will constitute a disobedience of the order and a contempt of court.

Other points are raised by counsel's brief, but in view of the conclusions reached as to the insufficiency of the petition and the invalidity of the order, it will be unnecessary to discuss them.

On October 23, 1934, relator moved to vacate the order theretofore entered by this court granting defendants' right to appeal and for a supersedeas; also that the petition of defendants be dismissed for want of jurisdiction. These motions were reserved to the hearing of said cause. It appears that a notice of appeal to the Supreme Court, dated February 20, 1934, was filed by all the defendants, including Gradle and Parowski, and notice of appearance was filed by relator on February 23, 1934. However, the record for review of the order, directing that the mandamus writ issue, was never lodged in the Supreme Court, but was filed here in connection with the petition for leave to appeal. Under the Civil Practice act (sec. 76, chap. 110, Cahill's 1933 Rev. Ill. Statutes), an appellant's right to appeal expires 90 days after the entry of the order or judgment complained of, unless his appeal is perfected within the number or amount, and this does not appear in any of the pleadings or other proceedings, the defect is fatal and will warrant the reversal of the judgment."

In People v. Brooks, 57 Ill. 142, 143, the court said:

"We think the writ defective, too, for lack of certainty. The writ must clearly show upon its face that it is the defendant's duty to execute it, and must, with great certainty, call the attention of the defendant to his duty. Tapping on Mandamus, 382."

These rules are well settled and we find no authority to the contrary in plaintiff's brief. In consonance with these rules the order is bad because it commands Grudis and Parevski, who are not required by law either to appoint or to certify eligibles, to restore the relator to his functions and duties, and also because it fails to specify with any particularity, as the authorities hold it should, what those duties are, so as to permit a clear determination later of what facts will constitute a disobedience of the order and a contempt of court.

Other points are raised by counsel's brief, but in view of the conclusions reached as to the insufficiency of the petition and the invalidity of the order, it will be unnecessary to discuss them.

On October 22, 1934, relator moved to vacate the order theretofore entered by this court granting defendants' right to appeal and for a supersedeas; also that the petition of defendants be dismissed for want of jurisdiction. These motions were reserved to the hearing of said cause. It appears that a notice of appeal to the Supreme Court, dated February 20, 1934, was filed by all the defendants, including Grudis and Parevski, and notice of appearance was filed by relator on February 25, 1934. However, the record for review of the order, directing that the mandamus writ issue, was never lodged in the Supreme Court, but was filed here in connection with the petition for leave to appeal. Under the Civil Practice act (sec. 76, chap. 110, Cahill's 1933 Rev. Ill. Statutes), an appellant's right to appeal expires 90 days after the entry of the order or judgment complained of, unless his appeal is perfected within the

90 days. If not perfected within that time, the right to review is waived, and thereafter review is by permission of the reviewing court only. Nothing was done in this case to perfect the appeal within the 90 days. Therefore, defendants lost their right to review, and later obtained permission to appeal under the provisions of section 76. In that situation there were not actually two reviews attempted, as relator contends, because one was abandoned through failure of defendants to file a record within the time fixed by the statute. All of these matters were presented and considered on the petition for leave to appeal and the answer then filed. Relator's motion will therefore be denied.

The petition for mandamus, being defective for the reasons herein stated, the judgment of the superior court will be reversed and the cause remanded, with directions to sustain the demurrer.

REVERSED AND REMANDED WITH DIRECTIONS.

Scanlan and Sullivan, JJ., concur.

90 days. If not perfected within that time, the right to review is waived, and thereafter review is by permission of the reviewing court only. Nothing was done in this case to perfect the appeal within the 90 days. Therefore, defendants lost their right to review, and later obtained permission to appeal under the provisions of section 76. In that situation there were not actually two review attempted, as relator contends, because one was abandoned through failure of defendants to file a record within the time fixed by the statute. All of these matters were presented and considered on the petition for leave to appeal and the answer then filed. Relator's motion will therefore be denied.

The petition for mandamus, being defective for the reasons herein stated, the judgment of the superior court will be reversed and the cause remanded, with directions to sustain the demurrer.

REVERSED AND REMANDED WITH DIRECTIONS.

Scanlan and Sullivan, JJ., concur.

75H

37734

AMERICAN NATIONAL BANK AND TRUST COMPANY OF CHICAGO, as successor trustee,
Complainant,
v.
HOTEL GRAEMERE, Inc., et al.,
Defendants.

J. ROSS LOGAN and FLORENCE B. LOGAN, his wife; THELMA GARNO, EDWARD J. PAULER, IDA KARLIN and MARY BUCHER,
Cross complainants,

AMERICAN NATIONAL BANK AND TRUST COMPANY OF CHICAGO, as successor trustee,
Appellant,
v.
J. ROSS LOGAN and FLORENCE B. LOGAN, his wife; THELMA GARNO, EDWARD J. PAULER, IDA KARLIN, MARY BUCHER and OSCAR WEINER, receiver,
Appellees.

APPEAL FROM SUPERIOR COURT, COOK COUNTY.

280 I.A. 626[1]

MR. PRESIDING JUSTICE FRIEND DELIVERED THE OPINION OF THE COURT.

This is an appeal by American National Bank & Trust Company, as successor trustee under a first mortgage securing bonds aggregating $1,800,000, from an order in Superior court consolidated cases Nos. 526216 and 553261, allowing Shulman, Shulman & Abrams, solicitors for certain bondholders, $3,500 fees for services claimed to have been rendered for Oscar Weiner, receiver.

In the first suit (hereinafter referred to as the foreclosure case) a decree of foreclosure was entered January 19, 1931. Thereafter, October 11, 1933, several bondholders filed an independent suit (hereinafter referred to as the bondholders' case) by Shulman, Shulman & Abrams, their attorneys, alleging fraud in the issuance

37734

AMERICAN NATIONAL BANK AND TRUST COMPANY OF CHICAGO, as successor trustee,
Complainant,

v.

HOTEL [illegible], Inc., et al.,
Defendants.

J. ROSS LOGAN and FLORENCE B. LOGAN, his wife; THELMA GAERO, EDWARD J. PARKER, IDA MARLIN and MARY BUCHER,
Cross complainants,

AMERICAN NATIONAL BANK AND TRUST COMPANY OF CHICAGO, as successor trustee,
Appellant,

v.

J. ROSS LOGAN and FLORENCE B. LOGAN, his wife; THELMA GAERO, EDWARD J. PARKER, IDA MARLIN, MARY BUCHER and OSCAR WOLNER, receiver,
Appellees.

APPEAL FROM SUPERIOR COURT, COOK COUNTY.

280 I.A. 626

MR. PRESIDING JUSTICE FRIEND DELIVERED THE OPINION OF THE COURT.

This is an appeal by American National Bank & Trust Company, as successor trustee under a first mortgage securing bonds aggregating $1,800,000, from an order in Superior court consolidated cases Nos. 526216 and 563261, allowing Shulman, Shulman & Abrams, solicitors for certain bondholders, $3,600 fees for services claimed to have been rendered for Oscar Wolner, receiver.

In the first suit (hereinafter referred to as the foreclosure case) a decree of foreclosure was entered January 19, 1931. Thereafter, October 11, 1933, several bondholders filed an independent suit (hereinafter referred to as the bondholders' case) by Shulman, Shulman & Abrams, their attorneys, alleging fraud in the issuance of the bonds involved in the foreclosure suit, a fraudulent purpose in the organization of the bondholders' protective committee, and praying that the decree of sale theretofore entered be decreed to be void, praying for an accounting, and that a new trustee and a receiver be appointed.

November 15, 1933, on motion of Shulman, Shulman & Abrams, solicitors for complainants, an order was entered in the bondholders' case, appointing Oscar Weiner receiver and fixing his bond at $50,000. This bond was never filed, probably because it was at the time impossible for the receiver to acquire physical control of the mortgaged property, which was in possession of the county collector as receiver appointed by the county court in a pending tax case.

After November 15, 1933, Weiner, in order to possess himself of the mortgaged property, negotiated for the surrender of possession by the receiver appointed by the county court, and consulted Meyer Abrams of the firm of Shulman, Shulman & Abrams, who, with Weiner, appeared before the county court on several occasions in an effort to gain possession of the premises for Weiner. Being unable to do so, however, Weiner instituted mandamus proceedings in the Supreme court against Edmund K. Jarecki, as Judge of the County court, to compel him to expunge the order appointing the county collector as receiver, and filed briefs in said proceedings, wherein Shulman, Shulman & Abrams appeared as his attorneys.

Up to January 27, 1934, Weiner had not qualified as receiver by filing his bond, and had not succeeded in obtaining possession of the mortgaged property. On that date, the American National Bank & Trust Co., as successor trustee, petitioned the court in the foreclosure case to be substituted as complainant. Order of substitution was entered as requested, and Oscar Weiner was again appointed receiver and his bond this time fixed at $500. He qualified as receiver on the same date by having his bond approved, and the court thereupon of the bonds involved in [illegible] fraudulent persons in the organization of the [illegible] protective [illegible], praying that the decree [illegible] be declared to be void, praying for an accounting, and that a [illegible] receiver be appointed.

November 1[illegible], 1934, on motion of Shulman, [illegible] solicitors for complainants, an order was entered in this [illegible] case, appointing Oscar Falner receiver and fixing his bond [illegible] $5,000. This bond was never filed, probably because it was [illegible] impossible for the receiver to acquire physical control of the mortgaged property, which is in possession of the county [illegible] receiver appointed by the county court in a pending tax case.

After November 15, 1935, Falner, in order to force a [illegible] sale of the mortgaged property, negotiated for the [illegible] possession by the receiver appointed by the county court [illegible] consulted Meyer [illegible] of the firm of Shulman, Shulman [illegible] with [illegible] appeared before the county court on several occasions in an effort to gain possession of the premises for [illegible] to do so, however, [illegible] instituted mandamus proceedings in the Supreme court against [illegible] Jarecki, as Judge of the county court, to compel him to expunge the order appointing the county [illegible] receiver, and filed [illegible] proceedings [illegible]

[illegible] January 17, 1936, [illegible] ceiver by filing his bond, [illegible] of the mortgaged property [illegible] Trust Co., as successor [illegible] name to be substituted [illegible] complainant, [illegible] was entered as requested, and Oscar Falner [illegible] receiver and his bond this time fixed at $50[illegible] on the same date by having his bond approved, and the court thereupon entered another order authorizing Weiner, as receiver, to retain Samuel Berke as his attorney. At the same time an order was entered consolidating the foreclosure case and the bondholders' case, under the title and number of the former proceeding.

Subsequent to the entry of these orders, and prior to February 28, 1934, the mandamus proceedings were dismissed by stipulation, Mr. Abrams and solicitors for complainants in the foreclosure case having obtained an agreement from the state's attorney to a voluntary surrender of possession by the county court receiver.

February 28, 1934, the Superior court entered an order in the consolidated cases, reciting that Weiner was then in actual possession of the premises, increasing his bond from $500 to $25,000, and ordering that his bond, which was then presented, be filed and approved.

April 23, 1934, Mary Bucher, by Shulman, Shulman & Abrams, her attorneys, filed a petition in the consolidated cases, alleging that she was the owner of a $500 bond, asking leave to intervene as a party complainant in the bondholders' case, and praying that an order be entered allowing reasonable compensation to Shulman, Shulman & Abrams, as attorneys for the receiver, for services performed by them in connection with the mandamus proceeding and the surrender of possession by the county court receiver. To this petition, American National Bank & Trust Co. filed an answer, denying that said attorneys were entitled to compensation from the receiver.

June 25, 1934, the Superior court entered the order appealed from, reciting that the cause came on to be heard upon the petition of Shulman, Shulman & Abrams, for the allowance of fees for services rendered by them on behalf of the receiver, reciting the performance of services, and ordering the receiver to pay said attorneys the sum of $3,500 in the due course of administration of the receivership, out of the funds on hand.

entered another order authorizing Weiner, as receiver, to retain Samuel Marks as his attorney. At the same time an order was entered consolidating the foreclosure case and the bondholders' case, under the title and number of the former proceeding.

Subsequent to the entry of these orders, and prior to February 28, 1934, the mandamus proceedings were dismissed by stipulation, Mr. Abrams and solicitors for complainants in the foreclosure case having obtained an agreement from the state's attorney to a voluntary surrender of possession by the county court receiver.

February 28, 1934, the Superior court entered an order in the consolidated cases, reciting that Weiner was then in actual possession of the premises, increasing his bond from $500 to $25,000, and ordering that his bond, which was then presented, be filed and approved.

April 25, 1934, Mary Buehler, by Chulman, Chulman & Abrams, her attorneys, filed a petition in the consolidated cases, alleging that she was the owner of a $500 bond, asking leave to intervene as a party complainant in the bondholders' case, and praying that an order be entered allowing reasonable compensation to Shulman, Shulman & Abrams, as attorneys for the receiver, for services performed by them in connection with the mandamus proceeding and the surrender of possession by the county court receiver. To this petition, Mercantile National Bank & Trust Co. filed an answer, denying that said attorneys were entitled to compensation from the receiver.

June 25, 1934, the Superior court entered the order appealed from, reciting that the cause came on to be heard upon the petition of Shulman, Shulman & Abrams, for the allowance of fees for services rendered by them on behalf of the receiver, reciting the performance of services, and ordering the receiver to pay said attorneys the sum of $2,500 in the due course of administration of the receivership, out of the funds on hand.

It is urged on behalf of Shulman, Shulman & Abrams that the receiver employed them to obtain possession of the premises from the county court receiver, and that they rendered valuable services to the receivership estate in connection with the mandamus proceeding and in obtaining the agreement of the state's attorney to voluntarily surrender possession. Substantially all their services were rendered prior to January 27, 1934, when Weiner was appointed receiver for the second time. It is urged, however, that the first appointment, November 15, 1933, was valid, and that the receiver then qualified by filing his bond, in the sum of $50,000, and was thereafter authorized, without the court's sanction, to retain attorneys to obtain for him possession of the premises from the county court receiver. The record discloses that no bond was filed by Weiner under the order of November 15, 1933. Counsel say that the bond was brought into court and left with the clerk. Apparently it was not filed, in order to avoid payment of premium to the surety on so large a sum, at a time when it was apparent that the receiver would not obtain possession of the property. Whatever the reason may be, the bond was not filed, and Weiner did not qualify as receiver until January 27, 1934, when he was appointed by a subsequent order. It has been held that until the bond is given, as required by the order of appointment, a receiver has no power to act. (Edgerly v. Blackburn, 140 App. Div. 419, 125 N. Y. S. 353; Edwards v. Edwards, L. R. 2 Ch. Div. 291; Crumlish's Adm'r v. Shenandoah Valley R. Co., 40 W. Va. 627, 22 S. E. 90; Johnson v. Martin, 1 Thom. & Cook (N.Y.) 504.) In Phillips v. Smoot, 1 Mackey (12 D. C.) 478, it was held that a receiver, appointed to take possession of property, who was required to give bond, could not legally dispossess a tenant until bond was given. The only conclusion to be reached from the state of the record and the authorities is that the order of November 15, 1933, never became effective.

It is urged on behalf of Shulman, Shulman & Abrams that the receiver employed them to obtain possession of the premises from the county court receiver, and that they rendered valuable services to the receivership estate in connection with the mandamus proceeding and in obtaining the agreement of the state's attorney to voluntarily surrender possession. Substantially all their services were rendered prior to January 27, 1934, when Weiner was appointed receiver for the second time. It is urged, however, that the first appointment, November 15, 1933, was valid, and that the receiver then qualified by filing his bond, in the sum of $50,000, and was thereafter authorized, without the court's sanction, to retain attorneys to obtain for him possession of the premises from the county court receiver. The record discloses that no bond was filed by Weiner under the order of November 15, 1933. Counsel say that the bond was brought into court and left with the clerk. Apparently it was not filed, in order to avoid payment of premium to the surety on so large a sum at a time when it was apparent that the receiver would not obtain possession of the property. Whatever the reason may be, the bond was not filed, and Weiner did not qualify as receiver until January 27, 1934, when he was appointed by a subsequent order. It has been held that until the bond is given, as required by the order of appointment, a receiver has no power to act. (Moberly v. Blackburn, 140 App. Div. 419, 125 N. Y. S. 385; Edwards v. Edwards, L. R. 2 Ch. Div. 291; Grantham's Adm'r v. Shenandoah Valley R. Co., 40 W. Va. 627, 22 S. E. 60; Johnson v. Martin, 1 Thom. & Cook (N.Y.) 504.) In Phillips v. Smoot, 1 Mackey (12 D. C.) 478, it was held that a receiver, appointed to take possession of property, who was required to give bond, could not legally dispossess a tenant until bond was given. The only conclusion to be reached from the state of the record and the authorities is that the order of November 15, 1933, never became effective.

The appointing order of January 27, 1934, recites that the $50,000 bond required by the order of November 15, 1933, was "withheld of record until the determination of the Supreme court of a mandamus proceeding now pending therein, involving the surrender of possession by the county collector as receiver, and until the disposition of said cause, in order to avoid the payment of a large premium on said bond," and it is now urged that the filing of the $500 bond on January 27, 1934, relates back to the original order of appointment. This contention, however, is untenable. There were in fact two separate orders, and the bonds fixed were of entirely different amounts. Since it is clear that no premium was ever paid on the $50,000 bond, the surety never became bound, and the bond not having been filed of record nor approved by the court, the receiver never became qualified to act until he complied with the second order appointing him, under which he filed bond and had the same duly approved by the court. Consequently, the services rendered for Oscar Weiner by Shulman, Shulman & Abrams subsequent to November 15, 1933, and prior to January 27, 1934, were for Weiner individually in connection with mandamus proceedings in the Supreme court and negotiations with the county court and state's attorney, culminating in the voluntary surrender of possession of the premises by the county court receiver, and whatever fees may have been earned by them for such services cannot be charged against the receivership estate, because there was no receivership estate until Weiner had qualified January 27, 1934, which was long after most of these services were performed.

It is urged as an additional ground for sustaining the order allowing fees that the receivership estate was greatly benefited by the services rendered. The order allowing the fees contains the following recitals:

The appointing order of January 27, 1934, recites that the $50,000 bond required by the order of November 15, 1933, was "withheld of record until the determination of the Supreme court of a mandamus proceeding now pending therein, involving the surrender of possession by the county collector as receiver, and until the disposition of said cause, in order to avoid the payment of a large premium on said bond," and it is now urged that the filing of the $500 bond on January 27, 1934, relates back to the original order of appointment. This contention, however, is untenable. There were in fact two separate orders, and the bonds fixed were of entirely different amounts. Since it is clear that no premium was ever paid on the $50,000 bond, the surety never became bound, and the bond not having been filed of record nor approved by the court, the receiver never became qualified to act until he complied with the second order appointing him, under which he filed bond and had the same duly approved by the court. Consequently, the services rendered for Oscar Weiner by Shulman, Shulman & Abrams subsequent to November 15, 1933, and prior to January 27, 1934, were for Weiner individually in connection with mandamus proceedings in the Supreme court and negotiations with the county court and state's attorney, culminating in the voluntary surrender of possession of the premises by the county court receiver, and whatever fees may have been earned by them for such services cannot be charged against the receivership estate, because there was no receivership estate until Weiner had qualified January 27, 1934, which was long after most of these services were performed.

It is urged as an additional ground for sustaining the order allowing fees that the receivership estate was greatly benefited by the services rendered. The order allowing the fees contains the following recitals:

"That the placing of the Receiver of this Court in possession was a direct result of the services rendered by said attorneys and that the appointment by this Court of the Receiver greatly benefited the Receivership Estate in that while the County Collector during the term that he managed the property only applied on taxes the sum of Seven Thousand ($7,000.00) Dollars and left the Estate in debt in the sum of approximately Fourteen Thousand ($14,000.00) Dollars, this Receiver was able to pay at a rate of Twenty Five Hundred ($2500.00) Dollars per month on taxes and also have a reserve fund on hand."

There is no competent evidence to support this finding. Counsel evidently made allegations to this effect in the petition for mandamus and argued the subject in their briefs filed in the Supreme court. Upon the hearing in the Superior court on the petition for the allowance of fees they offered in evidence copies of the mandamus petition and briefs. These documents do not substantiate the fact that the receivership estate was benefited; they are mere averments of the contentions of counsel and do not constitute proof. Upon the record of the case it remains a matter of conjecture whether the receiver appointed by the Superior court was more efficient than the county court receiver, and proof is lacking to show that the receivership estate was benefited.

Counsel for the American National Bank & Trust Co., who have prosecuted this appeal, call our attention to the fact that Shulman, Shulman & Abrams were at all times attorneys of record for alleged bondholders, and that when they assisted Weiner in gaining possession of the premises it will be presumed that they were acting in the interest of their clients, for whom they appeared, and should be compensated by their clients and not out of the receivership estate. A considerable portion of the brief is devoted to a discussion of this proposition and cases cited in support thereof. We think there is merit in the contention, but in view of the conclusions reached upon the other points, we believe it is unnecessary to discuss the point further.

For the reasons hereinabove stated, the order of the Superior court allowing $3,500 fees is reversed. REVERSED.

Scanlan and Sullivan, JJ., concur.

"That the placing of the Receiver of this Court in possession was a direct result of the services rendered by said attorneys and that the appointment by this Court of the Receiver greatly benefited the Receivership Estate in that while the County Collector during the term that he managed the property only applied on taxes the sum of Seven Thousand ($7,000.00) Dollars and left the Estate in debt in the sum of approximately Fourteen Thousand ($14,000.00) Dollars, this Receiver was able to pay at a rate of Twenty Five Hundred ($2500.00) Dollars per month on taxes and also have a reserve fund on hand."

There is no competent evidence to support this finding. Counsel evidently made allegations to this effect in the petition for mandamus and argued the subject in their briefs filed in the Supreme court. Upon the hearing in the Superior court on the petition for the allowance of fees they offered in evidence copies of the mandamus petition and briefs. These documents do not substantiate the fact that the receivership estate was benefited; they are mere averments of the contentions of counsel and do not constitute proof. Upon the record of the case it remains a matter of conjecture whether the receiver appointed by the Superior court was more efficient than the county court receiver, and proof is lacking to show that the receivership estate was benefited.

Counsel for the American National Bank & Trust Co., who have prosecuted this appeal, call our attention to the fact that Shulman, Shulman & Abrams were at all times attorneys of record for alleged bondholders, and that when they assisted Weimer in gaining possession of the premises it will be presumed that they were acting in the interest of their clients, for whom they appeared, and should be compensated by their clients and not out of the receivership estate. A considerable portion of the brief is devoted to a discussion of this proposition and cases cited in support thereof. We think there is merit in the contention, but in view of the conclusions reached upon the other points, we believe it is unnecessary to discuss the point further.

For the reasons hereinabove stated, the order of the Superior court allowing $3,500 fees is reversed.

REVERSED.

Scanlan and Sullivan, JJ., concur.

37789

76 A

SAMUEL PARKER JOHNSTON et al., Appellants, v. ALEXANDER W. HANNAH et al., Appellees.	)	APPEAL FROM CIRCUIT COURT, COOK COUNTY.

280 I.A. 626[2]

MR. PRESIDING JUSTICE FRIEND DELIVERED THE OPINION OF THE COURT.

Plaintiffs brought an action in deceit in the circuit court for false representations which are alleged to have induced them to acquire, by exchange, improved real estate in Chicago, known as Juneway Fireproof Garage. The cause was heard by the court without a jury, resulting in findings and judgment in favor of defendants, from which plaintiffs have appealed.

It appears from the evidence that in May, 1929, Samuel Parker Johnston and Olive Adams Johnston, his wife, owned improved real estate at 227-229 W. Washington street, Chicago, and defendants Alexander W. Hannah, Hazel H. Newton and Mabel H. McIntosh, his sisters, were the owners of improved property in Chicago, known as the Juneway Fireproof Garage. About a year before the transaction in question was consummated plaintiff Samuel Parker Johnston, who had for many years been engaged in the real estate business in this city, listed the Washington street property for sale or exchange with his broker, Trestler. The property was called to the attention of one Newton, of Ross & Newton, brokers for defendants. Negotiations were commenced for the exchange of the property for the Juneway Fireproof Garage. Trestler inquired about the tenant in the garage and Newton referred him to his partner, Ross, who stated that "he thought the man was a very good garage man, a very able man." This was

37760

SAMUEL PARKER JOHNSTON et al.,
Appellants,

v.

ALEXANDER W. HANNAH et al.,
Appellees.

APPEAL FROM CIRCUIT COURT,
COOK COUNTY.

260 I.A. 326

MR. PRESIDING JUSTICE FRIEND DELIVERED THE OPINION OF THE COURT.

Plaintiffs brought an action in deceit in the circuit court for false representations which are alleged to have induced them to acquire, by exchange, improved real estate in Chicago, known as Janeway Fireproof Garage. The cause was heard by the court without a jury, resulting in findings and judgment in favor of defendants, from which plaintiffs have appealed.

It appears from the evidence that in May, 1929, Samuel Parker Johnston and Olive Adams Johnston, his wife, owned improved real estate at 227-229 W. Washington street, Chicago, and defendants Alexander W. Hannah, Hazel H. Newton and Mabel B. McIntosh, his sisters, were the owners of improved property in Chicago, known as the Janeway Fireproof Garage. About a year before the transaction in question was consummated plaintiff Samuel Parker Johnston, who had for many years been engaged in the real estate business in this city, listed the Washington street property for sale or exchange with his broker, Troelter. The property was called to the attention of one Newton, of Ross & Newton, brokers for defendants. Negotiations were commenced for the exchange of the property for the Janeway Fireproof Garage. Troelter inquired about the tenant in the garage and Newton referred him to his partner, Ross, who stated that "he thought the man was a very good garage man, a very able man." This was reported to Johnston, who went out to look at the garage property several times before the contract was signed, investigated the neighborhood and talked to the tenant, Steele. Mrs. Johnston, who held title to the Washington street property, likewise visited the garage, examined the building and its surroundings, discussed with Steele, the tenant, the occupancy of the garage, and stated that "it looked neat and all that."

The contract for the exchange of the two properties was made April 18, 1929. Rentals and taxes were to be adjusted as of the date of delivery of deeds. Plaintiffs were to pay a broker's commission to Trostler, and defendants were to pay a like commission to Ross & Newton. After the contract had been signed, Johnston came to the office of defendants' attorney with his lawyer to discuss the matter of the lease and its terms. The original lease to Steele was for a term of seven years, beginning at a graduated monthly rental of $1,166.67, increasing to $1,333.33. Plaintiffs' attorney requested that the lease be redrawn with certain articles thereof written out in full. Defendants' attorney agreed thereto and procured a new lease, drawn and executed as suggested by plaintiffs' counsel. The parties met for the first time in the office of defendants' attorney when the transaction was to be consummated. A postponement was necessary because some question was raised in connection with the title, and they met again May 10, 1929, when the deal was closed. On this occasion defendants' attorney stated that "it was a good lease, and that he (Steele) was a good tenant, he was a thorough, experienced garage man, nothing to worry about on him." In computing the adjustments of rent and taxes in closing the deal either the defendant Hannah, or his attorney, stated that the rent for the month of May had been paid, also that deposits on account of taxes, except for one payment of $200 had been received, and computations were made accordingly. A few months after the transaction was closed Steele reported to Johnston, who went out to look at the garage property several times before the contract was signed, investigated the neighborhood and talked to the tenant, Steele. Mrs. Johnston, who held title to the Washington street property, likewise visited the garage, examined the building and its surroundings, discussed with Steele, the tenant, the occupancy of the garage, and stated that "it looked neat and all that."

The contract for the exchange of the two properties was made April 16, 1929. Rentals and taxes were to be adjusted as of the date of delivery of deeds. Plaintiffs were to pay a broker's commission to Tressler, and defendants were to pay a like commission to Ross & Newton. After the contract had been signed, Johnston came to the office of defendants' attorney with his lawyer to discuss the matter of the lease and its terms. The original lease to Steele was for a term of seven years, beginning at a graduated monthly rental of $1,166.67, increasing to $1,333.33. Plaintiffs' attorney requested that the lease be redrawn with certain articles thereof written out in full. Defendants' attorney agreed thereto and procured a new lease, drawn and executed as requested by plaintiffs' counsel. The parties met for the first time in the office of defendants' attorney when the transaction was to be consummated. A postponement was necessary because some question was raised in connection with the title, and they met again May 16, 1929, when the deal was closed. On this occasion defendants' attorney stated that "it was a good lease, and that he (Steele) was a good tenant; he was a thorough, experienced garage man, nothing to worry about on him." In computing the adjustments of rent and taxes in closing the deal either the defendant Hannah, or his attorney, stated that the rent for the month of May had been paid, also that deposits on account of taxes, except for one payment of $200 had been received, and computations were made accordingly. A few months after the transaction was closed Steele sold his leasehold and business to one Reid for $5,500 cash. Plaintiffs consented to the assignment of the lease to Reid, who then paid rent to plaintiffs.

When Steele took over the lease of the garage in August, 1928, there were some 38 or 39 cars therein and the building was dirty and run-down, requiring a substantial amount of capital to rehabilitate it. The inside of the garage was white-washed, the floors cleaned, and the air compressor, washer and other equipment repaired. In April and May, 1929, the garage was well filled, with an occupancy of approximately 160 cars, and was yielding a gross income of over $3,000 a month. All of the receipts were deposited in a bank account, and the rent money was paid out of the deposits.

As heretofore stated, the Washington street property had been listed for exchange or sale for about a year before the exchange was made. Defendants contend that its value was extremely doubtful and speculative, as evidenced by the fact that the defendant Hannah had disposed of the equity in the property for some lots of doubtful value before this proceeding was instituted. The $100,000 mortgage placed upon the property in connection with the exchange had been foreclosed with a deficiency decree of $10,000, and it is argued that plaintiffs were moved to make the exchange in order to "get out from under" a very doubtful parcel of real estate.

Plaintiffs maintain that they were defrauded by the following false representations:

(1) That Steele was the lessee under the terms of the written lease, whereas the lease was a sham, never enforced or intended to be enforced between Hannah and Steele, but served only to lure plaintiffs into making the exchange.

(2) That Steele had paid all rents accrued before the sale, whereas all rents were in fact not paid.

With reference to the first contention, the court found that the lease to Steele was a bona fide lease, correctly setting forth his obligations thereunder; that Steele was the sole proprietor sold his leasehold and business to [illegible] for [illegible] a sh[illegible] [illegible] little consented to the assignment of the lease to [illegible], who then paid rent to plaintiffs.

When Steele took over the le[illegible] [illegible] August, 1925, there were some 25 or 30 cars therein and the building was dirty and run-down, requiring [illegible] substantial amounts [illegible] to rehabilitate it. The inside of the garage [illegible] white-washed, the floors cleaned, and the old compressor, washer and other equipment repaired. In April and May, 1926, the garage was well filled, with an occupancy of approximately 150 cars, and was yielding a gross income of over $3,000 a month. All of the [illegible] deposited in a bank account, and the rent money was paid out of the deposits.

As heretofore stated, the [illegible] property had been listed for exchange or sale for about a year before the exchange was made. Defendants contend that its value was extremely doubtful and speculative, as evidenced by the fact that the defendants had disposed of the equity in the property for some lots of doubtful value before this proceeding was instituted. The $100,000 mortgage placed upon the property in connection with the exchange has been foreclosed with a deficiency decree of $[illegible], and it is argued that plaintiffs were moved to make the exchange in order to "get out from under" a very doubtful parcel of real estate.

Plaintiffs maintain [illegible] [illegible] [illegible] by the following false representations:

(1) That Steele was the [illegible] [illegible] of the written lease, whereas the lease was a sham, never entered, or intended to be made out between Hannah and Steele, [illegible] to lure plaintiffs into making the exchange.

(2) That Steele had paid all rents [illegible] to the [illegible] sale, whereas all rents were in fact not paid.

With reference to the first contention, the court found that the lease to Steele was a bona fide lease, correctly setting forth his obligations thereunder; that Steele was the sole proprietor of the garage business conducted in the demised premises and the lease w s exhibited to plaintiffs; and that the only representations made in regard to the garage business were that Steele was a competent and experienced garage man and that the garage was then doing a good business, both of which representations were found to be true. To support these findings the evidence discloses that Steele leased the garage property long before any negotiations were commenced for the exchange of properties. The lease refers on its face to a separate agreement between Steele, the tenant, and Hannah, the owner, relating to the payment of taxes, assessments, etc., by Steele; keeping of the premises and the buildings thereon in proper maintenance and repair, and also properly insured; that no lien would be allowed to be placed against the premises, etc. After Hannah had investigated plaintiffs' property, but before the contract of exchange was signed, he went to see Steele, who told him that he could place the garage on a paying basis if some additional capital were furnished. Plaintiffs contend that this additional capital was not advanced to Steele until the date when the exchange was made. The record discloses, however, that there was an express agreement between Hannah and Steele for a loan before any contract was signed. It is plaintiffs' contention that the lease between Hannah and Steele lacked good faith, and that the separate agreement herein referred to, under all attending circumstances, was made for the purpose of luring plaintiffs into making the exchange. The court found otherwise, however, and a careful examination of the record amply sustains the court's findings that the lease was fairly entered into, that it was a bona fide lease, that Steele was the sole proprietor of the garage business conducted in the demised premises when the lease was exhibited to plaintiffs, that the garage was then doing a good business, and that no representations were made with reference to the lease or the garage business which were in anywise untrue or fraudulent.

of the garage business was noted in the [illegible] premises and was [illegible] lease w[illegible] [illegible] to plaintiffs, and that the only representations made in regard to the garage business were that Steele was a competent and experienced garage man and that the garage was then doing a good business, both of which representations were found to be true. To support their finding the trial court states that Steele gave the garage property ten [illegible] before any [illegible] was commenced for the exchange of properties. The lease referred to [illegible] a separate agreement between Steele, the tenant, and [illegible], the owner, relating to the payment of taxes, assessments, etc., by Steele; keeping of the premises and the buildings thereon in proper maintenance and repair, and also properly insured; that no lien would be allowed to be placed against the premises, etc. After Hannah had inspected plaintiffs' property, but before the contract of exchange was signed, he went to see Steele, who told him that he could place the garage on a paying basis if some additional capital were furnished. Plaintiffs contend that this additional capital was not advanced to Steele until the date when the exchange was made. The record discloses, however, that there was an express agreement between Hannah and [illegible] before any contract was signed. It is plaintiffs' contention that the [illegible] between Hannah and Steele [illegible] agreement herein referred to, [illegible] made for the purpose of luring [illegible] plaintiffs. The court found otherwise, however, [illegible] the record amply sustains the court's finding that [illegible] entered into, that is [illegible] proprietor of the garage business [illegible] when the lease was exhibited to plaintiffs, [illegible] then [illegible] doing a good business, and that no representations were made with reference to the lease or the garage business which were in anywise [decep]tive or fraudulent.

With reference to the second representation alleged to have been made, relating to the payment of rent, the court found that at and before the sale defendants represented that Steele had paid the rents theretofore accrued and that when consummating the purchase plaintiffs believed and relied thereon. It appears from the evidence that no representations were made with reference to the rent prior to the signing of the contract for exchange of the properties. The only statements in regard to the payment of rent were made at the time of the closing of the deal and for the sole purpose of making adjustments between the parties. Plaintiff Samuel Parker Johnston testified that "in closing up the deal they said the rent for the month of May had been paid." Apparently the only significance of this statement was to effect adjustments in consummating the transaction, and for no other reason.

There is no contention that Hazel H. Newton and Mabel H. McIntosh in anywise participated in the transaction. The contract for exchange was made by Hannah alone, "as party of the first part," and he agreed "to cause to be conveyed" to plaintiffs the real estate in question. The record does not disclose by whom or in what manner title was held, nor how it was conveyed to plaintiffs. The contract seems to indicate that the title was held in trust, but the nature of the beneficiaries' interests does not appear. Certainly the beneficiaries took no part in the negotiations which resulted in the exchange. Insofar as the record discloses the beneficiaries knew nothing of the transaction. Under the circumstances, it cannot be fairly contended that Hannah was acting as agent for the other defendants, or that they "adopted or accepted the fruits" of the transaction.

Plaintiffs speak of the lease between Hannah and Steele as "a sham, never enforced or intended to be enforced." Nevertheless, plaintiffs accepted the benefits of this lease by collecting the rents with reference to the second representation alleged to have been made, relating to the payment of rent, the court found that at and before the sale defendants represented that tenants had paid the rents theretofore accrued and that when consummating the purchase plaintiffs believed and relied thereon. It appears from the evidence that no representations were made with reference to the rent prior to the signing of the contract for exchange of the properties. The only statements in regard to the payment of rent were made at the time of the closing of the deal and for the sole purpose of making adjustments between the parties. Plaintiff Samuel Parker Johnston testified that "in closing up the deal they said the rent for the month of May had been paid." Apparently the only significance of this statement was to effect adjustments in consummating the transaction, and for no other reason.

There is no contention that Hazel M. Hannah and Hannah M. McIntosh in anywise participated in the transaction. The contract for exchange was made by Hannah alone, as party of the first part, and he agreed "to cause to be conveyed" to plaintiffs the real estate in question. The record does not disclose by whom or in what manner title was held, nor how it was conveyed to plaintiffs. The contract seems to indicate that the title was held in trust but the nature of the beneficiaries' interests does not appear. Certainly the beneficiaries took no part in the negotiations which resulted in the exchange. Insofar as the record discloses the beneficiaries knew nothing of the transaction. Under the circumstances it cannot be fairly contended that Hannah was acting as agent for the other defendants, or that they accepted or received the fruits of the transaction.

Plaintiffs speak of the lease between Hannah and Steele as "a sham, never enforced or intended to be enforced." Nevertheless, plaintiffs accepted the benefits of this lease by collecting the rents for a period of three months and consenting to the assignment thereof to Reid when no defaults existed under the lease. Under the circumstances they cannot very well question the validity of the lease in the hands of Reid. They accepted Reid as a tenant by permitting the lease to be assigned to him, and were therefore estopped to question Steele's status as a bona fide tenant. (Macauley v. Dorian, 317 Ill. 126, 131; Springfield Marine Bank v. Marbold, 264 Ill. App. 446, 463.)

Another point urged by plaintiffs is that defendants deceived them as to the volume of business existing in the garage when the exchange was made. The record discloses that Hannah was in California when negotiations began. He had been there for upward of four months and visited the garage only once after his return before the transaction was closed. Steele testified that he had built up the garage business, so that in April and May, 1929, there were between 160 and 170 cars stored therein. Plaintiffs sought to rebut this evidence by showing that a number of cars had been moved into the garage to give it the appearance of full occupancy and deceive plaintiffs into believing that there were more tenants in the garage than the facts justified. Eugene Preather, a car washer, was offered as a witness, and testified to a conversation alleged to have been had between Hannah and Joe (Mr. Steele's brother-in-law) wherein Hannah said "There he is now, you tell him," and from Preather's testimony and the attending circumstances it is argued that fraud and deception were practiced on plaintiffs. Defendants denied the charge and the evidence relating thereto, and the court, who saw and heard the witnesses, found "that neither of the defendants nor anyone authorized by them, or acting with their knowledge, ever procured any automobiles to be placed in said garage, or ever procured any names, labels or signs to be placed upon stalls in the demised premises, or by any means made any representatfor a period of three months and consenting to the assignment thereof to Reid when no defaults existed under the lease. Under the circumstances they cannot very well question the validity of the lease in the hands of Reid. They accepted Reid as a tenant by permitting the lease to be assigned to him, and were therefore estopped to question Steele's status as a bona fide tenant. (Noensley v. Dorian, 317 Ill. 126, 131; Springfield Marine Bank v. Harbold, 264 Ill. App. 446, 463.)

Another point urged by plaintiffs is that defendants deceived them as to the volume of business existing in the garage when the exchange was made. The record discloses that Hannah was in California when negotiations began. He had been there for upward of four months and visited the garage only once after his return before the transaction was closed. Steele testified that he had built up the garage business, so that in April and May, 1929, there were between 150 and 170 cars stored therein. Plaintiffs sought to rebut this evidence by showing that a number of cars had been moved into the garage to give it the appearance of full occupancy and deceive plaintiffs into believing that there were more tenants in the garage than the facts justified. Eugene Prenther, a car washer, was offered as a witness, and testified to a conversation alleged to have been had between Hannah and Fox (Mr. Steele's brother-in-law) wherein Hannah said "There he is now, you tell him," and from Prenther's testimony and the attending circumstances it is argued that fraud and deception were practiced on plaintiffs. Defendants denied the charge and the evidence relating thereto, and the court, who saw and heard the witnesses, found "that neither of the defendants nor anyone authorized by them, or acting with their knowledge, ever procured any automobiles to be placed in said garage, or ever procured any names, labels or signs to be placed upon stalls in the demised premises, or by any means made any ....

were any patrons of said garage other than those who actually were bona fide patrons thereof."

It is urged by plaintiffs and their counsel on oral argument that when the lease was rewritten, and before it was executed, some changes were made therein with reference to the term of the lease and the rental provisions thereof. The lease as written is a lengthy document, and counsel on both sides admitted on oral argument that they had not carefully compared the documents at the time the new lease was executed. However, the legal matters were handled by attorneys for the respective parties, the required changes were made according to plaintiffs' request, the lease was re-executed and we find nothing in the circumstances which would justify the conclusion that there was any fraud in this branch of the transaction that would sustain a recovery for plaintiffs.

The general rule applicable to actions of this kind is well settled and concretely stated in Johnston v. Shockey, 335 Ill. 363, at 366, wherein the court states the elements required to be established by the party seeking to recover, as follows:

"An action for fraud and deceit must show six elements in order to afford relief: (1) The misrepresentation must be in form a statement of fact; (2) it must be made for the purpose of influencing the other party to act; (3) it must be untrue; (4) the party making the statement must know or believe it to be untrue; (5) the person to whom it is made must believe and rely on the statement; and (6) the statement must be material."

Moreover, the courts have uniformly held that it is incumbent upon the party charging fraud to prove the same by clear and convincing evidence. (McKennan v. Mickelberry, 242 Ill. 117, 134; Garrett v. Garrett, 343 Ill. 577; Gould v. Lewis, 267 Ill. pp. 569; Kuska v. Yankat, 341 Ill. 358.) In harmony with these decisions, it was incumbent upon plaintiffs to prove the various elements required and to establish fraud by clear and convincing evidence. A careful examination of the record, especially with reference to the particular charges of fraudulent representations as heretofore mentioned, leads to the were any patrons of said garage other than those who actually were bona fide patrons thereof."

It is urged by plaintiffs and their counsel on oral argument that when the lease was rewritten, and before it was executed, some changes were made therein with reference to the term of the lease and the rental provisions thereof. The lease as written is a lengthy document, and counsel on both sides admitted on oral argument that they had not carefully compared the documents at the time the new lease was executed. However, the legal matters were handled by attorneys for the respective parties, the required changes were made according to plaintiffs' request, the lease was re-executed and we find nothing in the circumstances which would justify the conclusion that there was any fraud in this branch of the transaction that would sustain a recovery for plaintiffs.

The general rule applicable to actions of this kind is well settled and concretely stated in Johnston v. Shockey, 356 Ill. 366, at 369, wherein the court states the elements required to be established by the party seeking to recover, as follows:

"An action for fraud and deceit must show six elements in order to afford relief: (1) The misrepresentation must be in form a statement of fact; (2) it must be made for the purpose of influencing the other party to act; (3) it must be untrue; (4) the party making the statement must know or believe it to be untrue; (5) the person to whom it is made must believe and rely on the statement; and (6) the statement must be material."

Moreover, the courts have uniformly held that it is incumbent upon the party charging fraud to prove the same by clear and convincing evidence. (McKennan v. Mickelberry, 242 Ill. 117, 124; Jarrett v. Garrett, 345 Ill. 577; Gould v. Lewis, 267 Ill. pp. 560; Kuska v. Vankat, 341 Ill. 358.) In harmony with these decisions, it was incumbent upon plaintiffs to prove the various elements required and to establish fraud by clear and convincing evidence. Careful examination of the record, especially with reference to the particular charges of fraudulent representations as heretofore mentioned, leads to the conclusion that plaintiffs failed to make out a case of fraud and deceit as charged.

The evidence upon which plaintiffs' claim for damages is predicated is found in the testimony of Samuel Parker Johnston, who stated that the garage on a replacement basis was worth about $140,000 to $150,000, and as a going business with a good lease paying substantial rental and including the good will thereof was worth close to $200,000, which was the figure upon which the exchange was made. Plaintiffs knew, of course, that they were getting a lease with no security for the payment of the rent, and no inquiry was made as to the financial responsibility of the tenant. Plaintiffs relied upon the statement that they were getting "a good lease." However, from this it cannot be assumed that the tenant was financially responsible to carry out his obligations. The provision in the lease requiring the monthly deposit of rents on account of taxes would indicate that plaintiffs did not rely on the tenant's financial responsibility, so much as the income from the property. The record sustains the contention that plaintiffs obtained a lease from a tenant who had a "good business," paying substantial rent, and having the good will thereof.

All the findings of the court are adverse to plaintiffs' claim, and we find no justifiable reason for disturbing these findings. Therefore, the judgment of the circuit court will be affirmed.

AFFIRMED.

Scanlan and Sullivan, JJ., concur.

conclusion that plaintiffs failed to make out a case of fraud and deceit as charged.

The evidence upon which plaintiffs' claim for damages is predicated is found in the testimony of Samuel Parker Johnston, who stated that the garage on a replacement basis was worth about $140,000 to $150,000, and as a going business with a good lease paying substantial rental and including the good will thereof was worth close to $200,000, which was the figure upon which the exchange was made. Plaintiffs knew, of course, that they were getting a lease with no security for the payment of the rent, and no inquiry was made as to the financial responsibility of the tenant. Plaintiffs relied upon the statement that they were getting "a good lease." However, from this it cannot be assumed that the tenant was financially responsible to carry out his obligations. The provision in the lease requiring the monthly deposit of rents on account of taxes would indicate that plaintiffs did not rely on the tenant's financial responsibility, so much as the income from the property. The record sustains the contention that plaintiffs obtained a lease from a tenant who had a "good business," paying substantial rent, and having the good will thereof.

All the findings of the court are adverse to plaintiffs' claim, and we find no justifiable reason for disturbing these findings. Therefore, the judgment of the circuit court will be affirmed.

AFFIRMED.

Feinberg, P.J., and Sullivan, J., concur.

37909

774

PEOPLE OF THE STATE OF ILLINOIS
ex rel. ULYSSES J. GRIM,
Appellant,

v.

RODNEY H. BRANDON et al.,
Appellees.

APPEAL FROM SUPERIOR
COURT, COOK COUNTY.

280 I.A. 626[3]

MR. PRESIDING JUSTICE FRIEND DELIVERED THE OPINION OF THE COURT.

Following the order of the superior court of February 28, 1930, directing the issuance of a writ of mandamus against defendants in a similarly entitled cause, No. 37698, relator filed a petition against defendants for a rule to show cause why they should not be punished for contempt of court for failure to comply with the mandamus writ. The petition was denied and relator appeals.

Our views as to the sufficiency of the petition in case No. 37698 are fully set forth in the opinion filed in that cause and are controlling as to this appeal.

Being of the opinion that the petition for mandamus was defective, and that the demurrer thereto should be sustained, no contempt proceedings can be predicated thereon. Therefore, the order of the superior court denying the petition for the rule to show cause is affirmed.

AFFIRMED.

Scanlan and Sullivan, JJ., concur.

[illegible]

PEOPLE OF THE STATE OF ILLINOIS
ex rel. WILLIAM J. KIRK,
Appellant,

v.

[illegible] A. DOUGHERTY et al.,
Appellees.

[illegible]

Following the order of the superior court of January [illegible], directing the issuance of a writ of mandamus against defendants in a similarly entitled cause, No. [illegible], relator filed a petition against defendants for a rule to show cause why they should not be punished for contempt of court for failure to comply with the mandamus writ. The petition [illegible] and **relator appeals.**

Our views as to the sufficiency of the [illegible] in cause **No. 37698 are fully set forth in the opinion [illegible] in that case** and need not [illegible] in this appeal.

Being of the opinion that the [illegible] for rule was defective, and that the [illegible] contempt proceedings can be [illegible] order of the superior court [illegible] **show cause is affirmed.**

Scanlan and Sullivan, JJ., concur.

18 H

37708

THE LIVE STOCK NATIONAL BANK OF CHICAGO (formerly known as Stock Yards Bank & Trust Company), Administrator de bonis non of the Estate of ANTHONY KLEIN, Deceased,
Appellant,

v.

CLARENCE MYROUP,
Appellee.

APPEAL FROM SUPERIOR COURT, COOK COUNTY.

280 I.A. 626

MR. JUSTICE SCANLAN DELIVERED THE OPINION OF THE COURT.

Plaintiff sued to recover damages for the alleged wrongful death of its intestate. At the close of plaintiff's evidence, the trial court, upon motion of defendant, directed the jury to find him not guilty. Plaintiff appeals from a judgment entered upon the verdict.

Plaintiff complains that under the evidence and the law the action of the trial court in directing a verdict was entirely unwarranted.

Plaintiff's evidence, that pertains to the accident, is, in substance, as follows: John Larson, twenty-three years of age, a machinist employed by the International Harvester Company, testified that he had known the deceased for five years and that he went to night school with him at the Fenger high school, located at the southwest corner of 112th and Wallace streets; that they attended school there on March 1, 1932, the day of the accident; that the entrance of the school is about forty feet south of the southwest corner of 112th and Wallace streets; that it had been raining very hard that evening but not constantly; that the "illumination" from

37708

THE LIVE STOCK NATIONAL BANK OF CHICAGO (formerly known as Stock Yards Bank & Trust Company), Administrator de bonis non of the Estate of ANTHONY KLEIN, Deceased,

Appellant,

v.

CLARENCE MYROUP,

Appellee.

APPEAL FROM SUPERIOR COURT, COOK COUNTY.

280 I.A. 626

MR. JUSTICE SCANLAN DELIVERED THE OPINION OF THE COURT.

Plaintiff sued to recover damages for the alleged wrongful death of its intestate. At the close of plaintiff's evidence, the trial court, upon motion of defendant, directed the jury to find him not guilty. Plaintiff appeals from a judgment entered upon the verdict.

Plaintiff complains that under the evidence and the law the action of the trial court in directing a verdict was entirely unwarranted.

Plaintiff's evidence, that pertains to the accident, is, in substance, as follows: John Larson, twenty-three years of age, a machinist employed by the International Harvester Company, testified that he had known the deceased for five years and that he went to night school with him at the Fenger high school, located at the southwest corner of 112th and Wallace streets; that they attended school there on March 1, 1932, the day of the accident; that the entrance of the school is about forty feet south of the southwest corner of 112th and Wallace streets; that it had been raining very hard that evening but not constantly; that the "illumination" from the street lights located on the southwest and northeast corners of the intersection was good; that he was the driver of an automobil which he had parked along the west curb of Wallace street, north of 112th street; that his car was the one parked third from the corner; that the first car north of the sidewalk on 112th street did not block the sidewalk; that there were also cars parked behind his auto "all the way up the street," all very close together, "bumper to bumper;" that all of the cars on the west curb faced south; that after the classes were over that evening at a quarter to ten, he met Anthony Klein, the deceased, on the first floor of the school, right inside the door; that Klein was dressed in a sheepskin coat, the collar turned up, and had no hat on; that he, the witness, Klein and Carl Benson were going home together; that they walked out of the building and then north on Wallace street, across 112th street; that he, the witness, crossed Wallace street and walked north past the two cars that were parked in front of his car; that the deceased was right behind him at the corner; that there were four doors to his automobile and he kept the two back doors locked "because they tried to steal the car once and they pulled the handle off the right hand door in front," so that it was necessary for the witness to go around to the left side of the car; that he walked from the northwest corner "alongside" of the two cars parked in front of his car and then walked to the left hand front door, the driver's door, of his car; that Carl Benson was ahead of him and got into the car from the street side, or left hand side of the automobile, and then got into the front seat of the car, which was a five-passenger sedan; that he, the witness, then got into the car and into the driver's seat; that the deceased was walking up the street right behind them; that he was behind them because his leg was hurting him; that witness was going to take the deceased home; that as he, the witness, got into the driver's seat and was just closing the door he saw the deceased the street lights located on the southwest and northeast corners of the intersection was good; that he was the driver of an automobil which he had parked along the west curb of Wallace street, north of 112th street; that his car was the one parked third from the corner; that the first car north of the sidewalk on 112th street did not block the sidewalk; that there were also cars parked behind his auto "all the way up the street," all very close together, "bumper to bumper;" that all of the cars on the west curb faced south; that after the classes were over that evening at a quarter to ten, he met Anthony Klein, the deceased, on the first floor of the school, right inside the door; that Klein was dressed in a sheepskin coat, the collar turned up, and had no hat on; that he, the witness, Klein and Carl Benson were going home together; that they walked out of the building and then north on Wallace street, across 112th street; that he, the witness, crossed Wallace street and walked north past the two cars that were parked in front of his car; that the deceased was right behind him at the corner; that there were four doors to his automobile and he kept the two back doors locked "because they tried to steal the car once and they pulled the handle off the right hand door in front," so that it was necessary for the witness to go around to the left side of the car; that he walked from the northwest corner "alongside" of the two cars parked in front of his car and then walked to the left hand front door, the driver's door, of his car; that Carl Benson was ahead of him and got into the car from the street side, or left hand side of the automobile, and then got into the front seat of the car, which was a five-passenger sedan; that he, the witness, then got into the car and into the driver's seat; that the deceased was walking up the street right behind them; that he was behind them because his leg was hurting him; that witness was going to take the deceased home; that as he, the witness, got into the driver's seat and was just closing the door he saw the deceased "alongside" one of the cars in front of witness's car; that he saw the deceased walking alongside the first car, the most southerly of the three cars, walking alongside of it as close as he could get to it, "a couple of inches" away from it; that he was facing directly north and walking in the street "toward us;" that the witness then saw him alongside of the second car, "the car directly in front of my car," and as the witness bent down to put the key in the ignition lock he heard a crash and saw the deceased lying on the ground; that he saw an automobile traveling south in Wallace street but "didn't see the actual hit;" that the southbound car passed his car "pretty close, about two feet or so," from the side of his car; that he heard the noise of the collision and then saw the deceased lying in the street. Questioned by the court, the witness stated that he saw Klein east of the parked cars and saw him walking in the street to the witness's car; that the car that hit Klein "finally came to a stop after it had passed the south corner of 112th street;" that "the car had gone across 112th street, the front wheels were past the south side of 112th street before it turned around and came back to the north;" that both streets are narrow; that he did not hear any horn blown before the accident occurred. "The Court: Hear a horn blown? Blew for what? Mr. Hulbert (attorney for plaintiff): For a pedestrian out in the street. The Court: Out in the street? Mr. Hulbert: Out in the street. The Court: What do you mean by that? According to your version, what you understand, a man must keep his horn blowing all the time, is that it? Mr. Hulbert: I don't know. All I know is what the statute of the State of Illinois provides. The Court: Yes, I know, I know." Upon cross-examination the witness testified that the lock on the right front door was jammed or broken and that he had latched the rear right door so that it could be opened only from the inside; that he, Benson and Klein left the school together; that it was raining at the time and they had no umbrellas;

"alongside" one of the cars in front of him [illegible] he saw the deceased walking alongside the [illegible] car; the [illegible] of the three cars, within [illegible] of it [illegible] close as he could get to it, "a couple of inches' away from it; that he was facing directly north and walking in the street "toward us"; that the witness then saw him alongside of the second car, "the car directly in front of my car," and as the witness bent down to put the key in the ignition lock he heard a crash and saw the deceased lying on the ground; that he saw an automobile traveling south in Wallace Street but "didn't see the actual hit;" that the southbound car passed his car "pretty close, about two feet or so," from the side of his car, that he heard the noise of the collision and then saw the deceased lying in the street. Questioned by the court, the witness stated that he saw Klein east of the parked cars and saw him walking in the street to the witness's car; that the car that hit Klein "finally come to a stop after it had passed the south corner of 11-th street;" that "the car had gone across 112th street, the front wheels were past the south side of 112th street before it turned round and came back to the north;" that both streets are narrow, that he did not hear any horn blown before the accident occurred. "The Court: Was there no horn blown? Blow for what? Mr. Hulbert (attorney for plaintiff): For a pedestrian out in the street. The Court: Out in the street? Mr. Hulbert: Out in the street. The Court: What do you mean by that? According to your version, what you and [illegible] mean [illegible] keep his horn blowing all the time, in the [illegible] don't know. All I know is what the statute of the State of Illinois provides. The Court. Yes, I know, I know." Upon cross examination the witness testified that the lock on the right front door [illegible] or broken and that he had latched the rear right door so that it could be opened only from the inside; that he, Bennen and Klein left the school together; that it was raining at the time and they had no umbrellas;

that he ran to the northwest corner so that he might get out of the rain as fast as he could; that Klein did likewise; that his car was parked about forty feet from the north crosswalk on Wallace street; that as he walked in the street to get into his car he saw the lights of the car coming southbound; that it was traveling to the right of the center of the road coming south; that on the east side of the street there were cars parked but no cars were parked on that side for a hundred feet north of 112th street; that there were trees along the parkway which overhung the street somewhat and the nearest street light was on the northeast corner of 112th and Wallace streets; that the streets were wet at the time and defendant's car came to a stop when the front wheels were south of the curb of 112th street; that he, Bensen and Klein knew the defendant and that the latter attended the Fenger high school but that he did not attend school that night. Carl Bensen, twenty-three years old, testified that he was a clerk at the First National Bank of Chicago; that he had known the deceased for many years; that he went to the Fenger high school with him and was there with him on the night of the accident; that as Larson, Klein and the witness left the school together it was raining and the witness went ahead to open the door of the car so that Klein and Larson could get in it easier; that the street lights on the northeast corner and the southwest corner of the intersection were lit that night; that he knew that the two back doors of the automobile were locked and that the handle of the right front door of the car had been broken off; that he walked from the school building to the northwest corner and then walked alongside of the two parked cars until he got "to the driver's seat of our car;" that their machine was the third one north of the corner and all of the cars on that side of the street were parked as close to the curb as possible; that when he got into the machine he sat in the right hand front seat; that before the accident happened he saw the deceased that he ran to the northwest corner so that he might get out of the rain as fast as he could; that Klein did likewise, went his car was parked about forty feet from the north crosswalk on Wallace street, that as he walked in the street to get into his car he saw the lights of the car coming southbound; that it was traveling to the right of the center of the road coming south; that on the east side of the street there were cars parked but no cars were parked on that side for a hundred feet north of 112th street; that there were trees along the parkway which overhung the street somewhat and the nearest tree to it was on the northeast corner of 112th and Wallace streets; that the streets were wet at the time and defendant's car came to a stop when the front was [illegible] south of the curb of 112th street; that he, Benson and Klein were [illegible] and that the latter attended the Fenger high school but that he did not attend school that night. Carl Benson, [illegible] years old, testified that he was a clerk at the First National Bank [illegible] that he had known the deceased for many years, [illegible] the Fenger high school with him and was there with him on the night of the accident; that as Larson, Klein and the witness left the school together it was raining, and the witness went ahead to open the door of the car so that Klein and Larson could get in it [illegible] that the street lights on the northeast corner [illegible] of the intersection were lit that night; that he [illegible] doors of the automobile were locked and [illegible] front door of the car and [illegible] broken [illegible] school building to the northwest corner [illegible] the two parked cars until he got to the driver's seat [illegible] that their machine was the third one north of the corner [illegible] the cars on that side of the [illegible] were parked as close to the curb as possible; that when he got into the machine he sat in the right hand front seat; that before the accident happened he saw the deceased walking in the street near the front of the car ahead of them and walking right alongside of the machine "as close as possible. Just a matter of inches away from this machine;" that the deceased was facing north and walking rather slowly; that he saw the deceased coming and turned to open the door, and "as I turned there was a loud crash. When I turned back I saw Anthony in the street lying down;" that the southbound automobile went about twenty to twenty-five feet before it stopped; that it stopped at the intersection where the sidewalk crosses; that the accident happened about 9:50 p. m. On cross-examination the witness testified that the high school is on the southwest corner of 112th and Wallace streets and the building stands back from the sidewalk; that the lights in the school building were lit at the time; that he ran ahead of the other two boys and got into the car; that he opened the rear door on the right hand side of the car; that there were cars parked on both sides of the street. Reinhold Schulz testified that he was a clerk of Company 1692, Camp Perkinstown, C. C. C., Wisconsin; that he had known the deceased for about six months prior to the accident; that the three of them were attending the high school evening classes; that he and his sister, on their way home, crossed Wallace street at its intersection with 112th street, in a northeasterly direction, from the southwest corner to the northeast corner; that all of the automobiles had their lights on and were ready to go, "it was pretty light," that the high school windows threw lights out into the street; that about three-quarters of the building was lit; that he saw the southbound automobile when it was about 160 feet north of him; that its lights were lit; that it traveled south until it was practically even with the sidewalk on the south side of 112th street before it stopped, or approximately 200 feet; that the car was traveling approximately twenty-five or thirty miles an hour; that other people were crossing the street at the time; that "the whole school was going out, some going down the

walking in the street near the front of the car ... of th m m,
walking right alongside of the machine "at close as possible. "But
a matter of inches away from this machine;" that the deceased was facing north and walking rather slowly; that he saw the deceased coming and turned to open the door, and "as I turned there was a loud crash. When I turned back I saw Anthony in the street lying down;" that the southbound automobile went about twenty to twenty-five feet before it stopped; that it stopped at the intersection where the sidewalk crosses; that the accident happened about 9:30 p. m. On cross-examination the witness testified that the high school is on the southwest corner of 112th and Allison streets and the building stands back from the sidewalk; that the lights in the school building were lit at the time; that he ran [illegible] of the other two boys and got into the car; that he opened the left door on the right hand side of the car; that there were cars park on both sides of the street. Reinhold Schulz testified that he [illegible] clerk of Company 1692, Camp Perkinstown, C. C. C., Wisconsin, that he had known the deceased for about six months prior to the accident; that the three of them were attending the high school evening classes; that he and his sister, on their way home, crossed Allison street at its intersection with 112th street, in a northerly direction, from the southwest corner to the northeast corner; that all of the automobiles had their lights on and were ready to go, "it was pretty light," that the high school windows threw lights out into the street, that about three-quarters of the building was lit; that he saw the southbound automobile when it was about 160 feet north of him; that its lights were lit; that it traveled south until it was practically even with the sidewalk on the south side of 112th street before it stopped, or approximately 200 feet; that the car was traveling approximately twenty-five or thirty miles an hour; that other people were crossing the street at the time; that "the whole school was going out, some going down the

street, some crossing the street. I crossed the street with my sister. Others were crossing the street in different directions;" there were quite a few people on the southwest corner, just coming out of school and crossing northward across 112th street; "there were people walking across, right across on 112th street;" that there were people walking straight east on one or both crosswalks on the north or south side of 112th street; that he saw the accident happen and heard the crash; "I heard a crash of glass. We were looking around facing west. Some one was lying there, so we walked over there. Sure enough, a boy was lying over there. A car had already passed there. It was on the south side of 112th street after the accident. Q. Where was this young man lying on the street? A. Lying, oh, about at the second car of the cars parked all along Wallace street bumper to bumper, lying at about the second car from the corner. * * * He was lying at the south end, I think, lying on his face." On cross-examination the witness testified that it was raining at the time and that he had an umbrella; that he and his sister were walking home at the time; that when he saw the car coming from the north he could see the lights and part of the car; that he kept his eye on the car all the time. "The Court: Do you call 25 miles an hour a fast speed? The Witness: Yes, sir, at that time when the school was letting out. I think that was going at a rather fast speed. Mr. White (counsel for defendant): I move that all the answer be stricken out and that the jury be instructed to disregard it. The Court: Strike it out." The balance of the testimony relates to matters that are not relevant to the instant contention.

After defendant moved for a directed verdict the trial court delivered the following opinion:

"The Court: Gentlemen of the jury, it is with some reluctance that the Court, at the close of the plaintiff's case, will give you a written instruction,, which is as follows:

"The Court instructs the jury to find the defendant, Clarence Myreup, not guilty.

6-

street, some crossing the street. I crossed the street with my sister. Others were crossing the street in different directions;" there were quite a few people on the southwest corner, just coming out of school and crossing northward across 112th street; "there were people walking across, right across on 112th street;" that there were people walking straight east on one or both crosswalks on the north or south side of 112th street; that he saw the accident happen and heard the crash; "I heard a crash of glass. We were looking around facing west. Some one was lying there, so we walked over there. Sure enough, a boy was lying over there. A car had already passed there. It was on the south side of 112th street after the accident. Q. There was this young man lying on the street? A. Lying, oh, about at the second car of the cars parked all along Wallace street bumper to bumper, lying at about the second car from the corner. * * * He was lying at the south end, I think, lying on his face." On cross-examination the witness testified that it was raining at the time and that he had an umbrella; that he and his sister were walking home at the time; that when he saw the car coming from the north he could see the lights and part of the car; that he kept his eye on the car all the time. "The Court: Do you call 25 miles an hour a fast speed? The Witness: Yes, sir, at that time when the school was letting out. I think that was going at a rather fast speed. Mr. White (counsel for defendant): I move that all the answer be stricken out and that the jury be instructed to disregard it. The Court: Strike it out." The balance of the testimony relates to matters that are not relevant to the instant contention.

After defendant moved for a directed verdict the trial court delivered the following opinion:

"The Court: Gentlemen of the jury, it is with some reluctance that the Court, at the close of the plaintiff's case, will give you a written instruction, which is as follows:

"The Court instructs the jury to find the defendant, Clarence Kyroup, not guilty.

"It is very rarely that the Court directs a verdict; but the Court has a duty to perform and cannot be governed by the mere consideration that this fine young man evidently came from a very fine family and has lost his life. There are two elements that are necessary to be established in a case of this kind: First, that the driver of the car, who under the law, is not permitted to testify, has no right to testify in this kind of a case; first, it must be shown that he was guilty of negligence which proximately caused this accident, and secondly, it must be shown, which is ordinarily a defense, that the deceased was not guilty of negligence which contributed to the injury.

"As a general rule, contributory negligence is a question of fact, but where it becomes in a case of this kind a question in the opinion of a court of law, and of which there is no dispute, then the Court is bound to exercise its discretion when it finds, as a matter of law, that the deceased was guilty of contributory negligence.

"The Court is of the opinion, gentlemen, that there is not any evidence at all of negligence on the part of the driver of this car. The evidence shows that he was going along on a rainy night at twenty-five miles an hour; he had absolutely no reason to suspect that a person would be walking along right in his pathway, not at an intersection but out into the street, on a rainy night, going along on the east side of these cars which were parked. There is not the slightest evidence that this defendant had any knowledge that anybody was in his path, nor had he any reason to suspect that anyone was in his path, and so this unfortunate accident happened in the manner it did; that the defendant violated no law that I know of. Of course, if he saw this man and failed to give warning in time, that would be a different situation, but no one claims that he saw this man; and the deceased could have just as easily - he was not required to do it - gone along on the sidewalk, crossed 112th street, gone on the sidewalk and entered this car on the west side of the car where the door would have been open and this unfortunate accident would not have occurred.

"So I say, with great reluctance, because neither of these elements were established in this case.

"First, that the defendant was guilty of any negligence; and second, that the deceased, as a matter of law, was guilty of no contributory negligence. You will therefore sign the verdict.

"Mr. Hulbert: Exception."

It is a well settled rule of law in this State that if there is any evidence in the record from which, if it stands alone, the jury could, without acting unreasonably in the eye of the law, find that all of the material averments of the declaration have been proved, then the cause should be submitted to a jury. (See Libby, McNeill & Libby v. Cook, 222 Ill. 206; McFarlane v. Chicago City Ry. Co., 288 Ill. 476; Walldren Express & Van Co. v. Krug, 291 Ill. 472. Many other cases to the same effect might be cited.)

"It is very rarely that the Court directs a verdict; but the Court has a duty to perform and cannot be governed by the mere consideration that this fine young man evidently came from a very fine family and has lost his life. There are two elements that are necessary to be established in a case of this kind: First, that the driver of the car, who under the law, is not permitted to testify, has no right to testify in this kind of a case; first, it must be shown that he was guilty of negligence which proximately caused this accident; and secondly, it must be shown, which is ordinarily a defense, that the deceased was not guilty of negligence which contributed to the injury.

"As a general rule, contributory negligence is a question of fact, but where it becomes in a case of this kind a question in the opinion of a court of law, and of which there is no dispute, then the Court is bound to exercise its discretion when it finds, as a matter of law, that the deceased was guilty of contributory negligence.

"The Court is of the opinion, gentlemen, that there is not any evidence at all of negligence on the part of the driver of this car. The evidence shows that he was going along on a rainy night at twenty-five miles an hour; he had absolutely no reason to expect that a person would be walking along right in his pathway, not at an intersection but out into the street, on a rainy night, walking along on the east side of these cars which were parked. There is not the slightest evidence that this defendant had any knowledge that anybody was in his path, nor had he any reason to suspect that anyone was in his path, and so this unfortunate accident happened in the manner it did; that the defendant violated no law that I know of. Of course, if he saw this man and failed to give warning to him, that would be a different situation, but no one claims that he saw this man; and the deceased could have just as easily - he was not required to do it - gone along on the sidewalk, crossed Fifth street, gone on the sidewalk and entered this car on the [illegible] of the car where the door would have been open and this unfortunate accident would not have occurred.

"So I say, with great reluctance, because neither of these elements were established in this case:

"First, that the defendant was guilty of any negligence; and second, that the deceased, as a matter of law, was guilty of no contributory negligence. You will therefore sign the verdict.

"Mr. Hulbert: Exception."

It is a well settled rule of law in this state that if there is any evidence in the record from which, if it stands alone, the jury could, without acting unreasonably in the eye of the law, find that all of the material averments of the declaration have been proved, then the cause should be submitted to a jury. (See Libby, McNeill & Libby v. Cook, 222 Ill. 206; McMillens v. Chicago City Ry. Co., 238 Ill. 476; Walldren Express & Van Co. v. Krug, 291 Ill. 472. Many other cases to the same effect might be cited.)

A mere statement of the evidence shows, in our judgment, that this case should have been submitted to the jury. In fact, defendant's counsel, in the oral argument, admits that the court's conclusions cannot be defended, but he argues that the judgment can be justified upon the following ground. Plaintiff's evidence fails to show the events immediately before and at the time of the accident, so that the jury would have to guess or speculate as to whether plaintiff was exercising care for his own safety immediately prior to and at the moment of the accident. We find no merit in this contention, as we are satisfied that the jury would have been warranted in finding that at the moment of the collision the deceased was walking alongside of the second machine "as close to it as possible. Just a matter of inches away from this machine," and that he was walking northward at the time, "coming toward my (Larson's) car." Benson testified that he saw the deceased coming in that manner and that as he (the witness) turned there was a loud crash. Larson testified that defendant's car passed his car "pretty close, about two feet or so," from the side of his car. When the witnesses reached the deceased he was lying at the south end of the second car. The argument that for aught that appears in the evidence the deceased might have, in the instant before the accident, stepped to the east and into the path of the oncoming southbound automobile is not a reasonable one. In the oral argument counsel for defendant admitted that the court was not justified in holding, as a matter of law, that the deceased was guilty of contributory negligence merely because he walked in the street to enter the automobile from its east side.

Plaintiff complains that the trial judge took an unwarranted part in the examination of the witnesses and made comments during the hearing of plaintiff's evidence that indicate plainly that he had made up his mind to direct a verdict for defendant long before plaintiff's

A mere statement of the evidence shows, in our judgment, that this case should have been submitted to the jury. In fact, defendant's counsel, in the oral argument, admits that the court's conclusions cannot be defended, but he argues that the judgment can be justified upon the following ground: Plaintiff's evidence fails to show the events immediately before and at the time of the accident, so that the jury would have to guess or speculate as to whether plaintiff was exercising care for his own safety immediately prior to and at the moment of the accident. We find no merit in this contention, as we are satisfied that the jury would have been warranted in finding that at the moment of the collision the deceased was walking alongside of the second machine "as close to it as possible. Just a matter of inches away from this machine," and that he was walking northward at the time, "coming toward my (Larson's) car." Benson testified that he saw the deceased coming in that manner and that as he (the witness) turned there was a loud crash. Larson testified that defendant's car passed his car "pretty close, about two feet or so," from the side of his car. When the witnesses reached the deceased he was lying at the south end of the second car. The argument that for aught that appears in the evidence the deceased might have, in the instant before the accident, stepped to the east and into the path of the oncoming southbound automobile is not a reasonable one. In the oral argument counsel for defendant admitted that the court was not justified in holding, as a matter of law, that the deceased was guilty of contributory negligence merely because he walked in the street to enter the automobile from its east side.

Plaintiff complains that the trial judge took an unwarranted part in the examination of the witnesses and made comments during the hearing of plaintiff's evidence that indicate plainly that he had made up his mind to direct a verdict for defendant long before plaintiff's evidence was completed upon the ground that the deceased was guilty of contributory negligence, as a matter of law, merely because he walked in the street to enter the car. From the tone of plaintiff's argument, it would seem that the judge who tried this case is not very apt to again try it, and, furthermore, in our determination of this appeal it is entirely unnecessary for us to pass upon the alleged conduct of the trial judge.

As we are satisfied that the trial court erred in directing a verdict for defendant at the close of plaintiff's case, the judgment of the Superior court of Cook county is reversed and the cause is remanded for a new trial.

REVERSED AND REMANDED.

Friend, P. J., and Sullivan, J., concur.

evidence was complete upon the point that the deceased was guilty of contributory negligence, as a matter of law, merely because he walked in the street to enter the car. From the tone of plaintiff's argument, it would seem that the judge who tried this case is not very apt to try it anew. Furthermore, in our determination of this appeal it is entirely unnecessary for us to pass upon the alleged conduct of the trial judge.

As we are satisfied that the trial court erred in directing a verdict for defendant at the close of plaintiff's case, the judgment of the superior court of Cook county is reversed and the cause is remanded for a new trial.

REVERSED AND REMANDED.

Friend, P. J., and Sullivan, J., concur.

794

37825

HARRY PRINGOURIS, also known as HARRY PAPPAS, by his mother and next friend, Akrivi Pappas, Appellant,

v.

GENERAL OUTDOOR ADVERTISING COMPANY, a corporation, Appellee.

APPEAL FROM CIRCUIT COURT, COOK COUNTY.

280 I.A. 627[1]

MR. JUSTICE SCANLAN DELIVERED THE OPINION OF THE COURT.

An action on the case in which a jury returned a verdict finding defendant not guilty. Plaintiff has appealed from a judgment entered upon the verdict.

The amended declaration alleges that on September 6, 1932, defendant was in possession and control of an advertisement structure and platform located on the northern part of a lot on the northwest corner of East 63d street and Eberhart avenue, Chicago; that the structure consisted of two main parts, a billboard space and a platform, the latter containing a walk or floor made of planks; that the platform was about 24 inches in width, 120 feet in length, and was made of boards or planks fastened or nailed on joists or supports; that at the west end it was about 35 inches in height, at the east end 42 inches, and in the middle 44 inches; that a child might easily climb on the platform; that defendants maintained the structure "unfenced and unguarded," and allowed and suffered the platform and floor to decay and to become dangerous by permitting and suffering a part or parts of the same to decay and to become and remain defective, unfastened, unnailed and disjoined; and "allowed and suffered one of the boards or planks of said floor and platform to become and remain defective, dilapidated, unfastened, unnailed

37828

HARRY KINGOU IS, also known as HARRY PAPPAS, by his mother and next friend, Krivi Pappas, Appellant,	APPEAL FROM CIRCUIT
v.	COURT, COOK COUNTY.
GENERAL OUTDOOR ADVERTISING COMPANY, a corporation, Appellee.	280 I.A. 627

MR. JUSTICE [illegible] DELIVERED THE OPINION OF THE COURT.

An action on the case in which a jury returned a verdict finding defendant not guilty. Plaintiff has appealed from a judgment entered upon the verdict.

The amended declaration alleges that on September 6, 1932, defendant was in possession and control of a [illegible] structure and platform located on the north in [illegible] of a lot on the northwest corner of East 63d street and [illegible] avenue, Chicago; that the structure consisted of two main parts, a billboard space and a platform, the latter containing a walk or floor [illegible] of planks; that the platform was about 24 inches in width, 12 feet in length, and was made of boards or planks fastened or nailed on joists or supports; that at the west end it was about 35 inches in height, at the east end 42 inches, and in the middle 44 inches; that [illegible] child might easily climb on the platform; that defendants maintained the structure "unfenced and unguarded," and allowed and suffered the platform and floor to decay and to become dangerous by permitting and suffering a part or parts of the same to decay and to become and remain defective, unfastened, unnailed and disjoined; and "allowed and suffered one of the boards or planks of said floor and platform to become and remain defective, dilapidated, unfastened, unnailed and unsupported on one end whereby said board or plank swung up and down on such end, when a child or children mounted thereon, like a springboard," and children who were permitted to be around the platform would, in consequence thereof "and of their childish instincts, or impulses, and lack of judgment, and experience, be exposed to great danger of falling off from said advertisement structure, platform and floor and from said board or plank of said floor and thereby injured;" that the structure and platform were so attractive to children of tender age as to amount to a strong inducement or implied invitation to them to ascend the same and play thereon; that it was situated in a populous section of Chicago where many children were in the habit of passing by, and that it could be seen and observed from the sidewalks at East 63d street and Eberhart avenue; that children were in the habit of ascending the structure and platform and playing thereon, all of which facts the defendant knew or could have known prior to the day of plaintiff's injuries; that ordinary care on the part of defendant required that it fence the structure and platform, or guard the same; "or it should not have allowed and suffered said advertisement structure and platform and said floor to decay and to become dilapidated, defective and dangerous to life and said board or plank of said floor to decay and to become and remain defective, unfastened, unnailed, unsupported and swinging on one end; or it should have maintained a watchman around or about the structure and platform to prevent children from climbing up the same and playing thereon, and from mounting, getting on and playing on or about said defective, unfastened, unnailed, unsupported and swinging board or plank of said floor as aforesaid;" that defendant negligently failed to fence, guard or repair the structure and platform for the purpose aforesaid, or to do any or either of these things; that plaintiff, about eight years of age on September 6, 1932, together with other children, ascended the platform as a consequence of the attractiveness thereof and

and unsupported on one end and whereby said board or plank swung up and down on each end, when a child or children mounted thereon, like a springboard," and children who were permitted to be around the platform would, in consequence thereof "and of their childish instincts, or impulses, and lack of judgment, and experience, be exposed to great danger of falling off from said advertisement structure, platform and floor and from said board or plank of said floor and thereby injured," that the structure and platform were so attractive to children of tender age as to amount to a strong inducement or implied invitation to ~~xxxxx~~ them to ascend the same and play thereon; that it was situated in a populous section of Chicago where many children were in the habit of passing by, and that it could be seen and observed from the sidewalks at East 63d street and Dorchester avenue; that children were in the habit of ascending the structure and platform and playing thereon, all of which facts the defendant knew or could have known prior to the day of plaintiff's injuries; that ordinary care on the part of defendant required that it fence the structure and platform, or guard the same; "or it should not have allowed and suffered said advertisement structure and platform and said floor to decay and to become dilapidated, defective and dangerous to life and said board or plank of said floor to decay and to become and remain a "movable, unfastened, unnailed, unsupported and swinging on one end; or it should have maintained a watchman around or about the structure and platform to prevent children from climbing up the same and playing thereon, and from mounting, getting on and playing on or about said "defective, unfastened, unnailed, unsupported and swinging board or plank of said floor as aforesaid;" that defendant negligently failed to fence, guard or repair the structure and platform for the purpose aforesaid, or to do any or either of these things; that plaintiff, about eight years of age on September 4, 1932, together with other children, ascended the platform as a consequence of the attractiveness thereof and commenced to play on it and on the swinging board, and while he was so engaged the swinging board broke and plaintiff fell off from said board or plank of the floor and from said structure and platform to the ground; that plaintiff was then and there exercising such ordinary care for his own safety as could be reasonably expected of a boy of his age, intelligence, mental capacity and experience; that as a direct result of the fall plaintiff sustained external and internal injuries, etc., to his damage in the sum of $25,000.

The advertisement structure was located on the northern part of a vacant lot located at the northwest corner of East 63d street and Eberhart avenue, Chicago. It had been leased by the owner to defendant, and was situated in a populous part of the city of Chicago. The lot was not fenced nor guarded, and there were no warning signs placed thereon. Plaintiff was eight years of age at the time of the accident. He and other children of the neighborhood were in the habit of playing on the lot and upon the platform of the structure. Children played on the loose board of the platform and jumped up and down on it. There was a walk, "a path where people cut across," the lot from 63d street to Eberhart avenue, used by children and adults. The testimony in respect to the use of the lot by children and adults was uncontradicted.

The main contention of defendant in support of the verdict is that "the plaintiff is not entitled to recover from the defendant as a matter of law because the alleged defective sign-board owned by the defendant did not attract the plaintiff to the premises. The plaintiff was, therefore, a trespasser at the time he was injured and despite the fact that he is a child he cannot recover." This contention has been determined, and adversely to defendant, in the case of Ramsay v. Tuthill Material Co., 295 Ill. 395. In its opinion the court states (pp. 399-402):

commenced to play on it and on the swinging board, and while he was so engaged the swinging board broke and plaintiff fell off from said board or plank of the floor and from said structure and platform to the ground; that plaintiff was then and there exercising such ordinary care for his own safety as could be reasonably expected of a boy of his age, intelligence, mental capacity and experience; that as a direct result of the fall plaintiff sustained external and internal injuries, etc., to his damage in the sum of $25,000.

The advertisement structure was located on the northern part of a vacant lot located at the northwest corner of East 63d street and Eberhart avenue, Chicago. It had been leased by the owner to defendant, and was situated in a populous part of the city of Chicago. The lot was not fenced nor guarded, and there were no warning signs placed thereon. Plaintiff was eight years of age at the time of the accident. He and other children of the neighborhood were in the habit of playing on the lot and upon the platform of the structure. Children played on the loose board of the platform and jumped up and down on it. There was a walk, "a path where people cut across," the lot from 63d street to Eberhart avenue, used by children and adults. The testimony in respect to the use of the lot by children and adults was uncontradicted.

The main contention of defendant in support of the verdict is that "the plaintiff is not entitled to recover from the defendant as a matter of law because the alleged defective sign-board owned by the defendant did not attract the plaintiff to the premises. The plaintiff was, therefore, a trespasser at the time he was injured and despite the fact that he is a child he cannot recover." This contention has been determined, and adversely to defendant, in the case of Ramsey v. Tuthill Material Co., 295 Ill. 395. In its opinion the court states (pp. 401-402):

"The law does not require the owner of premises to keep them in a safe condition for persons who come upon them without invitation, either express or implied, and merely for their own pleasure or to gratify their curiosity. 'An exception, however, to this general rule exists in favor of children. Although a child of tender years who meets with an injury upon the premises of a private owner may be a technical trespasser, yet the owner may be liable if the things causing the injury have been left exposed and unguarded and are of such a character as to be an attraction to the child, appealing to his childish curiosity and instincts. Unguarded premises which are thus supplied with dangerous attractions are regarded as holding out implied invitations to such children. "The owner of land where children are allowed or accustomed to play, particularly if it is unfenced, must use ordinary care to keep it in safe condition, for they, being without judgment and likely to be drawn by childish curiosity into places of danger, are not to be classed with trespassers, idlers and mere licensees."' City of Pekin v. McMahon, 154 Ill. 141.

"* * *

"It is not necessary, to make a defendant liable, that the attractive and dangerous thing should be visible from the street and that children should have been attracted to the premises by it. If an owner maintains dangerous conditions upon his premises to which he permits children to come he must use ordinary care to guard them against danger which their youth and ignorance prevent them from appreciating. There is no implied invitation from the mere existence of a dangerous attraction which is not discoverable off the premises, but if to the knowledge of the owner children habitually come upon his premises where a dangerous condition exists to which they are exposed, the duty to exercise care for their safety arises, not because of an implied invitation but because of his knowledge of unconscious exposure to danger which the children do not realize. The situation is different from that in the case of McDermott v. Burke, 256 Ill. 401, which the plaintiff in error has cited and relies upon. In that case the attractive thing was a pile of sand in the middle of the lower floor of a building which was in process of construction. The sand itself was not dangerous and had nothing to do with the injury which gave rise to the cause of action in that case. The injury was occasioned by a rope running over a sheave used in hoisting material at some distance from the sand. The rope and sheave were not attractive and the injured child was not playing with them but had merely rested his hand upon the rope and was injured when the machinery was started. It did not appear that the defendant, who was the contractor engaged in constructing the building, knew that the children were there or that they had been in the habit of coming there and playing in the sand. In this case it appears that for some time children had been in the habit of coming on the premises of plaintiff in error, playing in the sand on the ground, going up the ladder to the top of the elevated structure, jumping into the sand-bins, playing in the sand there, and going down through the openings in the chutes. This was known to the employees of plaintiff in error, who testified that they frequently told the children to stay away, but no effective means were taken to prevent their coming there; so that here the defendant, by taking no effectual means to prevent it, permitted little children, too young to have judgment and exercise care to protect themselves from danger, to play constantly about its premises where it knew that they were habitually exposed to danger which they did not realize and which was likely to result in serious injury or death

"The law does not require the owner of premises to keep them in a safe condition for persons who come upon them without invitation, either express or implied, and merely for their own pleasure or to gratify their curiosity. 'An exception, however, to this generalrule exists in favor of children. Although a child of tend r years who meets with an injury upon the premises of a private owner may be a technical trespasser, yet the owner may be liable if the things causing the injury have been left exposed and unguarded and are of such a character as to be an attraction to the child, appealing to h■ childish curiosity and instincts. Unguarded premises which are thus supplied with dangerous attractions are regarded as holding out implied invitations to such children. "The owner of land where children are allowed or accustomed to play, particularly if it is unfenced, must use ordinary care to keep it in safe condition, for they, being without judgment and likely ■ be drawn by childish curiosity into places of danger, are not to be classed with trespassers, idlers and mere licensees."' City of Pekin v. McMahon, 154 Ill. 141.

"* * *

"It is not necessary, to make a defendant liable, that the attractive and dangerous thing should be visible from the street and that children should have been attracted to the premises by it. If an owner maintains dangerous conditions upon his premises to which he permits children to come he must use ordinary care to guard them against danger which their youth and ignorance prevent them from appreciating. There is no implied invitation from the mere existence of a dangerous attraction which is not discoverable off the premises, but if to the knowledge of the owner children habitually come upon his premises where a dangerous condition exists to whi they are exposed, the duty to exercise care for their safety arises, not because o' an implied invitation but because of his knowledge of unconscious exposure to danger which the children do not realize. The situation is different from that in the c of McDermott v. Burke, 256 Ill. 401, which the plaintiff in error has cited and relies upon. In that case the attractive thing was a pile of sand in the middle of the lower floor of a building which was in process of construction. The sand itself was not dangerous and had nothing to do with the injury which gave rise ■ the cause of action in that case. The injury was occasioned by a rope running over a sheave used in hoisting material at some distance from the sand. The rope and sheave were not attractive and the injured child was not playing with them but had merely rested his hand upon the rope and was injured when the machinery was started. It did not appear that the defendant, who was the contractor engaged in constructing the building, knew that the children were there or that they had been in the habit of coming there and playing in the sand. In this case it appears that for some time children had been ■ the habit of coming on the premises of plaintiff in error, playing in the sand on the ground, going up the ladder to the top of the elevated a ature, jumping into the sand-bins, playing in the sand there, and going down through the openings in the chutes. This was known to the employees of plaintiff in error, who testified that they frequently told the children to stay away, but no effective means were taken to prevent their coming there; so that here the defendant, by taking no effectual means to prevent it, permitted little children, too young to have judgment and exercise care to protect from danger, to play constantly about its premises where it that they were habitually exposed to danger which they did not realize and which was likely to result in serious injury or death to some of them, and which actually has resulted so. Under such circumstances the owner of property is responsible for the injury which has occurred by reason of its negligence in failing to use adequate means to keep children away from the danger which it has created.

"* * *

"If a person engaged in any operation which is dangerous to others who come in contact with it, permits children who are incapable of appreciating the danger to come upon his premises where they are exposed to danger, there is certainly an obligation in humanity to take such means to prevent the injury, either by excluding them from his premises or protecting them while they are on his premises, as will be effective, and this obligation imposes upon him the legal duty to do those things. It was not error to refuse the instruction to find a verdict for the defendant."

(See also Wolczek v. Public Service Co., 342 Ill. 482, where the Ramsay v. Tuthill Material Co. case is approved and the entire subject reviewed.)

Plaintiff contends that the verdict is against the manifest weight of the evidence. Defendant's answer to this contention is that the principal question of fact in the case is whether or not the platform was in a defective condition; that plaintiff based his right to recover upon an alleged defective condition of the signboard and that the jury's verdict finding this question of fact against plaintiff is not against the manifest weight of the evidence. We have carefully examined all of the evidence bearing upon this material question of fact and we have reached the conclusion that the finding of the jury in that regard is manifestly against the weight of the evidence.

In the instant case the trial court, of its own motion, gave sixteen instructions to the jury and refused all instructions offered by plaintiff and defendant. The court instructed the jury as follows:

"* * * In order to find the defendant guilty, the plaintiff must prove by a preponderance of the evidence that the defendant negligently allowed the platform to be in a dangerous state of unrepair at and just before the time of the injury, the plaintiff must further prove by a preponderance of the evidence, that such condition of unrepair was the proximate cause of the injury in question, *and that the plaintiff himself used such care against injurying himself as a child of his years would ordinarily use.*" (Italics ours.)

to some of them, and which actually has resulted so. Under such circumstances the owner of property is responsible for the injury which has occurred by reason of its negligence in failing to use adequate means to keep children away from the danger which it has created.

" * * *

"If a person engaged in any operation which is dangerous to others who come in contact with it, permits children who are incapable of appreciating the danger to come upon his premises where they are exposed to danger, there is certainly an obligation in humanity to take such means to prevent the injury, either by excluding them from his premises or protecting them while they are on his premises, as will be effective, and this obligation imposes upon him the legal duty to do those things. It was not error to refuse the instruction to find a verdict for the defendant."

(See also Wolczek v. Public Service Co., 342 Ill. 482, where the Ramsay v. Tuthill Material Co. case is approved and the entire subject reviewed.)

Plaintiff contends that the verdict is against the manifest weight of the evidence. Defendant's answer to this contention is that the principal question of fact in the case is whether or not the platform was in a defective condition; that plaintiff based his right to recover upon an alleged defective condition of the signboard and that the jury's verdict finding this question of fact against plaintiff is not against the manifest weight of the evidence. We have carefully examined all of the evidence bearing upon this material question of fact and we have reached the conclusion that the finding of the jury in that regard is manifestly against the weight of the evidence.

In the instant case the trial court, of its own motion, gave sixteen instructions to the jury and refused all instructions offered by plaintiff and defendant. The court instructed the jury as follows:

"* * * In order to find the defendant guilty, the plaintiff must prove by a preponderance of the evidence that the defendant negligently allowed the platform to be in a dangerous state of unrepair at and just before the time of the injury, the plaintiff must further prove by a preponderance of the evidence, that such condition of unrepair was the proximate cause of the injury in question, and that the plaintiff himself used such care against injuring himself as a child of his years would ordinarily use." (Italics ours.)

And again:

"* * * It was defendant's duty to use ordinary care to keep the platform in a safe condition of repair; *and it was plaintiff's duty to use such care against injury to himself as a child of his years may be expected to use at the time and place in question.*" (Italics ours.)

No other instruction was given touching the care required of plaintiff. That these two instructions do not fully and accurately state the law governing the care that was required of plaintiff cannot be seriously questioned. The correct rule is that a boy of the age of the plaintiff is required to exercise that degree of care and caution that a boy of his age, intelligence, capacity and experience would exercise under the same or similar circumstances. But defendant contends that under the new practice act (sec. 67) plaintiff was bound to make specific objections to the court's charge and that the record shows that plaintiff made only a general objection to each of the instructions given by the court. The record does not support defendant's contention. It shows that at the conclusion of the court's charge plaintiff requested the court to give to the jury (*inter alia*) the two following instructions and that the court refused to give same to the jury:

"(1) When it is said in these instructions that the plaintiff must have been in the exercise of ordinary care at and prior to his injury, it is meant that degree of care and caution which an ordinarily prudent child of his age, capacity, experience and intelligence, as shown by the evidence, would exercise under like circumstances and like surroundings; that is to say, if a child does only what prudent children of like age, capacity, experience and intelligence would do under like circumstances and like surroundings, then the child has exercised ordinary care and is not guilty of contributory negligence.

"(2) The jury are instructed that a boy of the age of the plaintiff is only required to exercise that degree of care and caution that a boy of his age, intelligence, capacity and experience would exercise under the same or similar circumstances."

These two instructions correctly state the law, and the action of plaintiff in requesting the court to give the same was a sufficient compliance with the requirements of section 67. The court also instructed the jury that "contributory negligence means, negligence,

And again:

"... it was defendant's duty to use ordinary care to keep the platform in a safe condition ... [illegible] plaintiff's duty to use such care for his own safety as a child of his years may be expected to use at the time and place in question." (Italics ours.)

No other instruction was given touching the care required of plaintiff. That these two instructions do not fully and clearly state the law governing the care that was required of plaintiff cannot be seriously questioned. The correct rule is that a boy of the age of the plaintiff is required to exercise that degree of care and caution that a boy of his age, intelligence, capacity and experience would exercise under the same or similar circumstances.

But defendant contends that under the new practice act [illegible] plaintiff was bound to make specific objections to this charge and that the record shows that plaintiff made [illegible] objection to each of the instructions given by the court. The record does not support defendant's contention. It shows that at the conclusion of the court's charge plaintiff requested the court to give to the jury (Inter alia) the two following instructions and that the court refused to give same to the jury:

"(3) When it is held in these instructions that the plaintiff must have been in the exercise of ordinary care for his own safety at and prior to his injury, it is meant that degree of care and caution which an ordinarily prudent child of his age, capacity, experience and intelligence, as shown by the evidence, would exercise under like circumstances [illegible] is to say, if a child does not use that prudence [illegible] of like age, capacity, experience and intelligence [illegible] circumstances and like surroundings, then the child is not exercising ordinary care and is not guilty of contributory negligence.

"(4) The jury are instructed that a boy of the age of the plaintiff is only required to exercise that degree of care and caution that a boy of his age, intelligence, capacity and experience would exercise under the same or similar circumstances."

These two instructions correctly state the law and the action of plaintiff in requesting the court to give the same was a sufficient compliance with the requirements of section 67. The court also instructed the jury that "contributory negligence means, negligence, if any, on the part of the person injured, which contributed to cause the injury in question." Plaintiff contends that as the court failed to correctly state in its instructions the degree of care required of a child eight years old, this instruction was calculated to mislead the jury. We think there is merit in this contention.

After a careful consideration of the record we have reached the conclusion that justice requires that this case be retried.

The judgment of the Circuit court of Cook county is reversed and the cause is remanded for a new trial.

REVERSED AND REMANDED.

Friend, P. J., and Sullivan, J., concur.

if any, on the part of the person injured, which contributed to cause the injury in question." Plaintiff contends that as the court failed to correctly state in its instructions the degree of care required of a child eight years old, this instruction was calculated to mislead the jury. We think there is merit in this contention.

After a careful consideration of the record we have reached the conclusion that justice requires that this case be retried.

The judgment of the Circuit court of Cook county is reversed and the cause is remanded for a new trial.

REVERSED AND REMANDED.

Friend, P. J., and Sullivan, J., concur.

37737

80 A

AETNA ACCEPTANCE COMPANY,
a corporation,
Appellant,

v.

ANDREW STRIEFF,
Appellee.

APPEAL FROM SUPERIOR COURT, COOK COUNTY.

280 I.A. 627[2]

MR. JUSTICE SULLIVAN DELIVERED THE OPINION OF THE COURT.

This is an appeal by plaintiff, Aetna Acceptance Company, from a judgment entered on a finding for defendant, Andrew Strieff, in an action of fraud and deceit, tried by the court without a jury. Defendant filed no brief.

The declaration filed June 23, 1933, consists of two counts. The first alleges substantially that January 14, 1930, defendant falsely, fraudulently and knowingly entered into a written contract with Auburn Woodlawn Motors, Inc., (hereinafter referred to as the Sales Agency) for the purported purchase of an Auburn sedan automobile for the purported consideration of $2,158.84; that $652 thereof was falsely represented to have been paid in cash, leaving a balance of $1,506.84, which balance was evidenced by a conditional sales contract and note which provided that said balance shall be paid in twelve monthly installments of $125.57 each, together with interest at 7% after maturity; that defendant knew or by the exercise of reasonable care should have known that the Sales Agency, by its officers, agents and representatives, would negotiate, sell, assign and transfer the said conditional sales contract and note to plaintiff herein, who would rely upon the truth of defendant's statements and representations in said contract and note, and that plaintiff would be defrauded thereby; that defendant was not in fact the purchaser of said

37757

AETNA ACCEPTANCE COMPANY,
a corporation,
Appellant,

v.

ANDREW STRIEFF,
Appellee.

APPEAL FROM SUPERIOR
COURT, COOK COUNTY.

280 I.A. 627

MR. JUSTICE SULLIVAN DELIVERED THE OPINION OF THE COURT.

This is an appeal by plaintiff, Aetna Acceptance Company, from a judgment entered on a finding for defendant, Andrew Strieff, in an action of fraud and deceit, tried by the court without a jury. Defendant filed no brief.

The declaration filed June 23, 1933, consists of two counts. The first alleges substantially that January 14, 1930, defendant falsely, fraudulently and knowingly entered into a written contract with Auburn Woodlawn Motors, Inc., (hereinafter referred to as the Sales Agency) for the purported purchase of an Auburn sedan automobile for the purported consideration of $2,156.84; that $652 thereof was falsely represented to have been paid in cash, leaving a balance of $1,504.84, which balance was evidenced by a conditional sales contract and note which provided that said balance shall be paid in twelve monthly installments of $125.67 each, together with interest at 7% after maturity; that defendant knew or by the exercise of reasonable care should have known that the Sales Agency, by its officers, agents and representatives, would negotiate, sell, assign and transfer the said conditional sales contract and note to plaintiff herein, who would rely upon the truth of defendant's statements and representations in said contract and note, and that plaintiff would be defrauded thereby; that defendant was not in fact the purchaser of said automobile and did not intend to purchase it, but he executed the contract and note with a fraudulent intent and purpose on his part so as to enable the Sales Agency to wrongfully and fraudulently receive from the plaintiff the consideration for the purchase of said contract and note, and that it actually did receive from plaintiff $1,310; that plaintiff did not know and had no means of ascertaining the falsity of defendant's representations and conduct; that, on or about February 10, 1930, defendant again falsely and fraudulently represented that the terms and conditions of the contract and note were in all respects true, as a result of which plaintiff was put to considerable expense and sustained damages in attempting to retrieve the said automobile after it had been taken possession of by another finance company under a claim of prior right of possession or title; that no part of its original consideration has ever been repaid to plaintiff; and that the additional damages which it suffered were all caused by the fraudulent conduct of defendant.

The second count charges defendant with having perpetrated the frauds complained of in combination and conspiracy with certain officers, agents and representatives of the Sales Agency to enable that company to defraud plaintiff of $1,310, which it paid for said contract and note; and that on or about February 10, 1930, defendant fraudulently reaffirmed the representations contained in the contract and note with additional resultant damages to plaintiff.

After defendant's demurrer to the declaration had been overruled he filed a plea of the general issue.

Defendant, an engineer employed by the Illinois Central Railroad Company, earns from $230 to $250 a month. Two of his fellow engineers, James E. Hoke and Thomas V. Allison, with whom he had been acquainted many years, became interested in an automobile agency incorporated and doing business under the name of Auburn Woodlawn Motors, Inc., of which one Monroe was president. It automobile and did not intend to purchase it, but he executed the contract and note with a fraudulent intent and purpose on his part so as to enable the Sales Agency to wrongfully and fraudulently receive from the plaintiff the consideration for the purchase of said contract and note, and that it actually did receive from plaintiff $1,310; that plaintiff did not know and had no means of ascertaining the falsity of defendant's representations and conduct; that, on or about February 10, 1950, defendant again falsely and fraudulently represented that the terms and conditions of the contract and note were in all respects true, as a result of which plaintiff was put to considerable expense and sustained damages in attempting to retrieve the said automobile after it had been taken possession of by another finance company under a claim of prior right of possession or title; that no part of its original consideration has ever been repaid to plaintiff; and that the additional damages which it suffered were all caused by the fraudulent conduct of defendant.

The second count charges defendant with having perpetrated the frauds complained of in combination and conspiracy with certain officers, agents and representatives of the Sales Agency to enable that company to defraud plaintiff of $1,310, which it paid for said contract and note; and that on or about February 10, 1950, defendant fraudulently reaffirmed the representations contained in the contract and note with additional resultant damages to plaintiff.

After defendant's demurrer to the declaration had been overruled he filed a plea of the general issue.

Defendant, an engineer employed by the Illinois Central Railroad Company, earns from $230 to $250 a month. Two of his fellow engineers, James E. Hoke and Thomas V. Willison, with whom he had been acquainted many years, became interested in an automobile agency incorporated and doing business under the name of Auburn Woodlawn Motors, Inc., of which one Monroe was president. It appeared that defendant did not purchase and had no intention of purchasing an automobile from this concern, and made no payment on such a purchase, but that sometime prior to January 14, 1930, Hoke asked him to sign papers for what he called a "floor plan deal," for the purpose of assisting the Sales Agency to secure an Auburn automobile from the manufacturer or distributor of such cars, same to be displayed in the Sales Agency's show room and later sold. Defendant testified that Hoke brought him to the office of the Sales Agency, where he met Allison, who told him there was "nothing to worry about, it is perfectly all right" to sign the papers Hoke asked him to sign as a favor; that he was advised that the automobile would remain at the Sales Agency until it was sold and paid for in full, and that he would be thereby relieved of all obligation on the documents to be signed by him; and that, under these circumstances, he signed, without reading them, the papers which were presented to him in blank by Monroe.

A "floor plan deal" was explained to be a transaction whereby the Sales Agency paid 10% and the finance company 90% of the wholesale price of an automobile to the manufacturer for the delivery of same to the Sales Agency, which could not sell it without the consent of and a release from the finance company.

It developed that the documents executed by defendant did not concern a "floor plan deal" at all. One of the papers he signed for Monroe was a conditional sales contract for the purchase by him of an Auburn automobile from the Sales Agency for a purported consideration of $2,158.84, $624 of which was represented in such contract as having been paid in cash, the balance of the purchase price amounting to $1,506.84 to be payable by defendant in monthly installments of $125.57 each. The other paper signed was a note, which also evidenced and secured the deferred payments.

Plaintiff was advised by the Sales Agency that defendant

appeared that defendant did not purchase and, had no intention of purchasing an automobile from this concern, and made no payment on such a purchase, but that sometime prior to January 14, 1930, Hoke asked him to sign papers for what he called a "floor plan deal," for the purpose of assisting the Sales Agency to secure an Auburn automobile from the manufacturer or distributor of such cars, same to be displayed in the Sales Agency's show room and later sold. Defendant testified that Hoke brought him to the office of the Sales Agency, where he met Allison, who told him there was "nothing to worry about, it is perfectly all right" to sign the papers Hoke asked him to sign as a favor; that he was advised that the automobile would remain at the Sales Agency until it was sold and paid for in full, and that he would b thereby relieved of all obligation on the documents to be signed by him; and that, under these circumstances, he signed, without reading them, the papers which were presented to him in blank by Monroe.

A "floor plan deal" was explained to be a transaction whereby the Sales Agency paid 10% and the finance company 90% of the wholesale price of an automobile to the manufacturer for the delivery of same to the Sales Agency, which could not sell it without the consent of and a release from the finance company.

It developed that the documents executed by defendant did not concern a "floor plan deal" at all. One of the papers he signed for Monroe was a conditional sales contract for the purchase by him of an Auburn automobile from the Sales Agency for a purported consideration of $2,130.24, $624 of which was represented in such contract as having been paid in cash, the balance of the purchase price amounting to $1,506.24, to be payable by defendant in monthly installments of $125.57 each. The other paper signed was a note, which also evidenced and secured the deferred payments.

Plaintiff was advised by the Sales Agency that defendant

had signed the necessary papers for the purchase of the automobile. After investigating defendant's financial responsibility plaintiff advised the Sales Agency that it would discount defendant's note, and it thereafter purchased the contract and the note and paid the Sales Agency $1,310 therefor.

Plaintiff contends that it is entitled to recover the amount thus paid to the Sales Agency, as well as the additional damages sustained by it by reason of its payment of attorney's fees and other charges and costs in its unsuccessful endeavor thereafter to replevy the automobile.

We are of the opinion that there can be no question as to plaintiff's right to recover from defendant the $1,310 paid by it to the Sales Agency. Regardless of the question of whether defendant did or did not intend to commit a wrongful act when in his desire to do a favor for his friends he signed documents which he, an intelligent man, did not read, and which he was advised and thought would not obligate him financially, he cannot under the law escape liability for his conduct in placing within the hands of Monroe, president of the Sales Agency, the means with which to perpetrate a palpable fraud upon plaintiff.

It is not necessary in an action of this kind to show that defendant had any interest in the subject matter or that he received any benefit therefrom. (Weatherford v. Fishback, 3 Scam. 170; Eames v. Morgan, 37 Ill. 260; Endsley v. Johns, 120 id. 469; Leonard v. Springer, 197 id. 532.) Defendant is liable, not upon any idea of benefit to himself, but because of his negligent or wrongful act and consequent injury to the other party. (14 Am. & Eng. Ency. of Law, - 2d ed. - 153; Leonard v. Springer, supra.) Even though we assume that defendant intended no wrong, it is well settled that where one of two innocent parties must suffer, that one, whose conduct brought about or contributed to the injury, must bear the loss.

After a careful examination of all the evidence in

had signed the necessary papers for the purchase of the automobile. After investigating defendant's financial responsibility plaintiff advised the Sales Agency that it would discount defendant's note, and it thereafter purchased the contract and the note and paid the Sales Agency $1,310 therefor.

Plaintiff contends that it is entitled to recover the amount thus paid to the Sales Agency, as well as the additional damages sustained by it by reason of the payment of attorney's fees and other charges and costs in its unsuccessful endeavor thereafter to replevy the automobile.

We are of the opinion that there can be no question as to plaintiff's right to recover from defendant the $1,310 paid by it to the Sales Agency. Regardless of the question of whether defendant did or did not intend to commit a wrongful act when in his desire to do a favor for his friends he signed documents which he, an intelligent man, did not read, and which he was advised and thought would not obligate him financially, he cannot under the law escape liability for his conduct in placing within the hands of Monroe, president of the Sales Agency, the means with which to perpetrate a palpable fraud upon plaintiff.

It is not necessary in an action of this kind to show that defendant had any interest in the subject matter or that he received any benefit therefrom. (Weatherford v. Fishback, 3 Scam. 170; Jones v. Morgan, 37 Ill. 260; Endsley v. Johns, 120 Id. 469; Leonard v. Springer, 197 Id. 532.) Defendant is liable, not upon any idea of benefit to himself, but because of his negligent or wrongful act and consequent injury to the other party. (14 Am. & Eng. Ency. of Law, 2d ed. - 193; Leonard v. Springer, supra.) Even though we assume that defendant intended no wrong, it is well settled that where one of two innocent parties must suffer, that one, whose conduct brought about or contributed to the injury, must bear the loss.

After a careful examination of all the evidence in

the record, we think there is no merit to plaintiff's claim for additional damages claimed to have been suffered in connection with its unsuccessful effort to replevy the automobile.

The judgment of the Superior court is reversed and judgment is entered here for plaintiff and against defendant for $1,310.

REVERSED AND JUDGMENT HERE.

Friend, P. J., and Scanlan, J., concur.

-2-

the record, we think there is no merit to plaintiff's claim for additional damages claimed to have been suffered in connection with its unsuccessful effort to replevy the automobile.

The judgment of the Superior court is reversed and judgment is entered here for plaintiff and against defendant for $1,310.

REVERSED AND JUDGMENT HERE.

Friend, P. J., and Scanlan, J., concur.

37819

ANTONINA MYSLIWIEC,
Appellee,

v.

INDEPENDENT ORDER OF FORESTERS, a corporation,
Appellant.

APPEAL FROM MUNICIPAL COURT OF CHICAGO.

280 I.A. 627[3]

MR. JUSTICE SULLIVAN DELIVERED THE OPINION OF THE COURT.

Defendant, Independent Order of Foresters, seeks to reverse a judgment for $1,000 rendered against it in favor of plaintiff, Antonina Mysliwiec, in an action on a certificate of insurance issued February 20, 1924, on the life of her husband, Feliks Mysliwiec, by Modern Brotherhood of America, which merged with defendant December 14, 1931. The cause was tried by the court without a jury.

Plaintiff's statement of claim alleged substantially that the Modern Brotherhood of America (hereinafter referred to as the Brotherhood) agreed to pay her, as the beneficiary named in said insurance certificate, $1,000 upon the death of her husband; that the insured died June 4, 1933; that during his lifetime the deceased complied with all the covenants and conditions of the policy; and that she is entitled to recover $1,000 as provided in said policy from defendant, which had acquired the assets and assumed the obligations of the Brotherhood.

Defendant's affidavit of merits averred in substance that the insured had forfeited all rights under his policy by his failure to pay his contribution or assessment and dues for the month of January, 1933, on or before December 31, 1932, and that pursuant to the terms and conditions of said policy he stood

37819

ANTONINA MYALIWIEC,
Appellee,

v.

[illegible], a corporation,
Appellant.

APPEAL FROM SUPERIOR COURT
COOK COUNTY.

260 I.A. 627

MR. JUSTICE SULLIVAN DELIVERED THE OPINION OF THE COURT.

Defendant, Independent Order of Foresters, seeks to reverse a judgment for $1,000 rendered against it in favor of plaintiff, Antonina Myaliwiec, in an action on a certificate of insurance issued February 20, 1924, on the life of her husband, Feliks Myaliwiec, by Modern Brotherhood of America, which merged with defendant December 14, 1931. The cause was tried by the court without a jury.

Plaintiff's statement of claim alleged substantially that the Modern Brotherhood of America (hereinafter referred to as the Brotherhood) agreed to pay her, as beneficiary named in said insurance certificate, $1,000 upon the death of her husband; that the insured died June 4, 1935; that during his lifetime the deceased complied with all the covenants and stipulations of the policy; and that she is entitled to recover $1,000 as provided in said policy from defendant, which [illegible] the assets and assumed the obligations of the Brotherhood.

Defendant's affidavit of merits averred in substance that the insured had forfeited all rights under his policy by his failure to pay his contribution or assessment and dues for the month of January, 1933, on or before December 31, 1932, and that pursuant to the terms and conditions of said policy he stood *ipso facto* suspended January 1, 1933; that as a result of such suspension from membership all that his beneficiary was entitled to receive from defendant upon his death was $222 under certain extended and paid-up insurance provisions of the policy, which amount has been tendered to plaintiff and refused; and that after his suspension the insured had not been reinstated prior to his death.

It is claimed by defendant that under its constitution and laws deceased was automatically suspended December 31, 1932, for the nonpayment of his assessment for the month of January, 1933, and that, inasmuch as he had neither applied for nor been granted reinstatement within ninety days from the date of such suspension, he had forfeited his rights under his benefit certificate, except as to $222 extended or paid-up insurance.

The constitution and laws of the Independent Order of Foresters in force at the time of the insured's death contained the following provision:

"The required payments to the Order after initiation are due and payable by each member of the Order to the Financial Secretary of his Court, thirty-one days before the first day of each and every month, provided thirty days' grace shall be allowed for such payments. Upon failure to pay the required payments to the Order as aforesaid, within the period of grace, the member so failing shall *ipso facto* stand suspended from the Order. * * *"

It was further provided therein that a "beneficiary member suspended for nonpayment of his required payments to the order may, within ninety days after the date of his suspension, be reinstated, without ballot, into the court from which he was suspended and to his former status in the order" by presenting to the financial secretary of his court an application for reinstatement and a health certificate, both on prescribed forms, accompanied by a deposit of all payments in arrears, subject, however, to the approval of his application for reinstatement by the "medical board" and the "supreme chief ranger."

January 1, 1933, the records of the supreme secretary of defendant society showed that all payments required of the insured *ipso facto* suspended January 1, 1933; that as a result of such suspension from membership all that his beneficiary was entitled to receive from defendant upon his death was $222 under certain extended and paid-up insurance provisions of the policy, which amount has been tendered to plaintiff and refused; and that after his suspension the insured had not been reinstated prior to his death.

It is claimed by defendant that under its constitution and laws deceased was automatically suspended December 31, 1932, for the nonpayment of his assessment for the month of January, 1933, and that, inasmuch as he had neither applied for nor been granted reinstatement within ninety days from the date of such suspension, he had forfeited his rights under his benefit certificate, except as to $222 extended or paid-up insurance.

The constitution and laws of the Independent Order of Foresters in force at the time of the insured's death contained the following provision:

> "The required payments to the Order after initiation are due and payable by each member of the Order to the Financial Secretary of his Court, thirty-one days before the first day of each and every month, provided thirty days' grace shall be allowed for such payments. Upon failure to pay the required payments to the Order as aforesaid, within the period of grace, the member so failing shall *ipso facto* stand suspended from the Order. * * *"

It was further provided therein that a "beneficiary member suspended for nonpayment of his required payments to the order may, within ninety days after the date of his suspension, be reinstated, without ballot, into the court from which he was suspended and to his former status in the order" by presenting to the financial secretary of his court an application for reinstatement and a health certificate, both on prescribed forms, accompanied by a deposit of all payments in arrears, subject, however, to the approval of his application for reinstatement by the "medical board" and the "supreme chief ranger."

January 1, 1933, the records of the supreme secretary of defendant society showed that all payments required of the insured up to and including December, 1932, had been received, same having been transmitted by the financial secretary of his local court.

John P. Lang, the supreme secretary, testified that his home and office were in Toronto, Canada, that deceased was automatically suspended pursuant to the January, 1933, report of the financial secretary of his local court that he had not paid his January, 1933, assessment; and that, thereafter and prior to his death, the "head office" of defendant had received no application for his reinstatement or report of further assessments paid by him or in his behalf.

Walter Smyd, financial secretary of the local court of which insured was a member, testified that he had forwarded to the supreme lodge of defendant all payments necessary to keep deceased in good standing to December 31, 1933; that payments of monthly assessments and dues were thereafter made either by or for him on January 6, 1933, February 3, 1933, March 3, 1933, April 7, 1933, May 5, 1933, and June 2, 1933, the last payment having been made two days before his death June 4, 1933; that, notwithstanding the payment of January 6, 1933, he reported to the supreme lodge that deceased had failed to make his required payment for January, 1933; that, despite his report of the insured's failure to make such payment and his suspension because thereof, he continued to accept assessments and dues paid in his behalf; that deceased was in arrears in his payments practically since he joined the Brotherhood in 1924; that in April, 1932, he had suspended him because he was at that time ten months in arrears in the payment of his assessments and dues, but that he reinstated him the following month without the payment of any purported arrearages, and without any application for reinstatement or certificate of health; and that the assessments and dues paid for deceased in January, February, March, April, May and June, 1933, were neither forwarded nor reported [redacted] to the supreme lodge, but were up to and including [illegible]ber, 1952, had been received, thus having been transmitted by the financial secretary of his local [illegible].

John [illegible], the supreme secretary, testified that the head office [illegible] in Toronto, Canada, [illegible] received and automatically suspended [illegible] the [illegible] 1952, report of the financial secretary [illegible] had not paid his January, 1952, assessments; [illegible] thereafter and prior to his death, the "head office" of defendant [illegible] no application for his reinstatement or report of further assessments paid by him or in his behalf.

Walter [illegible], financial secretary of the local council of which insured was a member, testified that he had forwarded to the supreme lodge of defendant all payments necessary to keep insured in good standing to December 31, 1951; that payments of monthly assessments and dues were thereafter made [illegible] January 6, 1953, February 3, 1953, March 3, 1953, April [illegible], 1953, May 5, 1953, and June 8, 1953, the last payment having been made two days before his death June [illegible], 1953; [illegible] payment of January 6, 1953, he reported to the supreme lodge that deceased had failed to make his required payments for [illegible], 1952; that, despite his report of the insured's failure to make such payment and his suspension because thereof, he continued to accept assessments and dues paid in his behalf; that [illegible] in his payments [illegible] that in April, 1952, [illegible] ten months in arrears in the payment of his assessments [illegible] that he [illegible] purported arrearages, and without any application for reinstatement or certificate of health; and that the assessments and dues paid for deceased in January, February, March, April, May and June, 1953, were neither [illegible] nor reported to the supreme lodge, but were applied by him as payment of assessments and dues for March, April, May, June, July and ugust, 1932, for which months insured was in arrears to the local court.

Plaintiff testified that her husband had been suffering from tuberculosis for more than two years prior to his death, and that in the year 1933 he was confined to his home and bed most of the time; that she went to the "lodge" and made his payments in January, February, March, April and May, 1933; that she simply paid the money to Szmyd, he signed the book and she "went home;" that nothing was said upon any of these occasions about her husband's suspension or as to how the payments were credited. Her son made the June, 1933, payment, and merely looked to see that Szmyd signed the book, without examining his manner of crediting payment.

The insured was fully paid up on the records of the supreme lodge to December 31, 1932. Assessments were thereafter paid to the local court for him each month until his death June 4, 1933. Admittedly no notice was given him by the supreme lodge of his suspension for his alleged failure to make his January, 1933, payment. The evidence furnishes ample justification for disbelief of Szmyd's testimony that he notified insured sometime in February, 1933, of his suspension for failure to make his January, 1933, payment. Szmyd also testified that the beneficiary was advised of the suspension. It is incredible that plaintiff would continue to pay her husband's dues and assessments until almost the very day of his death with knowledge that he had been suspended from the society and that such payments after his suspension could not avail her to reap the benefits of his insurance.

We think that the acceptance of the payments made in insured's behalf in 1933, regardless of how they were applied by the financial secretary, should be considered as evidence tending to prove that the society recognized the membership of her husband as a continuing applied by him as payment of assessments and dues for March, April, May, June, July and August, 1933, for which month he was in arrears to the local court.

Plaintiff testified that her husband had been suffering from tuberculosis for more than two years prior to his death, and that in the year 1933 he was confined to his home and had most of the time; that she went to the local court and made his payments in January, February, March, April and May, 1933; that she always paid the money to Sandy, the clerk, who took and went home; that nothing was said upon any of these occasions about her husband's suspension or as to the payments made thereafter. She then made the June, 1933, payment, and we only look to see that Sandy signed the book, without examining his manner of crediting payment.

The insured was fully paid up on the records of the supreme lodge to December 31, 1932. Assessments were thereafter paid to the local court for him each month until his death June 4, 1933. And really no notice was given him by the supreme lodge of his suspension for his alleged failure to make his January, 1933, payment. The evidence further made justification to disbelief of Sandy's testimony that he notified insured sometime in February, 1933, of his suspension for failure to make his January, 1933, payment. Sandy also testified that the beneficiary was advised of the suspension. It is incredible that plaintiff would continue to pay her husband's dues and assessments until almost the very day of his death with knowledge that he had been suspended from the society and that such payments after his suspension would not revive or keep the benefits of his insurance.

We think that the acceptance of the payments made in insured's behalf in 1933, regardless of how they were applied by the financial secretary, should be considered as evidence tending to prove that the society recognized the membership of her husband as a continuing one and his benefit certificate as still in force. In our opinion it would be tantamount to the approval of conduct that savors of fraud to hold that a fraternal benefit order, one of its local courts, or an officer of same, could keep a member's suspension a secret from him and thereafter continue to accept the payment of assessments during his lifetime, and upon his death declare with impunity to his beneficiary that the member had been theretofore suspended and that she was not entitled to the full benefit of his insurance certificate. We think that this would be none the less true even though the financial secretary of the local court had advised the insured of his suspension and had thereafter continued to accept the payment of his assessments and dues from his beneficiary. e are impelled to hold that any right of defendant society under its contract of insurance with deceased to the forfeiture of his membership was waived by its acts and conduct, and by the acts and conduct of its subordinate council and officers.

Questions somewhat similar to those raised here were presented for our determination in Routa v. Royal League, 274 Ill. App. 152, where we said at pp. 165, 166-67:

"This contention of lack of authority on the part of representatives of the society to waive forfeiture provisions of its laws is untenable. In construing a similar by-law in Dromgold v. Royal Neighbors, 261 Ill. 60, the Supreme Court said:

"'The application for a benefit certificate and the by-laws of the society are to be considered a part of the contract between the society and the member. (Enright v. Knights and Ladies of Security, 253 Ill. 460.) Restrictions upon the power of an agent of an insurance company to waive any of the conditions of the contract or upon the manner of such waiver are themselves conditions of the contract, which may be waived the same as any other condition of the policy.'

"In Loman v. North American Union, 263 Ill. 304, on p. 312, the court held:

"'The law is well settled in this State that the provisions of the by-laws of mutual benefit societies of this character may be waived by the society; that the local lodge or council of such society is the agent of the supreme Lodge, and may waive such by-laws by accepting dues and assessments with full knowledge of all the facts constituting a violation of the rules of the order, or by other acts and conduct of its officers and agents of such a character as to induce a belief on the part of the insured that the society does not intend to exercise its right of forfeiture, but, on the contrary, recognizes the insured as a member of the society in good standing. (Jones v. Knights of Honor, 236 Ill. 113; Grand Lodge A. O. U. W. v.

one and his benefit certificate as still in force. In our opinion it would be tantamount to the approval of conduct that savors of fraud to hold that a fraternal benefit order, one of its local courts, or an officer of same, could keep a member's suspension a secret from him and thereafter continue to accept the payment of assessments during his lifetime, and upon his death declare with impunity to his beneficiary that the member had been theretofore suspended and that she was not entitled to the full benefit of his insurance certificate. We think that this would be none the less true even though the financial secretary of the local court had advised the insured of his suspension and had thereafter continued to accept the payment of his assessments and dues from his beneficiary. We are impelled to hold that any right of defendant society under its contract of insurance with deceased to the forfeiture of his membership was waived by its acts and conduct, and by the acts and conduct of its subordinate council and officers.

Questions somewhat similar to those raised here were presented for our determination in Kontz v. Royal League, 274 Ill. App. 155, where we said at pp. 165, 166-67:

"This contention of lack of authority on the part of representatives of the society to waive forfeiture provisions of its laws is untenable. In construing a similar by-law in Bromwold v. Royal Neighbors, 261 Ill. 60, the Supreme Court said:

'The application for a benefit certificate and the by-laws of the society are to be considered a part of the contract between the society and the member. (Wright v. Knights and Ladies of Security, 255 Ill. 460.) Restrictions upon the power of an agent of an insurance company to waive any of the conditions of the contract or upon the manner of such waiver are themselves conditions of the contract, which may be waived the same as any other condition of the policy.'

"In Jensen v. North American Union, 263 Ill. 504, on p. 513, the court held:

'The law is well settled in this State that the provisions of the by-laws of mutual benefit societies of this character may be waived by the society; that the local lodge or council of such society is the agent of the supreme lodge, and may waive such by-laws by accepting dues and assessments with full knowledge of all the facts constituting a violation of the rules of the order, or by other acts and conduct of its officers and agents of such a character as to induce a belief on the part of the insured that the society does not intend to exercise its right of forfeiture, but, on the contrary, recognizes the insured as a member of the society in good standing. Jones v. Knights of Honor, 236 Ill. 113; Grand Lodge A. O. U. W. v.

Lachmann, 199 id. 140.) For this purpose knowledge of facts received or communicated to its officers having authority to act in the premises, and whose duty it is to act in the premises, is imputed to the society. (Court of Honor v. Dinger, 221 Ill. 176; Walker v. American Order of Foresters, 162 I . pp. 30; O'Brien v. Catholic Order of Foresters, 172 id. 638.)' I I

"Waerness v. Independent Order of Foresters, 244 Ill. App. 211, held at pp. 217, 218:

"'The defendant earnestly contends that the local court, and in particular the financial secretary, under the by-laws was wholly without authority to waive any requirement of the by-laws relating to reinstatement. * * * The general rule, however, in this and other States, seems to be that the by-laws of a mutual benefit society, limiting the authority of its local organizations or officers in these respects, are unavailing where such local body or officer has apparent authority. Independent Order of Foresters v. Schweitzer, 171 Ill. 325; Zeman v. North American Union, 263 Ill. 304; Dremgold v. Royal Neighbors of America, 261 Ill. 60.'

"That the provisions contained in the by-laws, application, benefit certificate or any other portion of the contract of membership in a fraternal benefit insurance society providing for the forfeiture of such membership in certain events may be waived by the society has been settled by a long and uninterrupted line of decisions in this State. In Chicago Life Ins. Co. v. Warner, 80 Ill. 410, pp. 412, 413, the court said:

"'It is obvious that the provision in the policy, providing for a forfeiture for a nonpayment of the annual premium, was incorporated in the contract for the benefit of the insurance company. The policy did not necessarily become void, if the premium was not paid when due. The company had the undoubted right to waive the forfeiture, if it saw proper, and dispense with a prompt payment of the premium at the time it was due.

"'If this had been done by the insurance company in this case, then, notwithstanding the contract declares the policy void if the premium is not paid when due, the company cannot avail of the defense.'"

As heretofore stated, Szmyd testified that the insured was delinquent in the payment of his assessments practically all of the time since his benefit certificate was issued to him in 1924. In discussing the question of waiver of forfeiture of membership by a fraternal benefit society under such circumstances, in Railway Passenger & Freight Conductors' Benevolent Ass'n v. Tucker, 157 Ill. 194, our Supreme court said at p. 201:

"What acts will in all cases amount to a waiver of a forfeiture of membership in a mutual benefit society cannot be definitely stated, but conduct on the part of the society, which amounts to a recognition of a member's claim to the continuing rights of membership, will relieve him from the consequences of his default. The receipt of assessments after default in payment is a common form of waiver. The question of waiver is in most cases a question of fact for the jury. (16 Am. & Eng. Ency. of Law, page 83.) * * * Where, out of sixty-four payments made by the assured, sixty-three had been made after the time limited by the by-laws had expired, and no conditions were insisted upon for re-instatement, it was held, that such a course of conduct

Lachmann, 199 id. 140.) For this purpose knowledge of facts received or communicated to its officers having authority to act in the premises, and whose duty it is to act in the premises, is imputed to the society. (Court of Honor v. Dinger, 221 Ill. 176; Walker v. American Order of Foresters, 168 Ill. App. 50; O'Brien v. Catholic Order of Foresters, 172 id. 638.)'

"Yeazman v. Independent Order of Foresters, 244 Ill. App. 211, held at pp. 217, 218:

"'The defendant earnestly contends that the local court, and in particular the financial secretary, under the by-laws was wholly without authority to waive any requirement of the by-laws relating to reinstatement. * * * The general rule, however, in this and other States, seems to be that the by-laws of a mutual benefit society, limiting the authority of its local organizations or officers in these respects, are unavailing where such local body or officer has apparent authority. Independent Order of Foresters v. Schweitzer, 171 Ill. 325; Zeman v. North American Union, 263 Ill. 304; Drennold v. Royal Neighbors of America, 261 Ill. 60.'

"That the provisions contained in the by-laws, application, benefit certificate or any other portion of the contract of membership in a fraternal benefit insurance society providing for the forfeiture of such membership in certain events may be waived by the society has been settled by a long and uninterrupted line of decisions in this State. In Chicago Life Ins. Co. v. Warner, 80 Ill. 410, pp. 412, 413, the court said:

"'It is obvious that the provisions in the policy, providing for a forfeiture for a nonpayment of the annual premium, was incorporated in the contract for the benefit of the insurance company. The policy did not necessarily become void, if the premium was not paid when due. The company had the undoubted right to waive the forfeiture, if it saw proper, and dispense with a prompt payment of the premium at the time it was due.

"'If this had been done by the insurance company in this case, then, notwithstanding the contract declares the policy void if the premium is not paid when due, the company cannot avail of the defense.'"

As heretofore stated, Samyd testified that the insured was delinquent in the payment of his assessments practically all of the time since his benefit certificate was issued to him in 1926. In discussing the question of waiver of forfeiture of membership by a fraternal benefit society under such circumstances, in Railway Passenger & Freight Conductors' Benevolent Ass'n v. Tucker, 157 Ill. 194, our Supreme court said at p. 201:

"What acts will in all cases amount to a waiver of a forfeiture of membership in a mutual benefit society cannot be definitely stated, but conduct on the part of the society, which amounts to a recognition of a member's claim to the continuing rights of membership, will relieve him from the consequences of his default. The receipt of assessments after default in payment is a common form of waiver. The question of waiver is in most cases a question of fact for the jury. (16 Am. & Eng. Ency. of Law, page 83.) * * * Where, out of sixty-four payments made by the insured, sixty-three had been made after the time limited by the by-laws had expired, and no conditions were insisted upon for [illegible] was held, that such a course of conduct.

of the company estopped it from insisting upon a forfeiture for nonpayment within such time without giving personal notice, that thereafter prompt payment would be re uired. (Stylow v. isconsin Odd Fellows Mut. Life Ins. Co., 69 Wis. 224.)"

A fraternal benefit society will not be permitted to treat a benefit certificate as alive and in full force, and accept a member's money over a period of years in violation of suspension and forfeiture provisions of its contract until death occurs, and then for the first time by asserting a previous suspension seek to void the certificate and escape its liability. Neither will such an association be permitted to insist on a forfeiture of a benefit certificate issued by it for the alleged nonpayment of an assessment when due where its course of dealing with the member has led him to believe that the provision for forfeiture would not be relied upon. (Routa v. Royal League, supra.)

By reason of the conduct of the financial secretary of its local court in accepting six monthly payments of dues and assessments made in insured's behalf subsequent to the alleged forfeiture of his membership and his conduct in inducing the insured to believe that a forfeiture would not be relied upon, defendant will be held to be estopped from taking advantage of such forfeiture.

It is urged that plaintiff failed to prove the case alleged in her statement of claim. It is sufficient to state in answer to this contention that this is a fourth class action in the Municipal court in which no formal pleadings are required and the case is such as the evidence makes it.

Other points have been urged by both parties, but in the view we take of this cause we deem it unnecessary to discuss them.

For the reasons indicated the judgment of the Municipal court is affirmed.

AFFIRMED.

Friend, P. J., and Scanlan, J., concur.

of the company estopped it from insisting upon a forfeiture for nonpayment within such time without giving personal notice, that thereafter prompt payment would be required. (Sixlow v. Wisconsin Odd Fellows Mut. Life Ins. Co., 99 Wis. 384.)"

A fraternal benefit society will not be permitted to treat a benefit certificate as alive and in full force, and accept a member's money over a period of years in violation of suspension and forfeiture provisions of its contract until death occurs, and then for the first time by asserting a previous suspension seek to void the certificate and escape its liability. Neither will such an association be permitted to insist on a forfeiture of a benefit certificate issued by it for the alleged nonpayment of an assessment when due where its course of dealing with the member has led him to believe that the provision for forfeiture would not be relied upon. (Honts v. Royal League, supra.)

By reason of the conduct of the financial secretary of its local court in accepting six monthly payments of dues and assessments made in insured's behalf subsequent to the alleged forfeiture of his membership and his conduct in inducing the insured to believe that a forfeiture would not be relied upon, defendant will be held to be estopped from taking advantage of such forfeiture.

It is urged that plaintiff failed to prove the case alleged in her statement of claim. It is sufficient to state in answer to this contention that this is a fourth class action in the Municipal court in which no formal pleadings are required and the case is such as the evidence makes it.

Other points have been urged by both parties, but in the view we take of this cause we deem it unnecessary to discuss them.

For the reasons indicated the judgment of the Municipal court is affirmed.

AFFIRMED.

Bland, P.J., and Sanlms, J., concur.

37840

827

WILLIAM R. RUCHTY,
Appellant,

v.

E. L. RAMM and C. H. RAMM,
doing business as E. L.
RAMM CO.,
Appellees.

APPEAL FROM SUPERIOR COURT,
COOK COUNTY.

280 I.A. 624

MR. JUSTICE SULLIVAN DELIVERED THE OPINION OF THE COURT.

Plaintiff, William A. Ruchty, brought an action against defendants E. L. Ramm and C. H. Ramm, doing business as the E. L. Ramm Company, to recover from them $6,000, which he claims they obligated themselves to pay him for the purchase of his coal business. On defendants' motion the trial court at the close of plaintiff's case directed a verdict for defendants, upon which judgment was entered May 11, 1934. This appeal followed.

The declaration consists of two counts, the first of which is a common count alleging that on or about September 2, 1932, defendants became indebted to plaintiff in the sum of $6,000 for his coal business in LaGrange, Illinois, which plaintiff sold and delivered to them, and they purchased and accepted from him, promising to pay therefor $6,000; and that they have refused to pay the said sum or any part thereof.

The second count alleges that on or about September 2, 1932, plaintiff and one of the defendants acting for both signed the following written memorandum:

"I, Wm. Ruchty, sole owner of the Ruchty Coal Co. agree to sell my business to E. L. Ramm Co. with the understanding that conditions and terms be made September 10, 1932, or before; the sale price to be $6,000.

Wm. R. Ruchty,
Ed. L. Ramm."

37940

WILLIAM A. HUCHTY,
Appellant,

v.

W. L. HAMM and O. H. HAMM,
doing business as W. L.
HAMM CO.,
Appellees.

APPEAL FROM CIRCUIT COURT,

COOK COUNTY.

280 I.A. 682

MR. JUSTICE SULLIVAN DELIVERED THE OPINION OF THE COURT.

Plaintiff, William A. Huchty, brought an action against defendants W. L. Hamm and O. H. Hamm, doing business as W. L. Hamm Company, to recover from them $6,000, which he claims they obligated themselves to pay him for the purchase of his coal business. On defendants' motion the trial court at the close of plaintiff's case directed a verdict for defendants, upon which judgment was entered May 11, 1934. This appeal followed.

The declaration consists of two counts, the first of which is a common count alleging that on or about September 10, 1932, defendants became indebted to plaintiff in the sum of $6,000 for his coal business in LaGrange, Illinois, which plaintiff sold and delivered to them, and they purchased and accepted from him, promising to pay therefor $6,000; and that they have refused to pay the said sum or any part thereof.

The second count alleges that on or about September 10, 1932, plaintiff and one of the defendants wrote for both signed the following written memorandum:

"I, Wm. Huchty, sole owner of the Huchty Coal Co. agree to sell my business to W. L. Hamm Co. with the understanding that conditions and terms be made September 10, 1932, or before; the sale price to be $6,000.

Wm. H. Huchty,
Ed. L. Hamm."

It is further alleged that plaintiff's only business was the said coal business and that at said time it was also agreed between the parties that defendants were to pay plaintiff $3,500 September 10, 1932, and the balance in monthly payments for a period of one year; that plaintiff then delivered his business to defendants, which defendants accepted and thereafter carried on; and that defendants have failed and refused to pay plaintiff said $6,000 or any part thereof.

Defendants filed a plea of the general issue and a special plea which denied that they entered into any agreement with plaintiff for the purchase of his coal business for $6,000 or any other sum; that plaintiff delivered to them at any time his coal business; that they accepted such business or carried on same; and that they owed him any sum of money whatsoever.

Plaintiff was seventy-four years old and had been engaged in the coal business in LaGrange for nineteen years. His office was at the southeast corner of Lincoln and Tilton Avenues, and his coal yard occupied eight lots bounded by Lincoln avenue on the north, Tilton avenue on the west and the Indiana Harbor Belt Railroad on the east, where a switch track from the railroad entered the premises. He originally occupied these eight lots under a written lease from the railroad for one year and thereafter under a verbal lease from year to year, said lease to be terminated and the possession of the property surrendered upon ninety days notice. Plaintiff's current lease expired May 1, 1933. The three lots immediately south of the leased lots belonged to plaintiff. Adjoining these lots to the south was defendants' plant where they conducted a building material business.

Plaintiff testified that in the latter part of August, 1932, defendants told him that "they would give me so much money for my property," if they could secure a lease of the eight lots from the railroad company, and he said he would do all he could

It is further alleged that plaintiff's only [illegible] was the said coal business and that at this time it was also agreed between the parties that [illegible] defendants [illegible] to pay plaintiff $6,000 September 10, 1932, and [illegible] in monthly payments for a period of one year; that plaintiff then delivered his business [illegible] and that, which defendants accepted and thereafter carried on; and that defendants have failed and refused to pay plaintiff said $6,000 or any part thereof.

Defendants filed a plea of the general issue and a special plea which denied that they entered into any agreement with plaintiff for the purchase of his coal business for $6,000 or [illegible] that plaintiff delivered to them at any time his coal business, that they accepted such business or carried on same; and that they owed him any sum of money whatsoever.

Plaintiff was seventy-four years old and had been engaged in the coal business in LaGrange for nineteen years. His office was at the southeast corner of Lincoln and Tilton avenues, and his coal yard occupied eight lots bounded by Lincoln avenue on the north, Tilton avenue on the west and the Indiana Harbor Belt Railroad on the east, where a switch track from the railroad entered the premises. He originally occupied these eight lots under a written lease from the railroad for one year and thereafter under a verbal lease from year to year, said lease to be terminated and the possession of the property surrendered upon ninety days notice. Plaintiff's written lease expired May 1, 1932. The three lots [illegible] of the leased lots belonged to plaintiff. Adjoining these lots to the [illegible] defendants' plant where they conducted a building material business.

Plaintiff testified that in the latter part of August, 1932, defendants told him that "they would give me so much money for my property," if they could secure a lease of the eight lots to assist them in acquiring such lease; that on September 1, 1932, the defendants came to his office and asked him what he would take for his coal business and he replied that the least he would accept was $6,000; that on September 2, 1932, defendants again came to his office and C. R. Ramm wrote the instrument hereinbefore set forth in plaintiff's declaration, which was signed by E. L. Ramm and plaintiff in duplicate, each of them receiving a copy; that on September 5, 1932 (he later testified that this occurred September 8, 1932), the defendants advised him that they had orders for about 200 tons of coal "booked," some of which were from plaintiff's customers; that on the same day E. L. Ramm asked him "how he wanted his money," and he told him "3,500 in cash and the balance in one year," either in one payment or in monthly payments; that Ramm then stated "the money man was in Wisconsin fishing, and he expected him back on the 8th;" that on either September 6 or 7, 1932, he delivered to defendants a list of his customers and quit the coal business September 7, 1932; that also on September 7, 1932, he rented for use as a coal yard the three lots which he owned to one Swindle, who had theretofore been in the coal business about one block farther north; that September 8, 1932, defendants offered him $1,500 for his business and that after they told him they had already secured the lease to the eight lots he told them they could not have his business for $1,500; that he was notified September 10, 1932, by representatives of the railroad company to vacate the eight leased lots; that defendants and their attorney met plaintiff and his attorney by appointment at plaintiff's home on the evening of September 10, 1932, for the purpose of closing the deal, but were unable to agree upon the terms for the purchase and sale of his coal business; that on September 17, 1932, he vacated the leased lots, after removing therefrom the frame coal sheds and office, as well as the scale; and that he rebuilt such frame office and installed the scale on his own three lots, which he had rented to Swindle for the operation of a coal business.

to assist them in acquiring such lease; that on September 1, 1932, the defendants came to his office and asked him what he would take for his coal business and he replied that the least he would accept was $6,000; that on September 2, 1932, defendants again came to his office and C. R. Hamm wrote the instrument hereinbefore set forth in plaintiff's declaration, which was signed by E. L. Hamm and plaintiff in duplicate, each of them receiving a copy; that on September 5, 1932 (he later testified that this occurred September 8, 1932), the defendants advised him that they had orders for about 200 tons of coal "booked," some of which were from plaintiff's customers; that on the same day E. L. Hamm asked him "how he wanted his money," and he told him "$1,500 in cash and the balance in one year," either in one payment or in monthly payments; that Hamm then stated "the money man was in Wisconsin fishing, and he expected him back on the 8th;" that on either September 6 or 7, 1932, he delivered to defendants a list of his customers and quit the coal business September 7, 1932; that also on September 7, 1932, he rented for use as a coal yard the three lots which he owned to one Swindle, who had theretofore been in the coal business about one block farther north; that September 8, 1932, defendants offered him $1,500 for his business and that after they told him they had already secured the lease to the eight lots he told them they could not have his business for $1,500; that he was notified September 10, 1932, by representatives of the railroad company to vacate the eight leased lots; that defendants and their attorney met plaintiff and his attorney by appointment at plaintiff's home on the evening of September 10, 1932, for the purpose of closing the deal, but were unable to agree upon the terms for the purchase and sale of his coal business; that on September 7, 1932, he vacated the leased lots, after removing therefrom the frame coal sheds and office, as well as the scales; and that he rebuilt such same office and installed the scale on his own three lots, which he had rented to Swindle for the operation of a coal business.

Plaintiff contends that the document set forth in the declaration, which was received in evidence, is a contract for the sale of plaintiff's business to defendants for $6,000; and that, if it is not a contract but only an offer of sale, then there arose out of the acts of the parties an implied contract whereby defendants became obligated to pay plaintiff $6,000.

Defendants' theory of the case is that the document which plaintiff claims is a contract is nothing more than an offer by plaintiff to sell his business for $6,000; that this offer was so indefinite and uncertain that it could not be accepted so as to create a contract to purchase; that the offer was made with the understanding that the terms and conditions of the proposed sale were to be agreed upon by September 10, 1932; that a counter offer to pay him $1,500 was made by defendants; and that neither plaintiff's offer to sell nor defendants' counter offer to buy ever developed into a contract, either express or implied.

The principal question presented for our determination is as to the construction to be given to the written memorandum heretofore set forth. It was not a contract of purchase and sale; it was a mere offer made by plaintiff to defendants to sell his coal business to them for $6,000. This offer might have been revoked by plaintiff at any time before it ripened into a contract, express or implied. A casual examination of the document is convincing that it does not possess that mutuality and certainty requisite to an enforceable agreement. It specifies on its face that the proposed sale was subject to "the understanding that the conditions and terms be made September 10, 1932 or before." Defendants and their attorney met plaintiff and his attorney at plaintiff's home on the evening of September 10, 1932, for the purpose of closing the deal. Plaintiff, although present throughout this conference, testified that not one of several documents that were pre-

Plaintiff contends that the document set forth in the declaration, which was received in evidence, is a contract for the sale of plaintiff's business to defendants for $6,000; and that, if it is not a contract but only an offer to sell, then there arose out of the acts of the parties an implied contract whereby defendants became obligated to pay plaintiff $6,000.

Defendants' theory of the case is that the document which plaintiff claims is a contract is no more than an offer by plaintiff to sell his business for $6,000; that this offer was so indefinite and uncertain that it could not be accepted so as to create a contract to purchase; that the offer was made with the understanding that the terms and conditions of the proposed sale were to be agreed upon by the parties [illegible]; that a counter offer to pay him $1,500 was made by defendants; and that neither plaintiff's offer to sell nor defendants' counter offer to buy ever developed into a contract, either express or implied.

The principal question present for our determination is as to the construction to be given to the written memorandum heretofore set forth. It was not a contract of purchase and sale; it was a mere offer made by plaintiff to defendants to sell his business to them for $6,000. This offer might have been revoked by plaintiff at any time before it ripened into a contract, [illegible]. An examination of the document as containing the [illegible] so that mutuality and certainty requisite to an enforceable agreement. It specifies on its face that the proposal [illegible] subject to the understanding that the conditions are to be agreed [illegible] 1952 or before.) Defendants and their attorney met plaintiff and his attorney at plaintiff's home on the evening of Sept. [illegible], 1952, for the purpose of closing the deal. Plaintiff, although present throughout this conference, testified that not one of several documents that were produced by defendants' attorney and examined and discussed was shown to him, and that he heard nothing that was said except a controversy concerning his tax title to the three lots south of the eight leased lots. He stated, however, "they couldn't agree somehow or other. I don't know what it was, but I know they could not agree." The inability of the parties to agree on the terms and conditions of the sale precludes any claim that plaintiff's offer and the subsequent negotiations resulted in a valid express contract binding on anyone.

But plaintiff's insists that, even though the writing in question did not constitute an express contract, an implied contract for the purchase of his coal business for $6,000 resulted from defendants' conduct in securing the lease with plaintiff's acquiescence and assistance to the eight lots on which he previously had conducted his coal business, and his delivery to defendants of a list of his customers. We are of the opinion that this position is untenable.

Plaintiff had a verbal lease to May 1, 1933, of the eight lots in question, subject to termination on ninety days notice. He owned one delivery truck used in his coal business, and there was situated on the leased premises a frame office, frame coal sheds and a scale. The three lots which he owned were between the eight leased lots and defendants' property, upon which they conducted their building material business. If the negotiations for the sale of his coal business to defendants had been satisfactorily concluded, it is reasonable to infer that plaintiff was prepared to retire from that business, as he did anyhow. It is also reasonable to assume from the evidence that if the deal went through it was within the contemplation of the parties that plaintiff's coal business included not only his good will, but the office, sheds and scale on the premises, as well as the truck and the three lots. It is inconceivable that when plaintiff offered to sell his coal business he contemplated that his "business" comprised only his precarious interest in the lease, which he did not even assert duced by defendants' attorney and examined and discussed was shown to him, and that he heard nothing that was said except a controversy concerning his tax title to the three lots south of the eight leased lots. He stated, however, "they couldn't agree somehow or other. I don't know what it was, but I know they could not agree." The inability of the parties to agree on the terms and conditions of the sale precludes any claim that plaintiff's offer and the subsequent negotiations resulted in a valid express contract binding on anyone.

But plaintiff's insists that, even though the writing in question did not constitute an express contract, an implied contract for the purchase of his coal business for $6,000 resulted from defendants' conduct in securing the lease with plaintiff's acquiescence and assistance to the eight lots on which he previously had conducted his coal business, and his delivery to defendants of a list of his customers. We are of the opinion that this position is untenable.

Plaintiff had a verbal lease to May 1, 1953, of the eight lots in question, subject to termination on ninety days notice. He owned one delivery truck used in his coal business, and there was situated on the leased premises a frame office, frame coal sheds and a scale. The three lots which he owned were between the eight leased lots and defendants' property, upon which they conducted their building material business. If the negotiations for the sale of his coal business to defendants had been satisfactorily concluded, it is reasonable to infer that plaintiff was prepared to retire from that business, as he did anyhow. It is also reasonable to assume from the evidence that if the deal went through it was within the contemplation of the parties that plaintiff's coal business included not only his good will, but the office, sheds and scale on the premises, as well as the truck and the three lots. It is inconceivable that when plaintiff offered to sell his coal business he contemplated that his "business" comprised only his precarious interest in the lease, which he did not even assert when he was ordered to vacate the premises, and the list of his customers, without even his good will.

Plaintiff had, at best, but a brief uncertain tenure under his lease of the premises. When defendants first broached the purchase of plaintiff's business, they stated to him that they would consider it only in the event that they could secure a lease from the railroad company which owned the property. All that plaintiff said he could or would do concerning the lease was to suggest to the railroad officials that the lease be given to defendants. When plaintiff suggested to the railroad people that the lease be made with defendants, and when defendants secured the lease, it was in anticipation of the sale being consummated between the parties, as was the delivery of his list of customers by plaintiff to defendants.

The evidence is conclusive that defendants did not even receive the good will that usually accompanies the sale of a business. Without plaintiff's good will and with his active participation in the establishment of Swindler as a neighbor competitor of defendants in the coal business, even though he did deliver a list of his customers, it can hardly be said that same would be of much, if any, value to them.

We are of the opinion that the lease of the premises by defendants from the railroad company and the mere delivery to them by plaintiff of a list of his customers in anticipation of a valid contract between the parties did not constitute an acceptance of plaintiff's offer to sell his coal business as embodied in the written memorandum. It conclusively appears that the defendants neither accepted nor received plaintiff's coal business, and therefore no contract for the purchase of his business can be implied from the facts and circumstances disclosed by the record in this case.

Other points have been urged, but in the view we take of this cause we deem it unnecessary to discuss them.

For the reasons indicated the judgment of the Superior court is affirmed.

AFFIRMED.

Friend, P. J., and Scanlan, J., concur.

when he was ordered to vacate the premises, and the list of his customers, without even his good will.

Plaintiff had, at best, but a brief uncertain tenure under his lease of the premises. When defendants first broached the purchase of plaintiff's business, they stated to him that they would consider it only in the event that they could secure a lease from the railroad company which owned the property. At that plaintiff said he could or would do concerning that lease was to suggest to the railroad officials that the lease be given to them. When plaintiff suggested to the railroad people that the lease be made with defendants, and when defendants secured the lease, it was in anticipation of the sale being consummated between the parties, as was the delivery of his list of customers by plaintiff to defendants.

The evidence is conclusive that defendants did not even receive the good will that usually accompanies the sale of a business. Without plaintiff's good will and with his active participation in the establishment of Crindler as a neighbor competitor of defendants in the coal business, even though he did give a list of his customers, it can hardly be said that same would be of much, if any, value to them.

We are of the opinion that the lease o[illegible] by defendants from the railroad company and the mere delivery [illegible] by plaintiff of a list of his customers is insufficient [illegible] contract between the parties [illegible] plaintiff's offer to sell his coal business [illegible] memorandum. It conclusively appears that [illegible] accepted nor received plaintiff's coal business, and therefore no contract for the purchase of his business can be implied from the facts and circumstances disclosed by the record in this case.

Other points have been urged, [illegible] this cause we deem it unnecessary to discuss them.

For the reasons indicated the judgment of the superior court is affirmed.

AFFIRMED.

Friend, P. J., and Beamish, J., concur.

37959

RUBIE RIDDIFORD POWNER, Appellee,

vs.

WILLIAM E. POWNER, Appellant.

APPEAL FROM SUPERIOR COURT OF COOK COUNTY.

83 A

280 I.A. 625

MR. PRESIDING JUSTICE O'CONNOR DELIVERED THE OPINION OF THE COURT.

By this appeal the defendant seeks to reverse a decree of divorce entered in plaintiff's favor.

The record discloses that on February 6, 1934, plaintiff filed her complaint for divorce, charging that defendant had been guilty of extreme and repeated cruelty. Defendant in his answer denied the acts of cruelty charged against him, and denied that the parties were married on December 8, 1921, as alleged in the bill. He asked for a jury trial. A jury was impaneled to try the question of whether defendant had been guilty of the acts of cruelty charged. The case was heard June 22, 1934, on this question; the jury returned a verdict finding defendant guilty of extreme and repeated cruelty as charged in the complaint Afterward the court heard the case on the question of the property rights and the custody of the child of the parties, and July 26, 1934, a decree was entered in plaintiff's favor awarding her a divorce, the custody of the child and $200 "back support" for the minor child; that there was also due plaintiff for her solicitor's fees $37.50, which defendant was ordered to pay. No alimony was claimed and the decree forever released and discharged defendant in this respect.

The complaint alleged that the parties were married on the 8th of December, 1921, and defendant was charged with acts of cruelty on October 20, 1932, October 15, 1933, October 18, 1933, and November 15, 1933. On the trial of the case, on motion of plaintiff's attorney, plaintiff was given leave to amend her com-

37069

RUBIE RIDDIFORD POWERS,
Appellee,

vs.

WILLIAM E. POWERS,
Appellant.

APPEAL FROM SUPERIOR COURT
OF COOK COUNTY.

280 I.A. 625

MR. PRESIDING JUSTICE O'CONNOR
DELIVERED THE OPINION OF THE COURT.

By this appeal the defendant seeks to reverse a decree of divorce entered in plaintiff's favor.

The record discloses that on February 6, 1934, plaintiff filed her complaint for divorce, charging that defendant had been guilty of extreme and repeated cruelty. Defendant in his answer denied the acts of cruelty charged against him, and denied that the parties were married on December 8, 1921, as alleged in the bill. He asked for a jury trial. A jury was impaneled to try the question of whether defendant had been guilty of the acts of cruelty charged. The case was heard June 22, 1934, on this question, the jury returned a verdict finding defendant guilty of extreme and repeated cruelty as charged in the complaint. Afterward the court heard the case on the question of the property rights and the custody of the child of the parties, and July 26, 1934, a decree was entered in plaintiff's favor awarding her a divorce, the custody of the child and $200 "back support" for the minor child; that there was also due plaintiff for her solicitor's fees $57.50, which defendant was ordered to pay. No alimony was claimed and the decree forever released and discharged defendant in this respect.

The complaint alleged that the parties were married on the 8th of December, 1921, and defendant was charged with acts of cruelty on October 20, 1932, October 15, 1933, October 18, 1933, and November 18, 1933. On the trial of the case, on motion of plaintiff's attorney, plaintiff was given leave to amend her complaint by alleging that the date of the marriage was December 18, 1920, instead of December 8, 1921, as had theretofore been alleged. Plaintiff was also permitted to amend her bill by alleging another act of cruelty as having occurred on November 1, 1930.

About a month after the trial of the case and after the jury had returned its verdict, plaintiff on July 19, 1934, by leave of court, filed her amended complaint setting up the date of the marriage, the same charges of cruelty as she had set up in her original complaint, and more specifically praying for a decree of divorce. The prayer in the original bill was that the marriage "be annulled and set aside" and for general relief. The amendments to the original complaint, which the court permitted to be made on the hearing of the case before the jury, as above stated, were never in fact made, but both parties tried the case on the theory that the amendments had in fact been made. The amended complaint, however, inadvertently followed the original complaint in charging the date of the marriage and the acts of cruelty, therefore the act of cruelty charged on November 1, 1930, was not included in the amended complaint.

The defendant contends that "No ground for divorce was alleged in the original or amended complaint," and the argument seems to be that although plaintiff charged specific acts of cruelty in her complaint, "she could not claim that the assaults mentioned were of such an aggravated nature that they could be regarded as extreme and repeated cruelty. It is submitted therefore, that no cause for divorce was alleged in the complaint. The mere fact that a person is 'bruised' or even 'greatly bruised,' or is made 'sore' does not imply that she was treated with 'extreme cruelty.'" The complaint alleged that on the specific dates mentioned defendant struck plaintiff on the arms, body and face, leaving her sore and bruised, that he threw a lamp at plaintiff plaint by alleging that the date of the marriage was December 18, 1920, instead of December 8, 1921, as had theretofore been alleged. Plaintiff was also permitted to amend her bill by alleging another act of cruelty as having occurred on November 1, 1930.

About a month after the trial of the case and after the jury had returned its verdict, plaintiff on July 14, 1934, by leave of court, filed her amended complaint setting up the date of the marriage, the same charges of cruelty as she had set up in her original complaint, and more specifically praying for a decree of divorce. The prayer in the original bill was that the marriage "be annulled and set aside" and for general relief. The amendments to the original complaint, which the court permitted to be made on the hearing of the case before the jury, as above stated, were never in fact made, but both parties tried the case on the theory that the amendments had in fact been made. The amended complaint, however, inadvertently followed the original complaint in charging the date of the marriage and the acts of cruelty, therefore the act of cruelty charged on November 1, 1930, was not included in the amended complaint.

The defendant contends that "No ground for divorce was alleged in the original or amended complaint," and the argument seems to be that although plaintiff charged specific acts of cruelty in her complaint, "she could not claim that the assaults mentioned were of such an aggravated nature that they could be regarded as extreme and repeated cruelty. It is submitted therefore, that no cause for divorce was alleged in the complaint. 'The mere fact that a person is 'bruised' or even 'greatly bruised,' or is made 'sore' does not imply that she was treated with 'extreme cruelty.'" The complaint alleged that on the specific dates mentioned defendant struck plaintiff on the arms, body and face, leaving her sore and bruised; that he threw a lamp at plaintiff which struck her on the breast greatly bruising her; that he kicked her on the shin, bruising her, that he struck plaintiff, causing bruises on her body, face and arms. These allegations, if they were proved, are certainly sufficient to warrant the court in granting plaintiff a divorce. It was not necessary for plaintiff to allege in detail the evidence that she would adduce to prove the charges made.

Defendant next says that although plaintiff did not actually amend her complaint, as the court permitted her to do on the hearing, yet since both parties tried the case on the theory that such amendments had been made, the amendments will be regarded by the court as having been made. We think this is a sound contention and obviously plaintiff does not contend to the contrary.

A further point is made that plaintiff, by filing her amended complaint after the verdict (showing the date of the marriage to be December 8, 1921) which was inconsistent with the evidence which showed that the parties were married December 18, 1920, and eliminating the charge of cruelty of November 1, 1930, changed the charges of assault which were heard before the jury and altered the issues between the parties, "and therefore, she should be deemed to have abandoned all right to a decree for divorce on said verdict."

It is true that the pleadings in this case were very badly prepared by counsel for plaintiff. The original complaint alleged the parties were married on December 8, 1921. On the hearing before the jury the court allowed plaintiff's motion to amend her complaint by changing the date of the marriage to December 18, 1920, and adding the act of cruelty not referred to in the complaint, namely, November 1, 1930. Neither of these amendments was actually made although the case was tried on the theory that they had been made. About a month later plaintiff obtained leave to file an amended complaint, apparently with a view to praying more specifically for a decree of divorce which struck her on the breast greatly bruising her, that he kicked her on the shin, bruising her, that he struck plaintiff, causing bruises on her body, face and arms. These allegations, if they were proved, are certainly sufficient to warrant the court in granting plaintiff a divorce. It was not necessary for plaintiff to allege in detail the evidence that she would adduce to prove the charges made.

Defendant next says that although plaintiff did not actually amend her complaint, as the court permitted her to do on the hearing, yet since both parties tried the case on the theory that such amendments had been made, the amendments will be regarded by the court as having been made. We think this is a sound contention and obviously plaintiff does not contend to the contrary.

A further point is made that plaintiff, by filing her amended complaint after the verdict (showing the date of the marriage to be December 8, 1921) which was inconsistent with the evidence which showed that the parties were married December 16, 1924, and eliminating the charge of cruelty of November 1, 19[illegible], on which the charges of assault which were heard before the jury [illegible] between the parties, "and therefore, she should be deemed to have abandoned all right to a decree for divorce on such verdict."

It is true that the pleadings in this case were very badly prepared by counsel for plaintiff. The original complaint alleged the parties were married on December 8, 1921. On the hearing before the jury the court allowed plaintiff's motion to amend her complaint by changing the date of the marriage to December 1, 19[illegible], and adding the act of cruelty not referred to in the complaint, namely, November 1, 1930. Neither of these amendments was actually made although the case was tried on the theory that they had been made. About a month later plaintiff obtained leave to file an amended complaint, apparently with a view to praying more specifically for a decree of divorce and other matters; and in place of the amended complaint setting up the correct date of the marriage and the specific charges of cruelty concerning which evidence was produced before the jury, counsel apparently went back to the original complaint and made the same mistakes that were made in that complaint. So far as we have been able to ascertain, however, no point was made in this respect on the hearing. Both parties tried the case on the theory that plaintiff was seeking an absolute divorce; that she was alleging the marriage occurred December 13, 1920, and that defendant was guilty of cruelty, the first act being on November 1, 1930 Both parties having tried the case on this theory without complaint, defendant, after he has been defeated, will not be permitted in this court to shift his position and for the first time here contend that the evidence does not conform to the allegations of the amended complaint. The issues were properly tried and although the pleading was badly bungled, we will not disturb the decree so as to permit a better record to be made on a retrial of the case. Lyons v. Kanter, 285 Ill. 336

Defendant further contends that the verdict, finding the defendant guilty of extreme cruelty as charged in the complaint, is contrary to the evidence. And in support of this counsel say that plaintiff testified defendant assaulted her on November 1, 1930, and that she was corroborated by two witnesses as to this occurrence; that the second assault was on October 20, 1932; that plaintiff testified on that date she was driving with defendant, that he got angry and hit her over the arms and legs and left bruises; that she was not corroborated as to this occurrence, that plaintiff testified the third assault took place on October 15, 1933, when defendant threw and struck her with a "wrought iron lamp", which struck her in the breast. Plaintiff was corroborated in this matter by the testimony of the 11 year old daughter of the parties; that plaintiff testified the fourth assault occurred and other matters; and in place of the amended complaint setting up the correct date of the marriage and the specific charges of cruelty concerning which evidence was produced before the jury, counsel apparently went back to the original complaint and made the same mistakes that were made in that complaint. So far as we have been able to ascertain, however, no point was made in this respect on the hearing. Both parties tried the case on the theory that plaintiff was seeking an absolute divorce, that she was alleging the marriage occurred December 18, 1920, and that defendant was guilty of cruelty, the first act being on November 1, 1930. Both parties having tried the case on this theory without complaint, defendant, after he has been defeated, will not be permitted in this court to shift his position and for the first time here contend that the evidence does not conform to the allegations of the amended complaint. The issues were properly tried and although the pleading was badly bungled, we will not disturb the decree so as to permit a better record to be made on a retrial of the case. <u>Lyons v. Lantor</u>, 288 Ill. 336.

Defendant further contends that the verdict, finding the defendant guilty of extreme cruelty as charged in the complaint, is contrary to the evidence. And in support of this counsel say that plaintiff testified defendant assaulted her on November 1, 1930, and that she was corroborated by two witnesses as to this occurrence; that the second assault was on October 20, 1933, that plaintiff testified on that date she was driving with defendant, that he got angry and hit her over the arm with a lead and left bruises, that she was not corroborated as to this occurrence, that plaintiff testified the third assault took place on October 14, 1935, when defendant threw and struck her with a "wrought iron lamp", which struck her in the breast. Plaintiff was corroborated in this matter by the testimony of the 11 year old daughter of the parties; that plaintiff testified the fourth assault occurred

October 18, 1933, when defendant kicked her on the shin and bruised her. Plaintiff is also corroborated by the daughter as to this occurrence. Plaintiff testified that the fifth assault occurred November 15, 1933, when defendant pounded her and hit her on the face and body and left bruises; that she notified the hotel clerk where they were living; that a representative of the hotel called at the room. He testified that on the evening in question he received a call to go to the room occupied by plaintiff and defendant; that he "heard a commotion like somebody was knocked against the door," - that he heard plaintiff say, "Keep your hands off of me - leave me alone and get out of here," that a few minutes thereafter defendant came out and the witness followed him to the lobby; that a few minutes later plaintiff called him and he went to her room; she was crying and appeared to be upset; that plaintiff told him defendant had threatened to take her life.

Objection was made to this latter statement and the court told the witness to give the actual conversation. The witness then stated plaintiff told him defendant had "just beat her up" and threatened to kill her. There was no objection to this, nor any motion to strike out the evidence. The first part of the testimony of the witness, as to what he heard outside the room door and what he saw after going into the room, was competent evidence and the objection was properly overruled. His further testimony, out of the presence of defendant, as to what plaintiff told him was incompetent but it was not objected to. Defendant denied in detail all acts of cruelty charged against him.

The jury saw and heard the witnesses testify; it found that plaintiff was guilty of the acts of cruelty as charged in the complaint. This finding was confirmed by the chancellor, and upon a consideration of all the evidence in the record, we think the finding was warranted. Certain it is that we are unable to say the

October 18, 1933, when defendant kicked her on the chin and bruised her. Plaintiff is also corroborated by the daughter as to this occurrence. Plaintiff testified that the fifth assault occurred November 15, 1933, when defendant pounded her and hit her on the face and body and left bruises; that she notified the hotel clerk where they were living, that a representative of the hotel called at the room. He testified that on the evening in question he received a call to go to the room occupied by plaintiff and defendant; that he "heard a commotion like somebody was knocked against the door," - that he heard plaintiff say, "Keep your hands off of me - leave me alone and get out of here." that a few minutes thereafter defendant came out and the witness followed him to the lobby, that a few minutes later plaintiff called him and he went to her room, she was crying and appeared to be upset; that plaintiff told him defendant had threatened to take her life.

Objection was made to this latter statement and the court told the witness to give the actual conversation. The witness then stated plaintiff told him defendant had "just beat her up" and threatened to kill her. There was no objection to this, nor any motion to strike out the evidence. The first part of the testimony of the witness, as to what he heard outside the room door and what he saw after going into the room, was competent evidence and the objection was properly overruled. His further testimony, out of the presence of defendant, as to what plaintiff told him was incompetent but it was not objected to. Defendant denied in detail all acts of cruelty charged against him.

The jury saw and heard the witnesses testify. It found that plaintiff was guilty of the acts of cruelty as charged in the complaint. This finding was confirmed by the chancellor, and upon a consideration of all the evidence in the record, we think the finding was warranted. Certain it is that we are unable to say the finding was against the manifest weight of the evidence.

A further point is made that the court erred in decreeing "that back support for the child be paid to the plaintiff, and that defendant pay her permanent attorney's fees and money for the support of the child," and it is argued that the evidence shows defendant was indebted in a large amount and that plaintiff testified she had real and personal property but refused to give its value. We think there is no merit in this contention. Defendant had been living at expensive hotels and clubs; certainly the amounts he was ordered by the decree to pay are very small.

The decree of the Superior court of Cook county is affirmed.

DECREE AFFIRMED.

McSurely and Matchett, JJ., concur.

finding was against the manifest weight of the evidence.

A further point is made that the court erred in decreeing "that back support for the child be paid to the plaintiff, and that defendant pay her permanent attorney's fees and money for the support of the child," and it is argued that the evidence shows defendant was indebted in a large amount and that plaintiff testified she had real and personal property but refused to give its value. We think there is no merit in this contention. Defendant had been living at expensive hotels and clubs; certainly the amounts he was ordered by the decree to pay are very small.

The decree of the Superior court of Cook county is affirmed.

DECREE AFFIRMED.

McSurely and Matchett, JJ., concur.

38010

EDWIN D. BUELL, as Trustee, etc.,
(Plaintiff) Appellant,

vs.

WESTERN NEWS COMPANY,
(Defendant) Appellee.

APPEAL FROM CIRCUIT COURT OF COOK COUNTY.

84

280 I.A. 628[1]

MR. PRESIDING JUSTICE O'CONNOR DELIVERED THE OPINION OF THE COURT.

This action is brought by plaintiff to recover $125,287.19 claimed to be "the difference between the magazines delivered and those paid or accounted for." The defendant denied liability; there was a trial before the court without a jury, a finding and judgment in defendant's favor, and plaintiff appeals.

The record discloses that the DuPont Publishing Co., a corporation, published a monthly magazine known as "College Comics" and on December 11, 1925, wrote defendant a letter in which it appointed defendant, Western News Company, its agent for supplying the magazine to the trade. The letter stated that the DuPont company "further agree to bill this publication to the WESTERN NEWS COMPANY at 21½¢ per copy, and to pay all transportation in excess of one cent per pound on quantities shipped to Branches, and to credit all unsold copies at 21½¢ per copy, and to pay in addition 2 cents per pound to cover expenses on such unsold copies, ***

"This agency is given with the understanding that THE WESTERN NEWS COMPANY is to supply our publication to dealers" at certain designated prices, and that it would "send to dealers such quantities as may be agreed upon from time to time, with the privilege of returning all copies that they do not sell. ***

"THE WESTERN NEWS COMPANY is to make settlement for the first number delivered to them after receipt and publication of the FOURTH number, all subsequent numbers to be paid for on the

[illegible]

[illegible] L., as Trustee, etc., (Plaintiff) Appellant,

v.

WESTERN NEWS COMPANY, (Defendant) Appellee.

280 I.A. 628

This action is brought by plaintiff to recover $[illegible]7.19 claimed to be "the difference between the [illegible] delivered [illegible]

[illegible]

corporation, published a monthly magazine known as "[illegible]"

[illegible]

pointed defendant, Western News Company, [illegible] the magazine to the trade. [illegible] letter [illegible] company "further agrees to [illegible]

[illegible]

excess of one cent per pound on [illegible]

and to credit all unsold copies at [illegible]

addition 2 cents per pound to cover expenses [illegible]

copies.

[illegible]

certain designated prices, [illegible] quantities as may be agreed upon [illegible] the privilege of returning all copies that they do not sell. [illegible]

"THE WESTERN NEWS COMPANY is to make settlement for the first number delivered to them after receipt and publication of the FOURTH number, all subsequent numbers to be paid for on the same basis, all copies, regardless of date, returned prior to any or all payments to be deducted therefrom. In case the publication is discontinued, or the agency withdrawn the WESTERN NEWS COMPANY is to make such approximate settlements from time to time thereafter as the sales in their judgment may warrant, and final settlement four months after the date of the notice to dealers to return unsold copies. ***

"In the event of our not sending for and taking into our own custody all unsold copies within six months from date of publication, we authorize THE WESTERN NEWS COMPANY to dispose of all unsold copies which they may have on hand for what they will bring as old paper, and place the proceeds to our credit."

This letter was signed by the DuPont Company by its president, James Vincent Spadea, and apparently was accepted by the defendant, and both parties proceeded to carry out the terms of the letter, plaintiff publishing and delivering its magazine to defendant to distribute among news agents for sale.

August 1, 1926, the DuPont company was forced into bankruptcy, plaintiff was appointed trustee, and the publication ceased. During the time the magazine was being published and delivered to defendant, the DuPont company, in accordance with the letter above quoted from, billed the defendant for the magazine the total bills, amounting to $206,625.35, and from time to time defendant remitted to the DuPont company moneys aggregating $78,999.30. Defendant also made a charge for freight for copies of the magazine sent to the dealers of $2338.86. These two items total $81,338.16, which plaintiff deducts from the total amount billed to defendant as above stated, leaving a balance of $125,287.19, for which plaintiff sues.

Defendant made its last remittance December 22, 1926, to plaintiff, the trustee of the bankrupt, by sending its check for $1499.30, on the face of which the words, "Payment in full" were same basis, all copies, regardless of [illegible], returned prior to [illegible]

or all payments to be deducted [illegible]. In case the publication is discontinued, [illegible] is to [illegible] such approximate [illegible] after a the sales in their [illegible] way [illegible] ment four months after the [illegible] return unsold copies. ***

"In the event of our not [illegible] own custody all unsold copies within six months [illegible] publication, we [illegible] unsold copies which they may have on hand [illegible] as old paper, [illegible] to the proceeds [illegible] our credit."

This letter was signed by the Parent Company by its President, James Vincent Spadea, and apparently, was accepted by the defendant, and both parties proceeded to carry out the terms of the letter, plaintiff publishing, and delivering its magazine to defendant to distribute among news dealers for sale.

August 1, 1930, the Parent company [illegible] bankruptcy, plaintiff was [illegible] During the time the magazine was being published and delivered to defendant, the Parent company [illegible] letter [illegible] magazine [illegible] total [illegible] fendant remitted to the Parent company [illegible] $70,099.50. Defendant also [illegible] of the magazine sent to the dealers of [illegible] total $81,358.16, which plaintiff [illegible] billed to defendant as above stated, [illegible] a balance of $125,237.19, for which plaintiff sues.

Defendant made its last remittance December [illegible], 19[illegible], to plaintiff, the trustee of the bankrupt, by sending its check for $1669.50, on the face of which the words, "Payment in full" were written. Two days afterward plaintiff's counsel wrote a letter acknowledging receipt of the check, stating "This check is not at all satisfactory. You show on the statement, which you sent, that there was a balance due on October 23rd of $4923.48. You wrote me on October 21st that there then was a balance of $6476.78.

"I suggest that you get all your records in shape and I will arrange to have the Trustee go over your records with you for the purpose of ascertaining the correct amount due."

Three days afterward (December 27, 1926) defendant wrote plaintiff's counsel acknowledging receipt of the letter of December 24th, and saying: "In your letter of December 24th you acknowledge receipt of our check $1,499.30 in payment in full due the DuPont Publishing Co. and made payable to Edwin D. Buell, Trustee in Bankruptcy. Further, you say that the check is not at all satisfactory, and you mention some letters and balances.

"Under date of October 21st we wrote you that the account at that writing, showed a balance in favor of the publisher of $6,476.78. The following debits were placed against that credit balance, and invoices forwarded to the publishers office.

"October 21st,	To Hauling	$83.28
October 23rd,	Returns	1,415.34
October 23rd,	Returns	54.68
		1,553.30
Balance shown on statement rendered		4,923.48

Additional returns were charged against the above balance, as follows:

October 30th.	To Returns	51.67
30th		1,138.99
November 6th		719.97
13th		1,038.84
20th		279.63
December 4th		170.70
11th		15.34
18th		9.04
		$3,424.18
Check to balance -		$1,499.30."

written. [illegible]

acknowledging receipt of the check, stating "It is [illegible] not at all satisfactory. You show on the statement, which you sent, that there was a balance due on October 23rd of $4963.48. You wrote on October 21st that there then was a balance of $6476.78.

"I suggest that you get all your records in shape and I will arrange to have the Trustee go over your records with you for the purpose of ascertaining the correct amount due."

Three days afterward [illegible] defendant wrote plaintiff's counsel acknowledging receipt [illegible] of December 24th, and saying "In your letter of December [illegible] you acknowledge receipt of our check $1,4[illegible] in payment [illegible] the amount [illegible] Publishing Co. and made payable to [illegible] Trustee in Bankruptcy. Further, you say that the [illegible] is not satisfactory, and you mention some letters [illegible]

"Under date of October 21st we wrote [illegible] that the account at that writing, showed a balance in favor [illegible] of $6,476.78. The following debits were placed against that credit balance, and invoices forwarded to the [illegible]

"October 21st,	To Mailing	[illegible]
October 22nd,	Returns	1,415.54
October 23rd,	Returns	[illegible]
		[illegible]

Balance shown on statement rendered [illegible]

Additional returns were charged against the [illegible] others

October 30th.	To Returns	[illegible]
31st		[illegible]
November 6th		[illegible]
13th		[illegible]
20th		[illegible]
December 4th		[illegible]
11th		[illegible]
18th		[illegible]

Two days later, December 28, 1926, plaintiff's lawyer wrote defendant stating: "This is to acknowledge receipt of your letter of December 27th and the Trustee deposited your check for $1499.30, subject however, to the right of the Trustee to investigate this matter further in the future if he desires to do so."

Nothing further was done until nearly seven years thereafter when, on October 18, 1933, plaintiff brought this suit. About a month thereafter plaintiff filed a bill for discovery in the Circuit court of Cook county, in which it sought answers to certain interrogatories, only four of which are important.

One of these interrogatories was: How many copies of "College Comics" "were delivered" by the bankrupt to defendant, and another was, How many copies of "College Comics" "were billed" by the bankrupt to the defendant, "beginning with the month of February, 1925, to and including the month of July, 1926, setting forth the same separately by months and dates of billing?" Defendant answered showing that 961,048 copies of the magazine were delivered and bills for this number sent defendant, aggregating $206,625.35.

Another interrogatory asked for the cost of transportation "in excess of 1 cent per pound on quantities of said magazine shipped by The Western News Company to its branches," setting forth the same in detail. Defendant answered in detail, showing amounts aggregating $2338.86.

Another interrogatory was, "What cash payments were made by Western News Company" between February and July, 1926? Defendant answered this in detail, showing $77,500.

On the trial plaintiff introduced in evidence the interrogatories and the answers above mentioned and rested, from which it appears that plaintiff was charging defendant with the full billing

Two days later, December 29, 1926, plaintiff's lawyer wrote defendant stating: "This is to acknowledge receipt of your letter of December [illegible]7th and the Trustee deposited your check for $1499.3[illegible], subject however, to the right of the Trustee to investigate this matter further in the future if he desires to do so."

Nothing further was done until nearly seven years thereafter when, on October 18, 1933, plaintiff brought this suit. About a month thereafter plaintiff filed a bill for discovery in the Circuit court of Cook county, in which it sought answers to certain interrogatories, only four of which are important.

One of these interrogatories was "How many copies of "College Comics" "were delivered" by the bankrupt to defendant," and another was, How many copies of "College Comics" "were billed" by the bankrupt to the defendant, "beginning with the month of February, 1925, to and including the month of July, 1926, setting forth the same separately by months and dates of billing?" Defendant answered showing that 961,049 copies of the magazine were delivered and bills for this number sent defendant, aggregating $206,625.35.

Another interrogatory asked for the cost of transportation "in excess of 1 cent per pound on quantities of said magazine shipped by The Western News Company to its branches," setting forth the same in detail. Defendant answered in detail, showing amounts aggregating $2558.86.

Another interrogatory was, "What cash payments were made by Western News Company" between February and July, 1926?" Defendant answered this in detail, showing $77,600.

On the trial plaintiff introduced in evidence the interrogatories and the answers above mentioned and rested, from which it appears that plaintiff was charging defendant with the full billing price of the magazines, namely, $206,625.35, less certain costs of transportation and the $77,500 paid, to which it added the final check sent to plaintiff December 22, 1926, of $1499.30. No credit was given for any returned magazines, although Spadea, manager of the bankrupt, testified magazines were returned weekly and their number checked.

At the time plaintiff rested there was also in evidence a copy of the letter of December 11, 1925, written by the DuPont Publishing Co. to plaintiff, from which we have above quoted. Plaintiff contends that letter constitutes the contract between the parties, that it was "one of sale and return, and that the burden was on defendant to show first the right to return the particular copies, and then the actual facts of return. Neither of which showings was made;" that "Under such a contract, title in the magazines passed to the defendant upon delivery and billings by the plaintiff;" that "It was not enough for the defendant to sit idly by with its warehouses full of 'College Comics' and plead inability to sell. Before any copies were returnable it had to be shown, and shown by the defendant, that the copies sought to be returned were copies which the dealers could not sell." We think this contention cannot be sustained. We construe the letter or contract of December 11, 1925, to mean that the DuPont Co. appointed the Western News Co. as its distributing agent; that the magazines were not sold to the News company, but were merely delivered to it to be distributed, that when the magazines were sold by the dealers who were engaged in the business of selling magazines to the public, and when such dealers had remitted to the Western News Co. it would in turn remit the proper amount to the DuPont Co. There is nothing in the letter or contract that says the magazines were sold by the DuPont Co. to the Western News Co. On the contrary, that contract provides that the DuPont Co. agreed "to bill" the News company at 21½¢ per copy, price of the magazines, [illegible], $206,620.35, less actual [illegible] of transportation [illegible] paid, to which [illegible] check sent to plaintiff [illegible], 1926, of [illegible] was given for any returned [illegible] [illegible] [illegible] number [illegible].

At the [illegible] plaintiff [illegible] was also [illegible] as a copy of the letter of December 1, 1925, written [illegible] [illegible] [illegible] Co. to plaintiff, [illegible] [illegible] [illegible] parties, that it was "one of sale and return, and that the burden was on defendant to show first the [illegible] to return [illegible] [illegible] [illegible] [illegible] was made;" that "Under such a contract, [illegible] passed to the defendant upon delivery [illegible] plaintiff," that "It was not enough for the defendant to [illegible] with its warehouses full of 'College Comics' [illegible] [illegible] [illegible] [illegible] the defendant, that the copies [illegible] to be returned were [illegible] which the dealers could not sell." [illegible] be sustained. We construe the letter or contract of December 1, 1925, to mean that the DuPont Co. appointed the Western [illegible] [illegible] News company, but were merely delivered to it [illegible]; [illegible] in the business of selling magazines to the public, [illegible] dealers had remitted to the Western News Co. [illegible] the proper amount to the DuPont Co. There is nothing in the letter or contract that says the magazines were sold by the DuPont Co. to the Western News Co. On the contrary, that contract provides that the DuPont Co. agreed "to bill" the News company at 21½¢ per copy, and it agreed to pay all transportation charges in excess of 1¢ per pound on the magazines shipped to the branches or dealers and to credit all unsold copies at 21½¢ per copy. This was a mere matter of bookkeeping - keeping an account of the business - and does not show that the magazines were actually sold. Furthermore, the contract says that the Western News Co. is to supply the magazines "to dealers" at certain prices; that the News Company is to "send to dealers" such number of copies of the magazine as may be agreed upon between the News Company and the dealers with the privilege to the dealers of returning all copies they do not sell; that the News Company is to make settlements for the first number of copies of the magazine after receipt and publication of the fourth number; that all copies returned, regardless of the date, are to be deducted before payment is made; that in case the publication of the magazine is discontinued, final settlement must be made within four months after notice of such discontinuance has been given to the dealers to return said unsold copies. The contract further provides: "In the event of our not sending for and taking into our own custody all unsold copies within six months," the News Company was authorized to dispose of such unsold copies as old paper.

We think it obvious that it was not contemplated by the parties that the copies of the magazine were sold when they were delivered by the DuPont Company to the News Company. On the contrary, we think it appears that the News Company would be under no obligation to pay the Publishing company until and unless the magazines were sold by the dealers.

The cases of House v. Beak, 141 Ill. 290, and Belender v. Pearce, 238 Ill. App. 137, cited by plaintiff, are clearly distinguishable from the case at bar.

In the House case the facts were that merchants in Chicago sold goods to Lea & Co. Two accounts were kept of the transactions, and it agreed to pay all transportation charges in excess of [illegible] per [illegible] on the magazines shipped to the branches or dealers and to credit all unsold copies at 2½ [illegible] per copy. [illegible] are a matter of bookkeeping - keeping an account of the business - and does not show that the magazines were sold [illegible] [illegible], the contract says that the Western News Co. is to supply the magazines "to dealers" at certain prices [illegible] to "[illegible] dealers" such number of copies of the magazine [illegible] between the News Company and the dealers [illegible] dealers of returning all copies they do not sell, [illegible] Company is to make settlement for the first number of [illegible] the magazine after receipt and publication of the fourth number; that all copies returned, regardless of [illegible], are to be deducted before payment is made, that in case the publication of the magazine is discontinued, final settlement must be made within four months after notice of such discontinuance has been given to the dealers to return said unsold copies. The contract [illegible] provides "In the event of our not arranging for and [illegible] into our own custody all unsold copies which are returned, [illegible] [illegible] to dispose of such unsold copies [illegible] own account."

We think it obvious that it was not contemplated by the parties that the copies of the [illegible] were delivered by the DuPont Co. [illegible] [illegible] contrary, we think it [illegible] [illegible] obligation to pay the publisher [illegible] magazines were sold by the dealers.

The cases of [illegible], 1 [illegible] Ill. [illegible], and [illegible] v. Pearce, 238 Ill. App. 137, cited by plaintiff, are clearly distinguishable from the case at bar.

In the House case the facts were that merchants in Chicago sold goods to Lee & Co. Two accounts were kept of the transactions, one of them for goods sold and the other for goods consigned. A witness testified that the defendants were paid for the goods consigned when they were sold, "and what was not sold they would return." Plaintiff recovered in that case and on appeal to the Appellate court the judgment was affirmed on the ground that there was an account stated. The Supreme court also affirmed the judgment. Most of the discussion in the opinion was as to whether the books of account were admissible to prove the case. In passing on the question now before us the court said (p. 300): "The goods in question were not consigned to the defendants to be sold by the latter as agents of the plaintiffs, but the agreement between the parties was what is known as a contract 'on sale or return.'" In the instant case we think the News Company was but the distributing agent of the Publishing company. The magazines were not sold nor consigned; defendant was not to pay for the magazines when it received them; it was not expected to sell the magazines but only to distribute them to the dealers. Moreover, defendant was not bound under the contract to return the unsold magazines because the contract provided that the Publishing company should send for all unsold copies within six months, and if it did not do so the News Company was authorized to dispose of them as old paper.

In Belender v. Pearce, 238 Ill. App. 137, the question of the sale of a diamond ring was involved. Sutton, to whom the ring was delivered, never sold it but wore it himself. It was held the ring belonged to him and that his estate was liable.

In any view of the evidence in this case, plaintiff cannot recover. The undisputed evidence shows that the copies of the magazine were delivered by the DuPont Co. to the defendant during the spring and summer of 1926. August 1, 1926, the DuPont Co. was forced into bankruptcy. December 22, 1926, defendant sent its check to plaintiff, trustee in bankruptcy, for $1499.30, which was one of them for goods [illegible] and the other for goods consigned. A witness testified that the defendants were [illegible] for the [illegible] consigned when they were sold, "and what was not sold they would return." Plaintiff recovered in that case and on appeal to the appellate court the judgment was affirmed on the ground that there was an account stated. The Supreme Court also affirmed the judgment. Most of the discussion in the opinion was as to whether the books of account were admissible to prove the case. In passing on the question now before us the court said (p. [illegible]): "The goods in question were not consigned to the defendants to be sold by the latter as agents of the plaintiffs, but the agreement between the parties was what is known as a contract for sale or return." In the instant case we think the News Company was not the distributing agent of the Publishing company. The magazines were not [illegible] for consignment, defendant was not to pay for [illegible]. It received them; it was not expected to sell the magazines but only to distribute them to the dealers. Moreover, defendant was not bound under the contract to return the unsold [illegible] within [illegible] the contract provided that the Publishing company [illegible] for all unsold copies within six months, and if [illegible] the News Company was authorized to dispose of them as old paper.

In [illegible], the question of the sale of a die and ring was involved. [illegible] was delivered, never sold it but [illegible]. It [illegible] the ring belonged to him and that the [illegible] was [illegible].

In any view of the evidence in this case, plaintiff cannot recover. The undisputed evidence shows that [illegible] of the magazines were delivered by the DuPont Co. to the defendant during the spring and summer of 1926. August 1, 1926, the [illegible] was forced into bankruptcy. December 22, 1926 defendant sent its check to plaintiff, trustee in bankruptcy, for $1499.30, which was sent in full payment of the account. The words, "Payment in full" were written on the face of the chekk. A few days thereafter letters passed between the parties, from which we have above quoted, shewing that the defendant was tendering the check in full payment and that it was the correct amount. The last letter was written by plaintiff's lawyer December 29, 1926, in which he states that the trustee had deposited the check "subject however, to the right of the Trustee to investigate this matter further in the future if he desires to do so." Apparently the trustee did not desire to investigate the matter further, for after this letter was written nothing was done for almost seven years. In the spring of 1931 defendant, the distributor of a large number of other magazines, destroyed in the regular course of business all books and records up to and including 1929 except the ledger containing the account in question. The bookkeeper had died before the trial. The only evidence plaintiff adduced on the hearing was the answers made by defendant to plaintiff's interrogatories. In these interrogatories plaintiff asked defendant to state the number of copies of the magazine the DuPont Co. had delivered and the amount of the billings. It also asked the amount of freight chargeable against the DuPont Co., and the amount of the payments made by the defendant. The answers to these interrogatories were obtained solely from the ledger account kept by the News Company. In the interrogatories filed plaintiff did not ask defendant how many magazines had been returned. If he wanted to find out the true situation, good faith required that this question be asked, the answer would have shown that the account had been settled. It was stated when defendant sent its check December 22, 1926, and in letters above quoted from written a few days thereafter. It would be most unjust and inequitable to permit plaintiff to obtain from defendant's own book information from which plaintiff could claim there was a balance due, and then

sent in full payment of t e acc unt . . . . . . 1.11."
were written on the ... e . . ecame. A ... . -
ters passed between the parties, ... noted,
showing that the defendant was ... ... in full payment
and that it was the correct amount. ... ... was given
by plaintiff's lawyer December 2 , 19 , in which he states that
the trustee had deposited the check "without however, ... the right
of the Trustee to investigate this matter further in the future if
he desires to do so." Apparently the trustee did not ... to
investigate the matter further, for after this letter was written
nothing was done for almost seven years. ... ...
defendant, the distributor of a large ... ... magazines,
destroyed in the regular course of business all books and records
up to and including 1927 except the ledger ... ... account
in question. The bookkeeper ... ... The only
evidence plaintiff adduced on the ... ... was ... ... by
defendant to plaintiff's interrogatories ... ... interrogatories
plaintiff asked defendant to state ... ... of copies of the
magazine the DuPont Co. did deliver ... ... amount of the billings.
It also asked the amount of freight charges ... against the ... ont
Co., and the amount of the payments made by the defendant ...
answers to these interrogatories were obtained solely from the ledger
account kept by the News Company. In the interrogatories filed
plaintiff did not ask defendant how many ... ... been returned
If he wanted to find out the true ... ... filed
that this question be asked, the answer ... ... shown ... ...
account had been settled. It was at ... ... sent its
check December 22, 1926, as in letters above noted from written
a few days thereafter. It would be most unjust and inequitable to
permit plaintiff to obtain from defendant's own book information
from which plaintiff could claim there was a balance due, and then

object to the admission in evidence of the same book, which showed the account settled in full. We think the ledger was properly admitted in evidence. A. L. Neis, who was manager of defendant in 1926, but who was no longer connected with it at the time of the trial, testified that he was familiar with the pages of the ledger involved and that from this ledger defendant had made settlements with plaintiff during the course of its business dealings, that they were always found to be correct. In addition to this testimony, Joseph Spadea, circulation manager, was called by the defendant and testified that the Company regularly received statements from the defendant News Company of unsold magazines which it checked up and always found correct. There is no evidence to the contrary.

Plaintiff offered no books or records of the bankrupt nor did he call any witness who was connected with the DuPont Company before it was forced into bankruptcy, nor is there any showing why he failed to do anything in this regard. All that appears is that at the close of defendant's evidence it was stipulated that if the trustee were present he would testify that he "found no books (of the bankrupt) when he took possession." There was no showing what plaintiff did toward endeavoring to find the books or records, and it is obvious a concern doing business of the magnitude of that of the DuPont Company would have some records. It is also obvious that it must have had a number of employees. None of them was called by plaintiff, nor is there any explanation why he failed to do so. On the contrary, Joseph Spadea was called by defendant and testified that he was then living in Detroit but in the year 1926 was manager of the circulation department of the DuPont Company and that the account was correct.

object to the [illegible] of the same book, [illegible] the account settled in full. [illegible] the ledger was ad- mitted in evidence. [illegible] manager of defendant in 1896, but [illegible] no longer connected with it at the time of the trial, testified that he was familiar with the pages of the ledger involved and [illegible] with plaintiff during the course of its business dealings; that they were always found to be correct. In addition to this testi- mony, [illegible] circulation manager, was called by the defend- ant [illegible] the company regularly received statements from the [illegible] and it was [illegible] company to avoid mistakes [illegible] it checked up [illegible] always found correct. There is no evidence to the contrary.

Plaintiff offered no books or records of the [illegible] nor did he call any witness who was connected with the Dupont Company before it was forced into bankruptcy, nor is there any showing why he [illegible] to do anything in this regard. At that [illegible] that at the close of defendant's evidence it was stipulated [illegible] the trustee were present he would testify that he found no [illegible] (i. e. the bankrupt) when he took possession. [illegible] were [illegible] what plaintiff did toward [illegible] books or [illegible] and it is obvious a concern doing business of the magnitude [illegible] of the [illegible] company would have some records. It is [illegible] obvious that it must have had a number of [illegible] by plaintiff, nor is there any explanation why he [illegible] On the contrary, Joseph Speden was called [illegible] testified that he was then [illegible] was manager of the circulation department [illegible] the Dupont Company [illegible] that the account was correct.

A consideration of all the evidence in the record leaves no doubt that the account had been paid in full.

A great deal is said in the briefs of both sides as to whether the copies of the magazines returned to plaintiff were "unsold magazines." Just how a magazine which had been sold could be returned, we are unable to comprehend. Obviously the magazines returned could be nothing but unsold magazines. Under the contract defendant was not required, as plaintiff contends, to make an effort to go out and sell the magazines, or pay for them. And this was the construction of the parties, because there is evidence that magazines were returned without any objection made that defendant had not diligently tried to sell them. There is nothing to that effect in the contract nor in the record. Under any view of the law and the evidence in this case, the only judgment that could stand would be one for defendant.

The judgment of the Circuit court of Cook county is affirmed.

JUDGMENT AFFIRMED.

McSurely and Matchett, JJ., concur.

A consideration of all the evidence in the record leaves no doubt that the account had been paid in full.

A great deal is said in the briefs of both sides as to whether the custom of the magazine returned to plaintiff were "unsold magazines." Just how a magazine which had been sold would be returned, we are unable to comprehend. Obviously the magazines returned could be nothing but unsold magazines. Under the contract defendant was not required, as plaintiff contends, to make an effort to go out and sell the magazines, or any for them, and this was the construction of the parties, because [illegible] magazines were returned without any objection made that defendant had not diligently tried to sell them. There is nothing to that effect in the contract nor in the record. Under any view of the law and the evidence in this case, the only judgment that could stand would be one for defendant.

The judgment of the Circuit court of Cook county is affirmed.

AFFIRMED.

McSurely and Matchett, JJ., concur.

38098

NATIONAL LIFE INSURANCE COMPANY, a Corporation,
Appellee,

vs.

DIANA FELDMAN et al.,
Appellants.

APPEAL FROM SUPERIOR COURT OF COOK COUNTY.

857

280 I.A. 628²

MR. PRESIDING JUSTICE O'CONNOR DELIVERED THE OPINION OF THE COURT.

On October 14, 1933, the National Life Insurance Company filed its bill to foreclose a trust deed given to secure an indebtedness of $40,000, evidenced by a number of notes, some of which thadbeen paid. June 21, 1934, a decree of foreclosure was entered as prayed for. The decree approves the master's report and supplemental report, but neither of the reports is in the record before us. Afterward the master in chancery sold the property pursuant to the decree, and on December 3, 1934, filed his report of sale and distribution, showing a deficiency of $4189.91. On the same day certain defendants filed objections "to the Deficiency," one of the objections being that on January 2, 1934, complainant, the National Life Insurance Company, caused judgment to be confessed in its favor in the Municipal court against the makers of a $2,000 note secured by the trust deed in foreclosure, the judgment being for more th n $3,000 (the face of the note, interest, costs, etc.), and that the judgment was still outstanding and unpaid.

January 9, 1935, the master's report of sale and distribution and the objections thereto came on for hearing. The objectors introduced in evidence the judgment entered in the Municipal court as above stated; the court overruled the objections, entered a decree approving the report, found that there had been paid more than $1000 on the deficiency, and a deficiency decree was entered for the balance

38098

NATIONAL LIFE INSURANCE CO. [illegible], a Corporation, Appellee,

v.

DIANA [illegible] et al., Appellants

280 I.A. 628

[illegible] OPINION [illegible]

On October 24, 19[illegible], the National Life [illegible]

filed its bill to foreclose a trust deed [illegible] securing an in-

debtedness of $40,000, evidenced by a number of notes, [illegible]

which had been paid. June 2, 19[illegible]4, a decree of [illegible] was

entered as prayed for. The decree [illegible] report

and supplemental report, but [illegible] reports [illegible] the

report [illegible]

property pursuant to the decree, [illegible] filed

his report of sale and distribution [illegible]

$4189.91. On the same day certain defendants filed objections "to

the Deficiency," [illegible]

[illegible]

judgment to be confessed in [illegible] court

against the makers of a [illegible] and in

foreclosure, the judgment [illegible]

the note, interest, costs, [illegible] still

outstanding and unpaid.

January 9, 19[illegible] [illegible]

tion and the objections thereto [illegible]

introduced in evidence [illegible] as

above stated, the court overruled the objections, entered a decree

approving the report, found that there had been paid more than 1,00

on the deficiency, and a deficiency decree was entered for the balance of $3177.37.

Defendants complain only of the deficiency decree on the ground that they should have received credit for the amount of the judgment entered against them in the Municipal court for the reason that the amount of the note on which judgment was confessed in the Municipal court was also included in the foreclosure decree.

The judgment of the Municipal court was entered January 2, 1934, while the decree of foreclosure was not entered until June 21, 1934. The proper way for defendants to have raised their question was to produce their evidence before the master who was hearing the case or before the chancellor before the decree was entered. But waiving the question of procedure, we think there is no merit in the contention made. For many years it has been held by repeated decisions of our Supreme court that a mortgagee has several remedies which he may pursue to enforce the payment of his debt. Simultaneously or concurrently he may sue the mortgagor on the note, file a bill of foreclosure, etc. Rohrer v. Deatherage, 336 Ill. 450. Of course there can be but one satisfaction.

The payment of the judgment or the satisfaction of the decree discharges the indebtedness, but the judgment not having been paid there is no merit in defendants' contention and the decree of the Circuit court of Cook county is affirmed.

DECREE AFFIRMED.

McSurely and Matchett, JJ., concur.

of $3177.37.

Defendants complain only of the deficiency decree on the ground that they should have received credit for the amount of the judgment entered against them in the Municipal court for the reason that the amount of the note on which judgment was confessed in the Municipal court was also included in the foreclosure decree.

The judgment of the Municipal court was entered January [illegible], 1934, while the decree of foreclosure was not entered until June 21, 1934. The proper way for defendants to have raised this question was to produce their evidence before the master who was hearing the case or before the chancellor before the decree was entered. But waiving the question of procedure, we think there is no merit in the contention made. For many years it has been held by repeated decisions of our Supreme court that a mortgagee has several remedies which he may pursue to enforce the payment of his debt. Simultaneously or concurrently he may sue the mortgagor on the note, file a bill of foreclosure, etc. [illegible] Of course there can be but one satisfaction.

The payment of the judgment or the satisfaction of the decree discharges the indebtedness, but the judgment not having been paid there is no merit in defendants' contention and the decree of the Circuit court of Cook county is affirmed.

DECREE AFFIRMED.

McSurely and Matchett, JJ., concur.

38055

WILLIAM J. DOYLE,
Appellee,

vs.

THE PRUDENTIAL INSURANCE COMPANY OF AMERICA, a Corporation,
Appellant.

APPEAL FROM MUNICIPAL COURT OF CHICAGO.

280 I.A. 628[3]

MR. JUSTICE McSURELY DELIVERED THE OPINION OF THE COURT.

Defendant appeals from a judgment of $1500 entered upon a verdict in a trial wherein plaintiff brought suit upon insurance policies issued by defendant upon the life of Maggie Doyle, plaintiff's wife.

Defendant issued three policies on the life of Maggie Doyle, but subsequently, without additional premium, agreed to pay double indemnity in case of death "caused as a result of bodily injuries solely through accidental means." The insured died in August, 1933, and defendant paid to plaintiff the face amount of the policies. This suit is for the additional amount of insurance, plaintiff claiming that the insured met her death as a result of bodily injuries solely through accidental means. Defendant denied that she so came to her death, claiming her death was due to bronchial pneumonia and heart trouble, and the issue of fact in this respect was presented.

In May or on June 23, 1933, (both dates are given) insured was burned on her neck and shoulder, and plaintiff says this caused her death, which occurred on the 17th of August following. The evidence for plaintiff tends to show that on the morning of June 23rd, or in May, when plaintiff awakened, he saw that his wife's dress was on fire around her neck, caused, probably, by insured falling asleep with a lighted cigarette in her mouth which fell on her neck. She suffered three burns in the region of the shoulder; the largest was a second degree burn about three inches in length, about two inches

38055

WILLIAM J. DOYLE,
Appellee,

vs.

THE PRUDENTIAL INSURANCE COMPANY OF AMERICA, a Corporation,
Appellant.

APPEAL FROM [illegible] COURT OF CHICAGO.

280 I.A. 628

MR. JUSTICE McSURELY DELIVERED THE OPINION OF THE COURT.

Defendant appeals from a judgment of $1500 entered upon a verdict in a trial wherein plaintiff brought suit upon insurance policies issued by defendant upon the life of Maggie Doyle, plaintiff's wife.

Defendant issued three policies on the life of Maggie Doyle, but subsequently, without additional premium, agreed to pay double indemnity in case of death "caused as a result of bodily injuries solely through accidental means." The insured died in August, 1933, and defendant paid to plaintiff the face amount of the policies. This suit is for the additional amount of insurance, plaintiff claiming that the insured met her death as a result of bodily injuries solely through accidental means. Defendant denied that she so came to her death, claiming her death was due to bronchial pneumonia and heart trouble, and the issue of fact in this respect was presented.

In May or on June 23, 1933, (the dates are given) insured was burned on her neck and shoulder, which plaintiff says was the cause of her death, which occurred on the 17th of August following. The evidence for plaintiff tends to show that on the morning of June 23rd, or in May, when plaintiff awakened, he saw that his wife's dress was on fire around her neck, caused, probably, by insured falling asleep with a lighted cigarette in her mouth which fell on her neck. She suffered three burns in the region of the shoulder, the largest was a second degree burn about three inches in length, about two inches in width at the center, running to a point, there was also a burn on the back of the right shoulder over the shoulder-blade, somewhat smaller than the palm of the hand, on the back of the right upper arm there was a superficial burn about the size of a silver dollar, plaintiff applied vaseline and medicine to the burns; the insured did not remain in bed but prepared breakfast, no doctor treated the burns; for about ten days she applied medicines which plaintiff procured; a scab then formed which fell off about the first of August and she no longer suffered pain from the burns, she did her daily housework from the time she was burned until the date of her death. When plaintiff returned to his home August 17, 1933, he found his wife dead in bed. No autopsy was performed at that time and the death certificate made by the coroner's physician states that in his opinion the cause of death was the result of a second degree burn of the neck, a chronic myocarditis and a chronic nephritis.

In May of 1934, by agreement, the insured's body was disinterred and a post mortem examination made by Doctors Greenspahn, Moore and Richardson. Doctors Greenspahn and Richardson testified, giving in great detail the results of the autopsy. Both apparently agree that deceased had suffered from bronchial pneumonia. Dr. Greenspahn, in answer to a hypothetical question, said "that there might or could be a causal connection between the burn suffered *** in May of 1933 and her subsequent death in August, 1933." Dr. Richardson testified that he found that the deceased had bronchial pneumonia and gave his opinion that the burns alone could not be responsible for her death. The Doctor further said that a burn that remains open for fifty-one days is not necessarily severe but may be rather mild; that he had "never heard of a person dying from a burn of that size."

The plaintiff had the burden of proving that the insured

in width at the center, running to a point, there was also a burn on the back of the right shoulder over the shoulder-blade, somewhat smaller than the palm of the hand, on the back of the right upper arm there was a superficial burn about the size of a silver dollar; plaintiff applied vaseline and medicine to the burns, the insured did not remain in bed but prepared breakfast, no doctor treated the burns; for about ten days she applied medicines which plaintiff procured; a scab then formed which fell off about the first of August and she no longer suffered pain from the burns, she did her daily housework from the time she was burned until the date of her death. When plaintiff returned to his home August 17, 1933, he found his wife dead in bed. No autopsy was performed at that time and the death certificate made by the coroner's physician states that in his opinion the cause of death was the result of a second degree burn of the neck, a chronic myocarditis and a chronic nephritis.

In May of 1934, by agreement, the insured's body was disinterred and a post mortem examination made by Doctors Greenspahn, Moore and Richardson. Doctors Greenspahn and Richardson testified, giving in great detail the results of the autopsy; both apparently agree that deceased had suffered from bronchial pneumonia. Dr. Greenspahn, in answer to a hypothetical question, said "that there might or could be a causal connection between the burn suffered *** in May of 1933 and her subsequent death in August, 1933." Dr. Richardson testified that he found that the deceased had bronchial pneumonia and gave his opinion that the burns alone could not be responsible for her death. The Doctor further said that a burn that remains open for fifty-one days is not necessarily severe but may be rather mild; that he had "never heard of a person dying from a burn of that size."

* * * The plaintiff had the burden of proving that the insured

sustained bodily injury solely through external, violent and accidental means, resulting in the death of the insured. Plaintiff failed in this respect. The only evidence to sustain his claim was Dr. Greenspahn's opinion that there "might or could be" a causal connection between the burns and the insured's death. Mere surmise or conjecture that injuries might result in death cannot be regarded as proof of an existing fact or of a future condition that will result. Stevens v. Illinois Central R. R. Co., 306 Ill. 370.

In instructions to the jury it was assumed that there was evidence that if the "burn superinduced a condition * as myocarditis or disease of the heart or chronic nephritis, that is, a disease of the kidney, or pneumonia, then of course this plaintiff is entitled to recover." There is no evidence that the burn superinduced the disease of the heart or kidney, or pneumonia. The most that could be said was the testimony that there might be "a causal connection between the burn and the death."

Defendant says there was no evidence to show that the burn was caused by accidental means and therefore plaintiff's case is based upon a presumption that the burn caused the death, which is based upon the presumption that the burn was caused by accidental means. As we have said, the evidence tended to show that the insured fell asleep with a lighted cigarette, which set fire to the bed clothes and her garment, causing the burn. This was sufficient evidence that the burn was accidental, without the help of any presumption.

For the reason that the verdict was against the manifest weight of the evidence, and because of the misleading instruction referred to, the judgment is reversed and the cause is remanded.

REVERSED AND REMANDED.

O'Connor, P. J., and Matchett, J., concur.

sustained bodily injury solely through external, violent and accidental means, resulting in the death of the insured. Plaintiff failed in this respect. The only evidence to sustain his claim was Dr. Greenspahn's opinion that there "might or could be" a causal connection between the burns and the insured's death. Mere surmise or conjecture that injuries might result in death cannot be regarded as proof of an existing fact or of a future condition that will result. Stevens v. Illinois Central R. R. Co., 305 Ill. 370.

In instructions to the jury it was assumed that there was evidence that if the "burn superinduced a condition * as myocarditis or disease of the heart or chronic nephritis, that is, a disease of the kidney, or pneumonia, then of course this plaintiff is entitled to recover." There is no evidence that the burn superinduced the disease of the heart or kidney, or pneumonia. The most that could be said was the testimony that there might be "a causal connection between the burn and the death."

Defendant says there was no evidence to show that the burn was caused by accidental means and therefore plaintiff's case is based upon a presumption that the burn caused the death, which is based upon the presumption that the burn was caused by accidental means. As we have said, the evidence tended to show that the insured fell asleep with a lighted cigarette, which set fire to the bed clothes and her garment, causing the burn. This was sufficient evidence that the burn was accidental, without the help of any presumption.

For the reason that the verdict was against the manifest weight of the evidence, and because of the misleading instruction referred to, the judgment is reversed and the cause is remanded.

REVERSED AND REMANDED.

O'Connor, P. J., and Matchett, J., concur.

38104

NELLIE I. COGGER, Appellee,

vs.

THE PRUDENTIAL INSURANCE COMPANY OF AMERICA, a Corporation, Appellant.

APPEAL FROM MUNICIPAL COURT OF CHICAGO.

877

280 I.A. 628[4]

MR. JUSTICE McSURELY DELIVERED THE OPINION OF THE COURT.

Plaintiff suing upon a life insurance policy issued by defendant on the life of Ward C. Cogger, upon trial had a verdict for $2963.85, and the defendant appeals from the judgment for this amount.

Plaintiff alleged the death of the insured on April 26, 1926, and defendant argues that no such proof was made. It seems to be conceded that the insured disappeared on that date and has never since been heard of. Death will be presumed after seven years of disappearance. Kennedy v. Modern Woodmen, 243 Ill. 560.

The contested question is, Was there sufficient evidence for the jury to find that he died on or about the date he disappeared, namely, on April 26, 1926? Disappearance alone raises no legal presumption of death at the time of disappearance. There must be certain circumstances appearing from which it may be reasonably presumed that one is deceased on or about the date of disappearance. In Donovan v. Major, 253 Ill. 179, it is said that among the circumstances which give rise to a presumption of death are, threats to commit suicide, the condition of health, that one is afflicted with some disease likely to undermine his constitution, and generally one's habits, disposition, pecuniary circumstances and family relations are all proper for consideration. In Reedy v. Milligan, 155 Ill. 636, it was said the condition of health of a person when last seen becomes an important subject of inquiry, or any conditions from which a presumption as to the continuance or

62

38104

NELLIE I. COGGER,
Appellee,

vs.

THE PRUDENTIAL INSURANCE COMPANY OF AMERICA, a Corporation,
Appellant.

APPEAL MUNICIPAL
COURT OF CHICAGO.

280 I.A. 628

MR. JUSTICE McSURELY DELIVERED THE OPINION OF THE COURT.

Plaintiff suing upon a life insurance policy issued by defendant on the life of Ward C. Cogger, upon trial had a verdict for $2963.85, and the defendant appeals from the judgment for this amount.

Plaintiff alleged the death of the insured on April 26, 1926, and defendant argues that no such proof was made. It seems to be conceded that the insured disappeared on that date and has never since been heard of. Death will be presumed after seven years of disappearance. [illegible] v. [illegible] Woodmen, 243 Ill. 560.

The contested question is, Was there sufficient evidence for the jury to find that he died on or about the date he disappeared, namely, on April 26, 1926? Disappearance alone raises no legal presumption of death at the time of disappearance. There must be certain circumstances appearing from which it may be reasonably presumed that one is deceased on or about the date of disappearance. In Donovan v. [illegible], 253 Ill. 179, it is said that among the circumstances which give rise to a presumption of death are, threats to commit suicide, the condition of health, that one is afflicted with some disease likely to undermine his constitution, and generally one's habits, dispositions, pecuniary circumstances and family relations are all proper for consideration. In Reedy v. Millizen, 155 Ill. 636, it was said the condition of health of a person when last seen becomes an important subject of inquiry, or any conditions from which a presumption as to the continuance or destruction of life would arise, are proper to be considered. In <u>Whiting v. Nicholl</u>, 46 Ill. 230, it was said that the death of a person who had not been heard from for eight years would be presumed to have occurred soon after the time of his disappearance, from the fact that he had frequently declared his intention to commit suicide. And to the same effect are <u>Benjamin v. District Grand Lodge etc.</u>, 171 Cal. 260, and <u>Mutual Life Ins. Co. v. Louisville Trust Co.</u>, 207 Ky. 654.

The evidence tended to show that the insured, Ward C. Cogger, had been very sick for six weeks prior to his disappearance and was very melancholy, there was testimony that he had threatened to commit suicide, that he was very gloomy and in poor health. Plaintiff testified that the insured was an engineer for a box factory; that he left the house on the morning of April 26, 1926, as though he were going to work; she never saw him again and has heard nothing of or concerning him since that date, she advertised for him in the Daily News and had his disappearance broadcast; she went to many persons trying to locate him - to the secretary of his lodge; she went to all his relatives and every time she heard of someone unknown or unidentified she would go to the morgue; prior to the day of his disappearance he had been very sick for six weeks, was very pale, he would sit around for a couple of hours, he was very melancholy, would get up every night at two or two-thirty o'clock and want to shave or cook or read, or something else; he had crying spells almost every evening and seemed to be worn out. Another witness testified to the same effect, saying that about a month before he disappeared Cogger became very melancholy; "he would sit around and cry, and would say, 'I will be there'"; that he had these crying spells about three or four times a week and would get despondent over his sickness and say, "I am so despondent - I am going to end it all. I am going to tie a sack of coal to my destruction of life would arise, are proper to be considered. In Whiting v. Nicholl, 46 Ill. 230, it was said that the death of a person who had not been heard from for eight years would be presumed to have occurred soon after the time of his disappearance, from the fact that he had frequently declared his intention to commit suicide. And to the same effect are Benjamin v. District Grand Lodge etc., 171 Cal. 260, and Mutual Life Ins. Co. v. Louisville Trust Co., 207 Ky. 654.

The evidence tended to show that the insured, Ward C. Cogger, had been very sick for six weeks prior to his disappearance and was very melancholy; there was testimony that he had threatened to commit suicide, that he was very gloomy and in poor health. Plaintiff testified that the insured was an engineer for a box factory; that he left the house on the morning of April 26, 1926, as though he were going to work. She never saw him again and has heard nothing of or concerning him since that date. She advertised for him in the Daily News and had his disappearance broadcast; she went to many persons trying to locate him - to the secretary of his lodge; she went to all his relatives and every time she heard of someone unknown or unidentified she would go to the morgue; prior to the day of his disappearance he had been very sick for six weeks, was very pale; he would sit around for a couple of hours, he was very melancholy, would get up every night at two or two-thirty o'clock and want to shave or cook or read, or something else; he had crying spells almost every evening and seemed to be worn out. Another witness testified to the same effect, saying that about a month before he disappeared Cogger became very melancholy, "he would sit around and cry, and would say, 'I will be there'", that he had these crying spells about three or four times a week and would get despondent over his stomach and say, "I am so despondent - I am going to end it all. I am going to tie a sack of coal to my body and throw myself into Bubbly creek."

These were circumstances proper for the jury to consider in determining whether or not he committed suicide about the time of his disappearance. We cannot say that the jury's conclusion in this respect is manifestly against the weight of the evidence.

Defendant says that the policy was forfeited because of the failure to pay the premium which fell due April 21, 1927. By a period of grace the payment of the premium was extended to May 22, 1927. Although there is contrary evidence, there is sufficient to justify the jury in finding that the premium was tendered to defendant's representative on May 10, 1927, and again on May 19th, when the tender was made to one of defendant's assistant superintendents. There was believable testimony that both of these representatives refused to accept the premium, giving as a reason that they would not accept the money until plaintiff had produced Ward Cogger. The jury could weigh this evidence in the light of the testimony of Mr. Stubbe, one of defendant's representatives, that he did not know the Cogger policy was in existence and had never discussed the matter with Mrs. Cogger, but who retracted this when shown a paper in which he had noted the policy and also the disappearance of the insured. Defendant's refusal to accept the premium so tendered estopped it from declaring a forfeiture of the policy for nonpayment of this premium. Travelers' Ins. Co. v. Pulling, 159 Ill. 603; Wardlow v. Grand Lodge Brotherhood, 245 Ill. App. 142; Hatch v. Grand Lodge Brotherhood, 233 Ill. App. 495. Cases cited by defendant do not hold to the contrary.

The court refused to permit defendant to file an additional affidavit of merits in which it was alleged that Ward C. Cogger was not married to Nellie Cogger at the date of the issuance of the insurance policy. The record shows that she was married to the insured on March 20, 1924, and that they were not married but

engaged to be married when the policy was issued. The policy provides that it shall be incontestable after one year from date, except for non-payment of premium. Also, by statute, such a policy is declared to be incontestable after two years from its date, except for violations of certain conditions of the policy not material here. If defendant had the right to avoid the policy, that right expired long before Ward Collier disappeared. The court properly denied leave to file the additional affidavit of merits.

Complaint is made of the instructions, which were oral, but we are of the opinion that, taken as a whole, they fairly presented the law with reference to the evidence in the case. Moreover, defendant failed to specify any grounds for the objection to the instructions before the jury retired. Lichtenhan v. Prudential Ins. Co., 191 Ill. App. 412; Pecararo v. Halberg, 246 Ill. 95.

Upon the record we see no sufficient reason to reverse the judgment, and it is affirmed.

AFFIRMED.

O'Connor, P. J., and Matchett, J., concur.

engaged to be married when the policy was issued. The policy provides that it shall be incontestable after one year from date, except for non-payment of premium. Also, by statute, such a policy is declared to be incontestable after two years from its date, except for violations of certain conditions of the policy not material here. If defendant had the right to avoid the policy, the right expired long before Ward Conner disappeared. The court properly denied leave to file the additional affidavit of merits.

Complaint is made of the instructions, which were oral, but we are of the opinion that, taken as a whole, they fairly presented the law with reference to the evidence in the case. Moreover, defendant failed to specify any grounds for the objection to the instructions before the jury retired. [illegible] Co., 201 Ill. App. 402; [illegible], 248 Ill. [illegible]

Upon the record we see no sufficient reason to reverse the judgment, and it is affirmed.

O'Connor, P. J., and Matchett, J., concur.

38065

ARTHUR G. SCHROEDER,
Appellee,

vs.

MARIA MARX,
Appellant.

APPEAL FROM SUPERIOR COURT OF COOK COUNTY.

88 77

280 I.A. 629

MR. JUSTICE MATCHETT DELIVERED THE OPINION OF THE COURT.

This is an appeal from a decree of foreclosure entered December 7, 1934. The cause was heard upon exceptions to the report of a master to whom it had been referred. The exceptions were overruled and a decree entered finding that $34,962.38, with interest, etc., was due, and directing a sale in case of default in payment.

The bill was filed June 1, 1933. It averred the execution on November 10, 1934, of a principal note for $30,000, due five years after date, together with interest coupons, the execution and delivery of the trust deed on the same date, the execution of an extension agreement on November 7, 1929, extending the time of payment of the principal note for five years from November 10, 1929, and the execution and delivery of interest notes representing interest at six per cent payable semi-annually, which would accrue upon the principal note during the period of time for which it was extended.

The bill averred that interest coupon No. A-17 for $900 fell due May 10, 1933, and it was not paid, and such default continuing, complainant (as the extension agreement provided he might) declared the whole amount due and payable and filed the bill to foreclose.

The only defense averred in the answer of defendant was, in substance, that on or about March 1, 1933, complainant and his agent had agreed to reduce the rate of interest from six to three per cent.

38065

ARTHUR G. SCHROEDER,
Appellant,

vs.

MARIA MARX,
Appellee.

280 I.A. 629

MR. JUSTICE MATCHETT delivered [illegible]

This is an appeal from a decree of [illegible] entered December 7, 1934. The cause was heard [illegible] of a master to whom it had been referred. The [illegible] were overruled and a decree entered [illegible] etc., was due, and directing a sale in [illegible]

The bill was filed [illegible] on November 17, 1926, [illegible] years after date, together with [illegible] delivery of the trust deed [illegible] extension agreement [illegible] ment of the principal [illegible] and the extension [illegible] terest at six per cent [illegible] upon the principal [illegible] was extended.

The bill avers [illegible] fell due May 1st, 1930, [illegible] ing, complainant [illegible] the extension [illegible] clared the whole amount [illegible] close.

The only defense averred in [illegible] substance, that on or about [illegible] had agreed to reduce the rate of interest [illegible] three per cent.

Testimony to that effect was given by Victor C. Marx, son of defendant. He testified that the agreement was made with Ralph W. Hartwig, who had the notes for collection and to whom he was referred by complainant. The master found against this contention, and the chancellor approved his finding. We have read the entire testimony bearing on this issue and are persuaded that the finding of the master is correct. The burden was on defendant to establish this defense. Mr. Marx testified that Mr. Hartwig promised a reduction of interest in the amount of three per cent, but this promise is flatly denied by Mr. Hartwig. Victor Marx also testified that thereafter he tendered $450, being the amount of interest due according to the agreement for reduction, which was refused. This also is absolutely denied. If such tender was made, it was not kept open. Taxes on the premises are in arrears for several years and at about the time at which defendant claims the agreement to reduce the interest was made, defendant transferred a seven-eighths interest in the property to another who did not appear to defend.

Some complaint is made of the rulings of the master in the taking of the evidence, but neither the objections before the master nor exceptions before the chancellor stated any complaint in these respects. Defendant is not in a position to complain in this court. Springer v. Kroeschell, 161 Ill. 371; Hurd v. Goodrich, 59 Ill. 450.

There is no error in the record which would justify a reversal, and the decree is therefore affirmed.

AFFIRMED.

O'Connor, P. J., and McSurely, J., concur.

Testimony to that effect was given by Victor [illegible] Marx, son of defendant. He testified that the agreement was made with Ralph F. Hartwig, who had the notes for collection and to whom he was referred by complainant. The master found against this contention, and the chancellor approved his finding. We have read the entire testimony bearing on this issue and are persuaded that the finding of the master is correct. The burden was on defendant to establish this defense. Mr. Marx testified that Mr. Hartwig promised [illegible] of interest in the amount of three per cent, but this promise is flatly denied by Mr. Hartwig. Victor Marx also testified that he tendered [illegible] being the amount of interest [illegible] to the agreement for reduction, which was refused. This also is flatly denied. If such tender was made, it was not kept good. Taxes on the premises are in arrears for several years and [illegible] which defendant claims the agreement to reduce the interest was made, defendant transferred a seven-eighths interest in the property to another who did not appear to defend.

Some complaint is made of the ruling of the master in the taking of the evidence, but neither are objections [illegible] nor exceptions before the chancellor at [illegible] but in those respects. Defendant is not in a position to complain in this court. [illegible]

There is no error in the record which requires a reversal, and the decree is therefore affirmed.

O'Connor, P. J., and McSurely, J., concur.

38092

BERTHA WEISSKOPF,
Appellee,

vs.

GRAND LODGE OF THE UNITED STATES OF THE FREE SONS OF ISRAEL,
Appellant.

APPEAL FROM CIRCUIT COURT OF COOK COUNTY.

8277

280 I.A. 629[2]

MR. JUSTICE MATCHETT DELIVERED THE OPINION OF THE COURT.

Bertha Weisskopf, plaintiff in the trial court, is the daughter of Maurice Schnurdreher, who died June 8, 1934. She brought suit upon a life insurance policy for the sum of $1,000 issued by defendant fraternal insurance society in the lifetime of her father, claiming that she was designated in the policy as a beneficiary in the amount of $500. Her complaint alleged that her father was a member of the order in good standing at the time of his death. She attached to her complaint a copy of the constitution of the order. She averred that in conformity with section 140 of the constitution, Maurice Schnurdeher designated his then wife, Henrietta Schnurdreher for half of the amount and plaintiff the beneficiary of the other half, that he made no further designation in his lifetime, and that upon the death of Henrietta, which occurred prior to his death, the designation to her lapsed; that Maurice Schnurdeher thereafter married Rosa Schnurdeher, who survived him as his widow. The complaint averred that section 210 of the constitution of the defendant order provided that at least half of the benefit should go to the surviving widow. Plaintiff therefore prayed judgment for the sum of $500.

The answer of the society averred a loan to Maurice Schnurdreher in his lifetime of $22.02, which it claimed the right to deduct from any sum due under the certificate. The answer further averred that Maurice Schnurdreher on October 1, 1924,

38092

BERTHA WEISSBORD,)
Appellee,)

vs.

GRAND LODGE OF THE UNITED
STATES OF THE FREE SONS OF
ISRAEL,
Appellant.

230 I.A. 629

MR. JUSTICE [illegible] DELIVERED THE OPINION OF THE COURT.

Bertha Weissbord, plaintiff in the trial court, the daughter of Maurice Schnurdreher, who died June 3, 1926, brought suit upon a life insurance policy for the sum of $1,000 issued by defendant fraternal insurance society in the lifetime of her father, claiming that she was designated in the policy as beneficiary in the amount of $500. Her complaint alleged that her father was a member of the order in good standing at the time of his death. She attached to her complaint a copy of the constitution of the order. She averred that in conformity with section 140 of the constitution, Maurice Schnurdreher designated his then wife, Henrietta Schnurdreher for half of the amount and plaintiff the beneficiary of the other half, but he made no further designation in his lifetime, and that upon the death of Henrietta, which occurred prior to his death, the [illegible] to her lapsed; that Maurice Schnurdreher thereafter married Rose Schnurdreher, who survived him as his widow. The complaint averred that section 140 of the constitution of the defendant order provided that at least half of the benefit should [illegible] his widow. Plaintiff therefore prayed judgment for the sum of $500.

The answer of the society averred a loan to Maurice Schnurdreher in his lifetime of $82.07, which it claimed the right to deduct from any sum due under the certificate. The answer further averred that Maurice Schnurdreher on October 1, 1924, designated his then wife beneficiary for $1,000; that she thereafter died and Maurice married Henrietta, that on May 8, 1928, a new certificate was issued in which Henrietta was designated as beneficiary of the sum of $1,000; that on March 19, 1930, Maurice changed the beneficiary so as to designate that Henrietta should receive $500 and plaintiff, Bertha Weisskopf, his daughter, the sum of $500; that a new certificate was issued by defendant in accordance with this change.

The answer further states that Henrietta thereafter died and that Maurice Schnurdreher changed the face of the certificate by crossing out the name of Henrietta and interlineating the words "one thousand dollars"; that he also struck out the word "each" and wrote on the face of the policy, "O. K. Maurice Schnurdreher." The answer avers that by reason of this alteration the certificate became null and void; that the insured thereafter married Rosa and that no further changes were made in the certificate and no other certificate issued to him; that at the time of the death of said Maurice paragraph 211 of the constitution of defendant society was as follows:

"In the event of a benefit member failing to designate in the manner provided for in this Constitution to whom his or her death benefit shall be paid upon his or her demise, said benefit shall be paid as follows: (1) the widow or widower; (2) to the children, if no widow or widower survives; (3) to the parents if no widow, widower or children survive; (4) the brothers and sisters in equal proportions if no widow, widower, children or parents survive. If none of the above survive, said death benefits shall be paid to such beneficiaries as shall be entitled thereto under the laws of the State of New York."

The answer averred that the insured having failed to make any designation in the manner provided for in the constitution as to whom the death benefit should be paid upon his demise by reason of the provisions of said section 211, the benefit became payable to his widow, who was Rosa Schnurdreher, and that defendant paid her the death benefit and received a release therefor; that the certificate

2

designated his then wife beneficiary for $1,000; that she there-
after died and Maurice married Henrietta; that on May [illegible], 1928, a new certificate was issued in which Henrietta was designated as beneficiary of the sum of $1,000; [illegible] Maurice changed the beneficiary so as to designate that Henrietta should receive $500 and plaintiff, [illegible], the sum of $500, that a new certificate was issued to plaintiff in accordance with this change.

The answer further states that Henrietta [illegible] died and that Maurice Schnitzdreher [illegible] the face of the certificate by crossing out the name of Henrietta and interlineating the words "one thousand dollars", that he also struck out the word "[illegible]" and wrote on the face of the policy, "[illegible] Maurice Schnitzdreher." The answer avers that by reason of this alteration the certificate became null and void, that the insured thereafter [illegible] and that no further changes were made in the certificate and no other certificate issued to him, that at the time of the death of said Maurice paragraph XII of the constitution of defendant society was as follows:

"In the event of a benefit member failing to designate in the manner provided for in this Constitution who or what death benefit shall be paid upon his or her demise, said benefit shall be paid as follows: (1) [illegible] (2) to the children, if no widow or widower survives, (3) to the parents if no widow, widower or children survive, (4) [illegible] in equal proportions if no widow, widower, children or parents survive. If none of the above survive, [illegible] shall be paid to such beneficiaries as shall be entitled thereto under the laws of the State of New York."

any designation in the [illegible] as

issued by defendant, in and by which Henrietta Schnurdreher and Bertha Weisskopf became beneficiaries to the extent of $500 each, became null and void by reason of the changes made on its face by said Maurice, who failed to designate in the manner provided for in the constitution to whom his death benefit should be paid, and that the widow Rosa thereupon became entitled to the death benefit; that the last certificate issued provided that the death benefit should be paid to Henrietta, his wife, and to Bertha Weisskopf, his daughter, each in the sum of $500; that Henrietta died before Maurice, who thereafter married Rosa; that after the marriage Maurice failed to leave his widow one-half of the death benefit in conformity with section 210 of the constitution, and that in accordance with section 210, by his failure so to do he violated the provision and the certificate became null and void; that the death benefit became due to his wife Rosa in conformity with the provisions of section 211.

Plaintiff made a motion to strike the answer of defendant and for the entry of judgment on the ground that the facts set forth in the answer were substantially insufficient in law to constitute a defense. The motion was sustained. Defendant elected to stand by its answer, and judgment was entered for plaintiff and against defendant for $488.66.

It is argued, first, that the motion to strike should have been denied because the grounds therefor were not set up in sufficient particularity as required by section 45 of the Illinois Practice act (Cahill's Ill. Rev. State. 1933, chap. 110, sec. 45, par. 173) which provides:

"All objections to pleadings heretofore raised by demurrer shall be raised by motion. Such motion shall point out specifically the defects complained of, and shall ask for such relief as the nature of the defects may make appropriate, such as the dismissal of the action or the entry of a judgment where a pleading is substantially insufficient in law, or that a pleading be made more definite and certain in a specified particular, or that designated immaterial matter be stricken out, or that necessary parties be issued by defendant, [illegible]

Bertha Weisskopf [illegible]

became null and void by reason of [illegible]

said marriage, [illegible]

the constitution [illegible] should be paid, [illegible] that

the widow [illegible]

the last certificate issued provided [illegible] should

be paid to Henrietta, his wife, [illegible]

daughter, each in the sum of [illegible]

[illegible]

[illegible]

in conformity with section [illegible]

accordance with section [illegible]

the provision [illegible] that the

death benefit became due to [illegible]

provisions of section [illegible].

Plaintiff made a motion to strike the answer of defendant and for the entry of judgment on [illegible] forth in the answer were substantially insufficient [illegible] to constitute a defense. The motion was [illegible] stand by its answer, and judgment [illegible] against defendant for $488.60.

It is argued, first, that [illegible] been denied because the grounds [illegible] not set up in sufficient particularity as required by [illegible] tice act (Cahill's Ill. Rev. Stats. [illegible], sec. 45, par. 173) which provides:

"All objections to pleadings [illegible] shall be raised by motion. [illegible] the defects complained of, and shall ask for [illegible] as the nature of the defects may make appropriate, [illegible] of the action or the entry of a judgment where a pleading is substantially insufficient in law, or that [illegible] be made more definite and certain in a specified particular, or that designated immaterial matter be stricken out, or that necessary parties be added, or that designated misjoined parties be dismissed, and so forth."

No objection, apparently, was made on this ground in the trial court. The statement that the answer was insufficient in law did not leave defendant in doubt as to the issue before the court, which was squarely raised by the pleadings. If defendant deemed the pleading lacking in certainty, it should have moved that it be made more definite. It did not do so. Apparently, the point that the reasons stated were uncertain occurred to defendant for the first time after the case had been removed to this court. The point is without merit. Hitchcock v. Reynolds, 278 Ill. App. 559.

It is also argued that the deceased made no valid designation of his beneficiary under the provisions of the constitution of defendant, and that there being no valid designation, the benefit was payable to the widow under paragraph 210 of the constitution, which provides:

"It shall be compulsory for each benefit member who shall leave a lawful wife or husband surviving him or her, to leave such widow or widower at least one-half of the death benefit. Any designation violating this provision shall be null and void."

The insured did not, as we understand it, fail to comply with this provision. He had on March 18, 1930, in accordance with the laws of defendant, made a change in the designation of his beneficiaries, designating that his then wife Henrietta should receive $500 and his daughter Bertha $500, and a new certificate containing such designation was delivered to him. It is true that after the death of Henrietta he undertook to change the designation so as to give the entire $1,000 to plaintiff; that he undertook to do this by making the notations described upon the certificate; that these were never called to the attention of the society and were wholly ineffectual by reason of paragraph E of section 140 of the constitution, which is attached to the complaint as Exhibit "A" and added, or that designated misjoined parties be dismissed, and so forth."

No objection, apparently, was made on this ground in the trial court. The statement that the answer was insufficient in law did not leave defendant in doubt as to the issue before the court, which was squarely raised by the pleadings. If defendant deemed the pleading lacking in certainty, it should have moved that it be made more definite. It did not do so. Apparently, the point that the reasons stated were uncertain occurred to defendant for the first time after the case had been removed to this court. The point is without merit. Hitchcock v. Reynolds, 278 Ill. App. 389.

It is also argued that the deceased made no valid designation of his beneficiary under the provisions of the constitution of defendant, and that there being no valid designation, the benefit was payable to the widow under paragraph 210 of the constitution, which provides:

"It shall be compulsory for each benefit member who shall leave a lawful wife or husband surviving him or her, to leave such widow or widower at least one-half of the death benefit. Any designation violating this provision shall be null and void."

The insured did not, as we understand it, fail to comply with this provision. He had on March 13, 1930, in accordance with the laws of defendant, made a change in the designation of his beneficiaries, designating that his then wife Henrietta should receive $500 and his daughter Bertha $500, and a new certificate containing such designation was delivered to him. It is true that after the death of Henrietta he undertook to change the designation so as to give the entire $1,000 to plaintiff, that he undertook to do this by making the notations described upon the certificate; that these were never called to the attention of the society and were wholly ineffectual by reason of paragraph E of section 140 of the constitution, which is attached to the complaint as Exhibit "A" and which provides:

"No assignment or transfer of any certificate or any right thereunder or change of beneficiary named therein or any amount payable thereunder shall be valid or operative until the said certificate shall have first been surrendered and the consent in writing to such change shall have been indorsed thereon, duly signed by the Grand Master and attested by the Grand Secretary. Any assignment or transfer made in disregard of this provision shall be wholly void and of no effect."

Deceased's attempt to change the beneficiaries in this matter was wholly ineffectual to accomplish the purpose intended and so all the authorities seem to hold. Delaney v. Delaney, 175 Ill. 187; Freund v. Freund, 218 Ill. 189; Hodalski v. Hodalski, 181 Ill.App. 158; Thomas v. Thomas, 131 N. Y. 205; 45 Corpus Juris 194, sec. 156. Paragraph H of section 140 of defendant's constitution provides:

"If a member has heretofore designated or shall hereafter designate as beneficiary a person who predeceases him, such designation shall lapse and the amount so designated shall be payable in the same manner as though no designation thereof had been made, without, however, affecting any other designation that may have been made to one or more surviving beneficiaries."

There is no inconsistency, as we construe the same, between paragraph H of section 140 and section 210. The effect of paragraph H of section 140 is that the designation of Henrietta lapsed by reason of her death but that the other designation, which had been made of plaintiff as beneficiary for the other half of the policy, was not altered. Also, under section 210, Rosa as the surviving widow would be entitled to half of the death benefit.

For the reasons indicated, the court properly sustained the motion to strike the answer, and upon defendant standing by its answer, rightly entered judgment, which is therefore affirmed.

AFFIRMED.

O'Connor, P. J., and McSurely, J., concur.

which provides:

"No assignment or transfer of any certificate [illegible] thereunder or change of beneficiary [illegible] payable thereunder shall be valid [illegible] until the said certificate shall have first been surrendered [illegible] in writing to such change shall [illegible] signed by the Grand Master and attested by the Grand Secretary. Any assignment or transfer [illegible] shall be wholly void and of no effect."

Deceased's attempt to change the beneficiary [illegible] was wholly ineffectual to accomplish the purpose intended [illegible] the authorities seem to hold. [illegible]

[illegible] Paragraph 2 of section 180 of [illegible] provides:

"If a member has heretofore designated [illegible] designate as beneficiary a person who [illegible] without, however, affecting any [illegible] been made to one or more surviving [illegible]"

There is no inconsistency, as [illegible] paragraph 2 of section 180 [illegible] of section 140 is that the designation [illegible] reason of her death but that the other designation [illegible] made of plaintiff as beneficiary [illegible] was not altered. Also, [illegible] widow would be entitled to half [illegible]

For the reasons indicated, the court [illegible] the motion to strike the answer, and upon [illegible] its answer, rightly entered judgment [illegible] affirmed.

O'Connor, P. J., and Moriarty, J., concur.

90 H

38112

PEOPLE ex rel. EDWARD J. BARRETT,
Auditor of Public Accounts of the
State of Illinois,
Complainant,

v.

THE WEST SIDE TRUST & SAVINGS BANK,
a corporation,
Defendant.

IDA GORDON,
(Petitioner),
Appellant,

v.

WILLIAM L. O'CONNELL,
(Respondent),
Appellee.

280 I.A. 629[3]

APPEAL FROM SUPERIOR COURT, COOK COUNTY.

MR. JUSTICE MATCHETT DELIVERED THE OPINION OF THE COURT.

January 12, 1934, O'Connell was appointed receiver of the West Side Trust & Savings Bank by the auditor of public accounts. On or before that date, petitioner, Ida Gordon, was a depositor in the bank to the amount of $4,569. She filed a petition praying that the amount due her should be allowed as a preferred claim against the estate upon the theory that the bank held her deposit impressed by a trust in her favor. The receiver answered denying that petitioner was entitled to a preference, and the matter was heard upon the petition, the answer of the receiver and a stipulation of the parties as to the facts. The court denied the prayer for a preference and allowed petitioner's claim as a general one, and from that order petitioner has appealed.

The facts are undisputed. March 16, 1932, Abraham Gordon

[illegible]

PEOPLE ex rel. EDWARD J. BARRETT,
Auditor of Public Accounts of the
State of Illinois,
Complainant,

v.

THE WEST SIDE TRUST & SAVINGS BANK,
a corporation,
Defendant.

IDA GORDON,
(Petitioner),
Appellant,

v.

WILLIAM A. O'CONNELL,
(Respondent),
Appellee.

APPEAL FROM SUPERIOR
COURT OF COOK COUNTY.

280 I.A. 620

MR. JUSTICE MATCHETT DELIVERED THE OPINION OF THE COURT.

January 12, 1934, O'Connell was appointed receiver of the West Side Trust & Savings Bank by the auditor of public accounts. On or before that date, petitioner, Ida Gordon, was a depositor in the bank to the amount of $4,500. She filed a petition praying that the amount due her should be allowed as a preferred claim against the estate upon the theory that the bank held her deposit impressed by a trust in her favor. The receiver answered denying that petitioner was entitled to a preference, and the matter was heard upon the petition, the answer of the receiver and a stipulation of the parties as to the facts. The court denied the prayer for a preference and allowed petitioner's claim as a general one, and from that order petitioner has appealed.

The facts are undisputed. March 16, 1932, Abraham Gordon

died intestate, leaving as his only heirs and next of kin lbert Gordon, Max Gordon, Alta Gruskin, Olga Teinovitz and Ida Gordon, all of whom were of legal age and under no disability. The only asset in his estate was a savings account in the liquidating bank to the amount of $5,000 which stood in his name.

March 31, 1932, a meeting was held at the bank, where in the presence of Mr. Pflaum, who was assistant trust officer, all the other heirs executed and delivered to petitioner, Ida Gordon, an assignment transferring to her all their right, title and interest in this bank account. The bank was informed that there were no debts against the estate, and through its duly authorized officer, the bank agreed to pay the money in the savings account to Ida Gordon, without probate, upon being furnished with a surety bond to indemnify itself from any claims. The bank suggested that the National Surety Co. would execute such bond as was required, and petitioner procured a surety bond from that company in the amount of $5,000, and on or about May 15, 1932, delivered this surety bond to Mr. Pflaum, the assistant trust officer of the bank.

It is further stipulated that if the petitioner were present she would testify that she at that time said: "Mr. Pflaum, here is the surety bond that you require. Now I want my money." It is also stipulated that if Mr. Pflaum had been in court he would have testified that he replied, "You will have to leave the money in here for a year." There were present at the bank, Albert Gordon, brother of petitioner, and Olga Teinovitz, her sister. The bond in question is a part of the stipulation. It is dated May 11, 1932, signed and sealed by the claimant and executed by the National Surety Co., by its attorney-in-fact. It recites the death of Abraham Gordon, intestate, leaving heirs at law and next of kin as heretofore stated; that the assets of his estate consisted of a certain savings account No. 64,279, in the liquidating bank and in his name, with a balance of died intestate, leaving as his only heirs and next of kin Ida [illegible] Gordon, Max Gordon, [illegible] Druskin, Olga Teinovits and [illegible] Gordon, all of whom were of legal age and under no disability. The only asset in his estate was a savings account in the liquidating bank to the amount of $[illegible] then stood in his name.

March 31, 1932, a meeting was held at the bank, where in the presence of Mr. Pflaum, who was assistant trust officer, all the other heirs executed and delivered to petitioner, Ida Gordon, an assignment transferring to her all their rights, title and interest in this bank account. The bank was informed that there were no debts against the estate, and through its duly authorized officers, the bank agreed to pay the money in the savings account to Ida Gordon, without probate, upon being furnished with a surety bond to indemnify itself from any claims. The bank requested that the National Surety Co. write such bond as was required, and petitioner procured a surety bond from that company in the amount of $6,000, and on or about May 15, 1932, delivered this surety bond to Mr. Pflaum, the assistant trust officer of the bank.

It is further stipulated that if the petitioner were present she would testify that she [illegible] Mr. Pflaum, here is the surety bond that you require. [illegible] It is also stipulated that if Mr. Pflaum had been in court he would have testified that he replied, "You will have to leave the money in there for a year." There were present at the bank, Ida Gordon, [illegible] petitioner, and Olga Teinovits, her sister. The bond [illegible] [illegible] sealed by the claimant and executed by the National [illegible] its attorney-in-fact. It recites the death of [illegible] intestate, leaving heirs at law and next of kin as heretofore stated; that the assets of his estate consisted of a certain savings account No. [illegible], in the liquidating bank and in his name, with a balance of

$5,000; that Ida Gordon is desirous of obtaining the payment of the money to her without due administration of the estate; that the obligee has signified its willingness to pay the money to the principal upon being furnished with a bond of indemnity; that therefore the condition of the obligation is that if Ida Gordon will indemnify the bank "from and against any and all loss, costs and expenses which it might suffer or incur by reason of the payment of said money hereinbefore mentioned to her without due administration according to law of the estate of the said Abraham Gordon, deceased," then the obligation would be null and void, otherwise in full force and effect.

After the delivery of this bond a new passbook No. 180157 was issued by the bank in the name of Ida Gordon for the sum of $4,900, $100 having been deducted to pay the premium upon the bond. The passbook had an indorsement on it to the effect that withdrawals from this new account would require the counter-signature of the surety company. Thereafter, the bank allowed the withdrawal of $473.50 for a headstone on decedent's grave and for necessaries. The bank was closed March 3, 1933, at which time the passbook showed a credit in favor of Ida Gordon in the sum of $4,569.

The theory of claimant is that by reason of the demand upon the bank, while it was still open and doing business, for the payment of the amount due to her and the wrongful refusal of the bank to honor the demand, the bank thereafter held claimant's money impressed by a trust *ex maleficio* for the benefit of claimant; that she was thereby removed from the class of general creditors to which other depositors belonged and was entitled to the allowance of the amount due her as a preferred claim. The briefs in behalf of claimant indicate that there is some authority for the proposition upon which this demand is based. The courts of Missouri have so held in *Johnson* v. *Farmers' Bank of Clarksdale*, 223 Mo. App. 813, relying on decisions of the courts of that state in *Bank of Poplar Bluff* v. *Millspaugh*, 281 S. W. 733, 313 Mo. 412, and *Claxton* v. *Cantley*,

$4,000; that Ida Gordon is desirous of obtaining the payment of the money to her without due administration of the estate; that the obligee has signified its willingness to pay the money to the principal upon being furnished with a bond of indemnity; that therefore the condition of the obligation is that if Ida Gordon will indemnify the bank "from and against any and all loss, costs and expenses which it might suffer or incur by reason of the payment of said money hereinbefore mentioned to her without due administration according to law of the estate of the said Abraham Gordon, deceased," then the obligation would be null and void, otherwise in full force and effect.

After the delivery of this bond a new passbook No. 180157 was issued by the bank in the name of Ida Gordon for the sum of $4,900, $100 having been deducted to pay the premium upon the bond. The passbook had an indorsement on it to the effect that withdrawals from this new account would require the counter-signature of the surety company. Thereafter, the bank allowed the withdrawal of $473.50 for a headstone on decedent's grave and for necessaries. The bank was closed March 3, 1933, at which time the passbook showed a credit in favor of Ida Gordon in the sum of $4,369.

The theory of claimant is that by reason of the demand upon the bank, while it was still open and doing business, for the payment of the amount due to her and the wrongful refusal of the bank to honor the demand, the bank thereafter held claimant's money impressed by a trust ex maleficio for the benefit of claimant; that she was thereby removed from the class of general creditors to which other depositors belonged and was entitled to the allowance of the amount due her as a preferred claim. The briefs in behalf of claimant indicate that there is some authority for the proposition upon which this demand is based. The courts of Missouri have so held in Johnson v. Farmers' Bank of Clarksdale, 223 Mo. App. 15, relying on decisions of the courts of that state in Bank of Poplar Bluff v. Millspaugh, 281 S. W. 733, 313 Mo. 412, and Claxton v. Gentley.

297 S. W. 975.

Claimant also relies on Mallett v. Tunnicliffe, 102 Fla. 809, 136 So. 347, a case, however, which received much consideration but is clearly distinguishable, in that there the claimant was persuaded by the false and fraudulent representations of the officer of the bank to allow her deposit to remain when she was about to withdraw it. That case was before the court upon a demurrer to the petition of the claimant, and the facts set up in the petition showed the perpetration of an intentional fraud upon the claimant.

The claimant also relies very much upon dictum of our Supreme court in People v. Dennhardt, 354 Ill. 450. In that case the claim was allowed as a preferred one under an act defining the relations between banks and their depositors with respect to the deposit and collection of checks and other instruments payable in money, approved July 8, 1931. See Laws of Illinois, 1931, p. 675; Cahill's Ill. Rev. Stats., 1931, p. 177. The claim having been preferred under the provisions of that act the receiver upon appeal challenged the validity of the act itself upon the ground that it was unconstitutional, but the court held the act valid. The claimant was a township treasurer and as such deposited funds in a bank in East Moline, Ill., prior to the time it closed, drew a check upon his account for $4,653.38 and presented it to the bank for payment. The bank did not pay but in lieu thereof issued a draft on a Chicago bank to the order of the township treasurer. The bank of East Moline then marked the check paid and charged it to the drawer's account. On the same day the treasurer deposited the draft in another bank, which mailed it to the Chicago bank. On the following day the depositor bank was closed, and the Chicago bank thereupon refused to pay the draft, which it returned. Construing the act in question, the Supreme court said that under the provisions of par. 2 of sec. 15, the act was extended beyond the bank's agency to make collections of items entrusted to it.

-4-

297 S. W. 975.

Claimant also relies on Mallett v. Tunnicliffe, 102 Fla. 809, 136 So. 347, a case, however, which received much consideration but is clearly distinguishable, in that there the claimant was persuaded by the false and fraudulent representations of the officer of the bank to allow her deposit to remain when she was about to withdraw it. That case was before the court upon a demurrer to the petition of the claimant, and the facts set up in the petition showed the perpetration of an intentional fraud upon the claimant.

The claimant also relies very much upon dictum of our Supreme court in People v. Dennhardt, 354 Ill. 450. In that case the claim was allowed as a preferred one under an act defining the relations between banks and their depositors with respect to the deposit and collection of checks and other instruments payable in money, approved July 8, 1931. See Laws of Illinois, 1931, p. 678; Cahill's Ill. Rev. Stats., 1931, p. 177. The claim having been preferred under the provisions of that act the receiver upon appeal challenged the validity of the act itself upon the ground that it was unconstitutional, but the court held the act valid. The claimant was a township treasurer and as such deposited funds in a bank in East Moline, Ill., prior to the time it closed, drew a check upon his account for $4,655.38 and presented it to the bank for payment. The bank did not pay but in lieu thereof issued a draft on a Chicago bank to the order of the township treasurer. The bank of East Moline then marked the check paid and charged it to the drawer's account. On the same day the treasurer deposited the draft in another bank, which mailed it to the Chicago bank. On the following day the depositor bank was closed, and the Chicago bank thereupon refused to pay the draft, which it returned. Construing the act in question, the Supreme court held that under the provisions of par. 2 of sec. 15, the act was extended beyond the bank's agency to make collections of items entrusted to it.

The court said:

"The paragraph provides that, under the conditions stated, the assets of the drawee shall be impressed with a trust and no limitation is imposed respecting the person who presents the check or other instrument for the payment of money. By charging the drawer's account with the amount of the check or instrument presented, that amount is in effect taken from his account and held in trust by the bank for the legal holder of the check or other instrument. The defendant in error did not request the draft on the Continental Illinois Bank and Trust Company and his right to a preference became fixed regardless of the issuance of the draft. Under the facts shown by the evidence the statute specifically impressed the assets of the closed bank with a trust in favor of the defendant in error and he is entitled to a preference in payment over the bank's general creditors for the amount claimed."

It is apparent, we think, that the only question there before the court concerned the validity of the statute. In People v. Bryn Mawr State Bank, 273 Ill. App. 115, the precise question seems to have been before the third division of this court. In that case the claimant made a deposit in the bank on June 9, 1931. He then asked the receiving teller what his checking balance was and upon receiving the information drew a check on the bank for that amount, presented it to the teller and demanded payment. The teller told him the check must be "O. K'd." by an officer of the bank. The depositor then presented the check to the assistant cashier of the bank, who endorsed thereon his approval for payment. The depositor again presented the check to the receiving teller with the request that it be paid. The teller took a package of bills and began to count them but while so doing he was called to the telephone and when he returned told the depositor that the check would not be paid, that the bank was going to close and was in the hands of the State. The receiver insisted that under these facts the claimant had no right to priority of payment over general creditors, while the claimant depositor urged that he was entitled to such preference upon the same theory that is urged here, namely, that upon wrongful refusal to pay upon demand the bank became a trustee ex maleficio of his deposit so as to constitute it a trust fund. After reviewing

The court said:

"The paragraph provides that, under the conditions stated, the assets of the drawee shall be impressed with a trust and no limitation is imposed respecting the person who presents the check or other instrument for the payment of money. By charging the drawer's account with the amount of the check or instrument presented, that amount is in effect taken from his account and held in trust by the bank for the legal holder of the check or other instrument. The defendant in error did not request the draft on the Continental Illinois Bank and Trust Company and his right to a preference became fixed regardless of the issuance of the draft. Under the facts shown by the evidence the statute specifically impressed the assets of the closed bank with a trust in favor of the defendant in error and he is entitled to a preference in payment over the bank's general creditors for the amount claimed."

It is apparent, we think, that the only question there before the court concerned the validity of the statute. In People v. Bryn Mawr State Bank, 273 Ill. App. 415, the precise question seems to have been before the third division of this court. In that case the claimant made a deposit in the bank on June 9, 1931. He then asked the receiving teller what his checking balance was and upon receiving the information drew a check on the bank for that amount, presented it to the teller and demanded payment. The teller told him the check must be "O. K'd." by an officer of the bank. The depositor then presented the check to the assistant cashier of the bank, who endorsed thereon his approval for payment. The depositor again presented the check to the receiving teller with the request that it be paid. The teller took a package of bills and began to count them but while so doing he was called to the telephone and when he returned told the depositor that the check would not be paid, that the bank was "closed" to cross and was in the hands of the State. The receiver insisted that under these facts the claimant had no right to priority of payment over general creditors, while the claimant depositor urged that he was entitled to such preference upon the same theory that is urged here, namely, that upon wrongful refusal to pay upon demand the bank became a trustee ex maleficio.

the authorities the opinion of the court held that the trial court erred in directing the receiver to pay the amount of the claim as preferred, and the order was reversed, one of the Justices dissenting.

The same question came up before the same division of this court in People v. First Italian State Bank, Gen. No. 36384, not reported, decided October 10, 1934. Certiorari was denied by the Supreme court on February 21, 1935. The opinion of the majority of the court in that case said of claimants who had drawn checks on their account in the bank and demanded payment on several occasions before it closed, that they "can only be regarded as general creditors, and the fact of the demand did not establish their claim as a preferred claim to be paid prior to the claims of the general creditors."

In People v. Chicago Bank of Commerce, 275 Ill. App. 68, a similar question again came before the third division. It appeared that on June 24, 1932, the bank closed and Alfred F. Foreman was appointed receiver. Before closing and while acting as receiver in other cases the bank collected $12,920.65, which it mingled with the general assets of its own bank. The trial court found that the assets of the bank thereupon became impressed with a trust for this amount, which was allowed as a preferred claim. Miss Glynn, another depositor, filed a petition setting up that on the day before the bank closed she presented a check and demanded payment of her deposit, which was refused. She asked that her claim should be considered before the final disbursement to Foreman on his preferred claim. The order which allowed the Foreman claim also directed immediate distribution. Miss Glynn appealed and in the Appellate court argued that receiver Foreman was not entitled to preference. The court held that the bank as receiver having failed to keep the fund collected intact and mingled the same with its own assets, the fund was presumed to be in the assets of the bank when it closed the authorities the opinion of the court held that the trial court erred in directing the receiver to pay the amount of the claim as preferred, and the order was reversed, one of the Justices dissenting.

The same question came up before the same division of this court in People v. First Italian State Bank, Gen. No. 36884, not reported, decided October 10, 1934. Certiorari was denied by the Supreme court on February 21, 1935. The opinion of the majority of the court in that case said of claimants who had drawn checks on their account in the bank and demanded payment on several occasions before it closed, that they "can only be regarded as general creditors, and the fact of the demand did not establish their claim as a preferred claim to be paid prior to the claims of the general creditors."

In People v. Chicago Bank of Commerce, 278 Ill. App. 69, a similar question again came before the third division. It appeared that on June 24, 1932, the bank closed and Alfred L. Foreman was appointed receiver. Before closing and while acting as collector in other cases the bank collected $12,928.65, which it mingled with the general assets of its own bank. The trial court found that the assets of the bank thereupon became impressed with a trust for this amount, which was allowed as a preferred claim. Miss Glynn, another depositor, filed a petition setting up that on the day before the bank closed she presented a check and demanded payment of her deposit, which was refused. She asked that her claim should be considered before the final disbursement to Foreman on his preferred claim. The order which allowed the Foreman claim also directed immediate distribution. Miss Glynn appealed and in the Appellate court argued that receiver Foreman was not entitled to preference. The court held that the bank as receiver having failed to keep the fund collected intact and mingled the same with its own assets, the fund was presumed to be in the assets of the bank when it closed and was impressed with a trust. The opinion also said that the claim of Miss Glynn for a preference had been recognized in various jurisdictions, and: "If demand is made and refused, the bank holds such moneys ex maleficio as a trust for the benefit of the depositors who made the demand. This demand removes such depositor from the class of general creditors to which other depositors belong." The opinion cited Munn v. Burch, 25 Ill. 35, and other cases from the Missouri and Florida jurisdictions, and also relied upon the dictum in People v. Dennhardt, 354 Ill. 450. That part of the order finding Foreman to be entitled to a preference was affirmed, and that part of the order which directed immediate distribution was reversed and the cause remanded. A majority of the justices of the court, while concurring in the conclusion reached, declined to accede to the statement that Josephine Glynn was entitled to a preference, insisting that the merits of her claim were not before the court and should not have been passed on.

The sum and substance of it all seems to be that the specific question here raised has never been passed upon directly by the Supreme court, but that it has been squarely passed upon by the third division of this court contrary to the contention of the claimant, and that the Supreme court has declined to review that court upon that question by cериоrari. It is worthy of note, however, that the facts in this case as stipulated are not entirely inconsistent with the theory that the claimant did not imperatively demand the payment of her deposit. The stipulation of facts justifies the inference that it was a part of the entire agreement with the bank that the deposit must be left there for one year. That would be a period within which, if administration had been granted, creditors would have been required to file any claims that existed against the estate. Such condition would not have been unreasonable. There is an entire absence of evidence tending to she was impressed with a trust. The opinion also said that the claim of Miss Glynn for a preference had been recognized in various jurisdictions, and, "If demand is made and refused, the bank holds such moneys ex maleficio as a trust for the benefit of the depositors who made the demand. This demand removes such depositor from the class of general creditors to which other depositors belong." The opinion cited Mann v. Burr, 25 Ill. 35, and other cases from the Missouri and Florida jurisdictions, and also relied upon the dictum in People v. Gerhardt, 284 Ill. 150. That part of the order finding Foreman to be entitled to a preference was affirmed, and that part of the order which directed immediate distribution was reversed and the cause remanded. A majority of the justices of the court, while concurring in the conclusion reached, declined to accede to the statement that Josephine Glynn was entitled to a preference, insisting that the merits of her claim were not before the court and should not have been passed on.

The sum and substance of it all seems to be that the specific question here raised has never been passed upon directly by the Supreme court, but that it has been squarely passed upon by the third division of this court contrary to the contention of the claimant, and that the Supreme court has declined to review that court upon that question by certiorari. It is worthy of note, however, that the facts in this case as stipulated are not entirely inconsistent with the theory that the claimant did not imperatively demand the payment of her deposit. The stipulation of facts justifies the inference that it was a part of the entire agreement with the bank that the deposit must be left there for one year. That would be a period within which, if administration had been granted, creditors would have been required to file any claims that existed against the estate. Such condition would not have been unreasonable. There is an entire absence of evidence tending to shew deceit or fraud on the part of the bank, or any of its officers. The claimant did not object when the officer of the bank said that the money should remain on deposit in the bank for a year. On the contrary, she seems to have acquiesced in his construction of the agreement between claimant and the bank, and left her money in the bank until it closed. The preference of her claim would be most unfair to other depositors.

For these reasons the order of the trial court is affirmed.

ORDER AFFIRMED.

O'Connor, P. J., and McSurely, J., concur.

shew deceit or fraud on the part of the bank, or any of its officers. The claimant did not object when the officer of the bank said that the money should remain on depo it in the bank fo a year. On the contrary she seems to have acquiesced in his construction of the agreement between claimant and the bank, and left her money in the bank until it closed. The preference of her claim would be most unfair to other depositors.

or these reasons the order of the trial court is affirmed

ORDER AFFIRMED.

O'Connor, P. J., McSurely, J., concur.

38131

THOMAS B. ROBERTS, Receiver of West Town State Bank,
Appellee,

vs.

G. A. SCHILLINGER,
Appellant.

APPEAL FROM MUNICIPAL COURT OF CHICAGO.

280 I.A. 629[4]

MR. JUSTICE MATCHETT DELIVERED THE OPINION OF THE COURT.

On October 4, 1933, Roberts, receiver of the West Town State Bank, caused a judgment to be entered by confession against defendant upon three promissory notes executed by defendant on May 18, 1931, due 30 days after date. The notes were for $2050, $1500, and $1350, respectively, and contained power to confess judgment. The notes stated upon their face that they were secured by collateral in the form of $5,000 in real estate bonds, and gave the holder power to sell at public or private sale and to purchase the same at any such sale.

The bank was closed by the Auditor of Public Accounts on June 11, 1931, and Roberts was appointed receiver on July 21st. The judgment entered October 4, 1933, was for a balance claimed to be due in the sum of $2104.11, with attorney's fees of $166.24. Execution on the judgment issued to the bailiff of the Municipal court on October 6, 1933, and was returned unsatisfied January 5, 1934, the return stating that neither defendant nor his property was found.

October 12, 1934, plaintiff filed a creditor's bill of which defendant received notice by publication October 20, 1934. January 11, 1935, defendant presented its verified petition in the Municipal court, praying that the judgment be vacated and set aside, or opened up with leave to plead, the petition to stand as an affidavit of merits. This motion was denied on that date. January 14, 1935, defendant presented another verified petition in

38131

THOMAS B. ROBERTS, Receiver of West Town State Bank, Appellee,

vs.

G. A. SCHILLINGER, Appellant.

APPEAL FROM MUNICIPAL COURT OF CHICAGO.

290 I.A. 629

MR. JUSTICE MATCHETT DELIVERED THE OPINION OF THE COURT.

On October 4, 1933, Roberts, receiver of the West Town State Bank, caused a judgment to be entered by confession against defendant upon three promissory notes executed by defendant on May 18, 1931, due 30 days after date. The notes were for $2050, $1500, and $1350, respectively, and contained power to confess judgment. The notes stated upon their face that they were secured by collateral in the form of $5,000 in real estate bonds, and gave the holder power to sell at public or private sale and to purchase the same at any such sale.

The bank was closed by the Auditor of Public Accounts on June 11, 1931, and Roberts was appointed receiver on July 21st. The judgment entered October 4, 1933, was for a balance claimed to be due in the sum of $2104.11, with attorney's fees of $105.24. Execution on the judgment issued to the bailiff of the Municipal court on October 6, 1933, and was returned unsatisfied May [illegible], 1934, the return stating that neither defendant nor his property was found.

October 12, 1934, plaintiff filed a creditor's bill of which defendant received notice by publication October 2, 1934. January 11, 1935, defendant presented its verified petition in the Municipal court, praying that the judgment be vacated and set aside, or opened up with leave to plead, the petition to stand as an affidavit of merits. This motion was denied on that date. January 14, 1935, defendant presented another verified petition in support of a motion to set aside the order entered January 14th, and an order was entered denying this motion. From these orders defendant has perfected his appeal. The question for decision on the record is whether the court erred in refusing to open up the judgment.

In behalf of defendant it is contended that his petition showed diligence and a good defense on the merits. On the contrary, plaintiff contends that the petitions were both properly refused because defendant failed to show a meritorious defense to the action and because it appears that defendant was guilty of laches.

The law applicable to proceedings of this kind is well settled and has been stated repeatedly. Such petition is to be construed most strongly against the defendant who presents it. Auto Supply Co. v. Scene-in-Action Corp., 340 Ill. 196. If, thus construed, a meritorious defense is shown, in the absence of laches the motion should be allowed, otherwise, it should be denied. Kaehler v. Glaum, 169 Ill. App. 537; Sternberger v. Wright, 239 Ill. App. 490.

As already stated, the judgment here was entered October 4, 1933. Thereafter an execution issued and was returned unsatisfied. A creditor's bill was filed October 12, 1934, of which defendant received notice October 20th. Defendant's first motion to set aside the judgment was not filed until January 11, 1935. The first petition did not undertake to excuse the delay. The second petition states that defendant's first motion was denied for that reason; that the question of whether the petition stated a meritorious defense was not given consideration.

Upon the hearing of the second motion as tending to show diligence, defendant submitted the affidavit of his attorney, James H. Burr, who also represents one Helen M. Bott, a defendant to the support of a motion to set aside the order entered January 14th, and an order was entered denying this motion. From these orders defendant has perfected his appeal. The question for decision on the record is whether the court erred in refusing to open up the judgment.

In behalf of defendant it is contended that his petition showed diligence and a good defense on the merits. On the contrary, plaintiff contends that the petitions were both properly refused because defendant failed to show a meritorious defense to the action and because it appears that defendant was guilty of laches.

The law applicable to proceedings of this kind is well settled and has been stated repeatedly. Such petition is to be construed most strongly against the defendant who presents it. Auto Supply Co. v. Scene-in-Action Corp., 340 Ill. 196. If, thus construed, a meritorious defense is shown, in the absence of laches the motion should be allowed; otherwise, it should be denied. Koehler v. Glaum, 169 Ill. App. 537; Steinbrenner v. Wright, 223 Ill. App. 420.

As already stated, the judgment here was entered October 4, 1932. Thereafter an execution issued and was returned unsatisfied. A creditor's bill was filed October 15, 1934, of which defendant received notice October 20th. Defendant's first motion to set aside the judgment was not filed until January 11, 1935. The first petition did not undertake to excuse the delay. The second petition states that defendant's first motion was denied for that reason; that the question of whether the petition stated a meritorious defense was not given consideration.

Upon the hearing of the second motion as tending to show diligence, defendant submitted the affidavit of his attorney, James H. Burr, who also represents one Helen M. Bott, a defendant to the creditor's bill. The affiant states that on November 23, 1934, he presented a motion in the Circuit court to dismiss the creditor's bill; that the motion was denied on December 3, 1934; that he thereafter presented a motion in the nature of a demurrer pursuant to the provisions of section 45 of the Civil Practice Act; that this motion was presented December 21, 1934, and the hearing thereon set for January 14, 1935. The affiant further states:

> " ** that after filing the last mentioned motion in said Circuit court, he had occasion to examine the files in Case No. B-224250 in the Circuit Court of Cook County, in which case Thomas B. Roberts the Plaintiff herein was appointed Receiver of the West Town State Bank; that the said files are voluminous and much time was consumed in examining them; that during the examination of the said files affiant learned of facts that had not previously come to his knowledge, which facts in his judgment, constituted a complete defense to the plaintiff's claim herein."

The affidavit of Burr further says that he informed Helen M. Bott, one of the co-defendants of C. A. Schillinger, that a defense could be interposed in this case, and that a motion should be made under the rules of the Municipal court to open up the judgment by confession and for leave to plead; that he was then authorized to proceed to make the motion, and that he makes the affidavit for the purpose of showing that the delay was not unreasonable.

This affidavit significantly fails to state that affiant did not know of these supposed defenses prior to the examination of the files of the Circuit court which he made at that time, and it also fails to state when he first learned that the judgment by confession had been entered. The petitions of defendant also do not state when he first came to know that the judgment by confession had been entered. He may not have known of the judgment on the date of its entry, but he certainly does know when he first learned that it had been entered. It is apparent that defendant withholds that information. The fair inference from both affidavits is that defendant knew of the judgment on or about the date it was entered - October 4, 1933.

creditor's bill. The affiant states that on November 23, 1934, he presented a motion in the Circuit court to dismiss the creditor's bill; that the motion was denied on December 3, 1934, that he thereafter presented a motion in the nature of a demurrer pursuant to the provisions of section 45 of the Civil Practice Act; that this motion was presented December 11, 1934, and the hearing thereon set for January 14, 1935. The affiant further states:

> "** that after filing the last mentioned motion in said Circuit court, he had occasion to examine the files in case No. B-283250 in the Circuit Court of Cook County, in which case Thomas E. Roberts the Plaintiff herein was appointed Receiver of the West Town State Bank; that the said files are voluminous and much time was consumed in examining them, that during the examination of the said files affiant learned of facts that had not previously come to his knowledge, which facts in his judgment, constituted a complete defense to the plaintiff's claim herein."

The affidavit of Burr further says that he informed Helen M. Bott, one of the co-defendants of C. A. Schillinger, that a defense could be interposed in this case, and that a motion should be made under the rules of the Municipal court to open up the judgment by confession and for leave to plead; that he was then authorized to proceed to make the motion, and that he makes the affidavit for the purpose of showing that the delay was not unreasonable.

This affidavit significantly fails to state that affiant did not know of these supposed defenses prior to the examination of the files of the Circuit court which he made at that time, and it also fails to state when he first learned that the judgment by confession had been entered. The petitions of defendant also do not state when he first came to know that the judgment by confession had been entered. He may not have known of the judgment on the date of its entry, but he certainly does know when he first learned that it had been entered. It is apparent that defendant withholds that information. The fair inference from both affidavits is that defendant knew of the judgment on or about the date it was entered - October 4, 1933.

The question to be decided then is narrowed down to this: Whether having waited from that time to January 11, 1935, without any excuse, defendant is guilty of laches in failing to present his motion at an earlier time. In Sternberger v. Wright, 239 Ill. App. 490, a delay from April 14, 1925, to May 18, 1925; in Freeman v. Counsell, 203 Ill. App. 333, a delay from July 16, 1915, to September 30, 1915, was in each case held to preclude defendant. On the contrary in Solomon v. Dunne, 264 Ill. App. 416, it was held defendant was not precluded by a delay from December 9, 1930, to June 5, 1931, under the circumstances there appearing. However, it also appeared in that case that the power to confess judgment was void, and the opinion states that in such case the motion to set aside might be made at any time. It is not urged here that the power was void or illegal. In that case, it was pointed out that a proceeding of this nature is controlled by equitable principles and that the rule as to laches is based on the equitable maxim that equity aids the vigilant, not those who slumber on their rights.

Assuming, as we must, that defendant here had knowledge of the judgment at the time it was entered, we think it must be held the delay of defendant was inexcusable. Defendant not only knew the judgment was entered but also knew that plaintiff's creditor's bill based upon it was pending. Defendant is estopped by laches.

Moreover, the affidavit fails to state a meritorious defense. One of the alleged defenses is that plaintiff sold collateral and purchased the same for less than it was worth. The notes gave the holder thereof power to sell the collateral and authorized the holder to buy at such sale. Defendant in his petition does not state the circumstances under which the sale was made. He states that the collateral sold for $1300, but he does not state any facts from which the true market value of the collateral sold might be determined. He sets up as an alleged defense a supposed agreement

The question to be decided then is narrowed down to this. Whether having waited from that time to January 11, 1935, without any excuse, defendant is guilty of laches in failing to present his motion at an earlier time. In *Sternberger v. Wright*, 239 Ill. App. 490, a delay from April 14, 1925, to May 18, 1925, in *Freeman v. Connell*, 203 Ill. App. 335, a delay from July 16, 1915, to September 30, 1916, was in each case held to preclude defendant. On the contrary in *Solomon v. Dunne*, 264 Ill. App. 415, it was held defendant was not precluded by a delay from December 9, 1930, to June 5, 1931, under the circumstances there appearing. However, it also appeared in that case that the power to confess judgment was void, and the opinion states that in such case the motion to set aside might be made at any time. It is not urged here that the power was void or illegal. In that case, it was pointed out that a proceeding of this nature is controlled by equitable principles and that the rule as to laches is based on the equitable maxim that equity aids the vigilant, not those who slumber on their rights.

Assuming, as we must, that defendant here had knowledge of the judgment at the time it was entered, we think it must be held the delay of defendant was inexcusable. Defendant not only knew the judgment was entered but also knew that plaintiff's creditor's bill based upon it was pending. Defendant is estopped by laches.

Moreover, the affidavit fails to state a meritorious defense. One of the alleged defenses is that plaintiff sold collateral and purchased the same for less than it was worth. The notes gave the holder thereof power to sell the collateral and authorized the holder to buy at such sale. Defendant in his petition does not state the circumstances under which the sale was made. He states that the collateral sold for $1300, but he does not state any facts from which the true market value of the collateral sold might be determined. He sets up as an alleged defense a supposed agreement made by the bank to repurchase the bonds which had been put up as collateral at a discount of not more than two per cent, but such agreement has been held invalid as against public policy in Knass v. Madison Kedzie State Bank, 364 Ill. 554; Hoffman v. Sears Community State Bank, 366 Ill. 598; Awotin v. Atlas Exch. Nat'l Bank, 275 Ill. App. 530. The alleged sale of the collateral by Roberts, the Receiver, was held on February 20, 1933. Defendant does not deny that he had actual notice of the sale. He made no objection. The facts as stated in his petitions strongly tend to show that he acquiesced in this sale. The petitions do not allege either a meritorious defense or diligence in presenting his supposed defenses.

The trial court properly denied defendant's motions, and the orders denying the same are therefore affirmed.

ORDERS AFFIRMED.

O'Connor, P. J., and McSurely, J., concur.

made by the bank to repurchase the bonds which had been put up as collateral at a discount of not more than two per cent, but such agreement has been held invalid as against public policy in Hanna v. Madison Kedzie State Bank, 354 Ill. 554; Collman v. Sears Community State Bank, 356 Ill. 598; Awotin v. Atlas Exch. Nat'l Bank, 275 Ill. App. 530. The alleged sale of the collateral by Roberts, the Receiver, was held on February 20, 1933. Defendant does not deny that he had actual notice of the sale. He made no objection. The facts as stated in his petitions strongly tend to show that he acquiesced in this sale. The petitions do not allege either a meritorious defense or diligence in presenting his supposed defenses.

The trial court properly denied defendant's motions, and the orders denying the same are therefore affirmed.

ORDERS AFFIRMED.

O'Connor, P. J., and McSurely, J., concur.

88-3

21

AT A TERM OF THE APPELLATE COURT,

Begun and held at Ottawa, on Tuesday, the fifth day of February, in the year of our Lord one thousand nine hundred and thirty-five, within and for the Second District of the State of Illinois:

Prêsent-- The Hon. FRED G. WOLFE, Presiding Justice

Hon. FRANKLIN R. DOVE, Justice

Hon. BLAINE HUFFMAN, Justice.

JUSTUS L. JOHNSON, Clerk

RALPH H. DESPER, Sheriff

280 I.A. 629[5]

BE IT REMEMBERED, that afterwards, to-wit On APR 22 1935 the opinion of the Court was filed in the Clerk's office of said Court, in the words and figures following, to-wit:

Gen. No. 8823 Agenda No. 4

In the Appellate Court of Illinois

Second District

October Term, A. D. 1934.

City National Bank of Kankakee, Illinois, a Corporation, and C. B. Sawyer,
Defendants in error,

vs.

E. J. Tegge, Emma R. Tegge, Edward Lottinville, Trustee in Bankruptcy for E.J. Tegge, bankrupt, etc., et al,
Defendants in error
and
Maria Arp,
Plaintiff in error,

vs.

City National Bank of Kankakee, Illinois, a Corporation, et al,
Defendants in error.

Error to the Circuit Court of Iroquois County

WOLFE - P. J.

The City National Bank of Kankakee, Illinois, and C B Sawyer as trustee, filed their bill of complaint on February 17, 1930 to foreclose a trust deed given by E. J. Tegge under date of March 28, 1928, which trust deed was given to convey 120 acres of land in Iroquois County as security for a note of $6,000.00. Maria Arp and numerous others were made parties defendant to the bill, but all except Maria Arp were later dismissed. On March 21, 1930, Maria Arp filed an answer to said bill, and also a cross-bill seeking to foreclose a trust deed, given by E. J. Tegge and his brother to August Arp on March 2, 1918, for eighty acres of land covered by the trust deed to Sawyer. The trust deed was given to secure a note of $5,000.00. The original complainants answered the cross-bill. The other defendants were defaulted. A hearing was had on the bill, cross-bill and the answers thereto.

The trust deed, sought to be foreclosed by the cross-bill was given to August Arp to secure a note for $5,000.00, dated March 2, 1918, signed by E. J. Tegge, and W. F. Tegge, payable to the

No. 8823 In the Appellate Court of Illinois 4 - G. 30.

Second District

October Term, A. D. 1934.

City National Bank of Kankakee, Illinois, a Corporation, and C. B. Sawyer, Defendants in error,

vs

E. J. Tegge, Emma R. Tegge, Edward Lottinville, Trustee in Bankruptcy for E. J. Tegge, bankrupt, etc., et al, Defendants in error

and

Maria Arp, Plaintiff in error,

vs.

City National Bank of Kankakee, Illinois a Corporation et al, Defendants in error.

Error to the Circuit Court of Iroquois County.

WOLFE - J.

The City National Bank of Kankakee, Illinois, and C. B. Sawyer as trustee, filed their bill of complaint on February 17, 1930 to foreclose a trust deed given by E. J. Tegge under date of March 28, 1928, which trust deed was given to convey 120 acres of land in Iroquois County as security for a note of $6,000.00. Maria Arp and numerous others were made parties defendant to the bill, but all except Maria Arp were later dismissed. On March 21, 1930, Maria Arp filed an answer to said bill, and also a cross-bill seeking to foreclose a trust deed, given by E. J. Tegge and his brother to August Arp on March 2, 1918, for eighty acres of land covered by the trust deed to Sawyer. This trust deed was given to secure a note of $5,000.00. The original complainants answered the cross-bill. The other defendants were defaulted. A hearing was had on the bill, cross-bill and the answers thereto.

The trust deed, sought to be foreclosed by the cross-bill was given to August Arp to secure a note for $5,000.00, dated March 2, 1918, signed by E. J. Tegge, and W. F. Tegge, payable to the order of August Arp and Maria Arp, due March 2, 1923. At the maturity of this note a new note for a like amount was executed by the Tegges, payable to Maria Arp, due five years after date thereof. The original or first note was delivered to E. J. Tegge. On March 2, 1928, the debt was extended for a further period of five years, and Tegges executed a new note for $5,000.00 payable to Maria Arp and the note of March 2, 1923 was delivered to E. J. Tegge. No extension agreement in writing was placed on record giving notice of the extension of this mortgage debt. The Tegge Construction Company, which was not a corporation, but a name under which E J. Tegge did business, was heavily indebted to the complainant bank. On March 28, 1928, this indebtedness amounted to a sum in excess of $9,700.00. The bank was insisting upon a payment on this indebtedness and threatened to take legal proceedings to collect this debt or have Mr. Tegge secure the same. An arrangement was made whereby additional time and credit was to be extended Tegge upon his giving as additional security the note and trust deed sought to be foreclosed in the original bill. The note of Tegge evidencing the indebtedness to the bank, was surrendered by the bank to him upon the execution of the note and trust deed in question.

Prior to the closing of the new arrangement Tegge was required to submit an abstract of title to the lands which were to be given as security for his indebtedness to the bank. Tegge delivered an abstract to the bank, or to its attorneys, prior to the time the deal was consumated. The abstract was to be examined and approved before the new arrangement should be closed. Mr. Sawyer, attorney for the bank, examined the abstract and discovered a prior deed of trust in which the premises had been conveyed to August Arp as trustee to secure a loan on March 4, 1918. This was called to Tegge's attention and on this point Tegge's testimony is as follows: "They called me up and said, there was a cloud on the title " "Well", I said, "I know, I have been all through my papers and I saw the order of August Arp and Maria Arp, due March 2, 1928. At the maturity of this note a new note for a like amount was executed by the Tegges, payable to Maria Arp, due five years after date thereof. The original or first note was delivered to J. F. Tegge. On March 2, 1928, the debt was extended for a further period of five years, and Tegges executed a new note for $2,000.00 payable to Maria Arp and the note of March 2, 1923 was delivered to J. F. Tegge. No extension agreement in writing was placed on record giving notice of the extension of this mortgage debt. The Tegge Construction Company, which was not a corporation, but a name under which J. F. Tegge did business, was heavily indebted to the complainant bank. On March 20, 1929, this indebtedness mounted to a sum in excess of $9,700.00. The bank was insisting upon a payment on this indebtedness and threatened to take legal proceedings to collect this debt or have Mr. Tegge secure the same. An arrangement was made whereby additional time and credit was to be extended Tegge upon his giving as additional security the note and trust deed sought to be foreclosed in the original bill. The note of Tegge evidencing the indebtedness to the bank, was surrendered by the bank to him upon the execution of the note and trust deed in question.

Prior to the closing of the new arrangement Tegge was required to submit an abstract of title to the lands which were to be given as security for his indebtedness to the bank. Tegge delivered an abstract to the bank, or to its attorneys, prior to the time the deal was consummated. The abstract was to be examined and approved before the new arrangement should be closed. [illegible] Sawyer, attorney for the bank, examined the abstract and discovered a prior deed of trust in which the premises had been conveyed to August Arp as trustee to secure a loan on March 4, 1918. This was called to Tegge's attention and on this point Tegge's testimony is as follows: "They called me up and said, there was a cloud on the title." "Well," I said, "I know, I have been all through my papers and I saw the mortgage note there, and I supposed the mortgage note had been paid and released. I went there and told them I was sure I could get it released because I had the cancelled paper." August Arp, the original trustee had died, and Victor Wilson, who was Clerk of the Circuit Court and Recorder of Deeds of Iroquois County was his successor in trust. A release deed was prepared and Tegge took it and the original Arp note, which was in his possession, and presented them to Mr. Wilson for his signature Mr. Wilson executed the release and the same was placed on the record on March 29, 1928. On March 30, 1928 the bank's trust deed was filed for redord and the arrangement of the bank with Tegge was completed.

At the hearing the Chancellor found that the bank had a valid first lien on the premises, that its trust deed was recorded without its having knowledge or notice that Maria Arp claimed or asserted any right inthe premises by virtue of any trust deed, that at the time of the recording of defendant in error's trust deed the records disclosed an unencumbered title to the lands in question in E. J. Tegge, that the rights of all defendants were subordinate to the lien of the defendant in error, that defendant in error was entitled to foreclosure and that plaintiff in error, Maria Arp, had a second lien on the eighty acres covered by the August Arp trust deed, that the amount due defendant in error was $8,362.91 and the amount due plaintiff in error $6,125.69. A decree was entered in accordance with Chancellor's findings.

Plaintiff in error asks reversal of the decree on the ground that it is contrary to the law and the evidence, and that the Chancellor should have found and decreed that the plaintiff in error, Maria Arp, under the Arp trust deed, has a first and prior lien on the eighty acre tract of land in question, that the Chancellor should have granted the prayer of the cross bill for a decree of foreclosure, and that the court further erred in holding that defendant in error had a prior or first lien by reason of lack of knowledge or notice of the Arp trust deed.

mortgage note there, and I supposed the mortgage note had been paid and released. I went there and told them I was sure I could get it released because I had the cancelled paper." August Arp, the original trustee had died, and Victor Wilson, who was Clerk of the Circuit Court and Recorder of Deeds of Iroquois County was his successor in trust. A release deed was prepared and Tegge took it and the original Arp note, which was in his possession, and presented them to Mr. Wilson for his signature. Mr. Wilson executed the release and the same was placed on the record on March 29, 1928. On March 30, 1928 the bank's trust deed was filed for record and the arrangement of the bank with Tegge was completed.

At the hearing the Chancellor found that the bank had a valid first lien on the premises; that its trust deed was recorded without its having knowledge or notice that Maria Arp claimed or asserted any right in the premises by virtue of any trust deed; that at the time of the recording of defendant in error's trust deed the records disclosed an unencumbered title to the lands in question in R. J. Tegge; that the rights of all defendants were subordinate to the lien of the defendant in error; that defendant in error was entitled to foreclosure and that plaintiff in error, Maria Arp, had a second lien on the eighty acres covered by the August Arp trust deed; that the amount due defendant in error was $5,358.91 and the amount due plaintiff in error $8,125.69. A decree was entered in accordance with Chancellor's findings.

Plaintiff in error asks reversal of the decree on the ground that it is contrary to the law and the evidence; and that the Chancellor should have found and decreed that the plaintiff in error, Maria Arp, under the Arp trust deed, has a first and prior lien on the eighty acre tract of land in question; that the Chancellor should have granted the prayer of the cross bill for a decree of foreclosure; and that the court further erred in holding that defendant in error had a prior or first lien by reason of lack of knowledge or notice of the Arp trust deed.

The principle question in this case is, whether or not the bank at the time it accepted the trust deed from Tegge had notice, either actual or constructive, that the prior trust deed which he had given to the Arps was a valid lien on the property. In the case of Connor v. Wahl, 330 Ill. page 136, the Supreme Court, in discussing the law applicable to such case, use this language "An unbroken line of decisions holds that a release of a trust deed unauthorized by the terms of the trust, or by the cestui que trust, affects only the right of the original parties or subsequent purchasers with notice. Since in law the trustee has power to release a lien so as to re-vest the legal title in the grantors, even though he does so without the consent of the cestui que trust and in violation of the trust, it follows that the releases in question in this case, which were executed after the notes were due, were good as to plaintiffs in error, who had no notice of any lack of authority on the part of Renshaw to release the first and second trust deeds."

"The public records of conveyances and instruments affecting the title to real estate are established by statute to furnish evidence of such title. A purchaser has a right to rely upon the records unless he has notice or is chargeable with notice of some title, conveyance or claim inconsistent therewith. If reliance cannot be placed on the disclosures of the records relative to such title, then no one can purchase an interest in real estate free from the possibility that somewhere in the chain of title a mortgage or trust deed has been assigned and wrongfully released by the trustee."

This brings us to a discussion of the second proposition as to whether or not the defendant in error did have notice, either actual or constructive of the rights of Marie Arp at the time of the execution of the notes and trust deed from Tegge to the bank. As we have heretofore stated, the attorney for the bank discovered that there was an unreleased deed of trust on record that was many years

The principle question in this case is, whether or not the bank at the time it accepted the trust deed from Tegge had notice, either actual or constructive, that the prior trust deed which he had given to the Arps was a valid lien on the property. In the case of Connor v. Wahl, 330 Ill. page 136, the Supreme Court, in discussing the law applicable to such case, use this language "An unbroken line of decisions holds that a release of a trust deed unauthorized by the terms of the trust, or by the cestui que trust, affects only the right of the original parties or subsequent purchasers with notice. Since in law the trustee has power to release a lien so as to re-vest the legal title in the grantors, even though he does so without the consent of the cestui que trust and in violation of the trust, it follows that the releases in question in this case, which were executed after the notes were due, were good as to plaintiffs in error, who had no notice of any lack of authority on the part of Kenshaw to release the first and second trust deeds."

"The public records of conveyances and instruments affecting the title to real estate are established by statute to furnish evidence of such title. A purchaser has a right to rely upon the records unless he has notice or is chargeable with notice of some title, conveyance or claim inconsistent therewith. If reliance cannot be placed on the disclosures of the records relative to such title, then no one can purchase an interest in real estate free from the possibility that somewhere in the chain of title a mortgage or trust deed has been assigned and wrongfully released by the trustee."

This brings us to a discussion of the second proposition as to whether or not the defendant in error did have notice, either actual or constructive of the rights of Maria Arp at the time of the execution of the notes and trust deed from Tegge to the bank. As we have heretofore stated, the attorney for the bank discovered that there was an unreleased deed of trust on record that was many years past due. When Tegge's attention was called to this fact he stated he had the cancelled papers and thought the same has been paid and released and that he could easily procure a release deed. He at once took the original note which was secured by the trust deed of March 2, 1918 to the trustee who immediately executed a release deed and the same was filed for record. Under the circumstances it is our opinion that the bank had a right to rely upon the record as it then existed which showed that this deed of trust to the Arps was properly cancelled and released. The plaintiff in error did nothing to protect her rights but relied wholly upon the record of the original deed of trust. There was no extension agreement filed to give notice to the public that she claimed a lien on the premises. It was Tegge's ignorance of the fact, or his fraud that caused the loss to Maria Arp. When one of two innocent persons must suffer by reason of the fraud or wrong conduct of the other, the burden shall fall upon the one who put it in the power of the wrong doer to commit the fraud or do the wrong.

It is contended on the behalf of Mrs. Arp that the defendant in error in taking the trust deed from Tegge did not advance anything upon the faith of the Arp trust deed having been released and discharged of record. The record discloses that the Tegge Construction Company was largely indebted to the bank, that the bank was insisting upon the payment of this indebtedness, and threatening to take judgment or other legal proceedings to collect its debt, that the bank relying upon the execution of the deed of trust did not commence legal proceedings but extended the time of payment with additional credit to Tegge, that the bank surrendered Tegge's old note which it held of Tegge's and changed its position with reference to the collection of its claim against the Tegge Construction Company. We think that the release of the Arp deed of trust innured to the benefit of the defendant in error.

past due. When Tegge's attention was called to this fact it stated he had the cancelled papers and brought the same in and said he had released and that he could easily procure a release deed. [illegible] once took the original note which was secured by the first deed of [illegible] [illegible] who immediately executed a release deed and the same was filed for record. Under the circumstances it is our opinion that the bank had a right to rely upon the record as it then existed [illegible] was properly cancelled and released. The plaintiff in error had nothing to protect her rights but relied wholly upon the one [illegible] the original deed of trust. [illegible] [illegible] [illegible] loss to [illegible] one of two innocent persons must suffer by reason of the fraud or wrong conduct of another, the burden should fall upon the one who put it in the power of the wrongdoer to commit the fraud or do the wrong.

It is contended on the behalf of [illegible] that the defendant in error in taking the trust deed from Tegge did not [illegible] thing upon the faith of the Arp trust deed having been released or discharged of record. The record discloses that the Tegge Construction Company was largely indebted to the bank, that the bank was insisting upon the payment of this indebtedness, [illegible] judgment or other legal proceedings to collect this debt, that the bank relying upon the execution of the deed of trust did not commence legal proceedings but extended the time of credit with additional [illegible] to Tegge, that the bank surrendered the old note which it held of Tegge's and changed its position with reference to the collection of its claim against the Tegge Construction Company. We think that the release of the Arp deed of trust inured to the benefit of the defendant in error.

We cannot regard these parties as equally innocent as a matter of law. Both acted honestly and confided in Tegge. Neither had a bad motive for anything they did, or attempted to do, but Maria Arp by failing to record any extension agreement and allowing the indebtedness due her to remain on record as being long past due, was negligence of her own rights and she must suffer the consequences.

The judgment of the Circuit Court of Iroquois County is hereby affirmed.

Affirmed.

We cannot regard these parties as equally innocent as a matter of law. Both acted honestly and confided in Tegge. Neither had a bad motive for anything they did, or attempted to do, but Marie [illegible] by failing to record any extension agreement and allowing the indebtedness due her to remain on record as being long past due, was negligent of her own rights and she must suffer the consequences.

The judgment of the Circuit Court of Iroquois County is hereby affirmed.

Affirmed

} ss.

I, JUSTUS L. JOHNSON Clerk of the Appellate Court, in and of the State of Illinois, and the keeper of the Records and Seal thereof do hereby ; is a true copy of the opinion of the said Appellate Court in the above entitled cause.

In Testimony Whereof, I hereunto set my hand and affix the seal of said Appellate Court at Ottawa this ______________ day of ______________ in the year of our Lord one thousand nine hundred and thirty-______________

____

Clerk of the Appellate Court

8865

AT A TERM OF THE APPELLATE COURT,

Begun and held at Ottawa, on Tuesday, the fifth day of February, in the year of our Lord one thousand nine hundred and thirty-five, within and for the Second District of the State of Illinois:

Present-- The Hon FRED G. WOLFE, Presiding Justice

Hon. FRANKLIN R DOVE, Justice

Hon. BLAINE HUFFMAN, Justice.

JUSTUS L. JOHNSON, Clerk

RALPH H. DESPER, Sheriff.

280 I.A. 630

BE IT REMEMBERED, that afterwards, to-wit On APR 22 1935 the opinion of the Court was filed in the Clerk's office of said Court, in the words and figures following, to-wit:

No. 8865 Ag. 37

IN THE
APPELLATE COURT OF ILLINOIS
SECOND DISTRICT

October Term, A. D. 1935.

ALBERT LETTOW, a minor, by MARGARET FOX, his mother and next friend,
(Plaintiff) Appellee

vs.

IVAN M. SURKAMER, individually and doing business under the style and name of GLEN ELLYN CHECKER CAB COMPANY,
(Defendant) Appellant.

Appeal from the Circuit Court, DuPage County.

WOLFE -- P. J.

Suit was started by Albert Lettow, a minor, by Margaret Fox, his mother and next friend, against Ivan M. Surkamer, individually and doing business under the name and style of the Glen Ellyn Checker Cab Company, to recover damages sustained by the plaintiff because of the alleged negligence of the agent and servant of the defendant while driving the defendant's automobile in Glen Ellyn, Illinois, on July 27, 1932, when the automobile ran upon and against and struck the plaintiff who was riding a bicycle thereby causing the injuries complained of. The declaration consisted of four counts. The first count charges that on the day in question the defendant, by his agent and servant was operating an automobile commonly known as a taxicab, in a northeasterly direction on Loraine Avenue near its intersection with Kenilworth Avenue in Glen Ellyn; that on the same day the plaintiff was driving and riding a certain bicycle along Loraine Avenue and near its intersection with Kenilworth Avenue, and the defendant, through its agent and servant, carelessly, negligently, and improperly drove, used, managed, controlled and operated his automobile so that said automobile ran upon and against and struck the plaintiff and his bicycle with great force and violence. The second count charges wilful and wanton misconduct on the part of the defendant, but a demurrer was sustained

No 8865

[illegible] D DIST ICT

October Term, A. D. 1935

ALBERT LETTOW, a minor, by
MARGARET FOX, his mother and
next friend,
(Plaintiff) Appellee

vs.

IVAN M. SURKAMER individually
and doing business under the
style and name of GLEN ELLYN
CHECKER CAB COMPANY,
(Defendant) Appellant

Appeal from the
Circuit Court,
DuPage County

WOLFE - P. J.

Suit was started by Albert Letto[illegible] minor, by [illegible] his mother and next friend, against Ivan Surk[illegible] individually and doing business under the name and style of [illegible] Ellyn Checker Cab Company, to recover damages sustained by the [illegible] because of the alleged negligence of the [illegible] defendant while driving the defendant's automobile in [illegible] Illinois, on July 27, 1932, when the automobile [illegible] against and struck the plaintiff who was riding a bicycle [illegible] causing the injuries complained of. The declaration [illegible] four counts. The first count charges that on the day in question the defendant, by his agent and servant was operat[illegible] commonly known as a taxicab, in [illegible] Avenue near its intersection with [illegible] Avenue [illegible] that on the same day the plaintiff was driving [illegible] bicycle along Loraine Avenue [illegible] near its intersection [illegible] worth Avenue, and the defendant, through its agent and servant, carelessly, negligently, and improperly drove, used, managed, controlled and operated its automobile so that [illegible] automobile ran upon and against and struck the plaintiff and his bicycle with great force and violence. The second count charges wilful and wanton misconduct on the part of the defendant, but a demurrer was sustained to this count and the same was withdrawn from the consideration of the jury. The third count charges the defendant with driving his automobile at an excessive and high rate of speed, to-wit, 35 miles per hour, contrary to the provisions of the statute, and by reason of this excessive speed the accident was occasioned. The fourth count charges that the defendant was driving the taxicab to the left of the center of the beaten track of the street, contrary to and in violation of the provisions of the statute of the State of Illinois. To this declaration the defendant filed a plea of the general issue. The case was tried before a jury who found a verdict in favor of the plaintiff and assessed his damages at $10,000.00. The case is brought to this court by appellant to review this judgment.

There are nineteen errors relied upon for reversal, but, as this case will have to be reversed and remanded to the trial court, we will consider only two of the assignments. The first is "that the verdict is manifestly against the weight of the evidence."

Albert Lettow, the plaintiff, testified that he will be fifteen years of age on his next birthday; that he had no recollection of what took place on the day that he was hurt, that he neither remembers what kind of a day it was, when he left his home that day, where he went, nor that he was riding a bicycle. The other witnesses of the plaintiff testified as to what they saw after the accident occurred and the injuries the plaintiff received. At the time the accident occurred the driver of the taxicab was taking a lady named Mrs. Goyette to the station to take a train for Wheaton. The taxi driver and Mrs. Goyette were the only eye witnesses to this accident. Each testified as to what occurred just prior to and at the time of the accident. We see no useful purpose of reviewing the evidence in this opinion. We carefully read the record and are of the opinion that the verdict of the jury is manifestly against the weight of the evidence as it fails to show negligence on the part of the driver of the taxicab to this court [illegible]

of the jury. [illegible]

his automobile at an excessive and [illegible]

[illegible] miles per hour, contrary to the provisions of [illegible]

by reason of this excessive [illegible] the accident [illegible]

The [illegible]

cab to the left of the center of the [illegible]

contrary to and in violation of the provisions of the [illegible]

the State of Illinois. To this declaration the [illegible]

plea of the general issue. The case was tried before a [illegible]

found a verdict in favor of the plaintiff and assessed [illegible]

at $10,000.00. The case is brought to this court [illegible]

review this judgment.

There are nineteen errors [illegible] but,

as this case will have to be reversed and remanded [illegible]

court, we will consider only [illegible] of the [illegible] The first

is "that the verdict is manifestly against the weight of the

evidence."

Albert Lettow, the plaintiff, testified that he will be

fifteen years of age on his next birthday, that he had [illegible]

lection of what took place on the day that he was [illegible]

neither remembers what kind of a [illegible]

home that day, where he went, nor that he was [illegible]

The other witnesses of the plaintiff [illegible]

saw after the accident occurred [illegible]

received. At the time the [illegible] occurred the [illegible]

[illegible]

take a train for Benton. The taxi [illegible]

the only eye witnesses to this accident [illegible]

what occurred just prior to and at the time of the accident [illegible]

We see no useful purpose of reviewing the evidence [illegible]

We carefully read the record and are of the opinion that the verdict

of the jury is manifestly against the weight of the evidence as it

fails to show negligence on the part of the driver of the taxicab at the time this boy was injured.

The owner of the taxicab was placed on the witness stand by the defendant. In his testimony he stated he went to the scene of the accident, and to the hospital. He then called up his insurance agent to report the accident to him. This statement was given without objection, and was a voluntary statement on the part of the defendant. The defendant's counsel do not insist that there is any error committed which would be prejudicial to their client because of this statement, but they do insist that the closing argument of the attorney for the plaintiff was prejudicial to the defendant, especially in view of the amount of the verdict that was rendered by the jury. The remarks of the attorney for the plaintiff, stating that "Surkamer said that after he came back from the hospital he called up his insurance company." 'It is no business of yours how he pays or where he gets his money,' had no bearing upon the question as to whether the defendant was liable to the plaintiff for damages. This argument could be used for one purpose only, namely, to call the jury's attention to the fact that the defendant carried liability insurance. From the amount of the verdict in this case it seems to us that it was very prejudicial to the defendant.

The other errors assigned we have not attempted to discuss or pass upon, as the case will have to be reversed and remanded to the trial court for a new trial. The judgment of the Circuit Court of DuPage County is hereby reversed and the cause remanded.

Reversed and remanded.

at the time this boy was injured.

[illegible] by the defendant. In his testimony he stated he went to the scene of the accident, [illegible] to the hospital. He then called up his insurance agent to report the accident to him. This statement was given without objection, and was a voluntary statement on the part of the defendant. The defendant's counsel do not insist that there is any error committed which would be prejudicial to their client because of this statement, but they do insist that the closing argument of the attorney for the plaintiff was prejudicial to the defendant, especially in view of the amount of the verdict that was rendered by the jury. The remarks of the attorney for the plaintiff, stating that "Burkhamer said that after he came back from the hospital he called up his insurance company." "It is no business of yours how he pays or where he gets his money," had no bearing upon the question as to whether the defendant was liable to the plaintiff for damages. This argument could be used for one purpose only, namely, to call the jury's attention to the fact that the defendant carried liability insurance. From the amount of the verdict in this case it seems to us that it was very prejudicial to the defendant.

The other errors assigned we have not attempted to discuss or pass upon, as the case will have to be reversed and remanded to the trial court for a new trial. The judgment of the Circuit Court of DuPage County is hereby reversed and the cause remanded.

Reversed and remanded.

}ss.
I JUSTUS L. JOHNSON Clerk of the Appellate Court in and the State of Illinois, and the keeper of the Records and Seal thereof do hereby a true copy of the opinion of the said Appellate Court in the above entitled cause.

In Testimony Whereof, I hereunto set my hand and affix the seal of said Appellate Court at Ottawa this ________________ day of ________________ in the year of our Lord one thousand nine hundred and thirty- ____________

____

Clerk of the Appellate Court

8902

AT A TERM OF THE APPELLATE COURT,

Begun and held at Ottawa, on Tuesday, the fifth day of February, in the year of our Lord one thousand nine hundred and thirty-five, within and for the Second District of the State of Illinois

Present-- The Hon. FRED G. WOLFE, Presiding Justice

Hon. FRANKLIN R. DOVE, Justice

Hon. BLAINE HUFFMAN, Justice.

JUSTUS L. JOHNSON, Clerk.

RALPH H. DESPER, Sheriff.

280 I.A. 630[2]

BE IT REMEMBERED, that afterwards, to-wit On APR 22 1935 the opinion of the Court was filed in the Clerk's office of said Court, in the words and figures following, to-wit:

8902 Ag. 25

In the Appellate Court of Illinois

Second District

February Term, A D 1935

John Buffo,

Appellee,

vs.

Mutual Benefit Health and Accident Association,

Appellant.

Appeal from the Circuit Court of Winnebago County

WOLFE - P. J.

John Buffo, plaintiff, started suit in the Circuit Court of Winnebago County, against the Mutual Benefit Health & Accident Association to recover for accidental injuries he claims he sustained. The suit is based upon the terms and provisions of an Accident and Health Insurance Policy. The case was tried before a jury which found a verdict in favor of the plaintiff and assessed his damages at $960.00. After a motion for a new trial and arrest of judgment were overruled, judgment was entered on the verdict in favor of the plaintiff for this amount. From this judgment an appeal has been perfected.

The evidence shows that the plaintiff Buffo was riding in his own car which was being driven by his son. For some unexplained reason the truck stopped suddenly and the plaintiff was thrown against the wind shield, forcing his hand through it. The result was a deep cut on the back of his hand midway between the knuckles and the wrist, extending through the tendons almost to the bone. It was necessary to take twenty-five to thirty stitches to close the wound. The doctor who attended Mr. Buffo at the time of the injury was called as a witness and he gave his version of the extent of the injury, the treatment and the way the wound responded to the treatment and the condition of the plaintiff's hand at the time of the trial.

Ag. 35 8802

In the Appellate Court of Illinois

Second District

February Term, A D 1935

John Bulfo,
Appellee,

vs.

Mutual Benefit Health and Accident Association,
Appellant

Appeal from the Circuit Court of Winnebago County

WOLFE - P. J.

John Bulfo, plaintiff, started suit in the Circuit Court of Winnebago County, against the Mutual Benefit Health & Accident Association to recover for accidental injuries he claims he sustained. The suit is based upon the terms and provisions of an Accident and Health Insurance Policy. The case was tried before a jury which found a verdict in favor of the plaintiff and assessed his damages at $960.00. After a motion for a new trial and arrest of judgment were overruled, judgment was entered on the verdict in favor of the plaintiff for this amount. From this judgment an appeal has been perfected.

The evidence shows that the plaintiff Bulfo was riding in his own car which was being driven by his son. For some unexplained reason the truck stopped suddenly and the plaintiff was thrown against the wind shield, forcing his hand through it. The result was a deep cut on the back of his hand midway between the knuckles and the wrist, extending through the tendons almost to the bone. It was necessary to take twenty-five to thirty stitches to close the wound. The doctor who attended Mr. Bulfo at the time of the injury was called as a witness and he gave his version of the extent of the injury, the treatment and the way the wound responded to the treatment and the condition of the plaintiff's hand at the time of the trial.

~~hand at the time of the trial~~.

At the close of the plaintiff's evidence the defendant entered a motion for the court to direct the jury to find a verdict for the defendant. This motion was overruled and the case submitted to the jury. The defendant now insists that the court erred in overruling this motion, that plaintiff's given instructions numbered 1 and 2 are erroneous, that the court refused to give defendants proffered instructions numbered 1 and 2, and that the verdict and judgment are excessive.

This case, was before this court at the February term, 1934, and reported in Volume 274 Ill. App. page 114 At that time the court passed on the questions as to whether the plaintiff had given proper notice of his injury to the company, and also whether the instructions given, properly set forth the law applicable to the case We held that the trial court had committed no error in this respect. We reversed and remanded the case because the trial court had refused to give the proffered instruction of the defendant relative to its theory on which the plaintiff's recovery was limited. At the trial of the case the second time this instruction was given and the jury again found in favor of the plaintiff.

We have examined the given and refused instructions and it is our opinion that the jury was properly instructed relative to the law of the case. It is not disputed that the plaintiff had a severe cut on his hand, or that the wound became infected and blood poison developed. The doctor testified that blood poisoning following such an injury is not uncommon.

The jury being properly instructed, after hearing the evidence, it became a question for them to decide whether the plaintiff's disability arose from the injury he received or whether it was from a disease We cannot say that the verdict of the jury is manifestly against the weight of the evidence, and because we fully set forth the facts and discussion of the law in our [illegible] at the time of the trial.

At the close of the plaintiff's evidence the defendant entered a motion for the court to direct the jury to find a verdict for the defendant. This motion was overruled and the case submitted to the jury. The defendant now insists that the court erred in overruling this motion; that plaintiff's given instructions numbered 1 and 2 are erroneous, that the court refused to give defendants proffered instructions numbered 1 and 2, and that the verdict and judgment are excessive.

This case, was before this court at the February term, 1934, and reported in Volume 274 Ill. App. page 114. At that time the court passed on the questions as to whether the plaintiff had given proper notice of his injury to the company, and also whether the instructions given, properly set forth the law applicable to the case. We held that the trial court had committed no error in this respect. We reversed and remanded the case because the trial court had refused to give the proffered instruction of the defendant relative to its theory on which the plaintiff's recovery was limited. At the trial of the case the second time this instruction was given and the jury again found in favor of the plaintiff.

We have examined the given and refused instructions and it is our opinion that the jury was properly instructed relative to the law of the case. It is not disputed that the plaintiff had a severe cut on his hand, or that the wound became infected and blood poison developed. The doctor testified that blood poisoning following such an injury is not uncommon.

The jury being properly instructed, after hearing the evidence, it became a question for them to decide whether the plaintiff's disability arose from the injury he received or whether it was from a disease. We cannot say that the verdict of the jury is manifestly against the weight of the evidence, and because we fully set forth the facts and discussion of the law in our former opinion we have refrained from discussing them at this time We find no reversible error in this case and the judgment of the Circuit Court of Winnebago County is hereby affirmed.

Judgment affirmed.

}ss.

I JUSTUS L. JOHNSON Clerk of the Appellate Court in and the State of Illinois, and the keeper of the Records and Seal thereof do hereby a true copy of the opinion of the said Appellate Court in the above entitled cause.

In Testimony Whereof, I hereunto set my hand and affix the seal of said Appellate Court at Ottawa this ____________________ day of ____________________ in the year of our Lord one thousand nine hundred and thirty-________________

____

Clerk of the Appellate Court

8921

247

AT A TERM OF THE APPELLATE COURT,

Begun and held at Ottawa, on Tuesday, the fifth day of February, in the year of our Lord one thousand nine hundred and thirty-five, within and for the Second District of the State of Illinois:

Present-- The Hon. FRED G. WOLFE, Presiding Justice

Hon. FRANKLIN R. DOVE, Justice.

Hon. BLAINE HUFFMAN, Justice.

JUSTUS L. JOHNSON, Clerk

RALPH H. DESPER, Sheriff.

280 I.A. 630[3]

BE IT REMEMBERED, that afterwards, to-wit On APR 22 1935 the opinion of the Court was filed in the Clerk's office of said Court, in the words and figures following, to-wit:

8921 Ag. No. 34.

IN THE
APPELLATE COURT OF ILLINOIS
SECOND DISTRICT

February Term, A.D. 1935.

BERTHA RUST,
(Plaintiff) Appellee

vs.

Illinois Highway Transportation Co., a Corporation,
(Defendant) Appellant.

Appeal from the Circuit Court of Peoria County.

WOLFE * * P.J.

Bertha Rust, the plaintiff, started suit in the Circuit Court of Peoria County against the Illinois Highway Transportation Company, alleging that she was injured by reason of the negligence of the defendant in the operation of one of their buses. The declaration consists of three counts. The first count charges general negligence. The second charges that the defendant permitted their motor bus, in violation of the statute, to be parked and to stand stationery on a hard surfaced road so there was not ample room for two vehicles to pass upon the road or highway. The third count charges that the defendant was negligent in parking the motor bus on the hard surfaced road for a long space of time, to-wit, five minutes so that two vehicles could not pass thereon. To this declaration the defendant filed a plea of the general issue. Trial was had by a jury which resulted in a verdict of $800.00 for the plaintiff. The court entered judgment in favor of the plaintiff for this sum. From this judgment the defendant has perfected an appeal to this court.

The plaintiff lives in Pekin, Illinois, and she, in company with some of her friends had attended church in Peoria on the day of the accident. While driving from Peoria to Pekin on their

Gen. No. 34.   1298

SECOND DISTRICT

February Term, A.D. 1930.

BERTHA RUST,
(Plaintiff) Appellee

vs.   Appeal from the Circuit
                                       Court of Peoria County

Illinois Highway Transportation
Co., a Corporation,
(Defendant) Appellant.

WOLFE * * P.J.

Bertha Rust, the plaintiff, started suit in the Circuit Court of Peoria County against the Illinois Highway Transportation Company, alleging that she was injured by reason of the negligence of the defendant in the operation of one of their buses. The declaration consists of three counts. The first count charges general negligence. The second charges that the defendant permitted their motor bus, in violation of the statute, to be parked and to stand stationery on a hard surfaced road so there was not ample room for two vehicles to pass upon the road or highway. The third count charges that the defendant was negligent in parking the motor bus on the hard surfaced road for a long space of time, to-wit, five minutes so that two vehicles could not pass thereon. To this declaration the defendant filed a plea of the general issue. Trial was had by a jury which resulted in a verdict of $800.00 for the plaintiff. The court entered judgment in favor of the plaintiff for this sum. From this judgment the defendant has perfected an appeal to this court.

The plaintiff lives in Pekin, Illinois, and she, in company with some of her friends had attended church in Peoria on the day of the accident. While driving from Peoria to Pekin on their way home the collision occurred. The bus in question had stopped for a railroad, switch crossing on the hard road. It started again and went a short distance south of the railroad and stopped on the pavement, for a passenger to board the bus. The plaintiff was driving her car in a southerly direction following a Chevrolet car which was between the plaintiff and the bus. While the bus was standing on the hard road and when the Chevrolet was within a short distance of the bus the Chevrolet swerved suddenly to the left and the plaintiff became aware of the presence of the bus parked on the driveway. She could not swerve her Buick car far enough to the left to avoid a collision. The right side of the plaintiff's car struck the left rear end of the bus and the plaintiff received the injuries of which she complains.

The appellant does not seriously contend that they were not negligent in leaving the bus parked on the highway, but they do argue strenuously that the plaintiff was guilty of contributory negligence by running into the bus, and therefore, she should be barred from maintaining an action in this suit. Defendant also contends that the court erred in giving an instruction that if the plaintiff was placed in a position of danger by an emergency suddenly arising without her fault, that the plaintiff was not bound to use the same degree of care as otherwise would be required of her. We do not see how the jury could be mislead when the whole of the instruction is read, especially when it is considered with the other instructions given by the court.

While a court of review in reading the evidence might arrive at a different conclusion than that of the trial jury, it is a peculiar province of the jury to pass upon disputed questions of fact. We cannot say that this verdict is manifestly against the weight of the evidence, or that the judgment is excessive.

The Judgment of the Circuit Court of Peoria County is affirmed.

Judgment affirmed.

DOVE, J.

In my opinion the uncontradicted evidence in this record discloses appellee guilty of such contributory negligence as to bar a recovery.

way home the collision occurred. The bus in question had stopped for a railroad, switch crossing on the hard road. It started again and went a short distance south of the railroad and stopped on the pavement, for a passenger to board the bus. The plaintiff was driving her car in a southerly direction following a Chevrolet car which was between the plaintiff and the bus. While the bus was standing on the hard road and when the Chevrolet was within a short distance of the bus the Chevrolet swerved suddenly to the left and the plaintiff became aware of the presence of the bus parked on the driveway. She could not swerve her Buick car far enough to the left to avoid a collision. The right side of the plaintiff's car struck the left rear end of the bus and the plaintiff received the injuries of which she complains.

The appellant does not seriously contend that they were not negligent in leaving the bus parked on the highway, but they do argue strenuously that the plaintiff was guilty of contributory negligence by running into the bus, and therefore, she should be barred from maintaining an action in this suit. Defendant also contends that the court erred in giving an instruction that if the plaintiff was placed in a position of danger by an emergency suddenly arising without her fault, that the plaintiff was not bound to use the same degree of care as otherwise would be required of her. We do not see how the jury could be misled when the whole of the instruction is read, especially when it is considered with the other instructions given by the court.

While a court of review in reading the evidence might arrive at a different conclusion than that of the trial jury, it is a peculiar province of the jury to pass upon disputed questions of fact. We cannot say that this verdict is manifestly against the weight of the evidence, or that the judgment is excessive.

The judgment of the Circuit Court of Peoria County is affirmed.

with some of her 1 land Judgment affirmed.

the accident. While driving ...
In my opinion the uncontradicted evidence in this record
... guilty of such contributory negligence as to
... a recovery.

S, }ss.

I JUSTUS L. JOHNSON Clerk of the Appellate Court in and of the State of Illinois and the keeper of the Records and Seal thereof, do hereby g is a true copy of the opinion of the said Appellate Court in the above entitled cause.

In Testimony Whereof, I hereunto set my hand and affix the seal of said Appellate Court at Ottawa this________________day of ________________in the year of our Lord one thousand nine hundred and thirty-____________

____

Clerk of the Appellate Court

8876

AT A TERM OF THE APPELLATE COURT,

Begun and held at Ottawa, on Tuesday, the fifth day of February, in the year of our Lord one thousand nine hundred and thirty-five, within and for the Second District of the State of Illinois:

Present-- The Hon. FRED G. WOLFE, Presiding Justice

Hon. FRANKLIN R. DOVE, Justice

Hon. BLAINE HUFFMAN, Justice.

JUSTUS L. JOHNSON, Clerk

RALPH H. DESPER, Sheriff.

280 I.A. 630[4]

BE IT REMEMBERED, that afterwards, to-wit On MAY 1 1935 the opinion of the Court was filed in the Clerk's office of said Court, in the words and figures following, to-wit:

Gen. No. 8878 Agenda No. 11

In the Appellate Court of Illinois

Second District

February Term, A D 1935.

Eugene T. O'Neill and Charles J. O'Neill, partners doing business as O'Neill Brothers,

Appellants,

vs.

Whitaker Farmer's Elevator Company, a Corporation,

Appellee,

Appeal from the Circuit Court of Kankakee County

DOVE - J.

This is an action by appellants, O'Neill Brothers, holders of a note which was secured by a chattel mortgage on one thousand bushels of Indian corn, to recover the value of the corn from appellee, Whitaker Farmer's Elevator Company, a Corporation, the purchaser of said corn from Ed Rasmussen, the mortgagor. The cause was tried by the court, a jury being waived, and from a judgment in favor of appellee, the record is brought to this court for review by appeal.

It appears from the testimony that on February 28, 1930, Ed Rasmussen and his wife lived on a farm controlled by Mrs. Otto Weber and being indebted to the appellants in the sum of $802.32, executed and delivered to them a note for that amount, due January 1, 1931 and secured the payment of the same by executing and delivering to them a chattel mortgage on one thousand bushels of corn which Rasmussen had raised on the Weber land Approximately four hundred bushels of this corn was then in a crib near the residence on the farm where Mr. and Mrs. Rasmussen lived, and the balance had not been shucked, but was standing in the field near by. Certain other personal property not now in question was also covered by the mortgage. The mortgage conveyed to appellants "one thousand bushels of corn now in crib and field" and recited that the mortgagors were of

Gen. No. 8878 Agenda No. 11

In the Appellate Court of Illinois

Second District

February Term, A.D. 1935.

[illegible] T. O'Neill and Charles O'Neill, partners doing business as O'Neill Brothers,

Appellants,

vs.

Whitaker Farmer's Elevator Company, a Corporation,

Appellee.

Appeal from the Circuit Court of Kankakee County

[illegible] - J.

This is an action by appellants, O'Neill Brothers, holders of a note which was secured by a chattel mortgage on one thousand bushels of Indian corn, to recover the value of the corn from appellee, Whitaker Farmer's Elevator Company, a Corporation, the purchaser of said corn from Ed Rasmussen, the mortgagor. The cause was tried by the court, a jury being waived, and from a judgment in favor of appellee, the record is brought to this court for review by appeal.

It appears from the testimony that on February 28, 1930, Ed Rasmussen and his wife lived on a farm controlled by Mrs. Otto Weber and being indebted to the appellants in the sum of $802.32, executed and delivered to them a note for that amount, due January 1, 1931 and secured the payment of the same by executing and delivering to them a chattel mortgage on one thousand bushels of corn which Rasmussen had raised on the Weber land. Approximately four hundred bushels of this corn was then in a crib near the residence on the farm where Mr. and Mrs. Rasmussen lived, and the balance had not been husked, but was standing in the field near by. Certain other personal property not now in question was also covered by the mortgage. The mortgage conveyed to appellants "one thousand bushels of corn now in crib and field" and recited that the mortgagors were of

Sumner Township, Kankakee County, Illinois and contained the usual provisions for the mortgagors to retain possession of the chattels until default in the payment of the note. About June 27, 1930, Rasmussen sold to appellee for sixty-eight cents a bushel the one thousand bushels of corn covered by the mortgage, and delivered it to its grain elevator at Whitaker, two and one-half miles distant from the Weber farm where Rasmussen lived After the corn was delivered, appellee executed and delivered to Rasmussen on June 27, 1930 two checks aggregating $582.54, having previously advanced him on March 20, 1930 $37.00 and on June 11, 1930 $65.00.

It further appears from the evidence that for the crop year of 1929 Rasmussen had leased the premises upon which this corn was raised from Mrs. Weber, for which he was to pay her $1100 00 cash rent, one-half of which was payable September 15, 1929 and the remaining one-half was due February 15, 1930. At the time the corn was sold, all or at least a portion of this cash rent was unpaid.

Mr Rasmussen testified that Mr. Kahney, the manager of appellee, asked him at the time settlement was made for the corn to whom the corn belonged, and that he replied that it belonged to Mrs. Weber and himself, and that appellants had a mortgage on it. According to this witness that was all the conversation they had and thereupon Kahney gave the witness the check for $513.78. Mr. Rasmussen further testified that he didn't tell Mr. Kahney what he was going to do with the check, but that after he did receive it he went to Mrs. Weber's home with it.

Mrs. Weber testified that Rasmussen showed her the check which he received for the corn when he came to her home on June 27, 1930, but did not pay her any part of the rent that day, but later she went to his place and he wrote her a check for the balance that was left in the bank in his name She further testified that she "made some arrangement with him as to what ought to be done with the check the day he was in my home".

Sumner Township, Kankakee County, Illinois and contained the usual provisions for the mortgagors to retain possession of the chattels until default in the payment of the note. About June 27, 1930, Rasmussen sold to appellee for sixty-eight cents a bushel the one thousand bushels of corn covered by the mortgage, and delivered it to its grain elevator at Whitaker, two and one-half miles distant from the Weber farm where Rasmussen lived. After the corn was delivered, appellee executed and delivered to Rasmussen on June 27, 1930 two checks aggregating $582.54, having previously advanced him on March 20, 1930 $37.00 and on June 11, 1930 $65.00.

It further appears from the evidence that for the crop year of 1929 Rasmussen had leased the premises upon which this corn was raised from Mrs. Weber, for which he was to pay her $1100.00 cash rent, one-half of which was payable September 15, 1929 and the remaining one-half was due February 15, 1930. At the time the corn was sold, all or at least a portion of this cash rent was unpaid.

Mr. Rasmussen testified that Mr. Kahney, the manager of appellee, asked him at the time settlement was made for the corn to whom the corn belonged, and that he replied that it belonged to Mrs. Weber and himself, and that appellants had a mortgage on it. According to this witness that was all the conversation they had and thereupon Kahney gave the witness the check for $513.78. Mr. Rasmussen further testified that he didn't tell Mr. Kahney what he was going to do with the check, but that after he did receive it he went to Mrs. Weber's home with it.

Mrs. Weber testified that Rasmussen showed her the check which he received for the corn when he came to her home on June 27, 1930, but did not pay her any part of the rent that day, but later she went to his place and he wrote her a check for the balance that was left in the bank in his name. She further testified that she "made some arrangement with him as to what ought to be done with the check the day he was in my home."

H J. Kahney, the manager of appellee, testified that the corn which Rasmussen delivered was exactly one thousand bushels and that the purchase price was sixty-eight cents per bushel. That on March 20, 1930 Rasmussen gave Rook an order on appellee for $37.00 and on that day appellee gave Rook a check for that sum That on June 11, 1930 Rasmussen came in and said he had to have $65.00 and the witness gave him appellee's check for that sum. That on June 24, 1930 Rasmussen gave another order to pay the Advance Oil Company $68.76, so Rasmussen could pay for the gas for shelling the corn and a check for that amount, dated June 27, 1930, was issued by appellee to Rasmussen. That on June 27, 1930 Rasmussen stated he would have to have $513.78 to finish paying Mrs. Weber the rent, that the witness wanted to make the check out to Mrs. Weber but at the request of Rasmussen he made the check out to him, Rasmussen stating to Kahney that he would endorse it and give it to Mrs. Weber and by so doing it would be a receipt for his rent. Thereupon a check for that amount was given him. These four checks aggregated $4.54 more than the total amount due Rasmussen for the corn, and Mr. Kahney admitted that in making and delivering them to Rasmussen he disregarded Mrs. Weber's instructions and only did so because he relied upon the statements and promises of Rasmussen.

The foregoing is substantially all the evidence in this record concerning the same and delivery of the corn by Rasmussen, and the payment therefor by appellee, and it is the contention of counsel for appellee that on the day the corn was sold, Mrs Weber's lien for rent was superior to the lien of appellants under their chattel mortgage and that the evidence discloses that this superior lien was satisfied to the extent of the value of the corn which appellee purchased and that therefore appellants are precluded from recovering in this proceeding.

Appellants, while conceding that Mrs. Weber's lien was superior to that created by their chattel mortgage, insist that appellee,

H J Kenney, the manager of appellee, testified that the corn which Rasmussen delivered was exactly one thousand bushels and that the purchase price was sixty-eight cents per bushel. That on March 20, 1930 Rasmussen gave Rook an order on appellee for $37 00 and on that day appellee gave Rook a check for that sum. That on June 11, 1930 Rasmussen came in and said he had to have $65.00 and the witness gave him appellee's check for that sum. That on June 24, 1930 Rasmussen gave another order to pay the Advance Oil Company $66.76, so Rasmussen could pay for the gas for shelling the corn and a check for that amount, dated June 27, 1930, was issued by appellee to Rasmussen. That on June 27, 1930 Rasmussen stated he would have to have $513.78 to finish paying Mrs. Weber the rent; that the witness wanted to make the check out to Mrs Weber but at the request of Rasmussen he made the check out to him, Rasmussen stating to Kenney that he would endorse it and give it to Mrs Weber and by so doing it would be a receipt for his rent. Thereupon a check for that amount was given him. These four checks aggregated $4.54 more than the total amount due Rasmussen for the corn, and Mr Kenney admitted that in making and delivering them to Rasmussen he disregarded Mrs. Weber's instructions and only did so because he relied upon the statements and promises of Rasmussen.

The foregoing is substantially all the evidence in this record concerning the sale and delivery of the corn by Rasmussen, and the payment therefor by appellee, and it is the contention of counsel for appellee that on the day the corn was sold, Mrs Weber's lien for rent was superior to the lien of appellants under their chattel mortgage and that the evidence discloses that this superior lien was satisfied to the extent of the value of the corn which appellee purchased and that therefore appellants are precluded from recovering in this proceeding.

Appellants, while conceding that Mrs. Weber's lien was superior to that secured by their chattel mortgage, insist that appellee, took the day it was in purchasing this corn, committed a tort and as Mrs. Weber took no affirmative action in connection with her lien, she thereby waived it and in support of their contention that Mrs. Weber waived her lien, insist that the evidence does not disclose that the checks delivered by appellee to Rasmussen for this corn or the proceeds thereof were ever received by Mrs. Weber in satisfaction of her superior lien.

In support of the contention that Mrs. Weber waived her lien and acquiesced in the payment by appellee to Rasmussen, counsel for appellants cite Goeing v. Outhouse, 95 Ill. 346. It appeared in that case that Volney Carter had rented from appellants forty acres of land to be farmed in Indian corn, the landlords to receive one-fourth of the crop. Appellants issued a distress warrant, which was levied upon an undivided three-fourths of the forty acres of corn. The distress proceedings were instituted before a Justice of the Peace, who rendered judgment for the tenant. Upon appeal appellants recovered a judgment against Carter, the tenant, and a special execution was awarded against the property distrained. Pending these proceedings, appellees purchased the corn levied upon under the distress warrant and appropriated the same to their use. Thereupon the suit reported in 95 Ill. 346, supra, was instituted by appellants to recover damages for the alleged wrongful taking of the corn. The controverted question of fact was whether the landlord had waived his lien and the evidence disclosed that after the tenant had sold three-fourths of the corn raised on the landlord's premises, the agent of the landlords had a conversation with the purchaser and told him he had settled with the tenant and that nothing was due from him except that the landlord was to receive the remaining one-fourth of the corn which he was to gather at his own expense. The evidence further disclosed that while this conversation was had after the corn was purchased, it had not been paid for and the purchase money was not paid Carter until after this conversation with the agent of the landlord.

n purchasing this corn, committed a tort and as Mrs. Weber took
o affirmative action in connection with her lien, she thereby
aived it and in support of their contention that Mrs. Weber waived
er lien, insist that the evidence does not disclose that the checks
elivered by appellee to Rasmussen for this corn or the proceeds
hereof were ever received by Mrs. Weber in satisfaction of her
uperior lien.

In support of the contention that Mrs. Weber waived her lien
nd acquiesced in the payment by appellee to Rasmussen, counsel for
ppellants cite Cooling v. Outhouse, 85 Ill. 248. It appeared in that
ase that Volney Carter had rented from appellants forty acres of land
o be farmed in Indian corn, the landlords to receive one-fourth of
he crop. Appellants issued a distress warrant, which was levied upon
n undivided three-fourths of the forty acres of corn. The distress
roceedings were instituted before a Justice of the Peace, who render-
d judgment for the tenant. Upon appeal appellants recovered a judg-
ent against Carter, the tenant, and a special execution was awarded
gainst the property distrained. Pending those proceedings, appellees
urchased the corn levied upon under the distress warrant and appro-
riated the same to their use. Thereupon the suit reported in 85 Ill.
48, supra, was instituted by appellants to recover damages for the
lleged wrongful taking of the corn. The controverted question of
act was whether the landlord had waived his lien and the evidence
isclosed that after the tenant had sold three-fourths of the corn
aised on the landlord's premises, the agent of the landlords had
 conversation with the purchaser and told him he had settled with
he tenant and that nothing was due from him except that the land-
ord was to receive the remaining one-fourth of the corn which he
as to gather at his own expense. The evidence further disclosed
hat while this conversation was had after the corn was purchased,
t had not been paid for and the purchase money was not paid Carter
ntil after this conversation with the agent of the landlord.

Appellants also cite in this connection the case of Leeper v. Rogers Grain Co., 145 Ill. App. 424, which was also an action by a landlord to recover the value of corn raised upon his premises which the tenant sold to the defendant. The trial in the Circuit Court resulted in a verdict for the plaintiff which was reversed because the decisive question in the case was whether the landlord had waived his lien by consenting to or acquiescing in the payment by the defendant to the tenant of the proceeds derived from the sale of the corn and the given instructions which directed a verdict entirely ignored this issue.

The conduct of Mrs. Weber in the instant case is not analagous to the conduct of the landlords in the Goeing case, nor are the facts in the Leeper case at all similar to the facts in the instant proceeding. Both of those cases were suits instituted by landlords to enforce their liens. Mrs. Weber is the landlord in the instant case. She did nothing prior to the sale of the corn which can be construed as a waiver of her lien. She had theretofore told appellee not to pay the tenant for the corn, but when she found out her instructions had been disregarded and that the tenant had received the money, she went to the tenant, Rasmussen, and he paid her an undisclosed amount, which we are satisfied came from the sale of the corn, and made some arrangement which was satisfactory to both of them, and as a result of which no proceedings to enforce her lien were ever taken by her and she is not complaining in this proceeding.

We are inclined to believe from all the testimony in this record that so far as the check for $513.78 is concerned, Rasmussen, with Mrs. Weber's express or implied consent, retained it and placed it to his own credit and that subsequently all or at least a portion of the proceeds thereof were received by Mrs. Weber in satisfaction of her lien for rent, that to the extent of $513.78 Mrs. Weber's superior lien was discharged by money paid by appellee to Rasmussen for this corn upon which appellants had their mortgage and this being

Appellants also cite in this connection the case of Leeper v. Rogers Grain Co., 145 Ill. App. 424, which was also an action by a landlord to recover the value of corn raised upon his premises which the tenant sold to the defendant. The trial in the Circuit Court resulted in a verdict for the plaintiff which was reversed because the decisive question in the case was whether the landlord had waived his lien by consenting to or acquiescing in the payment by the defendant to the tenant of the proceeds derived from the sale of the corn and the given instructions which directed a verdict entirely ignored this issue.

The conduct of Mrs. Weber in the instant case is not analagous to the conduct of the landlords in the Goeing case, nor are the facts in the Leeper case at all similar to the facts in the instant proceeding. Both of those cases were suits instituted by landlords to enforce their liens. Mrs. Weber is the landlord in the instant case. She did nothing prior to the sale of the corn which can be construed as a waiver of her lien. She had theretofore told appellees not to pay the tenant for the corn, but when she found out her instructions had been disregarded and that the tenant had received the money, she went to the tenant, Rasmussen, and he paid her an undisclosed amount, which we are satisfied came from the sale of the corn, and made some arrangement which was satisfactory to both of them, and as a result of which no proceedings to enforce her lien were ever taken by her and she is not complaining in this proceeding.

We are inclined to believe from all the testimony in this record that so far as the check for $513.73 is concerned, Rasmussen, with Mrs. Weber's express or implied consent, retained it and placed it to his own credit and that subsequently all or at least a portion of the proceeds thereof were received by Mrs. Weber in satisfaction of her lien for rent, that to the extent of $513.78 Mrs. Weber's superior lien was discharged by money paid by appellees to Rasmussen for this corn upon which appellants had their mortgage and this being true, appellee has a defense to this proceeding to the extent of $513.78 As to the balance of $166.22 appellants are clearly entitled to a judgment.

We have not overlooked the other contentions of appellee wherein it is insisted that appellants' mortgage is invalid because it was not properly acknowledged by Mrs. Rasmussen, that the description of the mortgaged property was uncertain and that it was fraudulent as to appellee because the mortgaged property was consumable in use. There is, in our opinion, no merit in any of these contentions.

As this case was tried by the court, a jury having been waived, this court may under the provisions of the Civil Practice Act enter such judgment as should have been entered by the trial court.

The judgment of the Circuit Court is therefore reversed and judgment is entered in this court in favor of appellants and against appellee for $166.22.

Reversed and Judgment Here.

true, appellee has a defense to this proceeding to the extent of $813.78. As to the balance of $165.25 appellants are clearly entitled to a judgment.

We have not overlooked the other contentions of appellee wherein it is insisted that appellants' mortgage is invalid because it was not properly acknowledged by Mrs. Rasmussen, that the description of the mortgaged property was uncertain and that it was fraudulent as to appellee because the mortgaged property was consumable in use. There is, in our opinion, no merit in any of these contentions.

As this case was tried by the court, a jury having been waived, this court may under the provisions of the Civil Practice Act enter such judgment as should have been entered by the trial court.

The judgment of the Circuit Court is therefore reversed and judgment is entered in this court in favor of appellants and against appellee for $165.25.

Reversed and judgment here.

}ss.

I, JUSTUS L. JOHNSON Clerk of the Appellate Court in and of the State of Illinois, and the keeper of the Records and Seal thereof, do hereby ; is a true copy of the opinion of the said Appellate Court in the above entitled cause.

In Testimony Whereof, I hereunto set my hand and affix the seal of said Appellate Court, at Ottawa this ______________ day of ______________ in the year of our Lord one thousand nine hundred and thirty-______________

____

Clerk of the Appellate Court

AT A TERM OF THE APPELLATE COURT,

Begun and held at Ottawa, on Tuesday, the fifth day of February, in the year of our Lord one thousand nine hundred and thirty-five, within and for the Second District of the State of Illinois:

Present-- The Hon. FRED G. WOLFE, Presiding Justice.

Hon. FRANKLIN R. DOVE, Justice

Hon. BLAINE HUFFMAN, Justice.

JUSTUS L. JOHNSON, Clerk

RALPH H. DESPER, Sheriff. 280 I.A. 631

BE IT REMEMBERED, that afterwards, to-wit On MAY 1 1935 the opinion of the Court was filed in the Clerk's office of said Court, in the words and figures following, to-wit:

GEN. NO. 8899 AGENDA NO. 23

IN THE
APPELLATE COURT OF ILLINOIS
SECOND DISTRICT

February Term, A.D. 1935.

UP-STATE MOTORS, INC., a Corporation, and T. V. Vandergrift,

Appellees,

vs.

MERCHANTS INSURANCE COMPANY OF PROVIDENCE, a corporation,

Appellant.

APPEAL FROM THE CIRCUIT COURT OF LAKE COUNTY.

DOVE, J.

This was an action instituted on October 31, 1933 by Up-State Motors, Inc., a Corporation, and T. V. Vandergrift, before a Justice of the Peace of Lake County, against the Merchants Insurance Company to recover upon a policy of insurance issued by the defendant to the plaintiff Vandergrift, which insured Vandergrift from loss by fire or theft of a DeSoto automobile. The case was subsequently appealed to the Circuit Court, where a trial was had and at the conclusion of all of the evidence, the jury, in obedience to a peremptory instruction, returned a verdict in favor of the plaintiffs and against the defendant for $400.00, upon which judgment was rendered and the record is here for review by appeal.

It is first insisted by appellant that the evidence discloses that at the time the policy was issued the title of Vandergrift to the automobile was not unconditional, but that all the interest he had therein was that of a purchaser under a conditional sales contract from the Up-State Motors, Inc., which had, by the contract, reserved title in itself until the car was fully paid for. The evidence does disclose that Vandergrift purchased and obtained possession of the car covered by the policy from Up-

GEN NO 8899

IN THE
APPELLATE COURT OF ILLINOIS
SECOND DISTRICT

February Term, A D 1955.

UP-STATE MOTORS, INC , a Corporation, and T V Vandergrift,

Appellees,

vs.

MERCHANTS INSURANCE COMPANY OF PROVIDENCE, a corporation

Appellant

APPEAL FROM THE CIRCUIT COURT OF LAKE COUNTY

DOVE, J.

This was an action instituted on October 31, 1953 by Up-State Motors, Inc., a Corporation and T V Vandergrift, before a Justice of the Peace of Lake County, against the Merchants Insurance Company to recover upon a policy of insurance issued by the defendant to the plaintiff Vandergrift, which insured Vandergrift from loss by fire or theft of a DeSoto automobile. The case was subsequently appealed to the Circuit Court where a trial was had and at the conclusion of all of the evidence, the jury, in obedience to a peremptory instruction returned a verdict in favor of the plaintiffs and against the defendant for $400 00, upon which judgment was rendered and the record is here for review by appeal.

It is first insisted by appellant that the evidence discloses that at the time the policy was issued the title of Vandergrift to the automobile was not unconditional, but that all the interest he had therein was that of purchaser under a conditional sales contract from the Up-State Motors, Inc., which had, by the contract, reserved title in itself until the car was fully paid for. The evidence does disclose that Vandergrift purchased and obtained possession of the car covered by the policy from Up-

State Motors, Inc. at Waukegan, on July 7, 1932, paying therefor $150.00 in cash and executing a conditional sales contract by the provisions of which he obligated himself to pay the further sum of $370.20 in semi-monthly payments of $11.25 each. The evidence further discloses that on February 13, 1933 appellant issued its policy of insurance thereon, insuring Vandergrift for one year against loss by fire or theft to the amount of $400.00, that the application for this policy was given by Vandergrift to Lee Savage, an insurance solicitor then in the employ of Burt Love, that Vandergrift advised Savage of the true condition of the title, that Love was the agent of appellant and as such agent accepted Vandergrift's application, issued the policy, countersigned it and the policy was thereupon delivered to Vandergrift. While the policy contained a provision to the effect that it would be void unless the assured was the unconditional and sole owner of the subject of the insurance, we are of the opinion that notice given to Savage by Vandergrift of the true condition of the title was notice to appellant. Phenix Ins. Co. v. Hart, 149 Ill. 513, Guter v. Security Benefit Ass'n., 335 Ill. 174. But if this were not so, the conduct of appellant thereafter amounted to a waiver of its right to forefeit the policy for this reason. The evidence discloses that on March 29, 1933 the car was stolen at Little Rock, Arkansas, while Vandergrift was on a visit to his parents and he, Vandergrift, immediately wired Love and also Mr. Spero, an officer of the Up-State Motors, Inc., advising them of what had happened, and about April 1, 1933, Vandergrift returned to Waukegan, and in company with Mr. Spero, reported the loss personally to Love, who testified as a witness for appellees that he thereupon notified by phone the state agent of appellant and sent appellant a notice of loss signed by Vandergrift. The duplicate of this notice of loss was produced by Love upon the trial, identified by him and it is dated April 5, 1933, is signed by Love, states that appellants special agent had been advised of the loss and recites that there is a mortgage on the car payable to Up-State Motors, Inc. Thereafter H. T. Sharp,

State Motors, Inc. at Waukegan, on July 7, 1932, paying therefor $150.00 in cash and executing a conditional sales contract by the provisions of which he obligated himself to pay the further sum of $370.80 in semi-monthly payments of $11.25 each. The evidence further discloses that on February 13, 1933 appellant issued its policy of insurance thereon, insuring Vandergrift for one year against loss by fire or theft to the amount of $400.00, that the application for this policy was given by Vandergrift to Lee Savage, an insurance solicitor then in the employ of Burt Love, that Vandergrift advised Savage of the true condition of the title, that Love was the agent of appellant and as such agent accepted Vandergrift's application, issued the policy, countersigned it and the policy was thereupon delivered to Vandergrift. While the policy contained a provision to the effect that it would be void unless the assured was the unconditional and sole owner of the subject of the insurance, we are of the opinion that notice given to Savage by Vandergrift of the true condition of the title was notice to appellant. Phenix Ins. Co. v. Hart, 149 Ill. 513, Outer v. Security Benefit Ass'n., 335 Ill. 174. But if this were not so, the conduct of appellant thereafter amounted to a waiver of its right to forfeit the policy for this reason. The evidence discloses that on March 12, 1933 the car was stolen at Little Rock, Arkansas, while Vandergrift was on a visit to his parents and he, Vandergrift, immediately wired Love and also Mr. Spero, an officer of the Up-State Motors, Inc., advising them of what had happened, and about April 1, 1933, Vandergrift returned to Waukegan, and in company with Mr. Spero, reported the loss personally to Love, who testified as a witness for appellant that he thereupon notified by phone the state agent of appellant and sent appellant a notice of loss signed by Vandergrift. The duplicate of this notice of loss was produced by Love upon the trial, identified by him and it is dated April 5, 1933, is signed by Love, states that appellants special agent had been advised of the loan and points that there is a mortgage on the car payable to the Up-State Motors, Inc. Thereafter H. T. Sharp, an adjuster for appellant, came to Love's office and also to the office of Up-State Motors, Inc. and there had a conversation with Vandergrift and Spero and the parties arrived at a settlement and a proof of loss was made up and Sharp requested that it be sent by mail to appellant, which was done on May 24th Or 25th, 1933. On June 10, 1933 Sharp wrote Vandergrift and returned the proof of loss to him, stating in his letter "We are returning same (the proof of loss), inasmuch as the company has instructed us to reject this proof of loss due to irregularities and variances of facts, which have developed during the course of the investigation. * * * You will find attached proof of loss, which represents your equity in the car in the amount of $89.80, which, if you wish to sign and execute at this time, the company has authorized us to accept a proof of loss in settlement in the amount of $89.80. If you wish to accept this offer, kindly return this proof of loss by return mail". This offer was not accepted by Vandergrift and on October 4, 1933, appellant sent Vandergrift its check for $7.20, the premium paid for the policy sued on, stating in the letter which accompanied the check that on completing its investigation it found that "the insuring company had legal title to the car even before it was sold to T. V. Vandergrift and under the circumstances the policy was void from its inception, had no force or effect or existence and it is for this reason the premium is returned."

Appellant was advised of the fact that Up-State Motors, Inc. had title to this car within a few days after the car was stolen. It never denied liability on that ground but discussed the loss with the officers of Up-State Motors, Inc. and the interested parties arrived at a settlement and proof of loss was executed by Spero, an officer of Up-State Motors, Inc. and by Vandergrift, and thereafter mailed to appellant at the request of appellant's adjuster. This proof of loss was rejected, but not upon the ground that Vandergrift did not have title to the car insured. Appellant by its conduct has waived its right to deny liability on the ground that Vandergrift's title was not unconditional. Traders Mutual Life Ins. Co. v. Johnson, 200 Ill. 359.

an adjuster for appellant, came to [illegible]'s office [illegible] also to the office of Up-state Motors, Inc. and there [illegible] action. It Vandergrift and Spero and the parties arrived at a settlement [illegible] a proof of loss was made up and [illegible] by mail to appellant, which was done on May 4th (or 5th), 1952. On June 10, 1952 Sharp wrote Vandergrift and returned the proof of loss to him stating in his letter "We are returning same (the proof of loss), inasmuch as this company has instructed us to reject this proof of loss due to irregularities and a number of facts, which have developed during the course of the investigation. * * * You will find attached proof of loss, which represents our equity in the car in the amount of [illegible], which [illegible] sign and execute [illegible] any one authorized to accept a proof of loss in settlement in the amount of $57.00 [illegible] you wish to accept this offer, kindly return this proof of loss by return mail." This offer was not accepted by Vandergrift nor [illegible] October 4, 1953, appellant sent Vandergrift its check for $7.20, the premium paid for the policy sued on, stating in the letter which accompanied the check that on completing its investigation it [illegible] that "the insuring company had legal title to the car even before it was sold to T. V. Vandergrift and under the circumstances the policy was void from its inception, had no force or effect or existence and it is for this reason the premium is returned."

Appellant was advised of the fact that Up-state Motors Inc. had title to this car within a few days after the car was stolen. It never denied liability on that ground but processed the loss with the office of Up-state Motors, Inc. [illegible] parties arrived at a settlement and proof of loss was executed by Spero, an officer of Up-state Motors, Inc., and by Vandergrift, and thereafter mailed to appellant at the request of [illegible] its adjuster. This proof of loss was rejected, but not upon the ground that Vandergrift did not have title to the car insured. Appellant by its conduct has waived its right to deny liability on the ground that Vandergrift's title was not unconditional. Traders Mutual Life Ins. Co. v. Johnson, 200 Ill. 359

At the conclusion of the evidence offered by appellees, appellant sought to prove by the depositions of several witnesses certain transactions had by one C. F. McDonald in the State of Wisconsin with reference to a De Soto automobile.

It appears from the record that in December, 1930 C. F. McDonald owned a De Soto automobile, subject to a mortgage thereon held by the Auto Credit Company. On December 27th of that year he, McDonald, executed a Bill of Sale thereon to Wisconsin Acceptance Corporation and on the same day McDonald, as purchaser, and the Wisconsin Acceptance Corporation as seller executed a conditional sales contract. Under this agreement, McDonald agreed to pay the Wisconsin Acceptance Corporation $48.72 one month after the date thereof and $44.00 each month thereafter, continuing for eleven months.

Prior to July 7, 1932 which was the date of the transaction had between Vandergrift and Up-State Motors, Inc., at which time Vandergrift purchased the car covered by the policy sued upon and on December 4th, 1931, C. F. McDonald executed a note for $304.00 and secured the payment of the same by a chattel mortgage to The Time Acceptance Corporation. A part of the proceeds of this loan was used by Up-State Motors, Inc. to discharge the balance due the Wisconsin Acceptance Corporation under its conditional sales contract of December 27, 1930. The mortgage to the Time Acceptance Corporation described the car as one De Soto De Luxe automobile Motor No. C. F. 3113 D, factory car No. L 015 W.W. The note was to be paid in monthly installments of $25.35 each from January 4, 1932 to December 4, 1932 inclusive. This mortgage was filed in the Register's office of Milwaukee County, Wisconsin on December 5, 1931. McDonald paid the monthly installments for January, February, March, April and May 1932, the last payment being on May 18, 1932. The Time Acceptance Corporation had this car, with others, insured by the Rhode Island Insurance Company, and in August, 1932 the Rhode Island Insurance Company paid the Time Acceptance Company $177.50, the balance due under its chattel mortgage.

At the time of the transaction between McDonald and the Time Acceptance Corporation on December 4, 1931, there was a chattel

At the conclusion of the evidence offered by appellees, appellant sought to prove by the depositions of several witnesses certain transactions had by one C. F. McDonald in the State of Wisconsin with reference to a De Soto automobile.

It appears from the record that in December, 1930 C. F. McDonald owned a De Soto automobile, subject to a mortgage thereon held by the Auto Credit Company. On December 27th of that year he, McDonald, executed a Bill of Sale thereon to Wisconsin Acceptance Corporation and on the same day McDonald, as purchaser, and the Wisconsin Acceptance Corporation as seller executed a conditional sales contract. Under this agreement, McDonald agreed to pay the Wisconsin Acceptance Corporation $48.72 one month after the date thereof and $44.00 each month thereafter, continuing for eleven months.

Prior to July 7, 1933 which was the date of the transaction had between Vandergrift and Up-State Motors, Inc., at which time Vandergrift purchased the car covered by the policy sued upon and on December 4th, 1931, C. F. McDonald executed a note for $304.00 and secured the payment of the same by a chattel mortgage to The Time Acceptance Corporation. A part of the proceeds of this loan was used by Up-State Motors, Inc. to discharge the balance due the Wisconsin Acceptance Corporation under its conditional sales contract of December 27, 1930. The mortgage to the Time Acceptance Corporation described the car as one De Soto De Luxe automobile Motor No. C. F. 3113 D, factory car No. L 915 W.W. The note was to be paid in monthly installments of $25.33 each from January 4, 1932 to December 4, 1932 inclusive. This mortgage was filed in the Register's office of Milwaukee County, Wisconsin on December 5, 1931. McDonald paid the monthly installments for January, February, March, April and May 1932, the last payment being on May 18, 1932. The Time Acceptance Corporation had this car, with others, insured by the Rhode Island Insurance Company, and in August, 1932 the Rhode Island Insurance Company paid the Time Acceptance Company $177.50, the balance due under its chattel mortgage.

At the time of the transaction between McDonald and the Time Acceptance Corporation on December 4, 1931, there was a chattel mortgage on this automobile, having been executed by C. F. McDonald to the National Discount Corporation on September 4, 1931 to secure the payment of $300.00, which was payable in twelve monthly installments of $30.40 each. McDonald paid the monthly installments for the months of October, November and December, 1931 and also the installment for January, 1932. He did not pay the February, 1932 installment, but on or about March 4, 1932 he, McDonald, and the National Discount Corporation and the Up-State Motors, Inc. made some arrangements whereby McDonald's interest in the automobile was conveyed to the Up-State Motors, Inc. and the Up-State Motors, Inc. took possession of the car and completed the monthly payments thereon to the National Discount Corporation, the final payment being made on September 17, 1932. It was the contention of appellant that these transactions show that the Rhode Island Insurance Company had a lien upon this automobile by virtue of the fact that it paid, in August, 1932, to the Time Acceptance Corporation, the balance due upon its chattel mortgage. And that when it did so, it procured an assignment of that chattel mortgage and that Vandergrift took no title when he purchased from the Up-State Motors, Inc. because in March, 1932 when McDonald made his agreement with the Up-State Motors, Inc. and delivered the car to it, it was subject to the mortgage of September 4, 1931 in favor of the National Discount Corporation and also subject to the mortgage of December 4, 1931 to the Time Acceptance Corporation.

The evidence which appellant offered, had it been admitted, tended to prove that the National Discount Corporation mortgage of September 4, 1931 was satisfied by Up-State Motors, Inc. paying the amount due thereon in full. The mortgage dated December 4, 1931 executed by C. F. McDonald to the Time Acceptance Corporation described the mortgaged property as one De Soto DeLuxe Sedan automobile, motor number C. F. 3113 D, factory car number L. O. 15 W.W. It appears to have been filed in the Register's office of Milwaukee County, Wisconsin December 5, 1931. When this exhibit was offered in evidence before the Commissioner who took the depositions of the several witnesses and during the examination of Mr. Morris Wallesz, who testified that he mortgage on this automobile, having been executed by C. F McDonald to the National Discount Corporation on September 4, 1931 to secure the payment of $300.00, which was payable in twelve monthly installments of $30.40 each. McDonald paid the monthly installments for the months of October, November and December, 1931 and also the installment for January, 1932. He did not pay the February, 1932 installment, but on or about March 4, 1932 he, McDonald, and the National Discount Corporation and the Up-State Motors, Inc. made some arrangements whereby McDonald's interest in the automobile was conveyed to the Up-State Motors, Inc. and the Up-State Motors, Inc. took possession of the car and completed the monthly payments thereon to the National Discount Corporation, the final payment being made on September 17, 1932. It was the contention of appellant that these transactions show that the Rhode Island Insurance Company had a lien upon this automobile by virtue of the fact that it paid, in August, 1932, to the Time Acceptance Corporation, the balance due upon its chattel mortgage, and that when it did so, it procured an assignment of that chattel mortgage and that Vandergrift took no title when he purchased from the Up-State Motors, Inc. because in March, 1932 when McDonald made his agreement with the Up-State Motors, Inc. and delivered the car to it, it was subject to the mortgage of September 4, 1931 in favor of the National Discount Corporation and also subject to the mortgage of December 4, 1931 to the Time Acceptance Corporation.

The evidence which appellant offered, had it been admitted, tended to prove that the National Discount Corporation mortgage of September 4, 1931 was satisfied by Up-State Motors, Inc. paying the amount due thereon in full. The mortgage dated December 4, 1931 executed by C. F McDonald to the Time Acceptance Corporation described the mortgaged property as one De Soto Deluxe Sedan automobile, motor number 6. F. 3113 D, factory car number L. O. 15 W. It appears to have been filed in the Register's office of Milwaukee County, Wisconsin December 5, 1931. When this exhibit was offered in evidence before the Commissioner who took the depositions of the several witnesses and during the examination of Mr. Morris Wallock, who testified that he at the was secretary and treasurer of the Time Acceptance Corporation, the specific objection was made that the factory number shown on the mortgage was different than the factory number of the automobile in question. A general objection was also made to the effect that the testimony of the witnesses and this exhibit were immaterial, incompetent and irrelevant. Upon direct examination, Mr. Wallesz testified that in August, 1932 when he received the amount due his company under the chattel mortgage from the Rhode Island Insurance Company, he assigned the chattel mortgage to the Insurance Company. He had previously testified that the note for which the chattel mortgage was given had been turned over to the Nurnberg Adjustment Company. Upon cross examination he testified that he had signed an assignment of the chattel mortgage to the Rhode Island Insurance Company, but that he did not know where the assignment was and that there was nothing due from McDonald to the Time Acceptance Corporation. In this state of the record, we are clearly of the opinion that the testimony which appellant offered in the depositions of the several witnesses disclosed no defense in this proceeding. The policy sued on described the automobile as a De Soto sedan, serial number L. O. - 15-W.W. and the motor number as F. 3113 O. The description of the automobile in the mortgage which McDonald executed to the Time Acceptance Corporation gave its motor number as C. F. 3113 D. There is no proof in this record that the mortgaged automobile was the same automobile covered by the insurance policy sued upon, but assuming that it is, still the evidence discloses that the amount due the Time Acceptance Corporation under its note secured by a chattel mortgage has been paid and there is no proof that the note had ever been assigned to the Rhode Island Insurance Company and no competent proof that the mortgage had been assigned to it. What the record does disclose with reference to this chattel mortgage is that the last installment of the debt secured thereby matured December 4, 1932 and while at the time Vandergrift purchased this car from the Up-State Motors, Ins. all of the installments upon the note secured by the Time was secretary and treasurer of the Time Acceptance Corporation, the specific objection was made that the factory number shown on the mortgage was different than the factory number of the automobile in question. A general objection was also made to the effect that the testimony of the witnesses and this exhibit were immaterial, incompetent and irrelevant. Upon direct examination, Mr. Walless testified that in August, 1932 when he received the amount due his company under the chattel mortgage from the Rhode Island Insurance Company, he assigned the chattel mortgage to the Insurance Company. He had previously testified that the note for which the chattel mortgage was given had been turned over to the Nurnberg Adjustment Company. Upon cross examination he testified that he had signed an assignment of the chattel mortgage to the Rhode Island Insurance Company, but that he did not know where the assignment was and that there was nothing due from McDonald to the Time Acceptance Corporation. In this state of the record, we are clearly of the opinion that the testimony which appellant offered in the depositions of the several witnesses disclosed no defense in this proceeding. The policy sued on described the automobile as a De Soto sedan, serial number L. O. - 15-W.W. and the motor number as F. 3113 O. The description of the automobile in the mortgage which McDonald executed to the Time Acceptance Corporation gave its motor number as C. F. 3113 D There is no proof in this record that the mortgaged automobile was the same automobile covered by the insurance policy sued upon, but assuming that it is, still the evidence discloses that the amount due the Time Acceptance Corporation under its note secured by a chattel mortgage has been paid and there is no proof that the note had ever been assigned to the Rhode Island Insurance Company and no competent proof that the mortgage had been assigned to it. What the record does disclose with reference to this chattel mortgage is that the last installment of the debt secured thereby matured December 4, 1932 and while at the time Vandergrift purchased this car from the Up-State Motors, Inc. all of the installments upon the note secured by the Time

Acceptance Corporation mortgage had not matured, the last installment had matured more than three months before the policy sued on was issued, and default in making any payments thereunder occurred on May 18, 1932 and no further payments had ever been made thereafter, and it is not contended that appellees had any actual or constructive notice of the chattel mortgage to the Time Acceptance Corporation or its assigns. If, however, we assume that the chattel mortgage executed by McDonald to the Time Acceptance Corporation on December 4, 1931 did cover the automobile which Vandergrift purchased on July 7, 1932 and if we further assume that this mortgage was assigned to the Rhode Island Insurance Company in August, 1932, and that the insurance company was subrogated to the rights of the Acceptance Corporation, still the Rhode Island Insurance Company is not attempting to assert any rights in this proceeding which it may have acquired by virtue of the provisions of this chattel mortgage, and therefore the question that was presented in National Bond and Investment Co. v. Larsh, 262 Ill. App. 363, and in National Bond and Investment Co./v. Moss, 263 Ill. App. 187, does not arise upon this record. This is not a contest between the parties who seek to assert title or claim possession of an automobile, but is a suit brought to recover upon an insurance policy, and the defense sought to be interposed is that the insured was not the unconditional and sole owner of the subject of insurance.

In our opinion the trial court properly directed a verdict in favor of the plaintiff. There is no merit in appellant's contention that the amount of the loss was not proven. The only evidence in the record is that the car at the time of the loss had a fair, cash, market value of $400.00 and the court in its peremptory instruction directed a verdict for that amount.

There is no reversible error in this record and the judgment of the Circuit Court is therefore affirmed.

JUDGMENT AFFIRMED.

Acceptance Corporation mortgage had not matured, the last installment had matured more than three months before the policy sued on was issued, and default in making any payments thereunder occurred on May 18, 1932 and no further payments had ever been made thereafter, and it is not contended that appellees had any actual or constructive notice of the chattel mortgage to the Time Acceptance Corporation or its assigns. If, however, we assume that the chattel mortgage executed by McDonald to the Time Acceptance Corporation on December 4, 1931 did cover the automobile which Vandergrift purchased on July 7, 1932 and if we further assume that this mortgage was assigned to the Rhode Island Insurance Company in August, 1932, and that the insurance company was subrogated to the rights of the Acceptance Corporation, still the Rhode Island Insurance Company is not attempting to assert any rights in this proceeding which it may have acquired by virtue of the provisions of this chattel mortgage, and therefore the question that was presented in National Bond and Investment Co. v. Latan, 252 Ill. App. 583, and in National Bond and Investment Co. v. Loss, 265 Ill. App. 197, does not arise upon this record. This is not a contest between the parties who seek to assert title or claim possession of an automobile, but is a suit brought to recover upon an insurance policy, and the defense sought to be interposed is that the insured was not the unconditional and sole owner of the subject of insurance.

In our opinion the trial court properly directed a verdict in favor of the plaintiff. There is no merit in appellant's contention that the amount of the loss was not proven. The only evidence in the record is that the car at the time of the loss had a fair, cash, market value of $400.00 and the court in its peremptory instruction directed a verdict for that amount.

There is no reversible error in this record and the judgment of the Circuit Court is therefore affirmed.

JUDGMENT AFFIRMED.

S, }ss. I JUSTUS L. JOHNSON Clerk of the Appellate Court in and of the State of Illinois, and the keeper of the Records and Seal thereof do hereby g is a true copy of the opinion of the said Appellate Court in the above entitled cause.

In Testimony Whereof, I hereunto set my hand and affix the seal of said Appellate Court, at Ottawa, this____________day of ____________in the year of our Lord one thousand nine hundred and thirty-____________

____

Clerk of the Appellate Court

AT A TERM OF THE APPELLATE COURT,

Begun and held at Ottawa, on Tuesday, the seventh day of May, in the year of our Lord one thousand nine hundred and thirty-five, within and for the Second District of the State of Illinois:

Present-- The Hon. FRED G. WOLFE, Presiding Justice

Hon. FRANKLIN R. DOVE, Justice.

Hon. BLAINE HUFFMAN, Justice.

JUSTUS L. JOHNSON, Clerk

RALPH H. DESPER, Sheriff. 280 I.A. 631[2]

44

BE IT REMEMBERED, that afterwards, to-wit On MAY 17 1935 the opinion of the Court was filed in the Clerk's office of said Court, in the words and figures following, to-wit:

GEN. NO. 8856 AGENDA NO. 5.

IN THE

APPELLATE COURT OF ILLINOIS

SECOND DISTRICT

February Term, A. D 1935

AMALIA NIEMI, Administratrix of the Estate of August Niemi, Deceased, Appellee, vs. A. A. SPRAGUE and BRITTON I. BUDD, as Receivers, etc , Appellants	APPEAL FROM THE CIRCUIT COURT OF LAKE COUNTY

DOVE, J.

This is an action brought by the plaintiff as Administratrix of the estate of August Niemi, deceased, to recover damages for the alleged wrongful death of plaintiff's intestate. The complaint alleged that on January 29, 1934, plaintiff's intestate was driving an automobile in a westerly direction along Tenth Street in the City of Waukegan and that he was in the exercise of due care and caution for his own safety, that about 9 00 o'clock in the morning of said day, the defendants, by their servants and employees, negligently drove a passenger train so that it ran into the automobile which Niemi was driving and as a result thereof Niemi died. The negligence alleged was the high rate of speed at which the passenger train was being driven, the failure to sound a bell or [illegible]. NO. 8856 AGENDA NO. 5.

IN THE

APPELLATE COURT OF ILLINOIS

SECOND DISTRICT

February Term, A. D. 1935.

AMALIA NIEMI, Administratrix of the Estate of August Niemi, Deceased, Appellee, vs. [illegible] A. SPRAGUE and BRITTON I. BUDD, as Receivers, etc., Appellants.	APPEAL FROM THE CIRCUIT COURT OF LAKE COUNTY.

[illegible], J.

This is an action brought by the plaintiff as Administratrix of the estate of August Niemi, deceased, to recover damages for the alleged wrongful death of plaintiff's intestate. The complaint alleged that on January 29, 1934, plaintiff's intestate was driving an automobile in a westerly direction along Tenth Street in the City of Waukegan and that he was in the exercise of due care and caution for his own safety; that about 9.00 o'clock in the morning of said day, the defendants, by their servants and employees, negligently drove a passenger train so that it ran into the automobile which Niemi was driving and as a result thereof Niemi died. The negligence alleged was the high rate of speed at which the passenger train was being driven, the failure to sound a bell or blow a whistle, the failure to properly guard and protect the crossing except for a wig-wag signal and bell which was located at the soutwest corner of the crossing. The plaintiff further averred that because of the location of the wig-wag signal it did not provide a reasonably safe means of warning those who approached the crossing from the east, and further at the time of the collision the wig-wag signal and bell failed to function and operate. The answer of the defendants denied the material allegations of negligence and denied that the plaintiff's intestate was in the exercise of due care and caution for his own safety as alleged in the complaint. The cause was submitted to a jury, which returned a verdict finding the defendants not guilty. The trial court, on a motion of the plaintiff, set aside the verdict and granted a new trial and it is from this order that this appeal has been prosecuted.

The trial court was of the opinion that the court erred in including in its instructions suggestions 19 and 25 submitted by counsel for the defendants, that it erred in refusing the instructions suggested by the plaintiff numbered 1, 4, 5, 6 and 7, and that it was error to admit in evidence a photograph designated in the record as Exhibit No. 4 offered by the defendants and admitted in evidence over the objections of the plaintiff.

It is insisted by appellants that the material facts are undisputed, that the verdict of the jury was the only verdict that could have been permitted to stand upon the evidence, that there was no error committed by the court in its instructions or in the admission or rejection of evidence, and that the court therefore erred in awarding the plaintiff a new trial

The accident occurred in the City of Waukegan, a city of approximately thirty-five thousand people, where Tenth Street blow a whistle, the failure to properly guard and protect the crossing except for a wig-wag signal and bell which was located at the southwest corner of the crossing. The plaintiff further averred that because of the location of the wig-wag signal it did not provide a reasonably safe means of warning those who approached the crossing from the east and further at the time of the collision the wig-wag signal and bell failed to function and operate. The answer of the defendants denied the material allegations of negligence and denied that the plaintiff's intestate was in the exercise of due care and caution for his own safety as alleged in the complaint. The cause was submitted to a jury, which returned a verdict finding the defendants not guilty. The trial court, on a motion of the plaintiff, set aside the verdict and granted a new trial and it is from this order that this appeal has been prosecuted.

The trial court was of the opinion that the court erred in including in its instructions suggestions 19 and 25 submitted by counsel for the defendants, that it erred in refusing to instructions suggested by the plaintiff numbered 1, 4, 5, 6 and 7 and that it was error to admit in evidence a photograph designated in the record as Exhibit No. 4 offered by the defendants and admitted in evidence over the objection of the plaintiff.

It is insisted by appellants that the material facts are undisputed, that the verdict of the jury was the only verdict that could have been permitted to stand upon the evidence, that there was no error committed by the court in its instruction or admission or rejection of evidence, and that the court therefore erred in awarding the plaintiff a new trial.

The accident occurred in the City of Waukegan, a city of approximately thirty-five thousand people, where Tenth street crosses the railroad tracks of the defendants. The railroad tracks run north and south and Tenth Street east and west. Tenth Street is one of the main travelled streets of the city. Other than the usual stationery railroad crossing signal, the defendants had provided at this crossing at the southwest corner thereof a wig-wag signal. This signal consisted of a circular banner supported by a shaft running to a cross bar which is attached to an upright post approximately 14 feet high. The banner itself is located approximately 12 feet from the ground In the center of the banner there is a light and a bell mechanism is located near the top of the upright post. The signal is electrically operated and the normal operation of the signal consists of a simultaneous swinging back and forth of the banner with the flashing of the light and a ringing of the bell. This signal was normally put in operation automatically by north bound trains at a cut-in located 2659 feet south of the Tenth Street crossing, so that this signal would, if operating, be in operation during the time the train was travelling this 2659 feet. The evidence further discloses that on January 29th plaintiff's intestate had driven his two daughters from his home to school and it was upon his return trip home, driving west on the north side of Tenth Street, that the accident occurred. It was a controverted question of fact whether the wig-wag signal was functioning or not It was also a disputed question of fact as to the rate of speed at which the train was travelling and whether or not the whistle was sounding

The court instructed the jury at the request of appellants as follows "Even should you believe from the evidence that the wig-wag crossing signal at the place in question was not at the time operating, or that the whistle on the train was not sounded, still crosses the railroad tracks of the defendants. The railroad tracks run north and south and Tenth Street east and west. Tenth Street is one of the main travelled streets of the city. Other than the usual stationary railroad crossing signal, the defendants had provided at this crossing at the southwest corner thereof a wig-wag signal. This signal consisted of a circular banner supported by a shaft running to a cross bar which is attached to an upright post approximately 14 feet high. The banner itself is located approximately 12 feet from the ground. In the center of the banner there is a light and a bell mechanism is located near the top of the upright post. The signal is electrically operated and the normal operation of the signal consists of a simultaneous swinging back and forth of the banner with the flashing of the light and a ringing of the bell. This signal was normally put in operation automatically by north bound trains at a cut-in located 2659 feet south of the Tenth Street crossing, so that this signal would, if operating, be in operation during the time the train was travelling this 2659 feet. The evidence further discloses that on January 20th plaintiff's intestate had driven his two daughters from his home to school and it was upon his return trip home, driving west on the north side of Tenth Street, that the accident occurred. It was a controverted question of fact whether the wig-wag signal was functioning or not. It was also a disputed question of fact as to the rate of speed at which the train was travelling and whether or not the whistle was sounding

The court instructed the jury at the request of appellants as follows: "Even should you believe from the evidence that the wig-wag crossing signal at the place in question was not at the time operating, or that the whistle on the train was not sounded, still if you further believe from the evidence that the deceased, by the exercise of ordinary care in the use of his sense of sight, could have discovered the approaching train in question in time to have avoided a collision therewith, if he had looked therefor, and that ordinary care on his part, under all the facts and circumstances shown by the evidence, required him to so look, regardless of whether the crossing signal was operating or the whistle on the train was blown, then there can be no recovery in this case, and this is true notwithstanding you may further believe from the evidence, if you do so believe, that the deceased did not in fact look or see the approaching train before the collision".

Counsel for appellants insist that this instruction is supported by the cases of Greenwald v. B. & O. R. R. Co., 332 Ill. 627, Provenzano v. I. C. R. R. Co., 357 Ill.192, Goodman v. C. & E. I. R.R. Co., 248 Ill. App. 128 and that it was held proper in Flynn v. Chicago City R. R. Co., 250 Ill. 460. The instruction which the trial court refused to give in the Flynn case and which refusal was held reversible error by the Supreme Court is as follows: "If you believe from the evidence that the plaintiff by using his faculties with ordinary and reasonable care in looking out for danger, could have avoided injury on the occasion in question, and that he negligently failed to do so and thereby contributed to the injury, if you believe he was injured, then he cannot recover in this case." In our opinion this instruction differs materially from the one given in the instant case. In the instant case the phrase "if he had looked therefor" assumes that the deceased did not look for the train before attempting to drive over the crossing. Whether the deceased negligently failed to look for the approaching train and whether that negligent omission directly contributed to his death were questions of fact for the jury to determine. Chicago and Alton R. R. Co. v. Robinson, 106 Ill. 142.

If you further believe from the evidence that the deceased, by the exercise of ordinary care in the use of his sense of sight, could have discovered the approaching train in question in time to have avoided a collision therewith, if he had looked therefor, and that ordinary care on his part, under all the facts and circumstances shown by the evidence, required him to so look, regardless of whether the crossing signal was operating or the whistle on the train was blown, then there can be no recovery in this case; and this is true notwithstanding you my further believe from the evidence, if you do so believe, that the deceased did not in fact look or see the approaching train before the collision."

Counsel for appellants insist that this instruction is supported by the cases of Greenwald v. B. & O. S. W. R. Co., 332 Ill. 627, Provenzano v. I. C. R. R. Co., 357 Ill.192, Goodman v. C. & E. I. R.R. Co., 248 Ill. App. 138 and that it was held proper in Flynn v. Chicago City R. R. Co., 250 Ill. 460. The instruction which the trial court refused to give in the Flynn case and which refusal was held reversible error by the Supreme Court is as follows: "If you believe from the evidence that the plaintiff by using his faculties with ordinary and reasonable care in looking out for danger, could have avoided injury on the occasion in question, and that he negligently failed to do so and thereby contributed to the injury, if you believe he was injured, then he cannot recover in this case." In our opinion this instruction differs materially from the one given in the instant case. In the instant case the phrase: "if he had looked therefor" assumes that the deceased did not look for the train before attempting to drive over the crossing. Whether the deceased negligently failed to look for the approaching train and whether that negligent omission directly contributed to his death were questions of fact for the jury to determine. Chicago and Alton R. R. Co. v. Robinson, 106 Ill. 142.

The other instruction suggested by appellants and given by the court and which the trial court upon awarding a new trial held should not have been given is as follows: "One who has an unobstructed view of an approaching train, and by the exercise of ordinary care, could see the same approaching, if he had looked therefor, before getting into a place of danger therefrom, is not justified in not looking upon approaching a railroad track in reliance upon the assumption that if a train were approaching a whistle would be sounded or a crossing signal would be operating. No one may assume that there will not be a violation of the law or negligence of others and offer such assumption as an excuse for failure to exercise due care." In Greenwald v. C. & O. R. R. Co., supra, which was an action to recover damages to plaintiff's truck which was struck by one of defendant's trains at a street crossing intersection, the Supreme Court in sustaining the action of the trial court in directing a verdict for the defendant at the close of the plaintiff's case, in its opinion, after reviewing the evidence in the case, said "One who has an unobstructed view of an approaching train is not justified in closing his eyes or failing to look, or in crossing a railroad track in reliance upon the assumption that a bell will be rung or a whistle sounded. No one can assume that there will not be a violation of the law or negligence of others and then offer such assumption as an excuse for failure to exercise due care". What is there said must be read in connection with the facts as disclosed by the evidence in that case. No wig-wag crossing signal was involved in the Greenwald case, and it seems to us that the instruction given in the instant case told the jury that the deceased, as a matter of law, regardless of the surrounding circumstances had no right to place any reliance whatever upon this crossing signal which appellant had

provided as a means of warning. The evidence here disclosed that the deceased had used this crossing five or six times a day for a number of years and was familiar with it and with the signals appellant had provided and we are not prepared to say, as a matter of law, that it was wholly immaterial whether this wig-wag signal was working or not. It is true that Caroline Ewry, a witness for appellants, testified that she was a passenger on the train and observed the deceased as he approached the crossing, that he had both his hands on the steering wheel of his car and it appeared to her that he was staring straight ahead The motorman also testified that he first observed the deceased just for a second before the collision when his train was within forty feet of the point of the collision and that the deceased had both hands on the steering wheel of his automobile and appeared to be staring straight ahead.

In C. & N. W R'y. Co. v. Hansen, 166 Ill 623, the court stated that it cannot be held as a matter of law that a traveller is bound to look or listen because there may be various modifying circumstances excusing him from doing so. That a traveller may not be at fault in failing to look or listen if misled without his fault "It seems to us impossible", says the court, "that there should be a rule of law as to what particular thing a person is bound to do for his protection in the diversity of cases that constantly arise, and the question what a reasonably prudent person would do for his own safety under like circumstances must be left to the jury as one of fact " In C. & N. W. Ry. Co v Dunleavy, 129 Ill. 132, at page 148, the court says "Undoubtedly a failure to look or listen, especially where it affirmatively appears that looking or listening might have enabled the party provided as a means of warning. The evidence here disclosed that the deceased had used this crossing five or six times a day for a number of years and was familiar with it and with the signals appellant had provided and we are not prepared to say, as a matter of law, that it was wholly immaterial whether this wig-wag signal was working or not. It is true that Caroline Perry, a witness for appellants, testified that she was a passenger on the train and observed the deceased as he approached the crossing, that he had both his hands on the steering wheel of his car and it appeared to her that he was staring straight ahead. The fireman also testified that he first observed the deceased just a second before the collision when his train was within forty feet of the point of the collision and that the deceased had both hands on the steering wheel of his automobile and appeared to be staring straight ahead.

In C. & N. W. R'y. Co. v. Hansen, 166 Ill. 623, the court stated that it cannot be held as a matter of law that a traveller is bound to look or listen because there may be various modifying circumstances excusing him from doing so. That a traveller may not be at fault in failing to look or listen if misled without his fault. "It seems to us impossible", says the court, "that there should be a rule of law as to what particular thing a person is bound to do for his protection in the diversity of cases that constantly arise, and the question what a reasonably prudent person would do for his own safety under like circumstances must be left to the jury as one of fact." In C. & N. W. Ry. Co. v. Dunleavy, 129 Ill. 132, at page 143, the court says "Undoubtedly a failure to look or listen, especially where it affirmatively appears that looking or listening might have enabled the party [illegible] of the [illegible] whatever upon this [illegible] exposed to injury to see the train and thus avoid being injured, is evidence tending to show negligence. But they are not conclusive evidence, so that a charge of negligence can be predicated upon them as a matter of law There may be various modifying circumstances excusing the party from looking or listening, and that being the case, a mere failure to look or listen cannot, as a legal conclusion, be pronounced negligence per se"

In T H. & I. R. R. Co v. Voelker, 129 Ill. 540, at pages 552-3, the court says "It has frequently been said in judicial decisions in this State and elsewhere, that it is the duty of persons approaching a railway crossing, to look and listen before going upon the track, and that their failure to do so is negligence, but it will be found generally, though not uniformly, on examining the cases where such language occurs, that it has been used in discussing the duty as to care and caution in approaching a railway crossing, viewed as a mere question of fact, and not as a question of law. It is doubtless a rule of law that a person approaching a railway crossing is bound, in so doing, to exercise such care, caution and circumspection to foresee danger and avoid injury as ordinary prudence would require, having in view all the known dangers of the situation, but precisely what such requirements would be, must manifestly differ with the ever varying circumstances under which such approach may be made. Ordinarily of course the diligent use of the senses of sight and hearing is the most obvious and practicable means of avoiding injury in such cases, but occasions may and often do arise where the use of those senses would be unavailing, or where their non-use may be excused. The view may be obstructed by intervening objects or by the darkness of the night Other and louder noises, as is often the case in a city, may confuse

[illegible]ed to injury to see the train and thus avoid being in-
[illegible]ed, is evidence tending to show negligence. But they are [illegible] persuasive evidence, so that a charge of negligence can be [illegible]icated upon them as a matter of law. There may be various [illegible]ifying circumstances excusing the party from looking or listen-[illegible]g, and that being the case, a mere failure to look or listen [illegible], as a legal conclusion, be pronounced negligence per se".
[illegible] T. H. & I. R. R. Co. v. Voelker, 129 Ill. 540, at pages 552-3, [illegible] court says: "It has frequently been said in judicial decisions [illegible] this State and elsewhere, that it is the duty of persons approach-[illegible] a railway crossing, to look and listen before going upon the [illegible], and that their failure to do so is negligence, but it will [illegible] found generally, though not uniformly, on examining the cases [illegible] such language occurs, that it has been used in discussing [illegible] duty as to care and caution in approaching a railway crossing, [illegible] as a mere question of fact, and not as a question of law. [illegible] doubtless a rule of law that a person approaching a railway crossing is bound, in so doing, to exercise such care, caution [illegible] circumspection to foresee danger and avoid injury as ordinary [illegible] would require, having in view all the known dangers of the situation, but precisely what such requirements would be, must manifestly differ with the ever varying circumstances under which such approach may be made. Ordinarily of course the diligent use of the senses of sight and hearing is the most obvious and practicable means of avoiding injury in such cases, but occasions may and often do arise where the use of these senses would be unavailing, or where their use may be excused. The view may be obstructed by intervening objects or by the darkness of the night. Other and louder noises, as is often the case in a city, may confuse

the sense of hearing and render its use impracticable. The railway company, by its flagman or other agent or agency, may put the person off his guard and induce him to cross the track without resorting to the usual precautions The duty may be more or less varied by the age, degree of intelligence and mental capacity of the party, and by a variety of other circumstances by which he may be surrounded. It follows that no invariable rule can be predicated upon the mere act of failing to look or listen, but a jury, properly instructed as to the legal duty in respect to care and caution, of a person approaching a railway crossing, must draw from such act, in connection with all the attendant circumstances, the proper conclusion as to whether he is guilty of negligence or not." See also C P. J. & P. R'y Co. v Clough, 134 Ill. 586. C & A. R. R. Co. v. Pearson, 184 Ill. 386. Under these authorities, it was error for the trial court to have given the foregoing instructions. The other cases cited by appellants announce no different rule and we are of the opinion the trial court was justified in entering the order appealed from.

The plaintiff's suggested instructions, which the court refused to incorporate in its charge, are as follows "Whenever the death of a person shall be caused by wrongful act, neglect or default, and the act, neglect or default is such as would if death had not ensued have entitled the party injured to maintain an action and to recover damages in respect thereto, then and in every such case, the person who, or company, or corporation, which would have been liable if death had not ensued, shall be liable to an action for damages notwithstanding the death of the person injured. Every such action shall be brought by and in the names of the personal representatives of such deceased person " This is the sense of hearing and render its use impracticable. The railway company, by its flagman or other agent or agency, may put the person off his guard and induce him to cross the track without resorting to the usual precautions. The duty may be more or less varied by the age, degree of intelligence and mental capacity of the party, and by a variety of other circumstances by which he may be surrounded. It follows that no invariable rule can be predicated upon the mere act of failing to look or listen, but a jury properly instructed as to the legal duty in respect to care [illegible], of a person approaching a railway crossing, must draw from such act, in connection with all the attendant circumstances, the proper conclusion as to whether he is guilty of negligence or [illegible]. See also C. R. I. & P. Ry. Co. v. Clough, 134 Ill. 586. C. [illegible] R. R. Co. v. Pearson, 184 Ill. 386. Under these authorities, it was error for the trial court to have given the foregoing instructions. The other cases cited by appellants announce no different rule and we are of the opinion the trial court was justified in entering the order appealed from.

In the plaintiff's suggested instructions, which the court refused [illegible] in its charge, are as follows: "Whenever the death of a person shall be caused by wrongful act, neglect or default, and the act, neglect or default is such as would if death had not ensued have entitled the party injured to maintain an action and to recover damages in respect thereto, then and in every such case, the person who, or company, or corporation, which would have been liable if death had not ensued, shall be liable to an action for damages notwithstanding the death of the person injured. Every such action shall be brought by and in the names of the personal representatives of such deceased person." This is [illegible] an abstract proposition of law stating the statutory basis of plaintiff's action. In our opinion it was not reversible error to refuse this suggested instruction, and its refusal alone would not have warranted the granting of appellee's motion for a new trial. The second suggested instruction offered by appellee and which was refused is as follows "If you believe from the evidence that the servants of the defendants in charge of the train involved in this accident drove their train over this crossing at an unreasonable and unsafe rate of speed, considering all of the circumstances in this case, and the nature of the crossing, and that the collision resulting in the decedent's death was directly caused thereby, and that the decedent used ordinary care and diligence for his own safety, under all the circumstances in this case, then your verdict should be for the plaintiff." In support of appellee's contention that this was a proper instruction, the case of St. L. A. and T. H. R. R. Co. v. Odum, 156 Ill 78 is cited. The suggested instruction is materially different from the seventh instruction given in the cited case In the Odum case the instruction distinctly told the jury that before they could find for the plaintiff they must believe that defendant's servants were guilty of negligence In the instant case the suggested instruction did not require the jury to believe that the defendants were negligent but told the jury that if the defendants drove their train over this crossing at an unreasonable and unsafe rate of speed and decedent's death was directly caused thereby and he was using ordinary care for his own safety that then the plaintiff was entitled to recover

Suggested instruction number five is as follows "It was the duty of the defendants to use reasonable care to keep the [illegible] The an abstract proposition of law stating the statutory basis of plaintiff's action. In our opinion it was not reversible error to refuse this suggested instruction, and its refusal alone would not have warranted the granting of appellee's motion for a new trial. The second suggested instruction offered by appellee and which was refused is as follows: "If you believe from the evidence that the servants of the defendants in charge of the train involved in this accident drove their train over this crossing at an unreasonable and unsafe rate of speed, considering all of the circumstances in this case, and the nature of the crossing, and that the collision resulting in the decedent's death was directly caused thereby, and that the decedent used ordinary care and diligence for his own safety, under all the circumstances in this case, then your verdict should be for the plaintiff." In support of appellee's contention that this was a proper instruction, the case of St. L. A. and T. H. R. R. Co. v. Odum, 156 Ill. 78 is cited. The suggested instruction is materially different from the seventh instruction given in the cited case. In the Odum case the instruction distinctly told the jury that before they could find for the plaintiff they must believe that defendant's servants were guilty of negligence. In the instant case the suggested instruction did not require the jury to believe that the defendants were negligent but told the jury that if the defendants drove their train over this crossing at an unreasonable and unsafe rate of speed and decedent's death was directly caused thereby and he was using ordinary care for his own safety, that then the plaintiff was entitled to recover.

Suggested instruction number five is as follows: "It was the duty of the defendants to use reasonable care to keep the wig-wag signal provided by them at this crossing in good condition and in working order." Suggested instruction number six is: "If you believe from the evidence that the wig-wag signal located at this crossing was not operating at the time of this accident, and that the failure of said signal to operate was known, or in the exercise of reasonable care should have been known to the defendants, and that the decedent, August Nicci, was misled into attempting to drive his automobile over said crossing, by reason of the failure of said wig-wag signal to warn him of the approach of said train, and that he met his death as a direct result thereof, and that in driving over said crossing he acted as an ordinary prudent person would act under all the circumstances in this case, then it is your duty to find the issues for the plaintiff" Suggested instruction number seven is "Although the mere failure of the wig-wag signal provided for by the defendants at this crossing to operate, if there was such failure, would not, in itself, excuse the decedent from exercising ordinary care for his own safety in driving his automobile over this crossing, yet the existence of such a signal at this crossing and its failure to operate at the time of this accident, constituted an implied invitation to the decedent to drive his automobile over said crossing in safety, and if you find from the evidence that the decedent acted as a reasonably prudent person under all of the circumstances in this case in driving his automobile across said crossing and that the defendants were negligent in their failure, if any, to provide a reasonably safe and workable method of warning to the plaintiff of the approach of said train, and that the decedent met his death as a direct and proximate result of said negligence, if any, then your verdict should be for the plaintiff."

wig-wag signal provided by them at this crossing in good condition and in working order." Suggested instruction number six is:
"If you believe from the evidence that the wig-wag signal located
at this crossing was not operating at the time of this accident,
and that the failure of said signal to operate was known, or in
the exercise of reasonable care should have been known to the
defendants, and that the decedent, August Miemi, was misled into
attempting to drive his automobile over said crossing, by reason
of the failure of said wig-wag signal to warn him of the approach
of said train, and that he met his death as a direct result thereof,
and that in driving over said crossing he acted as an ordinary
prudent person would act under all the circumstances in this case,
then it is your duty to find the issues for the plaintiff". Suggested instruction number seven is: "Although the mere failure
of the wig-wag signal provided for by the defendants at this crossing to operate, if there was such failure, would not, in itself,
excuse the decedent from exercising ordinary care for his own
safety in driving his automobile over this crossing, yet the
existence of such a signal at this crossing and its failure to
operate at the time of this accident, constituted an implied
invitation to the decedent to drive his automobile over said crossing in safety, and if you find from the evidence that the decedent
acted as a reasonably prudent person under all of the circumstances
in this case in driving his automobile across said crossing and
that the defendants were negligent in their failure, if any, to
provide a reasonably safe and workable method of warning to the
plaintiff of the approach of said train, and that the decedent
met his death as a direct and proximate result of said negligence,
if any, then your verdict should be for the plaintiff."

Counsel for appellants state that it was the duty of defendants to give ample and timely warning of the approach of its train and whether they did this by use of the wig-wag signal or whistle was immaterial. That the evidence discloses timely warning was given, that the wig-wag was operating an hour before the accident, that there is no evidence that deceased paid any attention to the wig-wag signal and that there was no evidence upon which these instructions could be based. It is true that a witness for appellants testified that he was riding on one of appellant's trains and passed this crossing at eight o'clock on the morning of the accident and that this signal was working. There was other evidence that proved it was not working at seven o'clock or at nine o'clock that morning, which was the time of the accident and there is no evidence that any inspection was made between seven and nine o'clock. Whether the deceased was misled into attempting to drive across the tracks of appellant because of the alleged failure of the wig-wag signal to work was not susceptible of direct and positive proof. It would not have been an unreasonable inference, however, to be drawn from all the facts and circumstances in evidence that deceased would have been warranted in assuming that if the wig-wag signal was not operating no train was approaching. He was familiar with this crossing and the fact that there was a signal there which normally operated and began to function when trains approached the crossing from either direction and when they were a considerable distance from the crossing. Under all the facts and circumstances as they appeared in evidence in this case, appellee was entitled to some instructions along the lines suggested and no valid criticism of suggested instructions numbers five and six has been pointed out to us.

Counsel for appellants state that it was the duty of defendants to give ample and timely warning of the approach of its train and whether they did this by use of the wig-wag signal or whistle was immaterial. That the evidence discloses timely warning was given, that the wig-wag was operating an hour before the accident, that there is no evidence that deceased paid any attention to the wig-wag signal and that there was no evidence upon which these instructions could be based. It is true that a witness for appellants testified that he was riding on one of appellant's trains and passed this crossing at eight o'clock on the morning of the accident and that this signal was working. There was other evidence that proved it was not working at seven o'clock or at nine o'clock that morning, which was the time of the accident and there is no evidence that any inspection was made between seven and nine o'clock. Whether the deceased was misled into attempting to drive across the tracks of appellant because of the alleged failure of the wig-wag signal to work was not susceptible of direct and positive proof. "It would not have been an unreasonable inference, however, to be drawn from all the facts and circumstances in evidence that deceased would have been warranted in assuming that if the wig-wag signal was not operating no train was approaching. He was familiar with its operation and the fact that there was a signal there which normally operated and began to function when trains approached the crossing from either direction and when they were a considerable distance from the crossing. Under all the facts and circumstances as they appeared in evidence in this case, appellee was entitled to some instructions along the lines suggested and no doubt the giving of suggested instructions numbers five and six [illegible]

The trial court was further of the opinion that it was error to admit in evidence defendant's exhibit No. 4. This exhibit was a photograph of the railroad and adjacent territory. On the back of the exhibit were these words 'Looking southwest Camera middle of 10th Street 95 ft. east of east rail of north bound track. Moving train in picture The picture shows the train and a man standing on the right of way not far from the crossing facing toward the train with extended arm. The evidence discloses that the train involved in the accident was a three car train The train in the picture, the evidence discloses, is a two coach, north bound limited travelling on the same track as the train involved in the accident, and when the picture was taken, this train was 650 feet south of and approaching the tenth street crossing. Counsel for appellants say that this exhibit shows the situation as it existed on the day of the accident and is a demonstration that a train approaching this crossing from the south could be seen 650 feet south of the crossing from a point in tenth street 95 feet east of the east rail of the north bound track There is no evidence in the record that decedent's automobile was 95 feet east of the crossing when appellants' train was 650 feet south of the crossing From this photograph the jury would have been warranted in concluding that at a point 95 feet east of the crossing the deceased could have seen this approaching train for a distance of at least 650 feet The camera was stationary and the lens fixed while appellee's intestate was in a moving automobile as he approached this crossing In 27 A. L. R., 910, following the report of the case of Nunnelly v. Muth, 195 Ky. 352, cited in Burns v. Salyers, 270 Ill App 46, is an exhaustive annotation and from that case and the cases there cited, we are of the opinion this photograph should not have been admitted in evidence

The trial court was further of the opinion that it was error to admit in evidence defendant's exhibit No. 4. This exhibit was a photograph of the railroad and adjacent territory. On the back of the exhibit were these words: "Looking southwest. Camera middle of 10th Street 95 ft. east of east rail on north bound track. Moving train in picture." The picture shows the train and a man standing on the right of way not far from the crossing facing toward the train with extended arm. The evidence discloses that the train involved in the accident was a three car train. The train in the picture, the evidence discloses, is a two coach, north bound limited travelling on the same track as the train involved in the accident, and when the picture was taken, this train was 650 feet south of and approaching the tenth street crossing. Counsel for appellants say that this exhibit shows the situation as it existed on the day of the accident and is a demonstration that a train approaching the crossing from the south could be seen 650 feet south of the crossing from a point in tenth street 95 feet east of the east rail of the north bound track. There is no evidence in the record that deceased's automobile was 95 feet east of the crossing when appellants' train was 650 feet south of the crossing. From this photograph the jury would have been warranted in concluding that at a point 95 feet east of the crossing the deceased could have seen the approaching train for a distance of at least 650 feet. The [illegible] the visibility and the lens fixed while appellee's intestate was in a moving automobile as he approached this crossing. In [illegible], following the report of the case of Nunnelly v Muth, [illegible], and in Burns v. Sulyers, 270 Ill. App. 46, is an [illegible] and in that case and the cases there cited, [illegible] this photograph should not have been admitted in evidence.

Counsel for appellants finally insist that even conceding that there were erroneous rulings upon instructions and the admission of evidence, still the material facts are entirely undisputed, and that the jury returned the only verdict which would have been permitted to stand and that appellants are therefore entitled to have judgment entered upon this verdict. We have read this record and all of the material facts are not entirely undisputed. The trial court, as pointed out in this opinion, did not err in awarding appellee a new trial and that order is affirmed

ORDER AFFIRMED.

Counsel for appellants finally insist that even conceding that there were erroneous rulings upon instructions and the admission of evidence, still the material facts are entirely undisputed, and that the jury returned the only verdict which would have been permitted to stand and that appellants are therefore entitled to have judgment entered upon this verdict. We have read this record and all of the material facts are not entirely undisputed. The trial court, as pointed out in this opinion, did not err in awarding appellees a new trial and that order is affirmed.

ORDER AFFIRMED.

} ss.

I, JUSTUS L. JOHNSON Clerk of the Appellate Court in and of the State of Illinois, and the keeper of the Records and Seal thereof do hereby ; is a true copy of the opinion of the said Appellate Court in the above entitled cause.

In Testimony Whereof, I hereunto set my hand and affix the seal of said Appellate Court at Ottawa this____________________day of ____________________in the year of our Lord one thousand nine hundred and thirty-________________

____

Clerk of the Appellate Court

AT A TERM OF THE APPELLATE CO

Begun and held at Ottawa, on Tuesday, the seventh day of May, in the year of our Lord one thousand nine hundred and thirty-five, within and for the Second District of the State of Illinois:

Present-- The Hon FRED G. WOLFE, Presiding Justice.

Hon. FRANKLIN P DOVE, Justice

Hon. BLAINE HUFFMAN, Justice.

JUSTUS L. JOHNSON, Clerk

RALPH H DESPER, Sheriff.

280 I.A. 631[3]

BE IT REMEMBERED, that afterwards, to-wit On MAY 17 1935 the opinion of the Court was filed in the Clerk's office of said Court, in the words and figures following, to-wit:

GEN. NO. 8884 AGENDA NO. 14

IN THE

APPELLATE COURT OF ILLINOIS

SECOND DISTRICT

February Term, A. D. 1935

MARY ELIAS, Appellee, vs. NEW JERSEY INSURANCE COMPANY, a Corporation, of Newark, New Jersey, Appellant.	APPEAL FROM THE CIRCUIT COURT OF LA SALLE COUNTY

DOVE, J.

This is an action of assumpsit instituted by Mary Elias, against the New Jersey Insurance Company, The declaration, consisting of the common counts was filed December 29, 1932. Subsequently a bill of particulars was filed, reciting that on August 18, 1928, the defendant issued to the plaintiff its insurance policy insuring her against all loss or damage to her Dodge five passenger sedan caused by collision, that on July 7, 1929, this automobile so insured collided with another automobile, whereby the plaintiff sustained damages to the amount of $2,000.00, that on July 8, 1929, the plaintiff gave notice of her loss and on July 12, 1929, she delivered to defendant a particular account of her loss and thereafter on November 15, 1929, defendant promised to pay her the sum of

IN THE

APPELLATE COURT OF ILLINOIS

SECOND DISTRICT

February Term, A. D. 1933

ELIAS,

Appellee,

vs.

NEW JERSEY INSURANCE COMPANY, a Corporation, of Newark, New Jersey,

Appellant.

APPEAL FROM THE CIRCUIT COURT OF LA SALLE COUNTY

DOVE, J.

This is an action of assumpsit instituted by Mary Elias, against the New Jersey Insurance Company. The declaration, consisting of the common counts was filed December 29, 1932. Subsequently a bill of particulars was filed, reciting that on August 18, 192 , the defendant issued to the plaintiff its insurance policy insuring her against all loss or damage to her Dodge ive passenger sedan caused by collision, that on July 7, 1929, this automobile so insured collided with another automobile, whereby the plaintiff sustained damages to the amount of $2,0 0 00, that on July 8, 1929, the plaintiff gave notice of her loss and on July 12, 1929, she delivered to defendant a partial r ac ou t of he loss and th re after on November 15, 1929, defendant promised to pay her the sum of

$650.00 in full settlement of the damage she had sustained. A plea of the general issue was filed, a jury trial had resulting in a verdict and judgment in favor of the plaintiff and against the defendant for $539.00. From this judgment the record is brought to this court for review by appeal.

It appears from the evidence that appellee purchased a Dodge sedan in August, 1928, which on July 7, 1929, had been driven about 10,000 miles. During July, 1929, appellee was employed at the Clifton Hotel in Ottawa, Illinois, and on the 7th day of July she gave Ed Jacobs, a porter at the hotel, a note which authorized him to procure her car and take it to a garage where it was to be washed and polished. Instead of doing that, Jacobs drove the car, without appellee's knowledge or consent, to a place near Dwight, Illinois, on State Route No. 4, where he had a collision with another automobile and completely wrecked appellee's car. At the time of the collision, appellee carried collision insurance with appellant and theft insurance with the National Insurance Company, these policies were both in full force and effect on the date of the collision. The evidence further discloses that appellee notified D. J. Farrell, a resident agent for appellant, who lives in Ottawa, of the accident. Farrell notified appellant and Frank T. Gordon, an adjuster was sent out to interview appellee. Farrell and Gordon, on October 10, 1929, called on appellee at the home of Mrs. Wahl, her sister, in Streator, where appellee was then living. According to the testimony of appellee, there was a general discussion about the car at this meeting and Gordon there stated to appellee that the insurance company would pay her $650.00 for her car, which was satisfactory to her. Gordon then produced a paper and she signed it without reading it and did not know what was in it. She further testified that she had not seen the adjuster since that date except she

recognized him as being present in the court room at the trial. That she had not heard anything since then about a settlement and had not ever been paid anything. Mrs. Wahl, appellee's sister, testified that she was at her home and present when Gordon and Farrell called and upon that occasion she heard Gordon say his company would pay appellee $650.00 for her car. Farrell testified that there was no promise upon the part of Gordon to pay appellee, that there was a little discussion about signing a non-waiver agreement, that appellee kept this instrument before her for two minutes and then signed it and he, Farrell, witnessed her signature.

Frank T. Gordon, appellant's adjuster, testified that the instrument which appellee and he signed and which Farrell witnessed was a non-waiver and a loss and damage agreement: that he informed appellee of the contents of the agreement she signed and that he also told her he would not agree to pay her any sum of money and that he had no authority to make any adjustment with her. He further testified that his purpose in meeting her was to procure a non-waiver and loss and damage agreement signed by her. That a non-waiver agreement allows the company to make an investigation without an admission of liability and the loss and damage agreement states the amount of the loss and damage without admitting liability. According to his testimony he fully explained these instruments to appellee, that she read them and signed them and he signed them on behalf of appellant. This instrument which was so executed is as follows:

"NON-WAIVER AGREEMENT.

"It is mutually understood and agreed by and between Mary Elias of the first part, and New Jersey Insurance Company of Newark New Jersey and other Compan--- signing this agreement, part.... of the second part, that any action taken by said part... of

the second part in investigating the loss or ascertaining the amount of the sound value or loss and damage to the property of the part... of the first part, alleged to have occurred on the 8th day of July, 1929, shall not waive or invalidate any of the conditions of the policy of the part... of the second part, held by the party... of the first part, and shall not waive, invalidate or prejudice any rights whatever of either of the parties to this agreement.

"Notice is hereby given by the party... of the second part, and accepted by the party... of the first part, that the signer of this agreement for the part... of the second part, has no authority either express or implied, to waive or invalidate any of the conditions of the policy, or waive or invalidate any of the rights whatever of or to commit the party... of the second part. The intent of this agreement is to preserve the right of the parties hereto, and provide only for an investigation of the loss and claim, and the determination of the amount of the sound value and loss or damage without regard whatever to liability of the party,.. of the second part.

"Executed in duplicate this 10th day of October, 1929.

"New Jersey Insurance Co. by Wilson S. Levens & Co.
per F. T. Gordon

Mary Elias

"Witness: D. J. Farrell

"SOUND VALUE AND LOSS AND DAMAGE AGREEMENT

"Subject to and in conformity with the foregoing 'NON-WAIVER AGREEMENT,' and without regard whatever as to liability of the part... of the second part for said loss or damage, it is now further hereby agreed between said parties hereto, that the sound value and loss and damage is as follows:

"SOUND VALUE $500.00 LOSS AND DAMAGE $500.00

"Executed in duplicate this 10th day of October, 1929.
X Mary Elias
"New Jersey Insurance Co. by Wilson . Levens & Co.
per F. T. Gordon
"Witness: D. J. Farrell".

Appellee testified that she was thirty-six years of age at the time of the trial, that she signed these instruments and that she could read and write, but said that Gordon did not give her a duplicate thereof and in this particular she is corroborated by Farrell.

The foregoing is substantially all the evidence in this record and it is the contention of appellant that where the parties reduce their agreement to writing, such written agreement is the final consummation of their negotiations and the exact expression of their purpose and that the written instrument expresses the whole undertaking of the parties. This is a fundamental principle of law and so conceded by appellee, but appellee insists that the evidence discloses that appellee was induced to sign this non-waiver and loss and damage agreement by fraud and misrepresentation. That the misrepresentation made by appellant's adjuster induced appellee to believe that she was signing a compromise settlement agreement by the provisions of which appellant was to pay her $650.00 for the loss of her car. Appellee may have believed that the instrument Gordon signed was a promise by appellant to pay her $650.00 and that she signed it for the purpose of indicating her acceptance of that promise, but if such was her belief, it did not come from anything contained in the instrument itself and her counsel's claim that her signatures were obtained by misrepresentation by Gordon is not substantiated by her testimony and from all the evidence in this record, the verdict of the jury was unwarranted. If the jury believed the testimony of appellee and her sister, then appellant, on October 10, 1929, promised to pay appellee $650.00 in satisfaction of the loss she sustained under her insurance policy, yet the jury on January 23, 1934, returned a verdict in her favor for $539.00. All that appellee and her sister testify to is that Gordon stated his company would pay appellee $650.00. This was denied by Gordon and not testified to by Farrell, who was present. Neither appellee nor her sister testify that Gordon said there was anything in the agreement to

which she affixed her signatures that so provided. As a general rule a person cannot avoid a written contract into which he has entered on the ground that he did not attend to its terms, that he did not read the document which he signed, that he supposed it was different in its terms or that it was a mere form. 13 C. J. 370.

The trial court should have granted appellant's motion for a new trial and for this error the judgment is reversed and the cause remanded.

REVERSED AND REMANDED.

which the affixed her signatures that so provided. As a general rule a person cannot avoid a written contract into which he has entered on the ground that he did not attend to its terms, that he did not read the document which he signed, that he supposed it was different in its terms or that it was a mere form. 13 C. J. 370.

The trial court should have granted appellant's motion for a new trial and for this error the judgment is reversed and the cause remanded.

REVERSED AND REMANDED.

S, } ss.

I, JUSTUS L. JOHNSON Clerk of the Appellate Court in and
of the State of Illinois, and the keeper of the Records and Seal thereof do hereby
; is a true copy of the opinion of the said Appellate Court in the above entitled cause,

In Testimony Whereof I hereunto set my hand and affix the seal of said Appellate Court at Ottawa this __________________ day of __________________ in the year of our Lord one thousand nine hundred and thirty-____________

____

Clerk of the Appellate Court

AT A TERM OF THE ATE CO

Begun and held at Ottawa, on Tuesday, the th day of May, in the year of our Lord one thousand nine hundred and thirty-five, within and for the Second District of the State of Illinois:

Present-- The Hon. FRED G. WOLFE, Presiding Justice.

Hon. FRANKLIN P. DOVE, Justice.

Hon. BLAINE HUFFMAN, Justice.

JUSTUS L. JOHNSON, Clerk

RALPH H. DESPER, Sheriff. 280 I.A. 631

BE IT REMEMBERED, that afterwards, to-wit On MAY 17 1935 the opinion of the Court was filed in the Clerk's office of said Court, in the words and figures following, to-wit:

GEN. NO. 8907 AGENDA NO 41

IN THE

APPELLATE COURT OF ILLINOIS

SECOND DISTRICT

February Term, A. D. 1935

HANNA BECHTEL,
Appellee,
vs.
BYRON L. COLBURN, et al,
Appellants.

APPEAL FROM THE CIRCUIT COURT OF WOODFORD COUNTY

DOVE, J.

This proceeding originated by Hanna Bechtel filing her bill on May 2, 1932, to foreclose a trust deed executed by Jeff Rocke and Lucy Rocke and dated March 5, 1928. This trust deed covered eighty acres of land designated in this record as tract A and was given to secure the payment of six notes, three for $1000.00 each, two for $1500.00 each and one for $4000 00 Each note matured March 1, 1933, bore 5½% interest and was payable to the order of the makers and duly endorsed in blank by them Byron L. Colburn was named as trustee in the trust deed and the bill made him individually and as trustee and the makers of the notes parties defendant. Later, by amendment, William E. Gibson was made a party thereto

Byron L. Colburn individually and as trustee answered, admitting the allegations of the original bill as to the execution

GEN. NO. 8907 AGENDA NO. 41

IN THE

APPELLATE COURT OF ILLINOIS

SECOND DISTRICT

February Term, A. D. 1935.

HANNA BECHTEL, Appellee, vs. BYRON L. COLBURN, et al, Appellants.	)	APPEAL FROM THE CIRCUIT COURT OF WOODFORD COUNTY

DAVIS, J.

This proceeding originated by Hanna Bechtel filing her bill on May 2, 1932, to foreclose a trust deed executed by Jeff Peake and Lucy Rocke and dated March 5, 1928. This trust deed covered eighty acres of land designated in this record as tract A and was given to secure the payment of six notes, three for $1000.00 each, two for $1500.00 each and one for $4000.00. Each note matured March 1, 1933, bore 5½% interest and was payable to the order of the makers and duly endorsed in blank by them. Byron L. Colburn was named as trustee in the trust deed and the bill made him individually and as trustee and the makers of the notes parties defendant. Later, by amendment, William E. Gibson was made a party thereto.

Byron L. Colburn individually and as trustee answered, admitting the allegations of the original bill as to the execution of the Bechtel trust deed, but set up that on February 9, 1926, the Rockes were indebted to the Farmers State Bank of Eureka in the sum of $8100.00, and to secure the payment of the same they executed on that date a trust deed to Colburn as trustee on said tract A, which was recorded on February 9, 1926. The answer then alleges that the amount of this indebtedness had been, on March 2, 1931, reduced to $5900.00, and an extension agreement had been entered into extending the payment of this $5900.00 to March 1, 1933. The answer states that this $5900.00 note and the trust deed to secure its payment are held by the Farmers State Bank of Eureka and avers that it is a first and prior lien on tract A On September 7, 1932, Colburn as trustee and the Farmers State Bank filed their cross bill to foreclose this trust deed, which not only covers the eighty acres designated as tract A, but also another tract consisting of 132 acres, which also belonged to Rocke and which is designated herein as tract B.

Hanna Bechtel answered the cross-bill, denying that the Farmers State Bank trust deed was a prior lien on tract A and averring that in March 1931, and for many years prior thereto, Byron L. Colburn was an officer and in charge of the Farmers State Bank and her confidential financial adviser, and that a fiduciary relationship existed between her and Colburn. That in March, 1931, she purchased, at the solicitation and request of Colburn, the notes and trust deed described in her original bill upon his assurance that the trust deed so purchased was a first lien upon the land described therein. Subsequently the cross-bill of Colburn and the bank was amended by alleging that tract B was, on June 8, 1932, released from the operation of the bank's mortgage Appellee answered this amendment by alleging that at the time this release was of the Bechtel trust deed, but set up that on February 9, 1926, the Hookes were indebted to the Farmers State Bank of Eureka in the sum of $8100.00, and to secure the payment of the same they executed on that date a trust deed to Colburn as trustee on said tract A, which was recorded on February 9, 1926. The answer then alleges that the amount of this indebtedness had been, on March 4, 1931, reduced to $5900.00, and an extension agreement had been entered into extending the payment of this $5900.00 to March 1, 1933. The answer states that this $5900.00 note and the trust deed to secure its payment are held by the Farmers State Bank of Eureka and avers that it is a first and prior lien on tract A. On September 7, 1932, Colburn as trustee and the Farmers State Bank filed their cross bill to foreclose this trust deed, which not only covers the eighty acres designated as tract A, but also another tract consisting of 122 acres, which also belonged to Hooke and which is designated herein as tract B.

Hanna Bechtel answered the cross-bill, denying that the Farmers State Bank trust deed was a prior lien on tract A and averring that in March 1931, and for many years prior thereto, Byron L. Colburn was an officer and in charge of the Farmers State Bank and her confidential financial adviser, and that a fiduciary relationship existed between her and Colburn. That in March, 1931, she purchased, at the solicitation and request of Colburn, the notes and trust deed described in her original bill upon his assurance that the trust deed so purchased was a first lien upon the land described therein. Subsequently the cross-bill of Colburn and the bank was amended by alleging that tract B was, on June 8, 1932, released from the operation of the bank's mortgage. Appellee answered this amendment by alleging that at the time this release was executed the bank and Colburn had knowledge that appellee's mortgage was in full force and effect and that if the court should hold that appellee's mortgage was not a first lien on tract A that then the bank in executing the release on tract B should be decreed to have released pro tanto tract A from the operation of its mortgage.

On March 7, 1933, the cross-bill of Colburn and the bank was further amended and by this amendment it was alleged that on June 8, 1932, when the release to tract B was executed, William E. Gibson held notes of the Rockes aggregating $31,000.00, the payment of $11,000.00 of which was secured by a mortgage on tract B and the payment of the remaining $20,000.00 was secured by a mortgage on both tracts A and B. That the release of tract B was made at the request of Gibson who had obtained a deed from Jeff and Lucy Rocke in consideration of his (Gibson's) agreement to release the Rockes from any personal liability on their notes which he held. By this amendment cross complainants sought to have the release which had been executed on June 8, 1932, set aside and that both tracts be sold to satisfy all the incumbrances thereon and that the bank be decreed to have a first lien on both tracts.

Subsequently William E. Gibson answered the original bill and cross bill, alleging that he held notes dated March 5, 1928, aggregating $11,000.00 executed by Jeff Rocke and Lucy Rocke, the payment of which was secured by a mortgage on tract B, and was also the owner of notes executed by Jeff Rocke and Lucy Rocke on March 5, 1928, aggregating $20,000.00, the payment of which was secured by a trust deed conveying both tracts of land. By his answer Gibson admits that the Farmers State Bank of Eureka had a first mortgage on both tracts and that on June 8, 1933, the trust deed of the bank was released so far as tract B was concerned executed the bank and Colburn had knowledge that appellee's mortgage was in full force and effect and that if the court should hold that appellee's mortgage was not a first lien on tract A that then the bank in executing the release on tract B should be decreed to have released pro tanto tract A from the operation of its mortgage.

On March 7, 1933, the cross-bill of Colburn and the bank was further amended and by this amendment it was alleged that on June 8, 1933, when the release to tract B was executed, William E. Gibson held notes of the Rookes aggregating $31,000.00, the payment of $11,000.00 of which was secured by a mortgage on tract B and the payment of the remaining $20,000.00 was secured by a mortgage on both tracts A and B. That the release of tract B was made at the request of Gibson who had obtained a deed from Tell and Lucy Rooke in consideration of his (Gibson's) agreement to release the Rookes from any personal liability on their notes which he held. By this amendment cross complainants sought to have the release which had been executed on June 8, 1933, set aside and that both tracts be sold to satisfy all the incumbrances thereon and that the bank be decreed to have a first lien on both tracts.

Subsequently William E. Gibson answered the original bill and cross-bill, alleging that he held notes dated March 8, 1928, aggregating $11,000.00 executed by Tell Rooke and Lucy Rooke, the payment of which was secured by a mortgage on tract B, and was also the holder of notes executed by Tell Rooke and Lucy Rooke on March 8, 1928, aggregating $20,000.00, the payment of which was secured by a trust deed conveying both tracts of land. By his answer he admits that the Farmers State Bank of Eureka had a first mortgage on both tracts and that on June 8, 1933, the trust deed of the bank was released so far as tract B was concerned. His amendment to his

That the bank in releasing said tract B from the operation of its mortgage did so in order to relieve Jeff Rocke and Lucy Rocke from any personal liability under the notes held by Gibson. By his answer and cross bill, Gibson sought to foreclose the trust deeds which he held After the issues had been made up, the cause was referred to the Master, who reported the evidence and his conclusions. Upon the hearing on exceptions to the report of the Master, a decree was rendered finding that Colburn stated to appellee Hanna Bechtol that the notes which were traded to her were secured by a trust deed which was a first lien upon tract A, that said statement was untrue, that in making said statement and in selling and delivering the said notes to appellee, Colburn was acting as the agent of Gibson and also as the cashier and agent of the bank, that Colburn knew said statements were untrue and made them for the purpose of inducing appellee to purchase said notes and that by reason of the fact that Colburn was a representative of the bank in selling said notes to appellee the bank, in this proceeding, is estopped from asserting that its mortgage is a prior lien to the trust deed of appellee. The decree then held that appellee's trust deed was a first and superior lien on tract A and rendered the usual decree of foreclosure and sale. The decree also dismissed the cross bill of Colburn and the bank for want of equity, refused to vacate the partial release and reinstate the mortgage of the bank as to tract B and dismissed for want of equity the cross bill of Gibson. From this decree Colburn and the bank have brought the record to this court for review by appeal.

Appellants insist that the trust deed of the bank is a first lien upon tracts A and B, and that the chancellor erred in not vacating the partial release which it executed and which released tract B therefrom. Appellants further contend that the evidence disat the bank in releasing said tract B from the operation of its mortgage did so in order to relieve Jeff Hooks and Lucy Hooks from personal liability under the notes held by Gibson. By his answer and cross bill, Gibson sought to foreclose the trust deeds which he held. After the issues had been made up, the cause was referred to the Master, who reported the evidence and his conclusions. On the hearing on exceptions to the report of the Master, a decree was rendered finding that Colburn stated to appellee Nanna Bechtel that the notes which were traded to her were secured by a trust deed which was a first lien upon tract A, that said statement was untrue, that in making said statement and in selling and delivering the said notes to appellee, Colburn was acting as the agent of Gibson and also as the cashier and agent of the bank, that Colburn knew said statements were untrue and made them for the purpose of inducing appellee to purchase said notes and that by reason of the fact that Colburn was representative of the bank in selling said notes to appellee the bank, in this proceeding, is estopped from asserting that its mortgage is a prior lien to the trust deed of appellee. The decree then held that appellee's trust deed was a first and superior lien on tract A and rendered the usual decree of foreclosure and sale. The decree also dismissed the cross bill of Colburn and the bank for want of equity, refused to vacate the partial release and reinstate the mortgage of the bank as to tract B and dismissed for want of equity the cross bill of Gibson. From this decree Colburn and the bank have brought the record to this court for review by appeal.

Appellants insist that the trust deed of the bank is a first lien upon tracts A and B, and that the chancellor erred in not setting the partial release which it executed and which released tract B therefrom. Appellants further contend that the evidence discloses that Colburn was acting for Gibson and not the bank when he exchanged the Rocke notes to appellee for the notes which appellee then held and which are referred to in this record as the Benta notes that there is no evidence supporting the finding in the decree that Colburn, when he traded the Rocke notes and trust deed to appellee, was acting for the bank, and that the decree is clearly erroneous in finding the lien of the bank on tract A to be inferior to the lien of appellee, but that a decree should have been rendered foreclosing appellant's trust deed as to both tracts A and B.

Appellee insists that the evidence discloses that Byron L. Colburn was the cashier and principal owner of the Farmers State Bank, that William E. Gibson was a customer and loaned his money through the bank. That a conspiracy existed between the bank, Colburn and Gibson, the object of which was to sell the notes aggregating $10,000.00, which were secured by a second mortgage on tract A "to some trusting customer, such as Hanna Bechtel, upon the false representation that it was a first mortgage" that in pursuance of such conspiracy, Colburn sold the note secured by said trust deed to appellee, and therefore the bank is estopped from asserting in this proceeding that its trust deed is prior to the one held by appellee. It is further insisted by appellee that in the event this court finds adversely to her on the question of fraud and conspiracy, that then it should be held that the bank, by releasing its trust deed on tract B, released the same in favor of appellee as to tract A to the extent of the value of tract B

The evidence discloses that previous to February 20, 1920, Jeff Rocke owned tract A, which consisted of eighty acres of land, that on that day he acquired tract B as a part of the purchase price, he, Rocke, assumed the payment of an $8,000.00 mortgage closes that Colburn was acting for Gibson and not the bank when he exchanged the Rocke notes to appellee for the notes which appellee then held and which are referred to in this record as the Banta notes; that there is no evidence supporting the finding in the decree that Colburn, when he traded the Rocke notes and trust deed to appellee, was acting for the bank, and that the decree is clearly erroneous in finding the lien of the bank on tract A to be inferior to the lien of appellee, but that a decree should have been rendered foreclosing appellant's trust deed as to both tracts A and B.

Appellee insists that the evidence discloses that Byron Colburn was the cashier and principal owner of the Farmers State Bank; that William B. Gibson was a customer and loaned his money through the bank; that a conspiracy existed between the bank, Colburn and Gibson, the object of which was to sell the notes ag- [illegible], which were secured by a second mortgage on tract [illegible] unwitting customers, such as Hanna Boeckel, upon the false [illegible] that it was a first mortgage; that in pursuance of [illegible] conspiracy, Colburn sold the note secured by said trust deed to appellee, and therefore the bank is estopped from asserting in [illegible] proceeding that its trust deed is prior to the one held by [illegible] It is further insisted by appellee that in the event [illegible] finds adversely to her on the question of fraud and [illegible], then it should be held that the bank, by releasing [illegible] deed on tract B, released the same in favor of appellee [illegible] to the extent of the value of tract B.

[illegible] The evidence discloses that previous to February 20, [illegible] tract A, which consisted of eighty acres of [illegible] he acquired tract B. As a part of the pur- [illegible] assumed the payment of ax$8,000.00 mortgage thereon On March 1, 1920, Jeff Rocke and wife executed a trust deed on tract B to Colburn as trustee, to secure the payment of $10,000.00. On September 22, 1922, Jeff Rocke and his wife executed and delivered to Colburn their note for $11,500.00 payable to Colburn on or before two years after date. This note was secured by a mortgage on certain real estate located in Ohio. On March 24, 1927, this note and mortgage were assigned by Colburn to the bank. On February 9, 1926, Jeff Rocke and wife executed a trust deed conveying tracts A and B to Colburn as trustee, to secure the payment of the balance then due on this $11,500.00 note which was $8100.00. On March 5, 1928, Jeff Rocke and wife executed their several notes aggregating $41,000.00, all payable to the order of themselves and secured the payment thereof by their three trust deeds. One trust deed conveyed tract A to Byron L. Colburn, Trustee, and secured the payment of $10,000.00. The notes evidencing this amount are the notes held by appellee, the payment of which are secured by the trust deed, which forms the basis of this foreclosure proceeding. This trust deed was recorded at 10 25 A. M. March 8, 1928. The second trust deed named Colburn as trustee and conveyed tracts A and B to him and secured the payment of $11,000.00. This trust deed was filed for record on March 8, 1928, at 10 27 A. M. The third trust deed was also executed to Colburn as trustee, also conveyed tracts A and B and secured the payment of $20,000.00. This trust deed was filed for record on March 8, 1928, at 10 29 A M. This is the condition of the title to tracts A and B, as shown by the public records of Woodford County at the time appellee became the owner of her notes and trust deed

ereon. On March 1, 1920, Jeff Rooke and wife executed a trust
ed on tract B to Colburn as trustee, to secure the payment of
10,000.00. On September 24, 1926, Jeff Rooke and his wife executed
d delivered to Colburn their note for $11,500.00 payable to
lburn on or before two years after date. This note was secured
a mortgage on certain real estate located in Ohio. On March 24,
27, this note and mortgage were assigned by Colburn to the bank.
February 8, 1926, Jeff Rooke and wife executed a trust deed con-
ying tracts A and B to Colburn as trustee, to secure the payment
the balance then due on this $11,500.00 note which was $8100.00.
March 8, 1928, Jeff Rooke and wife executed their several notes
gregating $41,000.00, all payable to the order of themselves and
cured the payment thereof by their three trust deeds. One trust
ed conveyed tract A to Byron L. Colburn, Trustee, and secured the
yment of $10,000.00. The notes evidencing this amount are the
tes held by appellee, the payment of which are secured by the
ust deed, which forms the basis of this forced sale proceeding.
is trust deed was recorded at 10:26 A. M. March 8, 1928. The
cond trust deed named Colburn as trustee and conveyed tracts A
and B and secured the payment of $11,000.00. This trust deed
filed for record on March 8, 1928, at 10:27 A. M. The third
ust deed was also executed to Colburn as trustee, also conveyed
acts A and B and secured the payment of $20,000.00. This trust
ed was filed for record on March 8, 1928, at 10.29 A. M. This
s the condition of the title to tracts A and B, as shown by the
records of Woodford County at the time appellee became the
of her notes and trust deed.

The evidence further discloses that Gibson owns various tracts of real estate, is a farm supervisor, knew the Rocke land, did some of his banking business with the Farmers State Bank and arranged with Colburn that he would take the Rocke notes and the first two of the trust deeds, given to secure the payment of $21,000.00 that thereafter Colburn negotiated the loans and for the $10,000.00 notes secured by the trust deed on tract A, he, Gibson, advanced to Colburn $10,000.00. Gibson and appellee had no personal dealings. Acting through Colburn, these notes, aggregating $10,000.00 were exchanged for $1,000.00 cash and certain notes executed by Anna Banta aggregating $9,000.00 secured by a first trust deed on what is known in this record as the Banta farm, which notes and trust deed were held by appellee, she having purchased them from Colburn several years before the exchange was made. On March 2, 1931 an extension agreement was executed by Jeff Rocke and Lucy Rocke. This instrument recited the execution by them of the note of $11,500.00 on September 22, 1922, and the mortgage given to secure the payment of the same, the fact that on February 9, 1926, the amount due thereon had been reduced to $8100.00 and that the payment thereof had been secured by a trust deed on tracts A and B, the fact that the obligation had been further reduced to the sum of $5900.00, the payment of which by this instrument was extended to March 1, 1933. This instrument was duly acknowledged and filed for record on May 10, 1932. On June 8, 1932, Jeff Rocke and wife conveyed tract B to Gibson in consideration that Gibson would cancel their notes, Gibson having acquired the third trust deed and the notes for which it was given to secure.

The evidence further discloses that Gibson owns various tracts of real estate, is a farm supervisor, knew the Rocke land, did some of his banking business with the Farmers State Bank and arranged with Colburn that he would take the Rocke notes and the first two of the trust deeds, given to secure the payment of $21,000.00; that thereafter Colburn negotiated the loans and for the $10,000.00 notes secured by the trust deed on tract A, he, Gibson, advanced to Colburn $10,000.00. Gibson and appellee had no personal dealings. Acting through Colburn, these notes, aggregating $10,000.00 were exchanged for $1,000.00 cash and certain notes executed by Anna Bants aggregating $9,000.00 secured by a first trust deed on what is known in this record as the Bants farm, which notes and trust deed were held by appellee, she having purchased them from Colburn several years before the exchange was made. On March 2, 1931 an extension agreement was executed by Jeff Rocke and Lucy Rocke. This instrument recited the execution by them of the note of $11,300.00 on September 22, 1922, and the mortgage given to secure the payment of the same, the fact that on February 9, 1926, the amount due thereon had been reduced to $8100.00 and that the payment thereof had been secured by a trust deed on tracts A and B, the fact that the obligation had been further reduced to the sum of $5900.00, the payment of which by this instrument was extended to March 1, 1933. This instrument was duly acknowledged and filed for record on May 10, 1932. On June 8, 1932, Jeff Rocke and wife conveyed tract B to Gibson in consideration that Gibson would cancel their notes, Gibson having acquired the third trust deed and the notes for which it was given to secure.

As to what occurred when the exchange was made of the Banta notes and trust deed from appellee to Gibson for the Rocke notes and trust deed, the evidence is conflicting. Appellee testified that that the Banta notes were past due and that Mrs. Banta was unable to pay the interest. That she knew Colburn and had transacted business with him for five or six years and she went to him and he told her he had a mortgage he would trade her which he thought was better than the one she held that her mortgage was a first mortgage and she asked Mr Colburn about the Rocke mortgage and inquired of him 'Is this a first mortgage and is that all that is on the farm?' and Colburn replied "You may go to the court house and look it up or drive to the farm and look at it". She further testified that Colburn told her where the land was located, to whom it belonged and that there was nothing more against it that she took his word for it and did not look up the record. She further testified that Colburn told her that Gibson held a mortgage on a part of the Banta farm Linda Bechtel, a sister of appellee, testified that she resided in Eureka and to a certain extent looked after her sister's affairs, as her sister resided in Peoria that she had a conversation with Colburn and later went with her sister to the bank about March 2, 1931, and Colburn there told her and appellee and it was talked over that the interest on the Banta mortgage was in default and Colburn expressed his opinion that it would be a good trade for them to trade the Banta notes and mortgage for the Rocke note and mortgage She testified that her sister asked Colburn if the Rocke mortgage was a first mortgage and he said that it was

The husband of appellee testified that before the original bill in this case was filed he talked with Colburn and Colburn told him that there was this $10,000.00 first mortgage and a blanket mortgage of $20,000.00 on Mr. Rocke's land

As to what occurred when the exchange was made of the Bante notes and trust deed from appellee to Gibson for the Rooke notes and trust deed, the evidence is conflicting. Appellee testified that the Bante notes were past due and that Mrs. Bante was unable to pay the interest. That she knew Colburn and had transacted business with him for five or six years and she went to him and he told her he had a mortgage he would trade her which he thought was better than the one she held; that her mortgage was a first mortgage and she asked Mr. Colburn about the Rooke mortgage and inquired of him, "Is this a first mortgage and is that all that is on the farm?" and Colburn replied, "You may go to the court house and look it up or drive to the farm and look at it". She further testified that Colburn told her where the land was located, to whom it belonged and that there was nothing more against it; that she took his word for it and did not look up the record. She further testified that Colburn told her that Gibson held a mortgage on a part of the Bante farm. Linda Bushell, a sister of appellee, testified that she resided in Eureka and, to a certain extent looked after her sister's affairs, as her sister resided in Peoria; that she had a conversation with Colburn and later went with her sister to the bank about March 2, 1951, and Colburn there told her and appellee and it was talked over that the interest on the Bante mortgage was in default and Colburn expressed his opinion that it would be a good trade for them to trade the Bante notes and mortgage for the Rooke note and mortgage. She testified that she, the sister, asked Colburn if the Rooke mortgage was a first mortgage and he said that it was.

The husband of appellee testified that before the original bill in this case was filed he talked with Colburn and Colburn told him that there was this $10,000.00 first mortgage and a blanket mortgage of $20,000.00 on Mr. Rooke's land.

Mr. Colburn testified that about March 1, 1931, appellee and her sister left with him interest coupons on a $9,000.00 note secured by a mortgage on the Banta land. These coupons were payable at the Farmers State Bank and at that time the Farmers State Bank had no interest whatever either in the Banta note and mortgage or the Rocke notes and mortgage, other than the one which it is seeking to foreclose by its cross bill herein. According to Mr. Colburn, appellee and her sister Linda came to the bank and it was mentioned that Mrs. Banta was unable to pay the principal or interest which was then past due and Colburn suggested that it might be possible for them to exchange the Banta note for the Rocke note, which was then held and owned by Gibson that he did not talk to Gibson about the exchange until after he had talked to appellee and her sister and he denies that he stated to appellee or her sister that the Rocke loan was secured by a first mortgage on the premises According to this witness, the value of the Banta land, consisting of one hundred nine acres, a trust deed upon which secured the $9,000 00 mortgage, was at the time the papers were exchanged $45.00 per acre. There is no other evidence in the record as to the valuation of the Banta land. Colburn fixed the value of the tract A at $225.00 per acre. John Zimmerman, a witness, testifying on behalf of appellants, gave it as his opinion that tract A, on March 1, 1931, was worth $250.00 per acre, and the husband of appellee, testifying in her behalf, placed a valuation on the tract A in March, 1931, at between $150.00 and $175 00 per acre. Another witness fixed the value of tract A at that time at $165.00, another witness at $175.00 and another at $200.00 per acre

The foregoing is substantially all of the evidence in this record. While appellee insists that a conspiracy existed between the bank, Colburn and Gibson, there is no evidence in the

Mr. Colburn testified that about March 1, 1931, appellee and her sister left with him interest coupons on a $9,000.00 note secured by a mortgage on the Bants land. These coupons were payable at the Farmers State Bank and at that time the Farmers State Bank had no interest whatever either in the Bants note and mortgage or the Rocke notes and mortgage, other than the one which it is seeking to foreclose by its cross bill herein. According to Mr. Colburn, appellee and her sister Linda came to the bank and it was mentioned that Mrs. Bants was unable to pay the principal or interest which was then past due and Colburn suggested that it might be possible for them to exchange the Bants note for the Rocke note, which was then held and owned by Gibson: that he did not talk to Gibson about the exchange until after he had talked to appellee and her sister and he denies that he stated to appellee or her sister that the Rocke loan was secured by a first mortgage on the premises. According to this witness, the value of the Bants land, consisting of one hundred nine acres, a trust deed upon which secured the $9,000.00 mortgage, was at the time the papers were exchanged $45.00 per acre. There is no other evidence in the record as to the valuation of the Bants land. Colburn fixed the value of the tract A at $225.00 per acre. John Zimmerman, a witness, testifying on behalf of appellants, gave it as his opinion that tract A, on March 1, 1931, was worth $250.00 per acre, and the husband of appellee, testifying in her behalf, placed a valuation on the tract A in March, 1931, at between $150.00 and $175.00 per acre. Another witness fixed the value of tract A at that time at $165.00, another witness at $175.00 and another at $200.00 per acre.

The foregoing is substantially all of the evidence in this record. While appellee insists that a conspiracy existed between the bank, Colburn and Gibson, there is no evidence in the record to sustain this contention. The uncontradicted facts are that the bank held a first mortgage on both tracts A and B and had held a mortgage thereon for many years. That Gibson owned a junior lien on tract A to secure the payment of $10,000.00, for which he furnished the money to make the original loan. That he also owned another mortgage, which was a third lien on tract A and a second lien on tract B to secure the payment of $11,000.00. Appellee owned the Banta notes amounting to $9,000.00, secured by a first mortgage on one hundred nine acres of land, worth $45.00 per acre, and a second mortgage on eighty acres of land, the value of which does not appear from the evidence. Gibson owned a first mortgage on this eighty acres. Gibson had no interest as a stockholder or officer in the bank. Colburn was a stockholder and an officer in the bank, and appellee and Gibson were both customers of the bank. At the time of the exchange, appellee and Colburn discussed the fact that Gibson held other notes and mortgages on the Banta land and Colburn testified that in the conversation at the bank, it was mentioned that it might be necessary for appellee to foreclose her Banta mortgage in order for her to acquire title to the mortgaged premises, and that he there suggested to appellee, in the presence of her sister, that to avoid foreclosure of the Banta mortgage, an exchange of paper with Gibson, who was the owner of other loans of Mrs. Banta, might be effected. Neither appellee nor her sister denied this and it stands uncontradicted in this record. The weight of the evidence is that Colburn stated to appellee that the Hocke mortgage which she was accepting in exchange for the Banta notes and mortgage was a first lien on tract A, so the question presented for determination is whether the bank is estopped in this proceeding from asserting that it has a prior record to sustain this contention. The uncontradicted facts are that the bank held a first mortgage on both tracts A and B and had held a mortgage thereon for many years. That Gibson owned a junior lien on tract A to secure the payment of $10,000.00, for which he furnished the money to make the original loan. That he also owned another mortgage, which was a third lien on tract A and a second lien on tract B to secure the payment of $11,000.00. Appellee owned the Bentz notes amounting to $9,400.00, secured by a first mortgage on one hundred nine acres of land, worth $45.00 per acre, and a second mortgage on eighty acres of land, the value of which does not appear from the evidence. Gibson owned a first mortgage on this eighty acres. Gibson had no interest as a stockholder or officer in the bank. Colburn was a stockholder and an officer in the bank, and appellee and Gibson were both customers of the bank. At the time of the exchange, appellee and Colburn discussed the fact that Gibson held other notes and mortgages on the Bentz land and Colburn testified that in the conversation at the bank, it was mentioned that it might be necessary for appellee to foreclose her Bentz mortgage in order for her to acquire title to the mortgaged premises, and that he there suggested to appellee, in the presence of her sister, that to avoid foreclosure of the Bentz mortgage, an exchange of paper with Gibson, who was the owner of other loans of Mrs. Bentz, might be effected. Neither appellee nor her sister denied this and it stands uncontradicted in this record. The weight of the evidence is that Colburn stated to appellee that the Hooke mortgage which she was accepting in exchange for the Bentz notes and mortgage was a first lien on tract A, so the question presented for determination is whether the bank is estopped in this proceeding from asserting that it has a prior lien on tract A because its cashier, in effecting an exchange of securities among two of its customers, stated to one that the mortgage she was accepting in exchange for another security was a first mortgage, when as a matter of fact it was a second mortgage and the cashier knew that his statement was untrue?

Counsel for appellee insist that the actual exchange of the Banta notes and trust deed for the Rocke notes and trust deed was made by Colburn in the bank of which he was cashier and that appellee believed they belonged to the bank and that Colburn encouraged her in that belief and that she never learned that Gibson had any connection with the Rocke notes and trust deed until the evidence was produced before the Master. In her testimony appellee nowhere states that Colburn told her that the Rocke notes and trust deed belonged to the bank, and in her original bill, appellee, after alleging the execution of the several notes by Jeff Rocke and wife, represented to the court that she confided in the undertaking of Jeff Rocke and Lucy Rocke and accepted and received the notes and trust deed from them. In this proceeding she does not seek to rescind the transaction nor does she seek to recover damages from Colburn, but insists that because Colburn was cashier of the bank and had knowledge of the true condition of the title of the Rocke land and knew that the bank held a prior lien, that therefore in this proceeding the bank is estopped from insisting upon a priority. In support of this contention, counsel cite Bondy v Samuels, 333 Ill. 535, where it is held that the general rule of equitable estoppel is that where a party by his statements and conduct leads another to do something he would not have done, but for such statements and conduct, the guilty party will not be allowed to deny his utterances or acts to the loss or damage of the other lien on tract A because its cashier, in effecting an exchange of securities among two of its customers, stated to one that the mort- gage she was accepting in exchange for another security was a first mortgage, when as a matter of fact it was a second mortgage and the cashier knew that his statement was untrue?

Counsel for appellee insist that the actual exchange of the Banks notes and trust deed for the Rocke notes and trust deed was made by Colburn in the bank of which he was cashier and that appellee believed they belonged to the bank and that Colburn encouraged her in that belief and that she never learned that Gibson had any connection with the Rocke notes and trust deed until the evidence was produced before the master. In her testimony appellee nowhere states that Colburn told her that the Rocke notes and trust deed belonged to the bank, and in her original bill, appellee, after alleging the execution of the several notes by Jeff Rocke and wife, represented to the court that she confided in the undertaking of Jeff Rocke and Lucy Rocke and accepted and received the notes and trust deed from them. In this proceeding she does not seek to rescind the transaction nor does she seek to recover damages from Colburn, but insists that because Colburn was cashier of the bank and had knowledge of the true condition of the title of the Rocke land and knew that the bank held a prior lien, that therefore in this proceeding the bank is estopped from insisting upon a priority. In support of this contention, counsel cite Bondy v. Samuels, 333 Ill. 535, where it is held that the general rule of equitable estoppel is that where a party by his statements and conduct leads another to do something he would not have done, but for such statements and conduct, the guilty party will not be allowed to deny his utterances or acts to the loss or damage of the other party. Counsel also cite Lion Oil Co. v. Sinclair Refining Co., 252 Ill. App. 92, and Pfeffer v. Farmers State Bank, 263 Ill. App. 360, where it is held that a principal is liable for the torts, frauds, deceits or misrepresentations of an agent committed in the course of and within the scope of his employment. Counsel also cite Hunt v. Creer, 271 Ill. App. 223, where it is held that a cashier of a bank is a general agent for the transaction of the bank's business, and his information concerning a note in the possession of the bank is the information of the bank. There is no fault to be found with these authorities, but they are not applicable to the facts as disclosed by this record. Appellee exchanged the Barta notes and trust deed, which she held, for the Roche notes and trust deed, which in fact belonged to Gibson and of this appellee was advised. According to the evidence the bank in no way profited by the exchange, had nothing to do with it, and if its cashier made the statement attributed to him by appellee, it was made about a note not then in the possession of or owned by the bank and when made Colburn was not acting within the scope of his authority. American Guaranty Co. v. State Bank of East Lynn, 244 Ill. App. 16; Heiple, Receiver, v. Boyer, 264 Ill. App. 572.

If, therefore, the bank is not estopped from asserting its prior lien on tract A, what decree should be entered that is equitable to all the parties? As security for the principal sum of $5900.00, the bank holds a first mortgage on forty-seven acres of land in Paulding County, Ohio, and if the release as to tract B had not been executed, it would also have had a first lien on tracts A and B. Appellee only had a lien on tract A. It is only fair and just that the release of the bank's lien on tract B be party. Counsel also cite Lion Oil Co. v. Sinclair Refining Co., 232 Ill. App.92, and Pfeffer v. Farmers State Bank, 263 Ill. App. 300, where it is held that a principal is liable for the torts, frauds, deceits or misrepresentations of an agent committed in the course of and within the scope of his employment. Counsel also cite Hunt v. Green, 271 Ill. App. 223, where it is held that a cashier of a bank is a general agent for the transaction of the bank's business, and his information concerning a note in the possession of the bank is the information of the bank. There is no fault to be found with these authorities, but they are not applicable to the facts as disclosed by this record. Appellee exchanged the Renta notes and trust deed, which she held, for the Hocke notes and trust deed, which in fact belonged to Gibson and of this appellee was advised. According to the evidence the bank in no way profited by the exchange, had nothing to do with it, and if its cashier made the statement attributed to him by appellee, it was made about a note not then in the possession of or owned by the bank and when made Colburn was not acting within the scope of his authority. American Guaranty Co. v. State Bank of East Lynn, 244 Ill. App. 16; Helpie, Receiver, v. Beyer, 264 Ill. App. 572.

If, therefore, the bank is not estopped from asserting its prior lien on tract A, what decree should be entered that is equitable to all the parties? As security for the principal sum of $3900.00, the bank holds a first mortgage on forty-seven acres of land in Paulding County, Ohio, and if the release as to tract B had not been executed, it would also have had a first lien on tracts A and B. Appellee only had a lien on tract A. It is only fair and just that the release of the bank's lien on tract B be cancelled. No consideration passed therefor and no one is objecting to a decree so providing. The bank is clearly entitled to have its lien foreclosed on both tracts A and B. Appellee is also entitled to have her lien on tract A foreclosed. The decree should provide that each tract be sold separately and out of the proceeds derived from the sale of tract B, there should be paid the bank, to apply on the amount due it, a sum in the proportion which the amount it sells for bears to the amount derived from the sale of both tracts. In other words, if tract B sells for $18,000.00, the amount the Master found it was worth in March, 1931, and tract A sells for $16,000.00, the amount the Master found it was worth in March, 1931, then tract B should contribute 9/17ths of the amount of the indebtedness so found due the bank. The balance of the proceeds derived from the sale of tract B should be paid Gibson, who now has the legal title thereto. Gibson is entitled to have his $20,000.00 trust deed foreclosed in this proceeding as to Tract A, it being a lien thereon subject to the liens of the bank and appellee. The decree should also provide that in the event the bank's lien is satisfied in full out of the proceeds of the sale and appellee's lien is not satisfied in full, that then the bank shall deliver to appellee the trust deed or mortgage on the Paulding County, Ohio land, together with proper assignment thereof. This, we understand, the bank offers to do.

The decree of the Circuit Court of Woodford County is reversed and this cause is remanded with directions to that court to enter a decree in conformity with this opinion.

REVERSED AND REMANDED WITH DIRECTIONS.

cancelled. No consideration passed therefor and no one is objecting to a decree so providing. The bank is clearly entitled to have its lien foreclosed on both tracts A and B. Appellee is also entitled to have her lien on tract A foreclosed. The decree should provide that each tract be sold separately and out of the proceeds derived from the sale of tract B, there should be paid the bank, to apply on the amount due it, a sum in the proportion which the amount it sells for bears to the amount derived from the sale of both tracts. In other words, if tract B sells for $18,000.00, the amount the Master found it was worth in March, 1934, and tract A sells for $14,000.00, the amount the Master found it was worth in March, 1934, then tract B should contribute [illegible] of the amount of the indebtedness so found due the bank. The balance of the proceeds derived from the sale of tract B should be paid Gibson, who now has the legal title thereto. Gibson is entitled to have his $20,000.00 trust deed foreclosed in this proceeding as to tract A, it being a lien thereon subject to the liens of the bank and appellee. The decree should also provide that in the event the bank's lien is satisfied in full out of the proceeds of the sale and appellee's lien is not satisfied in full, that then the bank shall release to appellee the trust deed or mortgage on the [illegible] County, Ohio land, together with proper assignment thereof. [illegible] understand, the bank offers to do.

[illegible] reason the decree of the Circuit Court of Woodford County is reversed and this cause is remanded with directions to that court to enter a decree in conformity with this opinion.

REVERSED AND REMANDED WITH DIRECTIONS.

}ss.
I JUSTUS L. JOHNSON Clerk of the Appellate Court in and of the State of Illinois, and the keeper of the Records and Seal thereof, do hereby ; is a true copy of the opinion of the said Appellate Court in the above entitled cause.

In Testimony Whereof, I hereunto set my hand and affix the seal of said Appellate Court at Ottawa this________________day of ________________in the year of our Lord one thousand nine hundred and thirty-________________

____

Clerk of the Appellate Court

PUBLISHED IN ABSTRACT

Ernest Roy Nunes, Appellee, v City of Jacksonville, a Municipal Corporation, Appellant

Appeal from Circuit Court, Morgan County.

JANUARY TERM, A D 1935 280 I.A. 631

Gen No 8846 **Agenda No. 1**

MR JUSTICE FULTON delivered the opinion of the Court

This was an action of trespass on the case brought by Appellee against Appellant, the City of Jacksonville, a municipal corporation to recover damages for an alleged injury to certain lands of the Appellee growing out of the diversion of surface water by the Appellant upon the lands of the Appellee, which surface water, or any major portion thereof, did not naturally drain upon the premises of the Appellee

The declaration consisted of one Count which in detail averred substantially the facts above stated and to which declaration the Appellant filed a plea of not guilty The case was tried before a jury who returned a verdict in favor of Appellee for the sum of $525 00 Motion for a new trial was overruled upon Appellee remitting the excess of damages over $500 00 and judgment was entered on the verdict for that amount From this judgment Appellant prosecutes an appeal to this Court

The facts show that Appellee was the owner of ten lots in the Car Shop Addition to the City of Jacksonville, that Appellee lived in a house on one of his lots and farmed the other nine lots where he raised vegetables and cultivated raspberry bushes and strawberry plants He had owned the premises for about five years The testimony further shows that on September 15, 1932 the Appellant completed the construction of a 24-inch storm sewer, which commenced at the corner of East LaFayette Ave and North Clay Ave, running thence north on North Clay Ave to Hockenhull Street, thence East on Hockenhull Street to Beesley Ave, thence north on Beesley Ave, to east Walnut Street thence East on Walnut Street to Hackett Ave, thence north along Hackett Ave, to a catch basin and from the catch basin the water from this sewer flowed under the Burlington track through a 36 or 40 inch tile

and thence in a northeasterly direction down to, upon and across Appellees property by way of an open ditch

The Appellee claims that after the construction of the storm water sewer by Appellant the land of Appellee was wetter than before such construction and that he could no longer farm a substantial portion of said land, that after heavy rains the water stood on a portion of said land for long periods of time at a depth from 2½ to 3 feet and at an average width of 40 to 70 feet in the vicinity of the open ditch which ran in a northeasterly direction across Appellee's property In addition to the testimony of Appellee a witness, John Baptist, testified that he had lived in the vicinity of Appellee's property for over 25 years and that the water which naturally flowed down north Clay Ave, and accumulated at the corner of North Clay Ave, and Hockenhull Street did not flow upon Appellee's land before the opening of the storm sewer by the Appellant because the property immediately East and north of the intersection of North Clay Ave, and Hockenhull Street was higher than the level of said intersection He also testified that the market value of Appellee's land decreased $500 00 by reason of the construction of the storm sewer Another witness, Fred Tholen, for the Appellee testified that there was an 8 inch tile under the Appellee's property which prior to the opening of said sewer took care of all the water naturally flowing across said premises and that he had never seen water standing on said property before the construction of such sewer

E M Henderson, a civil engineer and witness for Appellant testified that the draw or open ditch across Appellee's land was 3 or 4 feet lower than the land on either side He also testified that the land level immediately east and north of the intersection of North Clay Ave, and Hockenhull Street was higher than at said intersection although the land level at the corner of Hockenhull Street and Beesley Ave, was lower than at the former intersection, further that the land drained by the storm sewer sloped generally north toward the Appellee's lots

Another witness for Appellant, James Vasconcellos, a former Superintendent of Streets for Appellant testified that the ground level at the corner of North Clay Ave, and Hockenhull Street was lower than the ground immediately east of said corner, and that water collecting at said corner prior to the construction of the storm water sewer would naturally drain to the west but that

the water ran across back yards and through a draw by nature to Appellee's land

The main controversy in the case is whether or not the Appellant has, by means of its storm water sewer, carried water upon Appellee's premises which did not naturally flow there It is the contention of Appellant that there is no evidence in the record to support the verdict of the jury and that the same was manifestly and palpably against the weight of the evidence, that therefor the Court erred in denying Appellant's motion for a directed verdict at the close of Appellee's testimony In support of its theory of the case the Appellant asked the Court to submit a special interrogatory to the jury which was as follows "Do the jury believe from the evidence that the water which is alleged to drain upon Plaintiff's premises, or any major portion of such water, naturally drain upon plaintiff's premises at the point where it is herein alleged that such water drains upon the Plaintiff's premises?" The jury answered the Special interrogatory in the negative

It is our judgment that there were sufficient facts developed in the testimony of the Appellee and his witnesses which tended to show that by reason of construction and operation of the storm water sewer Appellant carried additional water to the lands of Appellee which by nature did not naturally flow there While the testimony of the engineer for Appellant disclosed by the levels shown on Exhibit D-2 that there was a slope to the north of the lands drained by the storm water sewer it did not off set the testimony of Appellee's witnesses that the land level at the corner of North Clay Ave, and Hockenhull Street was lower than the lands immediately east and north of said intersection With a conflict in the testimony it was proper to submit this question of fact to the jury for their determination Both by their verdict and by their answer to the Special Interrogatory the jury definitely decided from the preponderance of the testimony that the water, which now flows over Appellee's property and floods the same, did not in the state of nature flow there

It is well settled in Illinois that the finding of a jury on questions of fact will not be disturbed by the Court unless the finding is the result of passion or prejudice or manifestly against the weight of the evidence *Hirch v Chicago Consolidated Traction Company*, 146 App 501 It is our opinion that the record in this case does not warrant the Court in setting aside the verdict of the jury upon this particular question and that there is sufficient evidence to sustain the verdict of the jury.

It is further urged by the Appellant that the verdict of the jury is excessive The only testimony as to damages was that of John Baptist called in behalf of Appellee He testified that the ten lots belonging to Appellee with the improvements were worth about $100 00 a lot prior to September 15, 1932, that since that date at least four of the lots were no longer tillable and that the flooding of said lands decreased the market value of said property to the extent of $500 00

Appellant offered no testimony on the question of value or damages so that the jury were limited to the testimony of Appellee's witnesses as to the amount of the damages It is our judgment there is testimony in the record to support a verdict of $500 00 and that the same should therefor not be disturbed

Finding no substantial error in the record the judgment of the lower Court is therefore affirmed

Affirmed.

(Five pages in original opinion)

(47818—4 35) 14

UBLISHED IN ABSTRACT

Werner C Vollrath, Appellee, v Joseph Bordenkecher, Appellant

Appeal from Circuit Court, DeWitt County.

JANUARY TERM, A D 1935

280 I.A. 632

Gen No 8869½ Agenda No. 4

MR JUSTICE FULTON delivered the opinion of the Court

This is a suit filed by Appellee to recover on a contract for the sale of a second hand automobile The Appellee's declaration consisted of the common counts and a bill of particulars It was alleged in substance that on May 10th, 1930, Appellee sold and delivered to the Appellant a second hand Buick automobile for the sum of $850 00 $800 00 was to be paid by Appellant's promissory note, due in one year, and the old automobile of the Appellant to be taken in at the sum of $50 00 The declaration further alleged that Appellant purchased the car but refused to deliver the note or to take the automobile

Appellee filed four pleas, first the general issue, second a plea of set-off, third a breach of warranty stating that Appellee warranted the said automobile to be sound and in as good condition as a new automobile and that on the contrary the said car was not sound and not in as good condition as a new car Fourth, that Appellee promised and represented that the automobile sold had only been driven a small number of miles to-wit 15,000 miles and was in as sound and good condition as a new automobile, but on the contrary had been driven a large number of miles, to-wit 46,000 miles and was not in good and sound condition The Appellee filed replications traversing the pleas

The cause was tried by a Jury, the proofs submitted and the verdict rendered found the issues for the Appellee and assessed Appellee's damages at the sum of Eight Hundred Dollars ($800 00), together with interest computed thereon at the rate of 5 per cent per annum from the 10th day of May, 1930, to February 9, 1934, and found the entire amount due to Appellee, the sum of Nine Hundred Fifty Dollars ($950 00) Appellant's motion for a new trial was overruled as was also his motion for judgment notwithstanding the ver-

that Appellant made out the check and the application blank but said, "I don't want to sign the note on the 13th," that he had had enough bad luck but that he would be back on the next day

Later the Appellee met the appellant after the automobile was fixed and returned to Appellant and the latter was requested to sign the note and frequently promised to do so and remarked as Appellee testifies that the automobile was satisfactory On June 1st, 1930, Appellant came to Appellee's garage and the two sat down on the running board of the car for a short conversation Appellant asked Appellee if he had a cheaper or smaller car in stock and remarked that he should have bought a cheaper car Appellant further said that he would not be able to get the four hundred dollars that he expected within thirty days and Appellee replied that he would give him more time On June 5th, Appellant drove the car to Appellee's garage and complained of a noise in the differential or rear end of the Buick and left the car at the garage for Appellee's inspection Some further repairs and replacements were made on the car and on June 10th or 11th the car was taken to Appellants residence Appellee stated that he had given the Appellant a new car guarantee which included ninety days service and that if any trouble developed he would fix the same without cost or expense to Appellant Later the Appellant brought the car back to Appellee and stated that he was not going to take the car Appellee stated that he had sold the car to Appellant and that it was there subject to his order

Two mechanics, who had been in the employ of the Appellee, testified to having worked upon the car at various times and about the repairs and replacements made Both testified that the car was in good mechanical condition One of them testified that Appellee told him to turn back the speedometer and that he did turn it back to 15,000 miles He further stated that he did not remember what mileage was shown by the speedometer at the time he turned it back

Appellants testimony contradicts the evidence of Appellee principally in the following particulars, that Appellee represented to Appellant on two or three different occasions that 15,000 miles was the complete mileage the car had ever been driven, that he had never driven the car fast and that nearly every time he took it out he had difficulty and trouble with it He was corroborated in this respect by passengers or guests

who had been out riding with him on different occasions He further testified that he did not remember of being in Appellee's garage on May 13th and denied that he told Appellee he would not sign a note because it was the 13th He further denied telling Appellee that the car was satisfactory or that he should have bought a cheaper car He testified that Appellee's mechanic told Appellant that he had turned the speedometer on the car back from 46,000 miles to about 15,000 miles

It was stipulated by counsel that the jury might be instructed under the Old Practice Act and the Court thereupon gave the jury ten instructions at the request of Appellee and three instructions in behalf of Appellant

The Appellant has assigned many errors in the record upon which he seeks reversal but contends principally that prejudicial evidence was admitted in behalf of Appellee over objection by Appellant, that competent evidence offered by Appellant was rejected, that the Court made prejudicial remarks in the presence of the jury, that the Court erred both in the giving and refusing of instructions to the jury

We have examined the testimony admitted over Appellant's objection about which he complains but do not find any serious error in the ruling on the part of the trial court Both mechanics for Appellee wer permitted to testify that the car was in good mechanical condition at the time they finished working on the same but we think both witnesses were qualified to express an opinion under the circumstances of this case It was perhaps improper for the Court to permit the witness Myers to testify, when asked what he found to be the trouble with the car, that it had been driven faster than it should have been after being reconditioned, but only a general objection was made to the question and no motion to strike the answer made by counsel for Appellant Appellant further complains that the witness Robb, one of the mechanics and a witness in behalf of Appellee, was handed a document purporting to be a Bill of Exceptions on a former trial of this case and permitted to turn to certain pages thereof for the purpose of refreshing his recollection as to Plaintiff's exhibit 5 Ordinarily it would be error to permit the witness to examine a Bill of Exceptions to refresh his recollection but in this case counsel for Appellant agreed that Plaintiff's exhibit 5 was an exact copy of the original exhibit, that the original

exhibit had been lost, and that it would not be necessary to offer proof necessary to introduce secondary evidence Under these circumstances Appellant can not avail himself of the objection made There were no other flagrant violations of the rules of evidence and we do not believe on the whole that Appellant can seriously complain of either the admission or exclusion of evidence in this case

We have examined the remarks of the trial court which the Appellant complains were of a prejudicial nature but can find nothing that would constitute serious error or which prevented the Appellant from having a fair trial before the jury

Appellant further complains that the Court gave two instructions being number 2 and number 9 at the request of the Appellee upon the subject of measuring, weighing and determining the preponderance of the evidence First, because of repetition and second because of the use of the words "you must" and "you will" It is not ordinarily good practice to encumber the record with instructions covering the same matters, differing only in verbiage but in these two instructions there is nothing to indicate whether they are given in behalf of the Appellant or Appellee and the repetition could do no more harm to one party than to the other therefore it was not error to give them *Schmafeld* v *P & E Ry Co*, 158 App 335 Our Courts have also approved of the use of the words "should" and "must" in instructions on credibility and preponderance of evidence, *Walters* v *Checker Cab Co*, 265 App 329

Objection is also made to the giving of Appellee's third, fourth, fifth and seventh instructions, not because they contain erroneous statements of the law, but because there is repetition and too many instructions on the same subject Number three instructed the jury concerning the breach of warranty set forth in the third special plea of the Appellant, and states that the burden of proof was upon Appellant to prove the breach of warranty Number four was a similar instruction concerning the fraud of the Appellee in representing the number of miles the automobile had been driven as set forth in the fourth special plea of the Appellant, and also places the burden upon Appellant to prove such fraud and misrepresentation Number five does not deal with burden of proof in any manner Number seven stated the general proposition that the Appellant must prove both the breach of war-

ranty and the warranty thereof by a preponderance of the evidence Because of the special pleas of the Appellant and the necessity of covering the same we do not consider there is over emphasis in these instructions concerning the question of the burden of proof

We have examined the other objections pointed out by Appellant to the given instructions on the part of Appellee and find that they contain correct statements of the law The refusal of instructions offered on the part of Appellant was justified and the giving of same would have been prejudicial to Appellee We do not find any reversible error in either the giving or refusing of instructions by the trial Court

In this case there was a sharp conflict in the testimony as to representations or warranties made by Appellee to Appellant, in the sale of the car in question, both on the condition of the car and on the number of miles it had been driven, but these were questions of fact to be determined by the jury, and the testimony on both sides was fairly presented We do not therefore feel like disturbing the finding of the jury unless the record discloses some serious error

The case has been tried three times in the Circuit Court and this is the second appearance in this Court Where a case has been tried before two juries, each of which found for Appellee, the Courts are more reluctant to reverse than where there has been only one verdict, and the error should be plain and clearly prejudicial to warrant a reversal *Oliver* v *Oliver*, 340 Ill 445 *City of Chicago* v *McNally*, 128 App 375

We do not feel that the errors complained of or which are found in this record are sufficient to warrant a reversal of this case and the judgment of the Trial Court should be affirmed

Affirmed

(Eight pages in original opinion.)

(47312—4 35) 14

Published in Abstract

Frank B Harrison, Appellant, v The First Christian Church of Hamilton, Illinois, et al., Appellees

Appeal from Circuit Court of Hancock County

January Term, A D 1935 280 I.A. 632[2]

Gen No 8879 **Agenda No 7**

Mr Justice Fulton delivered the opinion of the Court

Appellant filed a bill in Chancery to set aside the Will of his brother Henry S Harrison, deceased, on the grounds of mental incapacity and undue influence He was the only heir of the decedent but was joined as a complainant in said suit with one Cleota O Quick Later the bill was amended by dismissing Cleota O Quick as a party complainant and the bill was later amended and supplemented The lower Court sustained a demurrer to the Appellants Bill as amended and Appellant elected to stand by his bill and prosecuted an appeal to this court from the decree dismissing his bill for want of equity The only question therefore before this Court is whether or not the Circuit Court erred in sustaining this demurrer

The bill was filed on the 9th day of September A D 1933 and alleges that the decedent Henry S Harrison executed a purported Last Will and Testament on the 13th day of May, A D 1932 and afterwards on the 10th day of January A D 1933 became deceased Among the bequests provided for in the Will was one to his brother, the Appellant in this suit, for the sum of $5000 00 On the 28th day of February A D 1933 the Appellant, by written instrument, transferred and assigned and set over to Cleota O Quick all of his right, title and interest of every nature and description which he took by virtue of said Will, which assignment was duly sworn to and acknowledged by Appellant On March 27th, 1934 the defendants filed an answer denying the allegations of the amended bill as to mental incompetency and undue influence and alleging that the Appellant, because of the transfer of his interest in the said estate by the said assignment, was estopped from claiming that the Last Will and Testament of his brother was invalid, and that because of said assignment the Appellant has recognized the

validity of said Will and was not permitted, under the law, to maintain a bill to contest said Will The Appellant filed a motion to strike out that part of the answer relating to said assignment made by him to Cleota O Quick, which motion was overruled by the Court Appellant then filed exceptions to that part of the answer and these were stricken from the files by order of the Court Appellant then took leave of Court to file an amendment and supplement to his amended bill which was accordingly done on the 30th day of April A D 1934 In this amendment and supplement on which Appellant relies it sets forth that on February 28th, 1933, the date of said assignment, no order of the County Court had been entered admitting the Will of Henry S Harrison to Probate but that a purported order was entered by such Court admitting said Will to Probate on March 2nd, 1933, that an appeal from said order was taken to the Circuit Court of Hancock County, Illinois and an order entered in that Court on the 8th day of June A D 1933 admitting the Will to Probate, that because of such facts no rights had passed in any manner to the Assignee by virtue of said assignment, that the same had never been delivered to Cleota O Quick and that she acquired no rights thereunder Furthermore, that Appellant had not been informed that by making said assignment he would lose any rights to contest the Will of the decedent, that as soon as he was informed that the Executor questioned his right to contest the Will on account of such assigment the Appellant and the Assignee took steps to withdraw the assignment from the files of the County Court and procured an order from that Court allowing the withdrawal and that at the time of the execution of the assignment Appellant was not informed of the facts which he has since discovered justifying the contest

The Appellees interposed a demurrer to this amended and supplemental bill which was sustained and the bill dismissed for want of equity

It is contended by the Appellant that because of the reasons set forth in his amended and supplemental bill he should not be barred from contesting said Will In our judgment the fact that the Will had not been admitted to Probate when the assignment was made is wholly immaterial The bill discloses that the Will had been filed in the County Clerk's office, that a petition for Probate had also been filed, and all the preliminary steps taken for the purpose of a hearing on the Probate of said Will The bill further shows that

Appellant was fully aware of all the proceedings that had been taken in the County Court, was fully advised as to all the provisions of the Will at the time he made his assignment The bill further discloses that the assignment was left on record in the County Clerk's office from the 28th day of February, A D 1933 until some time in March, A D 1934, at which time it was withdrawn from the County Clerk's office because the Appellees had interposed said written assignment as a defense Our Courts have held that contingent interests and expectancies, although not assignable in law, may be transferred so as to be binding in equity by a contract made in good faith and for a valuable consideration *James* v *Binkley*, 206 Ill 547 By the execution of the assignment it seems to us that the Appellant accepted the provisions of the Will and therefore could not maintain his bill to contest the Will because he was not a party interested and not a proper party complainant *Fishburn* v *Green*, 291 Ill 350 "The rule has long been established that in equity proceedings the Plaintiff must show an actual existing interest in the subject matter of the suit at the time suit is brought " *McGovern* v *McGovern*, 268 Ill 138

The fact that the Appellant was not at the time of making the assignment informed that by reason thereof that he would lose any rights to contest the Will of said deceased does not give him any grounds for maintaining his action in this case This was clearly a mistake as to the law and the legal effect of the instrument signed by him which is no grounds for relief "A general mistake of law pure and simple is not adequate ground for relief because of such mistake *** where the terms of a written instrument were used deliberately and knowingly by the parties, even though under a misapprehension of their legal effect." *Tilton* v *Fairmount Lodge*, 244 Ill 617

The allegation in the amended and supplemental bill that the said assignment to Cleota O Quick was never in fact delivered and for that reason never became operative is a pure conclusion of the pleader The facts as stated in the bill show that the instrument was under seal, sworn to by Appellant, that it was on file in the Clerk's office for more than one year and that both the Appellant and Mrs Quick joined in an application to the County Court to have the instrument withdrawn These and other facts appearing in the bill are inconsistent with the conclusion of the pleader, that the assignment was never, in fact, delivered

We think the last allegation of the amendment to the bill to the effect that the Appellant was not informed of the facts, which he afterwards discovered, in relation to the contest of the Will at the time the written assignment was made is without merit At the time he filed the bill he was, or should have been, fully informed as to all of his legal rights and no steps were taken at that time to cancel or set aside the assignment

We believe that none of the allegations in the amended and supplemental bill were sufficient to avoid or overcome the assignment so as to entitle the Appellant to file a bill to contest the Will in question In our judgment the Appellant could not show an actual existing interest in the subject matter of the suit at the time his bill was filed and that the attempted withdrawal of the assignment and its cancellation did not establish right or authority to bring suit

We, therefore, hold that the decree of the Circuit Court sustaining the demurrer to the amended and supplemental bill and dismissing the same for want of equity was correct and that the said decree should be affirmed

Affirmed.

(Five pages in original opinion)

(47818—4 35) 14

PUBLISHED IN ABSTRACT

Arch M Ryan, Appellee v The Baltimore and Ohio Railroad Company, a Corporation, Appellant.

Appeal from Circuit Court, Piatt County

JANUARY TERM, A D 1935 280 I.A. 632[3]

Gen. No 8883 **Agenda No. 10**

MR JUSTICE FULTON delivered the opinion of the Court

This suit was brought by Arch M Ryan the Appellee against the Baltimore and Ohio Railroad Company, a corporation, Appellant, for the value of a horse alleged to have been injured upon the tracks of Appellant

The suit was originally tried before a Justice of the Peace and later on appeal in the Circuit Court of Piatt County There was a trial by a jury in the Circuit Court and a verdict returned for Appellee in the sum of $125 00 upon which judgment was entered and this appeal seeks to reverse such judgment

The testimony shows that the Appellant's railroad passes through Piatt County from east to west and at a point several miles east of LaPlace in said County the railroad crosses a creek Over this creek there is a railroad trestle or bridge one hundred feet in length and fifteen to eighteen feet above the stream or the banks adjoining same On the morning of May 10th, 1933, a west bound freight train arrived at this trestle bridge at four thirty-five A M There was in the cab of the engine at the time, the engineer, who was riding on the right side of the engine, a brakeman and the fireman It was just at the break of dawn and the condition of darkness and light was such that neither night or day signals were easily discernible At a point about four hundred feet east of the trestle the engineer and brakeman from the north side of the engine observed a couple of moving objects ahead upon the track It was soon apparent that the objects were horses and the engineer applied the emergency brakes The view of the horses was immediately lost by the engineer but when he last saw them one horse was out ahead of the other about ten feet The brakeman crossed the engine cab to the south side of the engine, leaned his body out of the opening between the engine and tender and looked ahead At the east end of the bridge he

saw the engine strike one of the horses on the track, he saw the other horse run out ahead on the trestle to about its center and jump off to the ground on the left The fireman testified to practically the same facts as he observed it from the left side of the engine They both testified that the horse which ran ahead on the trestle was twenty-five feet in advance of the one struck by the engine They both further testified that the engine did not come in contact with or strike the horse for which suit is brought The rear horse which was struck by the engine at the east end of the bridge was pushed by it to about the center of the bridge where the engine came to a stop The engine was then backed off the bridge thirty to forty feet and after the train had thus backed off the bridge there was blood and hair at the east end of the bridge

It is stipulated that full settlement has been made for the horse killed by the engine For a few days prior to the morning in question employees for the railroad had been doing some work on the bridge and there was testimony that the fence along the right-of-way adjoining the railroad was out of repair and that the wires fencing the right-of-way were down at the time of the accident and that Appellee's pasture in which these two horses were kept at night was not properly fenced One of the sons of the Appellee testified that the hairs found on the track east of the trestle was from the light brown horse which was the horse in question in this suit Another son testified that he could not identify the color of the hair on the track The horse for which suit was brought after leaving the trestle struck on the ground at or near the east bank of the creek leaving its imprint on the ground at a point where the trestle was about fifteen to eighteen feet high This horse was found by a son of the owner and seen by other witnesses about one hundred feet south of the trestle It was in bad condition, bleeding at the nose, very muddy on the right side and with a laceration on the right leg about fourteen inches from the ground

The proof was ample that the horse was worth One Hundred Fifty Dollars before the accident and about Twenty-five Dollars after the injury

It is contended by the Appellant that the verdict is contrary to the law and the evidence and should be set aside It urges primarily that under the facts proved in this record and the law applicable thereto the Appellant is not liable

There is a duty under the Statute of the State of

Illinois for railroads to fence their right-of-way and keep said fences in good repair Smith-Hurd R S Chap 114 Par 53 A part of that section reads "And when such fences or cattleguards are not made as aforesaid, or when such fences or cattleguards are not kept in good repair, such railroad corporations shall be liable for all damages which may be done by the agents, engines or cars of such corporations, to such cattle, horses, sheep, hogs or other stock thereon" The Appellant insists that where there is no collision or actual contact between the train and the animal, the railroad is not liable under this section The authorities seem to bear out this contention In the case of *C N W R R Co* v *Taylor* 8 App 108 the Court in construing this Statute said "The Statute in our opinion imports that the injury must be done directly by the agents, engines or cars In this case neither engine or cars did the injury, the injury was occasioned by the horse falling through the bridge and that was caused by the fright that he took by the engine and cars while in motion The Statute does not provide that the corporation shall be liable for injuries received by stock getting into culverts and on bridges in case the road is not fenced and kept in repair as required by statute, it only provides for the injuries done by the engines, cars or agents in connection therewith The Statute does not provide for injuries done by the agents, engines or cars indirectly It seems to us that a fair interpretation of the Statute requires us to hold that the injury must be done by direct contact by the agents, engines or cars before a recovery can be had under the Statute" The same principle of law is held in *Schertz* v *I B & W Ry Co*, 107 Ill 577 The Supreme Courts of the States of Missouri and Indiana have given similar Statutes the same construction *Lefferty* v *H & St J R R Co*, 44 Mo 291, *Ohio & Miss R R Co*, v *Cole* 41 Ind 331

The Appellee argues because the horse was injured, had a laceration on its leg, and because there was blood and hair on the track at the east end of the trestle that such proof tended to show that the horse was actually struck by the train, but such testimony opposed to by the positive evidence of the brakeman and fireman, both eye witnesses, that the horse in question ran out on the trestle, jumped off left side of the track, landed on the ground about the center of said trestle and that the engine did not come in contact with or strike the animal, was not sufficient in itself to support a verdict

The Appellee further insists that the Appellant railroad was liable because of its negligence in not using ordinary care for the prevention of the accident after the discovery of the horse on the track We think there was not sufficient evidence to show common law liability or the want of ordinary care and prudence on the part of Appellants agents The failure to blow a whistle or ring a bell at a point where there was no highway crossing was not a violation of any statutory duty The engineer was only required to act as a reasonably prudent man under the circumstances He applied the emergency brakes as soon as he saw the horses upon the track and did all in his power to stop and avoid injury to the horse in question It seems to us that he exercised all the care and caution that could reasonably be expected of any engineer similarly situated The actions of an engineer under like circumstances has been held not to be negligence in *P D & E Ry Co*, v *Reed*, 17 App 413, and *Peoria etc R R Co*, *v Champ* 75 Ill 577

Believing the verdict to be contrary to the law and the evidence and viewing the case as we do, the judgment of the Circuit Court will be reversed and the cause remanded

Reversed and Remanded.

(Five pages in original opinion)

(47818—4 35) 14

PUBLISHED IN ABSTRACT

Mary Ann Adams, Appellant, v William L Patton, Appellee.

Appeal from Circuit Court of Sangamon County

JANUARY TERM, A D 1935 280 I.A. 632[4]

Gen No 8888 Agenda No 13

MR JUSTICE FULTON delivered the opinion of the Court

This appeal is brought to reverse a judgment of the Circuit Court of Sangamon County dismissing the complaint of appellant on the motion of the Appellee with a nil capiat and judgment for Appellee for costs of suit

The complaint was filed on August 21st, 1934 charging that the Appellee had therefore received, without right, $2000 00 belonging to Appellant and still retained the same and also demanding judgment for $2000 00 and interest from May 7th, 1932, on which date it was alleged the Appellee had received said sum of money Appellee answered the complaint with a general denial and also a special affirmative defense, setting up the circumstances under which he received the money and relying on an order of the Probate Court of Sangamon County entered December 5th, 1932, which first authorized the Appellee to pay the money into Court and upon such payment directed Appellee "be released and discharged and fully acquitted of all further responsibility and liability" with reference thereto Secondly, it directed the Clerk to hold the money subject to the further order of the Court, and thirdly set for hearing on February 1st, 1933 separate petition for the allowance out of the fund of Attorneys fees to Appellee

The answer further alleged that Appellee in pursuance of said order did deposit the money with the Clerk on December 6th, 1932 where the same remained continuously on deposit up and during all of August 21st, 1934, the date on which this suit was brought, the answer further alleges that said order of the Probate Court had never been set aside, changed, modified or appealed from and that all the acts and doings of the Appellee had been in compliance with and in accord with said order The answer concluded with the aver-

ment that Appellee at the time of bringing the suit had no monies belonging to the Appellant and owed APPELLANT NO MONIES

Appellant moved to strike the affirmative defense insisting that the order of the Probate Court was ob tained ex parte and without the jurisdiction of the person of Appellant, and that such order had been reversed by the opinion of this Court in *Patton* v *Adams* filed April 11th, 1934

The Court denied the motion to strike and the Appellant then replied to the affirmative defense denying that the order of the Probate Court under date of December 5th, 1932, was made with jurisdiction of the person of Appellant, the answer further denied that the Probate Court had jurisdiction of the subject matter of that order and that the order of December 5th, 1932 was never appealed from and also denied that such order was valid and binding Appellant then sets up in justification of the foregoing conclusions the facts of the appearance of the Appellant in the Probate Court on February 14th, 1933 and all subsequent proceedings in said Court and that there was an appeal from the order of February 15th, 1933

The Appellant further sets up in her reply the proceedings on appeal in the Circuit Court and then sets forth the appeal from a judgment of the Circuit Court to the Appellate Court, also the assignment of errors and the formal judgment of the Appellate Court She further sets up in her reply that on August 22nd, 1934 the day after complaint was filed in this cause the Appellee procured an order directing the Clerk of the Probate Court to turn over to Appellee the deposit and that on August 23rd, 1934 the fund was actually turned over to Appellee

Appellant later amended her reply by setting up certain allegations of the original petition filed by Appellee upon which petition the Probate Court entered the order for deposit on December 5th, 1932

Appellee then moved the Court to dismiss the complaint and for judgment on the grounds that the matters in the reply and amended reply had already been passed upon adversely to Appellant upon her motion to strike the affirmative defense and because the facts set forth in the reply and the amendment did not set up any facts which met the affirmative defense as set up in Appellee's answer The Court sustained a motion to dismiss and for judgment, the Appellant elected to stand by the replication as amended, and the Court entered judgment of nil capiat and for costs,

from which judgment this appeal is prosecuted

The Appellant assigns various errors but the controlling question is whether or not the affirmative defense set up by Appellee in his answer was a bar to the action The facts disclosed by the pleadings show that on March 22nd, 1932 Appellee received a letter from the law firm of Follansbee, Shorey and Schupp of Chicago, Illinois enclosing correspondence from Thomas Elliott a solicitor of Newry, Ireland in which Mr Elliott claimed to be acting for Mary Ann Adams, Appellant, a resident of Ireland and asking to have full particulars concerning the Estate of Harriet Kerneghan, deceased, whose estate was being administered in the Probate Court of Sangamon County Appellee entered his appearance in the said Estate and performed valuable service in behalf of Appellant On May 7th, 1932 the Executor of the said Estate paid to Appellee the sum of $2000 00 which he remitted to the Chicago firm and they on May 9th, 1932 wrote the said Elliott advising him of the collection and sending receipts for Appellant to sign with the advice that upon the return of the receipts remittance would be made, less attorneys fees Appellant declined to sign the receipts and denied that she had retained Elliott as her solicitor and claimed that Appellee had no authority to represent her or to make the collection Appellee then filed his petition in the Probate Court of Sangamon County praying to be authorized to deposit the $2000 00 with the Clerk of said Court and asking to be paid $300 00 as attorneys fees On December 5th, 1932 said Court ordered the deposit to be made subject to the further order of that Court, and further set down the separate prayer of Appellee for an allowance of an attorney fee for February 1st, 1933 and directing that notice be sent by the Clerk to Appellant by registered mail of the hearing

Thereafter motion was made in such proceeding to strike the petition for lack of jurisdiction of the subject matter by the Probate Court Such motion was overruled by the Probate Court and order made for the payment of $300 00 for attorneys fees to Appellee On Appeal from that order to the Circuit Court of Sangamon County a hearing was had upon the said petition and an answer filed by the Appellant and an order entered by that Court allowing payment to the Appellee of $300 00 attorneys fees and leaving the balance of the funds in the hands of the Probate Clerk

Thereupon Appellant prosecuted an appeal to this Court and on April 11th, 1934 this Court held that the lower Court had no jurisdiction of said petition or the subject matter thereof and reversed the final order of the Circuit Court and remanded the cause to the Circuit Court with directions to dismiss the petition for want of jurisdiction Upon mandate being filed in the Circuit Court the petition was dismissed on August 21st, 1934

In the opinion of this Court on the prior hearing we held that the Probate Court was in no way concerned with the dispute that had arisen between the Appellant and the Appellee either as to whether he was employed or as to what his reasonable compensation for services should be Therefore, upon the dismissal of the petition in Probate Court the matter was left in exactly the same position it had been prior to the filing of such petition and the fund of $2000 00 was discharged from the claim of Appellee for the $300 00 but leaving the question of Appellees employment and the amount of his compensation still undisposed of Upon the filing of the mandate from this Court the Appellant had an immediate remedy by going into the Probate Court with a petition claiming that the fund should be paid over to her Since the Probate Court had in its exclusive charge the administration of the Estate and all of the assets thereof it was improper for the Appellant to bring a suit in the Circuit Court of Sangamon County until the orders of the Probate Court with reference to this fund had been completely disposed of

The replication of the Appellant therefore to the affirmative defense filed by Appellee did not set up facts which adequately met the affirmative defense, or which justified the conclusions set forth in the reply One good plea in bar to the entire action, confessed to be true, terminates the suit and defendant is entitled to judgment *Johnson* v *Wright*, **221 App 6**

We do not feel that any orders entered by the Pro bate Court of Sangamon County after the beginning of this suit are subject to review on this record

The action of the Circuit Court in sustaining the motion to dismiss the complaint and for judgment was proper and the judgment of nil capiat and for costs entered by the lower court should be affirmed

Affirmed

(Six pages in original opinion)

(47818—4 35) 14

PUBLISHED IN ABSTRACT

Lawrence Coon, Appellee v T W Doss, Appellant

Appeal from County Court of Macon County

JANUARY TERM, A D 1935 280 I.A. 633

Gen. No 8892 **Agenda No 16**

MR JUSTICE FULTON delivered the opinion of the Court.

This was a case involving the trial of the right of property in the County Court of Macon County, between the Appellee Lawrence Coon and the Appellant T W Doss At the conclusion of all the evidence the Court instructed the jury to find the issues for the Appellee and a judgment was rendered upon such verdict This appeal is prosecuted to reverse such judgment

The facts show that on August 9th, 1927, one Taylor Coon, the father of the Appellee, was indebted to the Croninger State Bank for the sum of $2000 00 and on the same date executed and delivered to said bank his note for that amount and thereafter made certain payments thereon On March 3rd, 1934 the bank sold and assigned the said note to the Appellant T W Doss On April 5th, 1934, Appellant caused a judgment to be entered by confession on said note in the Circuit Court of Piatt County for the sum of $904 45 being the balance then remaining due on said note and an execution was duly issued on said judgment

On June 30th 1934 the Sheriff of Macon County levied upon certain personal property which is involved in this suit as the property of said Taylor Coon, the maker of said note On July 11th, 1934 statutory notice was served by the Appellee upon the Sheriff for the trial of the right of property

On November 13th, 1930 Taylor Coon sold certain farm implements and chattels to his landlord William L Alexander Afterward on the same day and date, Alexander leased his farm to the Appellee and sold him the same chattels now in question All of said chattels have been in possession and control of the Appellee Lawrence Coon since November 13th, 1930

There is little dispute as to the facts in the case but Appellant contends that the transfer of the goods and chattels by Taylor Coon to William L Alexander on November 13th, 1930 was in violation of the provisions

of the Bulk Sales Act, that the provisions of that Act requiring notice to creditors was not complied with and therefore was void against creditors of Taylor Coon The question arises as to whether or not T W Doss, the Appellant, as the assignee of the Croninger State Bank could assert the same rights as the original creditors relative to the sale of the chattel property involved in this suit It is admitted that the Appellant was not a creditor on the date of the transfer "The Bulk Sales Act" is entirely statutory, is in derogation of common law, highly penal in its nature and therefore must be strictly construed The language of the act is, "That the sale *** shall be fraudulent and void as against the creditors of the said vendor ***" We believe this Statute is directed to the existing creditors at the time of the transfer and that it is not permissible to enlarge or expand the language of the Statute to mean subsequent creditors It has been held by our Courts that a Common Law assignment to a Trustee for the benefit of Creditors is not included within the scope of this Act, *Tibbets-Hewitt Grocery Co* v *Cohen*, 260 Ill App 276, nor are those holding unliquidated claims or tort actions or uncertain or contingent claims held to be creditors within the meaning of the Act *Harry B Smead Co* v *J Oliver Johnson*, 262 Ill App 385 In *Talty* v *Schoenholz*, 323 Ill 232 it was held that a chattel mortgage does not come within the Act

It is our opinion that the Act was passed for the benefit of and to protect existing creditors at the time of the transfer so that they could assert their rights in the property promptly as against fraudulent transfers There is nothing in this record which indicates that the transfers from Taylor Coon to William L Alexander and by him to Lawrence Coon were not bona fide The Appellant in this case purchased the note upon which the judgment is based along with a number of other notes from the Croninger State Bank nearly three and one half years after the transfer to Appellee We cannot believe that the Bulk Sales Act was intended to or does protect stale claims of this character in the hands of Assignees and that therefore the action of the County Court of Macon County in directing a verdict in favor of the Appellee was correct and in conformity with the law and the facts

Judgment of the lower Court is therefore affirmed

Judgment affirmed

(Three pages in original opinion)

(47313—4 35) 14

PUBLISHED IN ABSTRACT

Ray Morgan and Blanche Morgan, Appellees, v Louis F Brumer, Appellant

Appeal from Circuit Court of Tazewell County

OCTOBER TERM, A D 1934 280 I.A. 633[2]

Gen No 8854 **Agenda No 18**

MR JUSTICE ALLABEN delivered the opinion of the Court

Ray and Blanche Morgan commenced a replevin suit before W H Williams, a justice of the peace, on March 9, 1933, against Louis F Brumer, to recover possession of a radio to which they claimed ownership, and which they claimed was wrongfully detained by Brumer When the writ was served on him he gave a forthcoming bond and retained possession of the property The cause was originally set before the justice of the peace on March 14, 1933, and was continued first to March 18th and later to March 22, 1933, at which time the defendant made a "special and limited appearance for questioning jurisdiction of the court Motion denied" Witnesses were sworn and testimony heard, and the matter taken under advisement until March 24, 1933, at which time the justice entered judgment for return of the radio in question, and $15 attorney's fees From this judgment the defendant-appellant appealed to the Circuit Court of Tazewell County, and filed his bond in apt time A transcript was filed on April 10, 1933, as follows

"State of Illinois, }
County of Tazewell } ss

"In Justice's Court, Before W H Williams, Justice of the Peace Ray Morgan and Blanche Morgan v Louis F Brumer, Action, Replevin, Demand, $150 00

"Writ issued March 9, 1933, returnable March 14, 1933, 9 a m, and delivered to A J Gschwend to serve, March 9, 1933, returned by Constable A J Gschwend"

Then follows recitals as to the giving of the forthcoming bond by the defendant, the special and limited appearance of the defendant, the entering of judgment, the fixing of the appeal bond and approval of same,

and assessing the costs, concluding with the certificate of the justice of the peace which is as follows.

"State of Illinois, }
Tazewell County } ss

"I, W H Williams, a Justice of the Peace in and said county, do hereby certify, that the foregoing is a true and correct transcript of the judgment given by me in the above-entitled suit, and that said transcript, and the papers herewith accompanying, being six in number, and numbered one to six, inclusive, contain a full and perfect statement of all the proceedings before me, in the above-entitled cause

"In witness whereof, I have hereunto set my hand and seal, this 7th day of April, A D 1933
W H Williams (Seal), Justice of the Peace"

The exact wording of the transcript is not set out out as there is no controversy except as to whether or not an affidavit for replevin was filed before the writ was issued

On May 10, 1934, the defendant- appellant entered his limited and special appearance in writing in the Circuit Court, together with a motion to quash the writ of replevin and to dismiss the suit for the reasons (1) That the transcript did not show affirmatively that the justice of the peace had jurisdiction of said cause, (2) That the judgment of the justice of the peace was not a judgment and was illegal, ambiguous, uncertain, and entirely void, (3) That the certificate attached to the transcript recited that the transcript was a full and perfect statement of all the proceedings had before the justice of the peace, (4) That the justice of the peace who entered the purported judgment had no jurisdiction of either the subject matter or the persons

On May 10, 1934, the Circuit Court of Tazewell County denied the motion to quash the writ and dismiss the cause, to which the defendant-appellant excepted By leave of court plaintiffs, on May 10, 1934, filed an amended transcript on appeal, in substance as follows

"AMENDED TRANSCRIPT WRIT OF REPLEVIN

"May 10, 1934 Docket amended to speak the truth as follows March 9, 1933, affidavit for replevin filed as required by law Writ issued March 9, 1933, ordered and issued returnable March 14, 1933, at 9 o'clock a m and delivered to A J Gschwend, constable, to serve March 9, 1933"

Then follow recitals as to the giving of the forthcoming bond, and so forth, substantially in the same words as in the original transcript, concluding with the certificate of the justice of the peace which is as follows

"State of Illinois, }
} ss.
Tazewell County }

"I, W H Williams, a Justice of the Peace in and for said county, do hereby certify that the foregoing is a true and correct transcript of the judgment given by me in the above-entitled suit, and that said transcript and the papers herewith accompanying, being in number, and numbered from one to , inclusive, contain a full and perfect statement of all the proceedings before me in the above-entitled cause

"In Witness Whereof, I have hereunto set my hand and seal this 10th day of May, A D 1934

W H Williams,
Justice of the Peace

(Seal)"

On May 15, 1934, defendant-appellant entered a special and limited appearance and motion to quash service of the writ and to quash the amended transcript, dismiss said cause, and tax costs against the plaintiffs, for the following reasons (1) That the amended transcript, filed May 10, 1934, is not a correct transcript, (2) That the amended transcript shows that the original docket entries had been altered and changed on May 10, 1934, (3) That the entries made in the docket of the justice on May 10, 1934, were made without notice, knowledge, or consent of the defendant-appellant, (4) That the justice had no authority to alter, change or amend his docket entries, (5) That the original transcript contained a correct record of the entries on the docket of the justice at the time it was certified by the justice, (6) That neither the original nor the amended transcript show that a proper affidavit for replevin was ever filed with the justice

The Circuit court denied the above motion, to which order defendant-appellant excepted and elected to stand, and not to plead over On May 16, 1934, on hearing by the court, the defendant appellant being in default for want of a plea, evidence was heard, and the court found the issues for the plaintiffs, assessed the plaintiffs' damages at the sum of $45, and that the plaintiffs have return of the property replevied, and entered judgment as follows "Therefore it is considered by the Court that the property replevined

herein by virtue of the writ of replevin issued in said cause be returned to the said plaintiffs and that a writ of retorno habendo do issue herein for the return of said property and that the plaintiffs do have and recover of and from the defendant Louis F Brumer their said damages of $45 00 in form as aforesaid by the Court assessed, together with their costs and charges, in this behalf expended, and have execution therefor "

Defendant appellant excepted to the entering of the above order and judgment, and from said order and judgment has prosecuted his appeal to this Court He contends that the trial court erred, first, in overruling defendant-appellant's motion to quash the writ of replevin and dismiss the case, second, in overruling defendant-appellant's motion made after the filing of the purported amended transcript to quash the writ of replevin and dismiss the case, third, in refusing to quash the writ and dismiss the case, and in entering judgment against defendant-appellant for the return of the property replevied, and for damages and costs

Any person bringing an action in replevin shall before the writ issues file with the justice of the peace before whom the suit is commenced an affidavit showing that the plaintiff in such action is the owner of the property described in the writ and about to be replevied or that he is then lawfully entitled to possession thereof, and that the property is wrongfully detained by the defendant (Smith-Hurd Illinois Revised Statutes 1933 Chap 119, Section 4) Thus, the filing of the requisite affidavit prior to the issuance of the writ is jurisdictional, and if this were not done the justice of the peace never had jurisdiction of the subject matter of this suit in replevin If the justice of the peace had no jurisdiction of this replevin suit the Circuit Court on appeal had none (*Evans* v *Bouton* 85 Ill 579, *Abbott* v *Kruse* 37 Ill App 549) However, on appeal in the Circuit court, "it is the duty of the court to hear the evidence, without reference to the justice's docket, and to render judgment in the case, unless from the evidence it appears the justice had no jurisdiction of the subject matter " *Swingley* v *Haynes*, 22 Ill 214 *Rogers* v *Blanchard*, 2 Gilm R 335, *Ballard* v *Mc Carty*, 11 Ill R 501, *Vaughan* v *Thompson*, 15 Ill R 39 In determining whether or not the justice of the peace had jurisdiction the trial court need not look to the justice's transcript alone but may and should consider the proceedings before the justice and all the

papers certified by him accompanying the transcript (*Evans* v *Bouton, supra*) We direct attention to the fact that in the certificates of the justice to the original transcript he certifies that accompanying the transcript are six papers numbered 1 to 6, inclusive Nowhere in the abstract, nor in the original record is any mention made of these six papers These papers were certified by the justice of the peace no doubt in accordance with the provisions of the statute regarding appeals from justices of the peace and police magistrates to the circuit or county courts (Smith-Hurd Illinois Revised Statutes 1933 Chap 79, Section 116) In the absence of proof to the contrary we assume that these papers were filed with the clerk of the Circuit Court, and that among them was the affidavit upon which the replevin writ was issued This is borne out by the statement of counsel for defendant-appellant, on page 3, of his brief, in his comment on the amended transcript, wherein he says "Said amended transcript is not accompanied by any documents or other papers filed before said Justice of the Peace" An inspection of the certificate of the justice of the peace to the amended transcript shows that the justice of the peace did not fill in the blanks setting out any papers accompanying the amended transcript This was no doubt true because all the documents, being numbered from one to six, inclusive, as set forth in the certificate to the original transcript had been previously filed with the clerk

Every presumption favors the correctness of the decision of the trial court, and we will presume, in the absence of any showing to the contrary, that among the papers certified to the Circuit court by the justice of the peace, together with his original transcript was the affidavit in question, showing that the same was filed prior to the issuance of the writ of replevin The court had the right to consider the affidavit together with the transcript, and therefrom determine whether or not the justice of the peace had jurisdiction of this suit, and having so determined that he had, the trial court correctly overruled the defendant-appellant's motion to dismiss the suit This presumption is further borne out by the fact that the certificate made by the clerk to the record does not certify that the same is a complete transcript of the record in the office of the clerk of the Circuit Court of Tazewell county As a matter of fact the word "exhibits" is stricken out of the certificate and none of the evidence is included,

although the record affirmatively shows that evidence was heard, and that the court based his judgment on such evidence

After defendant-appellant's motion to quash the writ and dismiss the cause on account of an alleged defect in the original transcript was denied, plaintiffs, by leave of court, filed an amended transcript This amended transcript shows "May 10, 1934 Docket amended to speak the truth as follows March 9, 1933, affidavit for replevin filed as required by law " The transcript then proceeds with recitals substantially the same as contained in the original transcript

Defendant-appellant insists that the justice of the peace had no right or authority to amend his docket after he entered judgment, and that the trial court committed error in permitting this to be done Counsel cites in support thereof the cases of *St L B & S Ry Co* v *Gundlach*, 69 Ill App 192, *Merritt* v *Yates*, 71 Ill 636, wherein it is held that "To allow a justice to make alterations and changes in his record, at will, and according to his whim, would be fraught with evil and wrong and thus would be oppressive " With such a holding we are in hearty accord, but we believe it is permissible for the justice of the peace, like a court of record, to correct his records at any time where there is sufficient memoranda to clearly indicate that the justice's record was in error or incomplete This change was no doubt made upon an inspection of the affidavit itself, and it was proper for the trial court with knowledge of these facts to permit the amended transcript to be filed We further believe, inasmuch as we have previously held that the trial court had sufficient evidence before it to determine that the justice of the peace had jurisdiction of this case before the amended transcript was filed, that the filing of the amended transcript in no event would constitute reversible error

This disposes of all of the contentions raised by counsel for the defendant-appellant, except as to the judgment entered by the trial court We have decided that the trial court had jurisdiction of the parties and of the subject matter Defendant appellant elected to stand by his motion to quash the writ and dismiss the case, which had been properly overruled Evidence was then heard by the court, no part of which is before this Court The court found the issues for the plaintiffs, and assessed plaintiffs' damages at $45, ordered that plaintiffs have return of the property re

plevied and that a writ of retorno habendo issue, that costs be taxed against defendant-appellant, and that plaintiffs have execution therefor In the absence of a transcript of evidence which the trial court heard it will be presumed by this Court that the evidence was sufficient to justify the finding of the court, and the judgment thereon For the reasons heretofore set forth the judgment of the trial court is affirmed

Judgment Affirmed

(Eleven pages in original opinion)

(47812—4 35) 14

PUBLISHED IN ABSTRACT

Herbert Pleines, Appellee, v Carl J Loeseke, Executor of the Last Will and Testament of Henry Pleines, Deceased, Appellant

Appeal from Circuit Court of Tazewell County.

JANUARY TERM, A D 1935 280 I.A. 633[3]

Gen No 8858 **Agenda No 3**

MR JUSTICE ALLABEN delivered the opinion of the Court

This cause arose out of five sets of claims filed by Herbert Pleines against the estate of his father, Henry Pleines, Sr, deceased, amounting to $6,274 11 in the County Court of Tazewell County, in Probate Henry Pleines, Sr, died testate December 1, 1930, at the age of 74 He was survived by his three sons, Hugo Herbert and Henry, Jr At the time of his decease he was seized of 360 acres of land, which at the time of his demise was being operated by his two oldest sons, Hugo farming 160 acres and Herbert farming the home place consisting of 200 acres Henry Pleines, Sr, had lost his wife several years before his decease, and was living with his youngest son, Henry, Jr, on the home place His sister-in-law, a Mrs Zimmerman, kept house for them in the homestead Herbert lived in a bungalow on the 200 acres south of the homestead, and Hugo on the 160 acre farm which he operated not far from the home place At the date of Henry Pleines, Sr 's death a 120 acre tract of the home place was unencumbered, 80 acres of the home place was encumbered with a $3,500 mortgage, and the 160 acre tract occupied by Hugo was encumbered with an $8,500 mortgage By his will Henry Pleines, Sr, deceased, gave his oldest son, Hugo, the north 80 acres of the place which he then occupied, and to Herbert, the next oldest son, the south 80 acres of the farm occupied by Hugo, and 80 acres of the home place with the right given to Herbert to remove his dwelling and buildings across the road to the land devised to him These devises were to be subject to the existing mortgages The youngest son, Henry, Jr, was given the remaining 120 acre tract of the home place, which was unencumbered, together with certain personal property, but the devise to him was charged with the obligation of

paying the indebtedness of the estate and the costs of administration which, according to stipulation, consisted of claims filed in the amount of $8,026 49, exclusive of the costs of administration and exclusive of the claims of Herbert Pleines in the amount hereinabove set forth

The defendant-appellant, Carl Loeseke, a brother-in law of Henry Pleines, Sr , deceased, was appointed executor under the will of the deceased, and qualified Several weeks after the demise of Henry Pleines, Sr , an apparent disagreement developed between his sons Hugo was indebted to his father for about $4,500, for help given in paying certain debts, and for setting him up in the farming business Herbert who for some time had operated the home place claimed that he was to farm the land and his father was to pay for the seed, legumes, purchase a tractor, pay for an extra man, provide machinery for Herbert to work with, together with gas and horses, for which Herbert was to receive one-third of the increase and crop, and his father two-thirds After the appointment of the executor Herbert refused to give him a partnership accounting, or to make a settlement with him, or to give up the horses, cattle and machinery which he had, and further refused to turn over certain of his father's papers Subsequently Hugo joined Herbert in filing a bill in the Circuit Court of Tazewell County to contest their father's will, which bill was later dismissed, which suit further evidenced their dissatisfaction as to the property which they had received The horses in question, claimed by Herbert to be nine in number, were inventoried by the executor Later Herbert claimed the horses as his own, though he had listed them with the tax assessor for two previous years as his father's property Just before the expiration of the year for filing claims Herbert filed his claim against his father's estate for the amount of $6,274 11, claiming advancements made by him on behalf of his father for lumber and glass, tractor and machine repairs, hospital bills, telephone, seed, newspaper, provisions, seed corn testing, corn shelling, veterinary bills, repairs to implements, for money loaned in the amount of $1,450, pasture, cattle, shipping expense of cream, hay and straw, feed for his father's horses for the years 1924 to 1930, with interest on the latter item, totalling $3,779 44 The $1,450 item he claimed to be for money loaned for the purchase of tractor, and plow for the sum of $550, and to pay part of the cost of building his house, in the amount of $900 Some

of these items were abandoned upon hearing because of failure of proof The executor filed a petition for a citation against Herbert Pleines in the County Court for the claimant herein to account for property of the estate which it was alleged he had converted and refused to deliver to the executor, and for an accounting for cream checks, proceeds from sale of cattle, horses, crops, and other items belonging to the estate The County Court heard the five claims, and allowed the sum of $257 69 to the claimant, and awarded to the executor the horses and other chattels mentioned in the citation The claimant, Herbert Pleines, appealed to the Circuit Court, in two separate appeals, one on the claims, and the other relative to the citation On this appeal the executor asked to consolidate the causes, which motion the court denied A motion was then filed asking leave of setoff instanter, and this was allowed to the executor Whereupon all phases of the claim and all questions concerning the property of the estate claimed to have been converted by Herbert were heard before a jury who returned a verdict in the amount of $2,682 22 The claimant, Herbert Pleines, failed to have his claims offered in evidence on an appeal to the Circuit Court, and failed to have them set forth in the transcript of the proceedings on the appeal from the County Court An objection, and motion in arrest of judgment, were filed by the executor after the verdict, alleging that the claims filed in the County Court constituted the basis of liability of the estate and that as there was no legal basis for the verdict because the claims were not before either the court or the jury This motion was denied The court then allowed a motion of the claimant granting leave to the County Clerk to file an additional transcript instanter, to supply the record with the claims in question, to which motion the defendant excepted A motion was then made for a new trial by the defendant appellant, and the court suggested that the plaintiff-appellee remit $675 58 from the verdict, which plaintiff accepted The motion for new trial was overruled, and judgment entered by the trial court in the amount of $2,006 64, and costs, to be paid in due course of administration of the estate It is from this judgment that this appeal is taken by the executor

The credit for cattle admittedly sold by Herbert, together with milk, soy beans, and machinery converted by him amounts to $1,372 68 This amount is apparently undisputed, and is admittedly the estate's prop

erty The court took the position that regarding the evidence most favorably for the claimant he would be entitled to a total sum of $3,015 82, that the defendant-appellee was entitled to a credit of $1,008 18, and therefore, fixed the remittitur in the amount of $675 58, by deducting what the court believed due the claimant from the verdict returned by the jury

In an action such as the one at bar the burden is upon the claimant to show the nature and amount of his claim, by a preponderance of the evidence *Edwards* v *Harness* 87 Ill App 471 The claimant herein, Herbert Pleines, in order to establish his alleged claim caused to be introduced in evidence a series of checks showing payment for various items which constitute a part of his claim The record shows that witnesses testified that these items were paid them by the claimant and by the checks introduced in evidence, these items being variously for repairs to machinery, gas and oil, grinding feed, cemetery dues, newspaper, telephone, hauling soy beans, and the like They were Herbert Pleines' checks, signed by him and delivered by him for items which he had ordered, or services which were rendered to him There is nothing in the evidence, however, so far as this court can determine from the record that tends to show how Henry Pleines, deceased, was connected with these transactions We do not see how the checks introduced, or the testimony concerning them can be construed to evidence a debt of Henry Pleines, deceased, to his son, Herbert, without some further evidence to support the contention showing a definite connection between these expenditures, and the alleged agreement between Herbert Pleines, and his father The claims based on these checks were allegedly for items that Herbert's father had agreed to assume in their partnership arrangement, but there is nothing directly to show that this is true In the case of *MacKenzie* v *Barrett,* 148 Ill App 414, a claimant against an estate attempted to show an obligation of a deceased to him for money loaned by reason of checks made payable to the deceased The court in that case held that "A check on a bank is not evidence of the indebtedness of the payee to the drawer of the check On the contrary, it is evidence of the indebtedness of the drawer to the payee " Thus, in the instant case the effect of the checks of themselves, can only be to show an indebtedness owing by Herbert Plaines to the persons to whom the checks were made payable If there had been a book of account which the testimony of Mrs Zimmer-

man indicates was in existence at the time settlements were made between Herbert and his father, to support the claims made by him in connection with the payment by check it might be said that it would constitute the connecting link between the indebtedness of Herbert's father to him and the payments made by Herbert, and further, except in cases of money loaned, this book of account would have been admissible to show the items expended by Herbert for these various items allegedly in connection with the partnership agreement between himself and his father *Estate of Martine,* 233 Ill App 94 The book of account referred to was not introduced in evidence, and no other written memoranda of any kind was produced to support the claims made concerning the checks Two of the items for which claim is made were $900 used in building the house for Herbert Pleines and $550 used in the purchase of the tractor and plow, both of which items Herbert Pleines claimed he loaned to his father for the above purposes The witness Hugo Pleines admitted that his father borrowed and paid back these items by a banking transaction This testimony is corroborated by the cancelled notes marked paid at the bank

In this case there is also testimony to show that Herbert Pleines and his father made annual settlements This is furnished by Mrs Zimmerman, the housekeeper for Henry Pleines, Sr, deceased, who testified that Herbert came to the house with his book of account which he and his father went over It is also shown by the testimony of the operators of grain elevators who testified to settlements of grain accounts when crops were sold and that they were divided two-thirds to the father and one-third to the son This is also corroborated by Herbert Pleines himself who testified that he had heard the testimony of his brother and Mrs Zimmerman, with reference to his coming to his father's house to have settlements, and that he had various settlements with him Certainly this testimony must have some significance, and we are led to inquire why many of the items for which Herbert Pleines has filed his claim were not included in these settlements

It has been held that an adjustment and settlement of accounts between parties affords evidence that all items properly chargeable at the time have been included While it is true that it is not conclusive, still it requires clear and convincing proof that items properly chargeable have been unintentionally omitted by

the person who is seeking to recover *Bull* v *Harris,* 31 Ill 487, *Straubher* v *Mohler,* 80 Ill 21, *Hodge* v *Boynton,* 16 Ill App 525 So, in the instant case, while it may be said that the exact settlements which were made from time to time are not clearly set out, yet there is evidence of settlements, and the items or part of them for which the claimant seeks to recover were such as should have properly been settled at those times, and it is not shown, in our opinion, by any clear and convincing proof that those items in this case were unintentionally omitted

The attempt of the claimant here to establish his claims except as to the items for which checks are shown rests entirely upon the testimony of his brother Hugo An examination of this testimony reveals many contradictions, and a great deal of indefiniteness upon the part of the witness It is likewise clear that Hugo had a definite interest in seeing that his brother Herbert was successful in establishing his alleged claims The record shows that when he was asked if he had not testified in the County Court that he had an interest in the outcome of this action in the trial court he replied that he would not say that he had not made such an answer It is also noteworthy that the portion of the property which was devised to Henry, Jr, was subject to the payment of the claims allowed against the estate, that Hugo could not suffer from an allowance of Herbert's claim and Herbert would definitely benefit from it It would, therefore, appear that Hugo was prejudiced in favor of the claimant, a fact which we feel must be taken into account It is the well settled law of this State that the judgment of the jury as to the credibility of witnesses, which is their peculiar province, will not be allowed to stand if it appears to be clearly unreasonable (*Bunn* v *Third Nat*, 38 Ill App 76) or where the preponderance of the evidence does not support the verdict *Kirsch* v *Wolf,* 106 Ill App 639, *Huber* v *McGlynn,* 161 Ill App 69 Such we think is the case here for the reasons given

The trial court ordered a remittitur of $675 58 This remittitur was determined in the following manner The court determined that from the evidence the claim ant was entitled to $3,015 82 He further determined that the executor was entitled to a credit on his cross-complaint in the sum of $1,008 18 He subtracted the amount he determined as due on the cross complaint from the amount due on the claim which made the sum of $2,006 64 The jury returned a verdict in the sum

of $2,682 22 The court then subtracted from the ver dict, $2,682 22, the said sum of $2,006 64, the amount he determined was due under the evidence, and ordered a remittitur of $675 58 In determining the amount due on the cross-complaint the court evidently overlooked the fact that there was no dispute but that the said sum of $364 50 for machinery should be allowed in addition to the items which he did allow, in the sum of $1,008 18, which would make the total amount which was undisputed, and should have been allowed on the cross-complaint, at $1,372 68, so that on the theory adopted by the court $364 50 should have been added to the $675 58, to make up the remittitur, or a sum of $1,040 08, and the judgment should have been $1,642 14 In ordering a remittitur it is fair to assume that the court felt that the verdict rendered by the jury was not warranted by the evidence In this we believe he was correct But in determining the amount the court undertook to determine what the jury allowed for various items, and in so doing apparently overlooked the item of $364 50 mentioned above We feel that instead of attempting to correct an unreasonable verdict by the jury by way of a remittitur the trial court should have granted the motion for new trial made by the defendant-appellee in the trial court *Wabash R Co* v *Billings,* 212 Ill 37, *Ill Cent* v *Rothschild,* 134 Ill App 504

The record in this case consists of greatly in excess of 400 pages of testimony, much of which had to do with figures and disassociated items which it would be difficult for any juror to keep in mind Witnesses were called to the stand and then recalled after other witnesses had testified so that there was undoubtedly considerable confusion in the minds of the jury as to just what the testimony did prove Considerable testimony was admitted and later stricken All this we think tended to result in a verdict which was clearly not supported by a preponderance of the evidence, and for the reasons given the judgment of the trial court is reversed, and this cause is remanded for a new trial.

Reversed and remanded.

(Thirteen pages in original opinion)

PUBLISHED IN ABSTRACT

First State Trust and Savings Bank of Springfield, a Banking Corporation, Complainant and Appellee, (Frank H McKelvey, also appellee), v. Henry J Schaffer, Susie F Schaffer, Henry Fraase, Edward Fraase, et al, Defendants, Henry Fraase and Edward Fraase, Appellants.

Appeal from Circuit Court of Sangamon County.

JANUARY TERM, A D 1935 280 I.A. 633[4]

Gen No 8878 **Agenda No 6**

MR JUSTICE ALLABEN delivered the opinion of the Court

This case arose in connection with the foreclosure of a certain trust deed, dated March 1, 1924, and executed by Ella W Brainard to the First State Trust and Savings Bank of Springfield, as trustee, to secure her promissory notes in the principal amount of $25,000 Subsequent to the execution of the mortgage the said mortgagor died and an undivided two-thirds of her interest in the mortgaged premises subject to said trust deed through various mesne conveyances became vested in the appellants Henry F Fraase and Edward Fraase, on July 17, 1930 The immediate grantor of the appellants, Henry J Schaffer, as part of the purchase price for said premises had assumed and agreed to pay the trust deed in question when he took title The appellants, however, did not become personally liable for the indebtedness when the premises upon which the trust deed was a lien were conveyed to them by Schaffer Subsequent to the acquisition of title by the appellants a default occurred under the terms of the trust deed and thereafter, on the 29th day of March, 1932, the appellee bank filed its bill in the Circuit Court of Sangamon County to foreclose the trust deed

Among other things, the bill of complaint alleged that the trust deed pledged the rents, issues and profits of the real estate upon which it was a lien and provided for the appointment of a receiver to collect such rents, issues and profits during the pendency of such forclosure suit, and until the expiration of the time to redeem from any sale made under any decree of fore closure After the clause contained in the trust deed

conveying the real estate therein described appears the following verbiage "Together with the rents, issues and profits thereof" and in the body of the trust deed "And such court may, without notice, appoint a receiver to collect the rents, issues and profits of the said premises during the pendency of such foreclosure suit, and until the time to redeem from any sale, made under any decree foreclosing this trust deed shall expire" The bill prayed for an accounting and for the sale of the property according to the provisions of the statute, and that a receiver be appointed to take possession of the property and to collect the rents, issues and profits therefrom, and to apply the same under the direction of the court A decree of foreclosure was entered and the real estate sold pursuant thereto Upon sale by the Master the premises did not sell for an amount sufficient to satisfy the indebtedness and a deficiency decree in the amount of $4,039 85 was entered against Henry J Schaffer Thereafter the appellee bank filed a petition for the appointment of a receiver to take possession of the premises, and to collect the rents, issues and profits therefrom until the expiration of the redemption period, to manage the property, make needful and proper disbursements, and hold the net revenue, to be applied under the direction of the court

Over the objection of appellants the court entered an order on November 2, 1932, finding that the trust deed pledged the rents, issues and profits of the real estate as security for the mortgaged debt, that it provided for the appointment of a receiver to take possession and to collect the rents, issues, and profits from the real estate conveyed by the trust deed The order appointing such receiver directed him to take possession of said premises, and further vested him with the powers prayed for in the petition, and enjoined all parties, including the appellants, and the tenant on the premises from interfering with the receiver's possession

At the time the receiver was appointed the tenant occupying the premises was holding under a lease which expired on March 1, 1933, which lease provided for the payment of certain cash rents, and a share of the emblements The tenant continued in occupancy of the premises after the appointment of the receiver and the receiver collected the rents, issues and profits Subsequently the receiver filed his report of receipts and disbursements from the time of his appointment to June 30, 1934, showing a cash balance of $660 31,

1,700 bushels of corn, and a claim for cash rent The receiver asked for the approval of his report, and a direction to pay the cash balance, the corn and claims for cash rent, to the appellee bank on its deficiency decree The appellants filed objections to the receiver's report, claiming to be entitled to their proportionate part of the net rents held by the receiver The court overruled these objections, and entered an order approving the report of the receiver and ordering him to pay the assets in his hands to the appellee bank, to be applied upon the deficiency judgment against Henry J Shaffer Appellants excepted to this ruling, and prayed an appeal to this court

Appellants contend that the appellee bank is not entitled to the rents, issues and profits accruing prior to the time the receiver took possession Appellee on December 27, 1934, filed in this court a confession of partial error in which it admits that the court erred in ordering the receiver to pay the appellee rents accruing prior to the time receiver took possession Appellants further contend that the trust deed did not pledge the rents, issues and profits accruing during the period of redemption, and that the appellee bank as the holder of the deficiency decree was not entitled to have the rents, issues, and profits, accruing after the appointment of a receiver applied upon such de-decree unless provision was made therefor in the trust deed, that the absence of a finding in the decree of foreclosure that the trust deed did pledge such rents, issues and profits during the period of redemption should prevent the appellee bank from obtaining such rents

The first question before us is whether the language contained in the trust deed involved in this case was sufficient to constitute a pledge of the rents, issues and profits during the period of redemption The verbiage contained in the trust deed which appears to us to be pertinent to the decision on this question has been set out above We believe the law to be in this State that no particular or specific wording is necessary in the trust deed to constitute a pledge of the rents, issues and profits, and that the mere fact that such rents, issues and profits are conveyed as in the instant mortgage without anything further is sufficient to constitute such a pledge In the case of *Rohrer* v *Deatherage* 336 Ill 450 the court in discussing this question which involved a mortgage conveying certain lands "together with the rents, issues and profits thereof"

said "Under the express pledge contained in the mortgage of the rents, issues, and profits for the security of the debt, it was proper to appoint a receiver to collect the rents, issues, and profits" This shows beyond question that the language used in the trust deed held by appellee bank was an express pledge Likewise, in the case of *Owsley* v *Neeves* 179 Ill App 61, which case involved the foreclosure of a mortgage containing substantially the same provision with regard to the pledging of rents as in the case at bar, the court held that the provisions providing for the appointment of a receiver to collect the rents, issues and profits, together with the conveyance of them following a description of the property, did expressly convey them and that the parties were bound by the terms of the mortgage We further believe that the appellee bank as holder of a deficiency judgment is entitled to have the rents, issues and profits which accrue after the appointment of a receiver applied to the payment of its deficiency decree, regardless of whether any specific provision of the trust deed by its terms so provided In the case of *Rohrer* v *Deatherage,* cited above, Mr Justice Dunn in delivering the opinion of the court said "After condition broken, however, the mortgagee is, as between him and the mortgagor, the owner of the fee * * * After condition broken, ejectment may be maintained by the mortgagee against the mortgagor or those to whom he may have assigned the equity of redemption * * * Upon default in the condition of the mortgage the mortgagee has the right to possession against the mortgagor, his grantee, lessee, or any one claiming under him by any right In such case the mortgagee has several remedies which he may pursue to enforce the payment of his debt He may sue the mortgagor in assumpsit for a judgment upon the personal obligation, he may sue in equity for the foreclosure of the mortgage, or he may recover the possession of the mortgaged property by an action of ejectment These remedies are concurrent or successive, as the mortgagee may deem proper, and he may pursue any two or all three of the remedies simultaneously " If as the court says after condition broken ejectment may be maintained against the mortgagor or those to whom he may assign the equity of redemption and since the mortgagee may have concurrent remedies to effect the payment of the debt owed him and to obtain possession of the premises mortgaged it necessarily follows that being entitled to such possession he is also entitled to get the rents, issues and

profits and apply the same upon the mortgage indebtedness A court of equity properly lends its aid in effecting this result by the appointment of a receiver, and the application of the rents collected by the receiver upon the debt owed to mortgagee In the case of *Haas* v *The Chicago Building Society* 89 Ill 498 the court in its opinion said "We find the decided weight of American authority to be in favor of the proposition that the court may, even when the mortgage does not by express words give a lien upon the income derived from such property, appoint a receiver to take charge of it and collect the rents, issues and profits arising therefrom Such action will not be taken, however, unless it be made to appear the mortgaged premises are an insufficient security for the debt, and the person liable personally for the debt is insolvent, or at least of very questionable responsibility " Both of the latter requirements were met in the case at bar by allegations in the bill to foreclose and the petition for the appointment of a receiver Also in *Prussing* v *Lancaster* 234 Ill 462 the Supreme Court upheld the right of the mortgagee to have the rents applied upon a deficiency decree though no specific authority therefor was contained in the trust deed In passing upon this question in the Prussing case the court said "The premises did not sell for enough to satisfy the foreclosure decree, and there was a deficiency decree for $5,598 44 in favor of appellees In such case the practice is a proper one to apply to the satisfaction of such deficiency decree, through a receiver, the rents which may accrue upon the premises covered by the trust deed during the redemption period, and this may be done by a court of equity, although the trust deed is silent upon the subject of the application of the rents to the payment of any deficiency that may remain after the sale of the land covered by the trust deed " This case is followed by *First National Bank* v *Illinois Steel Co*, 174 Ill 140, and we feel that this quotation is a clear expression of the law in this State upon the subject, and our Supreme Court has even gone so far as to say that where the trust deed provided that the rents, issues and profits collected during the redemption period should be paid to the person entitled to a deed under a Master's certificate of purchase that they were properly applied to a deficiency decree entered and should not be paid to the holder of the Master's deed *Schaeppi* v *Bartholomae*, 217 Ill 105

The final contention of appellants that because the decree of foreclosure did not pledge the rents, issues

and profits the appellee bank should not obtain payment of them from the receiver is we think wholly without basis The absence of such a finding in the decree is immaterial for as has been pointed out in the cases above cited the appellee is entitled to such rents as the holder of the deficiency decree independently of any provision of the trust deed and further by reason of the fact that in the order entered on November 2, 1932, appointing the receiver in the case at bar the court specifically found that the trust deed in question pledged the rents, issues and profits of the premises mortgaged as security for the debt and provided for the appointment of a receiver to take possession of the real estate and to collect such rents issues and profits The only other question raised in this case which we believe deserves attention is when did the receiver take possession of the mortgaged premises The order appointing said receiver recites in part as follows "The said receiver is authorized and directed forthwith to take possession of all and singular the said property," and this part of the appointment we feel was equivalent to his taking possession on the date of the order of appointment since in addition to the above verbiage the order also enjoined all parties, including the appellants and tenants then in possession, from interfering in any way with the exercise of the powers and duties imposed upon the receiver by the order The mere fact that the receiver did not actually go into physical possession of the property at that time has no effect upon the order of his appointment, his right to collect rents as an officer of the court began with the day of his appointment, and from that date he was in possession In holding as we do that the receiver's authority to collect rents, issues and profits commences with the day of his appointment, it necessarily follows that all rents, issues and profits which accrued and were collected after that date must be accounted for by him and applied in satisfaction of the deficiency, and insofar as the order approving the application of rents, issues and profits which accrued on and after the date of the appointment of the receiver to the deficiency the same is correct and is hereby affirmed

It appears from the contentions of appellants, and the confession of errors filed in this court by appellee that certain rents, issues and profits which accrued prior to the receiver's appointment came into his hands Insofar as these items are concerned the order approving the application of said items to the satis-

faction of the deficiency is incorrect, and is set aside This court is unable to determine from the record what these items may be, because the items contained in the confession of error are not the only items disputed by appellants Therefore, this cause is reversed and remanded with directions to the trial court to determine what rents, issues and profits, if any, which accrued prior to the appointment of the receiver, came into his hands, and to order such distribution thereof to the various parties as their interests shall appear.

Affirmed in Part, Reversed and Remanded in Part With Directions

(Eleven pages in original opinion)

PUBLISHED IN ABSTRACT

Mary Elizabeth Keys, Plaintiff Appellee, v. Bert North, Defendant-Appellant.

Appeal from Circuit Court, Edgar County

JANUARY TERM, A D 1935 230 I.A. 633[5]

Gen. No 8891 **Agenda No. 15**

MR JUSTICE ALLABEN delivered the opinion of the Court

This is a suit for personal injuries brought by the plaintiff, Mary Elizabeth Keys, against the defendants, Bert North and Arthur North The declaration was in one count which is set forth in haec verba

"For that, whereas, on, to wit, the 27th day of September, A D 1931, the defendant Bert North was the owner of a certain automobile, to wit, a Ford sedan, then and there being driven in a southwesterly direction along and upon a certain public highway near the Town of Redmon, in the county and state aforesaid, and said automobile was then and there being driven by the defendant Arthur North, the son of the defendant Bert North, who then and there was the agent and servant of the defendant Bert North in the operation of said car

"That the plaintiff was then and there riding in said automobile upon the invitation of the defendants, and was then and there a passenger and guest of the defendants for the purpose of riding in said automobile to Paris, Illinois, and the defendant Bert North directed and instructed the said Arthur North, his son, to drive and operate his said automobile and take plaintiff to Paris, Illinois, that the defendants, in conveying the plaintiff to Paris, Illinois, did drive said automobile upon said certain public highway, which said certain highway was an old county gravel road, and that at that time it was full of ruts and with a lot of loose, soft gravel on it, and in such condition because of the ruts and the loose, soft gravel on it, that it was exceedingly dangerous to travel thereon with an automobile at a high rate of speed, without danger of the automobile leaving the road and overturning, and endangering the lives of pas-

sengers, and that the defendants then and there had full knowledge of the facts aforesaid, and were conscious of the danger of operating an automobile at a high rate of speed on said road in its then condition, and that the said defendants, not regarding their duties in the premises, and with a conscious indifference to the surrounding circumstances and conditions of said highway, and conscious that their conduct would naturally and probably result in injury to persons riding in said automobile, and with a conscious indifference for the safety of the plaintiff as a passenger in said automobile, did wantonly and wilfully operate said automobile in which the plaintiff was then and there riding on the day aforesaid at a high, dangerous and unsafe speed, to wit, in excess of sixty (60) miles per hour on said highway, and by reason thereof said automobile left said roadway, ran into a ditch, crossed a field, ran against a post and turned over, and thereby injured the plaintiff, and the plaintiff avers that by means of the premises aforesaid the defendants were guilty of willful and wanton misconduct in the driving and operation of said automobile, which then and there was a motor vehicle, and that the willful and wanton misconduct of the defendants as aforesaid contributed to the injury of the plaintiff, as hereinafter set forth

"And the plaintiff further avers that the injuries of the plaintiff, occasioned as aforesaid, were severe and permanent injuries, both externally and internally, and the plaintiff was greatly hurt, bruised and wounded, and divers bones in her body and limbs were broken, crushed and maimed, and she thereby then and there sustained severe and permanent injury to her limbs, chest, abdomen and spine and she thereby then and there sustained a severe and permanent injury to divers of her internal organs and a severe shock and injury to her nervous system and mental faculties, and she thereby became then and there sick, sore, lame and disordered, and so remained for a long space of time, to wit, from thence hitherto, during all of which time she suffered great pain, and will in the future so suffer, and she was, by reason of her said injuries, and will be, permanently hindered and prevented from attending to her affairs and duties, and she was compelled to, and she did, expend and become obligated to pay divers large

> sums of money in and about endeavoring to be cured of her said injuries in the amount of, to wit, two thousand dollars ($2,000 00), and she will in the future be obliged to lay out and expend divers large sums of money in and about endeavoring to be cured of her said injuries, sickness and disorders occasioned as aforesaid, to the damage of the plaintiff in the sum of, to wit, ten thousand dollars ($10,000 00), and, therefore, she brings this suit "

A demurrer to this declaration was overruled by the court, whereupon defendant, Arthur North, filed a plea of the general issue, and defendant, Bert North, filed a plea of the general issue, and a second plea, which is as follows

> "And for a further and second plea in this behalf the defendant Bert North says that the plaintiff ought not to have her aforesaid action against him, this defendant, because he says that at the time of the alleged accident to the plaintiff, as set forth in the declaration, this defendant was not managing, operating or driving the said automobile in question, but that at the time of the said accident, and prior thereto, the said automobile was under the sole management and control and was being driven solely and alone by the defendant Arthur North, and that at all the times mentioned in said plaintiff's declaration the said Arthur North was not the agent, servant or employe of this defendant, nor was the said Arthur North at any of said times mentioned driving or operating said automobile as the agent, servant or employe of this defendant, and of this this defendant puts himself upon the country, etc "

Trial was had on the pleadings as above set forth At the close of all of the evidence for the plaintiff motions for directed verdict were made on behalf of both defendants jointly and each defendant separately The reason assigned in each motion was "That said evidence is insufficient in law to support the cause of action set out in the declaration " All motions for directed verdict were refused by the court Plaintiff's motion to dismiss the suit as to the defendant Arthur North was granted No evidence was submitted by the remaining defendant, Bert North, and the case was submitted to a jury who found the defendant guilty and assessed plaintiff's damages in the sum of Six Thousand Dollars ($6,000) Defendant Bert North's motions in arrest of judgment, and

for a new trial were overruled, and judgment was entered on the verdict by the court It is from this judgment that defendant, Bert North, has prosecuted an appeal to this court

Defendant contends that the trial court erred in refusing to direct a verdict in favor of the defendants, in denying defendant's motion for a new trial, and in arrest of judgment, that the declaration is substantially and innately defective, that the evidence does not justify a finding of willful and wanton conduct on the part of the driver of the car, that the proof is not sufficient to charge the defendant, Bert North, with the acts of Arthur North, and that the verdict is contrary to the law and the evidence generally

The facts are substantially as follows On September 26, 1931, Mary Elizabeth Keys, plaintiff, who then resided at Paris, Illinois, went with Grace North, who was afterward married and was known as Grace Sunkell, to the North farm home to spend the night At that time Grace Sunkell was unmarried, twenty two years of age and lived with her parents, Mr and Mrs Bert North, and a brother, Arthur North, a minor On the morning of September 27, 1931, plaintiff and Grace Sunkell attended Sunday school and then returned to the North home About two o'clock that afternoon plaintiff and Grace Sunkell, in a Ford sedan, owned by defendant, Bert North, and driven by Arthur North, minor son of Bert North, started to take Mrs Sunkel to a Sunday school council meeting at Paris, and to take the plaintiff to her home in the same city They did not take the most direct road to Paris but did take a road which the Norths often used in going to and from Paris because Bert North had "a place on that road "

They proceeded some distance on this road when they came to a place where the road had loose gravel on it and had a number of ruts and holes in it It was a road which had room for two cars to pass This road was chucky and the gravel was loose The plaintiff looked at the speedometer on the car, and the speedometer indicated sixty two miles The plaintiff then said to the driver, "Arthur, you are going sixty-two " This was said in a warning way Whereupon the driver said, "It is good for another five" and stepped on the gas The car started to move faster and within a few seconds swerved, and turned over at the side of the road, severely injuring the plaintiff Inasmuch as no complaint is made that the verdict is excessive we will not set up the testimony as to the

injuries further than to say that they were severe, plaintiff was in the hospital on several osccasions for some time, and considerable amount of money was spent for hospital and medical services, also she was permanently injured

It appears that Bert North was the owner of two automobiles, a Chrysler and a Ford, that on the morning of the day of the accident Grace Sunkell asked for the Chrysler automobile, that her father, the defendant, stated he could not spare the Chrysler automobile, but told his minor son, Arthur, to take the plaintiff and Mrs Sunkell in the Ford car to Paris This is all the pertinent testimony that was offered on this point

It would appear from this testimony that defendant, Bert North, who was the owner of the Ford car, which was in the accident in question, by the directions which he gave to his son, Arthur, to take Mrs Sunkell and the plaintiff to Paris in the Ford car constituted Arthur as his servant or agent for that purpose This holding is not based on the theory of the so-called "family purpose" doctrine, but on the theory of direct agency It has been directly held by this Court in an opinion written by Mr Justice Eldredge in the case of *Smoot v Hollingsworth*, 265 Ill App 447, that a minor son who at the direction of his father was taking out of town guests of the family to the theater was engaged in the father's business and was the servant or agent of the father The son was acting under specific directions of his father and was as much the servant or agent of his father in driving the automobile as a hired chauffeur would have been It appears that the route taken to Paris was not the most direct route but it was one which was frequently used by the Norths in going to and from Paris, and was a much used public highway It does not appear that this route was taken for any personal purpose of Arthur North or either of the passengers other than in accordance with the instructions of the defendant Bert North, and we do not feel that there was such a variance from the general line of the instructions given, to take Arthur North outside of the limits of the directions given to him by Bert North We further consider that the contention that Arthur North was the servant of Mrs Sunkell is not supported by the evidence in any way Nowhere is there any evidence that she gave any directions of any kind as to where or how her brother was to drive the car in question

The evidence shows that a short time prior to the accident the automobile in which the plaintiff was rid-

ing was being driven at a rate of speed so that the speedometer indicated sixty two miles per hour, and Mrs Sunkell, who was properly qualified as a judge of speed, testified that in her opinion at that time the car in question was going at the rate of sixty miles per hour This was a gravel road with ruts and rutty places and lots of holes in it The road had loose gravel on it It was at this time that the plaintiff in a warning way called to the attention of Arthur North the speed at which they were travelling, to which he replied, "It is good for another five", whereupon he stepped on the gas and the car moved faster, and immediately thereafter the car swerved, ran over to the side of the road and turned over on its side

At the close of all the testimony the court struck out that part of the testimony of plaintiff, Mary Elizabeth Keys in which she testified that she looked at the speedometer and that it showed sixty-two miles an hour However, these same facts were brought out on cross examination by defendant's attorneys of Grace Sunkell, and are in the record for consideration, no motion having been made to strike such testimony by Grace Sunkell It is insisted that there is no evidence sufficient to be submitted to a jury that the driver of the car in question at the time in question was guilty of willful and wanton conduct With this we can not agree In considering a motion for a directed verdict the trial court should place that construction on the evidence most favorable to the party against whom the motion is made and give to that party also inferences most favorable to him, it is only where there is no evidence upon which the jury could without acting unreasonably in the eye of the law decide in favor of the party producing it, that a verdict may be directed *Offutt* v *World's Columbian Exposition Co* 175 Ill 472 We feel that if there is any evidence in the record fairly tending to show a gross want of care such as indicates a willful disregard of consequences or a willingness to inflict injury, that it is a question to be determined by the jury *Walldren* v *Krug* 291 Ill 472 In our opinion the opinion of Mr Justice Farthing in *Streeter* v *Hummichouse* 357 Ill 234, wherein it is said. " * * * the speed of the Dodge coupe and the other circumstances in evidence made it necessary for the trial court to submit the question of willfulness and wantonness to the jury" applies aptly to this case, and we hold that the court properly submitted the question of willfullness to the jury in this case

Finally it is insisted by the defendant that the declaration is innately and substantially so deficient as to not to support the verdict While it is admitted that where a demurrer is interposed to a declaration and overruled, and the defendant pleads over, any defect as to form is waived, nevertheless, it is here argued that because the declaration does not charge the existence of a duty on the part of the defendant to protect the plaintiff it is, therefore, so defective as not to be cured by verdict An inspection of the declaration shows that there is a charge of failure of the defendant to perform a duty, and an injury resulting therefrom The recitals in the declaration further show facts which place upon the operator of the car a duty toward the plaintiff Where that is done it is unnecessary to allege the duty in so many words An allegation of duty if the facts stated raise the duty is unnecessary, if the facts do not raise a duty the allegation of a duty is unavailing *C & A R Co* v *Clausen* 173 Ill 100

This is the second time this case has been tried A previous jury allowed plaintiff Five Thousand Dollars ($5,000) That verdict was set aside by this court for errors in procedure *Keys* v *North* 271 Ill App 119 The damages assessed by this jury in this case now before this court were Six Thousand Dollars ($6,000) No evidence was offered by the defendants in this case There is no complaint as to the giving or refusing of any instructions, or error committed by the trial court in the admitting or refusing to admit evidence There is no contention that the amount of this verdict is excessive

In our opinion no error was committed by the trial court in overruling defendant's various motions for a directed verdict, for a new trial, or in arrest of judgment, or in submitting this cause to a jury for a determination of the matters at issue There being no reversible error in this record, the judgment of the trial court is hereby affirmed

Judgment affirmed.

(Ten pages in original opinion)

PUBLISHED IN ABSTRACT

Robert Carl Sweeter, a minor, by William Carl Sweeter, his father and next friend, Plaintiff-Appellee, v Charles M Poole and Home Oil Co, a Corporation, Defendants, Charles M Poole, Appellant

Appeal from Circuit Court of Tazewell County.

JANUARY TERM, A D 1935. 280 I.A. 634

Gen No 8857 **Agenda No 2**

MR JUSTICE DAVIS delivered the opinion of the Court

The appellant, Charles M Poole, who was engaged in the trucking and transfer business at Muscatine, Iowa, had one of his trucks in transit between Bloomington, Illinois, and Muscatine, Iowa, on January 14, 1933 Elmer Jamison, an employe of appellant, was driving the truck and Robert Poole, a brother was a passenger They left Bloomington between 8 30 and 9 00 o'clock that evening with a load of empty beer kegs, on a concrete highway known as No 9, extending from the city of Bloomington westerly to the village of Morton, Illinois, passing through Deer Creek When they arrived at a point about two and one-half miles east of the village of Morton the truck ran out of gasoline and Jamison pulled it over to the side of the road and stopped

William C Sweeter, together with his wife, Leona Sweeter, and their infant son, Carl Sweeter, left Deer Creek in a Buick coach and traveled west towards the village of Morton, and when they arrived at the Buckeye school, which is about a quarter of a mile east of where Elmer Jamison had parked the truck, they saw a car turning around about one hundred feet from them and proceed west on the right hand side of the road, traveling about 25 miles per hour Sweeter was following, and the distance between the cars was between 75 and 100 feet When the car in front of Sweeter neared the point where the truck was parked it turned to the left and proceeded on west and Sweeter followed, and as the car in front got opposite to the truck the Buick car in which Sweeter, his wife and son were riding collided with the rear of that car and then skidded around and caught the rear corner of the truck, which bent the radiator back and the corner of the hood broke the wind shield and some of the glass flew

and cut the right eye of the plaintiff and severely injured him

This suit was instituted in the circuit court of Tazewell county on February 3, 1933, to recover damages for injuries sustained by the plaintiff, and the Home Oil Co, a corporation, and appellant, Charles M Poole, were named defendants, and on the trial of said cause the Home Oil Co was found not guilty by the verdict of the jury and damages were awarded in the sum of $2500 00 against appellant The court entered a judgment on the verdict in favor of the Home Oil Co and a judgment against appellant, Charles M Poole, in the sum of $2500 00, from which judgment appellant appealed

The cause was tried upon the amended declaration of the plaintiff, consisting of two counts, and the first and second additional counts to said amended declaration, and a plea of not guilty by each of said defendants

The first amended count charged the defendant, Charles M Poole, with general negligence in having stopped his truck after dark upon a paved public highway and permitting it to remain standing upon the paved portion thereof, and the defendant, the Home Oil Co, a corporation, with general negligence in unlawfully stopping its Dodge sedan upon a paved public highway in the night time and permitting it to remain standing thereon so there was not room to pass said truck and said Dodge sedan on said pavement, and by means whereof the automobile in which the plaintiff was riding came in violent collision and ran into and struck against said motor truck and said Dodge sedan, and the plaintiff was thereby injured

The second amended count charged the defendant, Charles M Poole, with having stopped his truck upon the paved portion of Route 9 in the night time and unlawfully allowed it to remain standing thereon, contrary to the form of the statute in such cases made and provided, and the defendant, the Home Oil Co, a corporation, with driving its Dodge sedan in a westerly direction along said highway, and when it reached the point where said motor truck was parked it unlawfully stopped said Dodge sedan on the concrete portion of said Route 9 by the side of said truck so there was not ample room for two vehicles to pass on said highway, contrary to the statute in such cases made and provided, and because thereof the car in which the plaintiff was riding came in violent collision with said truck and Dodge sedan and he was thereby injured

The first additional count to the amended declaration charged that the defendant, Charles M Poole, unlawfully stopped his motor truck on Route No 9 on the pavement thereof in the night time and allowed it to remain standing thereon in the lane where the plaintiff had the right of way, in such a position that there was not ample room for two vehicles to pass, and at more than one hour after sunset and more than one hour prior to sunrise, and that said defendant had no red light displayed at the rear of said truck, contrary to the statute of the State of Illinois, and that the defendant, the Home Oil Co, unlawfully stopped its Dodge sedan on the concrete portion of the highway by the side of said truck so that there was not room enough to pass said truck and said Dodge sedan, contrary to the statute, and the automobile in which plaintiff was riding on said highway in a westerly direction came in violent collision with said motor truck and Dodge sedan and the plaintiff was injured

The second additional count to the amended declaration charged the defendant with substantially the same negligence as alleged in the first additional count

From the evidence it appears that the plaintiff, Robert Carl Sweeter, was a boy of the age of about three years and that on January 14, 1933, between 10 00 and 10 30 p m, was riding with his father and mother, William C Sweeter and Leona Sweeter, in a Buick coach on State Highway, Route No 9, between Deer Creek and the village of Morton The paved portion of Route 9 was 18 feet in width with a black line running down the center with the usual shoulders on each side of the concrete

The driver of the truck testified that he pulled the truck over to the side of the road as far as possible and stopped

The testimony shows that the shoulder of the road sloped at this point At a point 4½ feet from the edge of the pavement there was a drop from the center of the pavement of 1/10 of a foot, at 6 9 feet there was a drop of approximately 9½ inches and at a point 8 feet and 9 inches there was a drop of 2 1 feet The pavement was covered with ice and it was very slippery and the shoulder at the point where the truck was stopped was old sod frozen solid and covered with ice

The driver of the truck went to a farm house and telephoned the co defendant, the Home Oil Co, to send out gasoline, leaving Robert Poole in the truck

He was a brother of the appellant and was a passenger in the truck The Home Oil Co sent out a five gallon can of gasoline in a Dodge sedan which was driven by the witness, Valentine Wick, who was accompanied by the witness, Sam Wanner The Dodge car was driven by Wick in an easterly direction, passing the standing truck, and proceeded on east about a quarter of a mile until it reached an intersection where it turned around and proceeded westerly on the right hand side of the pavement towards the truck At the time the Dodge sedan turned at the intersection and proceeded in a westerly direction the car in which appellee was riding, driven by his father, followed along behind the Dodge sedan at a distance of from 75 to 100 feet Shortly before the Dodge sedan got to the standing truck it turned to the left in order to pull up along side of the truck or pass it, and when the rear end of the Dodge was near the rear end of the truck the Buick car struck the back end of the Dodge car and skidded to the right and struck the rear or southeasterly corner of the truck

The witness, Valentine Wick, the driver of the Dodge car, testified that he turned to the left when he was 60 to 75 feet behind the truck, and that when he attempted to pass the truck he was struck from the back and that at that time he was traveling 10 to 15 miles per hour.

From the testimony of William C Sweeter, father of appellee, and driver of the car in which appellee was riding, it appears that the accident took place about a quarter of a mile west of the Buckeye School After the Dodge car turned around at this intersection he followed it on west at a distance of 75 to 100 feet from the car He saw a light on the rear of the Dodge car but saw no other light As the Dodge car turned to the left it was 10 to 15 feet from the truck and he was 75 to 100 feet behind it and he was looking straight ahead watching the Dodge car and then noticed the truck on the right hand side of the road, but saw no light on it The Dodge car stopped on the left hand side of the road When he saw the Dodge car turn to the left he applied his brakes and swung to the left hand side of the road and bumped into the Dodge car, and that at that time it was right along side of the truck, he was going about 15 miles per hour when he hit the Dodge car He testified, when I say the Dodge car stopped I mean that it either stopped still or it might have been moving slightly, when

he bumped into the Dodge the front end of the Buick swung around and caught the corner of the truck He got out of the car and took the boy, and his wife got out Just then another car came over the top of the hill and hit the corner of his car Henry Heinold and his wife and boy were in that car I and my wife and boy got into the Dodge sedan and were driven to Morton, to Dr Bryant's office The extent of the injury to plaintiff and the amount of damages awarded by the verdict of the jury are not questioned The different witnesses placed the truck in various positions, some testified that all of the truck was on the concrete, and some that it stood half on the concrete and half on the shoulder, but none of the witnesses testified that the truck was at any time to the left of the center line of the paved portion of the highway All of the front lights on the truck were burning, there were five lights in front, consisting of the two headlights and three green clearance lights, located on the top of the cab of the truck, there were four red lights on the rear of the truck, one being the rear tail light, located below, and three red clearance lights in the center of the extreme end of the body There was a good deal of controversy as to whether the rear lights were burning on the truck, some of the witnesses testifying that they did not see any lights, and some testifying that there were none and several of the witnesses testifying that there were lights burning The evidence leaves it in doubt as to whether the Dodge sedan stopped on the left hand side of the highway opposite the truck or whether it was in motion all of the time The father and mother of the plaintiff testifying that it stopped, or if it did not stop that it was just slightly in motion, the driver of the Dodge car testifying that he did not stop his car

It is contended by appellant that the trial court erred in overruling his motion for a directed verdict at the close of the plaintiff's evidence and at the close of all of the evidence, and in refusing the instructions tendered therewith, and in entering judgment upon the verdict after overruling appellant's motion for a new trial, that he was guilty of no negligence which was the proximate cause of plaintiff's injury, and that the driver of the car in which plaintiff was riding was guilty of the sole and only negligence which was the proximate cause of plaintiff's injury

Appellee insists that appellant was guilty of negligence in parking the truck on the pavement and in not having a red light displayed on the rear of the truck,

and that it was a question for the jury as to whether an emergency existed which warranted appellant in so leaving his truck, and the jury have found that appellant failed to take that degree of care and caution which an ordinarily prudent person would take on a slippery road at night where he was violating the law and creating a hazard for every one who might use that highway

On the night in question the pavement was covered with ice and it was very slippery The shoulder at the point where the truck was stopped was also covered with ice and sloping

It was not negligence per se for appellant to stop his truck upon the pavement, and whether it was in fact negligence to be so parked depends upon the facts as disclosed by the evidence

The statute provides that a driver of a vehicle shall not stop the same on any durable hard surface state highway, or allow it to stand in such position that there is not ample room for two vehicles to pass upon the road * * * except in a case of emergency * * * Cahill's Ill Rev St, 1933, chap 121, sec 161 (2)

This court in the case of *Collins* v *McMullin,* 225 Ill App 430, held "The mere act of leaving the automobile standing on the proper side of a public road, however, cannot be regarded as negligence It is a matter of common knowledge that it is not an infrequent occurrence to see an automobile standing in the public road Sometimes this occurs on account of an accidental break in the car or because of a puncture in a tire, or because the car has run out of gasoline Persons operating cars often have no choice about leaving a car standing in the road until a remedy for the mishap is found " See also, *Crawford* v *Cahalan,* 259 Ill App 14, *Frochter* v *Arenholz,* 242 id 93, *Sugru* v *Highland Park Yellow Cab Co*, 251 id 99

In view of the fact that the truck had no gasoline and of the icy condition of the highway and the sloping condition of the shoulder, appellant had no choice other than to stop the truck where it was standing, and under the law an emergency existed, and appellant can not be charged with negligence because of so stopping the truck and leaving it standing until such time as he could, by the exercise of reasonable diligence, procure an additional supply of gasoline *Crawford* v *Cahalan, supra*

As has been pointed out before, there was considerable conflict in the evidence as to whether the tail light or any other lights were burning on the rear of the

truck From the testimony of the witnesses, it appears that the Buick car was from 75 to 135 feet from the truck when Sweeter first saw it

Appellee contends that Sweeter, when he saw the Dodge car turn to the left and saw the truck ahead of him on the right hand side of the road, applied his brakes and swung to the left hand side of the road and bumped into the Dodge car which was along side of the truck, and that because there was no red light on the rear of the truck the Buick car had to turn out without sufficient warning That tail lights on the truck would have been visible a considerable time, while the Buick car was east of the school house, that because of insufficient warning the driver of the Buick car was compelled to suddenly turn to the left and in so doing he bumped into the Dodge car and skidded into the corner of the truck and plaintiff was injured and that the negligence of appellant in not having lights burning on the rear of the truck was the proximate cause of the injury to the plaintiff

Appellant asks the court to reverse the judgment without remanding the cause to the trial court for another trial Where the evidence is conflicting as it is in this case and that which is offered on behalf of plaintiff tends to establish his cause of action a reversal of a judgment for the plaintiff, without remanding the cause, would deprive the plaintiff of his constitutional right to a trial by jury

We have carefully considered all of the evidence and conclude that the verdict of the jury is against the manifest weight of the evidence, and the judgment is reversed and the cause remanded

Reversed and remanded

(Nine pages in original opinion)

PUBLISHED IN ABSTRACT

William M Below, Receiver for the First National Bank of Sidell, Illinois, a Corporation, Defendant in Error, v Carrie E McDowell, Fred M McDowell, James L Fish, Grace P Kayser and William Ray McDowell, Plaintiffs in Error

Writ of Error to the Circuit Court of Vermilion County

JANUARY TERM, A D 1935. 280 I.A. 634[2]

Gen No 8877 **Agenda No 5**

MR JUSTICE DAVIS delivered the opinion of the Court

The First National Bank of Sidell, Illinois, filed its bill of complaint in the circuit court of Vermilion county for the purpose of setting aside and removing out of the way of complainant's executions an alleged fraudulent warranty deed made by Carrie E McDowell to her sister, Jennie D Fish

Carrie E McDowell, Ruvilla McDowell, F M McDowell and Jennie D Fish were made parties defendant to said bill of complaint and answered the same, and the cause was referred to a special master in chancery to take the evidence and report the same together with his conclusions to the court

The master proceeded to take the testimony offered by the parties to said cause The defendant, Jennie D Fish, was called as a witness for complainant, and sometime after testifying she died intestate, and a supplemental bill was filed making James L Fish, her husband, and Grace P Kayser and Carrie E McDowell, her sisters, and Fred M McDowell and William Ray McDowell, her brothers, and Margaret McDowell, Lyda J McDowell and Julia Eva McDowell, her neices, and Roger E McDowell, a nephew, her only heirs at law, parties defendant Parker S Duffin was appointed guardian ad litem and filed an answer for Lyda J McDowell, Julia Eva McDowell and Roger E McDowell, minors

The master made a report to the court of the testimony taken and of his findings and conclusions, to which objections were filed by the defendants Said cause came on for a hearing upon the bill of com

plaint and answers, and the report of the master and exceptions taken thereto, and the court entered a de cree in accordance with the report of said master and ordered the defendants to pay to complainant the sum of $7850 53 with interest in twenty days, and in default thereof that said deed be set aside and be declared null and void and of no effect, except that the heirs of Jennie D Fish were decreed to have a first lien on the premises described in said deed in the sum of $633 75, and that writs of *fieri facias* issue upon the judgments of complainant and that the sheriff proceed to sell said real estate for the payment and satisfaction of the same, and that the said real estate be sold free and clear of said lien of the defendants thereon, and from the proceeds of said sale the defendants be paid said sum of $633 75 less any unpaid costs ordered to be paid by the defendants, and the balance be paid to complainant on its judgments, interest and costs

Plaintiffs in error sued out this writ of error to reverse said decree, and the complainant, the First National Bank of Sidell, Illinois, having been declared insolvent and William M Below having been appointed receiver for said bank he was made defendant in error

The errors assigned are That the court should have found that Carrie E McDowell by the making of the deed to the premises in question did not render herself insolvent, that the court should have found that Carrie E McDowell retained sufficient property to pay her debts, that the findings and report are contrary to and against the evidence, that the court erred in not dismissing complainant's bill for want of equity

By its bill, as amended, the complainant alleged that on December 28, 1928, it recovered a judgment in the circuit court of Vermilion county against Carrie E McDowell and Ruvilla McDowell for the sum of $5347 08, damages and costs of suit, and that on said day recovered a judgment in said court against Carrie E McDowell for the sum of $266 66, damages, and costs of suit, and also, on said day, recovered a judgment against F M McDowell and Carrie E McDowell for $2236 77 and costs of suit

That previous to the time of the rendition of said judgments the defendant, Carrie E McDowell, owned the land in question, that executions were issued on said judgments directed to the sheriff of said county, commanding him to cause to be made of the lands and tenements and goods and chattels of said defendants the amount of said damages

That prior to the rendition of said judgments and on, to-wit, November 17, 1928, said Carrie E McDowell made a pretended conveyance in fee of said real estate to Jennie D Fish, which was filed for record on November 17, 1928, in the recorder's office of Vermilion county, that said deed was made without any adequate consideration, that by the making and delivery thereof said Carrie E McDowell rendered herself insolvent and did not retain sufficient property to pay her debts, that said conveyance was not real, but a mere sham made with the intention of defrauding your orator and the other creditors of said Carrie E McDowell out of their just demands, that no consideration was paid by the said Jennie D Fish to said Carrie E McDowell for said conveyance, and that said premises are now held in trust by the said Jennie D Fish for the said Carrie E McDowell for her use and benefit and for the purpose of preventing a levy and sale of the same under and by virtue of the said executions, that said defendants have no property liable to levy and sale except said premises conveyed by Carrie E McDowell to Jennie D Fish

The complainant prayed that defendants answer said bill, and that upon a hearing said deed be set aside, vacated and declared null and void as to complainant and that it may be authorized to proceed on its executions and that the sheriff may be directed to proceed to levy upon, advertise and sell said premises for the payment and satisfaction of complainant's judgments The defendants answered denying the allegations of the bill

The master, among other things, found that on November 17, 1928, Carrie E McDowell owned the 57 acre tract of farm land, described in the bill of complaint, and being the property described in said deed from Carrie E McDowell to Jennie D Fish, and also owned an undivided one-sixth interest in a 75 acre tract of her father's estate and also a mortgage of $3,000 00 on an undivided one sixth interest in said 75 acre tract, and no other property, that the 57 acre tract at that time was worth $9,975 00, and the undivided one-sixth interest in said 75 acre tract was worth $2,125 00 and the $3,000 00 mortgage was of the same value, making a total of not to exceed $4,250 00, interest in the 75 acres

That Carrie E McDowell was, on November 17, 1928, indebted to complainant on three notes, of the total principal of $7475 09, and to her sister, Jennie D Fish,

in the sum of $633 75, that the deed of conveyance was made for the 57 acres of land, described in the bill of complaint, to her sister, Jennie D Fish, but without her knowledge, that judgments were recovered by complainant in the Circuit Court of Vermilion county on December 28, 1928, against Carrie E McDowell for the sum of $5347 08, $266 68 and $2236 77, and costs, upon which executions were issued and delivered to the sheriff of Vermilion county and were returned by him "no property found subject to levy," and are good valid judgments and remain in full force and effect, not reversed, satisfied or vacated, that in two of the said judgments complainant recovered against the other defendants, namley, Ruvilla McDowell and F. M McDowell, who had no property subject to levy We are of the opinion that the findings of the master are in keeping with the weight of the testimony in the case

Appellant insists that, after making the deed in question, Carrie E McDowell among other properties had a sixty acre farm and although on September 25, 1928, she had conveyed the same to W A McDowell, yet she was the owner of the equitable title to said real estate, as shown by certain contracts in evidence This 60 acre tract was encumbered with a $6000 00 mortgage

Appellant also insists that the value of the property owned by Carrie E McDowell, after having made the deed in question, was greater than the amount shown by the report of the master Appellant also insists that Carrie E McDowell retained sufficient property to pay all of her debts The value of the land conveyed by her to her sister, Jennie D Fish, as found by the master, was $9975 00, and from the evidence it appears that at that time she was indebted to her sister in the sum of $633 75, and that, except as to said sum of $633 75, said conveyance was voluntary on the part of said Carrie E McDowell

When, as in this case, a bill in aid of an execution which alleges that the conveyance sought to be set aside was made after the debt due complainant was incurred, but before judgment, that the conveyence was a sham, made without consideration, with the intention of defrauding the complainant and other creditors, and that the grantee holds the property in trust for the grantor in order to prevent its sale on execution, states a good cause of action *Andrews* v *Donnerstag*, 171 Ill 329

The bill filed in this case is a bill in aid of an execution and is not a creditor's bill The only purpose of this bill was to remove a fraudulent conveyance out of the way of the executions

As was said by our Supreme Court, in the case of *Rice Co* v *McJohn,* 244 Ill 264 "There is a clearly recognized distinction between these two classes of creditor's bills Under a bill in aid of an execution, the creditor may proceed as soon as he obtains judgment and before execution has issued, while, on the other hand, before he may proceed under a creditor's bill proper, he must exhaust his remedy at law by obtaining judgment, execution, and the return of the execution *nulla bona,* or unsatisfied in whole or in part (*Miller* v *Davidson,* 3 Gilm 578, *Dawson* v *First Nat Bank,* 228 Ill 577) The relief afforded by a bill in aid of an execution is of a different character from that afforded by a creditor's bill Under the former the only relief granted is to set aside the encumbrances, or the conveyances therein specified, as fraudulent, while, under the latter, any equitable estate of the defendant may be reached "

In the case of *Wisconsin Granite Co* v *Gerrity,* 144 Ill 77, our Supreme Court said "As between the parties, the conveyances are undoubtedly good, but as to those existing creditors it is different If the effect of the conveyances was to hinder and delay them in the collection of their debts, then, as to such creditors the conveyances are fraudulent and of no effort "

It clearly appears from the evidence that Carrie E McDowell was indebted to the First National Bank of Sidell in the sum of $7475 00, principal, prior to the 17th day of November, 1928, and on that day she conveyed to her sister, Jennie D Fish, 57 acres of real estate which she owned, which was unencumbered, and that the same was worth $9975 00, and that the only consideration for said conveyance was a debt owing to the grantee in said deed of the sum of $633 75, and that, at said time, she was the owner of other property of the value of only $4250 00, except as to an equitable interest in a 60 acre tract of land that was encumbered by a mortgage of $6000 00, and her interest in which could not be reached by levy of an execution and sale

The conveyance of said 57 acres of land for such a grossly inadequate consideration, together with the fact that the property remaining in her possession, was not sufficient to pay the debts which she had contracted, together also with the fact, as shown by the evidence, that she was largely indebted to other per-

sons, would make this conveyance fraudulent as to such creditors irrespective of her intentions when she made such conveyance

In the case of *Kennard* v *Curran*, 239 Ill 122, the court said "Actual insolvency is not necessary to render a voluntary conveyance void If a person largely indebted makes a voluntary conveyance and shortly after becomes insolvent, such conveyance will be held fraudulent A voluntary conveyance is fraudulent as to existing creditors even though the grantor retains property apparently sufficient in value to satisfy all of his creditors when it results that the property retained is not, in fact, sufficient to discharge all of his liabilities *Marmon* v *Harwood*, 124 Ill 104, *Patterson* v *McKinney*, 97 Ill 41 "

Under the allegations contained in the bill and the facts as disclosed by the evidence, it was unnecessary to have executions issued and returned *nulla bona*, or unsatisfied in whole or in part, and also unnecessary to allege and prove the exhaustion of its legal remedy before filing of its bill, but it was authorized to file its bill as soon as it had recovered its judgment

The evidence discloses that Carrie E McDowell, at the time this conveyance was made, was largely indebted and owed complainant over $7000 00, and that the value of the property retained by her at the time this conveyance was made was less than $5000 00, and also discloses that, when the executions were issued, the sheriff was unable to find any property upon which to levy to make the amount of the judgments held by the First National Bank of Sidell, and that the 60 acre tract of land in which she had an equitable interest was deeded by the holder of the fee to satisfy a mortgage placed on the same by her, and it is therefore clear that such conveyance was fraudulent as to the creditors and that the decree of the circuit court should be affirmed

Affirmed.

(Seven pages in original opinion)

PUBLISHED IN ABSTRACT

The Farmers Bank of Mt Pulaski, Illinois, Plaintiff and Appellee, v John C Weckel, Defendant and Appellant

Appeal from Circuit Court of Logan County

JANUARY TERM, A D 1935 280 I.A. 632

Gen No 8880 **Agenda No 8**

MR JUSTICE DAVIS delivered the opinion of the Court

The Farmers National Bank, of Mt Pulaski, Illinois, plaintiff and appellee herein, obtained a judgment by confession in the Circuit court of Logan county, in vacation, after the January Term, A D 1932, of said court, against Edward O Weckel, John C Weckel and Helen D Weckel for the sum of $2,628 10 and costs of suit, said judgment having been entered by the clerk of said court upon being presented with a narr and cognovit and a note payable to appellee executed by said defendants upon which was written a warrant of attorney, said note being for the principal sum of $2800 00, and upon which there was then due the said sum of $2628 10

At the May term of said court said judgment was opened up upon motion of appellant, John C Weckel, and he was given leave to plead After the issues were settled by the court, said cause went to trial upon the declaration of the plaintiff, to which a plea of the general issue was interposed and a special plea which alleged, in substance, that said Edward O Weckel was principal and John C Weckel and Helen D Weckel were sureties upon said $2800 00 note, and that appellee agreed with said Edward O Weckel, if he would pay $570 00 on the principal of said note and give to said bank a new note, signed by him and his wife, and a chattel mortgage on certain chattels belonging to the said Edward O Weckel, said bank would surrender the original note of $2800 00, signed by John C Weckel, appellant, that said Edward O Weckel and his wife, Helen D Weckel, did give to said bank a chattel mortgage and note and make payment on the principal of said note on consideration of said promise and that therefor the promissory note sued upon was satisfied and appellant became discharged from all liability upon it, and upon the replications of appel

lee to said special plea of appellant, alleging, first, that said Edward O Weckel did not deliver to it the said chattel mortgage and promissory note in full satisfaction and discharge of the prior note, and, second, that appellee did not make any such agreement with the said Edward O Weckel as was described in said plea, and that Edward O Weckel did not deliver the new note and mortgage

Upon a trial of said cause the verdict of the jury was in favor of appellant, and upon a motion for a new trial the court set aside the verdict of the jury and awarded a new trial On the second trial of said cause the jury returned a verdict in favor of appellee, a motion for a new trial made by appellant was overruled, and the court entered a judgment upon the verdict, ordering that the judgment rendered in favor of plaintiff and against defendants in said cause on the 4th day of April, 1932, in the sum of $2628 10 and costs of suit be confirmed, and that said judgment originally entered stand and remain in full force and effect, of said date, as previously rendered, and that it have execution of the same, from which judgment appellant appealed

Edward O Weckel testified that he was a farmer living near Beason, Illinois, that he was indebted to the First National Bank, of Beason, and that sometime prior to July 19, 1929, said bank obtained a judgment against him in the sum of thirteen or fourteen hundred dollars, that he had been dealing with the Mt Pulaski bank for a number of years, and at that time was indebted to said bank in the sum of about $1400 00, that after he had been served with an execution on the judgment obtained by the First National Bank of Beason he went to George Volle, cashier of the Farmers National Bank of Mt Pulaski and informed him that the bank at Beason had taken a judgment against him, and asked the assistance of the Farmers National Bank of Mt Pulaski, Illinois, that the cashier, Volle, obtained a statement from him of the property that he owned, and asked him if he could get his brother, John C Weckel, to sign the note with him, that he said he did not think that he could as John had refused to sign notes for him before John C Weckel was a farmer living near Champaign and Volle told Edward O Weckel that he had to go to Champaign in a day or two and would take him along and they would see if they could get John to sign the note They made the trip to Champaign, and on their way he was left at John's home while Volle went on

into town, when Volle returned he asked John to sign the note, and John told him he would not do it as it was not fair to his own creditors to sign Edward's note, and Volle told him he was only asking him to sign it for moral support and on account of the ruling o fthe bank, and after that John signed the note

George Volle testified that when Edward O Weckel made application to him for help they talked the matter over and found that it would take $2800 00 to pay off the Beason Bank judgment and cover the existing indebtedness to the Mt Pulaski Bank He demanded security of Edward and suggested that he might get his brother, John C Weckel, to go on the note, he told Edward he would let him have the money if John would go on the note, Edward said he could not get over to see John, and he told him that he was going to Champaign the next day and he could ride with him, and that they went over, and he left Weckel out at John's place, and then came back from Champaign in the afternoon and stopped and talked to John about Edward having a judgment taken against him by the Beason Bank and that he would have to have some help, and Edward asked John if he would sign the note to help him out, and John said he would, and he took a note out of his pocket, and Edward Weckel and John signed it there, and Edward said he would have Helen, his wife, sign it, and John said, "Ed, you ought to have a chattel mortgage to help kind of protect me on that, on your stuff," and Ed told him "All right, I will do that, that is all right," and that then Edward put the note in his pocket to take home to his wife to sign and said he would bring it back to Mt Pulaski and make out a chattel mortgage Volle also testified that he did not say at any time to John that "It is just a moral support and on account of the bank ruling," that shortly after they were at John's place Edward Weckel came to Mt Pulaski and he made out a chattel mortgage, which was acknowledged by Weckel and mailed back to the bank

John C Weckel testified that George Volle came to his house and wanted him to sign a note, and I told him, "No, I could not sign a note on account of my creditors," and he said if I would sign a note it would just be for the moral support and for the bank ruling, and he would take a chattel mortgage against the note I then signed the note, which is marked Plaintiff's Exhibit 1

Edward O Weckel testified that nothing further was said about the note until after it became due At

that time he went into the bank with a grain check and paid the bank $570 00, which was applied upon the note, that at that time Volle wanted a new note made out, and said he would hold it for John to sign and he told him that John would not sign another note

The matter ran along until the next April, when Volle called him into the bank and told him, if he would give him a new chattel mortgage covering his half of the crop which he had planted, that he would take the new note and the chattel mortgage, signed by him and his wife, and deliver the old note to him, and that he gave the bank a new note, signed by his wife and himself, and the new chattel mortgage, and when he went to the bank to obtain the old note Volle refused to give him the note signed by John, but gave him the old chattel mortgage and a $100 00 note, and said to him, "No I am not going to give it back," and I told him that he said he would return it, and he said, "Well, I am going to keep it"

Volle testified that he saw John about October 15th, 1930, and told him that the chattel mortgage had about run out, that the 90 days extension would run out in a few days and something had to be done about it, that John said he guessed it didn't make much difference anyway, and I told him Edward was getting some more money he needed to finish his corn shucking John said that he would try and get his sister Lydie to loan the money to Edward to pay the note, and also that Edward would have some money coming to him from his mother's estate In his testimony Volle denied that John said in that conversation that "It would be unjust to my creditors I signed the last one just for moral support, he said it was a bank ruling"

John C Weckel testified that he did not say on July 19, 1929, that Edward Weckel should give him a chattel mortgage to protect him, and that he did not tell Volle that Edward would have money coming out of his mother's estate

Volle further testified that Edward said he would take the new chattel mortgage and note and have Helen and John sign them and send them back to us, and I told him that after they were properly signed I would give him the old note I told Edward I would return the $100 00 note, but I would have to hold the old note until John signed the new one, and Edward said, All right A couple of weeks after we received the new note Edward was in the bank and I gave him the $100 00 note and the old chattel mortgage, but he did not say "You haven't returned the old note" Nor do I remember his making a demand for it

We have only set forth enough of the evidence to show it is sharply conflicting on the issues raised by the pleadings.

Among the errors assigned by appellant were the following that the motion for the new trial should have been allowed, that the verdict is the result of prejudice and of sympathy for the plaintiff, that the court erred in admitting improper and incompetent evidence on the part of appellee, that the court gave improper instructions upon request of appellee

Appellant complains of the first instruction given on behalf of the plaintiff, which is an instruction as to the credibility of the witnesses, and tells the jury that if they believe that any witness has knowingly and wilfully testified falsely as to any material matter or thing in this case, that then they have the right to disregard the entire testimony of such witness, except in so far as such witness might be corroborated, etc It it not the law that the entire testimony of a witness may be disregarded by the jury upon the ground that the witness knowingly and wilfully testified falsely as to any material thing or matter in the case, but only when such witness has knowingly and wilfully sworn falsely as to some matter material to the issues A witness may have sworn falsely to a material matter or thing, and at the same time not have sworn falsely to a matter material to the issue If a witness has knowingly and wilfully sworn falsely to some matter or thing material to the issue ir the case, he has committed perjury and is, therefore, unworthy of belief

It was held in *Zbinden* v *DeMaulin,* 245 Ill App 248, that an instruction that omits the statutory requirement that the false testimony be in reference to "a matter material to the issues or point in question," or words of equivalent meaning, is erroneous, citing *Young* v *People,* 134 Ill 37-39

In the case of *Cope* v *Brentz,* 190 Ill App 504, this court held that an instruction which informed the jury if any witness has knowingly and wilfully testified falsely to any "material facts or allegations," was erroneous, that it should have been "any fact material to the issue " In the case of *McQuillon* v *Evans,* 353 Ill 239, the court said, in reference to an instruction "While the instruction should have been limited to any matter material to the issue, we can not see where the defendant was unduly prejudiced by the giving of this instruction "

While it is true that the Supreme court held in that case that by the giving of such instruction the defendant was not unduly prejudiced, yet in cases where the evidence is conflicting upon material questions of fact, unless the instructions given on behalf of the successful party state the law with accuracy and are free from errors calculated to mislead the jury, such instructions are very apt to be unduly prejudicial to the opposite party This instruction did not limit the matter or thing to which the jury might believe the witness knowingly and wilfully testified falsely, to some matter or thing material to the issue, and they were thus free to disregard the testimony of such witness, if they believed he testified falsely as to some material matter or thing, even though it were not material to the issue, and so was prejudicial

Appellant complains of the second instruction given on behalf of the plaintiff, which was as follows "The court instructs the jury as a matter of law that when a note is held by the payee under claim that such note belonged to the said holder, then the law presumes that such note, if held by and in the hands of the payee, is unpaid and the burden of proof is upon the defendant to prove by the preponderance of the evidence that such note has been paid or discharged, as explained in these instructions "

This instruction is inaccurate and misleading This suit was instituted for the recovery of the amount due on the note in question Appellant was one of the makers of the note, and in defense of the action a plea of payment was interposed, in addition to the general issue, and in order that the plaintiff establish a presumption that the note was unpaid and cast the burden of proof upon the defendant to prove payment, something more was necessary than that such note be held by the payee under claim that it belonged to such payee

In an action on a note, the execution of which is not denied, when the plaintiff presents his note signed by the defendant, payable to the order of plaintiff, and the same is admitted in evidence by the court, then there is established a presumption that he is the owner of the note and entitled to recover the amount it calls for and a prima facie case is made and the burden is then upon the defendant to establish his defense of payment, but such prima facie case is not established by simply showing that a payee is in possession of a note payable to himself under the claim that the note belonged to such holder

If it be admitted that under the facts stated in such instruction, the law raises a presumption that a note is unpaid, yet the facts stated would not establish a prima facie case in favor of the plaintiff, and such presumption would prevail only in the absence of proof, and this is the extent to which it would reach and it would not cast the burden upon the defendant to prove his defense of payment by a preponderance of the evidence Such presumption would not be evidence and it could not be weighed in the scale against the evidence Presumptions are never indulged in against established facts and are indulged in only to supply the place of facts, as soon as evidence is produced which is contrary to the presumption which arises before the contrary proof was offered, the presumption vanishes entirely *Weger* v *Robinson-Nash Motor Co*, 340 Ill 81-89

The evidence discloses that Edward O Weckel and his wife, Helen, after the maturity of the note on which this suit was brought, executed and delivered to appellee a note and chattel mortgage for the amount due upon such note, said Edward O Weckel testifying that said note and chattel mortgage were delivered to and accepted by appellee in payment of said note sued upon

When this testimony was introduced, any presumption of law that the note was unpaid, which may have been raised by the mere fact that the plaintiff was payee and the holder of the note, vanished and the jury should not have been instructed as to such presumption

An instruction to the jury as to what the presumption of law is upon a question of disputed fact should not be given as it is extremely liable to mislead the jury *Guardian M L Ins Co* v *Hogan*, 80 Ill 35, *The People* v *Cochran*, 313 Ill 508-524

Complaint is also made of the sixth instruction given on behalf of the plaintiff The instruction is as follows

"The court instructs the jury as a matter of law that the possession of the promissory note offered in evidence, in the hands of the plaintiff at the time it was filed in the circuit court of Logan county, is evidence that such note was at such time unpaid and such evidence will prevail unless the defendant has proven by a preponderance of the evidence in this case that the said promissory note was, at the time or prior thereto, paid and discharged by an accord and satisfaction entered into between plaintiff and Edward O Weckel"

The production of the note in court by the plaintiff, signed by the defendant, payable to the order of plaintiff, created a presumption that the note was unpaid and that the plaintiff was the owner of the same and entitled to recover the amount called for, and upon its admission in evidence by the court made a prima facie case, or such a case as entitled the plaintiff to a judgment in the absence of any defense on the part of the defendant

This presumption that the note was unpaid would only be indulged in to supply the place of facts, and it is not evidence, and cannot be weighed in the scale against evidence

When the plaintiff made out its prima facie case, the defendant having interposed a plea of payment, the burden was cast upon him to overcome such prima facie facts by proving by a preponderance of the evidence that said note was paid, and the jury in arriving at their verdict were at liberty to consider the fact that the note was in the possession of the plaintiff, together with all of the other evidence introduced on the question of payment, and it was error to instruct the jury that such possession was evidence and evidence that would prevail, as it was the province of the jury to determine the weight that should be given to the evidence It was error to single out and isolated portion of the evidence and direct the attention of the jury to it and tell them to consider it

It is also said that the instruction contains the legal terms, "accord and satisfaction" without any explanation to the jury as to the meaning of such terms It has been said that "Jurors are not learned in the law, and the court should never instruct them in legal phrases not understood by a layman, by which they would be confused and mislead " *People* v *Csontos*, 275 Ill 402 408

Objection is also made to instructions 3, 5 and 7, given on behalf of plaintiff While they may not be strictly accurate, yet we are of the opinion that the inaccuracies are not of such a nature as to be unduly prejudicial to appellant

Instruction 5 tells the jury that if they believe that appellee made an agreement to surrender the note sued upon in exchange for a new note to be signed by appellant and others, and if they believe that appellant did not sign any such note, that they will find for appellee

Appellant insists that on the facts in the case there was a question of waiver and that it should have been

fair trial and the jury should be free to render its verdict uninfluenced by any immaterial or prejudicial matter

The fact that Edward O Weckel may have filed a petition in bankruptcy and had been adjudged a bankrupt was not material to the issues, and it was prejudicial to the defendant to have plaintiff persist in trying to have such evidence admitted over the objection of the defendant and the adverse ruling of the court We express no opinion as to the merits of the case as it must be reversed and remanded for another trial on account of the errors pointed out

Reversed and remanded.

(Twelve pages in original opinion)

(47818—4 36) 14

STATE OF ILLINOIS

APPELLATE COURT

FOURTH DISTRICT

FEBRUARY TERM A. D. 1935

TERM NO. 13.

AGENDA NO 14.

NORMAN MacLEOD,
Plaintiff--Appellee,

vs.

. W. HARRIS,
Defendant--Appellant

Appeal from the Circuit Court of Madison County.

280 I.A. 635

TONE, J:

This is an appeal from the Circuit Court of Madison County. On he first day of August, 1930, the parties hereto, entered into an agreement by which defendant appellant sold to plaintiff appellee his dental usiness in the city of Alton together with all equipment, good will etc. he sum of $1000 was the consideration for such sale. In the agreement f sale the parties covenanted and agreed in part as follows: "Party the first part covenants and agrees that he will not resume the busi-ss of dentistry in Alton for a space of two years from the date of reement herein (August 1, 1930), and then after that should he engage the practise, in the city of Alton, he will limit his practise exclu-vely to the extraction of teeth for a period of five years from said te".

On March 8, 1933, plaintiff appellee filed his bill in chancery leging a violation of the aforesaid part of said agreement on the part defendant appellant, damage caused by such violation and irreparable jury if the said defendant appellant were not restrained from further olating said covenant. A temporary injunction was issued on said bill. is case was before us before on a judgment of the Circuit Court of dison County finding defendant appellant guilty of contempt of court by e violation of said temporary injunction by practising dentistry in olation of his covenant with plaintiff appellee and against the express der of the court. We there affirmed the judgment of the trial court nding defendant appellant guilty of contempt and sentencing him to enty days in the county jail. (279 Ill. App. 127.)

Defendant appellant answered the bill denying all the material allegations thereof, and afterwards filed a special plea alleging that plaintiff appellee ought not to maintain his suit because he did not come into court with clean hands by reason of the fact that other interests had entered into said suit and wickedly intermeddled therewith, with the view to promote litigation and to excite quarrels between the parties; that the conduct of defendant appellant and said other parties was contrary to the statute of the State of Illinois. This plea on motion of plaintiff appellee was stricken from the files.

Before the filing of the answer an amended answer to the bill and amended bill defendant appellant filed his demurrer to said bill which, upon hearing, was overruled.

A hearing on the merits was had before the chancellor on the amended bill and amended answer thereto. The chancellor found the issues 'or plaintiff appellee and made permanent the injunction theretofor issued. 'his prohibits defendant appellant from engaging in the practice of lentistry except the extraction of teeth until the first day of August, 937. Defendant appellant brings this case here and assigns as errors he action of the court in striking his special plea, the entering of he final decree and the refusal of the court to admit proper evidence ffered by defendant appellant.

We do not think the court erred in striking the special plea. Said plea states many conclusions of the pleader, none of which are supported by allegations of fact from which the court can see that the atters complained of come within the classes denounced by the statutes r the holdings on champerty, maintainance or barratry. On the contrary he case on the face of the pleading shows that plaintiff appellee ad a clear right to support such suit in event of the violation of his ontract. The evidence shows and it is admitted by defendant appellant hat he did violate the contract. It would be difficult to conceive f how one in the position of plaintiff appellee could violate a criminal tatute in instituting a lawsuit under the facts and circumstances involved in this case. When plaintiff appellee violated his contract as he evidence shows that he did, plaintiff appellee had a perfect right o proceed against him as he did to prevent further violations. The law learly recognizes the right to pursue litigation of this character. ven though other parties might have encouraged him or assisted him in

the assertion of his rights under the contract, we cannot see how those facts would take from plaintiff appellee his right to pursue his remedy upon a matter of a specific breach of a specific contract. Such holding would be stretching the unclean hands theory to an unreasonable degree.

That defendant appellant breached his contract is beyond question. He admits that he did and he has already been punished for his conduct in that regard. It requires no further evidence on that subject. That contracts of the character of the one in question have been upheld and the parties thereto protected by courts of equity requires no review. If the contracts are reasonable as to time and place and terms and manifest intention of the parties relying thereon, even though such contracts maybe in restraint of trade they have been held valid and an forcible in equity. TARR v. STEARMAN, 264 Ill. 110---ANDREWS v. KINGSBURG, 212 Ill. 97----RYAN v. HAMILTON, 205 Ill. 191.

The contract under examination is not of an unusual character. Plaintiff appellee moved to Alton to engage in the practise of his profession. He had opportunity to buy out and did buy out the business, good will etc., of defendant appellant. He paid a valuable consideration therefor. Part of the consideration moving to him was the agreement by defendant appellant that he would not practise dentistry as prescribed by their agreement above set out. The contract on its face was reasonable and fair and in equity and good conscience it should have been lived up to by the parties. Defendant appellant failed and refused to keep his part of the covenant. Plaintiff appellee had a clear right in equity to have further breaches of said agreement enjoined.

It is argued that the evidence does not show that plaintiff appellee was damaged by the breach of the contract in question. The law presumes damages from violation of a contract of this character. Plaintiff appellee had a right under his contract to be free from the competition in dentistry of defendant appellant. When that contract was violated plaintiff appellee was damaged. A right was taken away from him. He was given a competitor in the person of the one man who agreed not to be a competitor. Each time that defendant appellant engaged in the practise of dentistry in violation of his contract he deprived plaintiff appellee of the right to be in a position to be offered the dental work which defendant appellant had.

It is argued that the limit upon the contract in question ex-ires by virtue of its own language on August 1, 1935. We cannot agree ith that contention. The language is "He will not resume the practise f dentistry in Alton for a space of two years from the date of the greement herein (August 1, 1930.) and then after that should he engage n the practise in the city of Alton he will limit his practise exclu-ively to the extraction of teeth for a period of five years from said ate." Said date does not, in our judgment, refer to August 1, 1930, ut rather refers to the date that is understood by the words, "after hat", which would be five years from August 1, 1932 and therefore on ugust 1, 1937.

It follows that in our judgment the trial court decided all questions involved correctly and that such decision and decree should e and it is hereby affirmed.

JUDGMENT AFFIRMED.

Not to be published in full.

[redacted] - Ill Unpublished O...

16

STATE OF ILLINOIS,
APPELLATE COURT,
FOURTH DISTRICT.

February Term, 1935.
Agenda 16.

280 I.A. 634

Gus Pahlman, Appellant, vs. The People, etc., at the Relation of Ida Wilson, Appellee.	)	Writ of Error to County Court of Randolph County.

EDWARDS, P. J.

This proceeding is to review a judgment of the county court of Randolph County, wherein Gus Pahlman, appellant, was adjudged to be the father of a bastard child. The sole ground urged for reversal is that the trial court failed to cause an issue to be made up, preceding the trial, as to whether appellant was the father of such child, in conformity with Sec. 4, Ch. 17, Smith-Hurd R. S., which section in substance requires that the court shall, at the time appointed for appearance and answer, cause an issue to be made up, whether the person charged is the real father of the child or not.

The record discloses that no formal issue was in fact made. It, however, shows that both parties, when the case was called, announced themselves ready for trial, that the trial proceeded, the jury were instructed, and later returned a verdict as follows "We the jury find that Gus Pahlman is the father of the bastard child of Ida Wilson," and that subsequent to the overruling of a motion for a new trial, judgment

was rendered on the verdict.

It thus appears that when the case was called for trial, appellant did not offer any objection to proceeding without a formal issue being made of record, nor did he question the jurisdiction of the court to enter upon the hearing under the circumstances, but participated in the trial as though there had been a formal joinder of issue.

The law is well settled in this state that a proceeding under the Bastardy Statutes, though criminal in form, is in fact a civil action. Rawlings v. The People, 102 Ill., 475, McCoy v. The People, 71 Ill., 111. That being such, the defendant may waive irregularities in process or procedure, and that going to trial, on the merits, amounts to such waiver; as held by this court in Rose v. The People, 81 Ill. App., 128.

The courts of Illinois have many times passed upon the effect of proceeding to trial in civil actions without the formation of, or a joinder in issue. In Devine v. Chicago City Ry. Co., 237 Ill., 278, the court said, at page 280: "We have also held that if the parties appear and go to trial without a plea being put in, it is such an irregularity as will be held waived and cured by the verdict under the Statute of Amendments."

The rule is stated to be, in Leroy State Bank v. Keenan's Bank, 337 Ill., 173, on page 193: "Where a party to a suit at law goes to trial the same as though the case was at issue, although the only pleadings are the declaration and a general and special demurrer, which are undisposed of and upon which no issue is joined, the error is waived, and the objection cannot be raised for the first time in a court of review."

In Loomis v. Riley, 24 Ill., 307, it is declared that where the parties proceed to trial without a formal issue being joined of record, they will be held to have consented to try the case as though the general

issue had been pleaded.

Section 7 of the Statute of Wills provides that when a bill is filed to contest the validity of any will which has been admitted to probate, "an issue at law shall be made up whether the writing produced be the will of the testator or testatrix or not, which shall be tried by a jury."

Godfrey v. Phillips, 209 Ill., 584, was a suit to set aside a will. No formal issue was made up as required by the statute; the parties went to trial without objection on such ground, and afterwards claimed it as error. The court said, on page 589: "It is urged that the court did not make up any issue at law to be submitted to the jury. Such an issue would have been, whether the instrument of September, 1900, was the last will and testament of Elizabeth Housh, and the objection is, that it was not formally, by decree, submitted to the determination of a jury. This is the precise question which was tried by the jury. It was the only issue presented by the bill and answer. No other issue could have been made up, and as appellants did not make this objection before entering upon the trial, where it could have been readily obviated, we will not consider it now."

Such situation was analagous to the instant case. The statute required the making up of an issue. The jury tried and decided the one and only possible issue, just as in this proceeding, also, no objection was made before commencing the trial, the same as here, when, if such objection had been made, the required issue could have been formed, as it manifestly would have been had appellant seen fit to urge same in time. He, however, chose to waive the irregularity and consented to trial, where the jury answered, in the affirmative, the only issue which could have been submitted to them under the statute. Within the rule, and for the reasons, stated in the authorities cited, we are of opinion that he is

now in no position to complain of the court's failure to make up the formal statutory issue.

Appellant relies upon The People v. Woodside, 72 Ill., 407, as an authority supporting his contention, a careful reading of which will disclose that a different question was involved than the one here presented. We do not regard the decision as applicable to this case.

For the reasons stated the judgment will be affirmed.

Judgment affirmed.

Not to be published in full.

STATE OF ILLINOIS

APPELLATE COURT

FOURTH DISTRICT

FEBRUARY TERM, A. D. 1935

Term No. 6 Agenda No. 9

LOUIS J. HERTEL, Trustee,
Plaintiff and Appellee,

vs.

SARAH A. REBHAN,
Defendant and Appellant,

GEORGE McCORMICK and FLOYD MARTIN,
Defendants and Appellees.

280 I.A. 634[5]

Bill to Foreclose Mortgage and for Receiver.

Appeal from the Circuit Court of St. Clair County.

Murphy, J:

June 15, 1928, Edward L. Rebhan and Sarah A. Rebhan, his wife, executed a note for $1600, payable to Walter J. Ruediger, trustee, due three years after date, and, on the same date, executed a mortgage purporting to secure the note, with Ruediger named as trustee. Within a year, Edward L. Rebhan died and by will, devised the property covered by the mortgage to Sarah A. Rebhan.

Louis J. Hertel, trustee, herein referred to as plaintiff, filed his suit against Sarah A. Rebhan, herein referred to as defendant, to foreclose the mortgage.

The complaint contains the usual averments of a complaint for the foreclosure of a mortgage. The allegations which are material to consider the points raised on this record are that the Rebhans became and were on the date of said note indebted to Walter J. Ruediger, trustee, in the sum of $1600 for money loaned and, being so indebted, made, executed and delivered

to Ruediger, trustee, the note and mortgage in question, that on the 9th day of July, 1928, for a valuable consideration, paid by the plaintiff, Ruediger executed and delivered to the plaintiff, a written instrument assigning to the plaintiff the mortgage, that the assignment was filed for record in the recorder's office of that county. It is alleged that at the same time and place that the mortgage was assigned, Ruediger undertook to assign the note to the plaintiff by indorsement on the back thereof but that by mistake the name of the plaintiff as assignee was not written in said indorsement but that instead thereof, Ruediger wrote his own name as assignee therein. It is alleged that since said assignment, plaintiff has been and still is the owner and holder of the note and mortgage.

Defendant filed an answer, denying that she and Edward L. Rebhan were indebted to Ruediger in any amount, alleges that the note and mortgage were executed and delivered to Ruediger without consideration and that they were executed and delivered to Ruediger for the purpose of raising money to pay a note of the Rebhans then owned by one William Schwartz. The Schwartz note was for the sum of $1600 and secured by mortgage on the same real estate described in the mortgage which is the subject of foreclosure in this suit, that Ruediger sold and assigned the note which had been delivered to him, embezzled the money derived from the sale of the note and failed to pay the Schwartz note, admits that the mortgage in this case was executed to secure the note described in the bill, admits that the mortgage instrument was assigned to the plaintiff but denys that the note was indorsed as required by statute to transfer legal title to plaintiff, denys that Ruediger's failure to make proper indorsement on the note was a mistake and avers that Ruediger is the owner of the note by indorsement and is a necessary party to the suit.

A decree was entered in accordance with a prayer of the bill and defendant Sarah A. Rebhan perfected her appeal to this court. As grounds for reversal of the decree, she urges that neither she nor her husband were indebted to Ruediger at the time of the execution and delivery of the note to him, that the note in question was never indorsed to plaintiff and that he has no right to foreclose this mortgage, that the indorsement on the note was not made by mistake and if it was a mistake, the decree did not undertake to correct the mistake, that defendant signed the note in the capacity of surety for her husband and that she is now discharged as such, that the plaintiff did not file his claim in the probate court against the estate of Edward L. Rebhan and that by virtue of the statute there can be no personal liability against said defendant on the note since the assets of the estate of said deceased was sufficient to pay said note in full.

The evidence shows that the Rebhans were indebted to William Schwartz on a note for $1500. The record discloses that the defendant by her answer and on cross-examination testified that the note and mortgage in question were executed and delivered to Ruediger so that he could dispose of the note and to enable Ruediger to pass title to the instruments when sale had been made, the defendant and her husband named him as payee and mortgagee and this together with the possession of the instruments and the authority given him clothed him with full power to make the sale and indorse the note as their agent. What Ruediger did in the sale and transfer of the instruments to plaintiff was within the scope of his agency and his dealings in the matter are as binding on the defendant as though she had transacted the business for herself. It is conceded that Ruediger sold the note and mortgage to plaintiff, collected the sale price and instead of using the proceeds for the payment of the

Rebhan note held by Schwartz, he applied it to his own personal use. This defalcation was by the agent of the defendant and plaintiff is in no wise liable for the loss. Defendant executed the mortgage containing a description of the note and a covenant to pay the same. Having negotiated the note and mortgage to plaintiff, she cannot now come into a court of equity and defend against the same on the grounds that she was not indebted to Ruediger when the note was given or that it is without consideration.

The contention is made that the indorsement in the note was not sufficient to pass the legal and equitable title to the plaintiff. Plaintiff testified that he had held the possession of the note since the date of the assignment of the mortgage to him in 1926; that he had paid Ruediger the purchase price of the note.

In Collins v. Ogden, 323 Ill. 594, 604, the court said, "It must be regarded as the settled law in this State that while an equitable interest in negotiable instruments payable to order may be acquired either by gift or contract without indorsement by the payee, the mere possession of negotiable securities payable to order and not indorsed by the payee, or if indorsed specially, not indorsed by the special indorsee, is not alone evidence of title, either legal or equitable, in the possessor, but the burden of proof is on the possessor to prove his equitable title by showing a delivery to him with the intent to pass title". We find that the evidence in this case is amply sufficient to prove that this note was delivered to plaintiff with the intent to pass title.

Defendant's contention that plaintiff's claim should have been filed against the estate of Edward L. Rebhan is without merit. In Waughop v. Bartlett, 165 Ill. 124, 129, the court said," The right of action of the mortgagee or legal

holder of a note is independent of the remedy given him by filing his claim in the probate court, and a failure to so present his claim in the probate court within two years will not of itself, bar a right of foreclosure of a note and mortgage not otherwise barred. Such a proceeding is not one against an estate nor is it one in personam. It is in the nature of a proceeding in rem to endorce certain security specially set apart for the indemnity of the holder of the note. In Karnes v. Harper, 48 Ill. 527, it is said (p.529) "In a proceeding to foreclose a mortgage in chancery the decree ascertains the sum due and orders the sale of the specific property for its satisfaction. It is in the nature of a decree in rem".

To sustain defendant's contentions would be to relieve her from the losses caused by the defalcations of her agent, Ruediger, and cast them upon the plaintiff. Under the evidence in this case, that would be unjust and inequitable. If, for no other reason, the decree in this case should be sustained under the application of the equitable rule that where one of two persons must suffer for the acts of a third, he who made it possible for such loss to occur must stand the consequences of the unlawful act of such third party.

Defendant further contends that there is such a variance between plaintiff's pleadings and proof that to sustain the decree, the pleadings would first have to be amended, is without merit.

The decree of the circuit court is affirmed.

Decree Affirmed.

Not to be published in full

STATE OF ILLINOIS

APPELLATE COURT

FOURTH DISTRICT

FEBRUARY TERM, A. D. 1935

Term No. 17 | Agenda No. 3

ST. CLAIR LOAN COMPANY, INC.
Plaintiff below, Appellant,

vs.

ELBERT PRITCHETT,
Defendant below, Appellee.

280 I.A. 635

APPEAL FROM THE
COUNTY COURT OF
WILLIAMSON COUNTY

Murphy, J:

This case was tried in the County Court of Williamson County on an appeal from a Justice of Peace The evidence shows that Clarence McNeish did on the 27th day of April, 1933, execute a note for $220, payable to Limerick Loan and Finance Company. This was the trade name under which G. L. Limerick was doing business. The note was payable in installments of $18.66, beginning on the 27th day of May following and each month thereafter, with interest thereon On the same date, McNeish secured the payment of the note by a chattel mortgage on a Ford truck. The mortgage was duly acknowledged and filed for record in the recorder's office of Williamson County, that being McNeish's residence. November 18, 1933, Limerick sold the note and mortgage to the appellant herein and it gave its check in payment therefor. G. L. Limerick indorsed the note without recourse to appellant on the same date. An assignment of the contract without recourse was indorsed upon the face of the mortgage.

March 19, 1934, appellant instituted in the justice court its replevin suit and seized the truck from appellee. Appellee was a constable of that county and was holding the truck by virtue of an execution issued by a Justice of Peace on a judgment against McNeish. The date of the judgment was January 12, 1934. The execution on which the sale was held was dated February 2, 1934. Appellant secured a judgment in the justice court but on a trial by jury in the county court, a verdict was returned in favor of appellee. Judgment was entered on the verdict.

The record, as filed in this court, does not show that the note, which the mortgage in question was given to secure, contained a notation that it was secured by chattel mortgage. Appellant's abstract did not abstract the note in full and made no reference to such a notation. February 18, 1935, appellee filed his brief and argument in this court in which he contends that the note did not bear the notation that it was secured by a chattel mortgage and that therefore it was void in the hands of an assignee. Four days thereafter, appellant obtained leave of this court to file its motion for diminution of record and attached three affidavits, one of them being the affidavit of the attorney for appellant. Each affiant avers that he saw the note introduced in evidence at the trial and that on the left end of the note was the indorsement "this note is secured by chattel mortgage" and attached to each affidavit is a printed form of a blank note, which each affiant swears is a copy of the note introduced in evidence. The affidavit of appellant's attorney states that some interested party, to affiant unknown, secured the note when it was in the office of the clerk of the county court and removed the notation on

the left end, that it was done subsequent to its admission in evidence and prior to the time it was copied into this record.

When appellant offered the note in evidence, the attorney for appellee announced that he had "no objection". It would appear that if the notation was not on the note at the time it was introduced in evidence, that appellee's attorney would have urged that, as an objection to its admission. For the purpose of this case, we need not determine how or by whom the notation was removed from the note, but, on this record, we are convinced that the notation was on the note at the time it was introduced in evidence in the trial court and we will treat the case as though it appeared in the record.

Appellee contends that there is no evidence proving the assignment of the note and mortgage to appellant prior to the institution of the suit. On the trial, appellant offered the note and mortgage in evidence and appellee made no objection to its introduction. Each of said instruments had an indorsement by the mortgagee Limerick to appellant. The evidence is that the indorsement on the note and the assignment on the mortgage was made November 18, 19[illegible] Appellant bought the note and mortgage from Limerick and paid for it by check. The date of the check is November 17, 19[illegible] Under this evidence, it is clear that the note and mortgage was assigned to appellant prior to the institution of the suit.

It is contended by appellee that there was no proof of demand made by appellant before the institution of the suit. The evidence is that the representatives of appellant presented the mortgage to appellee and demanded possession of the truck to which appellee replied that it was all over, that they had sold the truck.

In Kee & Chapell Co. v. Pennsylvania Co., 291 Ill. 248, a witness had testified that he had gone to the freight agent of appellant and told him there was a car-load of milk bottles going away which belonged to appellee and that he was going to take those bottles out, to which the reply was made that if he took them, he would have to do so legally. The court on page 255 said, "Even though this be considered not sufficient as a demand, it is sufficient to show that a demand would have been unavailing and therefore unnecessary, as the effect of appellant's statement was that it would not surrender the property without a writ being issued. While demand is usually necessary where the defendant comes into possession of the goods rightfully, yet where the circumstances show that demand would be unavailing such demand is not necessary. Cranz v. Kroger, 22 Ill. 74, Johnson v. Howe, 2 Gilm. 342." The instant case is controlled by the rule announced in the cited case.

Appellee contends that there was no proof that the note and mortgage were in default and that there is no proof that appellant acted under the insecurity clause of the mortgage. The evidence shows that the note and mortgage were past due had the monthly payments been made, as provided in the note and mortgage, it would not have been past due, therefore, under the evidence that it was past due, the reasonable conclusion is that there had been default in the payments. In addition, there is evidence that appellant notified appellee of its mortgage claim before appellee held the execution sale. Under this state of the record, there is ample proof that the debt was due. Even if it was not due,

appellant was warranted in seizing the truck under the insecurity clause in the mortgage.

Under the evidence in this case, the court erred in not directing a verdict for appellant.

The judgment of the lower court is reversed and the order will be entered by the clerk of this court that appellant shall have and recover of appellee the Ford truck as described in said mortgage instrument.

Judgment of the lower court is
reversed and judgment here.

Not to be published in full.

STATE OF ILLINOIS

APPELLATE COURT

FOURTH DISTRICT

FEBRUARY TERM, A. D. 1935

Term No. 19

Agenda No 18

ALBERT JONES,
Plaintiff-Appellee,

vs.

STONEWARE PIPE COMPANY,
A Corporation,
Defendant-Appellant.

APPEAL FROM THE
CITY COURT OF THE
CITY OF ALTON,
ILLINOIS.

280 I.A. 635[2]

Murphy, J:

In 1895, appellee was in the employ of appellant at its factory, where it was engaged in the manufacture of vitrified tile and pipe. In the course of his employment, appellee sustained an injury, resulting in the loss of his right hand above the wrist. He made a claim for damages and in December 24, 1895, the parties entered into a contract undertaking to settle and adjust appellee's claim. The contract is the subject matter of this litigation. This case was before this court at a previous term and we then reversed a judgment in favor of appellee and remanded the cause. 277 Ill. App. 18. Upon a retrial, the jury returned a verdict for appellee for $2000 and judgment was entered on the verdict.

When the case was here on the previous appeal, appellant sought a construction of the contract, which was inconsistent with the theory upon which it had tried the case and we held that its contention on construction was not available on appeal Other errors were assigned which were sustained.

One of the errors assigned is the court's refusal to give certain instructions and the correctness of the court's ruling in that regard is to be determined by the

construction given the contract.

The contract, after setting forth the date of appellee's injury and his claim for damages, provided that in consideration of his right of action to recover damages "the said Stoneware Pipe Company has agreed and hereby does agree to retain and keep the said party of the second part in its employ so long as the said party of the second part desires to remain in its employ, and to pay him for his services at the rate of not less than two dollars and fifty cents per day, of ten hours each, the said wages to be paid for the time the said party of the second part may be actually employed, * * * it being the understanding by this agreement that said party of the second part shall have and retain his position with said company so long as such employment is desired by him, and he is able to perform his proper duties, and that said party of the first part shall not have the right or power to discharge him or dispense with his services, except as hereinabove stated", which is referred to herein as paragraph one. This contract contained the further provision which is material here, "The said party of the first part also agrees that in case it, the said Stoneware Pipe Company, should at any time within ten (10) years from this date make an assignment for the benefit of its creditors, or be or become insolvent, or should it for an indefinite period shut down its works (it being understood that the term "indefinite period" shall not be taken to mean a shut down for the purpose of making necessary repairs in said plant or something of like character, but shall refer only to a general or complete shut down brought about by a combination with other parties or through outside causes), then in the event of any one of the above causes,

the said party of the second part shall have, and it is hereby expressly stipulated that he will have, a legal and subsisting claim against said company for a definite and certain sum to be fixed as follows That is to say, he shall be paid and shall receive the sum of four hundred and fifty dollars ($450.00) for each unexpired year of said term of ten years, for example, should said company make an assignment or should shut down its works at the expiration of one year from this date, or thereabouts, then the said party of the second part shall have a claim against said company for the sum of four thousand and fifty dollars, if at the expiration of two years then he shall have a claim for the sum of thirty-six hundred dollars, and so on in like manner, decreasing at the rate of four hundred and fifty dollars each year until the expiration of ten years aforesaid, after which time the said party of the second part shall have the right and the right only on continuous employment at the rate of two dollars and fifty cents per day.", which is referred to as paragraph two.

After the execution of the contract in 1895, the parties entered upon the performance of the same and it does not appear that any controversy arose over any of its terms or kind of employment appellee was to be given until appellant discharged appellee in 1931, when, by reason of the general economic condition in the country, it closed its plant. It has been closed since, except for the months of May, June and July, 1934, when the factory was operated and appellee was given employment for that period in accordance with the contract.

It is appellant's contention that the contract did not give appellee any right of employment while its plant

was closed for "outside causes", such as the general economic conditions. It is conceded that when appellant begins operating its plant that appellee could under the provisions of the contract be entitled to re-employment.

On the former appeal, we held that the contract was based upon a release of damages by plaintiff, that such release furnished a valid and sufficient consideration and that such contract is in the nature of a contract for permanent employment. It is proper for the court to take into consideration the surrounding circumstances and to place itself in so far as may be possible in the same situation as the parties who made the contract, so that it may view the circumstances as they viewed them and so it may judge the meaning of the words and their application to the things described as the parties judged and applied them. But, this does not give either party the right to establish a different contract from that expressed in the written agreement. Armstrong Paint Works v. Can Co., 301 Ill. 102. It is to be presumed that the parties introduced into the contract every material item and term and in construing it, the court will not add thereto another term about which the agreement is silent. Decatur Lumber Co. v. Crail, 350 Ill. 319, Sterling-Midland Coal Co. v. Coal Co., 334 Ill. 281 A provision in a contract cannot be given effect when the court is left to ascertain the intention of the parties upon such provisions by mere conjecture or guess. Woods v. Evans, 113 Ill 186 "The motives and intentions of the parties can only be known from the writing to which the contract is reduced, and no assumption which is contrary to the language used therein can be based upon any external consideration (Emerich Outfitting Co v. Siegel, Cooper & Co., 237 Ill. 610) The intention must be determined

from the language used in the instrument and not from any surmise that the parties used in the language to express an intention or meaning they had in mind but failed to express and if they have overlooked a condition which they would perhaps have provided for, if it had occurred to them, the court cannot guess at the provision they would probably have made and by construction read it into the instrument on the presumption that they would naturally have made such provision if they had thought of it." Green v. Ashland State Bank, 346 Ill. 174

In paragraph one, the term employment is to be "so long as the said party of the second part (appellee) desires to remain in its employ". The latter part of paragraph one provides, "it being the understanding by this agreement that said party of the second part (appellee) shall have and retain his position with said company so long as such employment is desired by him and he is able to perform his proper duties". These paragraphs are broad as to point of time the employment was to continue and the services to be rendered by appellee.

The evidence shows that at the time the contract was made, appellee was employed as a foreman, and appellant now contends that the contract should be construed as giving appellee the right only to be employed as foreman and since outside causes have prevented appellant from operating its factory that there has been no work as foreman for appellee, and, that he does not have a claim for damages in this case. This contract cannot be construed as giving appellee the right to be employed at any particular work and cannot be construed as limiting the work of appellee to that which he was doing at the time of the making of the contract. There were many different kinds of employment in plaintiff's factory and for the court to say that when the contract was drawn it was intended to limit the employment of appellee to the work at which he was then engaged

would be for this court to read something into the contract that the parties had not agreed upon. It is contended that the words "as heretofore" following the sentence "his said wages to be paid for the time the said party of the second part may be actually employed" refers to the kind of employment. We are of the opinion that the words "as heretofore" should be construed as referring to the payment of wages and not to previous employment.

Our construction of paragraph two which made provision for conditions therein named happening within ten years from contract date, has no application since the ten year period has long since expired. The language used at the conclusion of the paragraph "decreasing (that is the annual payment) at the rate of fifty dollars each year until the expiration of ten years aforesaid after which time the said party of the second part shall have the right and the right only of continuous employment at the rate of two dollars and fifty cents per day" should be construed as referring to employment after the expiration of the ten year period provided for in said paragraph two. The words "after which time" refers to the ten year period.

There was no error in the construction given the contract by the trial court and its refusal of appellant's instruction is sustained.

The final contention of appellant is that even though the contract should be construed as giving appellee a right to claim employment during the period when appellant's plant was closed, yet the verdict cannot be sustained for the reason that he has not proved by a preponderance of the evidence that he was able to perform the duties it had for him to perform. The only work appellant had during the period the factory was closed was of a general nature, such as caring for and handling horses, cutting weeds, laying brick in walks, loading and unload-

ing tile, moving debris, and night watchman Plaintiff testified that he could hitch and care for horses, guard premises, use a fire extinguisher, lay brick walks, use a scythe in cutting weeds and other similar labor He is corroborated by witnesses who saw him do such labor but the labor they observed him do was of short duration Appellant's witnesses testified that he could not perform labor such as appellant had for appellee to do This presented a question of fact for the jury and we cannot say as a matter of law that the verdict was not warranted by the evidence.

For the reasons assigned, the judgment of the lower court is affirmed

Judgment affirmed.

Not to be published in full.

70

STATE OF ILLINOIS

APPELLATE COURT

FOURTH DISTRICT.

MAY TERM A D.1935.

TERM NO 4

AGENDA NO. 8

280 I.A. 635[3]

MARY GRINDROD,
Plaintiff and Appellee
vs
WILLIAM E. KNOWLES,
Defendant and Appellant,

and

CORA B. KNOWLES, His Wife, AMOS MOOTRY and FORREST STANCEL,
Defendants and Appellees
and
MARY GRINDROD,
Plaintiff and Appellee
vs
WILLIAM E. KNOWLES,
Defendant and Appellant
and
CORA B. KNOWLES, His Wife, and JOHN HEILIG,
Defendants and Appellees
(Consolidated)

In Equity
No. 5970
(Foreclosure.)

Appeal from the Circuit Court of St. Clair County.

In Equity.
No. 5971
(Foreclosure)

STONE, J., In this case there are errors assigned and the Court's attention is called to proof so supporting such assignments that in the state of the record we feel warranted in reversing this case. The Appellee has made no attempt to answer these assignments, or to show any reason of any kind or character why the case should not be reversed. Appellee in that respect is in violation of the rules of this Court, and the cause should be reversed for that reason alone. We do not regard it as our duty to argue the cause of Appellee for her.

The decree is, therefore, reversed, and the cause is remanded to the Circuit Court of St. Clair County with instructions to that Court to dismiss the bill for want of equity

REVERSED AND REMANDED WITH DIRECTIONS

Not to be published in full

STATE OF ILLINOIS

APPELLATE COURT

FOURTH DISTRICT

FEBRUARY TERM A. D. 1935

TERM NO. 18. AGENDA NO. 17.

280 I.A. 635

LYNE ALLEN, Plaintiff-Appellee, vs. RAYMOND F. MOORE, Defendant-Appellant,	Appeal from the City Court of East St. Louis, Illinois.

TONE, J:

This is an appeal from the City Court of East St. Louis. It s from a judgment of the City Court in the sum of $2500.00 as damages or personal injuries received by Appellee on the night of May 29th, 933. The injuries were received by her about midnight of said night, n State Street in East St. Louis, while she was a guest in the automobile f Appellant. Riding with the parties to this suit at that time was nother couple. They were all riding in a one-seated car. The complaint lleges that Appellant wantonly and recklessly permitted the said utomobile to run off the public highway and strike a telephone post, hereby injuring the plaintiff, secondly, that the defendant was not ooking in the direction he was traveling and was not watching the road nd in all respects operated his said motor vehicle in a wanton and reck-ess manner, showing an utter disregard for the safety of others under ircumstances liable to cause great bodily injury, and did therby cause uch injury to Appellee in violation of the Statute.

The answer to the complaint denies all the material allegations. fter the evidence was heard an amended complaint was filed alleging ll the things alleged in the original complaint and in addition alleging hat Appellant at the time and place in question was driving his said otor vehicle upon the said public highway, passing through the closely uilt up portion of the said City of East St. Louis, at a rate of speed

reatly in excess of fifteen miles an hour, to wit, at the rate of forty-ive miles an hour, in utter disregard of the traffic and use of the way, nd so as to endanger the life and limb of others and so forth. No nswer was made to this amended complaint.

It is alleged by Appellant that the above amended complaint oes not state a cause of action by reason of the fact that there is no harge of wanton and wilful negligence in said complaint and that a guest n the position that Appellee was in cannot recover without such charge nd the proof supporting it.

The charge in the complaint uses the expression that the Statute ses in the proviso of the section providing for damages to guests. The ord "wilful" is not used. However, our courts, both Supreme and Appell-te, have so ofter held that wanton and wilful are to be used inter-hangeably in allegations in this class of cases, that it may be said o be the established rule of this State at this time. (Streeter vs. mrichouse, 357 Ill., 234., Ames vs. Armour & Company, 257 Ill. App. 449.)

In the latter case on page 457 the court said: "Defendant eeks to avoid liability upon the theory that the charge in the additional ounts of reckless and wanton conduct was not a charge of willful and anton conduct. We think that this is the refinement of distinction and at the charge of reckless and wanton conduct was tantamount to a charge willful and wanton conduct."

So it seems to us that the claim that the complaint is faulty the extent of not stating a cause of action, is not well taken, even it could be considered for the first time on appeal.

It is next urged that even though the complaint states a cause action, the evidence does not support the complaint or does not justify finding of wantonness and wilfulness on the part of Appellant which oduced the injuries to Appellee. Each case of this character must st upon its own facts, and when submitted to a jury the question is a estion of fact for the jury. This case was tried without a jury. such cases the finding of the Trial Court is entitled to the same ight by an Appellate Tribunal as if the facts had been found by a jury. oore vs. Molloy Company, 222 Ill. App. 295, Fisk vs. Hopping 169 Ill. 5, and Field vs. Chicago & R I Co., 71 Ill. 458.).

So the question before this court is whether or not the finding nd judgment of the Court are against the manifest weight of the evidence. f it is not, we may not disturb it.

In this case the evidence is uncontradicted that Appellant as riding with three passengers in a one-seated car; that it was on tate Street in the City of East St. Louis at midnight, a closely uilt up section of the City; that he started from the point from which e did start, in one direction, made a "U" turn and came back the other ay; that after that according to his own statement he was driving at the ate of forty-five miles an hour; that part of the time he was not watching in front of hi , but had his head turned looking and talking to the eople who were situated in the car; that when the crash came he made no ffort to use his brakes, that his car at this rate of speed traveled rom the west side of State Street across the slab it was on, across a treet car track in the middle of the street, across the other slab, and ff of the road and into a telephone pole, without any effort on his art to try to prevent injury. The facts indicate very strongly that ppellant was driving his car in such a manner as to be considered in tter disregard of the safety of the people whose safety he had assumed.

The trial judge saw the witnesses and heard them testify. He as in a better position to judge from the evidence how serious Appellant's ffense was under the circumstances. He has found and so ordered that ppellant at the time and place in question was acting in wanton and wil- il disregard of the life and limb of others. We cannot say that his nding was against the manifest weight of the evidence.

Appellant raises the theory of immenent peril. There is no ich condition shown by this record except that which Appellant created.

Appellee was seriously injured. No complaint is made that the idgment of the court is excessive. We find no error in the record. e judgment of the City Court of East St. Louis is affirmed.

JUDGMENT AFFIRMED.

Not to be published in full.

vs.) of Wayne County.

ALFRED A. SMITH,)

Appellant) 280 I.A. 636

STONE, J:

This suit was originally brought before a Justice of the Peace against Alfred A. Smith and Marshall Smith for damages for cutting 435 hedge trees off the land of the plaintiffs by the defendants. Judgment was rendered by the Justice in favor of plaintiffs for $391.50, April 22, 1933. From this judgment an appeal was taken by the defendants to the Circuit Court of Wayne County. A trial was had in said Circuit Court and the jury returned a verdict in favor of plaintiffs and against Alfred A. Smith for $400. Motions for new trial in arrest of judgment and for judgment notwithstanding the verdict were made and each was overruled.

Appellant brings the case to this court on appeal and assigns as errors the admission of improper testimony; the refusal of proper testimony; the denial of the various motions, the refusal of instructions offered by appellant and that the judgment is contrary to the law and evidence.

In 1875, Benjamine Jelley, being the owner of the North-east Quarter of the South-west Quarter of Section Sixteen (16), Town One (1) South, Range Seven (7) East of the Third Principal Meridian, in Wayne County, Illinois, set out a hedge fence row, on the same, some three or four feet east of the west line of this forty acre tract. One Kate Wolfe, at that time, owned the forty acre tract immediately west of Mr. Jelley's forty acres in the same section. In 1880 or 1881, J. C. Gilliland acquired title to the Wolfe forty acres

n 1889, conveyed it to appellant. Appellant has owned this forty cres of land eyer since. The appellees own the Benjamine Jelley forty cres, having acquired the same by descent from Mr. Jelley, their grand_ ather.

There was a rail fence on the west line of Mr. Jelley's forty cre tract, between the Wolfe forty acres and Mr. Jelley's forty acres ; the time the hedge fence row was set out by Mr. Jelley. The hedge ow was set out on Mr. Jelley's land far enough east from this rail ence, that he could plow and cultivate his hedge between the rail fence d the hedge row with a single horse and plow.

It is stipulated by counsel for the parties that the appellees e the owners of the Jelley forty acre tract--the North-east Quarter of e South-west Quarter of Section Sixteen (16), Town (1) South, Range ven (7) East of the Third Principal Meridian, in Wayne County, Illinois, d that they derived title thereto, by descent from Benjamine Jelley, eir grand-father; that the appellant is the owner of the North-west arter of the South-west Quarter of the same section--and that he has ned it since 1889.

The hedge row set out by Mr. Jelley had grown to large tree ze, when, in March of 1933, appellant cut the south half of the hedge w and made the trees into posts, whereupon appellees brought suit to cover the value of the trees which appellant cut and converted to his n use.

Appellant now claims ownership of the narrow strip of land tween the hedge row and the west line of the North-east Quarter of the uth-west Quarter of Section Sixteen (16) in question and the hedge quest on, by adverse possession, under Section one of the Limitations atute.

In this case two forty acres tracts of land are involved. ese tracts adjoin each other and are properly and geographically scribed in the pleadings herein. We shall for the sake of simplicity fer to them as the west forty and the east forty. Regardless of all aims and contentions, it was fairly stipulated between the parties at appellant owns the west forty and appellees own the east forty.

ırty with all of its appurtenances.

It remains therefore, but to find out where the true line ·viding these two forties is. There is little or no controversy but ıat the original line of division was accurately located by the survey- ', Winters, some three to five feet west of the hedge fence in question. ıpellant does not controvert that, but claims that he and his immediate 'antors had been in open, notorious and exclusive possession of the rip between this line and the hedge fence far longer and the period 'quired by the statute to vest title in them. He also claims that the ıdge fence in question had for many years been regarded by the respective 'ners of the tracts as the division fence. We would be inclined to ılieve that appellant on these questions had by his evidence, brought mself with the rule announced in Sgro vs. Kames 235 Ill. 577, were that ıe turning point in this case, but it cannot be. By his stipulation ıpellant lost his right to claim title to the tract in question by escription and agreed upon the actual line of division as the true ne. In Roberts vs. Bicks 223 Ill. 291 cited by appellant it was held ıat a half century's possession of land with reference to a boundary ne does not control where the evidence shows that shortly before the it plaintiff and defendant in order to ascertain the true boundary, ither being certain of its location, should bear the expense of a rvey and agreed to build a fence upon the new line.

It seems to us from the evidence, conclusive that the hedge ne was not the true line of division between those two complete forty re tracts; that the hedge fence in question was east of said true ne and therefore, upon the property of appellees. Appellant having reed by his stipulation that he owned only forty acres of land and at appellees owned the other forty he cannot be heard to show that by ason of his possessions he now ownes more than the forty acres of nd. It follows therefore, that the trial court did not err in refusing e instructions which, in effect, told the jury that appellant owned re land than what he had stipulated about. The jury were fully warran- d in finding that the hedge fence in question was upon the land owned appellees. Appellant therefore, had no right to destroy or dispose any part of it. The issue between the parties having been determined

ie jury as it was, and this court finding no error in the record
n would warrant a reversal of this case, the judgment of the Circuit
t should be and it is hereby affirmed.

JUDGMENT AFFIRMED.

Not to be published in full.

Lightning Source UK Ltd.
Milton Keynes UK
UKHW031850290119
336364UK00006B/103/P

9 780260 986856